SQL Success

Database Programming Proficiency

SQL SUCCESS

Database Programming Proficiency

Stéphane Faroult

SQL Success: Database Programming Proficiency

Published by RoughSea Limited, Registered in England & Wales No. 3625100
Copyright © 2013 by Stéphane Faroult

Copy Editor: Trevor Trotman
Cover Design: Charles Peele and Ida Lee
Cover image courtesy NASA/JPL-Caltech.
Illustrated and indexed by the author.

The cover fonts are Adobe's Source Sans Pro and Maven Pro by Vissol Ltd,
The text font is Quattrocento, the heading font is Quattrocento Sans, both by Pablo Impallari.
Inconsolata, by Raph Levien, is used for code, and Ampersand, by Denise Chan, is used for annotations (Aenigma Scrawl, by Aenigma Fonts, appears in some pictures).

This work is subjected to copyright. All rights are reserved by the Publisher, whether the whole or part of the material is concerned, specifically the rights of translation, reprinting, reuse of illustrations, recitation, broadcasting, reproduction on microfilms or in any physical way, transmission or information storage and retrieval, electronic adaptation, adaptation to computer software, or by similar or dissimilar methodology now known or hereafter developed. Exempted from this legal reservation are brief excerpts in connection with reviews or scholarly analysis, or material supplied specifically for the purpose of being entered and executed on a computer system, for exclusive use by the purchaser of the work. Duplication of this publication or parts thereof is permitted only under the provisions of the Copyright Law of the Publisher's location, in its current version, and permission for use must always be obtained from RoughSea. Violations are liable to prosecution under the respective Copyright Law.

Trademarked names, logos and images may appear in this book. Rather than use a trademark symbol with every occurrence of a trademarked name, logo or image we use the names, logos and images only in an editorial fashion and to the benefit of the trademark owner, with no intention of infringement of the trademark. Trademarked names usually appear printed in caps or initial caps. The use in this publication of trade names, trademarks, service marks, and similar terms, even if they are not identified as such, is not to be taken as an expression of opinion as to whether or not they are subject to proprietary rights.

While every precaution has been taken in the preparation of this book and if the advice and information in this book are believed to be true and accurate at the date of publication, neither the author, the editors nor the publisher can accept any legal responsibility for any errors or omissions that may be made, or for damages resulting from the use of information contained herein.

ISBN-13: 978-1-909765-00-9

Printing History:
July 2013 First Edition.

For information on translations, please email **rights@roughsea.com**

Contents

Preface

Qu'on ne dise pas que je n'ai rien dit de nouveau: la disposition des matières est nouvelle; quand on joue à la paume, c'est une même balle dont joue l'un et l'autre, mais l'un la place mieux.

Let no one say that I have said nothing new... the arrangement of the subject is new. When we play tennis, we both play with the same ball, but one of us places it better.

- Blaise Pascal (1623-1662)

One day I received an email from a database instructor who had read my (then) two SQL books[1] and was looking for something in the same spirit but at a beginner's level, for her students. She wanted to know whether I could recommend a textbook.

When I first learned SQL, thirty years ago, there was little literature available apart from course manuals and reference documentation. Since then, I hadn't had any reason for keeping abreast of the latest in database and SQL textbooks and, somewhat intrigued by this unusual request, I started looking around for the kind of textbook with which I would enjoy teaching beginners. I came back empty-handed. I certainly discovered database textbooks that were obviously quite good but which gave me the feeling of having been written for graduate students with a strong taste for theory and abstraction. I felt some commiseration for undergraduates, especially when they don't plan immediately to pursue an advanced degree in Computer Science. The almost universal use of the "Students and Courses" database, in spite of its obvious attraction to a college student, does very little to make the Boyce-Codd Normal Form and functional dependencies as thrilling as intended.

---

[1] *The Art of SQL* and *Refactoring SQL Applications*, both published by O'Reilly.

I then turned my attention to the more familiar ground of professional books, many of which are excellent, and I suggested a few titles to my correspondent. Unfortunately, the best professional books assume, by definition, that readers have some professional experience of Information Technology and they don't come with the ecosystem (exercises, test bank, slides, instructor notes, companion website) that faculty expects of textbooks.

My quest for a textbook practical enough to trigger the interest of students was, for me, like a trip down memory lane. I have been served advanced abstract courses, a long time ago and I can now invoke the statute of limitations to avow that, frankly, the very little that I was taught on databases as a graduate student was all Greek to me. It looked pretty boring and for someone who couldn't then run a C program without having a segment violation and a core dump, `select * from courses` didn't seem too challenging or interesting. I was quite able to regurgitate the theory I had been fed but I was unable to relate it to something that was either practical or non trivial. Theory, which is so illuminating when you apply it to the real life issues you are familiar with, is mostly lost on beginners with no practice. There were, for me, on one side database theory (hard and boring) and on the other side that language, SQL (easy and boring), and the only link between the two was boredom. I was wrong to think that databases were boring and that SQL was easy but it took me some time and some practice to discover it (and improve my C).

I hope to shatter no dreams but when you are a fresh IT graduate, at work, you aren't asked about theory. You are rarely asked to design a 50 table database in your first job, and you are never asked whether a query returns a), b), c), or d). What people expect of you, within the scope of programs that can really be in any domain, is to occasionally write SQL statements, sometimes quite complex ones, and to make them run faster because poor performance angers end-users. SQL is the second computer language of almost every professional developer. Everybody uses databases. I doubt that many people realize that every time they make a phone call, surf the web, shop at a supermarket, or take money from an ATM, SQL statements are executed. Suddenly when you are confronted with the beast, you understand that there is a tremendous gap between the theory that you were taught and the practice. I have seen lots of young, smart developers, who had been taught databases, struggling with database programming.

Don't read the preceding remarks as an apology of practical skills training; this book isn't a "How To" book, and I am a firm believer in fundamentals. There are few ways of teaching SQL that I dislike more than a soul-less presentation of syntax (I have had to endure this too, as a young professional). Simply, very often, the theory that is taught isn't what's relevant and I realized this in Edinburgh. My friend Peter

Robson[2] organizes seminars in Europe for Chris Date (of whom I speak in the second chapter of this book). Peter twice invited me to seminars given by Chris in Edinburgh and introduced us to each other. Contrasting the points of view of the theorist and of the practitioner was most interesting, and something I had long felt very confusedly, became clear during these advanced seminars. What Chris was showing with talent, is that the part of theory that is practically relevant, is either ignored or misunderstood by most people. The idea stuck with me. In the professional world, you find most developers looking, sometimes desperately, for SQL recipes and they don't even try to connect what they are trying to do, to what they were taught. Spend some time on database forums and you'll see the same pattern again and again. It's like people who have been taught the grammar of a foreign language in excruciating detail at school, only to have to resort to phrase books when they travel to a country where this language is spoken because even if they were taught to master grammar better than some natives, their knowledge is useless in daily life. Grammar is very important, as grammar is the art of avoiding ambiguity in what you write; I simply wouldn't start teaching my native French to someone with the agreement of past participles but rather keep it for advanced learners.

My most recent pedagogical experiments have been with database video tutorials that I had posted on Youtube (http://www.youtube.com/user/roughsealtd) and at that point in my quest, I suddenly realized that my video efforts had left me with a considerable amount of material, much of it unpublished, and that this material was perfectly suitable for classes. I provided the instructor with slides and scripts, which she boldly used with a textbook that had nothing to do with them, and her experience was so successful (if you except the disconnect with the textbook) that she convinced me to embark on writing a "true" textbook.

Objective of This Book

The objective of this book is to make a reader with no prior knowledge of databases (and possibly at this stage little or no knowledge of programming), able to write relatively complex SQL statements that are both correct and efficient, and able to do it, not through trial and error but through logical reasoning. It's ambitious. My aim has been to provide a sturdy foundation, both for people who contemplate advanced database studies, so that then they can solidly anchor theory in practice and improve their practice through theory, and for people who want to start coding professionally after closing this book. Needless to say, in either case, the reader will still have a lot of work to do to achieve mastery but although there is still a long road ahead, I hope that this book will provide a good start that will make the journey enjoyable.

[2] You may want to check Peter's site, http://www.justsql.co.uk

As a consequence, I have chosen to be light on theory; not in the sense that I give recipes to be followed step by step, which isn't my purpose. I am light on theory in the sense that I refer first of all to logic; that I have tried to avoid scary words when I could; and that I prefer talking about common sense rather than enunciating rules. I have attempted to be rigorous without theoretical posturing, and to prepare people to understand theory rather than to wrap the text in a formality that would discourage a beginner.

To concentrate better on what I believe to be important, I have also ignored a lot of things that are in my experience rarely used or that anybody can easily discover for themselves. Most people will never use the **atan()** SQL function (arc tangent, in case you were wondering), this is the only place where you will see it mentioned in this book. I have tried to avoid information overload (which has been challenging, with six different SQL products). The intention of this book is not to cover every aspect of the language but to cover everything that is of practical use and to explain it as well as I could, the "why" and not just the "how". In this respect, this book also covers topics that are sometimes considered to be "advanced".

There are several variants of the SQL language, just as there are several variants of English, and I have tried to stick to what is common to most variants. That was easier in some chapters than in others but I have always tried to inscribe variants within a common framework. My goal is first and foremost, to make you understand and master the basic concepts of SQL. Where necessary, I discuss the peculiarities of different dialects of SQL but this book doesn't claim to be a substitute for the online reference documentation of the product you are using. I have no doubt that if you gain a good understanding of the content of the book, you will be able to pass easily from one dialect to another, after a short phase of adaptation.

If You Like This Book ... or Not

I'd love to hear your opinion about this book, and the best way to do it is to review and rate it on the web, whether it's on your blog or on an online bookshop – I'll find it. It's through reviews that I'll hear your opinion and will be able to improve the book in a future edition. Other authors will probably read your review too and learn from what you liked or disliked about this book, especially if your feedback is specific and gives direction for what should be emulated or avoided in the future. Thank you in advance.

Intended Audience

This book was primarily written with undergraduate students in mind, whether they contemplate further studies or not. By students, I mean students enrolled in a general Computer Science or Information Systems program, as well as students enrolled in a professional development program. This book also targets professionals who need to upgrade basic SQL skills, in particular those wishing to prepare for a professional SQL certification. Although some elementary knowledge of Information Technology is expected (if you know what a spreadsheet is and if you have surfed the web, it should be enough), no prior knowledge of a programming language is assumed, except for a section of Chapter 8 and for the two last chapters.

Contents of This Book

This book is organized in twelve chapters and four appendices.

- Chapter 1, *Introduction to Databases*, explains the purpose of databases, and shows with an example how to organize data in different tables inside a database. It insists on the database features that allow a database management system to ensure that changes don't bring inconsistencies, and it introduces a number of terms frequently used by database professionals.
- Chapter 2, *Introduction to SQL*, briefly tells the history of what has become the language to query databases, then explains, with the most widespread database management products, how to connect to a database and create the tables needed to store data. It then briefly shows how to enter data in these tables and visualize table contents.
- Chapter 3, *Retrieving Data from One Table*, explores in detail how to retrieve data stored in a table by using filtering conditions, how expressions allow the displaying of values derived from what was stored, how to deal with missing data and combine data from several rows, and how to chain retrieval operations by nesting them.
- Chapter 4, *Retrieving Data from Several Tables*, explains what SQL databases are famous for, linking tables through common values to combine data coming from two tables or more. It also shows how to retrieve data that cannot be matched, how queries on one table can reference the result of queries on other tables, and how data from several tables can also be combined through set operations.
- Chapter 5, *Ordering and Reporting*, discusses how result sets obtained through the operations described in the previous two chapters can be ordered for reporting; how output can be limited to the first (or last) rows after ordering and how hierarchies and complex ranking schemes can be displayed. It also demonstrates interesting applications of these techniques.
- Chapter 6, *Fuzzy Searches – Method*, presents a number of advanced search techniques for textual information and explains the logical steps that should take you from the English specification of a data retrieval problem, to the SQL query performing the retrieval.
- Chapter 7, *Changing Data*, talks about the important database concept of transaction, about validating or cancelling changes, and how new rows can be added to tables, modified or deleted. It also explains how to perform some

common data management tasks, such as uploading the contents of data files into a database, and how to modify data in a table based on data contained in another table.

- Chapter 8, *Functions, Procedures and Triggers*, explains how you can create your own functions in a database for performing frequent complex computations; how successions of SQL operations that belong to the same business process can be stored as a single procedure; and how change operations in one table, can spark modifications in other tables through the mechanism of triggers. Some sections require programming knowledge but the bulk of the chapter is accessible to people who have no experience of computer programming other than chapters 1 to 7 of this book.
- Chapter 9, *Speeding up Queries*, discusses in depth, the important topic of indexes, how they can make database accesses much faster, why sometimes they bring no improvement, why writing your queries badly can prevent the database engine from using them, and how your knowledge of existing indexes can influence query writing.
- Chapter 10, *Views, Security and Privileges*, shows how complex queries can be stored and used as virtual tables called *views*; as these virtual tables can be, and frequently are, used for controlling what users can see in a database. The management of users' rights and the protection of data from prying eyes are also explored in this chapter.

The two last chapters assume knowledge of a programming language.

- Chapter 11, *Using SQL in Programs*, explains how programs written in a traditional computer language, send SQL statements to a database server, check whether the statement executed successfully, and retrieve data when appropriate. It insists on the factors that may impact performance or compromise security and gives two simple examples, one in Java and the other one in PHP.
- Chapter 12, *Project Launchpad*, is a showcase for the same mildly complex program written in different programming languages, accessing different database systems, and gives copiously annotated examples of programs that are run in a console (the kind of programs that are run at night for massive operations), programs with a graphical user interface, a program to be run by a web server and even a mobile application. These examples are intended to be used as skeletons for more ambitious projects.
- Appendix A explains, if you install a free database management server on your own computer, how you should set it up for practicing what is shown in this book.
- Appendix B provides information on the most useful built-in functions provided by the different database products covered in this book, and

discusses some interesting topics such as how to work with time information from different time zones.

- Appendix C gives detailed answers to the exercises found at the end of chapters 1 to 10 (there are no exercises for the two last chapters).
- Appendix D includes additional SQL code related to Chapter 8 (functions, procedures and triggers.)

Companion Web Site and Instructor Materials

This book comes with a companion web site at http://edu.konagora.com. The site is divided into a public section and a member section reserved for faculty, which contains many teaching aids as well as additional material. The public section contains small sample databases for the various database systems covered in this book, which you can download and install for practicing what is shown in the book. It also contains code samples, which are released under a BSD-3 license[3], and will hopefully spare you some typing. Finally, it hosts an SQL sandbox which allows you to practice what is shown in this book, on a database that has the same structure as the database used in the book but contains more data than the downloadable sample databases. You won't be able to do everything that is shown in this book (what is shown in Chapter 8 isn't supported, for instance) but you can do a lot without having to install a database on your computer.

Typographical Conventions

The following typographical conventions are used in this book:

Italic	is used to indicate arbitrary names, such as the names given to tables in a database. It's also used, usually between angle brackets, to indicate an arbitrary value in a command or something that can vary in the name of a file for instance. Finally, it's also used for emphasis in the text, in particular when some important term or expression is introduced.
Bold	is used to indicate words that have a special meaning in SQL, as well as for the names of built-in functions. It's sometimes used for emphasis, in code examples in particular.
`Constant width`	is used for computer code, commands, and file names.
Grayish script	is used for annotating code samples in a visually striking way.

[3] It basically means that the code is provided "as is" without any guarantee but you must respect the copyright of the authors and not claim it as your own, nor use the authors' names to promote work that you could derive from it. Otherwise you are free to do whatever you want with it.

Acknowledgments

This book would simply not exist without Sandra Peele, the instructor whom I mentioned at the beginning of this preface. I was indeed beginning to mull over writing a book but on a completely different topic (project postponed); I wasn't even thinking about writing an SQL textbook. The feedback Sandra provided in field testing of my materials was a tremendous help in determining the scope and level of this book.

I had very strong reviewers in Rudi Bruchez and Serge Rielau, both noted database experts, whose remarks and clarifications have made some chapters significantly better. One of the chapters that required the most work was the last one, with its numerous examples in multiple languages. The contributions of Rudi Bruchez (once again) for the C# version of the program, of Laurent Fourrier who refactored my original Java program and turned something that was more a textbook example into a more professional program, and of Eddie McLean who provided the Objective C/Cocoa version of the program much enhanced the chapter and allowed the book to cover a much wider scope than I could have done on my own. Michel Cadot did an excellent work checking solutions for the exercises. Philippe Bertolino and Jérôme Mizon reviewed the book and their encouraging comments were quite appreciated. The book also benefited from remarks and input from Dan Barba, Jerzy Letkowski, and John Watson. The final stage was Trevor Trotman's merciless copy-editing: any sloppiness in this domain can probably be assigned to a last minute change that I made. Finally, my warm thanks to Charles Peele for the original design of what you probably saw first: the cover, and to Ida Lee who reviewed and improved Charles's work and designed the back cover.

Introduction to Databases 1

> Everything is vague to a degree you do not realize till you have tried to make it precise.
>
> - Bertrand Russell (1872-1970)

This chapter covers

- The purpose of databases and their basic concepts
- How the relational model of databases was born
- An introduction to how to organize data into tables
- Important vocabulary used by database professionals

Database is a word that you hear often in the business world. In itself, it doesn't mean much - just a collection of data. What is data? It can be anything. Text, such as names, addresses, descriptions, comments, articles, regulations; it can be numbers, measurements, prices, any amount or quantity; it can be dates and times; it can be pictures, sounds and music, video. Data is worthless, unless you establish connections between different pieces of data and turn them into information. It's information that helps trigger action. It's by relating their visitors to interests that many web companies make money, selling targeted advertising. More mundanely, it's the connection between a title you select and a sound file that allows you to play the song you want on a device. It's also the connection between your phone number, the contract that you have subscribed to, the location of the numbers that you called, the duration of your calls and possibly the time you called that allows the telephone company to bill you.

Collecting data is nothing new. Book-keeping is as old as trade. Two thousand years ago Roman Emperors were organizing censuses but our era of information gave a completely different dimension to the collection of data. Databases, today, are everywhere. Literally. All the bills you receive are extracted from databases that record what you are billed for. When you receive junk-mail, whether it is email or regular mail, you can be sure that your address comes from a database. The cash register at the grocery is connected to a database that stores the prices of the different articles and computes how many are left in stock. Compositions and calorific values on your box of cereals come from a database that records nutrition facts. Your address book in your phone? A small database. Your bank accounts? Numbers in a database. Your taxes too. The courses you take are recorded in databases in the information systems of colleges. Your purchase of this book has been recorded in a database. Even if you have downloaded it illegally (it's not too late to do the right thing and buy it), you can be sure that at least the number of downloads has been recorded in a database somewhere.

Where We Come From

The SQL language that you will learn in this book is strongly associated with what is called a "relational database". It's helpful to understand databases to have some idea about why they were invented, and the numerous problems they solve.

In The Beginning There Was Chaos

The story of modern databases starts somewhere in the 1960s, almost prehistory. Computers then were very expensive tools for accountants at a few very large corporations, and managing data with them was a pain. For software developers, it was a lot of file opening, file reading, file writing, file closing, complicated operations to sort records that were written in sequence on magnetic tapes – or, sometimes, punched cards (or even punched paper tape). You had to manage errors when the data wasn't what you were expecting, sometimes simply because the operator had mounted the wrong tape by mistake. Soon enough technology evolved and as computers were both very expensive and very fast, systems were designed to allow several people to use the same computer at the same time, with the computer working for a fraction of a second for one user, then switching to another one, and so forth. This added new complications. When several users were working simultaneously on the same data, as airline reservation systems discovered, you could easily make a mess of your data and sell the same seat to two different people if you weren't careful and if there weren't components in your programs to regulate, like traffic-lights, the flow of operations.

Creative laziness has always been the greatest quality of a good software developer. It didn't take long before software developers understood that, instead of rewriting the same complicated operations every time, a large part of data management could be shifted to a full subsystem – a set of programs doing the boring and dirty work, which would interact with application programs. This was the beginning of database management systems (DBMS): programs that run on a "database server" and accept and process high-level commands that instruct the computer which data to return. These systems take care of file management. Most importantly, they also ensure that data remains consistent across changes, whether they are carried out by one user or many users working on the same data.

A DBMS has basically two purposes:

- Letting you store and change data in a controlled way that guarantees as far as possible that the data is, and remains, valid,
- Retrieving and returning data that was previously stored as quickly as possible to a requesting program.

The first database systems required painful crafting and even minor changes to the structure of the database were nightmarish. Fortunately this was going to change.

And Codd Created the Relational Model

Around 1970 an IBM researcher, Edgar Codd, had the insight that database systems could rely on mathematical foundations that would transform the craft into a science. Codd's work became the relational theory of databases. Most modern databases, and the SQL language that is used to query them, derive from Codd's pioneering work. DBMS products became RDBMS products, *Relational Database Management Systems*.

Codd thought that the most convenient way to visualize the storage of data was to represent information in a database as a collection of tables. One table is associated with each item you want to manage and the columns describe different pieces of data that you can collect (they are usually called *attributes*). For instance, a table may contain some information about people. One column will store the surname, another one the first name, a third one the birth date, a fourth one a picture, and so on. One row will associate data related to one item, in that case one person; that's where "relation" and "relational database" come from.

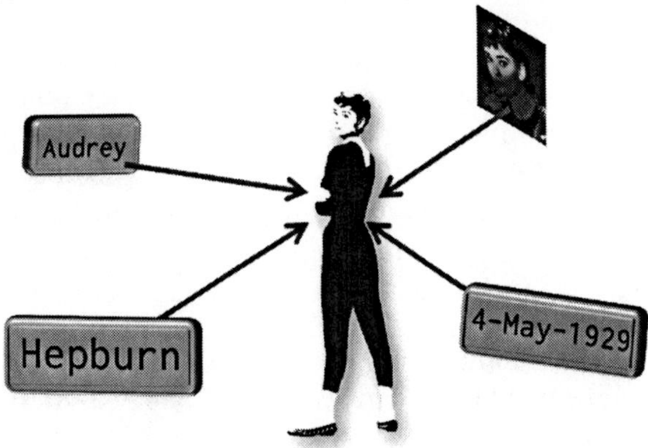

Figure 1.1: One row associates data related to one entity.

Each column always holds the same type of information but the order of columns is arbitrary. The order of rows in a table doesn't matter either. Once again, the only thing that counts is the association of the different pieces of data that constitute information; rows, columns and tables are just a convenient way to represent the association on a two-dimensional display such as a sheet of paper or a computer screen.

Codd's revolutionary idea wasn't the representation of datasets as tables. His real breakthrough was the idea that by representing datasets as tables, instead of storing data in hierarchical structures or by linking them in a complicated way as was customary at the time, you could operate on datasets in the very same way as you can operate on numbers, and crunch data in the same way as you crunch numbers. Instead of having operations such as addition, multiplication, subtraction and so forth, you would have operations that apply to datasets and transform one or several datasets into a new dataset in the very same way that when you add two numbers you get a new number. The correctness of results could be proved in the mathematical sense too. Understanding that datasets are, in a relational database, some strange kind of values, is probably the most important concept to understand – which very few people truly do. The result of a query comprises rows and columns, just like the contents of the tables that are queried. Datasets combined with datasets result in datasets.

If you have some knowledge of programming, tables are to datasets what variables are to values: containers that store something that usually changes over time (if they didn't, they wouldn't be called variables). Codd defined a number of operations that one could apply to datasets to create new datasets.
I am only going to mention the three most important ones, which are summarized in figure 1.2:

- What Codd called **selection**, which is extracting from a dataset a subset by applying a filtering condition to any of its attributes. For instance, retrieving from the dataset of all the people in the database, the subset comprising people born after 1980 or named Tom, or born after 1980 AND named Tom. That means finding only some rows, 'some' being anything between no rows and all the rows in the initial dataset.
- What Codd called **projection** (an allusion to geometry) which is simply the possibility of extracting some of the attributes and not all of them. For instance, you might want to extract from a table storing data about films, in which year the movie *Titanic* was released (1997) and care very little about the fact that it lasts 194 minutes – or vice versa. It's simply picking from a table only the columns you need to answer a particular question to get, so to speak, a "narrower" table.
- What Codd called **join**, which is the ability to link the data from one table to the data from another table through common values. For instance, if you have

a table that stores information about persons with a date of birth and a table that stores a list of Oscar recipients, you can find which movie got the Oscar of the Best Movie in the year a given person was born by "joining" the *person* table and the *oscar* table on the year, stipulating that the year values that you find in both tables must match.

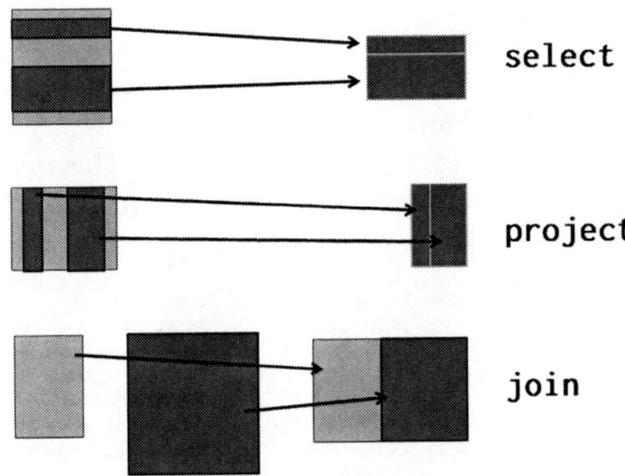

Figure 1.2: The three main relational operations.

Properly organizing the data that you want to manage is a key step when you begin to think about an application. You must know what items you want to manage – in this book we shall talk a lot about people and movies but for an on-line forum it might be topics, posts and members that write them, for a business it will be customers, articles, suppliers, purchase orders, invoices...

You must also know the attributes worth recording for each item and this entirely depends on your application. In the personnel database of a company, the fact that so and so is a passionate supporter of a particular sport team is of no relevance, even if it's very important to that person and if everyone in the office is aware of it. It may be a much more interesting fact to record as a characteristic of a customer in the database of an online-store that sells sport or sport-related articles. If you want to book a flight to travel from one place to another, most often you don't really care about the particular model of airplane in which you are going to fly. The company that operates the flight cares not only about the model, which tells it how many people it can carry, its autonomy and so on but also about the particular plane which must undergo maintenance operations at regular intervals. For an airline company, your flight will not only be an association between a schedule, a place of departure and a place of arrival but also an association between a particular airplane and a particular crew. And of course the view of an airplane taken by a company such as

Boeing or Airbus is completely different from the view of an airplane taken by an airline.

Once you know what you want to deal with, you have to organize it. Rather than giving you a load of theory that is beyond the scope of this book, I am going to show you how I have designed the small movie database that we shall use for examples.

Designing a Small Database

Tables in a database are very different from spreadsheets but let's start with a spreadsheet like figure 1.3 that contains information about a small number of classic movies: title, country, year, director and leading actors. This is a sample of the data that we need to manage; initially we shall model our main table after the spreadsheet.

	A	B	C	D	E	F
1	**Movie Title**	**Country**	**Year**	**Director**	**Starring**	
2	Citizen Kane	US	1941	welles, o.	Orson Welles, joseph Cotten	
3	La règle du jeu	FR	1939	Renoir, J.	Roland Toutain, Nora Grégor, Marcel Dalio, Jean Renoir	
4	North by Northwest	US	1959	HITCHCOCK, A.	Cary GRANT, Eva Marie SAINT, James MASON	
5	Singin' In the Rain	US	1952	Donen/Kelly	Gene Kelly, Debbie Reynolds, Donald O'Connor	
6	Rear Window	US	1954	HITCHCOCK, A.	James STEWART, Grace KELLY	
7	City Lights	US	1931	CHAPLIN, C.	Charlie CHAPLIN, Virginia CHERRILL	
8	The Third Man	GB	1949	Reed, C.	Joseph Cotten, Alida Valli, Orson Welles	
9	The Searchers	US	1956	Ford, J.	John Wayne, Jeffrey Hunter, Natalie Wood	
10	Ladri di biciclette	IT	1949	DeSica, V.	Lamberto Maggiorani, Enzo Staiola	
11	Annie Hall	US	1977	Allen, W.	Woody Allen, Diane Keaton	
12	On the Waterfront	US	1954	Kazan, E.	Marlon Brando, Eva Marie Saint, Karl Malden	
13	All about Eve	US	1950	Mankiewicz, J.	Bette Davis, Anne Baxter, George Sanders	
14	Casablanca	US	1942	Curtiz, M.	Humphrey Bogart,Ingrid Bergman, Claude Rains	
15	The Treasure of the Sierra Madre	US	1948	HUSTON, J.	Humphrey BOGART, Walter HUSTON, Tim HOLT	
16	High Noon	US	1952	Zinnemann, F.	Gary Cooper, Grace Kelly	
17	Some Like It Hot	US	1959	Wilder, B.	Tony Curtis, Jack Lemmon, Marilyn Monroe	
18						
19						

Figure 1.3: Data in a non-relational form.

Each row brings together a number of pieces of information that are the characteristics of a movie (usually called *attributes* of the movie). Whichever way you permute rows or columns, you still have exactly the same information in your database. What matters is that the different pieces of information on one row are related, and the titles of the columns define the relationship.

Identifying Rows

It makes no sense to have the same row repeated in a spreadsheet or in a table several times. It adds no information, the only thing it adds is a risk that one row is changed and not the other, and then you can't tell which one is up-to-date. An important step, when designing a database, consists in identifying the attributes that allow us to distinguish one row from another; and very often these characteristics are a subset of all the attributes. They are collectively called "the key". To know whether a column belongs or doesn't belong to the key is a question of knowing if a different value in the column would mean a completely different "fact" or simply an update that reflects a change of situation. For instance, in a table that stores information about people, replacing a picture of a person by another picture of the same person would be an update but if you assume that the current first name is correct, you cannot change it because the row would then refer to a different person. The first name is therefore a column that is part of the key. However, it cannot be the only key column, since several people can have the same first name and the first name alone isn't enough to identify precisely one person.

What is the smallest subset of attributes that uniquely identifies a movie?

You might think that a movie is identified by its title, but the title isn't enough because you have remakes. There are several movies based on the *Treasure Island* novel. If you talk about the *Treasure Island* movie, you must add another piece of information so that people understand that you are talking about one particular movie by that title and no other.
If you specify the title of a movie plus the name of the director, it will be sufficient in most cases but not always. If I tell you that I own a DVD of Alfred Hitchcock's *The Man Who Knew Too Much*, I must still add something because Alfred Hitchcock directed two movies called *The Man Who Knew Too Much*, one in 1934 and the other one in 1956.

Title, director and year may seem a better choice for uniquely identifying a movie - except that "director" isn't as simple a characteristic as it may seem. Some movies have several directors and it may lead to ambiguities. For instance, *Singin' In The Rain* was directed by Stanley Donen and Gene Kelly. We must be able to identify uniquely each movie, mistaking one movie for several is also a data management sin and we risk confusion if some people talk about *Singin' In The Rain* by Stanley Donen, others about *Singin' In The Rain* by Gene Kelly, or *Singin' In The Rain* by Stanley Donen and Gene Kelly - unless it is by Gene Kelly and Stanley Donen. It will not be obvious that everyone is talking about the same movie.

Title, country and year look a reasonable combination to uniquely identify a movie (I voluntarily ignore the fact that many movies are co-produced by companies from different countries and could legitimately claim multiple nationalities - it is reasonable to say that a movie has a "main country"). It is very unlikely, not least for commercial reasons, that two movies with exactly the same title will be produced the same year in the same country.
One can sometimes find several groups of characteristics that uniquely identify a row in a table; you are free to choose the group that you find the most convenient as the main identifier and this group of characteristics is called the "primary key".

NOTE I use 'group' very loosely. The 'group' may be a single characteristic.

Finding the Information

The ultimate goal of all databases is to be queried. That means that people will search the table to retrieve movies that satisfy some particular conditions, for instance movies by a given director.

Searching information inside a database isn't always as trivial as it looks. In a small spreadsheet it's easy to inspect the column of directors to spot the name that you are looking for, or you may wish to sort the rows by director first, so as to find the director name more easily. With a bigger spreadsheet you will want to filter by name. Searching in an SQL database is like filtering a spreadsheet. When you search in a database for the films directed by one specific person you must provide the director name. The database management system retrieves the relevant rows for you and what you specify for the search must match exactly, what is stored. It's much like the address book of your phone. You know that if you mistype a name when you register a new number in your phone, for instance 'Jhon' instead of 'John' if you don't correct the mistake you'll have to type 'Jhon' to retrieve John's number. It's exactly the same in any database.

If we want to retrieve all the movies that were directed by one given person, it's essential that the name that you provide exactly matches the contents of the table - whether you filter the rows in a spreadsheet or search a database and specify that the director attribute must be "HITCHCOCK, A.", you will only retrieve those movies for which the name of the director has been stored as "HITCHCOCK, A.", not as "HITCHCOCK", and definitely not as "Alfred Hitchcock". There are some ways to perform "fuzzy" searches that you will see later in Chapter 6 but search criteria and data must always match.

There may be a consistency issue with data that will in all likelihood be entered by different people at different times and must respect the same conventions. If you say when you populate your database that *North by Northwest* and *Rear Window* are "HITCHCOCK, A." movies, while *Strangers on a Train* is an "Alfred Hitchcock" movie, users who query the database will have a lot of trouble getting the full list of Hitchcock movies.

As a general rule, character fields that are free-form text are troublesome when they are used for searches. This is true for directors and this is also true for the leading stars. We must therefore define some kind of standard for storing names; storing first name and surname separately, in uppercase perhaps (we can change the case after retrieving the data to make it look better), or in lowercase with an initial capital - some DBMS products are case-sensitive, others aren't, and with other products case-sensitivity is optional. Standardization is a first step in the right direction but we still have a few problems to solve. The first one is typos. A user who mistypes a name may realize the mistake, check the spelling, and try again but there may be mistakes during data entry as well, which go unnoticed. If there are any misspellings inside the database, information that is misspelled will only be found by users making the same mistake when they query; not a desirable situation.

If we store data in a single, spreadsheet-like table, we shall never get rid of these problems if new data is regularly entered. To ensure that names are correctly stored, the best solution is to enter them only once (and if they are misspelled, it will be easily spotted and we'll have only one place to correct). This is where we are going to put to good use the join operation defined by Codd.

Let's see how it works. Suppose that we create a table of directors. In this table, we shall store first name, surname, and some biographical information. The key will be first name and surname and perhaps the birth date to distinguish between two people bearing the same name.

> NOTE In the film industry if you happen to have the same name as someone else you usually take a nom de guerre. If you are an actor named James Stewart and there is already someone famous named James Stewart, you change your name to Stewart Granger. If you are an actor called Michael Douglas and someone else is already known under your name, you have to call yourself something like Michael Keaton. If you are named after your dad like Douglas Fairbanks, 'Jr.' may be considered part of either the first name or the surname. It is therefore reasonable to consider that first name and surname are enough to identify unambiguously someone in a film database.

As we want to link movies and directors, and we want to avoid misspellings, we are going to use a code, a simple number that will be a synonym for the key and that we shall call *id*. Such an identifier is similar to your social security number (SSN): a short and convenient identification for administrative purposes. Users that query the database will ignore identifiers just as your friends ignore your SSN or as you ignore the serial number of your mobile phone; it's just something we add for our own convenience. It will be, technically speaking, a second key, as we shall assign different numbers to the different persons.

Inside the movies table we shall replace the identification of the director by the identifier. When a user wants to retrieve the titles and year of the movies directed by someone whose surname alone has been provided, the system will search the table of directors using the surname, will find the number associated with this director surname, then will use identifiers in the join operation to search the table of movies and find the relevant ones. If several directors have different first names but the same surname, several identifiers will be returned from the table of directors and all their films will be returned from the table of movies.

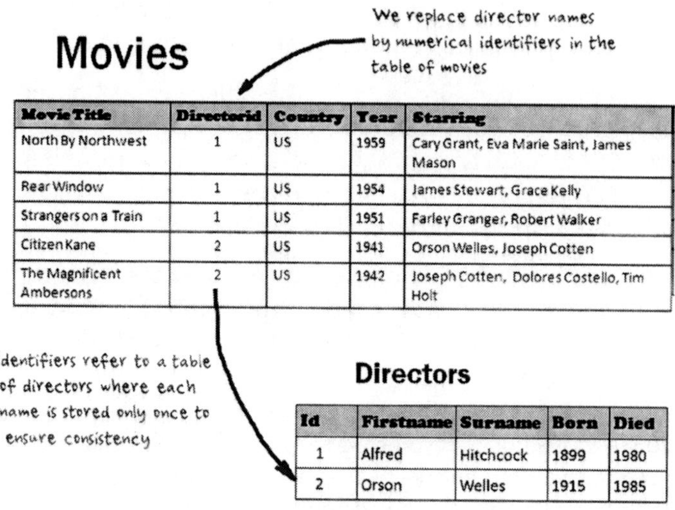

Movie Title	Directorid	Country	Year	Starring
North By Northwest	1	US	1959	Cary Grant, Eva Marie Saint, James Mason
Rear Window	1	US	1954	James Stewart, Grace Kelly
Strangers on a Train	1	US	1951	Farley Granger, Robert Walker
Citizen Kane	2	US	1941	Orson Welles, Joseph Cotten
The Magnificent Ambersons	2	US	1942	Joseph Cotten, Dolores Costello, Tim Holt

Id	Firstname	Surname	Born	Died
1	Alfred	Hitchcock	1899	1980
2	Orson	Welles	1915	1985

Figure 1.4: Isolating director data.

We can do something similar for actors.

Reorganizing Data

We still have a problem with the minority of movies that have more than one director, like *Singin' In The Rain*. Should we reserve two columns for storing director identifiers? That would mean joining on two columns, which can be done but isn't most convenient. But two isn't enough. There are many "anthology films", in which several loosely connected segments are directed by different authors. Some movies such as *New York Stories* have three directors (no less than Woody Allen, Francis Ford Coppola and Martin Scorsese). If you look at Italy, a country where anthology films were once very popular, you can find movies directed by even more people, such as *The Witches*, a 1967 movie in which Mauro Bolognini, Vittorio De Sica, Pier Paolo Pasolini, Franco Rossi and Luchino Visconti all directed a segment.

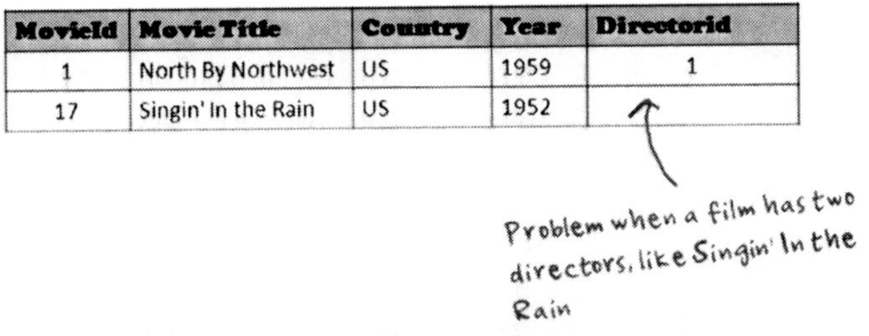

MovieId	Movie Title	Country	Year	Directorid
1	North By Northwest	US	1959	1
17	Singin' In the Rain	US	1952	

Problem when a film has two directors, like Singin' In the Rain

MovieId	Movie Title	Country	Year	Directorid1	Directorid2
1	North By Northwest	US	1959	1	
17	Singin' In the Rain	US	1952	27	53

BAD IDEA
There may be even more directors, and it's hard to put a cap.

Figure 1.5: Some movies have several directors and this can be a problem.

We have the same problem, even more acutely, with actors. How many actors should we record? The three leading actors only? What about a star-studded movie such as *The Longest Day*?

What if one day we decide to improve the database and record more actors, and perhaps the full cast? If we want to add more actor identifiers to the table we shall have to review all the existing queries to be able to search the new columns as well as the old ones.

Storing director and actor identifiers inside the movies table will make the evolution of the application very painful. This isn't therefore a good design and we must try harder.

First, as the real life key for movies may be a bit difficult to work with, we can do like we did for directors and actors, and use a numerical identifier *movieid* that will be used as a shorter alias for the title, year and country. It will make referring to a movie inside another table easier (in practice, these numerical identifiers can be automatically generated by database management systems).

If we add the movie identifier to the table of directors, we'll be able to solve the case of *Singin' In The Rain*, except that it won't work because usually one person has directed more than one movie. We have just shifted the problem from one table to the other.

Instead of having one column per director in the movies table or one column per movie in the directors table, the magic of Codd's relational theory allows us to have an intermediate table that will store director identifiers and movie identifiers and, through two joins, will allow us to link one director with several movies or several directors with one movie, if need be. We are going to call this table *directed_by* and it implements a link between the table of movies and the table of directors.

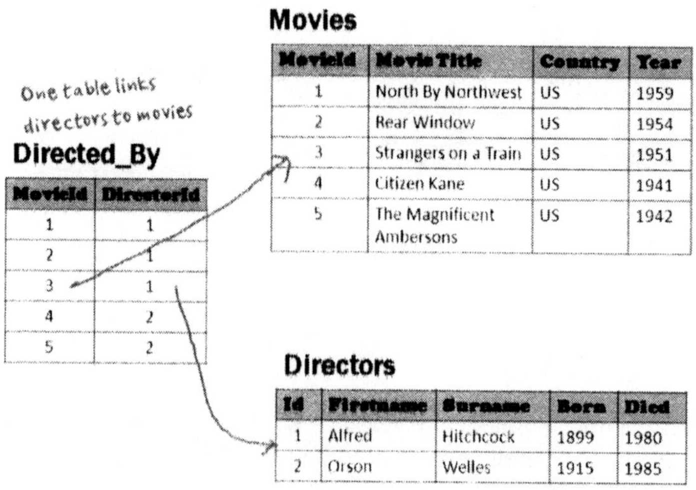

Movies

MovieId	Movie Title	Country	Year
1	North By Northwest	US	1959
2	Rear Window	US	1954
3	Strangers on a Train	US	1951
4	Citizen Kane	US	1941
5	The Magnificent Ambersons	US	1942

Directed_By

MovieId	DirectorId
1	1
2	1
3	1
4	2
5	2

Directors

Id	Firstname	Surname	Born	Died
1	Alfred	Hitchcock	1899	1980
2	Orson	Welles	1915	1985

Figure 1.6: Catering for the possibility of having several directors.

The directors will no longer be attributes of the movies but information about them is going to be transferred to other tables that will be linked by join operations to the *movies* table.

NOTE Everything I discuss about directors is of course valid for actors as well.

We have the movies, we have the directors, and the new table *directed_by* will record the fact that one person directed, at least partially, one movie. The unique combination of a director identifier and a movie identifier is the key of the new table. In the same way, we can also have a table called *played_in* that links the table that records actors to the *movies* table.

Now, we still have a problem. Orson Welles directed *Citizen Kane* but also played the leading character, and actors turned directors, or directors who occasionally or often play in their own movies are rather common - You can think of Charlie Chaplin, Woody Allen, Clint Eastwood and many others.

If we store directors and actors separately, biographical information will be duplicated, and if we update one table and forget the other one, we shall have inconsistencies - one table will say one thing, the other table will say something else, and we won't know which one is right.

What we really want is to merge the two tables and keep all the information about one person at a single location, in a table that we could call *people*, in which we can store directors and actors.

Let's modify our model one last time.

We could still keep *played_in* and *directed_by*, and make them link the *movies* table to the *people* table.

Another solution is to merge *played_in* and *directed_by* into a *credits* table that would hold a movie identifier, a person identifier and another attribute to tell in what capacity a person participated to the movie: actor or director. This last design is probably better if, in due course, we plan also to record who wrote the script, who composed the music, who was the photography director, who designed the set and so on ... which would otherwise require one additional link table per type of involvement. With one table, we can find cast and crew at one place and we have here a clean design, which guarantees data integrity and also allows evolution.

Movies

MovieId	Movie Title	Country	Year
2	Rear Window	US	1954
4	Citizen Kane	US	1941

Credits

MovieId	PersonId	Credited
2	1	D
2	3	A
2	4	A
4	2	D
4	2	A
4	5	A

People

Id	Firstname	Surname	Born	Died
1	Alfred	Hitchcock	1899	1980
2	Orson	Welles	1915	1985
3	James	Stewart	1908	1997
4	Grace	Kelly	1929	1982
5	Joseph	Cotten	1905	1994

By specifying how a person was involved (A)ctor or (D)irector, we can record easily directors who play in their films

Figure 1.7: Ready to create tables in a database.

I hope that this simple example will be enough to convince you of the importance of database design. I have introduced to you in a very informal way, the core of the sample database for this course, by trying to explain the thought process that leads to the organization of data.

In this process, I have:

- Defined what uniquely identifies one item that I am managing, such as a film or a person.
- Focused on having, in every column, only simple information that I can easily search. This is why I have separated first names and surnames and eliminated lists such as lists of actors.
- Tried to standardize data.
- Isolated important data such as the information about people in a different table to ease data maintenance and used numerical identifiers when I needed to reference this information in another table
- Taken special care of how many similar attributes an item can have: films may have more than one director, directors rarely make only one film, films usually have many actors and one actor can play in many movies.

In practice, as in my example, this process is usually iterative. Designing a database isn't easy, you can't always think of all the weird cases that may happen from the start and not everything falls into place at once. When you design a big database, it's also very often a team effort, and database designers communicate using a vocabulary (also shared with developers) that you need to know.

A Bit of Formalism

Database design is often presented to students with a relatively scary formalism. I have tried to avoid that and show you that good design is, first and foremost, the application of logic and common sense. All trades have their own jargon, the world of databases is no exception, and there are a few words that you will often hear in the corporate world when people discuss how best to store data in a database.

Entities

Some of the tables in a database correspond to "objects" that we want to manage and that have a number of attributes, like *movies* and *people*. These important objects are named *entities*. Entities have a life of their own. Besides entities, you have other tables, such as *credits*, that don't represent entities but relationships between entities. They may or may not have attributes (in our example, *credited_as* is an attribute of the relationship between a person and a film). The distinction between entities and relationships is sometimes subjective, and depends on the view that you have of data; one person's entity can be another person's relationship. For instance, if you are trying to design a sport database to register scores during an international tournament, you may consider that a team is an entity but for a club owner, a team is nothing more than a relationship between players at any given time. Modeling in terms of entities and relationships is very common, and the tables in a database are often represented as an *Entity/Relationship* (often shortened to *E/R*) *diagram*. Very crudely, those diagrams are basically what I have shown you here, boxes that represent tables and arrows that indicate how they are linked.

Cardinality

One often hears the word *cardinality* in relation to database design. Cardinality comes from a Latin word that means "essential" and is a word used in mathematics to describe the number of elements in a set; in this context it basically means "count" (but sounds more interesting). The cardinality of a column is its number of distinct values; the cardinality of a table is its number of rows, as a properly designed table contains no duplicates.

When discussing database modeling the word cardinality is also often associated with pairs of values that describe how many rows in one entity can match one row in another entity - for instance how many people can be linked to one movie or how many movies can be linked to one person. In that case, the values in the pair are picked in 0, 1 and *m* or *n* that stand for "an indeterminate number that can be more than one", and you will see references such as (1, n) or (m, n) (aka one-to-many or many-to-many) to qualify how many items can refer to another item. Let me explain. A (1,n) - or one-to-many - relationship is what would occur between the table of movies and a table of countries if we assume that one movie was produced by one single country (or at least one primary country); one movie will always be attached to one (and only one) country, while in one country an indeterminate number of movies (many) will be produced. Hence the one-to-many - (1, n) - link between *movies* and *countries*, which is nothing more than the minimum (one) and the maximum (indeterminate, can be more than one) number of films that can be related to one country. When you have such a relationship, it means nothing more in practice than that the country is an attribute of the movie (since we have no more than one) and is mandatory (we cannot have zero). An association between a movie and its original language would be of (0, n) cardinality (zero-to-many) because there are many movies in common languages but also silent movies which have no language at all. That means that a "language" attribute is optional and could be left undefined (we'll talk a lot about undefined attributes in the next chapters.)
A cardinality (m, n) is typically what you have between *actors* and *movies* - the cast of a movie is usually composed of several actors and one actor usually plays in several movies. Note that sometimes you have movies with no actors - think of an animated movie, or of a nature documentary. To implement a many-to-many cardinality, you need an intermediate table, like table *credits* in our example. If you

have a movie with no actors, there is no need to make any attribute optional - you will have no rows with role *A* for this movie in table *credits*.

Normalization

The whole process we have gone through from the spreadsheet to the final separation into three different tables with well-defined columns is known as *normalization*. One of the first steps we have done was to store first names and surnames separately, so as to make searches easier. Ensuring that one column contains only data that we can search or compare wholly, in other words having only one single piece of data in each column, is known as the **first normal form** (having to search one particular actor in thousands of lists of actors is the nightmare of every developer). It's a prerequisite of proper database modeling.
You also have further normal forms (**2nd**, **3rd**, and in some rare cases higher numbers) the only purpose of which is to ensure that

> *Each attribute that doesn't belong to the key is a fact related to the key, the whole key and nothing but the key*

as another pioneer of relational databases, Bill Kent, elegantly put it in a formula that is quoted very often.

> NOTE Not depending on a subset of the key is required by the 2nd normal form. For a table to be in 3rd normal form, additionally, an attribute mustn't depend on another attribute that doesn't belong to the key either.

Let me give you another example. Suppose that you want to organize an event about Asian cinema and you want to find the Asian movies in the database. We have recorded countries, but not continents. We could decide, to facilitate searches, to add another column to the *movies* table to store the continent but then we would violate the normal forms as defined by Bill Kent. What is the key? We have two keys, the numerical identifier, which is a technical key, and the real life key, title, country and year. Is the new continent attribute a fact about the key? Yes, in a way, but only about a part of the key - the country. If the country is specified, we know the continent (if you want to be pedantic and impress your audience, you can say that there is a *functional dependency* between continent and country - the country determines the continent). Neither the title nor the year has anything to do with the continent. The continent is not a fact about the whole key. That means that the continent shouldn't belong to the *movies* table but rather to another table *countries*, the key of which will be the country code and which will contain other country-related information such as the full country name, which may be more legible than a code in reports.

Talking about "normal forms" may look impressive but they are nothing more than formalized common sense. Checking Kent's rule when you think that you are done with organizing your data is probably the best way to check that you have nothing horribly wrong once you have the cardinalities right.

If you are interested by database design issues (and they are often very interesting, if not always easy to solve) I would advise you to take a look at Clare Churcher's book *Beginning Database Design* (disclaimer: I was the technical reviewer). It's very readable, under 250 pages, and covers design issue in much greater depth than I have done here.

To Remember

- Database management systems are independent programs devoted to managing data that dialogue with other programs. You find databases everywhere.
- The relational model devised by Ted Codd emerged as a mathematically based model in which tables store datasets on which you can operate.
- To design a database properly, you need at least one set of columns that uniquely identifies each row (the primary key) and other columns must correspond to a single "fact" about the key. You must be careful about how many similar attribute values you can associate with one key (cardinality).
- *Each attribute that doesn't belong to the key is a fact related to the key, the whole key and nothing but the key.*

Exercises

1. You want to put on-line on a website, the movie database that has been discussed in this chapter. You wish to build a community by letting people register as members on the site.
    a. Based on your own experience of websites, what type of information would you try to record for members and how would you identify them? In other words, what would a members table look like for the site? Specify which attributes would be mandatory and which would be optional.
    b. You want to allow members to post movie reviews, and/or to assign from one to 5 stars to a movie. Someone can review without rating or rate without posting a review. However, a member cannot rate or review a given movie more than once. How would you organize data?
2. You are working for an association that allows its members to borrow DVDs for a few days. We want to focus only on recording suitable DVD information. Firstly, you think that it would be a good idea to have several copies of popular movies so

that several people can borrow different DVDs of the same movie at once. Secondly, at the back of a DVD box you typically find this kind of information:

Special Features

* Behind-the-scenes mini-documentary

* Interactive Menus

* Theatrical Trailer

* Cast/Filmmaker Profile

* Scene access

LANGUAGES: English DTS 5.1 & Español Stereo Surround

SUBTITLES: English for the hearing impaired, Français, Português, Deutsch, Chinese, Thai & Korean

Color/118 Mins

Aspect-ratio: Widescreen

Not Rated

a. What information from the above would you choose to store in your database?

b. How would you organize the information that you want to manage

Introduction to SQL 2

Diese neue Tafel, o meine Brüder, stelle ich über euch.

This new table, O my brethren, I put up over you.

- Friedrich Nietzsche (1844–1900)

This chapter covers

- The origins and the main components of the SQL language
- Connecting to a database
- Creating a table
- Populating a table with data

I told you in the previous chapter that databases accept commands in a high-level language to store and retrieve data. The relational model invented by Codd demanded a language different from anything that existed. Among several contenders, one language emerged, SQL, the topic of this book.

A Structured Query Language

When Codd first conceived how you should organize data, his mathematical background made him use mathematical notation to express operations on datasets. He designed a language called Alpha, which remained a research project.

How SQL Was Born

At this time, the early 1970s, there was a lot of work going on to make computers more user-friendly. Alpha was certainly math PhD-friendly but IBM had a somewhat wider vision of user-friendliness. Two other young IBM researchers, Ray Boyce and Don Chamberlin, worked on creating a language that would provide a way to manage the new type of database imagined by Codd while at the same time remaining close enough to English to be usable by non-specialists (a database management system prototype, System-R, was developed at the same time.)

Boyce and Chamberlin came out with something that they called *Structured English Query Language*, or SEQUEL for short. The name SEQUEL was already a trademark of a British company, so it had to be abandoned and was further shortened to SQL. As *Query* in the name implies, the focus was on retrieving information. The authors of the language devised a simple syntax mimicking English for extracting data from tables:

SELECT followed by a list of columns to tell which attributes you want

then

FROM followed by a list of tables to tell where they come from

then

WHERE followed by conditions allowing to filter data.

The aim of Chamberlin and Boyce was primarily to allow "power users" to query a database, people who were professionals but who were neither software developers nor database specialists. SQL didn't strictly adhere to what Codd had designed and although over the years it became the dominant language, at one time it was just one among several competing ways to manage a database inspired by Codd's ideas.

- One can also mention QUEL (pronounced "kwel"), a language at the University of California at Berkeley in the INGRES project under the leadership of Eugene Wong and Mike Stonebraker (today's PostgreSQL is a direct descendent of INGRES), which also had a syntax directly inspired by English,
- and Query By Example (QBE), a graphical query environment imagined by another IBM researcher, Moshe Zloof, which has inspired tools still available several decades later (in Access in particular.)

One of the reasons for the success of SQL is perhaps that someone named Ed Oates read the specifications for the language when they were published by Boyce and Chamberlin in a scientific journal at the end of 1974. Oates talked about them to a friend, Larry Ellison, who had already read Codd's paper and had understood how revolutionary Codd's ideas were. Together with another friend, Bob Miner, a first rate software developer, they created a company, Software Development Laboratories. Working very hard with a fourth musketeer, Bruce Scott, who joined them shortly after, they managed to bring a database management system based on SQL to the market before IBM did. Their system was running on computers not made by IBM. They called their product Oracle and helped turn SQL into the standard language for querying databases.

The SQL Components

There are two main components in SQL. Before you can manage data, you must manage tables. An interesting feature of SQL (directly coming from Codd's original paper) is that the language allows you to create and modify both the containers (the tables identified when designing the database) and the contents (the data that you store into them).

- The subset of SQL used for creating tables is called *DDL* for *Data Definition Language* and mostly revolves around three keywords, **create**, **alter**, and **drop**.
- The subset of SQL used for accessing data is called *DML* for *Data Manipulation Language* with four main keywords, **insert**, **update**, **delete**, plus **select** for retrieving data (some consider that **select** is in a class of its own.)

NOTE One can add to the basic DML commands another one called **merge**, which you will see in Chapter 6. There are other components to the language than the two main ones; we'll see them in due course.

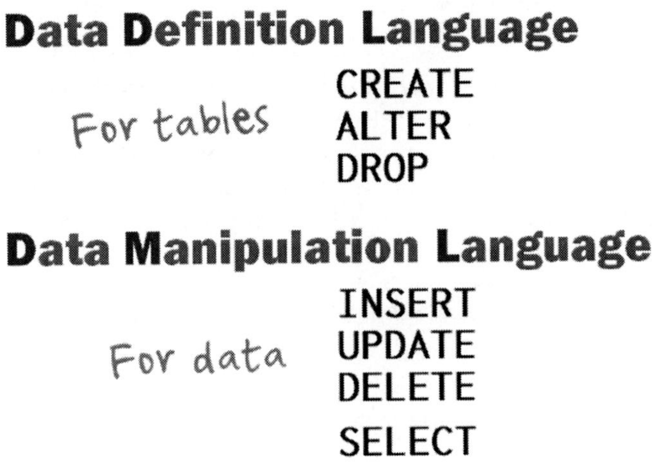

Data Definition Language

For tables: CREATE, ALTER, DROP

Data Manipulation Language

For data: INSERT, UPDATE, DELETE, SELECT

Figure 2.1: The two main components of SQL

All this looks very simple (and it's simple by design) and you must be wondering why there is such a fuss about SQL, why there is so much literature about it, and why this book still goes on for many chapters. The answer is that the apparent simplicity of SQL is deceiving. You can say that SQL is simple in the same way as you can say that playing chess is simple as it's no big deal to learn how to move each one of the six different pieces. It's combinations that are killing, and writing an SQL statement well can be pretty daunting. Writing good SQL is all the more difficult that paradoxically the slight liberties taken by its designers regarding the underlying theory require discipline with the language; it's much easier to obtain wrong results with SQL than with Codd's equations. SQL is an interesting language and sometimes fun to use but it has subtle pitfalls. Writing SQL well requires a very good understanding of its philosophy and a way of thinking that is very different from that used with procedural or object oriented languages.

A 2011 study carried out in Europe, Middle-East and Africa by Evans Data shows that more than 90% of developers spend part of their time coding in SQL with 37% of them spending at least a quarter of their time on SQL (with mixed results from what I have seen over the years).

There are many different DBMS products, each with its own SQL peculiarities. There are several SQL dialects just like British, Australian and American English are different dialects, each with its own words and expressions; but when you understand one, understanding the other doesn't require much effort - for the heart of the language at least. I'll try to stick to the common core as much as I can and I'll mention the main variants when needed so that you are ready to work with any of the main database products.

In this book, we'll start (logically) with **create**, then **insert** to show briefly how you can start populating a database. We'll then study the **select** statement in depth before returning to data manipulation proper and digging deeper in the data definition language. We'll also look at some other commands that are important but don't fall under either DDL or DML. Before anything else, let's see how you can access a database to run SQL statements.

Connecting To a Database

A database management system is an independent program that listens for commands, and then sends back either data or a status message. Very often, the DBMS runs on a different machine from the one where the program that issues the commands is running. A DBMS always comes with at least two ways to interact with it:

- One or several "client programs" that allow you to connect and interactively type SQL queries or statements (mostly for development or administrative tasks, because a DBMS, like an operating system, requires an administrator). Client programs are either simple command-line tools that you use in a terminal (such as *mysql* with the eponymous DBMS, *sqlplus* with Oracle, *clpplus* with DB2, or *psql* with PostgreSQL), or more sophisticated graphical tools (*SQL Server Management Studio* or Oracle's *SQL Developer*). Some independent graphical tools such as *Toad* or *SQL Squirrel* can connect to different database systems. Web-based tools are also available for most products.

- Client libraries containing functions allowing you to connect, to disconnect, to pass the text of an SQL statement to execute, and to get in return either a code indicating the outcome or, in the case of a query, a structure that describes the rows returned by the query and what they contain. You can call these functions from your own programs. The functions you call are either DBMS specific (which is usually the case when you program with a language such as C or C++), or generic layers that require DBMS-specific drivers but are otherwise independent from the DBMS (JDBC for Java, PDO for PHP, the Python database functions, perl ...) You also have some standard protocols such as ODBC that allow you to access any database from many different environments, including spreadsheets. With some languages you can also have "embedded SQL" - you mix a regular programming language with special statements that usually start with EXEC SQL. In that case, when you compile and link your program there is a special pass prior to compilation in which a utility program replaces the special statements in your code by calls to DBMS client functions.

Like everything else, you won't become familiar with SQL just by reading about it. You need an environment for practice. You will need a client program for running the examples and exercises in this book. Chapter 11 will show you how you can issue SQL statements from programs, in different languages.

A Work Environment for Practicing SQL

If you have no DBMS product already installed that you can access, you have several possible options.

- If you have the necessary rights to install software on a computer, you can install a database server on your machine. If you blindly accept all default options, it can be done relatively quickly once you have downloaded it. If you plan to study database administration after SQL, it will allow you to practice user management, backing up and restoring data and so on. Once again, several possibilities.
    - You can install a free, open-source DBMS. The two bigger names here are MySQL and PostgreSQL and are available both for Windows and Linux (or UNIX) environments. Unless you have immediate plans for using MySQL, I'd advise you to use PostgreSQL, simply because its SQL is closer to the standard than what MySQL implements. If you primarily want to develop web applications MySQL is a better choice because it's the DBMS that is most widely provided by web-hosting companies. I must also mention MariaDB (http://mariadb.org), which is compatible with MySQL.

  - If you target corporate IT, you should also be aware that all major DBMS vendors have free versions of their products with limits on the size of the database and without the most advanced features - none of which should be a concern for you before some time. If you know that you may have to work with Oracle, SQL Server or DB2 later, installing it to become familiar with its environment would be the best choice.

- If you don't want to install a full-blown DBMS, another possibility is a product such as Microsoft Access, also known as MS Access, which is somewhat in the same league as SQLite (which follows) with a much richer development environment that you won't use in this book. Free trial versions are available. However, its implementation of SQL is full of peculiarities.
- Even if you cannot install a product on your machine, you may have Firefox installed and you may have the right to install a Firefox plug-in. In that case, I would advise you to get the plug-in called *SQLite Manager*. SQLite is what is called an "embedded database". If you are just interested in learning SQL and if you want to create applications for mobile devices, this may be your best choice even though a number of features are missing from SQLite (at least at the time of writing, things evolve fast). SQLite is not a Database Management System in the sense that a *system* is a set of programs that run independently of any application. SQLite is a data manager that stores data in table format inside a single file (sometimes several files) and lets you manage it with SQL but doesn't run independently from your own programs. The product is small, free (it has been put in the public domain by its creator, Richard Hipp), supported by some very big names and is the "database" of choice for mobile applications.

  You can also download SQLite from http://www.sqlite.org and use it outside Firefox.
- If you can't install anything but have access to the internet, there is an SQL sandbox at http://edu.konagora.com, a site managed by the author of this book.

Appendix A provides information on how to set up a minimal clean environment if you choose to install a DBMS on your computer. You have, therefore, no excuse for not practicing what this book shows.

A stand-alone DBMS (as opposed to an embedded database) runs on a server on a network. To be able to access the database, a number of prerequisites must be satisfied:

- A client program must be installed on your machine.
- You must know the name of the machine that hosts the database (or its IP address, four dot-separated numbers between 0 and 255 such as

192.168.254.27). The name of the computer isn't enough, though. One machine may actually be a multi-purpose server, for instance being able to serve files or web pages as well as data. It's like a condominium with multiple apartments - each service has its own "address" within the server as a number called *port*. All DBMS products have one default port (for instance 1521 for Oracle or 1433 for SQL Server) but sometimes administrators choose to change it when they have, for instance, different versions of the same DBMS running concurrently on the same machine, or for security reasons. The port isn't the only thing you need. One database server often hosts several more or less independent databases, even when they are using the same version of the DBMS; it's a frequent occurrence on development servers - the exact meaning of "independent databases" varies from product to product. Each independent database has a name and you must specify the name of the particular database you want to connect to.

So, you must provide three pieces of information,

- the name of a machine,
- a port (if you don't specify it a preset value will be used)
- a database name (there may be a default for the database name too but not always).

Sometimes, part of the information is taken from a registry or environment variable, or an alias is used and the gory detail is read from a configuration file but basically this is what you need.

- As databases often contain sensitive information (anything from salaries and grades to medical data or trade secrets such as chemical formulas) you must prove that you are allowed to access it. The classical way to do so is to provide a username and a password that are unrelated to the operating system account you are using on your computer. In some cases you can be authenticated by the system you are logged onto (the fact that you are connected to that very computer that you are using is considered proof enough that you are the right person) or you can be authenticated by sophisticated mechanisms far, far beyond the scope of this book.

SQL without a Database Server

If you are using a product such as SQLite, there is no database server, no data shared with others, and there is no connection. If you are using it in a console, you just type `sqlite3` followed by a filename, for instance

```
sqlite3 mydata.dbf
```

If the file `mydata.dbf` exists, it will be opened. If not, it will be created and suitably initialized. If you are using SQLite Manager in Firefox, opening or creating a database similarly requires nothing more than providing a file name.

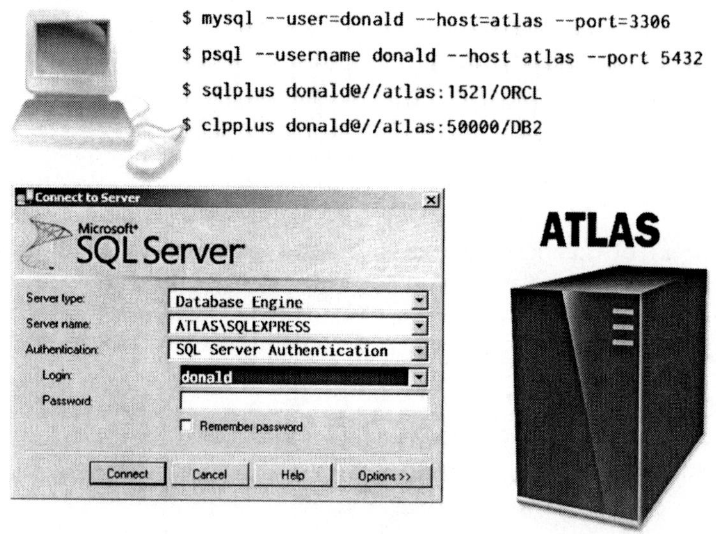

Figure 2.2: Connecting to different DBMS products

Successfully connected? Check Appendix A and be sure to have a clean work environment for your system. Then we can go on and create tables.

Creating Tables

If you are using a graphical interface, you'll have a "create table" option somewhere and you will be guided in table creation. Directly creating a table in SQL is easy, and you'll understand better what you are doing if you know how to perform the same task without the interface.

The command for creating a table is, logically enough, **create table** followed by the table name and followed by the specification of its columns in parentheses; **create** and **table** are called *SQL keywords*, words that have a special meaning in the language. SQL keywords can be typed in uppercase, lowercase or any combination, it doesn't matter. User-defined names in SQL obey a number of simple rules; what I'm saying here is valid for table names and column names, and any name that you can define in SQL (we'll see other database objects than tables later):

- The name length is limited. The actual limit varies with the product, 30 characters with Oracle, 64 with PostgreSQL, 128 with DB2 and SQL Server ...

- Names are not case-sensitive, which means that whether you type them in uppercase or lowercase you will always refer to the same table or column.
- Names must start with a letter and can only contain letters, digits, the underscore character, very often the dollar character, and sometimes the pound (also known as hash) character (#).

  When I say 'letter', let's quickly add that you are on a safer ground with unaccented letters from the standard Latin alphabet but most products will let you use for instance Chinese, Russian or Hindi characters to name a table – although without the suitable keyboard it may make the typing of queries challenging. Spaces are not allowed in names and names cannot be the same as an SQL keyword.

NOTE Some products also accept a name that starts with an underscore. MS Access has much looser restrictions than all other products; it allows spaces in names, for instance.

All preceding rules except the length limit can be violated if the name is placed in quotes, usually double quotes but once again some products may accept other types of quotes - or even square brackets with SQL Server. In most cases, a quoted name IS case-sensitive, can start with something other than a letter and can contain spaces. Quoted names are very rarely used.

NOTE Quoted names aren't necessarily case-sensitive with SQL Server.

A table name must of course be unique (within what is called a schema - more about schemas later in the book); in the same way you cannot have, which looks reasonable, two identically named columns inside a table.

Naming standards may vary from company to company but as names are not case-sensitive it's customary to use underscore characters in names to separate words; this is why in Chapter 1 I have called a table *directed_by* and not *DirectedBy*, which would have been an equally valid name. Once again, it's more a matter of custom than anything else.

Plural or Singular

There is some debate among people who design databases about whether table names should be in plural form (*movies*) or in singular form (*movie*). Proponents of plural see tables as collections of rows that each represents one particular item (or entity); supporters of singular see the definition of a table as a pattern that defines what one item looks like, very similar to what is called *class* in object-oriented programming (singular is very popular with people using object oriented languages). Interestingly, the sample databases provided by the major vendors use sometimes the singular convention, and sometimes the plural convention. I have used plural in this book, because it's plural that I have seen most often. One or the other isn't (or aren't) important; if you feel strongly about singular, use singular. What matters is consistency: if you have the choice, choose one standard, and stick to it. Otherwise, follow the rules in place.

Once the table is named, the minimum required to complete the table definition is, in parentheses, a comma-separated list of column names followed by their data types.

Data types are where SQL begins to get messy. Codd was insistent in his research papers on the idea of a *domain* that defines which values are valid for a column. Ensuring that only proper data ever makes it into the database was a priority for Codd. In their desire to have a language accessible to all, the designers of SQL considerably simplified the idea of domain to replace it with a data type taken from a small list of supported data types – text, number, date, binary ...; you can also find some product-specific data types, for geographical information, money or network addresses for instance. Some of these types are very strict about what they accept as valid data: if you try to enter an invalid date, for instance June 31st, into a date type, you will get an error but data types are a far cry from what Codd imagined.

Data Types

The names of data types vary widely from product to product. I am going to summarize what you can find – but for details about what one particular product supports, see the reference documentation for that product.

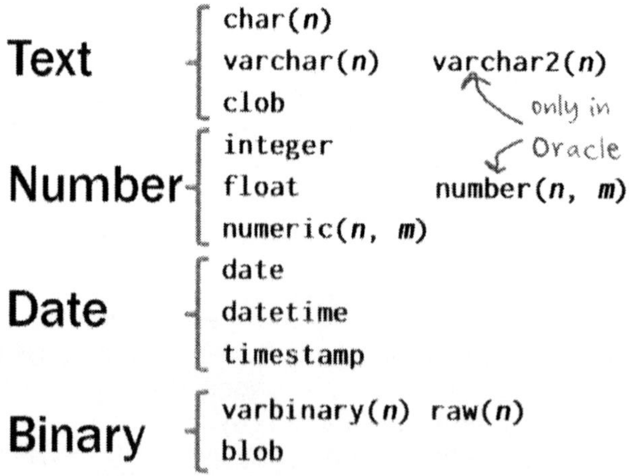

Figure 2.3: The jungle of data types (specific to Oracle on the right)

TEXT DATA TYPES

There are generally three categories of text data types:

- Fixed-length strings, which are defined by **char** followed by the length in parentheses, for instance **char(5)**; **char** alone is a short-cut for **char(1)**. Columns of type **char** are used for storing codes, for instance the two-letter code of a country or a state, or a zip code (even in countries where zip codes are composed entirely of digits, they have no numerical significance), or an extension number, or a one-letter status – whether for instance a bug reported by a customer has been analyzed, solved or rejected. Traditionally developers also often use a **char** column to store Y or N (or anything similar such as M/F for the gender) to indicate whether one object has or hasn't a predefined characteristic. Most products don't implement the **boolean** type available in PostgreSQL to store true/false values.

  Note that if you enter a four-digit code in a column defined as **char(5)** what will be actually stored in the table are the four digits followed by a space and if you try to enter something bigger than the predefined length, you will get an error.

- Variable-length strings, defined by **varchar** followed by parentheses enclosing the maximum allowed length, for instance **varchar(20)**.

  NOTE Oracle uses **varchar2** where everyone else is using **varchar**. The **varchar** data type is accepted by Oracle but not recommended because their implementation may in some cases not behave as you would expect when comparing values so if you get a creation script written for another DBMS, be careful. With some versions of Oracle, a **varchar** column will be automatically transformed into a **varchar2** but there is no commitment from Oracle that it will always be so.

  Unlike **char**, you must always specify a length for a **varchar**. With variable length strings, there is no padding with spaces; the database only stores what you have entered. You typically use this data type for names, addresses, descriptions, or codes that can vary in length. Like with the **char** data type, you get an error if you try to store something bigger than the maximum length.

  NOTE You may also encounter the **nvarchar** type. N stands for National; this is the data type used to store text written in a non-Latin character set.

- Very long strings, for which the standard data type is **clob**, an acronym for *Character Large OBject*.

  NOTE SQL Server uses **varchar(max)**, **text** is also common.

Those columns are used for storing news articles, blog entries and comments. Large chunks of text that aren't usually directly searched for specific content (although I'll elaborate more on this topic in a later chapter) but are more often associated to titles or tags that are stored in **varchar** columns and are the criteria used for retrieving the text information.

Numerical Data Types

There are also three broad categories of data types for numerical data.

- **integer**, often shortened to **int**, used for what you can count or what you consider as atomic – that cannot be split. For instance, data such as how many items you have in stock, grades on a 0 to 100 scale, sport match scores, or how many seconds people have spoken on the phone.

> NOTE There are variants (**tinyint**, **smallint**, **bigint**) depending on the order of magnitude of the numbers you want to store and mostly aimed at saving storage in very big databases. You can safely ignore variants while learning SQL.

- **float**, sometimes called **real** for, basically, numbers with a decimal part.

> NOTE There is also a **double** type which is to **float** what **bigint** is to **int**.

- **numeric**, sometimes called **decimal** , which is a special way to store numbers, with or without a decimal part.

  This data type ensures that you don't lose precision when you have a large number of digits and that you have no rounding errors when computing, which is important in financial applications. There is a slight performance penalty for scientific, computing-intensive processes with the **numeric** type, but this is hardly relevant to most database applications. Unless the DBMS supports a special **money** data type, **numeric** is a very good type for storing monetary amounts.

  The **numeric** type is usually followed by two numbers in parentheses, *precision* and *scale*. *Precision* specifies the maximum number of digits you will store and *scale* specifies how many decimal places you will have. Thus **numeric(8, 2)** allows you to store values between -999,999.99 and +999,999.99 (eight significant digits at most, two of them for the decimal part). If scale is zero or omitted - **numeric(8, 0)** or **numeric(8)** - you only store integer values.

  The maximum value for precision is very high, 31 for DB2, 38 for Oracle and SQL Server, 65 for MySQL, 1000 for PostgreSQL. If you specify neither precision nor scale, you can basically store any number, without any control on its order of magnitude.

As usual, Oracle does it differently. Although it "understands" most data types mentioned above, numerical columns are usually specified with the **number** data type (identical to **numeric**), with or without precision and scale; if you specify a column as **int** or **smallint** or **numeric** in Oracle, it will be automatically converted to **number** (without scale for integer values).

Date and Time Data Types

SQL also has special types for storing dates and times and they should be used because date validity is automatically checked. Don't do what one sees from time to time, storing dates and times in an **integer** column as the traditional UNIX number of seconds since January 1st, 1970. Moreover, all DBMS products implement a number of functions allowing us to display dates in a choice of different formats and to perform computations on dates – adding or subtracting days, computing the number of days between two dates and so on, which are very useful and very commonly used.

The most useful type is **datetime** that stores what it says (day, month, year, hours, minutes, seconds). It's simply called **date** in Oracle.

NOTE The SQL Server **datetime** also stores fractions of a second, down to a 0.003 second precision.

Most products other than Oracle also have a **date** type that stores no time and a **time** type that only stores a time. As the minimum precision of one second usually provided by the **datetime** type isn't always enough, there is also a **timestamp** type which is very similar but stores date and time with a much greater accuracy. DB2 has no **datetime**, only a **timestamp** type.

NOTE You can optionally specify the accuracy you need with a **timestamp**; thus, a **timestamp(0)** with DB2 has a precision of one second and is the exact equivalent of a **datetime** in other products.

NOTE The SQL Server equivalent of **timestamp** is called **datetime2**. This type is both more precise than **datetime** and has a greater range of values; the latter has no great practical interest unless you are a historian or a Sci-Fi author. Beware that the **timestamp** type that you may encounter in old versions of SQL Server (it's called **rowversion** in newer versions) isn't the same as with other DBMS products.

Some products (Oracle, PostgreSQL) implement the **interval** type that describes a time range. As a column data type, it's not very useful; it's more common to store a duration in seconds, minutes, hours or days in a numerical column. However, intervals often intervene in date arithmetic.

Binary Data Types

All products also have types for storing binary data such as multimedia data (images, sound, video). Just as with text, with many products you have one data type, equivalent to **varchar()**, for smaller binary data (**varbinary()** with MySQL, **raw()** with Oracle, **varchar() for bit data** with DB2) and one data type for large binary data, usually called **blob**; the **blob** acronym stands for *Binary Large OBject*, and is reserved for very large multimedia data, or big documents in formats that aren't pure text, such as PDF. SQL Server and PostgreSQL use a single type for binary data, called **varbinary()** in SQL Server and **bytea** in PostgreSQL. You won't see these data types in this book. Binary data is always handled by a special program.

Those four data type categories, text, numbers, dates, and binary data, are common to all products; some of them implement special data types to perform unusual controls, for managing geographical coordinates for instance.

Data types in SQLite

I need to single out one product: SQLite. In SQLite, you can give any name to a data type. You can say that a column is of type **integer**, **varchar(10)** or *bungabunga*, it makes no difference, you can store anything you want in it, and it can be longer than the specified length. Needless to say, SQLite is useless at protecting you against data entry errors, such as typing letter O instead of zero into an **int** column, and you'd better know exactly what you are doing when you are using SQLite. Comparing apples and oranges is something that SQLite will allow you to do, without any warning, and with the result you would expect.

There is however in SQLite a notion of *affinity*, which basically means that if you use a data type name commonly used with other products, SQLite will be able to guess if data is numerical or not, and store it accordingly. Dates in SQLite are another interesting case that is beyond the scope of this book. To summarize, with SQLite be consistent with your data type naming, and be very careful.

To create a table to store information about actors and directors, I can for instance create my table in the following way (I have aligned everything for legibility - use **varchar2** instead of **varchar** if you are using Oracle):

```
create table people (peopleid   int,
                     first_name varchar(30),
                     surname    varchar(30),
                     born       numeric(4),
                     died       numeric(4))
```

If you are using a graphical interface, you can click on the "Execute" or "Run" button. If you are using a command line interface, add a semi-colon and hit return (the semi-colon is what tells to your client program "I'm done with my SQL statement, send it to the server".)

NOTE In this book I'll omit the final semi-colons except when there are several distinct statements to execute in sequence.

I have defined the *born* and *died* columns as **numeric(4)** columns instead of **date** (or **datetime**) columns, simply because I am not interested by the precise date and just want to store the year as a four-digit number; with MySQL I could use a **year** data type that is non-standard.

The preceding statement is a valid SQL statement to create a table. It's also a very bad way to do it if you are serious about data management.

What is wrong? Many things.

Mandatory Columns

First of all, I must talk about something that Codd defined from the start and which has been hotly debated since – the representation of missing data. Codd specified that a relational system should have a particular way to represent the absence of a value. If you store in the table the name of a person who is alive, you cannot put a year in the *died* column; traditionally in IT people have used "special values" that have to be interpreted as "missing data" – for instance you could set *died* to 0 or -1 for someone who is alive but this wasn't satisfactory to Codd. There are some cases when what was thought to be a meaningless value becomes meaningful over time. Meaningful or meaningless depends on context: if we were storing information about historical characters, there was never any year 0 but we might one day store information about some king or queen, general or poet who died in year -1. Or you may store a one-letter status that comes from a system you don't control, use 'U' for undefined and be told one day that from now on 'U' will stand for 'Updated'.

Codd really wanted something different that in SQL is called **null** and means "no known value".

When you create a table, by default all columns must take a value of the specified type (with the exception of SQLite) or have no value. But you don't want to only have absent values. If you are storing something, you necessarily have data. Some columns must be mandatory, at least the columns that identify the row.

To specify that a column is mandatory, you follow the data type with **not null**. Deciding which columns are mandatory and which can be left unspecified is a question that you must ask yourself very early in the database design process.

In our table, *peopleid* is mandatory because it's what we will use to say that a person is credited in a movie. The surname is mandatory, we don't want to store anonymous actors or directors. The death year isn't, we don't want to record only dead people.

For the two remaining columns, it's more debatable. You might think that the first name is mandatory but remember that we will be storing actors, and some of them have a single stage name - Madonna played in some movies, Topol stars in *The Fiddler On The Roof.* You find many famous one-name actors in several countries, Italy (Toto), France (Arletty, Fernandel, Bourvil), India (Dharmendra, Kajol ...). A single stage name is even much more common among singers.

Therefore I won't make the first name mandatory and will state that when an actor is known under a single name, that single name will be considered as the surname.

When you take a decision such as this, it's essential to document it because it isn't uncommon that a stage name is actually a first name. Oracle, DB2 and PostgreSQL provide a **comment** statement that allows recording information about objects in the database; for instance:

```
comment on column people.surname is 'Surname or stage name'
```

You can also attach comments to tables with a statement

```
comment on table <tablename> is 'your comment'
```

All products also support comments inside SQL statements; those comments usually start with a double-dash and end at the end of the line.

The main difference between the two types of comments is that the first type of comment documents data definitions and is stored in the database, while a comment that starts with a double-dash merely documents an SQL command and is ignored when the command is run.

NOTE If you add comments to a **create table** statement, SQLite will save them with the full statement to a table called *sqlite_master.*

What about the birth year? Everybody has a birth year. Some people have been known to cheat with it but that's a different matter. However, if we make the information mandatory we won't be able to enter anyone in the database, even if we know that this person played in a movie or directed it, if we don't know their birth year.

Deciding whether the birth year information has to be mandatory or not isn't easy; it's a point that is debatable. I decided to make the birth year mandatory: I have very little biographical information in my database, I want people who enter data to do their homework and search the information before populating the database but an opposite decision could make sense as well. You'll often have to take this type of decision and it's harder to make when you know that the information exists, you know that we should have it but perhaps that it won't be available at the time of data entry.

I am going to drop and re-create my table (existing tables can also be modified):

```
drop table people;
create table people (peopleid   int not null,
                     first_name varchar(30),
                     surname    varchar(30) not null,
                     born       numeric(4) not null,
                     died       numeric(4));
```

It's slightly better but we are far from done. I told you in Chapter 1 that each row must be uniquely identified; we have here both the *peopleid* column and the (*first_name, surname)* pair that can be used to distinguish one row from another. But if you create the table as I have shown, the DBMS will not prevent you from inserting exactly the same data twice.

Constraints

In relational database theory, a dataset contains no duplicates by definition because each row in the dataset represents a "fact". A fact cannot be duplicated. If you insert into a table of movie stars information about the same actor twice, it will not create a new actor who is a clone of the existing one - you will have more data but exactly the same information in your database. The additional row will just pollute the database and give weird, and probably wrong, results in the programs that try to make sense of the data. Nevertheless, if you don't take care when designing your database, SQL will allow it.

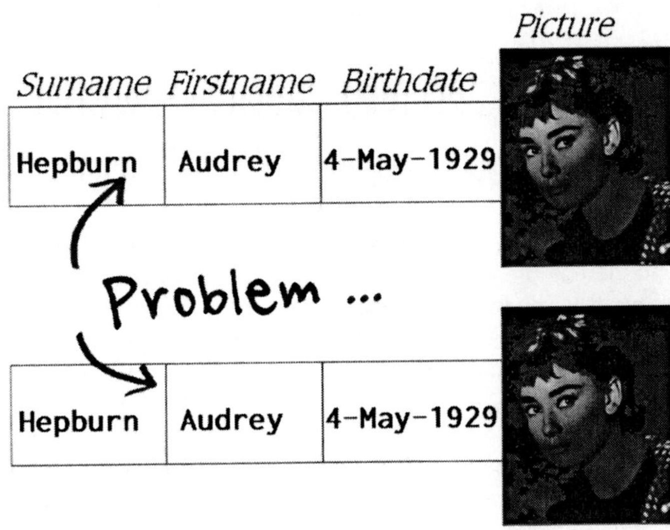

Figure 2.4: No duplicates (even of Audrey Hepburn)

While Don Chamberlin and his team were busy working on SQL, Ted Codd had been joined by another IBMer, Chris Date (like Codd, British-born) who played the role of an evangelist while working with him on the theory. Although SQL knew nothing of domains, Date pushed really hard to introduce *constraints* in SQL. Constraints are declarations that, as the name implies, constrain the data to a range of acceptable values much narrower than what the data type alone allows.

Constraints can be applied to a single column or to several columns – let me add sample constraints to table *people* to illustrate them.

```
drop table people;
create table people (peopleid   int not null primary key,     ① Specify the identifier
                     first_name varchar(30)
                         check (first_name = upper(first_name)),    ② Check case
                     surname    varchar(30) not null
                         check (surname = upper(surname)),        ③ Check case
                     born       numeric(4) not null
                                check (born >= 1850),             ④ Check years
                     died       numeric(4) check (died >= 1895),  ⑤ make sense
                       unique (first_name, surname));    ⑥ No duplicates
```

The constraint on *peopleid*① just says that it is the primary key, and enforces, first that *peopleid* is mandatory (it makes the **not null** redundant but keeping **not null** doesn't hurt), and second that we cannot have the same identifier in two different rows. The two **check** constraints ② and ③ on *first_name* and *surname* are easy to understand: **upper()** is an SQL function that converts to uppercase. The constraints ensure that I only store uppercase names.

NOTE Oracle, PostgreSQL and DB2 care about the case of text data. By default, SQL Server, MySQL and SQLite don't and the **check** constraint on the case will always return *true*.

I have derived the constraints on *born* and *died*④ and ⑤ from the history of cinematography – the very first film was shot by the Lumière brothers in 1895, and anybody who died before this date is unlikely to be credited, at least as director or actor (it's different for composers). Finally, the *unique* constraint ⑥ enforces that I cannot have the same first name and surname in two different rows; the combination (*first_name, surname*) must be unique, even if several people have John for first name or Hepburn, Douglas, Barrymore, Fonda, Redgrave or Khan for the surname.

When you run the **create** statement, with some products (PostgreSQL in particular) you may get notices about implicitly created indexes. Indexes are special structures that you will see at length later in this book and which are used for efficiently enforcing constraints.

Constraints such as a primary key and uniqueness are enforced by all DBMS products. For **check** constraints, it's a mixed bag. Some products will let you specify them but won't enforce them.

NOTE DB2 doesn't allow you to create a unique constraint on columns that aren't all mandatory because it won't control uniqueness if all values aren't defined (which arguably makes some sense). With DB2, you can make the first name mandatory and simply store an empty string ('') when people only have a stage name. Empty strings are considered the same as null with Oracle, not with other products.

NOTE MySQL up to and including version 5 doesn't enforce **check** constraints. However, MySQL implements some non-standard data types, such as the **enum** data type that allows us to control that a column can only take a limited number of values, which you would do with a **check** constraint with other products.

It's also possible with a **check** constraint to enforce that *died* is later than *born*, although constraints between attributes should be exceptional. Remember Bill Kent's rules – non key attributes are supposed only to qualify the key and not to be related to each other.

If **check** constraints are a "nice to have" feature, there is another type of constraint that is in practice much more interesting: *referential integrity* constraints. When you declare referential integrity constraints, you can ensure that the values contained in a column belong to a large set of values, stored in another table, that has been acknowledged as valid – for instance that a country or zip code actually belongs to a set of valid codes.

I am going to illustrate referential integrity, not with the *people* table, but with the *movies* table, which I can create in the following way:

```
create table movies (movieid       int not null primary key,
                     title         varchar(60) not null,
                     country       char(2) not null,
                     year_released numeric(4) not null
                                   check(year_released >= 1895),
                     unique (title, country, year_released))
```

I have made all columns mandatory (once again, a design choice) and the constraints I have defined are very similar to what I have defined for the *people* table. I haven't enforced the title to be in uppercase; searching for a several-word title is different from searching for a name, having the title in uppercase could help but less than with names, and I'll discuss advanced search techniques in Chapter 6.

I haven't enforced any case (lower or upper) for the country code either but for a different reason. Enforcing the case would be good but it would in no way guarantee that the code is a valid one. You could type in a country code SF in the required case and insert the data, when there is no country that is identified by the SF code. What we are going to do is to create what is called a *reference table* for countries, in which we are going to store all countries (or at least those for which we have films), their code, their name, and other relevant information such as the continent they belong to.

NOTE You may think of a continent problem with the Russian Federation. Modeling isn't easy.

The name is important information, because while you can easily identify the codes of some countries, you may be hesitating about many others and an American might think more readily of California when seeing CA than of Canada.

NOTE Canadian reader, be honest. Does Slovakia spring to mind when you see SK, or Peru when you see PE or the Netherlands when you see NL?

So, let's create a *countries* table:

```
create table countries(country_code  char(2) not null primary key,
                       country_name  varchar(50) not null,
                       continent     varchar(20),
                       unique(country_name))
```

As reference tables are filled once and for all by data administrators and then very rarely modified, you can have fewer constraints than when a table can be updated by many people.

Now that I have table *countries*, I can add a foreign key constraint to table *movies*:

```
create table movies (movieid        int not null primary key,
                     title          varchar(60) not null,
                     country        char(2) not null,
                     year_released  numeric(4) not null
                                    check(year_released >= 1895),
                     unique (title, country, year_released),
                     foreign key(country)
                        references countries(country_code))
```

The foreign key constraint says that when I store a value in column *country*, then it must match the value in column *country_code* of an existing row in table *countries*. We could have a foreign key constraint on several columns, in which case the parentheses after **foreign key** would enclose a comma-separated list of column names, and I should have exactly the same number of columns in a comma-separated list following the name of the referenced table. This would enforce that I must find a matching pair (or triplet, or ... depending on the number of columns involved.)

Several interesting points to note:

- The column that is referenced in a foreign key constraint (here column *country_code* of table *countries*) must necessarily be either the primary key of the referenced table or a column stated as unique by a constraint.
- A column on which you define a foreign key doesn't need to be mandatory. If there is nothing in it (null), it doesn't violate referential integrity. A referenced column that isn't a primary key but is only involved in a unique constraint can also contain a null, except with DB2; nulls are just "out of the game".

> NOTE As already mentioned, DB2 requires unique columns to be not null, in the sample database column *first_name* is mandatory with DB2 and when a person only has a single stage name an empty string ('') is stored in lieu of the first name.

- A foreign key constraint is necessarily between two tables, not more. However, distinct columns in one table can reference different tables. That would be the case with the *credits* table that says which person was involved in which movie. Inserting an identifier of a person we cannot find in the *people* table would make no sense, therefore we must define a foreign key constraint that only accepts identifiers of known people; ditto for the movie identifier and table *movies*.

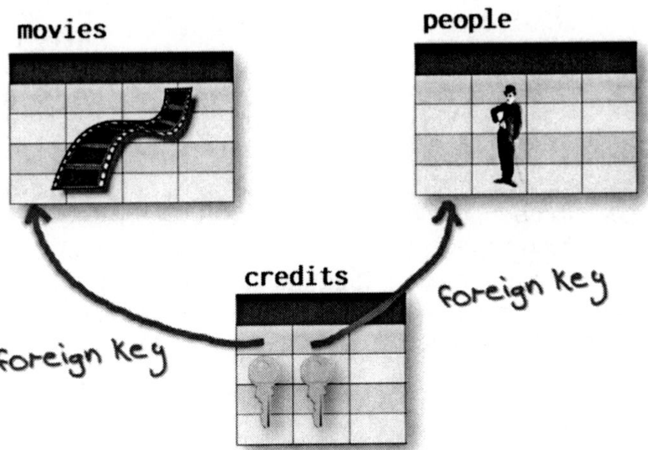

Figure 2.5: Foreign keys that are part of the primary key.

- Within one table, primary key and foreign key are unrelated notions. In the *credits* table again, the movie identifier and the person identifier are both part of the primary key, and are both foreign keys, as shown in figure 2.5. In some cases you can have a single column primary key that is also a foreign key.

- A foreign key constraint can sometimes reference another column from the same table.

As you can see, creating tables isn't simply a matter of defining a structure in a database; you must also define constraints that ensure the quality of data. This is a very important point because if we can be sure that data that is stored is correct and remains correct, it follows that there are many checks that no longer need to be coded into programs.

> NOTE For convenience it is common to check that manually-entered data at least looks right before being sent over to the DBMS. Most web forms usually perform a number of checks locally in javascript but a user can decide to disable javascript in the browser, and you should not rely on receiving valid data.

Programs become leaner, have fewer bugs and are easier to maintain. Properly modeling data and defining constraints may seem boring to developers who are eager to code but it's like preparing a wall surface before painting - if you don't do it well, cracks will appear much sooner than you would have expected. Because constraints are so important, I'll mention them over and over in this book - especially when we look at how to modify data.

A Quick Reminder About Keys

Keys are the columns that identify rows in a table. One row may contain several keys; for instance a course can be identified by its name and the department, or by a code; an actor can be identified by first name and surname, or by a numerical identifier *peopleid*. The different keys are sometimes called *candidate keys*, to express that all of them are equally valid candidates to identify one row. You choose arbitrarily one out of all candidate keys and define it as the *primary key*.. It's common practice, when the key is composed of several columns and when other tables need to refer to the rows, to add a numerical identifier that will be used as primary key; those artificial identifiers are called *surrogate keys*. Unique constraints should be created on all other candidate keys.

Foreign keys are not in a table keys in the same sense as primary or candidate keys: they are columns that can only take the values of keys (primary or candidate) in other tables and ensure data consistency between tables. It can happen that a foreign key is also a part of the primary key (as in table *credits*) or even is the full primary key but it's fortuitous.

Now that you know how to create tables, you can insert some data into them; this is a topic that we shall discuss in greater depth later in this book but let's see quickly how it can be done.

Inserting Data

As you have seen, the great idea of Codd was that you can operate on data sets in the same sense as you can operate on numbers. The **insert** command of SQL can be compared to addition: it allows you to add a dataset to an existing dataset.

When you have foreign key constraints, you must first populate the reference tables (sometimes, to initialize a database with data that is known to be clean, tables are first populated in any order without constraints, and constraints are defined afterwards). Let's start by inserting a few rows in table *countries*. A table that has just been created is empty; we have therefore an empty dataset, something we can compare to 0.

To add a one-row dataset to the existing dataset, we must pass to the database management system the following SQL command

```
insert into table_name (list of columns)
values (list of values)
```

We need not list the columns in the same order that we created them; remember that in the relational theory the order of the attributes is irrelevant, what matters is that they are related. However, the values that are provided must of course match, one for one, the columns in which we want them to be inserted.

Strings must always, in SQL, be specified between single quotes. If you want to insert a row into the table you have just created, you can for instance execute:

```
insert into countries(country_code, country_name, continent)
values('us', 'United States', 'AMERICA')
```

If you are using SQL Server (version 2008 and above), PostgreSQL, MySQL or DB2, you can insert several rows at once:

```
insert into countries(country_code, country_name, continent)
values('us', 'United States', 'AMERICA'),
      ('in', 'India', 'ASIA'),
      ('gb', 'United Kingdom', 'EUROPE'),
      ('it', 'Italy', 'EUROPE')
```

One thing that is important to remember is that while table and column names are not, usually, case-sensitive, anything that is stored inside a table is case sensitive with several products (Oracle, DB2 and PostgreSQL in particular). For these products, 'italy' in lowercase isn't the same as 'ITALY' in uppercase or 'Italy' with an initial capital. If you say that the *country_name* column must only contain distinct values, storing uppercase 'ITALY' after having stored 'Italy' will not violate the constraint and will not generate any errors. It is therefore important to store strings in a way that is consistent and very often programs sanitize user-input by converting it to a consistent case before storing it into a database. It's a good practice to follow even with a DBMS such as SQL Server or MySQL that isn't fussy about case.

Once you have a few countries you can start to insert rows in table *movies*, and see what happens when you violate constraints.

```
insert into countries(country_code,
country_name, continent)
values('us', 'United States', 'AMERICA')
```

```
select * from countries
```

Figure 2.6: Inserting data and checking the result.

You can check the contents of table countries by running

```
select * from countries
```

The next chapters will be devoted to more sophisticated queries.

On a practical note, if a string you want to store contains a quote, then you must double it. If you want to enter a classic 1960 Italian movie by Michelangelo Antonioni, *L'Avventura*, you have to type something such as

```
insert into movies(movieid, title, country, year_released)
values (123, 'L''Avventura', 'it', 1960)
```

The *movieid* value must of course be a value not yet present in the table. Note the doubled single quote in the title - only one will be stored in the table.

Each new row you insert changes the dataset that is stored in the table - the table is like a variable and the dataset it contains at one point in time is the value of this variable at this particular point in time.

Local settings may impact the way you enter numbers (particularly when there are decimals, some countries separate decimals with a comma rather than a dot) and dates. There are basically two ways to enter a date:

- As a string, in which case you should always specify the format you are using if several formats are acceptable (never rely on a "default format" that can be changed). For instance, use function **to_date()** with Oracle or DB2.
- As a result of a function, most commonly the one that returns the current date. This function has different names in different SQL dialects, and you shouldn't be surprised to meet variations. Oracle uses **sysdate**, MySQL **curdate()**, SQL Server uses **getdate()**, SQLite **date('now')** and so on. You must also be aware that most of these functions return what is usually called a

datetime - that is, they insert at any given moment, the current date and the current time, which is of course a different value from the current date and time five minutes ago but we shall talk about this again later.

As you have probably noticed, typing **insert** statements is rather tedious.

In practice, there are utilities or commands for bulk-loading data from external sources, for instance, data from a spreadsheet saved in the CSV format; I'll show you these types of commands in Chapter 7. More often than not, **insert** statements are run by a program. For instance, the data you enter into a web-form is sent over to a program that passes it to an **insert** statement.

Now that you have seen how tables are created and can be populated with data, we are going to discover the real power of SQL and of the **select** statement.

To Remember

- SQL is THE language for accessing databases; there are several dialects, with slight differences. It allows management of tables and data.
- Connecting to a database requires the name of the server, a port number, the name of a database and most often a username and a password for authentication.
- When you create a table, you must not only specify the data types of columns and whether they are mandatory but you must also specify constraints: at least a primary key.
- SQL keywords and identifiers of tables and columns are not case-sensitive but data that is stored can be case-sensitive and quotes must be doubled when inside a string.

Exercises

1. To enhance the database, it has been decided to add, as a one letter code, an indication about the genre of the movie - Drama, Comedy, Musical, Thriller, Action, ... with a reference table called *movie_genres* storing the acceptable codes and their meanings.
    a. Write the create statements for *movie_genres* and the modified *movies* table.
    b. Write two or three **insert** statements to add genres into *movie_genres*.
2. We want to design the tables for a forum. We have a table of members that stores a member id, a password, a screen name and a registration date. There must be one table that defines various broad categories (for instance, Database Topics, HTML, Javascript ...), a table of questions that will specify the forum to which the question relates, which member posted the question, when it was posted, the actual text of the question, and an indicator which shows whether the original poster considers the question answered or not. Finally, there is a table of answers,

with a reference to the question that is answered, who (which member) answered it, when the answer was posted, the text of the answer, and an indicator (which may be set by the original poster of the question) which shows whether this answer helped the original poster. Write the create statements for these four tables, if you need to make assumptions for data types justify them, identify primary keys, unique columns and foreign keys (ignore check constraints - all columns are mandatory).

Retrieving Data From One Table 3

If there's a row of any kind,
I find it easy to find.

- Otto Harbach (1873-1963) and Oscar Hammerstein II (1895-1960)

This chapter covers

- How to install the sample database
- How to return only some rows or columns from a table
- How to transform data before displaying it
- How to compute new results by aggregating rows

Now that you have seen how tables are created and can be populated with data, we are going to discover the real power of SQL and of the **select** statement. I suggest you download the script to create the sample movie database, available from `http://edu.konagora.com` with the resources associated with this book. Scripts are available for Oracle, SQL Server, MySQL, PostgreSQL, DB2 and SQLite, and are available for several character sets, *utf8*, *latin1*, and *ascii*. Character sets (or *charsets*) define how characters are coded on the computer. The sample data contains some accented letters and if the character set that was defined for the database doesn't match the character set of the script, accented characters won't appear as intended. On Linux and with MySQL, PostgreSQL and SQLite, *utf8* should display everything properly. With other products and in Windows environments, *latin1* should hopefully be properly understood with default settings; if all else fails, use the *ascii* charset file in which accented letters are replaced by their unaccented equivalent (scripts drop and recreate what has been created by each other). Scripts are named *moviedb_<dbms>_<charset>.sql* and zipped for download into one zip file for each DBMS.

Installing the Sample Database

To install the sample database you need, after having unzipped the downloaded file, to run the script that corresponds with your DBMS. However, this script will drop (and recreate) any table named *movies*, *countries*, *people* or *credits*. If you have already created tables with one of these names, I suggest that you rename them first before running the script - you may have use for these tables in a later chapter.

Renaming an Existing Table

I told you in Chapter 2 that three commands, **create**, **alter**, and **drop**, were used to manage tables. Unless you are using SQL Server, you can rename a table with **alter**, and the following syntax:

```
alter table old_name
rename to new_name
```

where, as you have probably guessed, *old_name* is the name you want to change (for instance *movies*) and *new_name* the name you want to give (for instance *my_movies*).

With SQL Server you must invoke a special command (a system procedure) to rename a table:

```
sp_rename old_name, new_name
```

Don't forget the comma.

Running a Script to Initialize a Database

You are now ready to run the installation script for your database. I'll talk much later about rights in a database but the account that you are using must be allowed to create tables and functions or procedures (see Appendix A).

If you are using a graphical interface, it will usually be enough to open the file through the usual File/Open menu navigation (alternatively, you may find, especially on a web interface, a choice called *Import*) and then click on the Execute button that you should find somewhere on the main menu.

Running a Script with a Command-Line Tool

If you are (like me) a command-line aficionado, the actual command to type depends on the product. First, unless you enjoy typing a full 60-character access path when you refer to a file, navigate to the directory where you have unzipped the .sql file, it will make your life easier.

Character Sets with Oracle

Even before connecting to the database, you must tell the DBMS what character encoding is used on your side so that it can convert to what is used inside the database. This is done by assigning a special value to what is called an *environment variable*. The name of this environment variable is NLS_LANG. It can be found in the registry on Windows and you set it at the shell prompt on a UNIX/Linux system. It is composed of three parts, a language name (for error messages) followed by an underscore and something known as *territory* (usually a country name), which mostly defines calendar characteristics (default date format, how weeks are numbered, and so on). Finally there is a dot and the character set, which sometimes has an Oracle-specific name (*latin1* is named WE8ISO8859P1 in Oracle). Just for creating the sample database, you can set language and territory to whatever you want. For instance, if you want to run the *utf8* script you can under Linux first type

```
export NLS_LANG=american_america.UTF8
```

Connect to the database as you must have done in the previous chapter. In what follows I replace the character set name by *xxxx* in the file names.
To run the script with Oracle you just need to type the following command at the prompt:

```
start moviedb_oracle_xxxx
```

or

```
@moviedb_oracle_xxxx
```

You don't need to type *moviedb_oracle_xxxx.sql*, SQL*Plus assumes by default that the file extension is .sql

The command is the same with DB2 and `clpplus` – except of course for the name of the file, which will be `moviedb_db2_xxxx.sql`.

With PostgreSQL's `psql`, the proper command is

```
\i moviedb_postgres_xxxx.sql
```

It's very similar with `mysql`:

```
\. moviedb_mysql_xxxx.sql
```

Here, the full script name is required, as it is with `sqlite3`, in which you must type

```
.read moviedb_sqlite_xxxx.sql
```

With SQL Server there is also a command line tool called *sqlcmd* that you can use in a DOS window as follows, assuming that the file is in the current directory:

```
sqlcmd  S <server name>  d moviedb  i moviedb_sqlserver_xxxx.sql
```

Alternatively, you can open `moviedb_sqlserver_xxxx.sql` in SQL Server Management Studio and execute the script.

Once you have loaded the sample data, you are ready to learn how to query the database.

Seeing What a Table Contains

The **select** command is used to return information; the rows returned by a **select** statement are known as the *result set* (unrelated to character sets...). At the end of the previous chapter, you saw that if you want to retrieve all the data that has been inserted into a table, the syntax is quite simple:

```
select * from <tablename>
```

For instance:

```
select * from movies
```

The * is a wildcard character that stands for "all columns". It's very convenient with an interactive tool because it doesn't require any prior knowledge of the table structure - you discover what the columns are when they are returned. However, using * is a practice that is strongly discouraged in programs because programs fetch data values into variables; you must know how many variables you need and whether they are string or number variables. As you'll see later in this book it is possible to alter tables so as to add columns, which may break a program that recklessly asks for "all columns". In a program, you should name the columns and separate the names with commas, as follows:

```
select movie_id, title, year_released, country
from movies
```

Once again, the order in which we list columns is irrelevant: whatever the order, it's the same information. `select *` returns the columns in the order they were created.

Now, remember what you have seen, which is that Codd's insight was to say that you can consider data sets like weird values, values to which you can apply operations that give you other derived data sets. In this view

```
select * from
```

is the same as displaying the contents of a variable or an array. The dataset you get is strictly identical to the dataset that the table currently holds. Convenient for seeing what the database contains but otherwise not madly interesting - especially when the table contains hundreds of thousands or even millions of rows.

Restricting the Result Set

The first operation that we can apply to a dataset is filtering the rows to obtain a result that is a subset of the original table. This is done by adding to the previous simple **select** statement, a clause that starts with **where** and lists a number of conditions that we want satisfied by the resulting dataset.

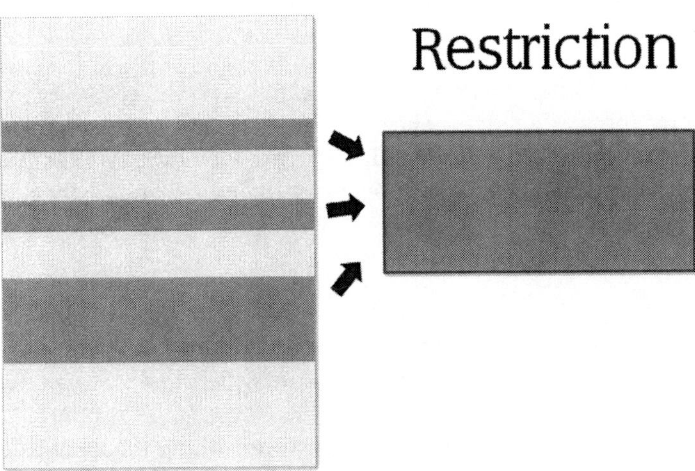

Figure 3.1: Restricting the result set

Simple Screening

Suppose you only want to list American movies. You simply have to type

```
select * from movies
where country = 'us'
```

Simple conditions are usually expressed as a column name (here *country*) followed by a comparison operator (here equal) followed by a constant (here 'us') – or the name of another column, in which case it means that we want check the value in one column against the value in the other column for the same row (something that will make more sense to you later in this book).

A common beginner's mistake is to confuse column names and values. Remember that dates and string values are always between single quotes (and don't forget that if they contain quotes, the inner quotes must be doubled). Column names are either, most commonly, unquoted or less commonly, between double quotes or square brackets with SQL Server.

NOTE Column names may also sometimes be between inverted quotes or square brackets, depending on the product.

If I write

```
select * from movies
where title = 'Title'
```

I am comparing (left hand side) the contents of the column named *title* to (right hand side) the value 'Title' to see if there is a movie thus named. If I write

```
where title = Title
```

I am checking if the contents of column *title* is equal to the contents of column *Title*, which is exactly the same since column names are not case-sensitive – title, Title, TITLE and TiTle all refer to the same column. There is always a title, it's always equal to itself, and the condition is always true and satisfied by ALL movies, whatever their title is.
If I write

```
where title = Jaws
```

then the SQL engine will think that the unquoted *Jaws* is a column name, try to compare the contents of column *title* to the contents of column *jaws*, which doesn't exist, and the query will fail and return an error.

Remember what I said previously, what is stored in the database is case-sensitive with many products. It is important that data is stored in a consistent manner. In the sample database, all proper nouns and movie titles are capitalized; everything else is in lower case.

At this point I'd like to show you something that you may find a bit stretched (it is stretched) but which will be of the utmost importance when we deal with more sophisticated queries. The dataset that results from the "list American movies" query really looks like the contents of a table. There are no duplicate rows and each row represents related information about one American movie. It could as well be the result of a query that would be a simple **select**, without any **where** clause, applied to a table that only contains American movies. This allows me to give you the first glimpse of the power of the relational model: you can chain queries and apply new operations, such as restrictions to the dataset obtained from a previous query. For instance, if you want to list all the American movies from the 1940s, you can use the query that returns American movies:

```
select * from movies
where country = 'us'
```

and use it in the **from** clause of another query as if it were a table, assigning the name *us_movies* to it (the name is usually called an *alias*):

```
select *
from (select * from movies
      where country = 'us') us_movies
where year_released between 1940 and 1949
```

NOTE Several products refer to a query used as if it were a table as a *derived table*. Oracle refers to an *inline view*, by reference to a database object that we shall see in a later chapter). It can also be referred to as a *nested query* or a *subquery in the **from** clause*.

To this virtual table that only contains American movies we apply a new restriction, using an SQL operator called **between** that, you have probably guessed it, includes the boundaries. It's really like if data were on an assembly line, with more refined filtering at each stage.

Now, an interesting fact is that we could have obtained exactly the same final result set (the set of rows returned by the SQL query) by first identifying the movies from the 1940s, and by then applying to our result set a condition that would have restricted the final result to American movies:

```
select *
from (select * from movies
     where year_released between 1940 and 1949) movies_from_the_1940s
where country = 'us'
```

You are probably beginning to understand what I said about Codd's insight that we could operate on datasets in the same way that we could operate on numbers, because comparing both ways of proceeding is very similar to comparing 2 + 3 to 3 + 2.

In practice, you will never chain operations on so simple a query. If you were to identify American movies from the 1940s in a big pile of DVDs, you would not first constitute a smaller pile of American movies for further scanning. If you were to select DVDs, you would check both conditions at once. Instead of nesting queries in embedded **from** clauses like I did, you can instead, chain conditions in the **where** clause with **and**, thus:

```
select * from movies
where country = 'us'
  and year_released between 1940 and 1949
```

It's shorter and easier to write.

NOTE In practice, whether you write the query as nested queries or by linking conditions makes no difference because all DBMS products include a software component called the *optimizer* that decides how best to return data.

You can also combine conditions with **or**, and negate them using **not**. If you are already familiar with programming, you are also probably already familiar with the combination of logical conditions (known as *Boolean algebra* after the 19th century English mathematician George Boole) and its numerous traps. If not, a couple of examples will give you an idea.

A first trap is that **or** linking two conditions in a **where** clause means that you want to see returned the rows that satisfy the first condition AND the rows that satisfy the second condition. If you want to display the American movies AND the British movies, you are going to write

```
select * from movies
where country = 'us'
   or country = 'gb'
```

It makes sense when you think about it but it's not immediately intuitive.

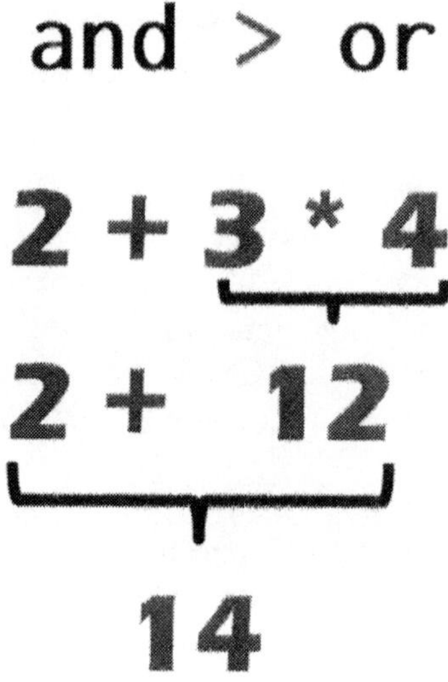

Figure 3.2: Comparing logical operator priority to arithmetic operator priority

A second trap is that **and** has a higher priority than **or** - actually, it works like multiplication compared to addition. If you see

2 + 3 * 4

You know that you must compute the multiplication first, because it has a higher priority, and then add 2 to the result to obtain 14.

If you write the following condition:

```
where country = 'us'
   or country = 'gb'
  and year_released between 1940 and 1949
```

you will get all the British movies from the 1940s, plus all the American movies irrespective of the year when they were released, because the stronger bond of **and** will be evaluated first. It may be what you wanted; if, however, you wanted to have a list of movies from the 1940s, either American or British, you should do what you would do with numerical expressions and use parentheses, thus:

```
where (country = 'us'
       or country = 'gb')
  and year_released between 1940 and 1949
```

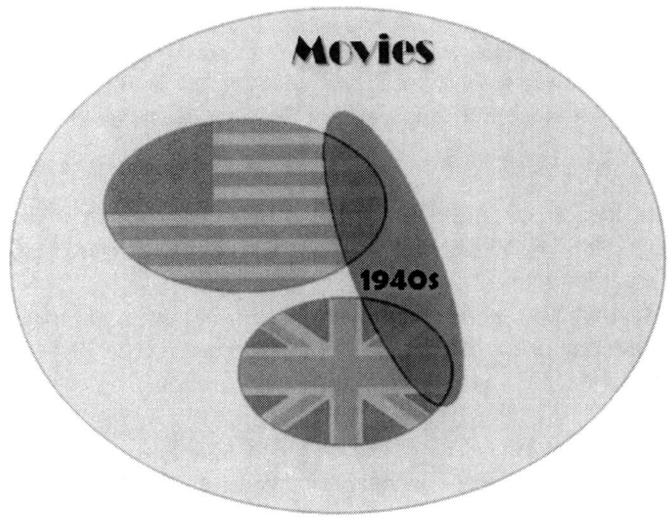

Figure 3.3: British and American movies of the 1940s.

Don't be afraid to experiment with **and**, **or** and **not**. Boolean expressions are the first stumbling block on the road to SQL mastery.

More Complex Conditions

SQL implements the comparison operators that you are familiar with:
Equal, different (expressed as **!=** or **<>**), and inequality operators, lesser than (**<**), greater than (**>**), lesser than or equal to (**<=**), greater than or equal to (**>=**).

Inequality

You shouldn't forget that inequality operators rely on ordering, and that ordering depends on the type of data being compared – alphabetical, numerical or chronological.

For example, the string '2' isn't smaller than the string '10', but bigger, because text data between quotes is ordered alphabetically; as character '2' comes after character '1', '2' comes after '10'. Comparing '2' with '10' works the same as comparing 'C' with 'BA'.

Following the same logic, the string '2-JUN-1883' is greater than '1-DEC-2056'. Date comparison is a frequent source of errors, because if you compare a date column to a string that for you represents a date, the DBMS products usually carry out implicit type conversions using a default date format - you can imagine the result if the DBMS implicitly uses the European date format (DD/MM/YYYY) when you are using the American one (MM/DD/YYYY) or the reverse.

NOTE I have met, in the tables of a big bank, a few transactions apparently recorded under the reign of Emperor Augustus (27 BC - 14 AD). The kind of thing that happens when constraints are loose and people enter a two digit year when the system expects a four digit year.

The default date format of DBMS products is unambiguous (it's usually something such as DD-MON-YYYY or YYYY-MM-DD) but a database administrator may change it to suit local customs better.

If we suppose that you have a date, say '18951228', as year, month and day (of course you can use any usual format, this one is known as the ISO format), to turn it into a real date for the DBMS, you use a *conversion function*.

NOTE ISO is the International Organization for Standardization and works, among other things, on definitions that everybody can agree on. You can also thank ISO for its work on SQL.

Conversion functions transform a character string into a date by specifying the pattern and you should always use them:

- With Oracle, DB2 and PostgreSQL `to_date('18951228', 'YYYYMMDD')`
- SQL Server can convert this format implicitly but it's better to use an explicit conversion with `convert(date, '18951228', 112)`

  NOTE SQL Server uses a number of numerical codes that describe date formats - 112 corresponds to the one I have used, 101 is the US format, 102 the format used in Britain and France, and so on.

- With MySQL `str_to_date('18951228', '%Y%m%d')`

I have already mentioned SQLite's cavalier handling of data types. SQLite will only understand that the string is a date if it is entered as YYYY-MM-DD (another standard international format), such as '1895-12-28'.

Dates in conditions are particularly tricky, even with equality. Very often, when rows are inserted into a table, the current date is recorded within the row; this is frequent in commercial operations and is the modern equivalent of the date rubber stamp. Suppose that you want a list of all the invoices that were issued exactly one week ago, and that you have a date column called *issued*. The natural way to write the query is to check the calendar, and type a query with a condition

```
where issued = <some date>
```

Frequently, such a query will return nothing, even if a large number of invoices were issued that particular day. Why? In many cases, when you associate a date with an event that you record in a database, you store not only the date but also the time down to the second. Sometimes programmers are careful either to use a **date** type without any time component or to remove the time part and only store the date part. When they don't, or when you also need the time, you'll have equality only when the constant you provide matches the exact moment when an invoice was issued, down to the second (or fraction of a second with a more precise date type). If your constant only mentions day, month and year, it's the same as saying day, month, year, and 0 hours 0 minutes 0 seconds, usually a time when there is no activity at all.

The error may be subtler because if you want all the invoices that were issued last week and say

```
where issued >= <Monday's date>
  and issued <= <Friday's date>
```

it will actually mean

```
where issued >= <Monday's date at 00:00:00>
  and issued <= <Friday's date at 00:00:00>
```

The first condition is fine, but the second condition isn't because you'll miss all of Friday's invoices. It may be harder to spot than returning no rows at all, especially if you are generating the report in a hurry to rush it to the boss.

Generally speaking, whenever you are interested by events that have occurred during a period of time, you should be careful to express this period as a *range* and be even more careful about the bounds. For instance, if you want records for which the values of a date column all fall within one given day, you should say that those values are between that date at 00:00:00 and 23:59:59 inclusive if the date includes a time element or, even better, greater than or equal to that date at 00:00:00 and strictly less than the next day at 00:00:00 (which frees you from considering what is the smaller unit of time that can be recorded).

NOTE I'll talk in more detail about how the various DBMS products store date and time information later in this chapter.

Special Operators

Even if you are familiar with programming, SQL implements a number of operators that you don't usually find in a programming language.

You have already met one:

```
year_released between 1940 and 1949
```

is a short-hand for

```
    year_released >= 1940
and year_released <= 1949
```

Note that both bounds are included, and that the first value that is provided has to be smaller than the second one if you want to see any data returned.

Another very useful short-hand notation is the clause: **in** followed by parentheses, which replaces a series of **or** conditions – thus

```
where (country = 'us'
       or country = 'gb')
  and year_released between 1940 and 1949
```

can also be written

```
where country in ('us', 'gb')
  and year_released between 1940 and 1949
```

You just give a comma-separated list of values that you want (as you shall see later, there are some even more interesting possibilities with **in**).

The advantage of an **in** list compared with a list of conditions connected by **or** is that it makes clear, without any further condition grouping, that the query will return American and British movies, and that they were released in the 1940s irrespectively of the country – assuming of course that this is what you want!

You can also use **not in**, for instance `country not in ('us', 'gb')` to signify that you want all the movies excluding those of American or British origin. Once again, don't hesitate to run a few tests.

There are some other operators that are unique to SQL. One of them is **like**, which performs simplistic pattern-matching on strings. **Like** allows comparing the contents of a character column with a pattern that can contain two wildcard characters.

- The first one is **%** that stands for "any occurrence of any character, including no characters at all"; it works exactly like * when you are looking for a filename.
- The second wild-card character is _ (underscore) that stands for "any single character".

For instance, you can find all the movies that contain no *a* in their title by typing

```
select * from movies
where title not like '%A%'
  and title not like '%a%'
```

As you have probably noticed, movie titles mix uppercase and lowercase characters. If you are working with a DBMS for which data is case-sensitive, you must take capitalization into account, otherwise you'll get the wrong results.

Alternatively, you can use a built-in function that converts (for instance) titles to uppercase and write

```
select * from movies
where upper(title) not like '%A%'
```

(no prize for guessing the existence of the **lower()** function)

I don't recommend this manner of writing queries. As you will see in a later chapter, applying functions to columns in the **where** clause isn't a very good practice, even though rather innocent in this particular example, and I'd rather advise you to use the previous format. Of course, if the DBMS is not case-sensitive for data,

```
where title not like '%A%'
```

is enough.

The **like** operator implements very coarse pattern matching; those of you who are regular-expression fiends will probably be happy to learn that some products implement some true regular-expression matching functions. For the rest of us, **like** works quite well.

The operator that is most particular to SQL is the one that deals with NULLs - missing values.

Figure 3.4: nulls in SQL are different.

If you have some experience of a language such as C++, Java or C#, to name but a few, you have probably coded some equality comparisons with *null* to check whether an object had been instantiated (or memory allocated). In these languages, *null* is a very special value, a marker. In SQL's case it's different; in fact, it can happen that a null isn't stored at all in a database - not even a special marker. The fact that it's null is derived from absence. Although you will often find people referring to "null values", **null** in SQL isn't a value, it's a missing value – it just means "I don't know what this piece of data is" (actually, it can also stand for "meaningless" or "not available").

Remember that SQL is a language that is data oriented. If you write a condition

```
where column_name = null
```

It reads "the rows for which the contents of *column_name* is equal to I haven't the slightest idea what" - which of course isn't very helpful. No rows can match such a vague condition and if in one row the column named *column_name* contains nothing (in other words, **null**) the condition that is tested isn't "is something unset equal to what means unset" but instead means "is something I don't know equal to something else I don't know" - which isn't true, generally speaking. One of the reviewers, Rudi Bruchez, suggested an excellent analogy: suppose that in the morning someone whose phone number is hidden calls you, that you miss the call, and that the caller leaves no message. Now, suppose that in the afternoon exactly the same story repeats itself. If I ask you to answer either yes or no, whether it was the same person both times, you'll have to answer no but if I ask you whether two different people called, you'll have to answer no as well. You cannot tell.
Let's say it in another way:

```
where column_name = null
```

is <u>never true</u>, even for rows where there is no value for *column_name*! In the *people* table, some actors have a single stage name and there is nothing in column *first_name*, but a query with a condition `where first_name = null` will return no rows. In the same way

```
where column_name <> null
```

is <u>also never true</u>, because you can never say whether something you know is equal to or different from something you don't know.

How can we check whether we have a known value in a column in a row then? Not by comparing it to something unknown but by stating "the value is not known" or "the value is known". This in SQL is expressed by conditions

```
where column_name is null
```

and

```
where column_name is not null
```

Beware of nulls, they are by far the most common reason why a query returns wrong results (when results are wrong and nulls are not to blame, it's usually duplicate rows). A good database design tries to reduce the number of optional columns to the minimum.

Returning Only Some Columns

We have so far returned full rows from the database. As you may have guessed when I recommended that you name columns in **select** statements instead of using * - and as perhaps you have already tried for yourself - you can query only some columns - for instance, you can run a query such as

```
select title, year_released
from movies
where country_code = 'us'
```

Checking the Structure of a Table

You can see very easily in all environments what the structure of a table looks like and which columns you can fetch. Most graphical tools present the structure of a database as a tree, with databases in which you have schemas, in which you have tables, in which you have columns (it displays information about other things too but we'll see them later).

> NOTE A brief description of database structures is given in Appendix A.

In three or four clicks you can see the names, data types and various characteristics of your columns.
With a command-line tool you also have simple commands to display the structure of a table.

- With Oracle (`sqlplus`), DB2 (`clpplus`) and MySQL (`mysql`) you just type **desc** (the abbreviation of *describe*), followed by the table name:

  ```
  desc movies;
  ```

  The semi-colon to terminate the command is required by `mysql`, optional with `sqlplus` and `clpplus`.

  > NOTE `sqlplus` and `clpplus` terminate SQL commands, which are sent and executed on the server "as is", by a semi-colon or by a / at the beginning of a line; but there are also commands, such as **desc**, which aren't directly run by the SQL engine and are optionally terminated by a semi-colon.

- With PostgreSQL (`psql`), it's

  ```
  \d movies
  ```

- And with SQLite (`sqlite3`)

  ```
  .schema movies
  ```

  will simply display the text of the **create** statement.

- With SQL Server

  ```
  sp_help movies
  ```

will tell you everything you always wanted to know about the table *movies*, although you'll probably find the graphical interface of SQL Studio more convenient.

Once you have the description of your table, you can decide which columns you want to return and which you want to ignore.

Computing Derived Columns

You can also return information that is derived from what is stored in the database - you can compute columns. You can add, subtract, multiply or divide combinations of numerical columns (or combinations of numerical columns and constants). You can format and perform computations on dates, most products come with an impressive set of built-in functions. You can concatenate strings; SQL Server uses **+** as the operator that concatenates strings, most other products use two vertical bars, and there is also a function **concat()** that concatenates its arguments. You can try the following example that concatenates columns from the database and text:

```
select title ||' was released in ' || year_released movie_release
from movies
where country = 'us'
```

NOTE If you are using MySQL or SQL Server 2012 or above write

```
select concat(title, ' was released in ', year_released) movie_release
```

With earlier versions of SQL Server replace each set of double bars with a plus sign, and convert the year to a string with `cast(year_released as char)`.

movie_release (which can be preceded by **as**) is an alias that you supply, a name given to the expression which is used by interactive SQL clients as a column heading.

NOTE Using **as** is considered to be a good practice. I don't always follow it.

If you can return computed columns, you'll understand easily that you can also apply filtering conditions to computed columns; however, there are very strong performance reasons that I shall explain later for avoiding it. In general, you can massage the data that you return almost as much as you want to present it to users or programs but inside the **where** clause you should try to apply functions and computations only to constants and to user input, not to columns. If your database has been properly designed and normalized, the data in your tables becomes the reference, the touchstone and you should massage constants and user input to make them look like what you store, not the opposite.

I mentioned very briefly that I'd present some functions. Before that, though, there is an SQL construct that isn't a function proper but is extremely useful for massaging data before displaying it: the **case ... end** construct. This construct is a kind of *if... then*

... else if ... else ... end statement that allows you to test for the value of columns in the current row and accordingly change, on the fly, what is returned. The **case ... end** construct is commonly used for making internal codes more user-friendly – for instance, a column named *color* that contains only 'Y' or 'N' values could be associated with each movie to specify whether it is a color or black and white movie. This indicator can be returned and displayed with

```
select ...,
       case upper(color)
         when 'Y' then 'Color'
         when 'N' then 'B&W'
         else '?'
       end as color,
       ...
from ...
where ...
```

The **upper()** function converts to uppercase and is there to ensure that uppercase and lower case Ys will be identically interpreted. If the value retrieved from the database is Y, then it is checked against expected values and when a match is found the associated label is displayed instead of the column value. If we encounter a null (or an unknown code), it can match no value and we display what is associated with **else**; and so on. The interesting question is of course "What happens if there is no **else** (which is optional) in the **case ... end** expression and we don't find a match?" The answer is that null is returned.

What you see here is the first and simplest way to use the **case ... end** construct: it takes the value of one column for the current row, tests it against values, and returns something else instead; here we return constants but we could as well return an expression based on the values of other columns from the same row.

There are times though, when checking a column for the values it contains simply doesn't work. You may want a more complicated condition, for instance, display the message 'very old American movie' for American movies that are older than 1940. Returning this message depends on the values of two columns (*country* and *year_released*), not one. In that case you have to use a variation on the **case ... end** construct, in which you don't name a column after the **case** keyword, implicitly testing it against the values named in the various **when** branches, but instead write an explicit condition in each **when** branch:

```
case
  when country = 'us' and year_released < 1940
          then 'very old American movie'
  else 'either more recent or not American'
end
```

NOTE **case** followed by a column name is referred to as *simple case expression*; if a condition, rather than a value, follows **when**, it's usually called *searched case expression*.

There is also an event where you are checking a single column and cannot use

```
case column_name
```

Do you remember how nulls cannot be compared to anything, including null?

```
case column_name
  when null then
  else …
end
```

will <u>NOT</u> work any more than a condition

```
where column_name = null
```

You have just seen that we can catch nulls in the **else** branch of the **case** construct:

```
case upper(color)
   when 'Y' then 'Color'
    when 'N' then 'B&W'
    else '?'
 end as color,
   …
```

What will happen indeed, is that the **else** branch will catch not only nulls but also invalid entries such as 'X' (which of course you couldn't have with a **check** constraint such as those discussed in Chapter 2 but you don't always have constraints where you would like them to be.)

Relying on **else** only works because we have a very limited range of valid values and we can enumerate them all. Suppose that you want to list the names of all actors and display next to their name 'alive and kicking' if they are still alive (that is if column *died* is null) and 'passed away' otherwise. Relying on **else** to catch nulls is near impossible because we would have to list in the **when** branches all possible values of *died*, existing ones plus those that the enrichment of the database will bring in, plus years in the future … That would be unmanageable.

In that case you must write the **case** in the same way as when the condition bears on several columns:

```
case
  when died is null then 'alive and kicking'
  else 'passed away'
end as status
```

Useful Built-In Functions

Listing all the various functions available in all DBMS products would be boring and pretty useless - the list of available functions is probably what I refer to most often in the documentation of the various DBMS products with which I have to work. I'll just mention for now the functions you use 90% of the time you need functions; I'll introduce a few others in the course of this book, when needed. I won't describe the parameters here in detail, just what the function does so that you know it exists (you'll find more information in Appendix B). You'll see some of them in action later in the book when I feel the need for them.

Numerical Functions

First, unless you have scientific computations to perform, you use very few numerical functions in SQL, even if most products document an impressive list. It is common to apply numerical operations to columns but the only numerical functions that are commonly used are **round()** and its close relative **trunc()** - the distinction is that **round()** returns the nearest value, **trunc()** the nearest smaller value.

> NOTE **trunc()** isn't available with SQL Server nor SQLite but an additional argument passed to **round()** with SQL Server achieves the same result.

String Functions

Several string functions are regularly used. You have seen **upper()** and **lower()**, several products also have an **initcap()** that capitalizes all words.

The classical **length()** function is sometimes useful, as well as **substr()** to extract substrings. Function **trim()** and its variants **ltrim()** and **rtrim()** that remove spaces (optionally other characters) respectively at both ends, on the left and on the right of a string are quite handy for sanitizing user input. I must also mention **position()** that locates the position of a character in a string (it can be helpful to check the validity of an email address in a **check** constraint for instance) and **replace()** to substitute characters for another set of characters inside a string. If you only know these functions you'll be able to do a lot of things.

> NOTE **length()**, **substr()** and **position()** are respectively called **len()**, **substring()** and **charindex()** with SQL Server; the same product implements **rtrim()** and **ltrim()**, but not **trim()**. Function **position()** is called **instr()** in Oracle and DB2. See the details in Appendix B.

Date Functions

The date function that is by far the most used is the function that returns the current date and time.

The name varies with the DBMS, Oracle and DB2 use **sysdate** (no parentheses), SQL Server uses **getdate()**, MySQL **current_timestamp()**, PostgreSQL **now()** and SQLite **date()**. You have variants (if you only want the date), sometimes you can use different synonym names, and for specifics, please refer to Appendix B and to the documentation of your favorite DBMS.

Some really useful functions are the functions that allow you to compute dates. If with Oracle, you add a number (not necessarily an integer) to a date, the number is interpreted as a number of days (with possibly a fraction of day). You also have **add_months()** that allows you to compute dates in the future or the past without having to worry about the number of days in a month. Other products have similar functions, **dateadd()** and **datediff()** with SQL Server, **date_add()** and **date_sub()** with MySQL.

For DB2 you can add or subtract integer values by qualifying them by a time unit, for instance `sysdate + 1 month` or `sysdate    2`. SQLite let you do this type of operations with function **date()**. PostgreSQL has a philosophy similar to DB2, instead of writing `1 month` you would write `interval '1 month'` – while MySQL also supports `+ interval 1 month`.

Another useful date function is **extract()** (available in most products, and known as **datename()** and **datepart()** in SQL Server) that allows you, as the name says, to extract various subcomponents from a date – the year, the month, the day, the hour ...

All products also provide formatting functions for displaying dates in a format that is familiar to your users.

Conversion Functions

The functions that I have just mentioned, which format a date, actually convert what is internally a date for the DBMS into a character string that looks more like a date to the end user (there are also functions for formatting numbers which are more rarely used).

> NOTE Number formatting is usually done in the program that issues SQL statements to retrieve data from the database more than in SQL itself.

Those date-formatting functions perform opposite operations to the functions I have already mentioned at the beginning of this chapter – **to_date()** for DB2, Oracle, and Postgres, **convert()** with SQL Server and **str_to_date()** with MySQL – that transform a string (representing a date) into what is really known internally as a **date** or **datetime** data type to the DBMS.

Another transformation that can be seen as a conversion function is a very useful function called **coalesce()** that takes two (sometimes more) parameters and returns the first one that isn't null. This function is convenient for returning default values. You can obtain the same result with a **case ... end** construct but **case** is more verbose. For instance you can write either

```
coalesce(status, 'Unknown')
```

or

```
case
  when status is null then 'Unknown'
  else status
end
```

Those are simple, and perfectly legitimate, conversions but you sometimes need a bit more juggling than you'd really like. In an ideal relational world all data would be stored with one unquestionable data type. In the real world the picture is fuzzier. Some people will store dates as text (big mistake) or a number of seconds from January 1st 1970 (lesser mistake but mistake nonetheless), others will store numerical codes as numbers (in many countries postal codes are only composed of digits) even if they have no real numerical meaning, others will store the same codes as text. You get apples and oranges, with oranges that aren't really oranges but apples disguised as oranges. You can change the type of a constant or column with function **cast()** (used as `cast(`*thing_to_change* `as` *target_datatype*`)`), assuming that the conversion makes sense (`cast('Hello World!' as integer)` fails).

Those are the most useful built-in functions. My use of 'built-in' is a hint that all DBMS products allow users to define their own functions, as you will see in a later chapter. Except in the case of SQLite that comes with a rather frugal set of built-in functions (but much easier ways to add one's own functions than most products, as a bug in your functions will only take down your application, not a server with 2,000 people connected), user-defined functions are much less necessary than most people believe. Read the reference documentation of functions just to have an idea about everything that is available for your DBMS; you will feel much less need to reinvent the wheel and a clever use of built-in function is usually much more efficient than what you can write as a user-defined function.

Portability

Another point I wish to underscore is that as you have seen, although available functionalities are, by and large, very similar among most products, there are huge syntactical variations – date arithmetic is possibly the most blatant example and date arithmetic is very widely used in enterprise-grade applications (it can be argued that most business applications are mostly managing dates and numbers.) There is an inescapable conclusion: application portability is something that is very difficult to achieve, if achievable at all. Unless you are only using extremely basic SQL statements and under-using your DBMS, porting an application from a DBMS to another DBMS requires much careful work; it doesn't matter if you are using a framework that claims that it will make your applications auto-magically portable, even with the cleverest of frameworks it will not be a matter of transferring application files, downloading and uploading data, and starting the application.

Where SQL Must Be Kept in Check

When I mentioned that you could select only some of the columns from a table, I omitted something: selecting only some columns raises a very important question. I told you that the theory that Ted Codd initially developed was mathematically grounded and allowed to operate on tables as if they were some kind of variables; I showed you that we could use the result of a query as if it were a table. Combining operations to drill into data is what is really interesting.

However, combining operations only works if we respect some rules. For instance if we have three variables x, y and z, and we write an expression such as z / (x + y), we can say that it is the same as dividing z by another variable that would hold the value stored in x plus the value stored in y. Except that it doesn't always work. If x + y is equal to zero, the division is impossible; if x + y is different from zero then we get a value that we can combine in an even more complex operation. In other words, we can go on chaining operations only when we respect some rules at each step (the rule here being "not dividing by zero").

The same thing happens with the relational theory. The table operations I am presenting here can be further combined if result sets present the same features as I have required of tables – namely, that we have no duplicates and that we have a set of columns that can be used to identify uniquely each row; features enforced in tables by constraints.

Results Don't Always Look Like Properly Designed Tables

If we only select some of the columns, then trouble looms not very far away. For instance, we can choose to return only the *country* column from the *movies* table:

```
select country from movies
```

You get the same country several times. Is it interesting information? No. I don't know what your gut reaction is when you see a list with several duplicated countries but it is probably one of two:

- Either you try to identify the different countries from which the sample database stores movies – that is, what matters to you is the presence of a country,
- Or you try to count how many times each country is recurring, trying perhaps to find out which are the countries with the most or least movies in the sample database.

The answer to either of the preceding questions is an interesting piece of information – the list with duplicates is just raw data, and it's not a "relation" in Codd's sense. The problem is that although we can define constraints on tables to ensure that they store proper information, we cannot pre-define constraints on query results – we must write our queries properly, so that what they return contains no duplicates. As soon as we don't return a full set of columns that has been declared as the primary key or unique, we may have duplicates.

The SQL language provides the means to return interesting information and even more importantly result sets that feature key columns and no duplicate rows, even when you select only some of the columns from a table; it is your responsibility as a developer to use these means, as the language doesn't constrain you.

Removing Duplicates

The **distinct** keyword allows you to suppress duplicates in a result set. It is used immediately after the **select** keyword and I suggest you try the following query and possibly some variations if you feel inspired:

```
select distinct country from movies
```

This is the query you should run if you only want to know the list of countries for which we have recorded movies.

Aggregating Rows

If you want to know how many movies are recorded per country, then you have another construct, which is slightly more complicated but is used very often in SQL queries: the construct that calls *aggregate functions*, usually associated with a **group by** clause.

You can list all films in table *movies* but you can also ask the DBMS to regroup them, for instance by country, and return only one row for each group but with meaningful information about the group, for example, how many films we have per group. It could as well be the oldest or most recent year of release or the first title in alphabetical order.

Let me show you how to write the query to count how many films we have per country:

```
select country, count(*) number_of_movies
from movies
group by country
```

This query will display next to each country code the number of movies for this country, and asks for a few comments: **count(*)** is what is called an *aggregate function*, because it is computed by aggregating several rows. ***** is a dummy parameter that stands for "the row" or "all the columns" as in **select ***; you can also use the name of a column as the argument. In this example, **count()** is associated with the *country* column which is the criterion for counting rows in the same group. Every column that appears alongside an aggregate function must also appear in the **group by** clause.

NOTE MySQL doesn't enforce this rule but you should respect it.

There may be one column as shown here, there may be several if you want sub-groups - for instance you may wish to see a count by country and year, which you'll write

```
select country, year_released, count(*) number_of_movies
from movies
group by country,
         year_released
```

Once again, all the columns that appear next to the aggregate function must also appear in the **group by** clause; they become the key of the result set.

You can also have no column at all next to the **count(*)** – in which case you need no **group by** clause. The result is just a single row indicating how many rows the table contains.

```
select count(*) number_of_movies
from movies
```

There is however an important feature of queries with **distinct** and aggregate functions that needs to be pointed out. Whenever your query returns all the columns, or at least the key columns that uniquely identify each row, the SQL engine can get rows, check whether they satisfy the various conditions specified in the **where** clause, then return or discard them and then proceed. By analogy with video on the web, we can say that the SQL engine can "stream" the result set. By contrast, looking for distinct values, or counting them, implies that the SQL engine must inspect all the values and sort them in one way or another in order to remove either duplicates or group results, even if it tries to find short-cuts. Nevertheless, introducing this type of operation in a query deeply influences the way the SQL engine will be able to process the query.

count(*) isn't the only aggregate function. There are three much used aggregate functions, **count()** is one of them. The two others are **min()**, which returns the minimum value in a group, and **max()**, which returns the maximum value. Less frequently used, **avg()** returns the average (you'll often want to wrap what **avg()** returns with the **round()** function to avoid long lists of pretty meaningless decimal digits). Unlike **count(*)**, the three functions **max()**, **min()**, and **avg()** demand a column name as argument; **min()** and **max()** can apply to any type of column for which the notions of minimum and maximum are meaningful; **avg()** can only take a numerical column as argument.

There are other aggregate functions that are much less used, such as **stddev()** that computes standard deviation; many products also have a built-in aggregate function for strings that allows one to build for instance a comma-separated list by concatenating column values from several rows.

To give you another example, if you want to list for each country in which year the earliest movie was released, you can write:

```
select country, min(year_released) oldest_movie
from movies
group by country
```

Thus, SQL provides all the means to return a dataset that has all the right properties to undergo further operations.

For example, you can nest the previous query into another query and limit the output to countries for which the oldest movie was released before 1940.

```
select *
from (select country, min(year_released) oldest_movie
      from movies
      group by country) earliest_movies_per_country
where oldest_movie < 1940
```

As with successive conditions that you link with **and**, there is a short-hand notation, which is the **having** clause, a condition added after the **group by** clause – and evaluated after the grouping operation. The previous query can also be written with a **having** clause that asks for the minimum (oldest) release year to be prior to 1940.

```
select country, min(year_released) oldest_movie
from movies
group by country
having min(year_released) < 1940
```

I'd like at this stage, to introduce a topic of great practical importance: performance. As I have told you, aggregate functions usually work by sorting the subsets of rows that are returned as a prerequisite to aggregation. The more data you have to sort, the more work the DBMS has to perform and the longer it takes. In this example, you could indifferently apply the **having** condition to the result of the aggregate function or to the column on which the **group by** operates. For instance you could write

```
select country, min(year_released) oldest_movie
from movies
group by country
having country = 'us'
```

But the difference with the query with the condition on the oldest release year is not only in the result returned. There is a big logical difference as well: when **having** is applied to the result computed by **min()**, the result of the aggregate function has to be computed before you can filter the rows you want to see, you cannot do otherwise. When **having** is applied to a column such as *country*, you could have first screened by country inside the **where** clause before aggregating, thus potentially operating on a much smaller amount of data and returning the result faster.

Before being first executed, queries run through an optimizer that tries to bring the different steps into an order that minimizes the work for the DBMS. Unfortunately not all optimizers have the same degree of sophistication; for some products, your applying **having** to the *country* column will result in filtering before the aggregation but for others this will not be the case. Therefore beware, and only apply **having** to what it was designed for, conditions applied to the result of an aggregate.

There is finally a last point with aggregate functions that must be underlined: how they behave with nulls. In general, if you execute an operation that combines known values and an unknown value, the result is indeterminate and you get a null. Aggregate functions behave differently: they simply ignore nulls. Thus, if you query the *people* table and check which is the maximum death year in the table

```
select max(died) most_recent_death
from people
```

The result is implicitly the same as if you had written an additional clause

```
where died is not null
```

NOTE SQL Server will issue warnings without the **where** condition, though.

Don't hesitate to try these queries.

The treatment of nulls by aggregate functions can lead to surprising results, especially with **count()**. As I've told you, **count()** can take as argument either * or a column name. Since, at least in a properly designed database, a table will always have a key that is not null (indeed it is a fundamental prerequisite that primary keys should never contain nulls), **count(*)** will always return the number of rows in the table; however, **count(*column_name*)** will return the number of rows for which *column_name* is not null, which may not be the same. You can check it by running the following query:

```
select count(*) people_count,
       count(born) birth_year_count,
       count(died) death_year_count
from people
```

To conclude on **count()**, I must also tell you that if you use it with a column name as argument, then this column name can be optionally preceded by **distinct** to count distinct values only once.

NOTE **count(distinct ...)** isn't supported in old versions of SQLite.

For example, if you want to count, per country, for how many different years we have movies in our database, you can use a **distinct** when you count the years.

```
select country, count(distinct year_released) number_of_years
from movies
group by country
```

This query returns exactly the same result as counting the rows from a result set obtained by using **distinct**.

```
select country, count(*) number_of_years
from (select distinct country, year_released
      from movies) t
group by country
```

If you have trouble understanding nested queries, I advise you to run the subquery alone to see what it returns.

A Relatively Complex Example

To begin to illustrate how one approaches an SQL problem, I am going to answer a question that is simple but that you might have trouble to translate in SQL: how many people in the sample database are both actors and directors? At the beginning of this chapter, I gave you a slightly contrived example where I was feeding the output of one query as the input for the next query, adding one **where** condition each time, chaining queries instead of chaining conditions with **and**. I am going to follow a similar pattern, except that this time the example isn't contrived.

Finding the Starting Point

Where are we going to find the information? Don't be misled by the 'people' in the question. We want directors who are also actors. The only place where we have the capacity in which people were involved in a movie is *credits*.

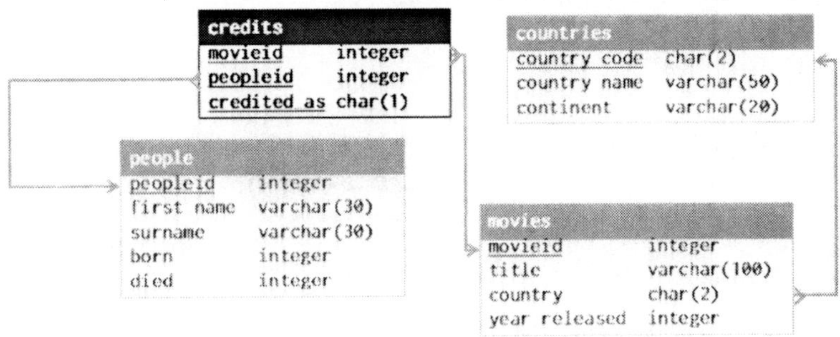

Figure 3.5: Identifying the table that contains the information.

For sure, there isn't much information about people in *credits* but since we just want to count them, an identifier is as good as extensive information. So we'll find the information in table *credits*. What do we need from this table? I have just mentioned it, *peopleid*, and of course, *credited_as* that tells us whether a person played in a movie or directed it. Do we need the movie identifier? No, it's irrelevant to the question. What defines the scope of data for the question we have to answer are therefore columns *peopleid* and *credited_as* from table *credits* but the primary key of *credits* is also composed of *movieid*, the film identifier. If I leave out part of the key and only collect two columns, I can, and shall, have duplicates since as soon as one person has played in different movies or has directed several movies I'll get identical values of *peopleid* and *credited_as* for each movie.

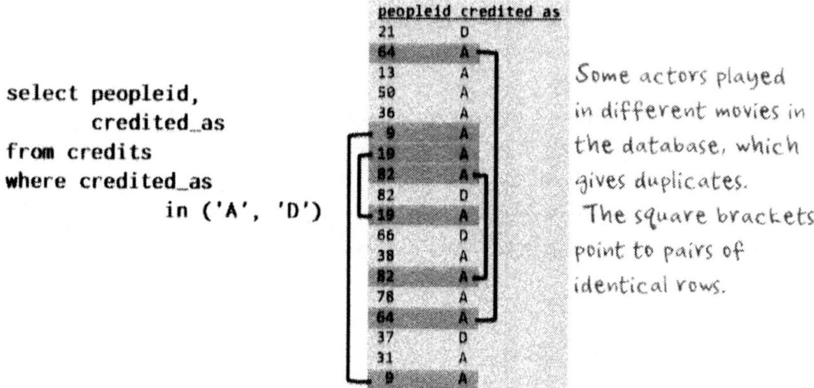

select peopleid,
credited_as
from credits
where credited_as
in ('A', 'D')
peopleid credited_as
21 D
64 A
13 A
50 A
36 A
9 A
19 A
82 A
82 D
19 A
66 D
38 A
82 A
78 A
64 A
37 D
31 A
9 A
Some actors played in different movies in the database, which gives duplicates.
The square brackets point to pairs of identical rows.

Figure 3.6: Getting duplicates when we omit the film identifier.

The keyword **distinct** is required to obtain a set of rows that has no duplicates, the primary condition to have a proper relation in Codd's sense, and to which the relational theory applies.

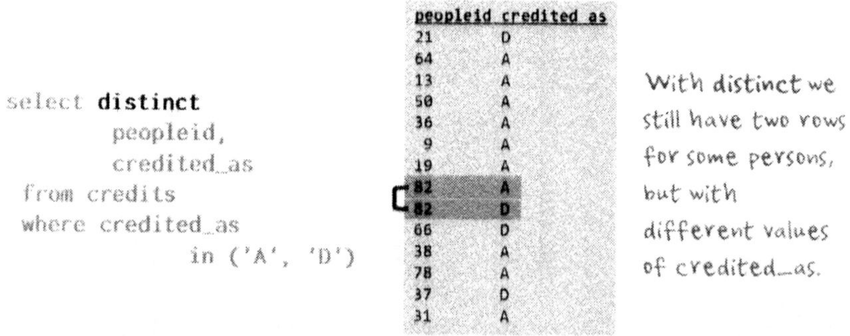

Figure 3.7: Using distinct to obtain a result without duplicates.

We obtain a result set that looks like a table: identifiers of people, and the capacities in which we find them in the database. Most people appear only as actors, or as directors, and on only one row. People who appear both as actor and director are the only ones that we'll find on two different rows.

A and D are the only different values we currently have in *credited_as*, and the **where** condition in the query may look unnecessary and somewhat luxurious but it is quite possible that one day we'll want to add the director of photography, or the executive producer, or stuntmen. It doesn't hurt to specify exactly what we want: it's part of the original question.

Drilling Down

We can call the result of the previous query *all_actors_and_directors*. I am sure that you have already seen the solution for identifying people who are both actors and directors: count in how many rows they appear, a result I shall call *number of roles* (*role* meaning here actor or director, not playing a character.)

```
select peopleid,
       count(*) as number_of_roles
from (select distinct
             peopleid,
             credited_as
      from credits
      where credited_as in ('A', 'D'))
           all_actors_and_directors
group by peopleid
```

peopleid	number of roles
9	1
13	1
19	1
21	1
31	1
36	1
37	1
38	1
50	1
64	1
66	1
78	1
82	2

Figure 3.8: Counting how many different positions are recorded for each person.

We must only keep those people who are recorded in the database with two different positions. As this is a condition on an aggregate, it must be expressed in a **having** clause.

```
select peopleid,
       count(*) as number_of_roles
from (select distinct
             peopleid,
             credited_as
      from credits
      where credited_as in ('A', 'D'))
           all_actors_and_directors
group by peopleid
having count(*) = 2
```

peopleid	number of roles
82	2

Figure 3.9: Only keeping people who both played and directed.

I don't need to return the count as a column, since I know it will be two. I could omit it; I need **count(*)** only in the **having** clause but when you build a query, it is often reassuring to return data that proves that everything is going as planned.

The Final Result

We get a new result set that has no duplicates and only contains the different people who are both actors and directors (I call it *acting_directors*). At this stage, obtaining the answer to the original question isn't too difficult.

```
select count(*) number_of_acting_directors
from (select peopleid,
             count(*) as number_of_roles
      from (select distinct
                   peopleid,
                   credited_as
            from credits
            where credited_as in ('A', 'D'))
                 all_actors_and_directors
      group by peopleid
      having count(*) = 2) acting_directors
```

number_of_acting_directors
1

Figure 3.10: Counting how many people in the database are both actors and directors.

And that's it. Nothing magical.

To Remember

- You restrict the number of rows that are returned from a table by listing conditions in a clause that starts with **where**.
- Conditions are comparisons between column values and expressions. Comparison operators are the usual ones plus a few others such as **between**, **like**, and **is null**.
- Conditions are combined with **and**, **or** and **not**. Parentheses are helpful.
- Comparisons with dates and nulls are tricky. You should explicitly state the format of dates, or use functions that return the current date and allow date computation.
- You can return only some columns and derive what you display from the actual data by computing expressions or applying functions to the columns; **case ... end** is a very useful construct for displaying data conditionally.
- If you don't return a key, then you may get duplicates. You remove duplicates either by using **distinct** or by using an aggregate function and **group by**. If you

don't, you are on the dark side of the relational theory (actually, you are outside the relational theory because relations contain no duplicate by definition).

Exercises

1. List the titles and years of release for all Indian movies released before 1985.
2. What are the titles of the American movies that we have in the database for the 1970s?
3. How many different people have a surname that starts with a K?
4. Write:
    a. A query to find how many people have the first name 'Peter' in the database.
    b. A query to find how many people have no first name.
    c. A query that returns two values, how many people have 'Peter' for first name and how many people have no first name.
5. A variant on the last example in the chapter: how many people have played in a movie that they have directed?

Retrieving Data From Several Tables

4

> Knowledge is of two kinds. We know a subject ourselves, or we know where we can find information on it.
>
> \- Samuel Johnson (1709 - 1784)

This chapter covers

- How to link tables through common columns
- How to return, as a single result set, data from tables that have no common values
- How to have conditions in a query that depend on the result of queries against other tables

You have seen in the previous chapter how you can select specific rows from a table, specific columns instead of full rows, how you can derive information with functions and operations from the data that is stored, and most importantly how you can do all this while obtaining result sets that have no duplicates, and retain keys. It is because result sets have the same characteristics as properly designed tables that we can chain operations, operating against result sets as if they were virtual tables, with the mathematical certainty that operations are logically valid.

It is time now to see how you can link tables together and pull data out of several combined tables or result sets. These operations are so powerful and have become so synonymous with relational databases that many people wrongly believe that's why they are called relational (the real reason is that they relate attributes in a row).

Joining Tables

We have seen in Chapter 2 that by creating referential integrity constraints you can guarantee that only valid values will be inserted into some specific columns. Common columns link the tables together but these common columns can also be used to bring together data from other columns from the linked tables. In Chapter 2, I introduced table *countries* and explained that knowing from the country code which country we are talking of isn't necessarily obvious, and that storing the country name in full in the reference table might be helpful. You probably have to be European to know that CH stands for Switzerland.

NOTE You probably also have to speak French to relate the CH code to *Confédération Helvétique* ... (the acronym officially comes from Latin.)

It's much better to return a country name instead of a country code when you want to display the country information for a movie.
The code stored in the *movies* table allows us to "pull" the name from the *countries* table.

Linking Two Tables Through Common Columns

Figure 4.1 will help you to remember what the tables in the sample database look like, with a data sample (the data sample just illustrates what data looks like, don't be surprised to see different data in the examples I give).

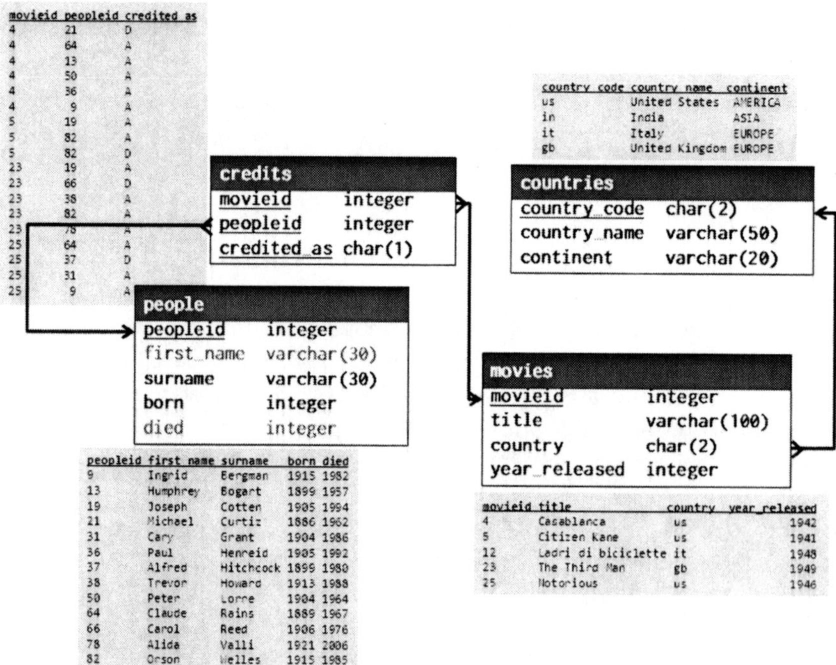

movieid	peopleid	credited as
4	21	D
4	64	A
4	13	A
4	50	A
4	36	A
4	9	A
5	19	A
5	82	A
5	82	D
23	19	A
23	66	D
23	38	A
23	82	A
23	78	A
25	64	A
25	37	D
25	31	A
25	9	A

country code	country name	continent
us	United States	AMERICA
in	India	ASIA
it	Italy	EUROPE
gb	United Kingdom	EUROPE

peopleid	first name	surname	born	died
9	Ingrid	Bergman	1915	1982
13	Humphrey	Bogart	1899	1957
19	Joseph	Cotten	1905	1994
21	Michael	Curtiz	1886	1962
31	Cary	Grant	1904	1986
36	Paul	Henreid	1905	1992
37	Alfred	Hitchcock	1899	1980
38	Trevor	Howard	1913	1988
50	Peter	Lorre	1904	1964
64	Claude	Rains	1889	1967
66	Carol	Reed	1906	1976
78	Alida	Valli	1921	2006
82	Orson	Welles	1915	1985

movieid	title	country	year_released
4	Casablanca	us	1942
5	Citizen Kane	us	1941
12	Ladri di biciclette	it	1948
23	The Third Man	gb	1949
25	Notorious	us	1946

Figure 4.1: The film database used in this book

If for instance you want to list the titles of all movies except American ones alongside the name of the country where they were produced and the year of release, you can type:

```
select title, country_name, year_released
from movies
     join countries
       on country_code = country
where country_code <> 'us'
```

which can return something such as:

```
title                  country_name        year_released
---------------------  ------------------  -------------
Bronenosets Potyomkin  Russia              1925
Ying hung boon sik     Hong Kong           1986
Sholay                 India               1975
Lawrence Of Arabia     United Kingdom      1962
The Third Man          United Kingdom      1949
Ladri di biciclette    Italy               1948
...
```

We return the first and third column from the *movies* table, while the second one comes from *countries*.

The **from** clause says which tables are our data sources and which column in table *countries* matches which column in table *movies*, and allows us to link them together. By doing so, we get access in our query to all the columns from *movies* and all the columns from *countries*. Columns from either table can appear in the **select** list or the **where** clause; it's exactly as if by joining the two tables we had a "larger" table, storing for each movie not only the country code but also the country name and the continent, to which you can apply the other operators, projection and selection (I have renamed *country* to *ctry*, *year_released* to *year* and *country_code* to *code* so that rows fit in the width of the page):

```
movieid  title                  ctry  year code  country_name     continent
-------  ---------------------  ----  ---- ----  ---------------  ---------
3        Bronenosets Potyomkin  ru    1925 ru    Russia           EUROPE
6        Ying hung boon sik     hk    1986 hk    Hong Kong        ASIA
7        Sholay                 in    1975 in    India            ASIA
9        Lawrence Of Arabia     gb    1962 gb    United Kingdom   EUROPE
10       The Third Man          gb    1949 gb    United Kingdom   EUROPE
11       Ladri di biciclette    it    1948 it    Italy            EUROPE
...
```

You might think that specifying the link between the two tables is a bit superfluous, since the foreign key constraint already says the same thing. However, joins and foreign key constraints have little in common; the first one is an operation allowing us to obtain a new result set from two (or more) result sets, while the second one refers to data validation. Remember that some DBMS products don't implement foreign key constraints; we can nevertheless perform joins in all of them.

NOTE Actually all products implemented joins in their first release, while referential integrity came (sometimes much) later.

You don't need foreign keys to perform a join. You only need to be able to compare the values contained in one column of a table with the values contained in one column of another table, which only requires that the two columns should have compatible data types.

NOTE If it makes sense you can use **cast()** to force the two columns to the same data type. Most products do it implicitly, which once in a while returns funny results to the unsuspecting developer.

You have probably seen birthday cards that list a number of notable events that occurred the year the potential recipient of the card was born. You could have a list of events with their dates, a list of people with their birth dates, and generate such a "On the year you were born ..." list of events by joining on the years (that you can extract from the dates). There is no reason for any referential integrity constraint between the two tables; yet you can join.

Which table is specified immediately after **from** and which table follows the **join** keyword (you can also find **inner join**, for reasons I shall explain later) doesn't matter; whether you specify *movies* or *countries* first changes nothing in the result because if there is no film for a country, the country will not appear in the joined result. It's like a multiplication, the order of two numbers that you multiply changes nothing to the value of the product. The **on** keyword introduces the join condition that defines a match; in some cases, a match is defined by the equality of several columns, and you can have for instance

```
on column1_from_table1 = column5_from_table2
and column2_from_table1 = column1_from_table2
```

In some (rare) cases, the comparison operator in the join condition may be something other than equality.

I told you in Chapter 3 that whenever we don't retrieve all the columns from the key or columns known as a unique combination, we should add either **distinct** or a **group by** clause to a query. As in the *movies* table, the title, year and country combination is unique, and as we have a one-to-one match between movie and country, we don't need either **distinct** or **group by** here – uniqueness is guaranteed.

To see how joins are used, let's consider how we would list the first name and surname of all directors in the database. First name and surname are pieces of information that we find in the *people* table; but the information that one person has directed a movie comes from the *credits* table.

We must therefore join them. To answer the question, we only need *first_name* and *surname* from *people*, *credited_as* from *credits* to identify directors – and *peopleid* in both tables to link them. Columns *first_name* and *surname* are unique in *people*, everything is clean on this side but if we omit *movieid* from what we return from *credits*, it means that we don't return the key from this table and we may have duplicates - and indeed, if a director has directed several movies, which is rather common, that director's name would appear as many times as he has directed movies in our database; **distinct** is required.

The start of the query is easy enough:

```
select distinct first_name, surname
from people
     join credits
```

Then we have a problem if we want to express the join condition in the same fashion as we did for the join condition between *movies* and *countries* (for which it was `on country = country_code`); if we write

```
on peopleid = peopleid
```

it becomes difficult to know to which *peopleid* we are referring- which one comes from table *people*? Which one comes from table *credits*? Or do we refer twice to the *peopleid* from table *people*? If we write our query this way, we are sure to get an error and a bitter complaint from our DBMS, which doesn't like ambiguity.

Most products implement three ways to write a query when the column used to link two tables bears the same name in both tables.

- The first one is to let the DBMS guess how tables are linked to each other. There is in the standard SQL syntax, this variation :

  ```
  select distinct first_name, surname
  from people
       natural join credits
  where credited_as = 'D'
  ```

  I strongly discourage you from using this syntax. If you write your join in this manner, the SQL engine is given a free hand to try to work out how to link the tables. I would have no issues if it were using foreign key constraints. The trouble is that it doesn't rely on defined constraints but on columns with identical names. If you don't enforce naming standards that are compliant with the SQL engine behavior with an iron fist, it will not be long before you get into trouble - for instance, there is nothing really shocking in having columns that have nothing to do with each other called *name* in various tables, such as in a *countries* table and in a *people* table; but the *people* table may also contain information about citizenship, thus linking to the country table. If what I have called *country_name* in table *countries* were more soberly called *name* and if I had a country code column in the *people* table to indicate citizenship, left to its own devices the DBMS would try to match on both the country code (named *ctry* in Figure 4-3 for lack of space) and *name*, when it should only be on the country code.

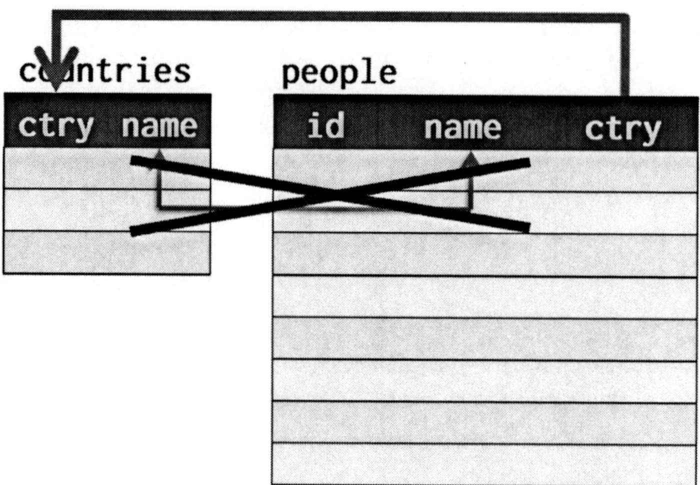

Figure 4.2: The dangers of natural joins.

- It is much better to specify in all cases how to join tables. When the column used to link the tables bears the same name on both sides, with most products you can simply write :

  ```
  select distinct first_name, surname
  from people
       join credits using (peopleid)
  where credited_as = 'D'
  ```

  (You may find between parentheses, a comma separated list if the tables are linked through several columns identically named in both tables).

  This way of writing the query is perfectly correct but, and this is more a matter of opinion and personal taste, I far prefer the following way of writing a join.

- The third way, supported by all products and my favorite, is to qualify column names with the table name and a dot, thus:

  ```
  select distinct first_name, surname
  from people
       join credits
         on credits.peopleid = people.peopleid
  where credited_as = 'D'
  ```

  In fact, my truly preferred way to write the query involves aliases. Table names can be laborious to type especially for three-finger typists like myself and we may need to prefix several columns to eliminate all ambiguities about the origin of data - as I have alluded, it's not impossible that we have *name* columns in several tables. You may remember that in the preceding chapter we assigned names to computed expressions, as well as to queries the output of which was used as the source for a new query. We can also assign a (short) alias to tables and write:

```
select distinct p.first_name, p.surname
from people p
     join credits c
       on c.peopleid = p.peopleid
where c.credited_as = 'D'
```

With most products, Oracle being an exception, you can also precede the table alias by **as** and write

```
select distinct p.first_name, p.surname
from people as p
     join credits as c
       on c.peopleid = p.peopleid
where c.credited_as = 'D'
```

I most often use a one or two character alias (three characters when I'm in a state of euphoria) and systematically prefix all columns by the alias corresponding to the table they come from; it documents the origin of data and makes maintenance much easier.

Why do I prefer using aliases? Many people recommend using the same name for columns in different tables when they correspond to exactly the same type of data. This recommendation has been applied here for *people* and *credits*, which is perfect for the syntax with **using ()**.

Although such a naming standard makes a lot of sense, finding as is the case in the sample database, a column named *country* in one table that matches a column named *country_code* in another table, doesn't deserve curses and very often you find in the same database, like here, some columns that are consistently named across tables and some columns that are not. It sometimes reflects several phases of development and different designers.

Besides, there are cases when it is impossible to match on columns that bear the same name; what I haven't said yet is that it's possible to join one table to itself (an operation known as a *self-join*) .

Suppose that in our *people* table we are interested in film dynasties, actors or directors who are the offspring of other famous actors or directors. We could redesign the *people* table and add two columns, *fatherid* and *motherid* so as to record in either or both the value of *peopleid* for, respectively, the father and the mother if they are people that we also have in the database (neither can be a mandatory column), as shown in figure 4.3. In such a case, there is no other way than to give different names to all three columns *peopleid*, *fatherid* and *motherid* which refer to the same type of data (a *peopleid* value) but on three different rows (Dad, Mom, and Junior). We need a join on differently named columns to trace genealogy.

peopleid	first_name	surname ...	fatherid	motherid
876	MICHAEL	REDGRAVE		
932	RACHEL	KEMPSON		
1234	VANESSA	REDGRAVE	876	932

```
select c.first_name || ' ' || c.surname as person,
       f.first_name || ' ' || f.surname as father
from people as c       -- child
     join people as f  -- father
       on f.peopleid = c.fatherid
```

Figure 4.3: A self-join on an extended *people* table.

I feel uncomfortable with the idea of statement syntax that depends on how columns are named, which is why I prefer not thinking too much and using the **on** syntax that always works, to specify explicitly matching conditions - and I standardize the way that I write queries, which I control, without relying on existing names that I rarely have the power to change.

Linking Many Tables

The result of a join is a dataset - to which, if it satisfies conditions such as the absence of duplicate rows, we can apply further relational operations, including other joins.

In a way reminiscent of successive **where** conditions that can be replaced by conditions linked by **and**, we can either nest the result of the join operation between parenthesis in the **from** clause and apply other join operations to it,

```
select something
from (select ...
      from table1
          join table2
            on join conditions) j
     join table3
       on table3.some_col = j.col
          ...
```

or we can list a succession of join operations in the same **from** clause as in this example:

```
select something
from table1
     join table2
       on join conditions
     a number of joins then
     join tablen
       on join conditions
```

followed by a **where** clause in which we can express filtering conditions on any of the tables (which can be named queries such as *us_movies*) in the **from** clause.

We will need at least two joins when we have, if you remember what you have seen in Chapter 1, a many-to-many relationship between two tables from which we want to return information. For instance, let's say that we want to display the title and the surname of the director for British films. The only way to link the *movies* table, where we find the title and the country, to the *people* table where we find the surname, is through the *credits* table, which moreover stores the "director" information.

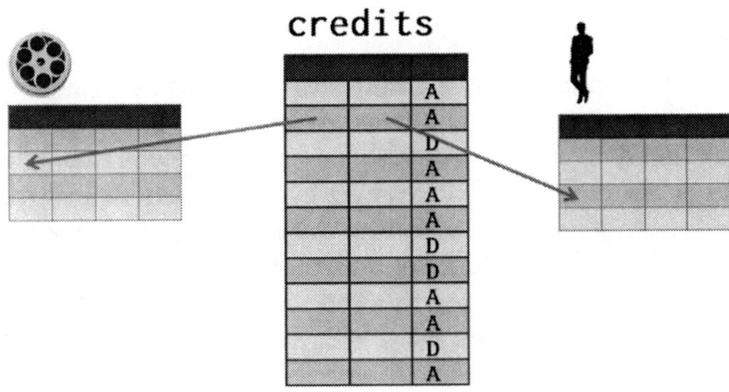

Figure 4.4: *movies*, *credits* and *people*.

One important point is that as the question is stated (title and director surname) we have no formal guarantee that what we return will contain no duplicate rows; even if this is unlikely, it isn't altogether impossible that the same person will direct several identically titled films (although in the case of Hitchcock's two *The Man Who Knew Too Much* movies, one is British and the other is American). There is at least one case in Indian cinema, with P.C. Barua who directed a *Devdas* in Bengali in 1935 and a *Devdas* in Hindi in 1936, plus a 1937 version in Assamese for good measure, with different people in the title role. Or it may happen that two movies with the same title are directed by two different people with the same surname - *Devdas* is a perfect example once again, with a 1955 version directed by Bimal Roy and a 1979 version directed by Dilip Roy. There are other interesting cases, such as movies directed by two brothers, for instance the Coen brothers in the US or the Dardenne brothers in Belgium. You've probably got the not-too-subtle message: we'll need either **distinct** or a **group by** and in this case it will best be **distinct**.

I can write my query:

```
select distinct m.title, p.surname
from movies m
     join credits c
       on c.movieid = m.movieid
     join people p
       on p.peopleid = c.peopleid
where c.credited_as = 'D'
  and m.country = 'gb'
```

and get something such as:

```
title              surname
------------------ ----------
Lawrence Of Arabia Lean
The Third Man      Reed
```

Even if this isn't the case in the example shown, you may be legitimately worried by the fact that the **distinct** might lose information. If we don't want to lose information, we need to return the year when the movie was released too (the country is fixed by the condition in the **where** clause, which means that with the year and the title we would get all three columns that uniquely identify a movie) and solve the *Devdas* problem. We should also return the first name (so that people are uniquely identified too), thus solving the Coen brothers problem. There is no issue with *credits*, since all columns from the primary key appear somewhere in the query. If we redefine the question, then we have a better answer:

```
select m.year_released, m.title, p.first_name, p.surname
from movies m
     join credits c
       on c.movieid = m.movieid
     join people p
       on p.peopleid = c.peopleid
where c.credited_as = 'D'
  and m.country = 'gb'
```

which would return instead of the previous, potentially information-lossy result:

```
year_released title              first_name surname
------------- ------------------ ---------- ----------
1962          Lawrence Of Arabia David      Lean
1949          The Third Man      Carol      Reed
```

As I have already mentioned, we can list tables in any order. When we write a **from** condition such as

```
from movies m
     join credits c
       on c.movieid = m.movieid
     join people p
       on p.peopleid = c.peopleid
```

we implicitly suggest that we start from *movies*, go through *credits* and end up with *people*, grabbing all the columns that are required by the query along the way. This isn't necessarily how the DBMS will process the query. I have put *credits* between *movies* and *people* for clarity and more or less documenting that it links the two tables but I could, as validly, have written:

```
from credits c
     join movies m
       on m.movieid = c.movieid
     join people p
       on p.peopleid = c.peopleid
```

The order doesn't matter at all. The SQL optimizer contemplates various combinations and tries to estimate how fast each possible way to run the query is likely to return the dataset. Then the optimizer settles for what it considers the fastest, possibly rewriting the query in the process before cutting to the chase. When the query is complex and when you are experienced enough, writing the query from the start in a way that is close to how it should be run may matter. For a relatively simple query as you see here, it doesn't.

You will probably encounter another, older syntax for joins. In the old syntax, all the tables (or aliased queries between parentheses) in the **from** clause are specified as a comma-separated list, and conditions that specify links are mixed up in the **where** clause with other conditions.
Thus this query

```
select m.year_released, m.title, p.first_name, p.surname
from movies m
     join credits c
       on c.movieid = m.movieid
     join people p
       on p.peopleid = c.peopleid
where c.credited_as = 'D'
  and m.country = 'gb'
```

can also be and is still frequently written like the following, with a list of tables in the **from** clause and join conditions in the **where** clause

```
select m.year_released, m.title, p.first_name, p.surname
from movies m,
     credits c,
     people p
where c.credited_as = 'D'
  and m.country = 'gb'
  and c.movieid = m.movieid
  and p.peopleid = c.peopleid
```

The advantage of the older writing is that it gives less preeminence to one table, and one understands perhaps more easily that listing tables in a different order changes nothing to the logic of the query. Its drawback, particularly when you have many joined tables, is that it makes for a rather confused **where** clause in which it's easier to forget a condition. If you forget a join condition, you obtain what is known as a Cartesian join, which is simply all possible combinations between the rows from one table and the rows from another table (it's also called a *cross join*).

NOTE Cartesian joins are named after René Descartes, a famous 17th century French mathematician and philosopher.

In any case, don't mix old and new join syntax, unless you absolutely want to uncover bugs in the SQL engine.

Now that you understand how to retrieve only some rows from tables, how to retrieve only some columns or derive column values, and how to join tables, you really know the foundations of SQL and we can go one step further.

Not Losing Rows

Let's modify slightly the query that associates directors with movie titles, and let's run it for Italian movies:

```
select m.year_released, m.title, p.first_name, p.surname
from movies m
     join credits c
       on c.movieid = m.movieid
     join people p
       on p.peopleid = c.peopleid
where c.credited_as = 'D'
  and m.country = 'it'
```

We may obtain:

```
year_released  title                            first_name  surname
-------------  -------------------------------  ----------  ----------
1966           Il buono, il brutto, il cattivo  Sergio      Leone
```

There is one possibly annoying fact that has very probably escaped you; not the fact that we may have several rows for movies with several directors (anthology films were once the rage in Italy) but something more serious - some Italian movies that have been recorded are missing from the list that shows the directors. There is an excellent reason for their absence: the director is unknown.

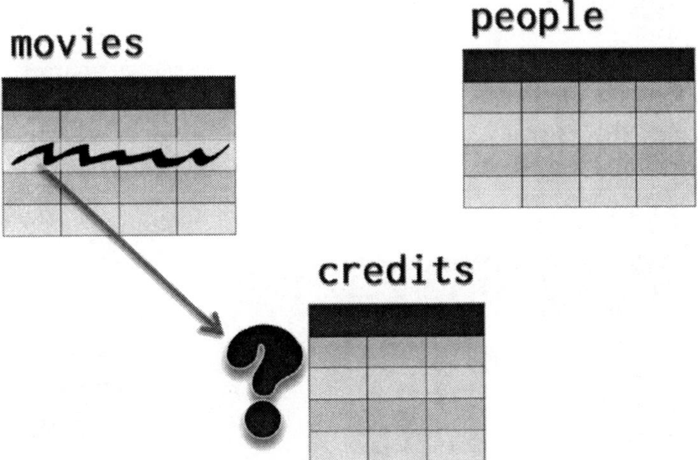

Figure 4.5: Disappearing rows when there is no match in *credits*.

When you join with an **inner join**, rows are returned when a match is found in both tables. If no match is found in the *credits* table for a movie, then this movie is ignored.
Perhaps that you'll find it easier to understand with the older syntax:

```
select m.year_released, m.title, p.first_name, p.surname
from movies m,
     credits c,
     people p
where c.movieid = m.movieid
  and p.peopleid = c.peopleid
  and c.credited_as = 'D'
  and m.country = 'it'
```

The join condition doubles as a filtering condition.

Having no reference at all to a movie isn't the same as not knowing who directed it. Is there a way to show all movies, with the director information when we have it? There are several ways to do it and SQL is somewhat infamous for the multiple ways, not always of comparable efficiency, that it offers to retrieve the same information.

In that particular case, the best way to answer the question is to use an *outer join* - and the presence of **outer** now explains why I mentioned that you can say **inner join** instead of **join** (and I'll use **inner join** for clarity from now on). With an **outer join**, we ask the SQL engine to return all values from at least one table and to supply nulls for the missing information when there is no match in the joined table. There are in theory three types of outer joins, **left outer join**, **right outer join**, and **full outer join**.

I have never found any use for the **right outer join** because all right outer joins can be written as left outer joins, and although I met someone who told me he used a full outer join once, this isn't statistically very significant over a quarter of century of database practice. Let's therefore concentrate our effort exclusively on the **left outer join**, the only one that is really used; when you have understood it well, you should be able to understand the others by yourself (if you really want to).

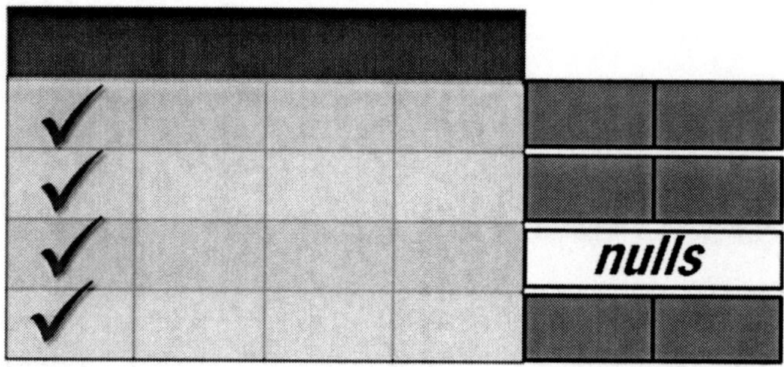

Figure 4.6: Replacement of missing data with null with an outer join.

As I've just told you, **left outer join** practically means "if there is no match, return the row but complete with nulls". For instance, let's display each country name, with the number of movies we have in the database for this country. In the sample database, not all countries have movies, therefore we need an outer join.

We have already computed, if you remember, the number of movies per country - per country code, actually, by using **count(*)** and a **group by**

```
select country as country_code, count(*) as number_of_movies
from movies
group by country
```

which (depending on the content of the database) may return:

```
country_code  number_of_movies
------------  ----------------
de                           1
fr                           3
gb                           2
hk                           1
in                           2
it                           2
jp                           1
nz                           1
ru                           1
se                           1
us                          17
```

If we join, with an **inner join**, the *countries* table to this perfectly suitable dataset, we'll get only those countries for which we have movies:

```
select c.country_name, x.number_of_movies
from countries c
     inner join (select country as country_code,
                        count(*) as number_of_movies
                 from movies
                 group by country) x
              on x.country_code = c.country_code

country_name       number_of_movies
------------------ ----------------
Germany                           1
France                            3
United Kingdom                    2
Hong Kong                         1
India                             2
Italy                             2
Japan                             1
New Zealand                       1
Russian Federation                1
Sweden                            1
United States                    17
```

However, if we replace the **inner join** with a **left outer join**

```
select c.country_name, x.number_of_movies
from countries c
     left outer join (select country as country_code,
                             count(*) as number_of_movies
                      from movies
                      group by country) x
              on x.country_code = c.country_code

country_name       number_of_movies
------------------ ----------------
Germany                           1
France                            3
United Kingdom                    2
Hong Kong                         1
India                             2
Italy                             2
Japan                             1
New Zealand                       1
Russian Federation                1
Sweden                            1
United States                    17
Finland
Bolivia
```

Then all countries appear.

Perhaps, for aesthetic reasons, it would be better to show zero rather than nothing when we have no movie from one country in the database – you have two options, with **case**:

```
select c.country_name,
       case
         when x.number_of_movies is null then 0
         else x.number_of_movies
       end as number_of_movies
from countries c
     left outer join (select country as country_code,
                             count(*) as number_of_movies
                      from movies
                      group by country) x
              on x.country_code = c.country_code
```

Alternatively you can use the more compact **coalesce()** function, which I briefly introduced in Chapter 3 and returns the first one of its parameters that isn't null:

```
select c.country_name,
       coalesce(x.number_of_movies, 0) as number_of_movies
from countries c
     left outer join (select country as country_code,
                             count(*) as number_of_movies
                      from movies
                      group by country) x
              on x.country_code = c.country_code
```

```
country_name       number_of_movies
------------------ ----------------
Germany                           1
France                            3
United Kingdom                    2
Hong Kong                         1
India                             2
Italy                             2
Japan                             1
New Zealand                       1
Russian Federation                1
Sweden                            1
United States                    17
Finland                           0
Bolivia                           0
```

I told you previously, that the order in which tables were mentioned in the **from** clause doesn't really matter – this is true for **inner joins**, not for **outer joins**. I have compared **inner joins** to multiplication, I could compare **outer joins** to division: the order of operands matters.

With a **left outer join**, the table you want to see fully (the table for which you want to see all rows that pass the screening conditions in the **where** clause), is the first one that appears in the **from** clause. If you prefer it, when you add a table with an **inner join** to a **from** clause, it can potentially reduce the number of rows in the result set of the query if no match is found. A table that is left outer joined doesn't filter out anything from the table to which it is joined, it just adds data when available. However, this table becomes somewhat ancillary and we no longer have the symmetry of inner joins.

Placing Conditions at the Right Place

I wrote a query to return the names of the directors of British movies, let's slightly modify the question to return the titles of British movies and, if available, the name of the director(s). Before I show you in detail the **left outer join**, I'd like to point out an **inner join** subtlety.

I have written the original query to return information about directors of British movies as follows, starting with the *movies* table, then joining *credits* to it, then joining *people* to *credits* and adding the filtering conditions first on the *credited_as* column that belongs to *credit*, then on the *country* column that belongs to *movies*:

```
select m.year_released, m.title, p.first_name, p.surname
from movies m
     join credits c
       on c.movieid = m.movieid
     join people p
       on p.peopleid = c.peopleid
where c.credited_as = 'D'
  and m.country = 'gb'
```

It might return:

```
year_released  title               first_name  surname
-------------  ------------------  ----------  ----------
         1962  Lawrence Of Arabia  David       Lean
         1949  The Third Man       Carol       Reed
```

Somehow it says "get the credits for all the movies, bring back almost everything and just keep British movies and directors". It's short for a subquery that would list for each movie all people that are credited, out of this dataset retrieve only British movies, and for these movies only people who are credited as directors:

```
select a.year_released, a.title, a.first_name, a.surname
from (select m.year_released, m.title, m.country,
             p.first_name, p.surname, c.credited_as
      from movies m
           inner join credits c
              on c.movieid = m.movieid
           inner join people p
              on p.peopleid = c.peopleid) a
where a.credited_as = 'D'
  and a.country = 'gb'
```

There is another way to contemplate the query, though, which is to say "find the identifier of each movie director, find all British movies, then get the director's name".

It could be written as follows:

```
select m.year_released, m.title, p.first_name, p.surname
from (select movieid, year_released, title
      from movies
      where country = 'gb') m
     inner join (select movieid, peopleid
                 from credits
                 where credited_as = 'D') c
        on c.movieid = m.movieid
     inner join people p
        on p.peopleid = c.peopleid
```

The first subquery, labeled *m*, only returns British movies, for instance:

```
movieid     year_released  title
----------  -------------  ------------------
         9           1962  Lawrence Of Arabia
        10           1949  The Third Man
```

The second subquery, labeled *c*, only returns identifiers of movies and of their directors, for instance:

```
movieid     peopleid
----------  ----------
         1           1
         2          29
         3          18
         4          33
         5          13
         6           7
         7          20
         8          37
         9          25
        10          15
      ...
       115         359
       116         348
       114         356
       119         378
       120         381
```

Joining the two intermediate result sets provides the year when the movie was released, its title and the identifier of the director(s), and a final join with *people* supplies the names.

The point is that with an **inner join**, you can consider

- that tables are joined together, then screening applied to the result,
- or that screening is applied first and what remains joined later.
- It is even possible to mix both operating modes: a condition can be applied to one of the tables to produce a small result set, which can be joined to another table before the application of further screening conditions.

... None of this really matters from a logical point of view. At least, it doesn't matter as long as we don't care about movies, the director of which is unknown.

It's different with **left outer joins**, therefore pay attention where conditions are applied.

For example let's start with the query that joins first, then filters the resulting rows:

```
select a.year_released, a.title, a.first_name, a.surname
from (select m.year_released, m.title, m.country,
             p.first_name, p.surname, c.credited_as
      from movies m
           inner join credits c
              on c.movieid = m.movieid
            inner join people p
              on p.peopleid = c.peopleid) a
where a.credited_as = 'D'
  and a.country = 'gb'
```

I am going to concentrate on the nested query that is called *a* in the previous example. As I've told you, the big question with a **left outer join** is to decide how to do it - which table we want to see in full, because it has to come first in the **from** clause, and which tables will be "extended" with nulls. Because of referential integrity constraints, the *credits* table can only contain values of *movieid* and of *peopleid* that exist, respectively, in the *movies* and *people* tables. That means that we cannot have a row for the director in *credits* and miss the corresponding individual in *people* - integrity constraints wouldn't allow that. If we don't have the director of a movie, it must be because we have no corresponding row in table *credits* for this movie. The subquery in the **from** clause must therefore be written with *movies* first and an outer join on *credits*.

```
select m.year_released, m.title, m.country,
       p.first_name, p.surname, c.credited_as
      from movies m
           left outer join credits c
              on c.movieid = m.movieid
           inner join people p
              on p.peopleid = c.peopleid
```

That's not enough, though - suppose you get a movie without known director. We return the row from *movies*, then the **left outer join** completes with nulls that should be returned from the *credits* table. Yes, but then we join with *people*, we join on the *peopleid* column that must match the value from *credits*. If we get, courtesy of the **left outer join**, null from *credits*, then the **on** condition of the **inner join** cannot be satisfied since null equals nothing, and because we have an **inner join** the row disappears altogether. Conclusion, we don't need one but TWO **outer joins**:

```
select m.year_released, m.title, m.country,
       p.first_name, p.surname, c.credited_as
      from movies m
```

```
          left outer join credits c
             on c.movieid = m.movieid
          left outer join people p
             on p.peopleid = c.peopleid
```

```
year_released  title              country  first_name  surname    credited_as
-------------  -----------------  -------  ----------  ---------  -----------
...
         1949 The Third Man       gb       Orson       Welles     A
         1949 The Third Man       gb       Joseph      Cotten     A
         1949 The Third Man       gb       Carol       Reed       D
         1949 The Third Man       gb       Alida       Valli      A
         1949 The Third Man       gb       Trevor      Howard     A
         1948 Ladri di biciclete  it
         1941 Citizen Kane        us       Orson       Welles     A
         1941 Citizen Kane        us       Orson       Welles     D
         1941 Citizen Kane        us       Joseph      Cotten     A
         1985 Das Boot            de       Wolfgang    Petersen   D
...
```

Note that we won't have any equality on null – but since equality on null will not work, the second **left outer join** will return a null to match it – it becomes deeply philosophical!

Except that if we write the full query

```
select a.year_released, a.title, a.first_name, a.surname
from (select m.year_released, m.title, m.country,
             p.first_name, p.surname, c.credited_as
      from movies m
           left outer join credits c
              on c.movieid = m.movieid
           left outer join people p
              on p.peopleid = c.peopleid) a
where a.credited_as = 'D'
  and a.country = 'gb'
```

we shall see no difference with the query with only inner joins because the screening condition on the type of involvement (*credited_as*) will not work with nulls. We can think of different ways to fix this. One is to cater for the result of the **left outer join** in the **where** clause and say "I want the row if *credited_as* is either D or null"

```
select a.year_released, a.title, a.first_name, a.surname
from (select m.year_released, m.title, m.country,
             p.first_name, p.surname, c.credited_as
      from movies m
           left outer join credits c
              on c.movieid = m.movieid
           left outer join people p
              on p.peopleid = c.peopleid) a
where (a.credited_as = 'D'
       or a.credited_as is null)
  and a.country = 'gb'
```

Well, this query is logically wrong. The answer follows but try to guess without cheating how it can fail.

What can go wrong is that it's perfectly possible that, for some films, we have no information about the director but we have the names of a few stars – after all, we associate actors more easily than directors with movies.

If you want, just try what it gives – think of a British film not yet in the database, for which you know one actor (who may already be in the database).

> NOTE If your brain refuses to remember a British film, any James Bond movie will do the trick.

Insert a row for this film in *movies*, insert if needed a row for the actor in *people*, then insert a row containing the values of *movieid*, *peopleid* and 'A' in the *credits* table.

What will happen? For this film the two left outer joins will not fire – they will behave like regular inner joins, since we can join *credits* to *movies* and *people* to *credits*. Only trouble is, what we get for *credited_as* is only 'A' – neither 'D' nor null, the row is filtered out by the condition, and the movie disappears in spite of the left outer joins. Interestingly, the behavior will be the same if we rewrite the query in a more compact way, without a nested query in the **from** clause:

```
select m.year_released, m.title, p.first_name, p.surname
from movies m
     left outer join credits c
        on c.movieid = m.movieid
     left outer join people p
        on p.peopleid = c.peopleid
where (c.credited_as = 'D'
       or c.credited_as is null)
  and m.country = 'gb'
```

Is this an SQL bug? No, logical behavior, and the correct result from the wrong SQL code to answer the question.

The question was "get me all the titles of British movies and give me the director name if available". The previous SQL expression means "get me the movie titles and the names of the people involved, then display British movies for which a director is known or no people are found". Not the same thing.

However, if I start from the version of the query with inner joins in which I first filter movies on the country and (this is what is important) the *credits* table on the director role:

```
select m.year_released, m.title, p.first_name, p.surname
from (select movieid, year_released, title
      from movies
      where country = 'gb') m
     inner join (select movieid, peopleid
                 from credits
                 where credited_as = 'D') c
```

```
      on c.movieid = m.movieid
   inner join people p
      on p.peopleid = c.peopleid
```

I am in a situation that matches the question much more closely - here I have a subquery that returns directors only. If I left outer join this subquery, instead of the *credits* table, I truly answer the question "return directors or nothing if directors are not available". This query will give the result I want:

```
select m.year_released, m.title, p.first_name, p.surname
from (select movieid, year_released, title
      from movies
      where country = 'gb') m
     left outer join (select movieid, peopleid
                      from credits
                      where credited_as = 'D') c
        on c.movieid = m.movieid
     left outer join people p
        on p.peopleid = c.peopleid
```

The thing to remember is that with left outer joins filtering conditions must be much closer, in a way, to tables than with inner joins. In the previous example, the condition on the country can just as easily be in a nested query or in a global **where** clause. Not the condition on *credited_as*. Be extremely careful about where your filtering conditions are applied because it is very easy to get wrong results that aren't obviously wrong, and programming bugs that are very hard to spot for the inexperienced eye. If we know neither the director nor any actor, the wrong query gives the right result - by chance.

Classifying Joins

To conclude on joins, I'd like to point out something that may not be very relevant as far as the syntax is concerned but which can be very important for performance in complex queries.

Joins fall into one of two categories:

- they can participate in the filtering,
- or they can be here merely as qualifying joins that return additional information.

For instance, suppose that when you query the movie database, you have a condition on a country name. In that case the join with the *countries* table is a filtering join because the condition on the country name will limit the number of acceptable country codes and therefore directly impact the rows you return from the *movies* table. If you just want to return the country name because it's more user-friendly than a country code and have no condition on a column from countries that cannot be found in another table, then you just have a qualifying join. It would not necessarily be so if we might have country codes in *movies* that are NOT in the *countries* table because then finding them in *countries* would be significant; this isn't the case here because we have integrity constraints; the question is to know whether finding a match in the joined table is meaningful or not.

If we want to find movies for which we know at least one director or actor, we can join with *credits* and then the join becomes significant because if we know of no person who was involved in a movie, then this movie will not be retrieved. When you have a **left outer join**, it is always a qualifying join unless you have a condition on the absence of a match - an **is null** condition.

The key criterion for deciding whether we have a filtering or a qualifying join is the answer to the question: if we remove the join, can the query return MORE rows? If the answer is yes, then the join filters. Otherwise it's a qualifying join.

The distinction isn't that important in theory but very important in practice. If you want queries to run fast, in the succession of relational operations that take you from the source data to your final result, you should identify early the dataset you want to retrieve; that means that filtering joins should appear as early in the process as possible. On the contrary, there is no need to return additional information, for instance the country name, for rows that will be ultimately discarded because they don't satisfy another condition. That would be performing work for no reason. Therefore, qualifying joins should be specified late in the process, when you know exactly what you're returning.

Set Operators

There is a way other than joins to return data from several tables. First of all, when I have combined relational operations so far, it has mostly been starting from a big set of data (such as all the movies in the database) and getting, after one or several relational operations, a subset of the original data, possibly enriched by data obtained from other tables through joins.

When I introduced the combination of conditions in the **where** clause, I pointed out that **and** was, in a way, a short-hand for cascading filtering conditions applied in succession to result sets - each condition subtracting rows from the previous step.

Then I introduced **or** without further ado - but then, if I retrieve American movies from the 1940s:

```
select * from movies
where country = 'us'
  and year_released between 1940 and 1949
```

and then if I retrieve American AND British movies from the 1940s:

```
select * from movies
where (country = 'us'
       or country = 'gb')
  and year_released between 1940 and 1949
```

the second result set cannot be considered a restriction of the first one – it's exactly the opposite of a restriction, since it returns MORE rows; it's the data set equivalent of an addition. It's even possible to make a query return a result set that contains more rows than any of the tables involved.

SQL implements a number of operators that are collectively known as *set operators*. You may have seen (or overheard) at school a little bit of set theory, Venn diagrams and all that. It's precisely what set operators implement.

Union

The best known of these set operators is **union** and is precisely the operation that adds a data set to another data set. When we want American movies from the 1940s and British movies from the 1940s, we can execute separately two queries, one for the American movies, one for the British movies, and mix just before serving. That's what **union** does:

```
select movieid, title, year_released, country from movies
where country = 'us'
  and year_released between 1940 and 1949
union
select movieid, title, year_released, country from movies
where country = 'gb'
  and year_released between 1940 and 1949
```

Advantage compared to **or**? In this example, none. Actually, **or** might be faster because here we have two queries to execute instead of one, and then we have to merge the results. But the interesting characteristic of **union** is that the tables that are queried need not be the same – which is why I have said that there are other ways than joins to return data from several tables. The only demand of **union** is that the same number of columns is returned from each query and that data types are compatible between columns in the same position, so that we get a result set that not only looks like but is a regular data set.

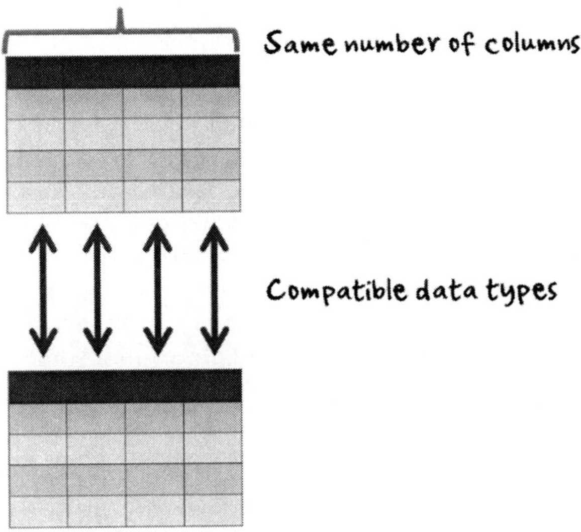

Figure 4.7: The requirements of set operators.

Suppose that you rent out films and that your catalog is stored in the *movies* table. A very good friend of yours, in a different country, has a catalog of films that aren't readily available in your own country. These can be rented to some of your best customers provided they are willing to wait for them. You have a list of your friend's movies in a table called *premium_movies*.

Regular customers only query *movies* - and your best customers may query

```
select 'regular' as class, movieid, title, year_released
from movies
union
select 'premium' as class, movieid, title, year_released
from premium_movies
```

Now an important point to note. In the examples I have given to you, the result sets generated by the two queries have an empty intersection (in plain English, no common rows) - we are merging together two data sets that cannot contain identical rows since there are constant values ('regular' and 'premium') that are different in both queries. Generally speaking, however, there might be a non-empty intersection; to put it another way, as constraints can only enforce that rows are unique within one table, it's not impossible that some rows might be returned by a query and some identical rows returned by the other query. Yuk, duplicate rows! That might completely derail subsequent queries, because then we'd be off the tracks laid down by the relational theory. Therefore, very logically, **union** eliminates duplicates and from a practical standpoint, to eliminate duplicates we need an additional operation, which may be costly if many, many rows are involved.

When you know - or more to the point when you are absolutely certain that there cannot be common rows in the different result sets that you combine, then you should use **union all**. The additional **all** keyword instructs the SQL engine to skip the duplicate removal part, which can result in a noticeable performance gain. I assume of course that all individual queries are properly written and that none of the result sets returns duplicate rows. In all the examples I have provided so far, I would have used **union all** because a movie is either American or British but not both, and because in the rental example the presence of a different constant value for *class* in each part of the query makes duplicates impossible, even if some *movieid* values are common, and even if some movies can be found in both collections with the same identifier.

You often see in SQL tutorials that **union all** is what you use when you want to keep duplicates; this is, of course, erroneous advice. You never want duplicates; duplicates aren't information you can do anything with. You use **union all** when you know that you cannot have duplicates. There are some cases, though, when apparent duplicates must be kept; this is what happens when you compute aggregates on a series of history tables.

History tables are tables that have the same structure (or almost the same structure) as the tables that record current activity but store past data. The reason for using history tables is that data that is active is usually only a fraction of all data that is kept. Think of telecom companies. Each time you make a phone call, a database somewhere records which number you have called and the duration of the call; by knowing whether you have made a local or long distance call, whether you have called a land-based or cell phone (they have different numbers in most countries), the telecom company will be able to bill you. Once bills are paid, the data detail becomes of no interest to the company but it must be kept for several reasons - all companies must keep archives, bills may be contested, and the company must keep some proof to back up its claims. There are also legal reasons; if the police track a criminal, they may be interested in checking who that criminal has called in the past months, or even years, to identify possible accomplices, and companies must keep detailed records by law. Telecom companies are therefore stuck with absolutely gigantic databases and detailed data that quickly loses any business relevance but must be kept. The problem with databases, whether they are gigantic or small, is that they must be very regularly backed up to protect against data loss in case of hardware failure or accident such as a fire or a flood; and most standard backup utilities operate against disk volumes, directories, files ... not the rows that have been modified in the past 24 hours.

NOTE Some database backup utilities, which are product specific, are able intelligently to backup the most recent changes; this is known as an incremental backup. Usually companies use a combination of different backup types, for instance an incremental backup during the week and a full backup on week-ends - but I am straying from the topic of this book.

Those copy operations can take a very long time and backing up an active database (telecom companies never sleep) isn't a simple operation. Hence the idea of transferring data that is no longer active to "history tables" that are backed up once and for all, and keeping smaller active tables that only store current data.

Suppose that a company applies a very simple archiving strategy that consists, at the end of each year, in archiving somewhere data from *last_year_data*, a table that contains the data for the previous year, then dropping this table, then renaming *current_year_data* to *last_year_data*, before finally recreating a brand new and empty *current_year_data* table. That would allow you to keep between one and two years of data continuously online.

Let's say that our data is made of a number of views per day for movies in a video-on-demand application and that we want a report that provides for each movie in the catalog the sum of last year's views, plus the year-to-date views.

One way to proceed is first to unite the query that computes last year's views and the query that computes this year's views to get two subtotals per film:

```
select movieid, sum(view_count) as view_count
from last_year_data
group by movieid
union
select movieid, sum(view_count) as view_count
from current_year_data
group by movieid
```

then to process the result set through a second **sum()** and **group by** to get the grand total per film:

```
select x.movieid, sum(x.view_count) as view_count
from (select movieid, sum(view_count) as view_count
      from last_year_data
      group by movieid
      union
      select movieid, sum(view_count) as view_count
      from current_year_data
      group by movieid) x
group by x.movieid
```

This query can potentially give a wrong result and once again the error may be pretty hard to detect: suppose that last year one film was watched 2,356 times and that so far this year it has been watched exactly the same number of times. For **union**, two rows with the same *movieid* associated with the very same number are duplicates and one should be eliminated. As a result, for this particular film, the final report would display only half the real figure, an error lost among many perfectly correct figures. In such a case, you must use **union all**, not because we want duplicates - once again, we never want duplicates - but because the rows are "technical duplicates", identical rows with different meanings. What I would advise you to do is to write the query as follows, with a label that I call here *period* in the inner query:

```
select x.movieid, sum(x.view_count) as view_count
from (select 'last year' as period,
             movieid, sum(view_count) as view_count
      from last_year_data
      group by movieid
      union all
      select 'this year' as period,
             movieid, sum(view_count) as view_count
      from current_year_data
      group by movieid) x
group by x.movieid
```

Even if my label doesn't appear at the outer level, the presence of the *period* constant makes technical duplicates impossible, justifies the presence of **union all** and documents the fact that even if *movieid* and *view_count* are identical in both parts of the union, this isn't redundant information and we are actually talking about different things.

Intersect and Except (aka Minus)

Of all the different set operators, **union** is the best known and the most widely used but all products also implement **intersect**, which returns the common part of two data sets and most products implement **except** (called **minus** with Oracle) which returns a data set minus its intersection with a second data set. Both **intersect** and **except** return a result without duplicates; some DBMS products allow an additional **all** qualifier, very rarely used.

> NOTE One can actually wonder about the meaning of duplicates with **intersect** and **except**. If it's understandable that the union of two data sets without duplicates can in some circumstances result in duplicates, there is no way to obtain duplicates in the intersection of two datasets without duplicates, nor in their difference. If duplicates show their ugly heads in such a set operation, the real problem is probably elsewhere.

Intersect and **except** can be useful but in practice, and unlike **union** that has no equivalent, the functionality they provide can often be achieved more easily by using, respectively, **inner join** and **left outer join** -- or sometimes even something else.

You probably remember the final example in Chapter 3, where I found how many people in the database were both actors and directors by writing:

```
select count(*) number_of_acting_directors
from (select peopleid, count(*) as number_of_roles
      from (select distinct peopleid, credited_as
```

```
          from credits
          where credited_as in ('A', 'D')) all_actors_and_directors
    group by peopleid
    having count(*) = 2) acting_directors
```

Another solution would have been to take the people that could be found both in the list of actors and in the list of directors using **intersect** and count them:

```
select count(*)
from (select distinct peopleid
      from credits
      where credited_as = 'D'
      intersect
      select distinct peopleid
      from credits
      where credited_as = 'A') acting_directors
```

This query looks simpler than the query presented in the previous chapter and you may find it more legible. However, in terms of efficiency, it requires two separate passes on table *credits* (one to find directors and one to find actors) and would be, on a very large table (on the sample database it makes no noticeable difference) slightly slower.

Suppose, for example, that we want the country codes that are both in *movies* and in *countries*. Can you write the query using a set operator?

We can write

```
select country_code
from countries
intersect
select country
from movies
```

Note that since we have several movies from the same country, the second data set is not a "clean" data set and it would be better to write

```
select country_code
from countries
intersect
select distinct country
from movies
```

The final result will be the same in all cases simply because **intersect** will have removed the duplicates but by removing them as early as possible in the process we reduce the volume of data we have to operate on at the next stage.

We can also write

```
select c.country_code
from countries c
     inner join (select distinct country
                 from movies) m
        on m.country = c.country_code
```

However, I have just tried to fool you. None of these queries is the correct way to answer the question. The best query to answer the question is simply this one,

```
select distinct country
from movies
```

as there is a referential integrity constraint between *movies* and *countries*, which implies, by definition, that the values of *country* in *movies* are a subset of the values of *country_code* in *countries*. This example illustrates very well, a common mistake which is to write a complicated query to check data consistency that is built, or can be built, by design in the database.

The countries that don't appear in the list of movies can be obtained by either

```
select country_code
from countries
except        ← minus with Oracle
select distinct country
from movies
```

or a **left outer join** between the codes in *countries* and the codes in *movies*, with the additional condition that there must be no match:

```
select c.country_code
from countries c
     left outer join (select distinct country
                      from movies) m
             on m.country = c.country_code
where m.country is null
```

In practice, the fact that there must be an identical number of columns and of similar types in all query-components of a set operation is often a severe hindrance for **intersect** and **except**. If you want, for instance, to return the country name instead of the country code in the preceding examples, the set operators require an additional join with table *countries*. With joins, you just take the preceding query and only have to replace the country code by the country name.

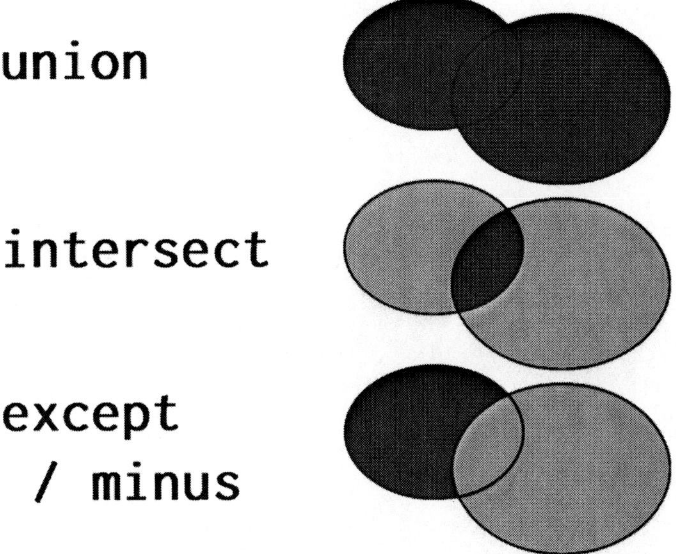

Figure 4.8: A summary of set operators.

Subqueries

I have shown you from the start, that the result of a query can be nested into another query and further processed as if it were a plain table but the **from** clause isn't the only place where you can have a nested query (subquery). You can also have subqueries in the *select list*, that is the list of attributes (stored or derived) that you return in your query, and you can have subqueries in the **where** clause.

Before I get down to the details, I must introduce a new twist: *correlation*.

Correlation

So far, I have taken a very global approach to the processing of data sets; when we join data, we say that we join by matching on one column (or several columns); we ignore individual rows.

But it's also possible to take a microscopic view of joins, by saying that when we join table *B* to table *A* on column *col*, then for each row in *A* we want information from *B* from the row or rows that match the value in *col* for the current row in *A*. It's not as "pure" a vision of data as when we operate in bulk on datasets but in some cases it can ease the construction of complex queries.

I will give you an example. We have seen that to list the title, year of release and country of all movies except American ones, all you had to write was

```
select m.title, m.year_released, c.country_name
from movies m
     join countries c
       on c.country_code = m.country
where m.country <> 'us'
```

You can write a functionally equivalent query by fetching, for each row in *movies*, the matching row from *countries* as a kind of dedicated query that fetches the proper country name:

```
select m.title,
       m.year_released,
       (select c.country_name
        from countries c
        where c.country_code = m.country) as country_name
from movies m
where m.country <> 'us'
```

In such a case, the subquery is said to be *correlated* because the subquery contains a reference, as *m.country*, to the current row of the outer query. That means that the subquery will be executed for each row that will be returned by the outer query. If the query should ultimately return very few rows, it can be a good way to proceed. If the query returns many rows, assuming that the SQL optimizer doesn't rewrite the query behind your back, it can become terribly ineffective because each row that is returned will trigger a little extra work before the truly complete row can be displayed. When a subquery is used in a **from** clause, it is never correlated – the query is executed only once. How the SQL engine then processes joins is a different matter, several different algorithms are available.

Strictly speaking, subqueries in the *select list* aren't equivalent to an **inner join** but to a **left outer join** because if we find no match, then the subquery returns nothing, which becomes null in the result set. Of course, returning null cannot happen in the example I have provided because of integrity constraints that ensure that all values in column *country* of table *movies* have a match in table *countries*.

Subqueries in the *select list* are, in my view, much less interesting than subqueries in the **where** clause.

NOTE I use subqueries extensively but almost never in the *select list*. There are however, some cases when they are required; there is an example in Chapter 12.

In the **from** clause, subqueries are uncorrelated; in the *select list*, they are correlated. In the **where** clause, they can be either.

NOTE Strictly speaking, you could have an uncorrelated query in the *select list* that returns the same value for all rows.

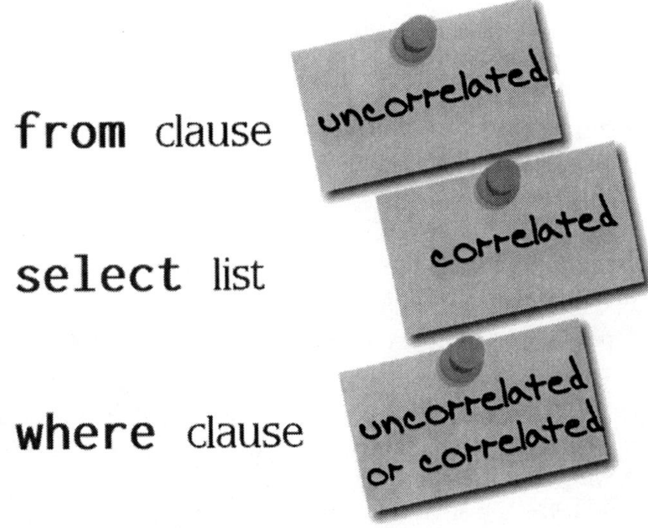

Figure 4.9: Correlation and subquery location.

Subqueries in a Where Clause

I introduced at a relatively early stage of this book, the condition **in** followed by a comma-separated list of values as an alternative to a series of **or** conditions. To refresh your memory, I told you that

```
select country, year_released, title
from movies
where (country = 'us'
       or country = 'gb')
  and year_released between 1940 and 1949
```

could also be written

```
select country, year_released, title
from movies
where country in ('us', 'gb')
  and year_released between 1940 and 1949
```

What is really interesting is that you can substitute for a comma separated list, a subquery that returns a single column; it makes the condition much easier to express when we cannot easily enumerate values.

For instance, if the question were "what are the European movies in the database?" one convenient way to answer it would be

```
select country, year_released, title
from movies
where country in (select country_code
                  from countries
                  where continent = 'EUROPE')
```

Some products even support conditions on several columns, as in

```
(col1, col2) in (select col3, col4
                 from t
                 where ...)
```

In such a case, the requirement is that several values match at once.

There are several points worth noting.

- Firstly, it's possible to write an **in ()** subquery that is correlated. Don't!
- Secondly, when a subquery is used in an **in ()** clause, duplicate values are ignored. It makes sense, as if you write an explicit comma-separated list of constants, repeating one changes nothing in the result. Where it matters, though, is when you wish, for any reason, to move the subquery up from the **where** to the **from** clause and for instance, instead of the following query with **in ()**

  ```
  select country, year_released, title
  from movies
  where country in (select country_code
                    from countries
                    where continent = 'EUROPE')
  ```

  you can write that query with a join

  ```
  select m.country, m.year_released,m.title
  from movies m
       inner join (select country_code
                   from countries
                   where continent = 'EUROPE') c
          on m.country = c.country_code
  ```

  An important question then raises its head: is the identifier that is returned in the subquery unique? Is the subquery that I have named *c* a valid relation in Codd's sense?

  I advise you always to stick to the same rule: whenever you have a subquery, wherever it appears in the query, if the odds of getting duplicate values are demonstrably nil (as here, since the column we return is the primary key), don't use **distinct** because it requires additional work. If there is the faintest chance you ever get duplicates, then use **distinct**, even if the subquery appears inside an **in ()** clause; explicit is always better than implicit when it comes to maintenance.

NOTE There is a school of thought that considers that it's better in **in ()** subqueries to let the SQL engine deal with duplicates and leave it have free rein. While I respect this position, my experience is that when queries become really complex the more explicitly you state what you need, the better.

Once again, the other question to ask yourself besides "can the subquery return duplicate rows?" is "can the subquery return null?"

Remember that an **in ()** is similar to a series of equality conditions linked by **or**. If you have a null in the list, the result of an equality condition with null is never true, since you cannot say that something you know is equal to something you don't know; if you have an "**or** something" that evaluates to false in a succession of logical propositions, then it changes nothing in the final result.

A famous India-born British logician of the 19th century, De Morgan, proved a number of laws that direct the negation of complex logical expressions. In particular, if an **in ()** clause is equivalent to a series of equalities linked by **or**, then a **not in** is equal to a series of inequalities linked by **and** – `country_code not in ('gb', 'us')` is the same as `country_code != 'gb' and country_code != 'us'`. Here things become interesting because if you have a null, neither equality nor inequality with null is true, as we have already seen you cannot say whether a value you know is different from a value that you don't know – it might be the same one, you have no way of knowing. Of course when conditions are linked by **and**, as soon as one condition isn't true the whole series becomes false.

It's with subqueries that you can most often meet interesting cases. Suppose you want to return information about all people who don't bear the same first name as someone who was born before 1950. Among the various options you have to write a query that answers this question, using **not in ()** may look like a simple, elegant and attractive writing, as in this query

```
select *
from people
where first_name not in (select first_name
                         from people
                         where born < 1950)
```

As it happens, there are in the sample database some people with a null first name who were born before 1950 – and the query returns nothing.

NOTE Some old SQLite versions simply ignore nulls in subqueries. The recent versions behave as described here – and as the other DBMS products.

Hence a piece of advice: whenever you have a subquery, wherever it appears in the query, ensure that it cannot return null. If the column that is returned isn't mandatory, add a condition

```
and column is not null
```

such as

```
select *
from people
where first_name not in (select first_name
                         from people
                         where born < 1950
                           and first_name is not null)
```

In case you are wondering, you can also replace a **not in ()** with a subquery in a **where** clause by the same subquery in the **from** clause. You have to use a **left outer join** and explicitly specify that you didn't find a match, as this:

```
select p.*
from people p
     left outer join (select first_name
                      from people
                      where born < 1950) p2
             on p2.first_name = p.first_name
where p2.first_name is null
```

You might think that a subquery that returns null values in this position causes less collateral damage but the query as a whole still returns a wrong result, although for a different reason from before. You will not waste your time trying to understand why, exactly, you have a wrong result...

What happens is that the query returns all the people who have a null first name, irrespective of when they were born – the problem doesn't come from the null in the subquery but from the null in the outer query.

When you retrieve someone who has a single stage name (say Dharmendra, born in 1935) and has therefore a null first name, there cannot be any equality with anything on the join condition between the null first name and any first name from someone born before 1950. There is not even equality between the row corresponding to Dharmendra retrieved from *people* aliased by *p* and the row corresponding to Dharmendra retrieved from the subquery aliased by *p2*. Null is equal to nothing at all, not even null because you can't decide whether something you don't know is equal to something you don't know.

As a result, a row retrieved for Dharmendra from *people* aliased by *p* will find no match in the subquery and as we have no match the left outer join will return null for the only column normally retrieved by *p2*. The condition in the **where** clause will be true and the row will be selected, even if implicitly we would expect to retrieve only the names of people born after 1950.

To correct the query the best solution is probably to add a condition `and p.born >= 1950` which will return people born after 1950 who have a null first name and filter out those born before 1950.

The operator that you use most often with a subquery in a **where** clause is **in ()** but when a subquery returns only one row (for instance an aggregate result) you can also use a classical comparison operator such as = or >. You may also find in text books (I don't remember having ever seen them in corporate programs in more than 20 years) operators **> any (*subquery*)** or **> all (*subquery*)**. The idea behind **any** or **all** is actually comparing with the minimum and the maximum values in the result set of the subquery; it's much easier to think about minimum and maximum than about the range of all the values returned by a subquery, which would explain why people usually return an aggregate function in their subqueries and use a simple comparison.

I told you that in a **where** clause you could have correlated as well as uncorrelated subqueries; so far, I have only shown uncorrelated subqueries. It is now time to talk about correlated queries.

As you have seen with queries in the *select list*, a correlated subquery includes conditions that reference values from the current row of the outer query. There are two conditions which I haven't mentioned so far, that are used with correlated subqueries. They are **exists** and its negation, **not exists**. The way you use **exists** is that you write

```
and exists
```

followed by a subquery that references the current row. If this subquery returns at least one row, the condition is satisfied. Otherwise it fails. Of course, it's the exact opposite with **not exists**.

Let's see this condition in action. If you want to find the titles of movies in which there is an actor who was born in 1970 or later, you can write

```
select distinct m.title
from movies m
where exists (select null
              from credits c
                   inner join people p
                      on p.peopleid = c.peopleid
              where c.credited_as= 'A'
                and p.born >= 1970
                and c.movieid = m.movieid)
```

In this query, you have in the subquery a reference to the current value of *movieid* in the outer query: it's a correlated subquery.

I hope that seeing `select null` made you start, especially after all the trouble we have just had with nulls. Actually, since the only thing that matters is whether the subquery returns something, and not what it returns, it doesn't matter if you write

```
select c.movieid
```

or

```
select p.surname
```

or

```
select 1
```

or

```
select 'Insert anything here'
```

`select null` is commonly used to emphasize that what the query returns doesn't matter.

I guess you see how it all works: the *movies* table is scanned, and for each row the current value of *movieid* is fed into the subquery that is fired and, depending on whether the subquery returns or doesn't return any row, the title is returned or skipped.

However, that's where once again things become interesting, you can just as easily write an uncorrelated query to obtain the same result; I just need to remove the correlated equality from the **where** clause of the subquery, render to the outer query what belongs to the outer query and use as a *select list* of the subquery what belongs to the subquery, with a **distinct** since several actors in the same movie can be born in or after 1970:

```
select distinct m.title
from movies m
where m.movieid in (select distinct c.movieid
                    from credits c
                         inner join people p
                            on p.peopleid = c.peopleid
                    where c.credited_as = 'A'
                      and p.born >= 1970)
```

If at this stage you don't feel utterly confused, I suggest you read again the whole part of this chapter that deals with subqueries. In a nutshell, correlated subqueries can be used instead of uncorrelated subqueries in the **where** clause and vice-versa, and both can be replaced by joins with subqueries in the **from** clause. What should you use then? The expert's answer to this type of question is always a thoughtful "it depends". At the risk of spoiling the topic, let me just say that performance may be noticeably different, and that it depends on volume and indexing, and I'll talk more about this in Chapter 9. There are also some cases that you will see in Chapter 10 that require the use of a subquery rather than a join.

Let me now introduce in the next chapter the last aspect of query syntax that I have left so far untouched: ordering.

To Remember

- Joins allow us to link tables on common values (usually columns involved in joins are foreign keys but not always). Inner joins only return data when there is a match; left outer joins complete with nulls missing matches and allow rows without matches to appear.
- With left outer joins the order of tables matters in the **from** clause, to the contrary of what happens with inner joins.
- Set operators, **union**, **intersect** and **except**, called **minus** in Oracle, are another way than joins to combine data that comes from two distinct datasets. To combine datasets with a set operator, columns from both datasets must match in number and type. **union** adds a functionality that no other operator provides. Inner joins and left outer joins are often more convenient than **intersect** and **except** respectively.
- You can have subqueries in the *select list*, in the **from** clause or in the **where** clause

  Subqueries in select lists are correlated, in **from** clauses they are uncorrelated and in **where** clauses they can be both. Beware of nulls everywhere but especially in subqueries.

Exercises

1. Which actors in the database appear in at least two movies?
2. Write a query that only returns the oldest movie in the database (hint: you need a subquery on the same table as the outer query)
3. Write a query that returns the people involved in the oldest movie, with their role (actor/director)
4. Of all the people in the database who are no longer alive, who died the oldest?
5. Who are the actors who played in films from different countries?

Ordering and Reporting 5

> Order was the dream of man.
>
> - Henry B. Adams (1838-1918)

This chapter covers

- How to present the result of a query, in order
- How to limit the number of rows returned
- How to deal with parent-child relationships between rows (hierarchies)
- How to answer some tricky questions and generate complex HTML output straight from SQL

Let me say it again: ordering is a notion that is completely foreign to the relational theory. What matters to relational theory is data. Whether the first name appears before or after the surname in the *people* table is meaningless. Even in the select list of a query it doesn't matter much because most often the data that is returned is handled by a program that may display the data whichever way it wants. In the same way, whether Cary Grant is stored before or after Ingrid Bergman in the movie database is perfectly irrelevant; whether Cary Grant is returned before or after Ingrid Bergman in a query is no more relevant. Facts matter, not how they are presented.

Nevertheless, we poor humans would be really inefficient at managing information if it were dumped to us in random order; which is why in almost all cases, the result set you finally pass to the end user, is a result set in which there is some relative ordering of rows.

Sorting Data

It is important to understand that in everything that I am going to present now, we have gone beyond the truly relational part of the database query. We have our dataset. Perhaps, as you will see, we may still discard some rows before presenting the result - and possibly many of them but by and large, the bulk of the work is done and we have found all the rows we want.

The Basics

The clause that orders a result set is **order by**, that comes last in a simple SQL query (as you will soon see, you may find **order by** in a nested query.) You can list and order by year, the titles and year of release of all the films in the database with the following query:

```
select title, year_released
from movies
order by year_released
```

It's important to understand that it really is the *result* of the query that is sorted, not the table itself. The table will be untouched by the operation. As a matter of consequence, you can order the result of *any* query: something as simple as a list of the films from one particular country, or something frankly more complicated such as the list of the films in which people played who were born after 1970, with a subquery that correctly restricts the result set:

```
select m.title, m.year_released, m.country
from movies m
where m.movieid in (select distinct c.movieid
                    from credits c
                         inner join people p
                            on p.peopleid = c.peopleid
                    where c.credited_as = 'A'
                      and p.born >= 1970)
order by m.year_released
```

You can also sort the result of a join, such as once again the list of films with people born after 1970, to which you add the country name retrieved from table *countries*:

```
select c.country_name,
       m.title,
       m.year_released
from movies m
     inner join countries c
     on c.country_code = m.country
where m.movieid in
  (select distinct c.movieid
   from credits c
        inner join people p
        on p.peopleid = c.peopleid
   where c.credited_as = 'A'
     and p.born >= 1970)
order by m.year_released
```

If you want to sort on several columns, you specify a comma-separated list of columns; if two rows have the same value in the first column, the second one is compared to determine which one should be displayed first, and if values are still equal comparison moves further down the list. You can also specify **desc** after the column name to make the sort descending, that is from the highest value to the lowest, instead of the default ascending order (which can be explicitly specified by using **asc** – that nobody uses.)

For instance, the previous list of films can be listed by country name and for each country from the most recent to the oldest movie, and finally by alphabetical order of titles:

```
select c.country_name,
       m.title,
       m.year_released
from movies m
     inner join countries c
     on c.country_code = m.country
where m.movieid in
   (select distinct c.movieid
    from credits c
         inner join people p
         on p.peopleid = c.peopleid
    where c.credited_as = 'A'
      and p.born >= 1970)
order by c.country_name,
         m.year_released desc,
         m.title
```

For the record, the lazy can also replace column names (or expressions) in the **order by** clause by ordinal numbers specifying which column: 1 for the leftmost one and so on. You could write in the previous example

```
order by 1, 3 desc, 2
```

I don't recommend this numbered notation because if you ever wish to display the columns in a different order, you may more easily miss that the **order by** clause also needs to be changed and it frequently leads to errors. It's much better to give a shorter alias to a column or expression and refer to this alias (instead of the actual column name) in the **order by** clause. You can refer to column aliases in the **order by** clause (to the contrary of the **where** clause) because the **order by** is always evaluated in an SQL query after the *select list* has been analyzed. An SQL engine starts by analyzing the **from** clause, at which point *table* aliases are known, then the **where** clause (which is why you can refer in conditions to aliases defined in the **from** clause), then **group by**, then **having**, then the *select list* which may define column aliases, then the **order by** where you can refer both to table and column aliases.

Sorting Subtleties

Syntax is fairly obvious for **order by**. Of course, you shouldn't forget that as with superior or inferior comparisons, ordering depends on the data type. If you apply function **cast()**, the ordering may be different.

Nulls, which cannot be compared with anything, can be returned either before or after everything else depending on the DBMS.

NOTE Oracle and PostgreSQL allow overriding the default behavior by appending to the **order by** clause either **nulls first** or **nulls last**.

Figure 5.1 shows how nulls are sorted by default with different DBMS products.

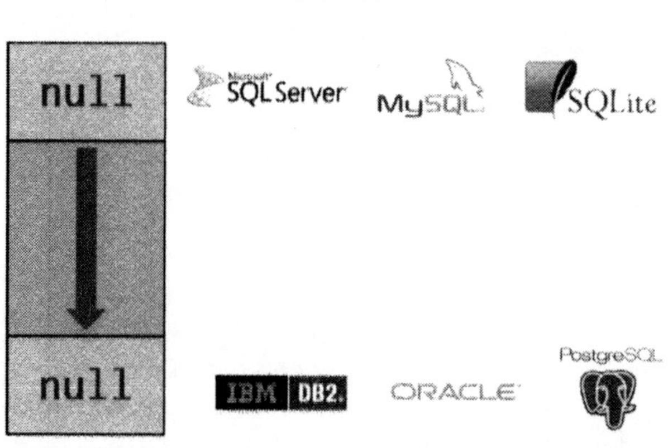

Figure 5.1: Sorting nulls.

In the particular case of text you must also be aware that case and accented letters (once again) may be a problem. Inside the computer, letters and characters are coded numerically; if the numbering of letters matches the alphabetical order, the order is respected only when the case is the same (upper case A has a code smaller than upper case B, but lower case A has a code greater than uppercase Z), and accented letters have codes that, not only don't fall in the same ranges of values as non accented letters but may depend on countries, or at least wide regions such as Western Europe.

You won't be surprised if I tell you that trying to sort a column that contains names in Latin, Greek, Cyrillic and Chinese characters will group names written in the same character set together. The names will not be sorted in the same order as they would have been sorted if all of them had been transcribed to the Latin alphabet but there is ample scope for trouble with Latin characters alone. If our DBMS is case-sensitive to data when ordering, everything that starts with an uppercase letter may be displayed before anything that starts with a lowercase letter (hence the need to standardize case). Then there is the problem of special letters and more importantly the cultural habits linked to ordering.

In Sweden, *ö* is considered to be greater than *z*, the opposite is true in Germany or Austria, where *ö* is supposed to appear with *o* (even if the code for *ö* in the computer is greater than the code for *p*). Besides, in the same country the common ordering may be different for phonebooks and dictionaries. The local, and cultural, set of rules for ordering letters is known as the *collation order*. A database always has a default collation order (which can be changed by an administrator) that is used for sorting text.

NOTE And yes, the default collation is Swedish for MySQL.

Several products (SQL Server, MySQL, PostgreSQL) allow us to specify at the column level in a **create table** statement, the collation to use for this column in the following way

```
create table ... (
        some_text_column varchar(100) collate <collation name> not null,
        ...)
```

The collation name is product specific; *utf8_bin* is a relatively safe generic choice with MySQL, *Latin1_General_100_* with SQL Server (SQL Server uses the same collation names as the Windows system).
Specifying the collation for a column when a table is created ensures that sorting this column will follow the collation specified.

Oracle doesn't have this option. If you want to specify a special collation for a column with Oracle, you must do it when sorting the column, by using a function called **nls_sort()** that takes as first parameter the name of a text column and as second parameter the name of a collation. You can use

```
order by nls_sort(some_text_column, '<collation name>')
```

instead of simply ordering by the column name.

NOTE NLS stands for **N**ational **L**anguage **S**upport. SQL Server also allows specifying the collation in the **order by** clause.

You may sort on a column that doesn't belong to the list of columns that are returned; this is particularly interesting with dates because very often you want to return a formatted date. When you format a date, you convert it to a character string, which you can only order alphabetically, not chronologically.

If I call the function that formats a date column, *date_format()* (generically, all products use differently named functions), a query such as

```
select date_format(a_date_column) as event_date, ...
from ...
where ...
order by event_date
```

will display the rows in chronological order, only if the format that is applied to the date is something such as YYYY/MM/DD, for which alphabetical and chronological order are identical.

```
select date_format(a_date_column) as event_date, ...
from ...
where ...
order by a_date_column
```

will always return rows in chronological order, irrespective of the format.

As I have shown you with the use of **nls_sort()** with Oracle, you can sort on the result of a function, or of an expression. The **case ... end** construct is commonly used to display results with an ordering that doesn't match any "natural" order.

movies

movied	title	country	year_released
1832	Gone With The Wind	us	1939

credits

movied	peopleid	credited_as
1832	237	A
1832	312	A
1832	742	P
1832	128	D

people

peopleid	first_name	surname	born	died
237	Clark	Gable	1901	1960
742	David	Selznick	1902	1965
312	Vivien	Leigh	1913	1967
128	Victor	Fleming	1889	1949

Figure 5.2: Crediting the producer.

For instance, suppose that we add to the *credits* table the names of producers, with a code P in column *credited_as* and that we want always to display movie credits in the following order:

1. Director(s)
2. Producer(s)
3. Actors

with names alphabetically ordered within each category. We cannot sort by *credited_as*, because none of A, D, P (the standard, ascending order) nor P, D, A (the descending order) matches the order we want. All we need to do is use a **case ... end** to 'transcode' the values of *credited_as* into something that we can sort as needed:

```
case credited_as
  when 'D' then 1
  when 'P' then 2
  when 'A' then 3
end as sort_key
```

We could have this expression in the *select list* and use it as the sort key but then, unless we nest the whole query as a subquery in the **from** clause, it would appear in the result. In fact, we just need to use the **case** expression in the **order by** clause:

```
order by case credited_as
           when 'D' then 1
           when 'P' then 2
           when 'A' then 3
         end,
         surname,
         first_name
```

A **case ... end** expression can also be used to improve the sorting of surnames. Some common abbreviations may ruin alphabetical order - for instance, *McLeod* should appear before, not after, *Maddox*, because it derives from *MacLeod*, *StClair* should appear before, not after, *Sellers*, because it stands for *SaintClair* (a fact happily ignored by many computerized systems). Abbreviation issues can be solved by enforcing stringent standards for data entry. You would also expect to find *von Stroheim* listed at *S*, not at *V*, and you have similar issues with Dutch names that start with a *van* followed by a space or French names that start with a *de* followed by a space. A solution is to store *Stroheim (von)* instead of *von Stroheim*. This will require a bit of juggling if you ever want to fetch the concatenation of the first name and of the surname, because *Erich Stroheim (von)* is probably not what you'll want to see but it makes correct surname ordering natural.

More often than not you will not have had a say in deciding how data has been stored. If a surname has been stored as *von Stroheim* (even as *Von Stroheim* if standardization of names is heavy-handed), you can still fix the ordering of surnames with a **case** expression, something such as the following that checks whether the surname starts with *von<space>* or *de<space>*, in which cases this prefix is stripped for ordering:

```
order by case
           when lower(substr(surname, 1, 4)) = 'von '
                then substr(surname, 5)
           when lower(substr(surname, 1, 3)) = 'de '
                then substr(surname, 4)
           else surname
         end
```

NOTE All products except Oracle and SQLite support a **left()** function which is most convenient for extracting the beginning of a string (the leftmost characters, when writing from left to right). A function call such as `substr(surname, 1, 4)` can also be written `left(surname, 4)`.

This will make names starting with *von* or *de* and a space appear where they should.

Limiting Output

It's quite frequent that after having retrieved a result set and ordered the rows for human consumption, you don't want to display all of the rows. There are at least two common cases when you want to limit output:

- When you want to give the answer to a question such as "What are the three oldest American movies in the database". To answer such a question, you need to apply a selection operation to get all American movies – and this is the only purely relational operation in the retrieval process. Then, the "three oldest" bit of the question requires sorting by year of release before limiting the output to the first three movies in the sorted list.
- When you want to page across many rows of results. This is typically what you see on a merchant site when you search on a broad category of articles and get a result set of several hundred (or more) items. You can usually sort that result set by "relevance", price, sales or customer rating. As it is not only time and resource consuming but also completely useless to return the full list, when everyone knows that users will inspect the first 20 or 30 results at most, only one page of rows is returned initially and buttons allow you to fetch on demand the next batches of rows, with respect to the specified ordering.

title ▾	country	year_released
Inglourious Basterds	us	2009
Jaws	us	1975
La Belle et la Bête	fr	1946
Ladri di biciclette	it	1948
Lawrence of Arabia	gb	1962
Le cinquième élément	fr	1997
Les Visiteurs du Soir	fr	1942
Mary Poppins	us	1964
On The Waterfront	us	1954
Pather Panchali	in	1955

1 2 3 4

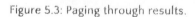

Figure 5.3: Paging through results.

There are several ways to limit output in pure SQL. I am going for now, to present the "historical" way to do it, which is still much in use. Later in this chapter, I'll also discuss newer, and in my view better, ways to do it. With the historical way, anarchy reigns. Several SQL engines (DB2, MySQL, PostgreSQL, SQLite) support a **limit** keyword. When I told you that **order by** comes last, this wasn't absolutely true: **limit** comes last, both in the text of a query and in execution order, which happens to follow the order of the different clauses (except for the *select list*):

where -> **group by** -> **having** -> *select list* -> **order by** -> **limit**

The **limit** keyword is followed by either simply one integer value, for instance if we want to display the three oldest American movies we can write:

```
select title, year_released
from movies
where country = 'us'
order by year_released
limit 3
```

or **limit** can be followed by an integer value, **offset** and another integer value that specifies the number of rows to skip – if I want to display all the movies in the database ordered by year of release and title on pages of 10 movies, I can display page 3 with this query that skips the 20 rows presumably already displayed on pages 1 and 2:

```
select year_released, title, country
from movies
order by year_released
limit 10 offset 20
```

NOTE Additionally, MySQL and DB2 also support the syntax **limit** ***<offset>, <count>***.

DB2 also implements **fetch first** *<count>* **rows** that works exactly as **limit** *<count>* and appears at the same place in a query (that is, after the **order by**) but has no reference to an offset. SQL Server specifies the limit with still another keyword, **top**, which appears not at the end of a statement but at the beginning, between a possible **distinct** and the first column to be returned from the database.

NOTE There are variants of **top**, such as **top with ties**, which may return more rows than specified if the values used for sorting are found several times, and **top** *n* **percent**.

Thus, the query to return the three oldest American movies would be written in Transact-SQL:

```
select top 3
       title, year_released
from movies
where country = 'us'
order by year_released
```

No offset here either for versions of SQL Server prior to SQL Server 2012.

NOTE Transact-SQL, or T-SQL, is the SQL dialect common to SQL Server and Sybase.

From SQL Server 2012, there is a new clause **offset** ... **fetch** ... that must be written after the **order by** clause and which is exclusive of **top**.

```
select title, year_released
from movies
where country = 'us'
order by year_released
offset 0 rows
fetch next 3 rows only
```

Oracle implements the same syntax, starting from Oracle 12c.

The query that displays the third of a list of 10 film pages would be

```
select year_released, title, country
from movies
order by year_released
offset 20 rows
 fetch next 10 rows only
```

Oracle implements no special clause to limit output before Oracle 12c. However, whenever you retrieve information from a source with Oracle, the first row obtained is internally numbered as 1 and the counter is increased as rows are retrieved. This internal counter can be accessed in a query as a pseudo-column called **rownum**.

Where things become tricky is that numbering, as I have said, is assigned to rows as they are retrieved - something which happens before you sort them, because to sort rows you must have retrieved the full set.

NOTE You will see in a later chapter that it is sometimes possible to store, and therefore retrieve, rows in a pre-defined order but this is an implementation trick on which you should never rely, as a database can be completely reorganized for perfectly legitimate reasons.

If you write with Oracle

```
select title, year_released
from movies
where country = 'us'
  and rownum <= 3
order by year_released
```

You will retrieve three American movies and display them in chronological order but they won't be the three oldest ones - they will be the first three movies that were retrieved from the table.

> NOTE If they also happen to be the three oldest ones, go and buy a lottery ticket immediately.

To retrieve the three oldest movies, you must filter on a **rownum** computed from a sorted source - which you can obtain by wrapping the sort in a subquery:

```
select title, year_released
from (select title, year_released
      from movies
      where country = 'us'
      order by year_released) sorted_us_movies
where rownum <= 3
```

As a side note, there is no guarantee when an **order by** clause appears in a subquery that the final result will be sorted in the same way. This is what will happen here but if you wanted to join the new dataset to *credits* and *people* to display the name of the director(s) next to the title, there is no guarantee that the rows will still be sorted by year - actually, it is highly likely that they won't be because the join process will bring turbulences. If you want the result to be sorted, the only clause that can guarantee the order is a final

```
order by year_released
```

at the outmost level.

Multiple sort operations inside a query are one of the possible ways to skip rows for paging when the DBMS natively offers no such possibility.

If you want to skip 20 rows and display the next 10 rows it practically means that

1. You need to identify the result set which represents the global scope of your query (such as "all American movies" - or possibly "all movies", in which case there is no selection operation on the table).
2. You sort this result set.
3. You fetch the first 30 rows: 20 that will be quietly discarded and 10 that will be shown.

Let's start by fetching, with SQL Server for instance, the first 30 rows:

```
select top 30
       year_released, title, country
from movies
order by year_released
```

Out of these, we only want to display, on page 3 if we show 10 movies per page, the 10 most recent ones - which are indeed another series of "top 10" movies but on a criterion that is the reverse of the previous one.

```
select top 10
       year_released, title, country
from (select top 30
             year_released, title, country
      from movies
      order by year_released) top_30
order by year_released desc
```

This query gives us the movies to display on page 3 – except that they are "wrongly" ordered. All we need is a kind of flip-flop operation that sorts them back as wanted (as this sort operates on a very small number of rows, it isn't a costly operation):

```
select *
from (select top 10
             year_released, title, country
      from (select top 30
                   year_released, title, country
            from movies
            order by year_released) top_30
      order by year_released desc) my_page
order by year_released
```

In the case of Oracle the logic is significantly different. A query such as

```
select year_released, title, country
from (select year_released, title, country
      from movies
      order by year_released) sorted_movies
where rownum between 21 and 30
```

returns no rows at all. The reason is that **rownum** is computed on the fly when rows are selected. We cannot have a row with a **rownum** equal to 21 if prior to it we haven't returned 20 rows that have successfully taken **rownum** values 1 to 20. We must first "materialize" the virtual **rownum** values by returning them as a part of a data set:

```
select rownum as rn, year_released, title, country
from (select year_released, title, country
      from movies
      order by year_released) sorted_movies
where rownum <= 30
```

This query provides us with a new data source, to which we can apply a regular filtering condition:

```
select year_released, title, country
from (select rownum as rn, year_released, title, country
      from (select year_released, title, country
            from movies
            order by year_released) sorted_movies
      where rownum <= 30) top_30
where rn >= 21
order by rn    ← To be on the safe side ...
```

Limiting the output doesn't technically require the presence of an **order by** clause but returning only a part of a result set without ordering makes little sense.

Hierarchies

Sometimes, no column or combination of columns can provide the ordering you want. A typical example would be a forum: let's say that a first user creates a new topic by posting a question and that other users post answers. You'll probably want to display the various posts chronologically, until someone comments, not on the original question but on one of the comments, to contradict or clarify it, thus starting a heated discussion that, if it attracts some troll, can last for a while. Then the order becomes anything but obvious because you basically want posts to be displayed in a chronological order, unless they are an answer to another post. If this is the case, then you have a new thread in which you want all answers to the same post to be in chronological order. All this at any depth. Hierarchies may be complicated, I have covered the topic in more detail in another book but I am going to present briefly some available solutions.

> NOTE I have devoted a full chapter to the topic of hierarchies in *The Art of SQL*, published by O'Reilly. The *Art of SQL* isn't a book for beginners, it assumes a few years of SQL practice.

Figure 5.4 shows how posts might be ordered in a forum.

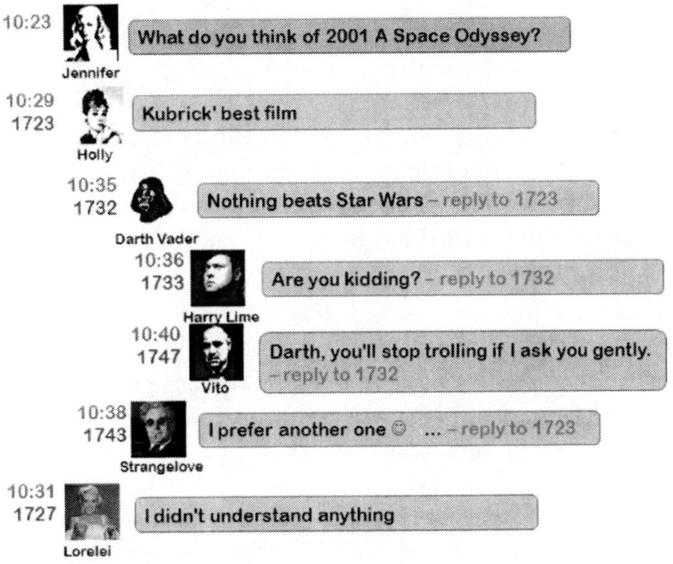

Figure 5.4: Post ordering on a forum.

Storing Ancestry

In the type of forum that I have just described, we have what is called a tree structure: a hierarchy of posts each linked to a "parent" post (the message that is answered directly). One of the best technical answers that one can give, in the absence of any product-specific feature to support trees in one way or another, is to store in a string the "ancestry" of a row, considered as an attribute - the identifier of the parent, of the parent of the parent, and of all the "ancestors" up to the root, the row that has no parent. Sorting by ancestry keeps threads related to the same post together.

Storing a list of numerical identifiers in a string isn't without dangers when you want to sort - as I have maintained, numerical and alphabetical comparison, and therefore sort, don't obey the same rules. Sorts will not give the result you expect unless you format identifiers, giving them a fixed length and padding with zeroes on the left hand side, using string functions or a number formatting function.

NOTE Number formatting is more usually handled in programs that issue SQL statements than in SQL itself, except in cases similar to this one.

Let's see how it works in practice. Suppose that the table that stores answers to a topic has the following structure:

```
create table forum_posts(postid       int not null primary key,
                         ancestry     varchar(1000),
                         topicid      int not null,
                         posted_by    int not null,
                         post_date    datetime not null,
                         message      text not null)
```

You can probably guess most referential integrity constraints. When a message is posted as an answer to an existing message (as opposed to an answer to the original topic), it must add the identifier of the answered message to its own ancestry - and in fact not only the identifier but the full ancestry of the answered message too. The ancestry of the new message becomes

```
concat(<ancestry of the answered message>,
       lpad(cast(<identifier of the answered message> as char), 10, '0'))
```

Function **lpad()** adds to the left of its first argument, as many occurrences of its third argument (a space by default) that are required to obtain a string the number of characters of which are the second argument.

NOTE Alternatively you can use product-specific functions such as **to_char()** with Oracle, DB2, or PostgreSQL. With SQL Server, `substring('0000000000', 1, len(cast(postid as char)) - 10) + cast(postid as char)` can replace `lpad(cast(postid as char), 10, '0'))`.

My padding to 10 digits implies that I don't expect to have 10 billion or more rows in my table (the maximum *postid* value will be 9999999999); if you are more ambitious than I am, you can pad to more digits. The size I gave to the *ancestry* column also assumes that I don't expect a discussion to develop to a depth (answer to answer to answer ....) of more than 100 levels, which looks reasonable to me especially if the forum is moderated; once again, this can be adjusted as needed.

Sorting with

```
order by concat(coalesce(ancestry, ''),
                lpad(cast(postid as char), 10, '0'))
```

should return all the threads suitably sorted (I assume that the post identifiers always increase with time).

Storing a carefully formatted ancestry is convenient for ordering, for finding all the "descendants" of a post and for finding all the "ancestors". It becomes less convenient when a moderator decides that a discussion should be better attached to a different topic and wants to prune a sub tree here and graft it there because then we have to modify the ancestry of each and every row that is logically moved but otherwise it's a rather efficient method.

Oracle's connect by

NOTE DB2 can be configured to support **connect by**.

Alone among all DBMS suppliers, Oracle long ago implemented an SQL extension to walk hierarchical structures. It only requires us to store as an attribute of each row, the identifier of the parent row - not the full ancestry as previously explained. What Oracle has implemented can arguably be described as a very special **order by** in which the ordering is permanently readjusted by a kind of join between the current row and the row that was retrieved before it. If I take the forum example once again, my table only needs to have the following structure (with Oracle data types):

```
create table forum_posts(postid          number not null primary key,
                         answered_postid number,
                         topicid         number not null,
                         posted_by       number not null,
                         post_date       date not null,
                         message         varchar2(2000) not null,
                        foreign key(answered_postid)
                           references forum_posts(postid))
```

There should be other foreign keys than the self-referencing one but I just focus on this particular table.

In an Oracle **connect by** query what is important is that, we have at any time, access to the values in the very last row that was retrieved with the keyword **prior**. Instead of having an **order by** clause, the last row that was retrieved determines the next row to retrieve using a **connect by** clause:

```
connect by answered_postid = prior postid
```

Whenever a column name is preceded by the **prior** keyword, it refers to the column from the row that was retrieved before the current one. It's really like a join condition between two successive rows: I want to retrieve a message that refers to the same topic as the previous one and which was posted as an answer to the previous message. The difference between this and a regular join is that when no rows are found, Oracle will automatically backtrack and branch to the next row that should logically be fetched, until all rows have been retrieved.

> NOTE Perhaps it is worth noting that a **connect by** query may return more rows than the table contains. If we retrieve the parent before the child, saying `connect by parent_id = prior id`, then we'll have the same number of rows as in the table because each child row only has one parent. If we retrieve the child before the parent with `connect by id = prior parent_id`, then a parent row with multiple children will be retrieved several times, leading to, guess what, duplicates. However, the information that interests us is not what a row contains but how rows relate to one another. Just don't apply a relational operation to such a query result...

The reference to the previous row is naturally meaningless for the very first row that is returned and we must specify with a **start with** clause how we prime the pump:

```
start with answered_postid is null
       and topicid = ...
```

Last issue, what about posts that are answers to the same message - posts that have the same "parent"? We wish to order them by post identifier but we need to specify it:

```
order siblings by postid
```

So, all I need to do is replace a simple **order by** with the following:

```
connect by answered_postid = prior postid
start with answered_postid is null
        and topicid = ...
order siblings by postid
```

There is a subtle difference of behavior between **order by** and **connect by**: as I have told you, **order by** operates after screening for all of the **where** conditions. This isn't true with **connect by**: conditions in the **connect by** and **start with** clause truly determine which rows will be retrieved. If a row doesn't satisfy a **where** condition, it will be retrieved by the query but skipped and not displayed; **connect by** is a kind of "order as you go" operation, not something that operates on a well defined result set.

ORACLE

```
select message, ....
from forum_posts ...
connect by answered_postid = prior postid
start with answered_postid is null
       and topicid = ...
order siblings by postid
```

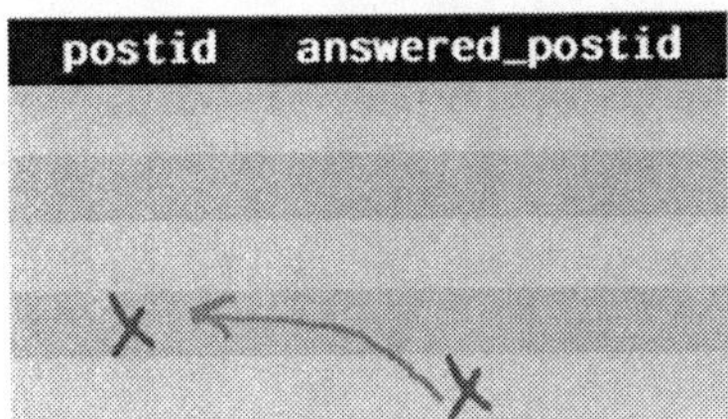

Figure 5.5: Oracle's connect by.

A special pseudo-column similar to **rownum** and named **level** tells us at what depth in the tree the current row can be found (when we store the path, the depth can be derived from the length of the path); this value is often used in computing how many spaces to add to the left for proper indenting.

Recursive Queries

DB2, SQL Server, PostgreSQL, Oracle (since version 11gR2) all implement a special construct that is complex but very interesting for managing hierarchical structures: recursive SQL queries. If you are an experienced programmer, you probably know what recursion is. If not, recursive processes are processes in which you start with something that is usually trivial to compute, then use the freshly computed value to compute the next one, then use this next one to compute the one that follows, and so on until you hit a predefined value that stops the recursion. When you program a recursive function, it calls itself.

Like Oracle's **connect by**, recursive SQL queries don't require the full ancestry of a post, you just need to record the identifier of the answered ("parent") post. The definition of a recursive query comes first, before the **select** that uses it, and is preceded by the **with** keyword (PostgreSQL demands **with recursive**.)

NOTE It is possible to have a non recursive **with** statement, in which case there is no list of columns, for instance `with myquery as (select …)`. It just defines an alias for a query expression that will be used, possibly at different places, in the select statement that follows the **with** clause (it's sometimes referred to as Common Table Expression, or CTE.)

The body of the recursive part is a **union all** query. The first part of the union corresponds to the trivial starting point, from which everything else is derived (equivalent to Oracle's **start with**.) When we write a recursive query, this first part is always fetching either the rows that have no parent rows (the "root" of the trees), or the rows that have no children rows (the "leaves" of the trees).

Then comes the **union all**, and the second part of the union, which is the interesting one. In this part, the table that is searched is joined to the recursive query, which represents the rows that have been retrieved (equivalent to Oracle's **connect by**.)

Once the recursive query has been defined, we can query it as if it were a table with a predefined row order.

```
with q(postid, message) as
     (select postid, message
      from forum_posts
      where answered_postid is null
        and topicid = ...
      union all
      select f.postid, f.message
      from forum_posts f
           inner join q
              on f.answered_postid = q.postid)
select *
from q
```

IBM DB2. SQL Server PostgreSQL ORACLE

Figure 5.6: A recursive query example.

The snag with recursive queries, which is why I won't say much on the topic, is that they operate by layers - returning all rows at the same level, one after the other, before moving to the next level. For instance, if I just return the identifier of posts and the identifier of the "parent" post with this query, computing the level in the tree:

```
with q(postid, answered_postid, level) as
  (select postid, answered_postid, 1 level
   from forum_posts
   where answered_postid is null
     and topicid = ...
   union all
   select child.postid, child.answered_postid, parent.level + 1
```

```
  from forum_posts child
       inner join q parent
          on parent.postid = child.answered_postid)
select * from q
```

I get something like this

```
postid answered_postid level
------ --------------- -----
1723                       1
1727                       1
1732              1723     2
1743              1723     2
1733              1732     3
1747              1732     3
```

Oracle implements a special clause (**search depth first**) to make a recursive query behave like a **connect by** query but as a **connect by** is much easier to write and understand, if ordering is your main concern you are better off with a **connect by**. It is possible to order the output of a recursive query even without Oracle's extension but it's rather complex. Recursive queries may be quite useful for complex computations; they can be used for computing cumulative values for instance, but this goes somewhat beyond the scope of this book. For ordering purposes, working with them is awkward unless their "natural order" is precisely what you need.

Window Functions

Window functions were introduced in the SQL standard in 2003; not all products implement them (you won't find them in MySQL 5 and the previous versions, nor in SQLite 3); some products implement more window functions than others.

NOTE Different vendors give them different names; they are called analytic functions in Oracle and OLAP functions in DB2 (OLAP is an acronym for **O**n-**L**ine **A**nalytical **P**rocessing).

The SQL functions that we have seen so far are of two kinds: standard functions that take as parameters values from one row (or no parameters at all, such as the function that returns the current date) and return another, derived, value for that same row, and aggregate functions that return one single value for a group of rows.

NOTE Standard functions are usually called *scalar functions*.

Window functions are hybrid functions: they return one result for each row in the result set, not for several rows like aggregate functions but this result isn't only computed from the values in the row but from values found in several rows. Unlike the other SQL functions, window functions only appear in what is called the *select list* – they must appear between **select** and **from**. If you want to apply a condition to what is returned by a window function, the solution is simple: you wrap the query where it appears as a subquery to which you can apply a **where** clause.

Although you may find their syntax a bit jarring at first, window functions, when they are available, are most convenient for reporting. I'm going to explain to you the hard-core of window functions, which you will find everywhere that window functions are available, before showing you some interesting uses.

There are two main categories of window functions, which I'll call non-ranking and ranking functions. Let's start with non-ranking functions.

Non-Ranking Functions

Non-ranking functions are, for the most part, a variation on aggregate functions.

Aggregate functions are great and good but the problem is that with aggregate functions you lose the detail. Let's take an example. If I ask you to give the year of the oldest movie per country (column *country* in table *movies* is actually a country code but let's keep things simple), I'm sure you'll come out very fast with a solution:

```
select country, min(year_released) earliest_year
from movies
group by country
```

That was easy. Now, if I ask you what are the title and year of the oldest movie for each country, you can probably come up with a solution too but it's not as easy:

```
select a.country, a.title, a.year_released
from movies a
     inner join (select country,
                        min(year_released) earliest_year
                 from movies
                 group by country) b
        on b.country = a.country
       and b.earliest_year = a.year_released
```

Your own solution may be slightly different but the basic idea is certainly the same: using the query that returns the earliest year per country and joining the result to the same table. This is why I said that you lose the detail: with the aggregate, the title must disappear because in the result of a query with an aggregate function you can only have the aggregate result, here the year, and the columns that are used to define the subset of rows on which the aggregate operates, and in this case it's the country code. To answer the question, you need two explicit passes over the same data: one to find the earliest year, one to retrieve the detail.

All aggregate functions have, when window functions are supported, an equivalent window function that allows you to see simultaneously on the same row, both aggregate and detail without any join.

The syntax for all window functions is as follows:

```
func(parameters) over (magic clause)
```

The *magic clause* specifies how the function is applied. For instance, if we want the release year of the oldest movie per country, we are going to write

```
min(year_released) over (partition by country)
```

The **partition by** denotes as **group by** how we define the subset of rows for which we must find the minimum value. However, there is no grouping proper, for the remainder of the row – this function can be called when returning each and every row, and you can have on the same row the detail AND an aggregate result without any join, as in this example:

```
select country,
       title,
       year_released,
       min(year_released) over (partition by country) earliest_year
from movies
```

which (depending on data in your tables) gives something like:

```
country title                          year_released earliest_year
...
gb      Lawrence Of Arabia                      1962          1949
gb      The Third Man                           1949          1949
hk      Ying hung boon sik                      1986          1986
in      Sholay                                  1975          1955
in      Pather Panchali                         1955          1955
it      Ladri di biciclette                     1948          1948
it      Il buono, il brutto, il cattivo         1966          1948
...
us      On The Waterfront                       1954          1941
us      The Sound of Music                      1965          1941
us      Jaws                                    1975          1941
us      Doctor Zhivago                          1965          1941
us      Mary Poppins                            1964          1941
us      Blade Runner                            1982          1941
us      Annie Hall                              1977          1941
us      Casablanca                              1942          1941
us      Goodfellas                              1990          1941
us      Citizen Kane                            1941          1941
us      Inglourious Basterds                    2009          1941
us      The Dark Knight                         2008          1941
us      The Shawshank Redemption                1994          1941
us      The Godfather                           1972          1941
us      Pulp Fiction                            1994          1941
us      Schindler's List                        1993          1941
us      Star Wars                               1977          1941
```

When you see the result of this query, finding the oldest movie per country becomes fairly easy. Do you see the solution?

You just have to wrap the previous query inside a condition on the years, saying that the year when the movie was released is actually the same year as for the oldest movie – you will notice that we may have several movies for the same country that satisfy the condition:

```
select m.country,
       m.title,
       m.year_released
from (select country,
             title,
             year_released,
             min(year_released)
                over (partition by country) earliest_year
      from movies) m
where m.year_released = m.earliest_year
```

This syntax is perhaps only marginally simpler than the join – there may be a significant performance gain sometimes but so far we are only interested in writing queries the best we can. Here we have a single pass over the table, even if it's admittedly a more complicated single pass than what we have seen so far.

When there are additional conditions, you must be careful as to whether they are applied before or after the reporting function. For instance, among the oldest movies of each country pick the one you like least from a country for which there are several movies. Once you have made your choice, you can say "I want the list of the oldest movies but I don't want this one to appear" and write this query:

```
select m.country,
       m.title,
       m.year_released
from (select country,
             title,
             year_released,
             min(year_released)
                over (partition by country) earliest_year
      from movies
      where title <> ' ...') m
where m.year_released = m.earliest_year
```

Magically, the movie that will now appear as the oldest one for this country will be in fact the second oldest – this is a very important point, the reporting function only applies to the rows that are selected through the **where** clause. It gives the same result as the following query with a join on the aggregate result:

```
select a.country, a.title, a.year_released
from movies a
     inner join (select country,
                        min(year_released) earliest_year
                 from movies
                 where title <> '...'
                 group by country) b
        on b.country = a.country
       and b.earliest_year = a.year_released
```

If you had put the condition in the outer query, that is if you had written this query, with the restriction on the title at the same level as the condition on years:

```
select m.country,
       m.title,
```

```
       m.year_released
from (select country,
             title,
             year_released,
             min(year_released)
                over (partition by country) earliest_year
      from movies) m
where m.year_released = m.earliest_year
  and m.title <> '...'
```

Then you would have had no result at all for this particular country unless several movies were released in the earliest year. It behaves exactly like the following query:

```
select a.country, a.title, a.year_released
from movies a
     inner join (select country,
                        min(year_released) earliest_year
                 from movies
                 group by country) b
        on b.country = a.country
       and b.earliest_year = a.year_released
where a.title <> '...'
```

You should note that it's perfectly valid to have an empty **over** clause, for instance

```
min(year_released) over ()
```

Like with an aggregate function without any grouping by any column, an empty **over ()** clause simply means that the function is applied to all the rows returned by the query. A window function with an empty **over ()** clause can be useful for computing a percentage. Let's say that you want to compute, not only how many movies we have per country in the database but which percentage of the movies each country represents.
A first query to compute the number of movies per country:

```
select c.country_name,
       coalesce(m.cnt, 0) cnt
from countries c
     left outer join (select country,
                             count(*) cnt
                      from movies
                      group by country) m
       on m.country = c.country_code
order by c.country_name
```

then I wrap it to compute the percentage:

```
select country_name,
       cnt,
       round(100 * cnt / sum(cnt) over (), 0) percentage
from (select c.country_name,
             coalesce(m.cnt, 0) cnt
      from countries c
           left outer join (select country,
                                   count(*) cnt
                            from movies
                            group by country) m
```

```
                  on m.country = c.country_code) q
order by country_name

country_name   cnt percentage
-------------- --- ----------
Bolivia          0          0
Finland          0          0
France           3          9
Germany          1          3
Hong Kong        1          3
India            2          6
Italy            2          6
Japan            1          3
New Zealand      1          3
Russia           1          3
Sweden           1          3
United Kingdom   2          6
United States   17         53
```

The equivalent query, without using a window function, would use a type of join that I have just mentioned in Chapter 4 called a **cross join**. A **cross join** has no join condition, it just generates all possible combinations of rows between the two tables that it links; it's also called a *Cartesian join*. For a percentage we need to compute separately the total (a single row result) and to combine it with every row, without any join condition, therefore with a **cross join**:

```
select country_name,
       cnt,
       round(100 * cnt / t.movie_count, 0) percentage
from (select c.country_name,
             coalesce(m.cnt, 0) cnt
      from countries c
           left outer join (select country,
                                   count(*) cnt
                            from movies
                            group by country) m
                 on m.country = c.country_code) q
     cross join (select count(*) movie_count
                 from movies) t
order by country_name
```

Ranking Functions

Ranking functions have no associated aggregate functions and the most important ranking functions take no parameters: the action is entirely defined by what you put inside the **over** clause. There are three main ranking functions, **row_number()**, **rank()** and **dense_rank()**. They all operate in a similar way. The first thing to define when you talk about ranking is of course how you order items to rank them. This goes to the **over** clause as an **order by**; and before the **order by**, you can also specify a **partition by** that says within which group you want to order.

An example will immediately make all this easier to understand: suppose that you want to assign a number to movies within each country, so that the most recent one is numbered 1, the second most recent one 2 and so on. First you identify the movies from the same country, then for each country you number the movies by the year they were released, from the most recent to the oldest one within each group.

```
select title,
       country,
       year_released,
       row_number()
        over (partition by country
              order by year_released desc) rn
from movies
```

title	country	year_released	
Casablanca	us	1942	5
Blade Runner	us	1982	2
On The Waterfront	us	1954	4
Lawrence Of Arabia	gb	1962	1
Annie Hall	us	1977	3
Goodfellas	us	1990	1
The Third Man	gb	1949	2
Citizen Kane	us	1941	6
Bicycle Thieves	it	1948	1
The Battleship Potemkin	ru	1925	1
Sholay	in	1975	1
A Better Tomorrow	hk	1986	1

Figure 5.7: Ranking movies by age within each country.

In SQL you first list the columns you want from the table, then you add the **row_number()** ranking function, you specify the groups with **partition**, then the ordering, and you're done.

```
select title,
       country,
       year_released,
       row_number()
                over (partition by country
                      order by year_released desc) rn
from movies
```

You can specify several columns, separated by commas, in both the **partition by** and **order by** parts of the **over** clause.

The difference between **row_number()**, **rank()** and **dense_rank()** is merely the way ties are numbered. Suppose there's a sporting competition in which two folks are in a tie for the third position. What will be the rank of the guy who didn't make it on the podium? With **row_number()**, ties are ignored and within a group the number of a row is always one more than the previous row in the group, even if the value that is used for ordering is the same in the two rows. Who will be number 3 and who will be number 4 is unpredictable if the number of points that is used for ranking is the same for both. It depends on whose name is the first retrieved from the table. For **rank()**, same number of points means same rank but then, the guy who follows is numbered 5. We have a gap in the ranks after ties. If we don't want any gap, then we use **dense_rank()** that still assigns the same rank to two rows with the same value but will then increase the rank of the next row by one only. In a way, **rank()** counts how many rows were returned before the current one when there is no tie; **dense_rank()** counts how many higher scores were returned. Table 5.1 shows what was obtained with the three functions when ordering countries by decreasing number of films on a sample database.

Country	Number of films	row_number()	rank()	dense_rank()
United States	39	1	1	1
India	7	2	2	2
Italy	4	3	3	3
France	4	4	3	3
United Kingdom	3	5	5	4
Hong Kong	1	6	6	5
Russia	1	7	6	5
Sweden	1	8	6	5
Japan	1	9	6	5

Table 5.1: A comparison between row_number(), rank() and dense_rank() when ordering countries by decreasing number of films.

I told you when I discussed how to limit the output of a query that there were better ways to do it than using **limit**, **top**, **fetch first**, **offset** ... **fetch** ...., or **rownum**: adding a ranking window function, usually wrapped in another query, allows you to limit output and skip rows by filtering on the output of this function, using a syntax that isn't product-specific.

> NOTE I must refine what I am saying here: using keywords such as **limit**, **top**, and so forth, provides the query optimizer with some information about the amount of data you really want, which sometimes can help it doing something really clever but in most cases, you'll find window functions to be both very flexible and very efficient.

The raw limit settings that you can define with the old fashioned syntax are equivalent to **row_number()** - they count rows and ignore ties, which is great for paging but not so for answering true ranking questions. Window functions provide much more flexibility.

When you are able to assign row numbers or ranks, it becomes very easy to answer questions that would have been extremely difficult to answer efficiently otherwise, such as which are the two most recent movies for each country. By taking the preceding query that numbers films by age within each country (actually, you may prefer using **rank()** to using **row_number()**), by wrapping this query inside another query and applying a condition to the rank or row number you can very easily solve the problem:

```
select c.country_name, m.title, m.year_released
from (select country,
             title,
             year_released,
             rank() over (partition by country
                          order by year_released desc) rnk
      from movies) m
     inner join countries c
      on c.country_code = m.country
where rnk <= 2
order by c.country_name, rnk
```

NOTE I am only showing you here the most common uses of window functions. They can do more and allow us for instance, to base computations not only on groups as defined by the values in some columns but on a moving window of rows that come before or after the current one, according to a sort key. This allows us, among other things, to compute moving averages in financial or statistical applications. All products also implement other window functions, which are often convenient short-hand notations for combinations of the basic functions shown in this chapter.

Window functions have a much wider scope of application than most people imagine. I want to show you how a combination of ranking and non ranking reporting functions can help us generate from SQL, proper HTML tags when you want to display the result of a query on a web page in an attractive way.

If you are unfamiliar with HTML, HTML pages comprise an indefinite number of pairs of tags. A tag usually looks usually like *<tag>*, then the text that must appear in a particular way follows, then you usually find an end tag that looks like *</tag>*. Tags are interpreted by browsers for rendering the page; the tags can be nested to multiple levels, which makes them powerful.

In this example I'll use only three pairs of tags:

- **<h1>** ... **</h1>** that surrounds what we want to see appear as a main header,
- **<ul>**... **</ul>** that surrounds a bulleted list,
- and **<li>** ... **</li>** that indicates a bulleted item in a list.

What I'd like to display is first a header made up of the country name, then a bulleted list with all the movies for this country sorted in alphabetical order - something like Figure 5-n:

Figure 5.8: A bulleted list of movies on an HTML page.

Getting this lay-out in my browser requires that I generate something that looks like the following sample, with the country name between a pair of **h1** tags, then the list of movies between a pair of **ul** tags, and finally each title between a pair of **li** tags. Note that HTML ignores carriage returns but will insert one after all of our closing tags; therefore it doesn't matter whether tags are or are not on the same line.

```
<h1>India</h1>
<ul>
  <li>Pather Panchali</li>
  <li>Sholay</li>
</ul>
```

Generating the list of country names and movie titles is something that we know how to do with a join but we have a problem with the tags. For instance, for each country, we must output the header with the country name and the "beginning of list" tag before outputting the first movie, and the first movie only. We must also output an "end of list" tag after the last movie for the country, and this one only. That can be tricky and very often people will run complicated logic inside a program that will execute SQL queries to process what is returned. In fact, we can generate everything as it is needed in SQL, and keep the calling program extremely simple.

Let's start by writing a join between *movies* and *countries*:

```
select c.country_name,
       m.title
from movies m
     inner join countries c
             on c.country_code = m.country
order by c.country_name, m.title
```

Then we can add a **row_number()** so as to identify which is the first movie, by title, for each country. I wrap the query with the reporting function inside another query because in the end I don't want the row number to be displayed but let's display it now to understand the mechanics better:

```
select x.rn,
       x.country_name,
       x.title
from (select c.country_name,
             m.title,
             row_number() over (partition by c.country_name
                                order by m.title) rn
      from movies m
           inner join countries c
                   on c.country_code = m.country) x
order by x.country_name, x.title, x.rn
```

By using the **case** construct and concatenating HTML tags as simple strings in the query, we can generate what is appropriate each time we start a list for a new country:

```
select case x.rn
         when 1 then '<h1>' || x.country_name || '</h1><ul><li>'
         else '<li>'
       end || x.title || '</li>' html
from (select c.country_name,
             m.title,
             row_number() over (partition by c.country_name
                                order by m.title) rn
      from movies m
           inner join countries c
                   on c.country_code = m.country) x
order by x.country_name, x.title, x.rn
```

That looks good, except that there is no ending tag for the list and if we try to output an ending tag before showing the country name, then we have a problem with the very first and very last rows returned by the query. What we need is something that tells us "this is the last row in the series" in the very same way as the value of 1 for *rn* tells us "this is the first row in the series"; but the number of movies per country varies.

The solution therefore is simply to count how many rows we have for each country, so that the comparison of *rn* with this value tells us whether the current row is the last one for this country. We can add the counter very easily, by using the window function variant of **count()**:

```
select case x.rn
         when 1 then '<h1>' || x.country_name || '</h1><ul><li>'
         else '<li>'
       end || x.title || '</li>' html
from (select c.country_name,
             m.title,
             row_number() over (partition by c.country_name
                                order by m.title) rn,
             count(*) over (partition by c.country_name) cnt
      from movies m
           inner join countries c
                   on c.country_code = m.country) x
order by x.country_name, x.title, x.rn
```

From there, it isn't very difficult to add a second **case** construct that appends a closing tag where needed:

```
select case x.rn
         when 1 then '<h1>' || x.country_name || '</h1><ul><li>'
         else '<li>'
       end || x.title || '</li>'
       || case x.rn
            When x.cnt then '</ul>'
            else ''
          end html
from (select c.country_name,
             m.title,
             row_number() over (partition by c.country_name
                                order by m.title) rn,
             count(*) over (partition by c.country_name) cnt
      from movies m
           inner join countries c
                   on c.country_code = m.country) x
order by x.country_name, x.title, x.rn
```

Here we are and we get a query, the result set of which would make a perfect answer to an AJAX request if you are into this type of programming...

If you think that the **case** constructs make the query hard to read, you could as well return the values of *rn* and *cnt* to a program and handle the conditional logic there. The nice thing is, though, that the developer would not have to worry about checking the values in each row against the values returned by the previous row - the database would return simple, good, reliable data, which is in truth all you want from a database.

Faking Ranking Functions with MySQL

If a non-ranking function can be replaced by a probably slightly slower but otherwise equivalent join with an aggregate query, obtaining the same functionality as a ranking function when no window function is available is more challenging. I have seen it recommended to use a correlated query, to count for each item that you want to rank (for example a movie), how many similar items are greater or smaller in respect to the value on which you want to rank (for examples how many movies were released earlier) within the same group (for example for the same country). This is a fine way to proceed if you are ready to launch the query before heading home on Friday evening and need the result by Monday morning - those kind of queries are terribly slow because you need to count and count and count the same values, over and over and over again. There are two reasonably efficient ways to simulate ranking functions with a MySQL version such as MySQL 5.x that lacks them: one involves using variables that are used for performing computations inside the query. I won't talk about this method because from an SQL view point it's rather dirty, the kind of thing that makes me give a quick glance around me to check that nobody is watching before coding it.

Emulating Window Functions with MySQL

If you are interested in this topic I published in 2007, on an O'Reilly website, **onlamp.com**, a two-part in-depth article about the emulation of window functions with MySQL. Here are the links to part 1:

http://onlamp.com/pub/a/mysql/2007/03/29/emulating-analytic-aka-ranking-functions-with-mysql.html

and part 2:

http://onlamp.com/pub/a/mysql/2007/04/12/emulating-analytic-aka-ranking-functions-with-mysql.html

The other one is slightly less efficient but much cleaner even though it involves functions that are specific to MySQL, and even though it has a restricted scope of application.

We can, with a **group by** and a join, display easily with MySQL 5.x, the title of the oldest movie per country. If we want to display the titles of the two oldest movies per country, then it becomes more difficult.

When window functions are available the following query that we have seen previously is probably the best way to answer the question:

```
select c.country_name, m.title, m.year_released
from (select country,
             title,
             year_released,
             rank() over (partition by country
                          order by year_released desc) rnk
      from movies) m
     inner join countries c
      on c.country_code = m.country
where rnk <= 2
order by c.country_name, rnk
```

For MySQL, a relatively elegant way to answer the same question, is to use the two specific functions, **group_concat()**, an aggregate function that concatenates values from several rows into a comma-separated (by default) string, and **find_in_set()** that returns the position of a value in a comma-separated string.

The aggregate function **group_concat()** accepts, like the **over ()** clause of ranking window functions, an optional **order by** specification, for instance

```
select country,
       group_concat(year_released
                    order by year_released desc) list
from movies
group by country
```

You'll notice that although *year_released* is an integer value, not text, I haven't converted it; I could have used `cast(year_released as char)` but conversion is automatically handled by MySQL.

One problem: the list that is generated has a finite length. By default, this length is of 1024 characters; I need five characters per movie (four digits for the year plus one comma) which means that if I have more than 204 movies for one country MySQL will not be able to store the year for the 205th oldest movie nor any movie that was released before it. It will not make the query fail but it will generate a warning and the values that don't fit in the resulting string will be quietly dropped. The 1024 character limit can be increased but whatever you do, one day or another you will hit the limit. Does it matter? I tend to think that for many problems, it doesn't matter too much. Sadly, when in any domain you rank 4,367th, nobody cares, irrespective of the personal achievement. In practice, people are interested in a limited number of values either at the top or at the bottom of a sorted list.

Function **find_in_set()** returns the position of its first element in its second element, a comma separated list. Therefore we can obtain the rank of movies with the following query:

```
select c.country_name,
       m.title,
       m.year_released,
       find_in_set(m.year_released, l.list) rnk
from movies m
     inner join (select country,
                        group_concat(year_released
                                     order by year_released desc) list
                 from movies
                 group by country) l
        on l.country = m.country
     inner join countries c
        on c.country_code = m.country
```

Wrap the query once again and we get the two most recent movies per country:

```
select country_name,
       title,
       year_released,
```

```
        rnk
  from (select c.country_name,
               m.title,
               m.year_released,
               find_in_set(m.year_released, l.list) rnk
        from movies m
             inner join
                (select country,
                        group_concat(year_released
                                     order by year_released desc) list
                 from movies
                 group by country) l
                on l.country = m.country
             inner join countries c
                on c.country_code = m.country) x
  where rnk between 1 and 2
  order by country_name, rnk
```

I bring to your attention the fact that, if I have written `rnk between 1 and 2` and not `rnk <= 2` as I did with the window function, it's not out of an irrepressible need to be fanciful. In fact, if I look with **find_in_set()** for one of those unfortunate movies that were so old that their identifiers weren't stored in the list for lack of space, the function will return 0. I must only return valid ranks.

What I have written here is equivalent (at least for the most recent 204 movies of each country) to **rank()**. I could obtain a result equivalent to **dense_rank()** by using a **distinct** inside the **group_concat()** function:

```
group_concat(distinct year_released
             order by year_released desc)
```

I could obtain a result equivalent to **row_number()** by building a list of movie identifiers instead of years (and of course by looking for the movie identifier in function **find_in_set()**):

```
group_concat(movieid
             order by year_released desc)
```

HTML Graphs

Another interesting example that uses window functions for unusual reporting is the SQL-generation of an HTML bar-chart. To generate a bar in HTML, I use a single-row, two-column table. On the left-hand side, I'll set the background color of the cell to be the color of the bar. On the right-hand side, the background color of the cell will be the background color of my 'graph' as a whole, so that it indicates emptiness. I'll compute the width relatively to the maximum value in my chart: if I want to draw a bar that represents 70% of the maximum value, then I'll say that the left-hand cell takes 70% of the width of the table and that the right-hand cell takes 30% (what I need to add to the left-hand value to obtain 100). That's for one bar. For a full bar chart I shall need another two-column table but this time, with as many rows I have values to chart. I'll say that the left-hand cells take 20% of the width of the table, and

I'll use them for labels. The right-hand cell will take the remaining 80% of the width of the table and will store another nested table - the bar I have described previously - that will expand so as to fill 100% of the cell.

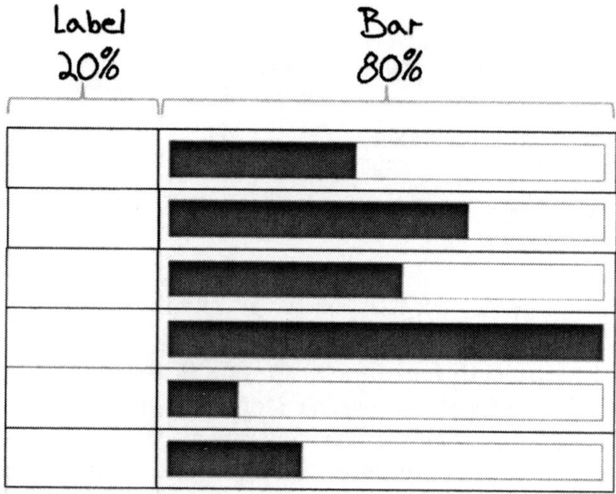

Figure 5.9: Structure of a HTML bar chart.

With such a template defined, I can "draw" an HTML graph with an SQL query that returns only three columns: a label, a value, and the value expressed as a percentage of the maximum value, something that I can easily obtain with a window function.

We have seen in Chapter 4 how to display the number of movies in the database per country:

```
select c.country_name,
       coalesce(x.number_of_movies, 0) as number_of_movies
from countries c
     left outer join (select country as country_code,
                             count(*) as number_of_movies
                      from movies
                      group by country) x
               on x.country_code = c.country_code
```

We need to compute each value as a percentage of the maximum value - the ratio of the detail (the value) to an aggregate (the maximum), a typical window function case. I wrap the previous query in a subquery, compute the ratio with the window function and I multiply the ratio by 100, before rounding it to have an integer value between 0 and 100, then order by country name:

```
select country_name,
       number_of_movies,
```

```
        round(100 * number_of_movies
              / max(number_of_movies) over (), 0) percentage
from (select c.country_name,
             coalesce(x.number_of_movies, 0) as number_of_movies
      from countries c
           left outer join (select country as country_code,
                                   count(*) as number_of_movies
                            from movies
                            group by country) x
             on x.country_code = c.country_code) y
order by country_name
```

I have the data I want but I want to display it in HTML. HTML means opening and closing tags; from the point of view of SQL, that means that I will have something special to do for the first row (at least an opening tag) and for the last one (at least a closing tag). I am going to add to the previous result a call to **row_number()** to identify the first row and a **count(*) over ()** to get the total number of rows, and be able to detect the last row by comparing the row number to this value:

```
select country_name,
       number_of_movies,
       round(100 * number_of_movies
             / max(number_of_movies) over (), 0) percentage,
       row_number() over (order by country_name) rn,
       count(*) over () cnt
from (select c.country_name,
             coalesce(x.number_of_movies, 0) as number_of_movies
      from countries c
           left outer join (select country as country_code,
                                   count(*) as number_of_movies
                            from movies
                            group by country) x
             on x.country_code = c.country_code) y
order by country_name
```

I wrap this query into another query and apply some rather simple logic:

- For the first row, and for the first row only, I display the tags that start a HTML page, a title and the beginning of a frameless-table that spreads over 80% of the page and that I center.
- For all rows I generate a regular HTML table row, with the first column that occupies 20% of the width of the outer table and displays the country name and a second table that occupies the remaining 80% and contains a bar. As a refinement, I put into the title attribute of the cell that represents the bar, the actual number of movies, so that it is displayed as a bubble whenever I move the cursor over the bar.
- For the final row, and for the final row only, I close all tags that need closing.

Here is the SQL Server version of the query, with + that indicates the concatenation of text; use || with Oracle, PostgreSQL or DB2. I specify the style of HTML elements as an attribute, which isn't good practice (I should have a **class** attribute and define the style of the class in a CSS file) but I wanted to have in the output, everything in one single piece, and as compact as possible. Consider it as an SQL example, not an HTML one:

```
select case rn            ① Check for the first row
            when 1 then
                 '<html><body>'
                 + '<h1>Number of movies per country</h1>'
                 + '<table width="80%" style="border:none;margin:auto">'
            else ''
        end
        + '<tr><td width="20%">' + country_name      ② For all rows
        + '</td><td width="80%">'
        + '<table width="100%"><tr>'
        + '<td style="background-color:grey" width="'
            + cast(percentage as varchar(5))
            + '%" title="' + cast(number_of_movies as varchar(10))
                                                    ③ Set the value as "title"
            + ' movies"> </td>'
         + '<td width="'                            Complementary empty cell
            + cast(100 - percentage as varchar(5))
            + '%"> </td></tr></table></tr>'
         + case rn                                  ④ Finish up
               when cnt then '</table></body></html>'
               else ''
            end html
from (select country_name,
               number_of_movies,
               round(100 * number_of_movies
                  / max(number_of_movies) over (), 0) percentage,
               row_number() over (order by country_name) rn,
               count(*) over () cnt
        from (select c.country_name,
                     coalesce(x.number_of_movies, 0) as number_of_movies
              from countries c
                   left outer join (select country as country_code,
                                           count(*) as number_of_movies
                                    from movies
                                    group by country) x
                      on x.country_code = c.country_code) y) z
order by country_name
```

We display the page and table header ① for the first row only, but we display the label (country name) ② and bar for all rows, setting ③ the actual value as "title" so that it is displayed when the cursor hovers over the bar, and ④ we finish the table and the page with the last row.

If you copy the output of this query to a file called graph.html and open the file in a browser, you get what is shown in Figure 5-10.

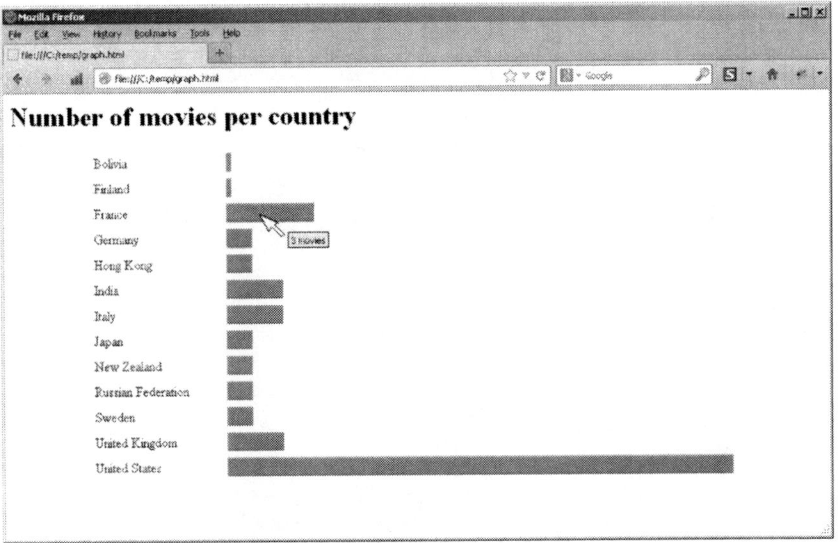

Figure 5.10: An SQL-generated HTML bar chart.

Needless to say, you can modify the query to display values as labels rather than in a bubble, or design the graph in a more fancy way but the principle is there, and you can graph almost anything by just changing the inner query.

To Remember

- Ordering has nothing to do with the relational theory and applies to a result set defined by relational operations.
- The **order by** clause therefore comes last and specifies how rows are ordered, and whether ordering is ascending or descending. The number of rows returned can be limited, in ways that are very dependent on the product.
- The main database management systems implement the standard window functions, which are either non-ranking or ranking.
- Non-ranking functions are variations on aggregate functions but allow us to see detail and aggregate on the same row. Unlike non-ranking reporting functions, ranking functions bear no relationship to aggregate functions
- The difference between the three main ranking functions, **row_number()**, **rank()** and **dense_rank()** is the way they process ties. The combination of ranking and non-ranking reporting functions is very effective to run complex reports as a single SQL statement.

Exercises

1. List all the people who are recorded as alive in the database and were born in 1965 or later by age, from oldest to youngest.
2. List continents with the number of movies per continent, ordered by decreasing number of movies.
3. Who are the three actors who appear in the most movies in the database? (warning: trick question)
4. List all directors alphabetically and the title of their earliest movie.
5. The following query:

```
select c.country_name,
         m.title,
        m.year_released
from countries c
       inner join movies m
      on m.country = c.country_code
order by c.country_name, m.title, m.year_released
```

would return something that looks like this:

```
country_name title                          year_released
------------ ------------------------------ -------------
...
France       La belle et la bête                     1946
France       Le cinquième élément                    1997
France       Les Visiteurs du Soir                   1942
Germany      Das Boot                                1985
Hong Kong    Ying hung boon sik                      1986
India        Pather Panchali                         1955
India        Sholay                                  1975
Italy        Il buono, il brutto, il cattivo         1966
Italy        Ladri di biciclette                     1948
Japan        Shichinin no Samurai                    1954
New Zealand  The Lord of the Rings                   2001
...
```

How would you write the query to display the country name only for the first film of each country? The goal is to obtain

```
country_name title                          year_released
------------ ------------------------------ -------------
...
France       La belle et la bête                     1946
             Le cinquième élément                    1997
             Les Visiteurs du Soir                   1942
Germany      Das Boot                                1985
Hong Kong    Ying hung boon sik                      1986
India        Pather Panchali                         1955
             Sholay                                  1975
Italy        Il buono, il brutto, il cattivo         1966
             Ladri di biciclette                     1948
Japan        Shichinin no Samurai                    1954
New Zealand  The Lord of the Rings                   2001
```

...

6. JSON (JavaScript Object Notation) is a popular data exchange format on the web.

    NOTE See http://www.json.org/

    The general format for dumping a table (or the result of a query) in JSON is

    ```
    {"tablename":[
       {"column_name1":value,"column_name2":value, ...,"column-namen":value},
       ...
       {"column_name1":value,"column_name2":value, ...,"column-namen":value}
     ]}
    ```

    Curly brackets surround the whole table output, which includes the table name. The whole set of rows is between square brackets and the values on each row are returned between curly brackets as a comma-separated list of "column name":value pairs. String values must be between double quotes like the column names.

    Basing your query on the HTML-generating queries and writing explicitly in the query, the table name and the column names, can you write a query to output table *countries* in JSON format?

Fuzzy Searches - Method 6

Où l'Indécis au Précis se joint

Where the Wavering weds Precision.

- Paul Verlaine (1844-1896)

This chapter covers

- How to search when criteria such as names are misspelled
- How to search a long text and find the best match
- How to search in various languages
- How to think and solve a query problem

Life would be easy if we only had to search for numerical values and dates but we often have to search for text too, and here the fun begins. However carefully we may try to normalize data, searching for text is surprisingly difficult and even the sample database can demonstrate it. Anybody can find easily films by John Ford but many people will stumble over the spelling of Steven Soderbergh, Joseph Mankiewicz, John Gielgud or Aki Kaurismäki, and not find what they are looking for, if we look for strict equality between user input (the search criterion) and what is stored in the database. Many names aren't written the way they are pronounced, accented letters get in the way (should we search for Roland Joffé or Roland Joffe?) and we run into deep, deep trouble with transcriptions in Latin characters of names originally written in a different script: a common Chinese name such as 周 can be rendered as Zhou, Chou, Chu, Chau, Chow, Chiew, Chiu and other variants. This is a problem that has long plagued (and is still plaguing) hospitals; when people arrive at Emergency they aren't usually in a state which allows them to calmly spell their name, and they are sometimes brought in by good Samaritans who hardly know them. Finding whether there is already a medical file relative to an incoming patient can be challenging.

Therefore, identifying rows in a table that match-more-or-less-but-not-quite the criteria that have been provided, is an activity that keeps programmers busy. As soon as a match isn't perfect, then comes the question of quantifying how much the result found differs from what was asked. Quantifying allows us to rank with window functions, and to select the best match.

NOTE The problem of "Identity Management" has spawned an entire industry, with software products to handle phonetic spelling, common errors and typos, and so on. If you have ever received two copies of exactly the same mail with a slight difference in your name and address, you have already experienced the problem.

Similarly Sounding Names

A commonly adopted solution for searching names is the use of function **soundex()**, available in most products.

NOTE **soundex()** isn't implemented by default in PostgreSQL but it's available in an optional module; SQLite must be built with a special option to include it.

The algorithm of **soundex()** predates information technology and was developed at the end of the 19th century for US censuses. Basically, the first letter of the name is retained, any *h*, *w* or vowel is dropped from the remainder and the remaining consonants are replaced by a digit, the same digit if they are likely to sound similar (for instance *p* and *b*, or *n* and *m*); successions of identical digits are replaced by a single one, and the result is either truncated to four characters, or right-padded with zeroes up to four characters; some variants of the algorithm exist.

NOTE No truncation occurs in the MySQL version of **soundex()**. If you want the full details about the soundex algorithm, you'll find them a few pages into the 6th chapter of volume 3, *Searching and Sorting*, of Donald Knuth's classic *Art of Computer Programming* (Addison-Wesley).

One way to perform a fuzzy search is to look for surnames for which soundex values match the soundex value of the searched value instead of looking for equality between surname and searched value.

Suppose that someone erroneously looks for *Orson Wells*. "Wells" is converted by the **soundex()** function to W420 but the rub is that if we look for names with this soundex value, we'll get not only *Welles*, but also *Willis* and *Wallach* for instance. We therefore need to rank the "possible surnames" we get by their likeliness to be the right one. If provided, the first name may give a clue. If not, we need to compute some kind of "distance" between what we have found and what was input and select the closest result.

One of the most famous definitions of a distance between two names is the one proposed in 1965 by the Russian mathematician Vladimir Levenshtein and known, not surprisingly, as the *Levenshtein distance* – it is based on the number of unitary letter changes required to transform one name into another one. The same optional module in PostgreSQL that contains **soundex()** provides a **levenshtein()** function; a quick web search will provide you with the source of user-defined functions (that we'll see in Chapter 8) that implement it for other DBMS products.

Alternatively, you can use something less sophisticated but faster. For instance, there is a commonly available function that I didn't mention in Chapter 4 named **translate()**. This function takes three arguments: the value it is applied to, a string value that is nothing more than a list of characters to change into something else, and another string value equal in length to the first one, that contains characters to substitute, one for one, for the characters in the second parameter (**translate()** is a shorthand for applying a series of **replace()** calls that would change one letter each). Let's take the "Wells" query as an example. We can substitute each letter from the input by, for instance, a dash in the surnames returned by the soundex search (a suitable number of dashes can be automatically generated by a function such as **repeat()** or **rpad()** depending on your DBMS):

```
translate(surname, 'Wells', '-----')
```

NOTE With DB2 the second and third parameters are inverted.

Each one of the letters present in the second parameter will be replaced by a dash in column surname. This will generate '------' for *Welles*, '-i--i-' for *Willis*, and '-a--ach' for *Wallach*. Then you can use **replace()** to replace dashes by nothing, compute the length of what remains, compute a **rank()** ordered by this length, and only retain rows of rank one, which seem to be the less different ones.

NOTE With Oracle if you suppress all characters from a string the length is null, not zero but you have **coalesce()** to turn null to zero.

It must be stressed that **soundex()** is strongly Anglo-centric. It does nothing for the silent final letters of French (*Renault*, soundex R543, and *Renaud*, soundex R530, sound exactly the same in French). *W* is dropped with vowels because it sounds like *oo* in English but it sounds like an English *v* in German, a language in which *v* itself sounds like *f* and where *j* would be more vowel-like; even if Austria and Spain were once part of the same Empire, *j* and *v* could hardly sound more different than in German and Spanish. *Gi* sounds like *z* in Vietnamese; and consonants are not always what they seem to be; a Spanish double *l* sounds like *y* (at least in Spain, it's different in Argentina), and sometimes in French as well (the French word for *straw*, *paille*, sounds like 'pie', not like 'pell'). The Dutch word for a dyke (an important word in the Netherlands) is pronounced as in English but written *dijk*. I could give many examples; the idea of something written "sounding like" is very dependent on a language (and sometimes on regional variants of a language) and its graphical conventions. Conversely, you can easily find names in different languages that have the same **soundex()** value and don't sound the same at all, such as the cities of Wuppertal in Germany and Weybridge in England. It would be quite easy to adapt **soundex()** to different languages but by construction it is and can only remain language dependent.

Even with plain Anglo-Saxon names, **soundex()** isn't bullet-proof. English (probably under the pervert influence of the French) also has its silent letters, as Charles Laughton might have testified, as well as every foreign youth lost in central London and meeting incomprehension when enquiring about how to get to Lei-ces-ter Square.

NOTE Leicester Square is pronounced "Lester Square". *Leicester* (L223) and *Lester* (L236) have different soundex values, by the way.

It's not immediately obvious to an English-learner nor to **soundex()** that *Knight* and *Nite* sound the same, *Thomson* has a soundex value of T525 and *Thompson* a value of T512. To summarize, **soundex()** is an OK solution in English but not more than that and may have to be reinforced by additional fuzzy search techniques - such as some of the techniques that I am going to discuss soon.

Searching Titles

If spelling errors make finding director or actor names difficult, opportunities for mistakes and approximations widen to Cinemascope dimensions when it comes to identifying films by title. Movie titles usually contain spaces, sometimes contain punctuation. An operator such as **like** will help you find *Oliver!* if you are searching for movies the title of which is `like 'Oliver%'` instead of being equal to 'Oliver'. However, carefully padding user input with % characters and replacing spaces and punctuation with % characters as well, will be of little help if people search for *A Lady Disappears* instead of *A Lady Vanishes*, or for *Space Oddissey 2001* (besides, performance will be dreadful, as you'll understand in Chapter 9.)

The problem we have with titles is of course a common one, which applies as well to topics (or answers) on a forum, or blog posts. For blogs and forums (as well as video or picture sites) people often use *tags*, simple words that allow a broad categorization, which are stored in a separate table and act as references. But tags cannot be applied to film titles, nor are they suitable for sophisticated searches in text columns that contain more than a single normalized word.

The solution to searching movies by title is called *full-text search*. Full-text search is offered by most products, although in the case of MySQL before version 5.6 you have to choose between the ability to run full-text searches on the text columns of a table and the ability to define foreign key constraints on that same table (as far as I am concerned the choice is quickly made: I'll go for referential integrity any time if the table isn't ancillary).

NOTE Full-text search availability requires special compiling options when building SQLite.

Full-text search always requires some product-dependent set-up, with product-dependent operators, and explaining how to use it with Oracle or SQL Server would take me outside the scope of this book. Rather, I am going to discuss the basic principles of full-text search and show you how to implement a simplified but functional version, which (I hope) you may find interesting from an SQL point of view, as the technique can be applied to solve various classes of problems.

Implementing Full-Text Search Lite

Let's take an example. I want to be able to perform some kind of full-text search on the title of *2001: A Space Odyssey*. All the process I am going to describe can either be performed by the program that inserts data into the database, or by programs coded inside the database and activated by operations on tables - they are called *triggers* and I'll show you some examples in Chapter 8.

I first need to isolate all the different words that compose the title, an operation known as *tokenizing* that generally consists of several steps:

1. Get punctuation signs out of the picture by replacing them with spaces. My example would become *2001 A Space Odyssey*.
2. If I am processing text that may contain accented letters, I should also replace accented letters or letters particular to one language (such as the German *es-zet*, ß) with their unaccented equivalent, which may be several characters; no change for my example.
3. Turn all the words to uppercase, thus getting *2001 A SPACE ODYSSEY*.
4. Store separately, for instance in an array, all the words that are separated by one or several spaces.

During the last step, I may want to discard words that aren't significant enough, such as *A*, *AN*, *THE* or *OF*, and which are specified in what is usually called a "stop list". However I would urge caution if you are processing multilingual titles because a word that isn't significant in one language may be very significant in another language where it has a completely different meaning; *THE* might be *thé* (tea) in French, not a common word in a film title. It's usually relatively safe though to get rid of one-letter words.

The final result with my example would therefore be an array containing {'2001', 'SPACE', 'ODYSSEY'}. At this point, I am going to insert each one of these words and the identifier of the movie into a different table known as the full-text index - as a book index, it associates words with a number, in that case not a page number as in a book but a movie identifier. I may create this table as follows:

```
create table movie_title_ft_index
              (title_word    varchar(30) not null,
               movieid       int not null,
               primary key(title_word, movieid),
               foreign key (movieid) references movies(movieid))
```

Note that I'll store each word from the title only once for each movie, even if it appears several times, such as in Lubitsch's *To Be Or Not To Be* - my primary key definition will prevent us from storing the same word twice for the same movie; if you are a purist you can add a counter to say how many times a word appears in a title but it's not necessary. A foreign key constraint, though, is necessary.

Using Full-Text Search Lite

Suppose that a user looks for *2001, a space odyssey*. What I am going to do is first apply the same processing I applied to titles in the first place, thus obtaining an array {'2001', 'SPACE', 'ODYSSEY'}. I can build this array into a comma-separated list so as to find all the movies, the title of which contains at least one of the words entered by the user:

```
select movieid
from movie_title_ft_index
where title_word in ('2001', 'SPACE', 'ODYSSEY')
```

and as this query will obviously return three rows for *2001: A Space Odyssey* I am going to count how many times I find a movie, which will give me a clean result:

```
select movieid, count(*) as hits
from movie_title_ft_index
where title_word in ('2001', 'SPACE', 'ODYSSEY')
group by movieid
```

This search may return, besides the movie identifier for Stanley Kubrick's classic film, the movie identifiers of movies containing *space* in their title such as *Plan 9 from Outer Space*, or perhaps some fairly obscure South Korean Sci-Fi B-movies such as *Reptile 2001*, or other movies containing *Odyssey*. The number of hits in the previous query will help me to select the most likely films:

```
select movieid
from (select movieid,
             rank() over (order by hits desc) as rnk
      from (select movieid, count(*) as hits
            from movie_title_ft_index
```

```
            where title_word in ('2001', 'SPACE', 'ODYSSEY')
            group by movieid) q1) q2
where rnk = 1
```

I will then have to join the result of this query to the *movies* table to return the best candidate titles and if the user had misspelled *Odyssey*, I would still have found the right film. We may have several candidates that all have the same number of words in common with user input, and we may still want to refine our search of the best candidate. If a user looks for *Casablanca*, the algorithm above will find with no problem Michael Curtiz's famous 1942 movie, an exact match but it will also return the Marx Brothers' *A Night in Casablanca*, which we may want to return as well just in case but not as the first choice. Several tactics are possible, I would probably settle for something simple such as ordering by `abs(length(<user input>) - length(title))`. I didn't mention in my (voluntarily short) list of SQL functions in Chapter 3, the numerical function **abs()**, which returns the absolute value – in other words, the value of the difference without any sign. The expression with **abs()** that I have written is short for

```
case
  when length(<user input>) > length(title) then
       length(<user input>)   length(title)
  else length(title) - length(<user input>)
end
```

Such an ordering would practically mean that I would list first, movies the title of which is closest in length (whether shorter or longer) to the user input.

Improving Full-Text Search Lite

The mechanism explained above gives reasonably accurate results; as long as people can spell *2001*, they should be able to locate *2001: A Space Odyssey* but it's necessary that we have at least one word right in the title, which may still be a problem with very short titles. People can also have the title basically right but use the plural where the original title is singular or vice versa. They may use a synonym by mistake, such as *disappears* instead of *vanishes* and, after having thought about people who spell badly, it would only be fair to think of people who can spell and may have trouble finding *Inglourious Basterds*.

Adding Words

Actual full-text search engines can be complicated beasts and instead of simply isolating words as I have suggested, they store *stems*, a technical term to describe a word free of any declination; in other words a noun will always be stored (for instance) as singular and recognized even in the plural, a verb will be stored as an infinitive and recognized in any tense, and the system will know whether two words belong to the same family. It implies an in-depth, and therefore language-dependent, knowledge of grammar, and most full-text search engines are independent subsystems that run in the background, continuously looking for and analyzing data that has just been inserted or updated. Without trying to compete with these systems, it's quite possible, to store in the table that is used as the full-text index, alternative words or spellings that are associated with the same movie as the original word; and if (always the ranking problem) you want to give more weight to the original word, you can add an integer column named *original* to the *movie_title_ft_index* table and set its value to 1 when the word is as found in the title and 0 otherwise.

If for instance one of the umpteen movie versions of *Wuthering Heights* is identified by *768*, you can store

```
title_word  original       movieid
WUTHERING       1             768
WOOTHERING      0             768
WUHTERING       0             768
WUTHERNG        0             768
```

If you not only count hits but also sum up values in the *original* column, you will be able to refine the order in which you display the results found.

The ideal case is of course when you don't have to imagine and store typos by yourself but when you can have your fat-fingered users doing it for you. When you have found a title, it's possible to compare the words that don't match between actual title and user input, measure their "distance" using the techniques discussed previously and, if you find words that are close enough, insert the mistyped words as possible alternatives, not only for the movie found but for all movies that contain the same word. Over time, your movie search engine will be able to say to users "Hmmm, are you sure you don't mean ....?" and you will be on your way to becoming a new Google. I mentioned when I discussed the virtues and flaws of **soundex()** that it had to be reinforced by other techniques; storing typos (and possibly computing their own soundex values) is certainly a way to do it.

Going Global

The sample database stores the original movie title in the Latin alphabet. Lovers of great and powerful old movies of shameless political propaganda are unlikely to search for the 1925 Russian movie called *Bronenosets Potyomkin*. In fact, if your database is searchable from the Internet, you are going to have two categories of people:

- Those with the right keyboard, who will search for ***Броненосец Потёмкин***, and
- Those with a different keyboard, who will try to find *Battleship Potemkin*, or *Panzerkreuzer Potemkin*, or *El acorazado Potemkin*, or *Le cuirassé Potemkine* or *Patyomkin páncélos* – or even المدمرة بوتمكين You get the idea.

The tactics I used to store word title variants can be used to store the words of a title in different languages – if you are careful to create the column that contains the various words as an **nvarchar** column rather than a **varchar** one to be able to accommodate multiple scripts. You can even add another column to specify the language of the word; and of course when I say "word", I mean of course "character" in a language that uses ideograms such as Chinese. On the web, a browser sends to a web server, among other things, its language settings; the language can be an additional way to tailor the ordering of the result. You can, if you wish, create a new table that contains a *movieid*, and alternative titles under which this movie was released but the only thing that really matters, is finding the words in the table that serves as full-text index because that is what drives searches.

NOTE A film can be released under different names in countries (or provinces in that case) that officially speak the same language. *Honey I Shrunk the Kids* was released as *Chérie, j'ai rétréci les gosses* in France and *Chérie, j'ai réduit les enfants* in Québec for the reason that any French-speaking Canadian will gladly explain to you after having stopped laughing.

Multilingual searches are increasingly common and many people fail to take account of them correctly from the start. The tourism industry is an area where multilingualism must been built-in, even without any more "fuzziness" than managing common typos. Someone trying to book a trip to a major tourist destination such as Venice will type Venice, Venise, Venedig or Wenecja without even thinking that the real name of the city is Venezia – it's only by having a single table that stores all possible variants and links them to the same city that you will be able to search efficiently and cater to the touristic appetites of more and more people.

How to Think a Query Problem

As we are closing on the (major) topic of writing **select** statements, it's time to try to define more explicitly the thought processes we navigate in the development of an SQL query. I have tried all along in this book to show you, step by step, how I was growing my queries and very often wrapping a query into another query to obtain the final results in a kind of nested Russian dolls approach, working from the inside toward the outside.

In a book, the solution to even the hairiest problem always looks simple and, while not always obvious, at least logical. It's like being taken several times to a place by someone who knows the road well. One day, you are left to your own devices and on the road you thought you knew, suddenly the landmarks no longer feel so familiar. It's very frustrating for people who have just finished an SQL course and think they have understood syntax, suddenly to wonder where to start (past **select**) when they have to cope with a real SQL problem.

I want to try to give you guidelines for writing queries and not only queries against the sample database. Back in 1637, René Descartes famously redefined science and philosophy, with his *Discourse on the Method.* I have much more modest ambitions (and much less cerebral firepower) than Descartes but I shall try in this section to sketch broadly in a few paragraphs, not tips, not recipes but something of a method for writing queries. I don't believe in magical recipes that you blindly follow step by step. If such an approach would work, it would already have long been coded into a program but there are principles that can bring enough light to dissipate the haze.

NOTE Many programs generate SQL statements and work relatively well for simple ones but get these programs against the ropes and you quickly reach their limits.

A Method

The very first point to understand, and I have done what I could to show it, is that, unless the problem is very simple (such as "Which are the British films in the database?"), you don't usually jump straight from a question to an SQL expression, even if that was the original hope of Chamberlin and Boyce, the creators of SQL. Writing a query is very much an iterative process, with a number of steps that is more or less proportional to the complexity of the question. Descartes advised, in his second precept, to "*divide each one of the difficulties I would examine into as many parts as possible, and as would be required to best solve these difficulties*". The principle is as valid today as it was four centuries ago and with an SQL problem you should always try to identify the little queries hidden inside the big one. For each query, little or big, try to apply the following steps.

Step 1: The Data You Are Working With

A query problem always contains two specifications that are more or less clearly expressed: the columns that need to be returned (the expected output), and what defines the subset of the database from which the data must be extracted (the input). You will never be asked to return either every column from the database or all rows from all tables.

The data you are asked to return and the data that defines the rows that you are processing may not be stored as such in the database; it may be derived, either through simple functions, or aggregate functions, or window functions if you are using a DBMS that supports them. But you must be able to identify from the plain English (or any other language) requirements, the basic data that delineates your scope. It may be an unglorified way to look at information technology and data processing but in some ways a query problem is like trying to replicate a dish without the recipe after going to a restaurant – the first step is identifying the ingredients that enter into the dish.

NOTE Many people could argue that cuisine is a much higher art form than programming...

Once you have found which are the basic ingredients, then you must identify the tables where you find them, which is usually easy but other tables will probably join the fray. If I ask you to return film titles and the names of the people involved, *people* and *movies* obviously belong to the scope but so does *credits* because the only link between *people* and *movies* goes across *credits*. When two tables in the scope aren't directly linked through common columns, then tables that are like stepping stones on the path between the two tables also belong to the scope.

Once you have the tables, check the columns that you need; those that you return, those that intervene (directly or indirectly) in **where** clauses, those that are required for joins and ordering.

At this stage, you are like a sculptor looking at a big block of Carrara marble and wondering how to turn it into a statue.

Step 2: Consider Aggregates as Separate Queries

The next step is considering whether aggregates will appear at some point in the query; you'll find hints in the expression of the question. Clues that point to aggregates are:

- Explicit words that naturally suggest an aggregate function (sum, total, count, number of, maximum, minimum, smallest, earliest, biggest, latest, current, most recent), usually associated to categories (per this or by that),
- Generally speaking any superlative (most, least)

If aggregates are needed to answer the question, consider if it is possible to compute at least some aggregates independently.

Step 3: The Main Filter

It is time to turn your attention to the criteria that are provided to filter the rows – they will rarely be explicit (I have always referred to British movies, not the movies for which the code found in *country* column is *gb*) but when you have a good understanding of tables, translation to SQL is easy. You must identify the criterion that is the most significant; this means the criterion that reduces by as much as possible the number of rows, the most efficient filter.

Step 4: Core Joins

I mentioned in Chapter 4 the distinction between *filtering joins* that may reduce the number of rows in the result set and *qualifying joins* that only add information to each row that is retrieved. Core joins are filtering joins and these are the joins that you should consider at this stage. Retrieve from each table involved in filtering joins all the columns that are needed but forget about other tables. This is especially important if some aggregation or sort is required: you don't want to burden yourself with data that will be discarded later.

As we have seen in Chapter 4, joins can sometimes be written as subqueries (if their only function is filtering by checking the existence of data in another table), whether uncorrelated – **in (select ...)** – or correlated – **exists (....)**. You will see in Chapter 9, what can decide you in favor of one type of method or the other. For the time being, don't worry about it, switching between the different methods isn't very difficult.

Check that your result satisfies the "no duplicate" test – not that your particular query returns no duplicate from the data you are running it against but that it never can return duplicates. Check that, if it were a table, you could identify the primary key. If you were processing a query inside the global query, consider it as a new table, and restart from Step 1.

Step 5: Apply Polish

Join with tables that are joined simply for adding information, check again that you have no duplicates, order rows, and possibly limit the number of rows. You are done.

Using the Method

I'm going to illustrate the method with three examples – two that I have made up and use the sample database and one that corresponds to a real, practical problem, and which I have adapted from a database forum question.

Example 1

Find the titles and the directors of movies for which we have three actors or more.

- Step 1: The scope

  "Titles" means table *movies*.

  "Directors" means actually first names and surnames, therefore table *people* but it also means some particular involvement in the movie, which I find in table *credits*.

  "Actors" associated with a count means that we are interested by the type of involvement, not by the actual person; therefore table *credits* only.

  We aren't provided with any specific input.

  To summarize: we need *movies*, *people*, and *credits* twice (from two different viewpoints).

- Step 2: Aggregates

  "three actors or more" is an obvious reference to a count. Can we identify by a separate query, movies that have three actors or more? We have seen this type of query in Chapter 3:

```
select movieid
from credits
where credited_as = 'A'
group by movieid
having count(*) >= 3
```

No other aggregate.

- Step 3: The Main Filter

  There is no particular condition in the question, other than the condition on the count. As a result, what will drive the (final) query is actually the preceding aggregate.

- Step 4: Core Joins

  Because of referential integrity constraints, the *movieid* values returned by the aggregate necessarily have a match in table *movies*. The join between the aggregate and *movies* is, by design, a core join. However, we have seen that we don't necessarily have the name of the director. If we have the names of three actors and no name for the director, do we want the movie to appear in the result or not? The question is vague on this topic. The reasonable answer is probably yes, with no director name. Therefore what refers to the director(s) doesn't belong to the core joins, finding no director will not change the number of rows displayed in the result set, it will just affect the information displayed in a row.

  We can write a first, incomplete, version of the query that returns the same number of rows that the final query should return:

```
select m.movieid, m.title
from (select movieid
      from credits
      where credited_as = 'A'
      group by movieid
      having count(*) >= 3) m0
    inner join movies m
      on m.movieid = m0.movieid
```

  No need to iterate and restart from step 1 since we are not working at this stage on a subquery but on the structure of the main query.

- Step 5: Polish

  The qualifying joins – a left outer join with *credits* to find directors when known, followed by another left outer join with *people* to retrieve their first name and surname.

  We may have a problem though – do we want to display the internal movie identifier to the end user? Probably not. In that case the query can return what appears as duplicates, remember Hitchcock's two *The Man Who Knew Too Much*, or P.C. Barua's three *Devdas*. Although this combination isn't officially declared as a key, it's probably safe to say that title, director(s) and year of release are enough to identify a film without any ambiguity and, for convenience, I'm going to sort the final result alphabetically by title.

```
select core.title, core.year_released, p.first_name, p.surname
from (select m.movieid, m.title, m.year_released
from (select movieid
      from credits
      where credited_as = 'A'
      group by movieid
      having count(*) >= 3) m0
    inner join movies m
       on m.movieid = m0.movieid) core
left outer join credits c
   on c.movieid = core.movieid
  and c.credited_as = 'D'
left outer join people p
  on p.peopleid  = c.peopleid
order by core.title,
         core.year_released,
         p.surname
```

EXAMPLE 2

Which is the decade for which we have the most European movies?

- Step 1: The scope

  "Decade" refers to a range of years, therefore to the *movies* table. "European" requires the *countries* table. We don't need anything else since the two tables are directly linked.

  The only specific input is that the continent is 'EUROPE'.

- Step 2: Aggregates

  "The most" means obviously an aggregate to count in a first step. Now the interesting question is how are we going to group? By "decade" but we need to derive the decade from the year.

Finding the Decade to which a Year Belongs

There are two ways to find the decade of a release year:

If the DBMS supports the **trunc()** function, we can compute `trunc(year_released/10) * 10`. 1943, 1946 and 1949 (for instance) will respectively give 194.3, 194.6 and 194.9, which once processed by **trunc()** will all give the integer value immediately smaller, 194, and of course 1940 once multiplied by 10. If we have no **trunc()** and no equivalent function such as **floor()**, we have one way for the mathematically inclined, which is to compute `round(year_released/10    0.5) * 10`. With the previous values, 194.3 – 0.5 will give 193.8 that rounds up to 194, 194.6 – 0.5 gives 194.1 that rounds down to 194, and 194.9 – 0.5 gives 194.4 that also round down to 194. Without the – 0.5, the first value would have rounded down to 194 and the two others up to 195.

The other way to do it is to transform the year into a string, keep the first three digits and replace the last one with a '0':

```
substr(cast(year_released as char(4)), 1, 3) || '0'
```

or with SQL Server

```
left(cast(year_released as char(4)), 3) + '0'
```

Whether you work with a decade that is an integer number or text changes nothing – it's just for grouping.

I'll use **trunc()**. So, let's get all European movies with their decade (I'm returning *title*, *country* and *year_released* merely for control)

```
select trunc(m.year_released/10) * 10 as decade,
       m.year_released,
       m.country,
       m.title
from movies m
     inner join countries c
        on c.country_code = m.country
       and c.continent = 'EUROPE'
```

I could as validly, instead of joining tables, have used a subquery in the **where** clause returning all country codes for European countries.

The aggregate itself becomes:

```
select decade, count(*) as cnt
from (select trunc(m.year_released/10) * 10 as decade
      from movies m
           inner join countries c
              on c.country_code = m.country
             and c.continent = 'EUROPE') european_movies
group by decade
```

- Step 3: The Main Filter

  None – it's already in the aggregate.

- Step 4: Core Joins

  None

- Step 5: Polish

  Order by decreasing count and only retain the first one; for instance (adapt to your DBMS):

```
select decade
from (select decade, count(*) as cnt
      from (select trunc(m.year_released/10) * 10 as decade
            from movies m
                 inner join countries c
                    on c.country_code = m.country
                   and c.continent = 'EUROPE') european_movies
      group by decade) decade_count
```

```
order by cnt desc
limit 1
```

Don't forget that if I use **limit** I ignore ties.

NOTE You can get ties with **top 1 with ties** with SQL Server.

Once again, whether I should or shouldn't ignore ties wasn't specified in the original question and can be open to debate. If I want ties, I can for instance, if the DBMS recognizes it, use the window function **rank()**:

```
select decade
from (select decade, rank() over (order by cnt desc) rnk
      from (select decade, count(*) as cnt
            from (select trunc(m.year_released/10) * 10 as decade
                  from movies m
                       inner join countries c
                          on c.country_code = m.country
                         and c.continent = 'EUROPE') european_movies
            group by decade) decade_count) decade_ranking
where rnk = 1
order by decade
```

EXAMPLE 3

(I have reverse-engineered a poor query corresponding to a real-life problem which was posted to a forum. I have slightly changed the tables).

Get the title and file name of the 10 videos that have the most categories in common with the currently watched video (say video with id 1234) to propose them in a side bar, and among these, list videos from currently active partners first.

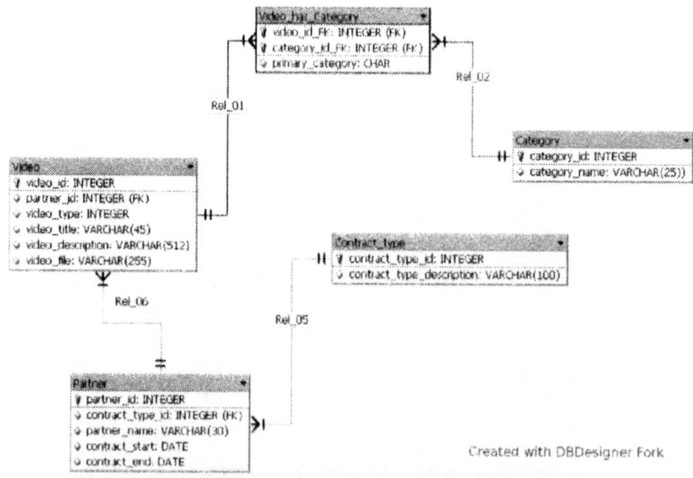

Figure 6.1: An extract from the database of a video website

Videos belong to categories, one of which may be flagged as the primary category. Videos may be associated, via the *partner_id* column, with partners who have a sponsorship contract with the website.

- Step 1: The scope

  We have a specific input value – the identifier of the video currently being watched but we only need to find for this video, the categories to which it belongs, which are in table *video_has_category*, no need for table *category*. For the videos that we want to find we also need *video_has_category* but video file name and title are information that we find in table *video*. We have the information about partners in table *video*. However, the problem refers to "currently active partners" – and partner contracts have a start and an end date, which we only found in the *partner* table. There is no particular requirement about the contract type and we can ignore the associated table.

- Step 2: Aggregates

  "The most categories in common" implies counts of categories and an ordering of counts. Let's for now just consider finding the categories of the current video:

  ```
  select category_id
  from video_has_category
  where video_id = 1234
  ```

  The requirement is to find videos that have at least some categories in common; the problem is very similar to what we have seen earlier in this chapter, finding movies the title of which contains certain words. We need a self join on *video_has_category*, once to retrieve the categories of the current video (the query above), and once to find the other videos with at least one common category. I am going to assign aliases much longer than my standard but, hopefully, explicit:

  ```
  select searched.video_id, searched.category_id
  from video_has_category watched
       inner join video_has_category searched
          on searched.category_id = watched.category_id
  where watched.video_id = 1234
    and searched.video_id <> watched.video_id
  ```

  We don't care about the specific *category_id* values, all we need is count how many categories we have per candidate video:

  ```
  select searched.video_id, count(*) as cnt
  from video_has_category watched
       inner join video_has_category searched
          on searched.category_id = watched.category_id
  where watched.video_id = 1234
    and searched.video_id <> watched.video_id
  group by searched.video_id
  ```

- Step 3: The Main Filter

  Now we have here an interesting case. The only input (the identifier of the currently watched video) has already been used to obtain the aggregate of Step 2. The result of Step 2 can therefore be considered as our new starting point, and our main filter becomes "videos the ids of which are returned by the query obtained in Step 2".

  We want the top 10 videos. If this were the only requirement, I would write something like this:

```
select video.video_title,
       video.video_file
from (select searched.video_id, count(*) as cnt
      from video_has_category watched
           inner join video_has_category searched
              on searched.category_id = watched.category_id
      where watched.video_id = 1234
        and searched.video_id <> watched.video_id
      group by searched.video_id
      order by cnt desc
      limit 10) top_ten_videos
     inner join video
        on video.video_id = top_ten_videos.video_id
order by top_ten_videos.cnt desc
```

  I am limiting the number of videos returned to 10 in the subquery, so that my join operates against these ten videos only - I avoid joining a larger number of rows and retrieve information I'll later discard - and in the end I sort again because the join will likely change the order.

  But I can't do that because there is an explicit requirement to list first videos associated with active partners. If I limit the videos returned in the subquery to ten, I have no information about partners. If some videos with an associated partner have as many categories in common as videos without a partner, I risk retaining the wrong ones.

- Step 4: Core Joins

  As a consequence of the previous remark, the core join is between the subquery obtained in Step 2 and the *video* table - but without any attempt at this stage to limit the number of rows because I'd risk limiting it wrongly.

```
select video.video_title,
       video.video_file
from (select searched.video_id, count(*) as cnt
from video_has_category watched
     inner join video_has_category searched
        on searched.category_id = watched.category_id
where watched.video_id = 1234
  and searched.video_id <> watched.video_id
group by searched.video_id) candidate_videos
     inner join video
        on video.video_id = candidate_videos.video_id
```

- Step 5: Polish

  Although the join with the *partner* table is required for ordering, it doesn't affect the number of rows returned by the query – it belongs to the really last stage.

```
select v.video_title,
       v.video_file
from (select searched.video_id, count(*) as cnt
      from video_has_category watched
           inner join video_has_category searched
              on searched.category_id = watched.category_id
      where watched.video_id = 1234
        and searched.video_id <> watched.video_id
      group by searched.video_id) candidate_videos
     inner join video v
        on v.video_id = candidate_videos.video_id
     left outer join partner p
        on p.partner_id = v.partner_id
       and p.contract_start <= <current_date>     Use the suitable function ...
       and p.contract_end >= <current_date>
order by candidate_videos.cnt desc,
         case
           when p.partner_id is not null then 1
           else 2
         end
limit 10
```

In such a case, it is very likely that it truly is **limit** (or equivalent) that we want; we probably don't care very much about ties but much more about having a list of suggestions with a consistent length. However, the ordering might give birth to serious discussion: here, the primary criterion for ordering is the number of categories in common; when the number of categories is the same, then partners come first. What if we find twelve videos with five common categories, none of them from a partner, and if we have partner videos with only four common categories? Should business imperatives dictate that we bump them up the charts, and should we permute the ordering expressions? But what if we only find partner videos with one common category and we have more than ten of them? If we propel to the front, videos that aren't very relevant simply because of commercial agreements, don't we risk alienating users? A compromise could be giving simply more weight to partner videos, for instance using this **order by** clause:

```
order by candidate_videos.cnt * case
                                  when p.partner_id is not null then 1.2
                                  else 1
                                end desc
```

As you can see, answers often spawn more questions.

To Remember

- Names and text are, in practice, difficult to search in databases. Function **soundex()** is helpful with English names but imperfect. Many systems implement full-text search subsystems which can be extremely useful for searching long pieces of text such as articles.
- The core idea behind fuzzy searches is to break what is searched into "atomic" pieces for which exact matches are searched, then counting exact matches and ordering so as to find the best match overall; this technique is widely used.
- Complex queries are built bit by bit. First determine from required output and provided input, with what tables you are working. Consider whether aggregates are needed and consider them as separate queries. Identify the criteria that drive the query and core joins. Ancillary joins, sorts, etc. belong to the last stage.

Exercises

1. Blogs, picture and video sites commonly use tags, which are very similar in their usage to words extracted from a title - for instance, a table *picture_tags* will contain a picture identifier *pic_id*, and a text column *tag* that contains a word used to qualify the picture. The same picture will be associated with several tags.

   How would you write a query to retrieve the identifiers of all pictures associated with tags WINTER and FOG but not associated with tag SNOW?

2. As stated, the third example demonstrating the application of a sound method for writing a query has been taken from a forum. Here are the comments by (presumably) the project manager who posted the query and the query he or she posted (slightly massaged - I have renamed some tables and columns and removed an ancillary condition):

   As my developer hasn't completely mastered SQL and its subtleties I am posting this query here looking for help.

   This query displays the 10 first videos having the greatest number of categories which are similar to the video being watched (in this example video 81). The current query takes 3 seconds with 2,700 videos on a rather powerful server, we find this a bit slow.

   ```
   SELECT DISTINCT
          video_id,
          video_type,
          video_title,
          video_description,
          video_idPartner,
          video_urlMini,
          video_dateValid,
          partner_valid,
   ```

```
       partner_redirection,
        ( SELECT COUNT(Y.v_belongs_c_idVideo) AS NbSimilar
          FROM  v_belongs_c  Y
          WHERE Y.v_belongs_c_idVideo=81
            AND Y.v_belongs_c_idCategory IN
              (SELECT Z.v_belongs_c_idCategory
               FROM v_belongs_c Z
               WHERE Z.v_belongs_c_idVideo=video_id)) as Counter,
        ( SELECT category_singular
          FROM category,
               v_belongs_c X
          WHERE X.v_belongs_c_idVideo=video_id
            AND X.v_belongs_c_default=1
            AND category_id=X.v_belongs_c_idCategory )
                    as category_singular
FROM category,
     v_belongs_c A,
     video
     LEFT JOIN partner
            ON video_idPartner=partner_id
WHERE (A.v_belongs_c_idCategory IN
          (SELECT W.v_belongs_c_idCategory
           FROM v_belongs_c W
           WHERE W.v_belongs_c_idVideo=81)
       AND video_id=A.v_belongs_c_idVideo)
 AND (video_idPartner=0
      OR (partner_valid=1
          AND partner_redirection<>1))
 AND video_valid=1
 AND video_id<>81
ORDER BY Counter DESC
LIMIT 10
```

There are in this query, a number of things that are plain wrong, even though the syntax is correct. Can you see the big mistake which means that many more rows than expected by the developer are processed and how it was "fixed" (as in "sweeping the dirt under the rug")?

That's what happens when people try to throw everything into the query at once.

Changing Data 7

All things must change
To something new, to something strange.

- Henry Wadsworth Longfellow (1807-1882)

This chapter covers

- What a transaction is in the context of database operations
- Inserting data, row by row, from other tables or from a file
- Updating and deleting data
- Consistency controls achieved by constraints

The **select** statement is the really "big piece" of the SQL language. When you master **select**, you fear nothing; everything else is simple by comparison. It's now time to see how data can be managed and changed. We have seen in Chapter 2 how to insert data row by row, so that we could get started. In this chapter, we'll study in more detail **insert** and more generally speaking how to load data into tables, as well as **update** and **delete** that I also mentioned in Chapter 2; in the process I'll tell you about other topics such as generating identifiers, some interesting features of the **create** statement and so on. Before I take you further I'd like to introduce a very important notion, which is the notion of *transaction*.

Transactions

You know what a transaction is in the real world: an exchange between two parties, usually of some goods against money. Let's say that you go to the grocery to buy some fruit. The grocer prepares a bag, you proffer a bank-note, the grocer hands you the bag and gives you your change. The transaction is finished and everyone is happy. Unless you discover that some of the fruit is rotten and insist on cancelling the transaction and getting your money back; or if you try to run away with the bag without paying; or if the grocer tries to cheat you on the change.

My point is that for a transaction to complete successfully there is a succession of independent actions and controls that must all succeed. A database transaction is a similar suite of operations that must all complete successfully, or not at all. It represents a single, logical unit of work.

Changing data in a table can fail for various reasons: the most common is violating a constraint but you may also run out of disk space, hardware can fail all of a sudden... Incidents don't happen very often, actually they are rather rare but with the incredibly high number of operations that are often executed (many companies insert millions of rows into their tables daily), even something that has very low odds of happening, eventually happens. It's bad enough when an SQL change operation fails; it's worse when it happens in the middle of a transaction after some of the related changes have succeeded.

The archetypal database transaction example is a money transfer between two accounts, say between a checking account and a savings account: the balance that is recorded for your current account must be decreased and the balance that is recorded for your savings account must be increased by the same amount. This requires two separate database operations. If for one reason or another something goes wrong somewhere in the middle - for instance there may be a cap that you are not allowed to exceed on how much you can hold in this particular high-interest savings account - everything must be cancelled and your current account mustn't be debited.

NOTE These savings accounts with a ceiling on how much you can deposit exist in some countries (government-sponsored schemes).

We can also take as an example what we saw in the preceding chapter, i.e. storing the various words of a title in an ancillary table, for finding films more easily, even when the title entered isn't the exact title. If a new film has successfully been inserted into the *movies* table, it may happen that we fail to insert some of the title words into the table we use as a full text index. It's probably better in such a case to cancel everything, fix the problem and perform the whole operation again because otherwise some searches may yield wrong results.

Databases know how to manage transactions. Many products require that we start a transaction by issuing a command such as

`begin transaction` (`start transaction` with MySQL)

Oracle and DB2 will automatically start a transaction, unless you already are in one, as soon as you issue a statement that changes the content of a table.

When the transaction completes successfully, we must issue a command to confirm the changes: **commit**. The **commit** statement validates all the changes that have been performed in the transaction and formally ends it, making the new consistent state permanent; it's the equivalent of an *OK* button. If anything goes wrong, then you (or your program) should issue a **rollback** statement, the equivalent of a *Cancel* button. Rollback will cancel ALL CHANGES since the beginning of the transaction and return the database to the consistent state it was in immediately before the transaction started. That way, if we have a money transfer that fails, rollback will automatically restore all initial balances as they were before the transaction started and the program doesn't need to undo what it did. It's a very powerful feature that participates in the mission of the database management system, to ensure that data remains consistent through the good times and the bad. There are other implications with transactions, especially in relation to what is called *concurrency*, simultaneous access to the same data by several people. When you and several other users are interested in the same information at the same time and you change the data, as long as no changes have been "committed", the system still shows the previous value to other users because you could change your mind and issue a **rollback.** Likewise, as long as you haven't committed a change, other users are prevented from modifying the same rows (in some rare cases the same table); they don't get an error but their **update** statements are blocked and put into a waiting line, executing once you have committed or rolled back your changes. The issues related to protecting data from simultaneous (or near simultaneous) changes are often referred to as *locking* because data is "locked" by active transactions. These issues are complex and outside the scope of this book. Just remember that when you start a transaction, you should aim to finish it as soon as possible to let other users access the data.

Beware that products that demand an explicit statement to start a transaction are by default in *autocommit mode*. This means that every single statement that changes the database starts a kind of light transaction the scope of which is restricted to the statement. If the statement fails, all changes are immediately rolled back (remember that a change operation applies globally to the table; you may want to increase the values of a numerical column and break a constraint on the maximum value for some rows only); if the statement succeeds, the result is automatically committed and cannot be undone unless you run another statement to perform an inverse operation.

As we step through the different commands and if you are testing them while reading this book, do not hesitate to issue, from time to time, a statement to start a transaction, run changes, then either **commit** or **rollback** and see how it affects the content of tables.

There is one point though that you should be aware of and it's an important one. With Oracle and MySQL, whenever you change the structure of the database, for instance when you create a table, any pending transaction is automatically committed, and there is no possible rollback (although Oracle has some facilities for having several data definition language commands all succeed or all fail). This is one reason why changes to the database structure and changes to the data should be kept strictly separated in programs - a good practice even when the data definition language statements can be part of a transaction.

What Changing Data Means

When we modify data, we switch from a consistent state of the database where tables contain some values, to another consistent state where some of the values will have changed. If several operations are required to go from one consistent state to another, they must be embedded in a transaction but to say that some of the values have changed doesn't mean that values have been replaced by other values in rows. It means that tables no longer contain exactly the same data. It may be the result of inserting new rows, modifying existing rows, or deleting rows.

When Updating is Inserting

It's interesting to note that the view that the end user has of an operation is rarely what really happens. Changing an existing row, for instance, is most often applied to values that were previously undefined or that represent a status. Other columns get updated rarely, other than to correct a data entry error; or if they get updated, it implies that either you don't care about previous values, or that you have stored them already. I'll give you some practical examples.

When I presented transactions, I mentioned the archetypal transaction example in which the balance of a current account is decreased and the balance of the savings account is increased. This example, while useful in understanding transactions, is not what really happens. What happens is that a table will record movements and that two rows will be inserted into this table, one to indicate a debit from the current account with a date and an amount, and one to indicate that the savings account is credited, with a date and an amount.

With little regard for realism, many textbooks illustrate data update with a salary raise applied to some rows in a table called *employees*. Changing a salary value in a row almost never happens in the real world: when we update something, we lose track of the previous value. We don't want to lose track of a previous salary; we'll probably need to know what it was and when it was changed for filing tax returns; the salary history is needed when negotiating a raise; we may need the previous values for statistics too, computing how much the global salary mass has changed over time. What we will do instead of changing a *salary* attribute in an *employees* table, is to have an *employee_salary_history* table that associates a salary and a date with the identifier of an employee. When the salary is raised, a new row is inserted and the current salary becomes the most recently inserted one. The only thing that can be updated is, perhaps, an indicator saying 'current salary' which may make queries simpler to write.

What appears as an update may also not be one, when members can vote on a video, or can vote in a forum on the usefulness of answers provided by other members. We could have a column called *number_of_votes* associated with each item that people can vote for, and increase its value each time someone votes but then, we couldn't prevent people from cheating and voting multiple times to "stuff the e-ballot box". If we want to prevent people from congratulating themselves time after time, then we must have a special table that associates with the identifier of the item, the identifier of each member who has voted for it, and add to this table a unique constraint enforcing that a member can only vote once for each item. The number of votes will be computed with an aggregate function. What you might think of as a value update will be an insert - a change to the database as a whole indeed but not an attribute value change.

When Deleting is Updating

While what appears as value updates to end-users are often inserts behind the scene, what appears as a row deletion in an application is often, in fact, a status update.

I mentioned the *employees* table. Employees are never deleted because there is a lot of information associated with each employee in other tables. When you are laid-off, you are not removed from the *employees* table; your *termination_date* attribute just gets updated.

If you consider a merchant website, over the life of the site, many articles will come and go: they may be discontinued, replaced by other, newer items that offer better performance and more bells and whistles for the same price, or the management may decide to cut-off a line of articles because they aren't profitable enough. Will the articles be physically removed from the *articles* table when they are no longer sold? The answer is no. The reason is simple: the article will probably have been ordered a number of times when it was officially for sale. Orders mean that you have rows in an *orders* table referring to this article, as well as to a customer, and in all likelihood a referential integrity constraint between tables *orders* and *articles*. If you remove the article from the table of articles, you will violate integrity constraints (actually, the DBMS will prevent you from doing it), unless you remove all orders that refer to this article. That would mean that you would lose the record of your commercial activity, as well as of the relationship with your customers; nobody with any business sense would want to do that, and therefore you'll simply update a *status* attribute associated with the article, saying it's no longer for sale.

You may however contemplate updating the price of an item when it increases or (more rarely) decreases but then, this implies that with each past order you have also

recorded the price paid. If not, any attempt to compute revenue figures by summing up orders multiplied by the (current) price will give the wrong result.
In conclusion, while inserts are usually what they seem to be, give some thought to other statements that modify the content of tables.

Inserting data

We have already seen in Chapter 2 the **insert** statement that is used to populate a database, and we have already used the syntax **insert into** *table name* followed by a list of columns, **values** and a list of comma-separated values enclosed by parentheses, or (except with Oracle) several such lists separated by commas.

We can omit the list of columns after the table name; in that case the SQL engine assumes that the values you pass must be inserted one by one in the columns of the table, in the order columns were listed when the table was created. Not naming columns in an **insert** statement is a bad practice in a program, for exactly the same reason as using **select *** instead of naming columns is a bad practice; you have no guarantee that alterations to the table or database reorganizations will always keep the order the same - after all, the order of columns doesn't matter.

Default Values and System-Generated Identifiers

An interesting question is, what happens when you specify and provide values for some but not all of the columns in the table? If you provide no values then when you query the table you probably won't be surprised to discover a null in the column - "no value" is what null stands for. If you omit a mandatory column, the **insert** statement will fail, unless a default value was defined for the column. I didn't mention it in Chapter 2 because it isn't fundamental and in practice it's a feature that isn't used as much as you might expect but a **create table** statement allows us to define default values, using the syntax

```
create table <table_name>
            (...
             <column_name>    <data type>
                   default <default_value> not null,
             ...)
```

Default values are more commonly used for initializing indicators that take a simple value such as Y or N, or for automatically recording when a row was inserted by indicating as default value the function that retrieves the current date and time. In spite of the convenience of default values, many people, me included, prefer simply making the column mandatory and coding directly into their **insert** statements, either a default constant value or a function call; that way you understand better when you read the program, what you ultimately get in the table. When a value isn't explicitly set, you don't always realize that there might be a default value defined.

There is however one particular type of default value that is very interesting: automatically generated identifiers, such as the *peopleid* or *movieid* values that you find in the sample database. Finding the highest used number and adding one is definitely a bad idea for two reasons: first it would increase the amount of work to be performed by requiring a data retrieval before each insertion, and secondly, more importantly, when you have several concurrent accesses to the database it's quite possible that two users trying to insert one or several rows at the same time would see (briefly) the same maximum current value. In that case they would try to insert duplicate primary key values, which would necessarily result in failure for one of the two users.

This is why all DBMS products provide a way to generate identifiers with optimized mechanisms that guarantee that two concurrent requests will return distinct values. I must stress the fact that if the identifiers are guaranteed to be unique, and if usually values are increasing over time, there is no guarantee that there will be no gaps in the numbers. People sometimes worry about having no gaps, and reusing unused values; this is often a pointless concern. System-generated identifiers are simply shorter and more convenient aliases for what uniquely identifies a row when the real-life key is a combination of several long columns; nothing more. It has no intrinsic value; it's not a "real" attribute especially as if you load the same data into two different databases it is quite possible that internal identifiers will end up taking different values in the two databases.

NOTE Some databases are automatically replicated to a different location for security reasons and in such a context you need to be very careful with automatically generated identifiers. Either they are generated on the master database and not on the replicated database, simply being copied from the master database; or automatically generated identifiers are excluded from the replication mechanism and the replicated database won't be a strict copy of the original one, which may cause problems with foreign keys. You may also have problems with identifiers when you try to aggregate data coming from several independent databases. For the record, there are functions that generate (very long) identifiers called GUIDs (**G**lobally **U**nique **ID**entifiers) that are guaranteed to be unique identifiers across databases.

Gaps may occur when a transaction is rolled back and a generated number is ultimately discarded; suppose for instance that *movieid* in table *movies* is automatically generated. If you check the maximum value of *movieid*, try to insert a new film with an nonexistent country code, then correct the code and insert the film again, you may notice by checking the new maximum *movieid* value that the failed **insert** will have "consumed" an identifier. Gaps may also occur when a database is shut down and restarted, because for performance reasons, identifier generation occurs in volatile memory before the requests are received; some ready-to-be-

assigned values may be lost during a shut down. Don't worry about running out of numbers – maximum values are truly astronomical and you may generate thousands of identifiers per second continuously for a few centuries before you reach the maximum possible value.
Two main mechanisms are used by DBMS products to generate automatically numerical identifiers: sequences and auto-incrementing columns.

SEQUENCES

Oracle, DB2, PostgreSQL and SQL Server (from SQL Server 2012) implement a special database object (in the same way as a table is a database object), a number generator that is called a *sequence* and exists independently from tables. The syntax for creating a sequence couldn't be simpler:

```
create sequence <sequence name>
```

People rarely specify anything else, although it is possible to specify a start value, an end value, an increment value (which can be negative) and whether you want to restart from the start value after you have reached the end value. By default, the start value is one, the end value is unlimited (and can be considered unlimited in practice), and the increment is one.
When a sequence has been created there are only two ways to use it:

- Either you make it generate a new value,
- Or you want to retrieve the last value that was generated in your session; this implies of course that you have previously asked for a new value. Retrieving the last (current) value is especially useful for foreign keys that must reference a freshly generated value in another table.

  For instance, if I insert a new film in the *movies* table, asking for a new system-generated *movieid* value produced by a sequence named (for instance) *movies_seq*, I can insert the director into the *credits* table by referring to the latest generated value for *movieid* even if I don't exactly know the actual value.

All three products use comparable but different syntaxes for referring to a new value and to the current value for the session:

- With Oracle, you obtain a new value by invoking *<sequence_name>*.**nextval** and you refer to the current value with *<sequence_name>*.**currval**
- With DB2, you refer to a new value by **next value for** *<sequence_name>* and to the current one by **previous value for** *<sequence_name*. SQL Server uses the same syntax as DB2 for generating the next value.

NOTE In SQL Server 2012 there is no easy way to retrieve the current value of a sequence. If you need to reference the current value, it's better to use the procedures that you will see in Chapter 8; in a procedure the generated value can be saved to a variable and used in several statements.

- With PostgreSQL, you get a new value by calling **nextval('*<sequence_name>*')** and the current one by calling **currval('*<sequence_name>*')**. Notice that, contrary to the other products, the name of the sequence is given between single quotes.

Those expressions are similar to function calls and take the place of a value in an **insert** statement. They can also be used in the list of columns of a **select** statement. If you ask in a **select** statement for the next value of a sequence and if the query returns several rows, each row will contain a different value.

AUTO-INCREMENTING COLUMNS

SQL Server, MySQL and SQLite use a different approach, in one way less flexible but easier to use, by defining, in the **create table** statement, a column as a system-generated numerical identifier; there can be only one such column per table.

NOTE It is possible with SQL Server, to specify a starting value and an increment as with sequences.

Instead of defining in the *movies* table:

```
create table movies
      (movieid int not null primary key,
       ...)
```

You just need to define *movieid* as follows (once again, syntax varies)

- With SQL Server

  ```
  movieid int not null identity primary key
  ```

- With MySQL

  ```
  movieid int not null auto_increment primary key
  ```

  Alternatively a more compact version is

  ```
  movieid serial primary key
  ```

  NOTE The two expressions aren't strictly identical, as a **serial** value is a **bigint** instead of an **int** – which basically is geek-speak to say that you can enter even bigger numbers but **int** is enough for most applications. The difference is important for foreign keys, which for MySQL must have exactly the same data type as the referenced column.

- With SQLite, the case is slightly different. Rows in a SQLite table are always numbered internally with a kind of built-in hidden auto-incrementing column. If you say

  ```
  movieid integer primary key
  ```

> Then you push this column, which normally stays in the wings, into the limelight and give it the name *movieid*; as by design this column always has a value, **not null** is implicit. From a practical viewpoint, it behaves as with other products.
>
> You should be careful that although SQLite is usually reckless with data types, in this particular case the type has to be exactly **integer** to make apparent the auto-numbered internal column; **int** will not do it. The reverse is also true: if you want an integer primary key but don't want it to be automatically assigned by SQLite, you should specify its type as **int**, not **integer**.

With an auto-incrementing column, you just omit the name of the column from the **insert** statement and it will automatically take a different value for each row, as if it were a default value. To solve the problem of inserting values in tables linked by a foreign key constraint, products that use auto-incrementing columns all provide functions (or system variables) that return the last value that was generated by your session - these functions allow you to get the freshly minted *movieid* value required to insert for instance the identifier of the director in table *credits*. With SQL Server, you'll refer to **@@identity** (the **@@** prefix indicates a system variable) or **scope_identity()**, with MySQL **last_insert_id()**, and with SQLite **last_insert_rowid()**. Beware that contrary to the sequence-based approach to generating identifiers, the value you get with any of these functions is the last that was generated across all tables; there is no way to specify that you want the last value your session generated for such and such table, except with SQL Server that has a function **ident_current()** that takes as a parameter, a table name between quotes - `ident_current('movies')` will always return the last generated *movieid* value, even after you have added new people.

Best of Both Worlds

PostgreSQL has an interesting and original approach that actually combines sequences and auto-incrementing columns. Although internally it uses sequences, it allows us to attach a sequence to a column (in PostgreSQL-speak, the column is said to *own* the sequence). The result is that if you ever drop the table, the sequence will be automatically dropped with it. More interestingly, it supports, like MySQL, a **serial** pseudo data type. If when you create table *movies* in PostgreSQL you declare

```
movieid serial primary key
```

the DBMS will automatically create a sequence named *movies_movieid_seq*, attach it to column *movieid* and set the default value of *movieid* to **nextval('***movies_movieid_seq***')**, thus making the behavior identical to what it would be with SQL Server or MySQL. PostgreSQL also provides a **lastval()** function that returns the last value that was generated across all sequences , exactly like **@@identity** or **last_insert_id()**.

DB2 allows something roughly similar, if you declare the *movieid* column as follows:

```
movieid int generated as identity primary key
```

and it provides a function called **identity_val_local()** to retrieve the last generated value; unfortunately this function doesn't return a value in some cases, which means that sequences are a safer choice.

NOTE **generated as identity** has also been introduced in Oracle 12c.

NOTE **identity_val_local()** only works with the simple **insert ... values()** statements that we saw at the beginning of this book. As you'll see soon, there are interesting ways to insert several rows at once, and then **identity_val_local()** returns null.

It should be noted that, prior to Oracle 12c, Oracle is the odd DBMS out, as it strictly uses sequences and it doesn't allow a reference to *<sequence_name>*.**nextval** as the default value for a column (this is allowed from Oracle 12c, but not in earlier versions). A recurring question on forums or mailing lists has long been "how can I simulate an identity/auto_increment column with Oracle ", to which someone was always quick to suggest a trigger-based solution (I'll talk about triggers in the next chapter). I must say that I tend to read this kind of question as "how can I drive an Oracle screw as if it were a SQL Server/MySQL nail". The difference between writing

```
insert into movies (title, year_released, country)
values (....)
```

and

```
insert into movies (movieid, title, year_released, country)
values (movies_seq.nextval, ....)
```

is, to say the least, slim and in my view doesn't justify spending time on camouflage that moreover, slows operations down. I hope that at this stage in the book you have a better idea about how products have slightly different means of performing the same function and that you have given up on the quixotic dream of writing code that runs without modification against any DBMS product; people who want to port an application written for one DBMS to a different DBMS usually seize the opportunity to review it in depth.

Inserting the Result of a Query

As you must have noticed, entering data into a table row by row is very tedious when you do it manually; what happens usually is that people fill a data entry form and the program they are running passes this data to an **insert** statement that is executed in the background. There is another syntax for massive insertions, which is

most commonly used for migration, data restructuring and big database maintenance operations. This syntax is the **insert ... select** construct.
insert ... select is very simple to understand: as with **insert ... values** you first specify the name of the table and the columns you are going to insert into, but instead of the **values** line, you just write a **select** statement, the columns of which must match the columns that are listed. Needless to say, the "columns" in the select list can be, and often are, expressions or constants. That allows you to copy and transform massive amounts of data between tables in a single statement. If you had created and begun to populate some tables when I taught you about the **create table** statement and if you have renamed them as I suggested at the beginning of Chapter 3, then you can add their content to the sample database by running **insert ... select** statements such as

```
insert into movies(title, country, year_released)
select title, country, year_released
from my_movies
```

I mentioned that some products allow the insertion of several rows at once in one statement with **insert ... values ...**, and some don't. The **insert ... select ...** construct is a way to work around the **insert ... values ...** limitation. With Oracle if you want to run a single statement to insert two rows, instead of executing two inserts in the same transaction, you cannot write as you could with SQL Server or PostgreSQL

```
insert into my_table(col1, col2, col3)
values (val1, val2, val3),
       (val4, val5, val6)
```

but you can write

```
insert into my_table(col1, col2, col3)
select val1, val2, val3 from dual
union all
select val4, val5, val6 from dual
```

Table *dual* is a special dummy one row, one column table used in Oracle when you want to use a **select** statement that doesn't actually return data from the database.

NOTE Like Oracle, DB2 (which accepts a multi-row **insert ... values ...**) always wants a **select** to be **from** a table and the table equivalent to *dual* with DB2 is *sysibm.sysdummy1* (welcome to the cool world of corporate IT). Other products accept **select** statements without a **from** clause such as `select 2 + 2`.

Loading a Data File

Loading a table from another table doesn't tell us how the source table was populated in the first place. There aren't that many ways for data to arrive into a database.

- It comes in from the network, with at the other end of the line someone who has filled in some kind of form and pressed 'Send', or possibly another computer sending data.
- Or it has been computed (not very common).
- Or it has been loaded from a file.

Loading data from files, even if at first sight the activity looks unglamorous, is used frequently and often presents interesting challenges. Any new application requires the loading of a copious amount of reference data before going live, whether it's a list of geographical places (such as table *countries* in the sample database; many applications require reference lists of regions or cities), people directories, phone prefixes, currencies, references of articles for sale, ranges of valid credit card numbers for control, and so on. For many other applications, file loading is not only part of take off but also of cruising. Whether you want to load log files for analysis or files that are transmitted regularly from other computers, many systems dedicated to analysis and decision support rely on file loading.

When files are binary files (which means that if you try to open them in a text editor you'll only see gobbledygook) there is no other way to load them than using a program that knows how to interpret the format, connects to the database and inserts records. In the very common case when data files are readable text files, then you have several possibilities. If I omit the case of exotic character sets and fancy encoding (which I'll ignore as it would take us too far), there is only one difficulty with text files: a text file is nothing but a series of bytes that encode printable characters, interspersed with special markers that indicate line breaks (what is inserted in the file when you hit the return key in a text editor). The snag is that different systems use different conventions for line breaks: on the one hand you have Windows that indicates a line break with two characters, traditionally represented as \r\n. The first character (\r) is called "carriage return" and means "back to the beginning of the line" (name and meaning hark back to the glorious days of the typewriter). The second character (\n) is called "line feed" and means "jump to the next line". On the other hand, UNIX (and Linux) systems use a single character, the line feed character (\n). So, if you try to read on Windows in a product such as Notepad, a file that was generated on a UNIX system, Notepad that looks for \r\n pairs will find none and only see one long line with non printable \n characters that it will represent with little squares.

NOTE WordPad is cleverer than Notepad and will understand correctly a text file created on a UNIX system.

Conversely, if you open in a UNIX editor a file that was created under Windows, the editor will indeed find the \n characters it's looking for, but the \r will sometimes appear (usually as `^M`) as parasitic characters at the end of each line.

It's very frequent that you load onto a system a file that was generated on another system. When you download some reference data from the internet, from a governmental website for instance, you have no guarantee that it was generated on the same platform you are using. Products that run both on Windows and UNIX systems usually ignore \r characters that precede a \n and strip them; whichever the origin of the file the content is correctly loaded in the database. Operations are a bit more difficult with SQL Server, which lives in its own Windows bubble. There are utility programs (*unix2dos* and *dos2unix*) for converting between formats but it is also possible to load the files directly - if you are careful enough, as I'll show you.

CSV Files

The CSV (**C**omma **S**eparated **V**alues) format is simple and, for that reason, popular. You just have on every line the data to be loaded as a row, with commas between the different attributes; for instance:

```
Casablanca,us,1942
Sholay,in,1975
```

The C in CSV has become over time a misnomer, as people often refer to CSV file when the separator isn't a comma. Because commas are sometimes part of the text string that's being delimited, tabs or vertical bars (less common inside text fields) are frequently used as separators. An alternative to using a different separator from a comma is enclosing a field that may contain a comma with a pair of special characters such as double quotes. All DBMS products make loading data from a CSV file into the database a relatively easy operation. What is usually required is that:

- You have created a table with as many columns as you have separated values in the file, with the proper data types
- The number of separators in the file is constant. If a value is missing, you still have two successive separators (or if the missing value is the last one on the line, the line is terminated by a separator)

Let's say that you have found on the web, a CSV file named *us_movie_info.csv* that lists, for some American films only, the title between double quotes, the year, the running time in minutes and *B* if the film is in black and white or *C* if it is in color.

NOTE A sample file is available for download from http://edu.konagora.com.

Running time and color are interesting pieces of information that are so far absent from the *movies* table and, thinking about a future enhanced version of your application, you decide to load this data into the database. For this purpose, you start by creating a table called *us_movie_info* with four columns, *title*, *year_released*, *duration* and *color* with the right data types, and you define the pair (*title*, *year_released*) as the primary key. For instance:

```
create table us_movie_info
    (title          varchar(100) not null,
     year_released  numeric(4) not null,
     duration       int not null,
     color          char(1) not null,
     primary key(title, year_released))
```

NOTE **varchar** is **varchar2** with Oracle.

First of all, one has to understand where the file to upload is located in relation to the database; when you are connected to a database you aren't usually logged in on the machine where the database server is located; you are entering your commands from a client computer, and communicate with the database server via a network. If you issue a database command, whether it is a **select** or an **insert** command, the text of the command is sent to and executed by the database server. If you issue a command that loads a file, the command is also sent to and executed by the database server - but refers to a file which may already be on the server or which is initially located on the user's client computer. The file location is a critical point that often determines which command to use for loading.

MySQL

MySQL has a special load command:

```
load data [local] infile '<filename>'
into table <tablename>
```

Without the optional **local** keyword, the SQL engine understands that the file is located on the same host as the database server. If the filename isn't a full path, the file will be looked for at a default place, for instance `/var/lib/mysql/`*<database name>* on a Linux system. If you specify **local**, then the client program will first transparently read and transfer the file to the machine that hosts the database before sending the command to load it.

By default, **load** expects the fields to be separated by tabs. As they are separated by commas in the sample datafile, you must specify it next:

```
fields terminated by ','
```

and as the title is enclosed by ", you must also tell it. Otherwise (in the best case) the " characters would be understood as part of the title and loaded into the database or (the worst case) a comma found inside a title would be understood as a separator and MySQL would get confused with the various fields, would try to load text in numerical columns and the load would fail. You specify that " are here just to enclose titles and must be stripped when loading into the table by adding:

```
optionally enclosed by '"'
```

Thus, assuming that you have created table *us_movie_info* and that the file to load is located in the current directory (on a Linux system as you may guess from the file path), you can load the sample file with

```
load data local infile './us_movie_info.csv'
into table us_movie_info
fields terminated by ','
optionally enclosed by '"'
```

There are other options. One common occurrence is a file, the first line of which describes the fields (headers) and mustn't be loaded; you can skip it by adding

```
ignore 1 lines
```

> NOTE There are actually many more options - those are the options you should find most useful but check the reference documentation.

SQL Server

SQL Server supports several possible options. When the file is accessible from the server (it can be on a network disk) you can use the **bulk insert** command:

```
bulk insert <tablename> from '<full path to file>'
```

Like with MySQL, the default field separator is a tab. You can specify many options, by indicating **with** followed by a list of parameters between parentheses. As I have mentioned previously, with SQL Server you must be careful about the origin (Windows or UNIX) of the file. With the example file you must for instance specify that the delimiter is a comma and as the sample file was created under Linux you must specify that lines are terminated by a single line feed character, the standard on UNIX systems, and not the traditional carriage return/line feed that is the Windows standard and the default for **bulk insert**.

There are other interesting options with **bulk insert**, for instance if you must skip one header line - in other words, start loading from the second line - you can specify the additional option `firstrow=2`.

Unfortunately specifying field and line terminator will not mean that you can load the file by snapping your fingers. First problem, if you type

```
bulk insert us_movie_info from 'C:\temp\us_movie_info.csv'
with (fieldterminator = ',', rowterminator='\n')
```

the load may still fail, for a reason that isn't immediately obvious. If you say that the row terminator is '\n', it may indeed be interpreted by SQL Server as "Oh, wait, what they <u>really</u> mean is '\r\n'" and the operations fails for the reason that, as the file contains no \r and SQL Server looks for \r\n to separate lines, it sees only one big line. If you want to specify that the line is terminated by a line feed character and nothing else because, how heretical it may be in the Microsoft world, the file was created under Linux, then the safe way to specify the row terminator is to give what is called its hexadecimal code, which you see in the following statement:

```
bulk insert us_movie_info from 'C:\temp\us_movie_info.csv'
with (fieldterminator = ',', rowterminator='0x0a')
```

Second problem, you will have the joy to discover that while the loads worked this time, all the titles in the table are surrounded by double quotes. We'll soon see how to remove them but it can be a problem when loading. This isn't the case in the sample data file but it sometimes happens that a title contains a comma (for instance *Goodbye, Mr. Chips* or *Sex, Lies, and Videotape*). If the comma inside the title is understood as a regular separator and SQL Server tries to load *Lies* in the column supposed to store the year and *and Videotape* in the duration, you can expect some trouble.

The solution is to specify how to map the file to a table, not just by giving terminators but by describing precisely the file structure in what is called a *format file*

A format file is a text file that you create with a text editor and that explains in detail how to map the content of the file to your table. It contains two header lines, plus as many lines as there are fields in the data file.

- The first line contains a version number (9.0 for SQL Server 2005, 10.0 for SQL Server 2008, 11.0 for SQL Server 2012 and so on).
- The second line contains the number of fields in the data file
- Then there is one row per field, with, separated by spaces:
  1. the number of the field in each line (the leftmost is one),
  2. the data type in the file (SQLCHAR will do very well with a text file),
  3. 0 - this field is used for some special formats where the field is preceded by its length and specifies how many bytes are used for the length. With a plain text file it will always be 0,
  4. the maximum length of the data for that column in the file (it doesn't need to be the actual maximum - just something that is big enough to accommodate the longest value),
  5. the separator that indicates the end of the field (the last one is special: it contains the line terminator, "\r\n" for a file created under Windows, "\n" for a file created under Linux - in a format file SQL Server doesn't try to replace "\n" by "\r\n" ,
  6. the number of the column in the table that maps to this field,
  7. the name of the column in the table
  8. and the column collation (the rules for sorting) - "" means that I use the default collation.

To load my example file into SQL Server 2012, I can use the following format file:

```
11.0                                    ← That means SQL Server 2012
4                                       ← Number of fields in the file
1 SQLCHAR 0 150 "," 1 title ""          ← Field description
2 SQLCHAR 0 4 "," 2 year_released ""
3 SQLCHAR 0 3 "," 3 duration ""
4 SQLCHAR 0 1 "\n" 4 color ""
```

If you save this format file as *us_movie_info.fmt* in the same directory as the data file, you can load the data with

```
bulk insert  us_movie_info from 'C:\temp\us_movie_info.csv'
with (formatfile='C:\temp\us_movie_info.fmt')
```

The problem is that this format file does nothing to solve the problem of commas in the title. The solution here is to say that what terminates the first field isn't a comma but a double quote followed by a comma. As the terminator must itself be specified between double quotes, the double quote in the terminator must be preceded by a \

```
11.0
4
1 SQLCHAR 0 150 "\"," 1 title ""
2 SQLCHAR 0 4 "," 2 year_released ""
3 SQLCHAR 0 3 "," 3 duration ""
4 SQLCHAR 0 1 "\n" 4 color ""
```

The first double quote at the beginning of each line will still be loaded but commas in titles won't be misinterpreted.

There is however no option with **bulk insert** to load a local file to a distant database server. For this purpose, you must use a command-line utility called **bcp** (**B**ulk **C**o**P**y) to which you can provide connection information (as well as, obviously, the name of the file, the name of the table to insert into, and the format file, that **bcp** understands.)

But when the file is accessible from the database server, there is an even better option than **bulk insert**. You can create with a very special function called **openrowset()**, a virtual table that maps to the file and lets you query the file with SQL as if it were a real table – needless to say you won't be able to do everything you would do with a table and you may find that performance lacks luster here and there but you can use it in a query:

```
select *
from openrowset(bulk 'C:\temp\us_movie_info.csv',
                formatfile='C:\temp\us_movie_info.fmt') as virtual_table
```

(*virtual_table* is an arbitrary name that I give to the expression – I have to give a name.)

You see that **openrowset()** takes two arguments, **bulk** followed by the filename and a second argument **formatfile=**, followed by the location of the format file that allows us to map the datafile to the virtual table. If you run this query with the format file I have described, you will see the file as if it were a table - once again with a double quote before each title.

The beauty of **openrowset()** is that you can use the virtual table as the source for an **insert ... select ...** statement and in the process omit columns from the source file, or apply SQL functions and transform data at the same time as you load it. For instance if I want to remove the double quotes and change the color indicator to *Y* for color and *N* for black and white when loading into table *us_movie_info*, the content of file *us_movie_info.csv*, I just have to run:

```
insert into us_movie_info(title, year_released, duration, color)
select replace(title, '"', '') title,
       year_released,
       duration,
       case color
         when 'B' then 'N'
         when 'C' then 'Y'
       end color
from openrowset(bulk 'C:\temp\us_movie_info.csv',
                formatfile='C:\temp\us_movie_info.fmt') as virtual_table
```

It's common that we get files that don't quite match tables that are used by the application. Very often people load datafiles into work tables known as *staging tables* that have exactly the same structure as the data file, and once data is loaded it can be massaged. Creating a virtual table with **openrowset()** allows us to bypass at least some staging.

As a side-note, format files allow describing much more sophisticated formats than CSV; they may also describe formats such as XML, which is a popular data exchange format.

ORACLE

Contrary to MySQL or SQL Server, Oracle has no built-in SQL command to load a file. There are two main options with Oracle:

- Creating an *external table*, which is a mapping of a datafile to a virtual table in the same spirit as what one can do on SQL Server with **openrowset()** but in a rather different way. First, Oracle doesn't allow you to read data from anywhere on the server; you can only read from a directory that has been registered under an arbitrary name *<dirname>* in the database by a DBA, using a command such as:

  ```
  create directory <dirname> as '<path to the directory>'
  ```

  This isn't enough. The DBA must moreover give read and write access to the account that wants to create an external table:

  ```
  grant read, write on directory <dirname> to <account name>
  ```

NOTE I'll tell you much more about the **grant** command in Chapter 10.

It may surprise you to need a write access when you just want to read from a file. What happens is that when you 'read' from an external table you actually load the datafile, which results in the writing of a log file that summarizes the outcome of the load operation. The process may also write other files that contain lines that failed to map into the virtual table (for instance because the data type didn't match).

NOTE It is possible to specify, for files that are written, directories other than the directory you read from when defining the external table, but I am trying to keep things simple.

Once the directory exists and I have all the required privileges, I can create my external table. For instance let's say that my file is the sample datafile, that it's located (on a Linux system) in directory */var/input_dir*, and that I'm connected to Oracle as user *SQLSUCCESS*. The prerequisites are that a DBA has executed the two following commands to register the directory as *input_dir* in the database and to give access to it to the account I am using:

```
create directory input_dir as '/var/input_dir';
grant read, write on directory input_dir to SQLSUCCESS;
```

If those prerequisites are satisfied, I can use the following syntax, that starts like a regular **create table** statement but specifies in the **organization external** clause, where to find the file and write the logs, how records are delimited in the input file and how fields are delimited within each record, and finally the name of the file -

```
create table virtual_us_movie_info
          (title          varchar2(150),
           year_released  number(4),
           duration       number(3),
           color          char)
organization external (default directory input_dir
   access parameters
      (records delimited by newline
       fields terminated by ','
              optionally enclosed by '"')
   location ('us_movie_info.csv'))
```

Note that the **newline** in `records delimited by newline` refers to the usual line termination on the system where Oracle is running - in my example it will be the simple linefeed (\n) of UNIX and Linux systems. It would be carriage return/line feed (\r\n) on Windows. If you are trying to load the sample datafile (created on a Linux system) on Windows, you must write

```
records delimited by '\n'
```

The external table becomes a permanent object of the database, which can be useful when loading a file that always bears the same name as a recurrent operational task (typically when you receive every night from other computers, files that must be uploaded).

- When the file isn't located on (or accessible from) the same machine as the database server, the solution is to use, as with SQL Server, a special utility, which is run from the operating system prompt, called *sqlldr* (the official name is *SQL*Loader*, *sqlldr* is the actual command that you run). SQL*Loader takes as input a *control file* that describes the mapping in a syntax that closely resembles the MySQL **load** command

NOTE MySQL copied Oracle that cloned the syntax of a DB2 utility.

```
load data
infile '<full path to file>'
insert
into table <tablename>
fields terminated by '<separator>'
   [optionally enclosed by '...']
(<comma separated list of column names>)
```

For instance on Windows:

```
load data
infile 'C:\temp\us_movie_info.csv'
insert
into table us_movie_info
fields terminated by ','
      optionally enclosed by '"'
(title, year_released, duration, color)
```

Note that even when loading a Linux file under Windows, there is no specification of how lines are terminated - SQL*Loader does the right thing.

If you save these commands to a control file, for instance *sqlldr.ctl*, you can load the file into a local or remote database by running it in a command window:

```
sqlldr <username>/<password>@<connection data> control=sqlldr.ctl
```

SQL*Loader is a very powerful utility that supports many formats.

PostgreSQL

Command **copy** in PostgreSQL is similar to **load** with MySQL; there is, though, a major difference: there is no **local** keyword to specify that the file isn't located on the server but instead is on the machine where the client program is running. With the command line client, *psql*, there is however a very simple way to load a local datafile, which is to use the command **\copy** instead of **copy**. Commands that are preceded by a backslash (\) in `psql` are `psql` commands, not SQL commands. This means that instead of being sent as is to the database server for processing, a command that

starts with \ is interpreted by the client program. Therefore, **\copy** is run locally, can read the file locally and sends the data to the server for insertion.
Depending on the location of the file, you'll execute either

```
copy <table name> from '<full filename>'
```

or

```
\copy <table name> from '<full filename>'
```

Note that PostgreSQL takes a purist view of CSV and considers (correctly) that a tab separated file isn't a CSV file but a text file; a text file in which fields are separated by tabs is what is expected by default. If the file to be loaded is really comma separated, you should append to the preceding command

```
with (format csv)
```

NOTE Old version of PostgreSQL used **with csv**.

In that case the default separator becomes a comma and (by default) fields may optionally be surrounded by double quotes. Once again, there are many possible options.

DB2

DB2 has a philosophy similar to MySQL, although with db2 **load** is a utility, not an SQL command (the difference is only important in programs). The same syntax is used independently of the location of the file but a special keyword specifies whether the file is located on the server or on the client side. If the file is on the database server, you simply say **load**; if the file is on the client side, you say **load client**.
The general syntax is

```
load [client] from '<path to file>' of del insert into <tablename>
```

The **del** doesn't stand for "delete" as it often does but for *delimited* and is meant to specify the type of file that is being loaded – a text file in which the different fields are delimited by one character. Unlike most products, the default delimiter is a comma and by default, text is expected to be surrounded by double-quotes, which makes loading the sample datafile very easy, as all the default options are the right ones. However, if your separators are tabs you must specify the delimiter by using the not-so-user-friendly:

```
load from '<file>' of del modified by coldel0x09 insert into <tablename>
```

coldel stands for **col**umn **del**imiter and the delimiter is usually appended (without any space) to **coldel**. It doesn't work for a tab, though and you have to replace the tab by the special code *0x09* that means *tab* to geeks. This in retrospect gives a measure of the achievement of Chamberlin and Boyce when they created SQL and tried to define with it, a language usable by a population not uniquely composed of avid readers of IBM reference documentation.

SQLite

The case with SQLite is much easier than with the "real" DBMS products, as there is no server – the client and the server are one. All you need to do with SQLite is first create the table to load into, with the same number of columns as there are fields in the datafile, then specify the separator in the file with

```
.separator '<separator>'
```

then issue the command

```
.import '<filename>' <tablename>
```

Unless you run an old version of SQLite, double quotes enclosing text won't be loaded.
As the separator that is set by `.separator` is used for both input and output (it's also used for separating columns when running a **select**), you may want to reset it to the default vertical bar after import.

OTHER TYPES OF READABLE FILES

As already mentioned, several utilities support formats other than CSV files (with a loose understanding of "C"), such as XML, or files in which the various columns start at fixed positions. You may encounter other formats in which, what should be a single row in the target table, will be recorded as a variable number of rows in the input file, such as for instance:

```
firstname: Gene
surname: Kelly
born: 1912
died: 1996
firstname: Debbie
surname: Reynolds
born: 1932
firstname: Donald
surname: O'Connor
born: 1925
died: 2003
```

NOTE If you have ever had the curiosity to take a look at the source of an email message, you may recognize similarities.

If you don't want to write a specific program to load this data, one reasonable "programming lite" approach consists in transforming the content of the source file into regular SQL **insert** statements that can then be run from a command-line client. This solution can work very well even when there are thousands of rows to load. Many scripting languages are usable for this purpose and if you are already familiar with one, stick to it. I have grown particularly fond of *awk*, a UNIX utility of which you can also find Windows versions. The syntax for processing a file with *awk* is

```
awk  f <awkscript> <input_file>
```

Because the command displays the transformation of *<input_file>* on the screen, you usually redirect the output of the command to a file. *Awk* reads the input file line by line, stores the current line in a variable called *$0* and considers that parts of the line that are separated by spaces (one or several spaces - you can specify that separators are something other than spaces) are the interesting bits, and they are assigned to variables called *$1*, *$2*, ... up to the last one. A variable called *NF* holds the number of chunks found in the line.

Thus, with the first line in the previous example, $0 would hold "firstname: Gene" (the full line), $1 would hold " firstname:", $2 would hold "Gene", and NF would be set to 2.

An *awk* script is composed of a succession of patterns, followed by an action between curly brackets that applies to the lines in the file that match this pattern. If there is no pattern, the action applies to all the lines in the file that is processed.

I am going to use a "no pattern" action only, plus two special patterns, **BEGIN** that indicates an initialization part which is run only once before the first line is processed, and **END** that indicates a finalization part which is run only once, after the last line is processed.

The structure of my script will therefore be the following:

```
BEGIN { ... }    ← Initialization part, run once
{ ... }          ← Main part, applied to all lines
END { ... }      ← Finalization part, run once
```

Inside the curly brackets, you find commands terminated by semi-colons that are very similar to what you can find in C, Java, PHP or javascript. If you know (however sketchily) any of these languages, you shouldn't have much trouble with a basic use of *awk*, as presented here.

In the initialization part I set to 0, an indicator I call *pending* which will tell me whether I need to output an **insert** statement and I initialize variables that will hold the two columns that can have no value, *fname* (the firstname, not a filename) and *died*. I don't initialize *fname* to "null" because I really need to know if it's empty or not, and if it isn't then it must be quoted. Finally, and very importantly if you are not using Oracle or DB2, I start a transaction (I am using here **begin transaction**, it should be **start transaction** with MySQL). If I don't, my load will be much slower and if the load fails it will be much more difficult to correct the data and restart. Don't be afraid of loading many, many rows in a single transaction - some people load millions of rows in one shot.

In the main part which is executed for every line in the input file, I first ignore empty lines by checking the number of fields **NF**, then I check the first "token".

> NOTE A much better use of awk would be to use patterns rather than check the first token for each line. I am not trying to use awk cleverly but to show a logic that can be converted easily to another scripting language.

If it's "firstname:" or "surname:", if I have something to output, I display an **insert** statement with the values collected so far. Because a name, first name or surname, may be composed of several tokens ("Jamie Lee" or "Del Toro" for instance), I concatenate the different bits I find in my line into a variable and remove the initial space I have added. Then I apply to the name, a procedure called **gsub()** that works like **replace()** in SQL (except that it directly modifies its third argument, the affected string) to turn any single quote into two single quotes. It's much easier for the years of birth and death.

In the finalization part, I display an **insert** statement if there is anything pending and (important), I commit the transaction.

Here is the full code:

> NOTE Once again, this isn't an elegant *awk* script. It could be written in a smarter and more compact way with patterns and functions but this version is relatively easy to adapt to another scripting language.

```
BEGIN {
      pending = 0;          ← Indicate than nothing is pending processing
      fname = "";           ← Initialize attributes that aren't mandatory
      died = "null";
      printf("begin transaction;\n");   ← Don't forget the transaction
}
{
 if (NF > 0) {      ← If the line isn't empty
   if ($1 == "firstname:") {   ① Check the first token
     if (pending == 1) {    ← Flush the data for the previous person
       printf("insert into people(first_name,surname,born,died)\n");
       if (length(fname) == 0) {  ← First name can be absent
         printf("values(null,'%s',%s,%s);\n", sname, born, died);
       } else {
         printf("values('%s','%s',%s,%s);\n", fname, sname, born, died);
       }
       fname = "";          ← Reset variables after flush
       died = "null";
       pending = 0;
     }
     for (i = 2; i <= NF; i++) {  ← Take care of multi-part names
       fname = fname " " $i;
```

```
      }
      fname = substr(fname, 2);   ← Skip the space added at the beginning
      gsub("'", "''", fname);     ② Replace single quotes by two single quotes
    } else {
      if ($1 == "surname:") {
        if (pending == 1) {     ← Flush the data for the previous person
          printf("insert into people(first_name,surname,born,died)\n");
          printf("values(null,'%s',%s,%s);\n", sname, born, died);
          fname = "";           ← Reset variables after flush
          died = "null";
        }
        sname = ""
        for (i = 2; i <= NF; i++) { ← Take care of multi-part names
          sname = sname " " $i;
        }
        sname = substr(sname, 2); ← Skip the space added at the beginning
        gsub("'", "''", sname);   ② Replace single quotes by two single quotes
        pending = 1;    ← Surname means a row to insert
      } else {
        if ($1 == "born:") {
          born = $2;
        } else {
          if ($1 == "died:") {
            died = $2;
          }
        }
      }
    }
  }
}
END {
     if (pending == 1) { ← Flush the data for the previous person
        printf("insert into people(first_name,surname,born,died)\n");
        if (length(fname) == 0) {
           printf("values(null,'%s',%s,%s);\n", sname, born, died);
        } else {
           printf("values('%s','%s',%s,%s);\n", fname, sname, born, died);
        }
     }
     printf("commit;\n"); ← Don't forget the transaction
}
```

In awk as in C and languages derived from C you test for equality ① with '=='. Some versions of awk allow the replacement of nested 'if' clauses by a 'switch' clause similar to an SQL 'case'. Both constructs could be avoided by associating actions with each separate pattern. The **gsub()** call ② modifies its 3rd parameter, replacing every occurrence of the first parameter by the second parameter.

I have saved the sample data to a file called *actor_info.txt* and here is what running the script above (saved as *awkscript*) displays:

```
$ awk -f awkscript actor_info.txt
```

```
begin transaction;
insert into people(first_name,surname,born,died)
values('Gene','Kelly',1912,1996);
insert into people(first_name,surname,born,died)
values('Debbie','Reynolds',1932,null);
insert into people(first_name,surname,born,died)
values('Donald','O''Connor',1925,2003);
commit;
```

As you can see, the quote in O'Connor has been correctly doubled. With Oracle, there would be no **begin transaction** but there should be a reference to a sequence to assign new values to the *peopleid* identifier.

Let's come back now to pure SQL and see how data can be changed once stored in the database.

Updating data

It happens quite often that data is inserted into a table and then never changed but it is also common that data has to be updated to reflect changes to the facts that are described. We aren't living in a static world. This is a rather sad example but in our movie database actors and directors die and we may have to set the *died* column to the current year when we learn from the media of such an event.

The Update Statement

To change the values in existing rows, there is a single command: **update**.
You just type **update** followed by the name of the table you want to change, then **set**, the name of a column you want to change and the new value that you want to assign to this column. If the column isn't mandatory, you can assign null to it (as in most computer languages, the equal sign in the **set** clause doesn't mean equality but assignment). If you want to change several columns in the same rows at once, then you should follow the first assignment by a comma, a new assignment and so on. The **set** keyword appears only once.
Finally, you must say which are the rows that you want to update. If you leave the update statement without any condition, it applies to all the rows in the table.

Simple Updates

I am calling *simple updates* changes in which I replace one or several values by either a constant or the result of an expression. For instance, if when loading file *us_movie_info.csv* into a table you loaded some double quotes with the titles, you can clean-up the data with

```
update us_movie_info
set title = replace(title, '"', '')
```

You'll notice that you can define, as in this example, the new value (on the left-hand side of the equal sign) as a function of the previous value (on the right-hand side). All titles will be modified. If you need to apply changes to a subset of the table, you use exactly the same kind of **where** clause as you use in a **select** statement.

You may have noticed for instance that the case used for titles isn't always consistent in table *movies*; you may make it more consistent by updating the table manually, for instance

```
update movies
set title = 'Il Buono, Il Brutto, Il Cattivo'
where title = 'Il buono, il brutto, il cattivo'
```

(You could also say `where movieid = ...`)

There are cases such as this one when you want to update a single row, and then using the primary key is fine. But one thing that you should always keep in mind is that **update** is designed to change datasets, not to change one by one, a series of rows retrieved by a prior query (which unfortunately you see done very often). The dataset affected by **update** can just be a one-row (or zero rows) dataset but updating a single row is just a particular case.

I mentioned in the previous chapter that surnames starting with 'von ' usually mess up sorts and that it may be more convenient for sorting to store 'Stroheim (von)' or 'Sternberg (von)' instead of 'von Stroheim' or 'von Sternberg' in the *people* table. A command such as

```
update people
set surname = substr(surname, 4) || ' (von)'
where surname like 'von %'
```

will process all people whose name starts with 'von ' at one go (as usual, `substring(surname, 4, len(surname))` instead of `substr(...)` and + instead of `||` with SQL Server, and `concat()` instead of `||` with MySQL.)

Complex Updates

Updates become trickier when the update depends on values in a table other than the one that is updated. As a general rule, unless the condition is very simple, run updates in transactions; if something goes wrong and you update many more rows than expected (client tools usually say how many rows were affected) you'll be able to roll back the changes. If the **where** condition reaches a complexity that takes you out of your comfort zone, write first a **select** statement that returns (or at least counts) the rows you want to update.

I am going to illustrate complex updates by creating a new, improved version of table *movies* called *movies_2* (the sequel) that will be identical to *movies* but with two additional columns, *duration*, an integer column, and *color*, a char column. I'm going to update both these new columns (when possible) with data loaded from *us_movie_info.csv*.

NOTE It is possible to add columns to an existing table with the command **alter table** and this is what people usually do when applications evolve and new attributes are needed. I could modify *movies* and not create *movies_2*. For instance, I could add a *duration* column to table *movies* with

`alter table movies add column duration int` with PostgreSQL, DB2 and SQLite
`alter table movies add duration int` with Oracle, MySQL, and SQL Server

(It's also possible with most products to use **alter table** to add or drop constraints)

However, a table copy will give us more freedom to mess with the data...

Although column *color* will bear the same name in tables *movies_2* and *us_movie_info*, I'll store in column *color* of *movies_2* the value *Y* if the film is a color movie (code *C* in *us_movie_info*) and *N* if it's in black and white (code *B* in *us_movie_info*).

If you are using Oracle, you should first create a sequence

```
create sequence movies_2_seq
```

Then you can create the table:

```
create table movies_2
        (movieid       <dbms specific> primary key,  ① See notes that follow
         title         varchar(60) not null,         ← varchar2 with Oracle
         country       char(2) not null,
         year_released int not null,                 ← number(4) with Oracle
         duration      int,                          ← number(3) with Oracle
         color         char,
         foreign key(country) references countries(country_code))
    Add "Engine=InnoDB" with MySQL
```

What I have indicated as **<dbms specific>** should be:

- **number** with Oracle
- **int identity** with SQL Server
- **int generated as identity** with DB2
- **serial** with PostgreSQL and MySQL
- **integer not null** with SQLite

This table can be initially populated with:

```
insert into movies_2(title, country, year_released)
select title, country, year_released
from movies
```

or, for Oracle:

```
insert into movies_2(movieid, title, country, year_released)
select movies_2_seq.nextval, title, country, year_released
from movies
```

The identifiers that will be generated will be different from the original ones and if I were one day to completely replace *movies* with *movies_2*, I should change the values in table *credits* accordingly, but we won't need *credits* or *people* for what we are going to do with *movies_2* in this book.

You can naturally update columns *duration* and *color* manually and say for instance

```
update movies_2
set duration = 188,
    color = 'Y'
where title = 'Sholay'
  and country = 'in'
```

Now the problem is updating *movies_2* with the information you can find in *us_movie_info*. As very often happens when you try to aggregate data from various sources, you have no exact match – even if you only consider American movies, some films in *movies_2* will not be found in *us_movie_info*, and vice versa.

Such an update bears a great resemblance to a **select** statement – you need to retrieve information from a source table (or sometimes several tables) before using it to change the target table. I have stressed how nulls and duplicates could make the result of a query completely wrong; the same danger lurks here and it's much more serious than with queries. If you update a table wrongly, the information that is stored will be false and most queries that will refer to the table, even flawless queries, will return wrong results. When constraints are properly defined, it's difficult to mess up data with an **insert** statement. It's incredibly easy with a complex **update**, and I shall illustrate it after having shown you how to write a complex **update** statement with the various products.

While the **update** statement that involves a single table is more or less standard across DBMS products, creativity blossomed for updates that require several tables. With all products, the value that you assign to a column can be the result of a subquery that is correlated to the table being updated. In a query, a correlated subquery refers to the current row that is inspected; in an update, it refers to the current row being updated.

SQLite

SQLite is a clumsy product when it comes to updating tables with data coming from other tables. Unfortunately, in SQLite you cannot assign an alias to the table that is updated; this forces us to prefix with the full table name in the subqueries. Also, there is no other way with SQLite, than to run as many correlated subqueries as there are columns to update:

```
update movies_2
set duration = (select duration
                from us_movie_info i
                where i.title = movies_2.title
                  and i.year_released = movies_2.year_released),
    color = (select case color
                      when 'C' then 'Y'
                      when 'B' then 'N'
                    end color
             from us_movie_info i
             where i.title = movies_2.title
               and i.year_released = movies_2.year_released)
```

If I run the statement as it is written above, I'm in for a nasty surprise: as there is no **where** clause, the **update** statement applies to all rows in the table. What will happen when I process the row that contains *Sholay*, which I have just manually updated? *Sholay* is an Indian film with no information in *us_movie_info*, the two subqueries will return nothing, which as always translates to null. I'll assign null to *duration* and *color* and erase the values I had previously set.

If I don't want to lose any information I already have, I must restrict with a **where** clause the scope of the **update** statement, firstly by saying precisely that I only update American movies, and secondly by saying furthermore, that the only American movies I am willing to update are those found in *us_movie_info* - I might have found the running time of some other American movies from a different source:

```
where country = 'us'
  and exists (select null
              from us_movie_info i2
              where i2.title = movies_2.title
                and i2.year_released = movies_2.year_released)
```

When you take a look at the **update** statement as a whole, you see that for each row that you update, you fetch the same correlated row from *us_movie_info* three times, which is performing a lot of operations for nothing. The subquery in the **where** clause might be uncorrelated if the "join" between *movies_2* and *us_movie_info* were on only one column (the title). Then we could write:

```
where country = 'us'
  and title in
          (select title
           from us_movie_info)
```

Unfortunately, because of possible remakes, it will be the pair (*title, year_released*) that will ensure that we are really talking about the same film in both tables. With SQLite the query has to be correlated and fired for each American movie in table *movies_2*.

Although the statement will be fast on small tables, it might be rather slow on big tables (on the other hand, when you have really big tables, SQLite isn't the best choice.)

Oracle and DB2

Oracle and DB2 share several features. The first (minor but comfortable) one is that they allow us to assign an alias to the table being updated. The second one, much more important, is that they allow us to set the values of multiple columns at once from the result of a correlated subquery. The third one, no less important, is that they also support matching a parenthesized list of columns to an **in (...)** uncorrelated subquery that returns as many columns as are present in the list. Nothing will explain it more clearly than an example:

```
update movies_2 m
set (duration, color) = (select duration,
                                case color
                                   when 'C' then 'Y'
                                  when 'B' then 'N'
                                end color
                         from us_movie_info i
                         where i.title = m.title
                           and i.year_released = m.year_released)
where m.country = 'us'
  and (m.title, m.year_released)
      in (select title, year_released
          from us_movie_info)
```

We are running one correlated subquery for each American movie in table *movies_2*, and we also run a subquery that isn't correlated (and will therefore run only once and not for each row) in the **where** clause. The **update** statement will be reasonably fast.

PostgreSQL and SQL Server

PostgreSQL and SQL Server implement a very similar syntax. This syntax is inspired by the old syntax for joins that I mentioned in Chapter 4, in which the various tables that are joined appear as a comma separated list in the **from** clause, and the conditions that chain tables together (and are usually specified after **on**) appear in the **where** clause. The table (or tables) that are used as data providers are listed in a **from** clause between the **set** clause and the **where** clause, and the join conditions are in the **where** clause together with real screening conditions (such as the condition on the country in this example):

```
update movies_2
set duration = i.duration,
    color = case i.color
              when 'C' then 'Y'
              when 'B' then 'N'
            end
from us_movie_info i
where i.title = movies_2.title
  and i.year_released = movies_2.year_released
  and movies_2.country = 'us'
```

As the join is an inner join, it is guaranteed that only rows in *movies_2* that have a match in *us_movie_info* (which isn't the case with *Sholay*) will be affected and there is no need for a subquery in the **where** clause.

NOTE To be fair to Oracle, if some, extremely stringent, conditions are satisfied (they aren't here) it allows us to update the result of a nested query which can be a join. In that case it doesn't need a subquery in the **where** clause either.

MySQL

MySQL allows a syntax in which you can also join other tables to the table that is updated but in a way that is much closer to the syntax of the **select** statement, and in which the newer join syntax is allowed (as well as table aliases):

```
update movies_2 m
       inner join us_movie_info i
          on i.title = m.title
         and i.year_released = m.year_released
set m.duration = i.duration,
    m.color = case i.color
                when 'C' then 'Y'
                when 'B' then 'N'
              end
where m.country = 'us'
```

It's probably the cleaner syntax of all SQL dialects – except that as you will see, you must be extra cautious with your primary keys.

How Things Can Go Horribly Wrong

I have been very cautious with the identification of my films – remember that they are identified by title, year and country in real life (as opposed to joins in SQL statements and to foreign keys, for which I rely on the internal identifier *movieid*.)

Let's suppose now that I hadn't been as cautious, simply relying on the title and that there are remakes in either *movies_2*, the table I am updating, or *us_movie_info*, my source for the running time, and whether the movie is in color or in black and white.

I am going to add two movies into *movies_2*, the 1934 *Treasure Island* starring Wallace Berry and Jackie Cooper and the 1950 film by the same name but with Robert Newton and Bobby Driscoll. To *us_movie_info*, I only add one line concerning the 1934 movie, saying that its running time was 103 minutes and that it's a black and white movie.

When you run a **select** statement in which you only join on the title, for instance this one:

```
select m.title, m.year_released, i.year_released, i.duration, i.color
from movies_2 m
     inner join us_movie_info i
        on i.title = m.title
where m.title like 'Treasure%'
```

you can easily spot the mistake when the same row from *us_movie_info* is associated with two distinct rows from *movies_2*:

```
title             year_released  year_released  duration   color
----------------- -------------- -------------- ---------- ------
Treasure Island             1934           1934        103 B
Treasure Island             1950           1934        103 B
```

When you run the **update** and forget the condition on the year, exactly the same thing happens – without any warning. Both films in *movies_2* will get the same running time and color attribute. For one of them it will be wrong.

The other, no less interesting case, is when *movies_2* only contains the 1976 remake of *King Kong* and *us_movie_info* contains data about both the 1976 remake (134 minutes, color), and the original 1933 movie (100 minutes, black and white.) In that case, this query:

```
select m.title, m.year_released, i.year_released, i.duration, i.color
from movies_2 m
     inner join us_movie_info i
        on i.title = m.title
where m.title = 'King Kong'
```

will return what follows:

```
title             year_released  year_released  duration   color
----------------- -------------- -------------- ---------- ------
King Kong                   1976           1933        100  B
King Kong                   1976           1976        134  C
```

The outcome of the **update** statement will then depend on how you write it. If you assign to your attributes in table *movies_2*, values retrieved by correlated subqueries, then the update will fail. For instance, Oracle will tell you:

```
ORA-01427: single-row subquery returns more than one row
```

You cannot assign to a variable (or return in a select list) the result of a subquery that returns more than one row (returning no rows however, is allowed – it becomes null.) But if the update is through a join, the result of the preceding query will help you understand that the various durations and color attributes found in *us_movie_info* will be used in turn to update the single row in *movies_2*, and what the row will store ultimately are the last values used for updating it. You stand a 50% chance of recording in your database that the 1976 King Kong is a 100 minute black and white movie and to quote *Dirty Harry*:

> *You've got to ask yourself one question: Do I feel lucky?*

Of course, nothing of this need happen if you correctly join on title <u>and</u> year of release (<u>and</u> country if the source table contains movies from various countries).

I hope that these examples will help you understand why I have been so insistent about primary keys, not having duplicates and always getting result sets to which

Codd could have delivered a "true relation" stamp of approval. Even if it's less obvious in **update** statements than in **select** statements, the same rules and the same logic apply; and developers should, when writing **update** statements, be as paranoid (if not more so) about keys as when writing queries.

Another important point is that, although from a technical point of view all columns can be updated, from a logical point of view I would remind you that updating a key column, that is, a column that identifies one row, alone or in combination with other columns, makes no sense at all. Indeed, it violates a fundamental tenet of relational theory. If it's not the same identifier, then it's not the same item. Many products explicitly prevent you from modifying a primary key; if it's possible, you should really keep in mind that updating an identifier isn't an update - it's shorthand for deleting the row identified by the old identifier, and inserting a new row identified by the new identifier.

The Merge Statement

It's frequent that you combine **update** and **insert** in a process: you get a list of values that more or less correspond to what you already have - by "more or less" I mean that most of the data contains new values that refer to items that have to be updated but you may get information about so far unknown items. It may happen when you are uploading on a merchant site, the new catalog of a supplier; it may happen when you update in a bank, the closing price of shares or financial products. You probably have most of the information already but you may have been provided with new products.

We have a similar situation with the sample database. Table *us_movie_info* contains information about films that are absent from *movies_2* and rather than just updating information for the films we already know, we may seize the opportunity to add new films to the database, postponing the search for director/actor information to a later stage. The question then becomes one of scanning *us_movie_info*, updating films in *movies_2* when we know them, and inserting them when we don't (an operation sometimes called *upsert*). Most beginner developers, code their process exactly as I have just described it, scanning, searching, updating or inserting but that's not how you should do it. Rather than wasting time coding a slow procedure, you should use the power of SQL to perform such a process - it will be faster to write and much (much!) faster to run.

Most products implement a **merge** command that is officially part of the SQL standard and is written as follows

```
merge into <table>
using <source>
on (<join condition>)
when matched then
     <update statement>
```

```
when not matched then
   <insert statement>
```

Beware that the join condition in a **merge** may be required to be enclosed between parentheses, contrary to what happens in a regular join.

NOTE In some versions Oracle complains about a missing **on** keyword when it is in fact there and when Oracle actually wants parentheses.

With tables *movies_2* and *us_movie_info*, I can write the following, pushing *us_movie_info* into a subquery so as to write the **case ... end** expression transforming the value of column *color* only once, instead of repeating it in the **update** and in the **insert** sub statements:

```
merge into movies_2 m
using (select 'us' as country,
              title,
              year_released,
              duration,
              case color
                when 'C' then 'Y'
                when 'B' then 'N'
              end as color
       from us_movie_info) i
      on (i.country = m.country
     and i.title = m.title
     and i.year_released = m.year_released)
when matched then
     update
     set m.duration = i.duration,
         m.color = i.color
when not matched then
     insert(title, year_released, country, duration, color)
     values(i.title, i.year_released, i.country, i.duration, i.color)
```

If you are running Oracle the **insert** sub statement should read:

```
     insert(movieid, title, year_released, country, duration, color)
     values(movies_2_seq.nextval , i.title, i.year_released,
            i.country, i.duration, i.color)
```

MySQL implements a non-standard extension to the **insert** statement as a clause called **on duplicate key update** that specifies what to do when a unique constraint (not necessarily the primary key constraint) is violated.

The preceding example can be written, with MySQL:

```
insert into movies_2(title, year_released, country, duration, color)
select title, year_released, country, duration, color
from (select title,
             year_released,
             'us' as country,
             duration,
```

```
            case color
              when 'C' then 'Y'
              when 'B' then 'N'
            end color
      from us_movie_info) i
on duplicate key update
 movies_2.duration = i.duration,
 movies_2.color = i.color
```

SQLite implements something simpler and more limited but similar in spirit, an **insert or replace**. You could write here

```
insert or replace into movies_2(title, year_released,
                                country, duration, color)
select title, year_released, country, duration, color
from (select title,
             year_released,
             'us' as country,
             duration,
             case color
               when 'C' then 'Y'
               when 'B' then 'N'
             end color
      from us_movie_info) i;
```

As a general rule, fixing a constraint violation once it has been detected is relatively costly when it happens for many rows. If the bulk of the process is composed of updates, you should consider whether it wouldn't be faster to do what you should do when a DBMS implements neither **merge** nor any specific command; certainly not painfully inspecting rows one by one but within one transaction:

- running first an **update** of the target table based on the values in the source table as I have described under *Complex Updates*,
- followed by an **insert ... select ...** that identifies the new rows through an outer join between the source table and the target table:

```
insert into movies_2(title, year_released, country, duration, color)
select i.title, i.year_released, 'us', i.duration,
       case i.color
         when 'C' then 'Y'
         when 'B' then 'N'
       end
from us_movie_info i
     left outer join movies_2 m
       on m.title = i.title
      and m.year_released = i.year_released
      and m.country = 'us'
where m.movieid is null
```

Deleting data

As I stated at the beginning of this chapter, very often what appears to be a deletion is nothing more than a status update saying that a row should now be ignored. Unfortunately the problem with keeping data is that it grows and grows and you end up with such massive amounts of data to search, that the performance of some query collapses. Most people try to keep the volume of operational data under control (I mean data that you use in your daily operations), by implementing archival processes. On a regular basis, older data in fast growing tables is copied to special history tables that may themselves, be written to a different physical device at a later stage. Once data has been safely copied then the rows are deleted from the main table.

I mentioned earlier in this chapter that when you move money from one account to another, you don't have two updates, one for each account balance but two inserts with the amount transferred, one recorded as a debit operation from the source account and one recorded as a credit operation to the target account. The balance of each account can be computed as the sum of all credits minus the sum of all debits.

Computing the balance each time you check it, is fine for recent operations but impractical in the long run; a bank cannot compute every time, all the operations over 30 years or more, for a senior, long term customer. Besides, it is likely that s/he no longer cares very much about how much s/he paid for that T-shirt back in September 1990. The problem is exactly the same for telecom companies and the details of phone calls, or Internet Service Providers and the details of web activity.

What usually happens is that on a regular basis, big programs are run that compute the balances that you have on your statements. When you ask for your balance, it isn't computed as the sum of all credits minus the sum of all debits since you first signed up but the sum of all credits minus the sum of all debits since the last time when the balance was computed, a result which is added to this balance. The detail of operations (or calls) will be kept for a limited amount of time (possibly three months or one year - long enough to check claims in case of disagreement). Older details will be archived for a longer period and, after some kind of statute of limitations has been reached, finally destroyed.

Sometimes, older data is aggregated and those aggregates replace the detail; this often happens with data that is kept for statistics. For instance, you may keep track of the number of visits to a web site but if you are interested in measuring the traffic, after a while you may no longer be interested in the detail but simply in how many hits you got per hour and country. After a few months you may still be interested in traffic figures per day or week but not per hour because you just want to analyze trends. Regular processes will compute aggregates with an increasingly coarser grain as you step back in time, insert those aggregates, then delete the rows used to compute them.

Deleting rows is probably the simplest operation in SQL. You just need to specify

```
delete from tablename
where ...
```

The **where** clause specifies the rows you want to delete and can be as complex as you like, including correlated or uncorrelated queries with references to other tables. The standard way to proceed is only to have references to other tables in subqueries and nothing else, although some products implement a kind of join for **delete** statements as well as for **update** statements.

There is no reference here to columns, since you can only delete full rows. I would advise you always to run a **delete** statement in a transaction; you can hope to correct, however painfully, a wrong update but when a row is gone, it's gone. If you omit the **where** clause, then all rows from the table are deleted, unless of course doing so violates constraints. Even if you have a **where** clause it may happen that you have forgotten a condition, or badly written it, and you sometimes have an 'Ooooops' moment when the DBMS reports the number of rows that were affected. That is when you often feel grateful for the existence of **rollback**. Running prior to the **delete**, a **select** that tests which or how many rows would be deleted, is also a commendable caution for one-off operations.

There is another, much more brutal, way to remove rows from a table but it applies to all the rows in a table.

> NOTE In fact (but this is beyond the scope of this book) some tables may be composed of sub tables called *partitions* that can be individually emptied.

The operation cannot be rolled back because it is considered a part of the data definition language (like **create** and **drop**) and not part of the data manipulation language (like **insert**, **update**, or **delete**.) The command is

```
truncate table <tablename>
```

and is more or less equivalent in effect to dropping a table and recreating it empty.

> NOTE In practice the big difference with dropping and recreating is that all the ecosystem linked to a table, triggers, indexes, grants, all things you will see in the following chapters, is preserved with **truncate**.

For massive amounts of data execution is much faster than a **delete** because, as there is no rollback, there is no need to save the rows temporarily, until the transaction is successful and committed. It is better to seek advice from a database administrator before using this kind of statement.

Constraints

You must remember that from the beginning of this book, I have strenuously insisted on the necessity of having constraints in a database - constraints that ensure that identifiers are unique and constraints that ensure that values in a column belong to an acceptable range or set of values. Constraints are your guarantee that data remains, at any point, consistent in the database and since constraints are defined in the database, they are active for any operation that changes the data. If one change violates a constraint, it fails, and you just have to issue a **rollback** statement if it happens in the middle of a transaction. If you have no constraints or if they were loosely defined, changes will go through. A referential constraint has a double purpose: it prevents us from inserting into a table, a value absent from the table that is referenced (error messages usually refer to "no parent row"), and it prevents us from deleting from a reference table, rows that are referenced by rows in other tables (error messages will mention the existence of "child rows").

A number of constraints have been implemented in the sample database to ensure consistency. Be very careful if you are using SQLite though because foreign key enforcement isn't necessarily active; you should issue, immediately after opening the SQLite data file:

```
pragma foreign_keys = on;
```

With MySQL, I'll remind you that for foreign keys to be enforced, both the referencing table and the referenced table must have been created with the special (MySQL specific) clause `Engine=InnoDB` (InnoDB tables can co-exist in a database with tables that use a different "storage engine".)

If foreign keys are enforced, a movie cannot be from a country that is absent from the *countries* table; or you cannot have a row in *credits* that references a non-existing movie or a non-existing individual; or you cannot remove someone from table *people* who is credited in a movie. Don't hesitate to try to create inconsistencies on purpose - they shouldn't get through (hopefully).

If I try to run the following statement:

```
insert into movies_2(title, country, year_released)
values('Test', 'SF' , 1066)
```

Error messages vary in helpfulness:

- DB2 will tell you that

  ```
  The insert or update value of the FOREIGN KEY
  "<account_name_here>.MOVIES_2.SQL120527233716560" is not equal to any value of
  the parent key of the parent table.
  ```

- For Oracle, it's

  ```
  ORA-02291: integrity constraint (<account_name_here>.SYS_C007275) violated -
  parent key not found
  ```

- SQL Server is a bit more talkative:

  ```
  The INSERT statement conflicted with the FOREIGN KEY constraint
  "FK__movies_2__countr__5AEE82B9".
  ```

```
The conflict occurred in database "movies", table "dbo.countries", column
'country_code'.
```

- So are PostgreSQL:

```
ERROR:  insert or update on table "movies_2" violates foreign key constraint
"movies_2_country_fkey"
DETAIL:  Key (country)=(SF) is not present in table "countries".
```

- And MySQL:

```
ERROR 1452 (23000): Cannot add or update a child row: a foreign key constraint
fails (`movies`.`movies_2`, CONSTRAINT `movies_2_ibfk_1` FOREIGN KEY
(`country`) REFERENCES `countries` (`country_code`))
```

- While SQLite soberingly states:

```
Error: foreign key constraint failed
```

If you ignore SQLite, you'll notice that all products have given a name to the constraint - a name relatively understandable in the case of PostgreSQL; bordering on the understandable with SQL Server and MySQL; and shamelessly cryptic with Oracle and DB2. Unfortunately, the less explicit the name, the fewer details we get about the column that violated the constraint. It's common for a table to have many foreign key constraints and some typos aren't obvious. If users choose values from drop-down lists, data entry mistakes will be limited but if they type in values, anything can happen.

I haven't mentioned it thus far but it is possible, and advisable, to name constraints (and more particularly **foreign key** constraints and the much less used **check** constraints), by preceding the definition of a constraint by **constraint** *<name>*, for instance:

```
create table movies_2
        (movieid    ...
         ...
         color          char,
        constraint movies_2_country_fk
           foreign key(country) references countries(country_code))
```

As the name of the constraint is returned in the error message, you can even try to be explicit and take advantage of the possibility of having spaces in a name when it's enclosed in double quotes:

```
create table movies_2
        (movieid    ...
         ...
         color          char,
        constraint "country code must be in COUNTRIES"
           foreign key(country) references countries(country_code))
```

However, this is often made impractical by two factors:

- The fact that constraint names must be unique, like table names,

- The limitation on the maximum length of an object name, especially with Oracle that has the shortest limit at 30 characters (the example above would be too long for Oracle)

While a constraint name that includes table name and column name (possibly abbreviated) may still appear mysterious to the layman, the helpdesk will be grateful to you for having provided clues.

To Remember

- Changes to a database are grouped by logical units of work called *transactions*. Transactions are terminated explicitly by **commit** that validates, or **rollback** that cancels all the changes, or they are terminated implicitly by structural changes that validate changes.
- Updates and deletes aren't always what they appear to be.
- A significant part of inserts into a database are performed through file uploading.
- Primary keys and the absence of duplicates are as important, if not more so, in statements that change data as in queries. Constraints don't protect against everything.
- Just as **select** returns a data set; insert, **update** and **delete** operate on data sets, which may contain any number of rows between zero and all the rows in the table. Don't think "row" or "record" but try to think globally.
- Changes to a database cannot violate integrity constraints.

Exercises

1. Write (and if possible execute) the statements required to add to the movies database information about *The Sea Hawk*, a 1940 American movie directed by Michael Curtiz (1886-1962), starring Errol Flynn (1909-1959), Brenda Marshall (1915-1992), and Claude Rains (1889-1967). Try to do it in as few statements as possible.
2. Make everybody in the people table three years younger ... and cancel the change!
3. Which sequence of statements would you apply, to remove from the database anything that refers to France?
4. Many sources of reference data are available on the web - including from Intelligence agencies. The NGA provides geographical information on several countries, in the format specified on this page:

   http://earth-info.nga.mil/gns/html/gis_countryfiles.html

   Create a suitable table, and then pick one country on this page:

   http://earth-info.nga.mil/gns/html/namefiles.htm

   download the data and load it into your database.

Functions, Procedures and Triggers

8

"

Well," said Owl, "the customary procedure in such cases is as follows. "What does Crustimoney Proseedcake mean?" said Pooh. "For I am a Bear of Very Little Brain, and long words Bother me."

- Alan Alexander Milne (1882-1956)

This chapter covers

- What are the procedural extensions to SQL
- Defining your own functions in SQL
- Combining several SQL operations in a single procedure
- Defining automatic operations when data is changed

I am going to touch in this chapter, on the topic of procedural extensions to the SQL language. Those extensions are programming languages built on top of SQL and run by the SQL engine. They allow us to define our own functions, usable in SQL statements like built-in functions; they also allow us to create procedures that are stored in the database and group for execution several SQL statements, chained by a logic which can be sophisticated; and finally, they allow us to create *triggers*. Triggers associate with an **insert**, **update**, or **delete** statement, a procedure that must be automatically run before, while or after the database is affected by the statement but in any case within the scope of the operation.

I don't intend here to cover exhaustively the topic of programming stored procedures, far from it. Many a thick book has been written on Oracle's PL/SQL alone, and I'll try to sketch a general introduction to procedural extensions to SQL. Rather than detailing the various features, I'll try to give you guidelines about when and why you should use functions, procedures and triggers. I'll start with a bit of historical background so that you understand how these extensions were born and integrated into SQL, which I think is important to understand how we got to where we are. I'll follow with examples of a simple function and a (relatively) simple procedure. For those of you who have an interest in traditional procedural programming, I'll give slightly more sophisticated examples in a section than can be skipped by the others. I'll conclude the chapter with triggers.

Although stored procedures are usually associated with "programming" in people's minds, most examples in this chapter require hardly more programming expertise than what you have acquired so far in this book. It's important that you understand the principles and don't get lost in the details (there are unfortunately many details in this chapter, as products differ markedly in their implementation of comparable features). I give examples with only one DBMS product each time because I didn't want to overburden the chapter. You'll find the same examples with the other products in Appendix D, where the code is commented and annotated.

Procedural Extensions to SQL

Procedural extensions to SQL are, I believe, very often misunderstood and as a direct consequence, badly used. Some of the worst database code I have seen was in stored procedures and what I find worrying is that in most cases that bad code had been written by people who honestly believed that they were following "good practices" and performing a jolly decent job instead of being wrecked by guilt.

Stored procedures are excellent for many tasks but they must be used in conformance with the general philosophy of SQL and this is really an area where you meet the Good, the Bad and the Ugly.

A Bit of Historical Background

SQL wasn't, any more than Rome, built in one day and it took many years to arrive at SQL as described in this book. To give you a time-line I can probably take no better example than Oracle. Oracle was the first commercially available SQL DBMS, the first to implement many features and, after having started life as a clone of IBM research projects, was the one which began to some extent to set the tone for other products.

The initial implementation of SQL was in all "historical" pioneering products, a very pale shadow of Codd's ideas.

NOTE The first main products that called themselves "relational" were System R (never a commercial product), Oracle, Ingres, SQL/DS (IBM's first commercial product) and Informix.

Some, and saying most would hardly be exaggerating, key features had been omitted. It took 15 years (and seven versions) for Oracle to implement referential integrity. Queries nested in a **from** clause (which I have used again and again in this book and were implicitly present in Codd's equations), first showed up in Oracle in the mid

1990s, a couple of years after referential integrity and more than a quarter of a century after Codd's original paper.

> **NOTE** Prior to the nested queries in the **from** clause that Oracle call "inline views" you had to create permanent views, which you'll see in Chapter 10.

Recursive queries took 23 years to appear in Oracle (although DB2 and SQL Server had implemented them several years earlier and, as reported in Chapter 5, Oracle had its own mechanism for managing tree structures almost from the beginning).

The fact that a feature isn't implemented in the core of the DBMS engine doesn't make it less necessary: controlling data consistency has to be done, even when you cannot define foreign keys. What the DBMS engine couldn't check was checked in the programs, for instance, verifying before inserting a new film, that the country code could indeed be found in table *countries*.

Many of the early interactive database access programs developed with Oracle were built with a tool called IAD, an early "application development framework", which made it very easy to develop forms for querying and updating tables; coding in minutes what could have required hours or days with other development environments.

> **NOTE** IAD stands for Interactive Application Development and the product, after much improvement, was later renamed SQL*Forms.

As IAD was gaining acceptance, the need for doing more than simply designing screens, sending statements and getting back data or return codes became more pressing. Oracle implemented in their development tool, procedural logic: condition testing, loops and error management, the bread and butter of programming, which allowed consistency checking and building robust applications. For performance, sending a whole procedure to the server for execution was far better than a talkative dialogue over the network between application and database, with one sending statements and the other returning data - especially in iterative processes. Adding to the DBMS, the possibility of running a number of statements sent as a block, of taking this or that action depending on the outcome of each statement and iterating on operations was relatively easy to implement, when compared with adding referential integrity to the DBMS engine. While core Oracle developers were addressing the challenge of implementing key new features at the heart of the DBMS, a procedural extension was taking on a life of its own to solve immediate issues, and after a period as a kind of plug-in feature, ended up being implemented in the DBMS engine at the same time as referential integrity. By then, you could write a complicated procedure, store it into the database and run it by just providing to the DBMS, the name of the procedure and the parameters it expected. Besides, in the late 1980s, external pressure was applied to Oracle by an aggressive newcomer in the market, Sybase, which was particularly strong on stored procedures with a special, extended version of SQL called Transact-SQL (also known as T-SQL) - the code base of Sybase was soon acquired by Microsoft who grew it into SQL Server.

People started using procedures in their database applications intensively, and were also using them to code critical features then missing from SQL, or to fix blatant performance issues.

Unfortunately Pandora's box had been opened. Procedural extensions allow one to do a lot of things that may be commendable in another context but are alien to the set approach that is so central to relational processing. Alongside genuinely useful and smart procedures, up popped a lot of questionable code. While the procedural crowd was re-programming joins and aggregate functions with loops, their object-oriented counterpart, having been told "databases are easy - tables are just like classes and you store each object as a row", were busy creating "methods" that were returning a single column value when provided with the primary key value (I have seen all of this in production in very large corporations). A lot of time and energy has been devoted to write stored programs that are useless in the SQL world, and worse than useless - damaging.

SQL First

This preamble is of course not meant to say that stored procedures are bad, quite the opposite; there are many cases when you should use them, and I'll try to give you some examples but you shouldn't use them to do what you can do in plain SQL. As a general rule, stored procedures and functions are better kept focused and simple. Tom Kyte, who is Senior Technology Architect at Oracle, says that his mantra is:

- You should do it in a single SQL statement if at all possible.
- If you cannot do it in a single SQL statement, then do it in PL/SQL (as little PL/SQL as possible!)

While I heartily agree with Tom's general message (and not only for Oracle), I don't quite agree with the wording *if you cannot do it in a single statement*, because "*you*" represents a rather mixed crowd. *I cannot do it in a single SQL statement* doesn't exactly have the same meaning for Tom Kyte as it does for a fresh college graduate. I'd rather say that if you cannot do it in a single SQL statement, you should first ask someone more experienced than yourself, ask on mailing lists and forums where people seem to know what they are talking about, and only resort to procedures when you have done your homework. You'll probably learn more than one interesting fact that you didn't know in the process, even if a procedure or function is, all things considered, the best solution.

Perhaps you are wondering why it's better to write one big SQL statement than a procedure that contains several simpler statements, combined by traditional programming logic. One simple analogy will help you to understand. A database server is like a shop assistant that has to go to the back of the store each time to fetch what the program wants to see. The analogy holds even if you are running a stored procedure inside the SQL engine - it's just that the back of the store is on the same floor and doesn't necessitate climbing a flight of stairs. Imagine you are buying shoes and can't decide between different models. If you ask to see all the models that interest you at the same time, it will involve far less work for the shop assistant and it will also be quicker for you (besides, the shop assistant knows how everything is stored in the back, which you don't, and won't have to climb up the same step-ladder three times). If you ask for one model, try it, then ask for another one, you'll spend much more time waiting, the shop assistant will be able to serve far fewer customers - and will drop dead from exhaustion by the end of the day.

Alternatives to Procedural SQL Extensions

I shall only talk in this chapter of the procedural extensions to SQL, which as I said previously are special programming languages built on top of SQL. Most products also allow creation of functions in other, more classical languages, such as C, Java and Visual Basic. A key difference between procedural extensions to SQL and other languages is that extensions to SQL are run by the SQL engine itself, with little or no direct interaction with the operating system. For DBMS products vendors, the difficulty with stored procedures is that they run in the context of the database server. When a program that runs alone is buggy and crashes, it's annoying but damage is limited. When a procedure that runs in the context of a database server is buggy and crashes, the SQL engine must handle all the errors, even the most lethal ones, and keep running. Otherwise, the faulty procedure risks taking down the whole database server and possibly thousands of connected users who never called the buggy procedure. There is a big containment issue that is difficult to solve technically, especially with plug-in functions written in a low level language such as C that belongs to the "great power, great responsibility" category; user-written code must be sand-boxed. DBMS products vendors have enough to do with their own bugs without having to fend off bugs introduced by their customers. In general, procedural SQL extensions deliver a good compromise in terms of performance, ease of programming, integration with SQL and security, which is the reason for their popularity.

SQL Server and .NET

SQL Server goes rather far in the containment direction with the Common Language Runtime (CLR), a component of the .NET framework which allows the use of any .NET language such as C# or Visual Basic for adding functions to SQL while keeping the database server safe.

SQLite allows us to add our own functions but they must be written in a traditional language such as C or PHP; of course there is no containment issue with SQLite as there is no shared database server.

You would be mistaken in believing that procedural extensions to SQL are very simple, quick-and-dirty languages. In fact, they combine features derived from SQL and features that you find in very "serious" languages. Oracle's PL/SQL was inspired by ADA, a language once selected by the American Department of Defense for its robustness, and in turn both PL/SQL and T-SQL served as yardsticks for later implementations of SQL procedural extensions.

The Basics

Stored functions and stored procedures, even if they look similar, are different beasts, with different purposes. While both can be written in the same language, stored in the database in the same way, and are both passed parameters when called, the main difference is that stored functions return a value (or an array of values or even a table), while procedures don't.

> NOTE Procedures can, in some circumstances, modify the parameters they are passed but you don't want to do that very often as it may be confusing in a program.

Most importantly, functions and procedures are used differently, which impacts how they should be written. Stored functions are mostly used like built-in functions, inside queries. Procedures are used to pack together a number of statements that logically belong together.

Syntax varies a lot from product to product once past the basics, which are

- that a function definition starts with **create function** *<funcname>* (names follow the same rules as for tables and columns) followed by a parenthesized list of expected arguments and the specification of the type of data that the function returns,

and

- that all the action takes place between **begin** and **end** keywords (those keywords aren't always necessary when the function is very simple as in the example that follows).

With most products you can define a procedure with

create procedure *<procname>*

Not with PostgreSQL, which only recognizes functions (including, I hasten to say, functions that return nothing and are just procedures by another name.) If the spirit is the same, the letter is very different between Oracle and PostgreSQL on one side, DB2 and MySQL on another side, and SQL Server.

A Simple Oracle Function Example

NOTE The commented code for this example with products other than Oracle is given in Appendix D.

I mentioned in Chapter 5 that for sorting purposes, a surname such as 'von Stroheim' was better stored as 'Stroheim (von)', and I have shown to you in Chapter 7 how to update table *people* to change such surnames.

NOTE The other solution is to remove prefixes such as 'von ', 'de ', 'van ' in the **order by** clause as shown in Chapter 5.

However, I have also told you in Chapter 5 that when you want to return the first name and the surname together, 'Erich Stroheim (von)' is probably not what you want to see.

If you want to display the name properly, you must first check whether the first name is null, replace it with an empty string if this is the case, otherwise append a space to it before concatenating the processed surname. To process the surname, you look for an opening parenthesis; if none is found, there's nothing to do, otherwise you must bring to the front of the name, whatever is between parentheses (without the parentheses), add one space and concatenate what remains. With Oracle (it doesn't look any simpler in another SQL variant) it gives something like this:

```
select case
         when first_name is null then ''
         else first_name || ' '
       end
       || case instr(surname, '(')
            when 0 then surname
            else trim(')' from substr(surname, instr(surname, '(') + 1))
                 || ' '
                 || trim(substr(surname, 1, instr(surname, '(') - 1))
          end full_name
from people
order by full_name
```

When you have written such a complex expression to transform data and when you know that you may have to use it in different queries, you are grateful when you can save it for reuse as a function. You can call the function *full_name()*, let it take two parameters (the first name and the surname) and return a single full name that looks right. Because (as you will see) parameters passed to a function or procedure can be directly used in SQL statements inside the procedure, they must never take the same name as a column. If they did, the SQL engine wouldn't know whether you are referring to the column or to the parameter value. It is common to give parameters "special names" (this is actually enforced by SQL Server, which wants parameter names to start with @). With products other than SQL Server, it's a good habit to use a special prefix such as *p_* (for *parameter*).

> NOTE You might also encounter variables named *@something* in MySQL but they are used to hold values for the duration of your session; they aren't linked to a function like SQL Server *@something* variables.

While the expression to rewrite surnames is complex, the function itself is very simple – it's nothing more than an alias for a complicated combination of built-in functions, without any logic of its own.

In a function, with the exception of SQL Server for which it is optional (but recommended), statements are terminated by a semi-colon, a symbol which in most interactive command line database clients indicates that an SQL statement is complete and can be sent to the server. This may be a problem when typing in a function, because if the client program sends at the first semi-colon, what you have typed so far, the SQL engine will receive only a syntactically incomplete chunk of function. The various products adopt different strategies for avoiding sending fragments of functions to the server.

For all products, arguments in a function are defined as a name followed by a data type. With Oracle (and PostgreSQL) you don't need to specify a length for parameters, even when the data type is **varchar2**. You can also specify a data type in a function not explicitly but implicitly, by saying something that means "same type as this column in that table". For instance, with Oracle I can say that the argument that corresponds to the first name (and that I call *p_fname*) is some text:

```
create function full_name(p_fname varchar2, ....
```

or I can say that the argument is of the same type as column *first_name* in table *people* by specifying *<table name>.<column name>* and adding the suffix **%type** (identical syntax with PostgreSQL):

```
create or replace function full_name(p_fname people.first_name%type, ...
```

The first style is better when you are writing a very generic function like this example, which could just as well be applied in another project, to the content of a table called *employees* or *students*. The second style is better for functions that are specific and closely linked to a table; if during the development phase data types are modified (a previously numeric code may be redefined as a string of characters, for instance), the impact on the code already written is reduced.

After the parenthesized list you must specify the data type of the function itself, or more precisely the data type of the value that it returns. Oracle uses

```
return <data type>
```

NOTE All other products I am talking of in this book want an **s** at **returns**:

returns *<data type>*

Then follows a single (mandatory) **as**, optionally the definition of local variables (more about them later) and the body of the function between **begin** and **end**. SQL*Plus (if you are using it) stops interpreting a semi-colon as the termination of a statement as soon as you have started typing **create function** (or **create procedure**). The body of the function is limited in that case, to a simple **return** (without an **s** with all products) followed by the expression. Here is the function with Oracle:

Simple user-defined function, Oracle version

```
create function full_name(p_fname varchar2, p_sname varchar2)   ① Parameters
return varchar2       ② Data type of what the function returns
as
begin
  return case
           when p_fname is null then ''
           else p_fname || ' '
          end ||
          case instr(p_sname, '(')
            when 0 then p_sname
            else trim(')' from substr(p_sname, instr(p_sname, '(') + 1))
                 || ' '
                 || trim(substr(p_sname, 1, instr(p_sname, '(') - 1))
          end;   ← End of the 'case' clause
end;   ← End of the function
```

Parameters ① must be given special names; this isn't important here but in procedures you use them in SQL statements and they must have names that are different from column names. Lengths need not be specified, nor when giving the data type ② of the value returned by the function. Note that here Oracle says "return", all other products say "returns".

If you are using SQL*Plus rather than SQL*Developer for creating the function, you must type a / in the first position of the next line, then hit the return key to send it to the database. Adding a semi-colon would merely be understood as an empty, do-nothing, statement.

Beware that if you mistype something in an Oracle stored procedure, you will get a warning but you need to issue

```
show errors
```

to make Oracle tell you the details.

Although it isn't that difficult to understand how to write a function in one dialect once you know how to do it in another dialect, there are a significant number of syntactical variations between products as you can see in Appendix D.

Once the function has been created, calling it is the same in all products but one:

```
select full_name(first_name, surname) as full_name
from people
order by full_name
```

The exception is SQL Server that requires the function name to be prefixed by the name of the owner of the function and a dot. If you haven't specified anything special when creating the function, this owner will be *dbo* and to call the function you'll write

```
select dbo.full_name(first_name, surname) as full_name
from people
order by full_name
```

NOTE **dbo** stands for **D**ata**B**ase **O**wner and is called the default schema (see Appendix A for a brief introduction to the structure of a database).

What You Shouldn't Do in Functions

You can do much more in a function than simply returning a complex expression as in the previous example. All procedural extensions to SQL allow us to test conditions, iterate with loops, handle errors, use variables and even arrays in functions, and retrieve data from tables into variables with the **select ... into ...** construct that we'll see in action next, and with *cursors*, which allow fetching the result of a query row by row (I'll talk about cursors later in this chapter).

You should be most cautious about the cultural mismatch between the row-by-row world of procedures (or object-by-object world of object-oriented programming) and the relational world where you think in data sets (more precisely, data sets with no duplicates). They don't mix any better than water and oil and, although you meet this type of function very often - they are called *look-up functions* -, you should not write functions that return a single value retrieved from the database. Calling such a function in an SQL statement instead of using a join makes it extremely difficult for the DBMS to optimize its operations and fetch data efficiently. You should always use joins instead.

A Simple SQL Server Procedure Example

Procedures are perfect for packing together, all the various statements that are needed to perform a unitary business operation. Besides (and this is a topic I'll develop in a later chapter) you can give users the right to modify tables exclusively through procedures, without having the right to run an **insert**, **update**, or **delete** statement directly against the tables involved, which ensures that they have to use a procedure to execute some critical operations. The procedures and functions you write can be called from other procedures.

The process of adding a film to the database is complicated if you want to do it well: you won't just simply add one row to table *movies*, it's likely that at the same time you'll want to add director and main actors. That will mean, in practice, looking up table *people* to find the identifiers of these people, then inserting rows into table *credits* to record their involvement in the film, as well as whether they were playing, directing, or both.

Let's create a limited procedure (this is a "no programming knowledge required" version) that I'll call *movie_registration()* and to which I'll pass the following parameters:

- A title,
- A country name,
- A release year,
- A (single) director name, passing separately first name and surname,
- A first actor name, passing first name and surname as for the director,
- A second actor name, specified in the same way as the other two people.

Having a very large number of parameters isn't very good programming (it's easy to get confused and miss a parameter). I could pass names as *surname,firstname* instead of passing separately first name and surname for each person. I could even pass a list of directors or of actors by using special characters as separators between the names of different people. I am just showing you a moderately complex example and in that case the multiple parameters make the code easier.

As there are major differences in the way stored procedures are written, I'll first explain the general logic before giving the code, for SQL Server in this chapter, and for other products in Appendix D.

Registering a Film: the Logic

The first operation we'll do is insert a row in table *movies*; the only required information that isn't passed as a parameter, is the country code (we'll give a more user-friendly name instead) but we can insert the row as an **insert ... select ...** that retrieves the country code from table *countries* by using the country name that is supplied.

We can expect three possible outcomes:

- We successfully insert one row
- The movie has already been inserted before, we violate the unique constraint on (*title, year_released, country*) and the error makes the procedure fail.

- The country name that has been provided couldn't be found in the *countries* table and no rows were inserted.

The case we must particularly take care of is the third one. Remember that an **insert** operation is the relational equivalent of an addition – we are changing the contents of a table by adding to it a data set, containing an indeterminate number of rows. If we insert into the *movies* table the result of a **select** that returns no rows, we are adding an empty data set. Adding an empty data set, while of dubious usefulness, is no more an error than adding zero to a number. In that case, the successful relational operation is a failure with regards to our expectations.

Fortunately, all products provide facilities for:

1. Finding out how many rows were affected by the latest **insert**, **update** or **delete** statement.
2. Generating an error and interrupting the procedure if no rows were inserted.

If the operation was successful and a row was inserted, a new identifier for the movie was generated. If we aren't using an explicit sequence but an automatically incremented integer column for *movieid*, it's better to store its value in a safe place, something known as a *variable* (if you have no prior experience of programming, consider it as a named box to hold values with a specific data type.)

Saving Generated Identifiers to Variables

You should always retrieve and save the latest identifier immediately after it has been generated if you need to refer to it in your procedure. It will not be the case in the example but most often several identifiers are generated in the course of a procedure and merely referring to the last generated one is a recipe for failure.

Like parameters, variables can be used in SQL statements in place of values - expressions and comparisons use the value the variable holds and, like parameters, variables can't have the same name as a column because that would make statements ambiguous for the SQL engine. SQL Server demands that variables, like parameters, have a name that starts with @. With other products, developers frequently prefix variable names with a letter and an underscore to indicate the type, which ensures that variable names follow a pattern of their own. All that matters is that there is no ambiguity.

For a variable to be used in a program, you must first bring it into existence by defining what the data type of the values that you will store in it will be; in the jargon, it must be *declared*. Variable declaration is performed at the beginning of the procedure. Storing a value in a variable is an operation known as *assignment* and you can store into a variable, a constant value, the value returned by a function call, or a value retrieved from the database.

Let's return to the insertion of a film. Once you have inserted a new row into table *movies* and you know the internal identifier of the new movie, you can record into *credits* the involvement of the different people with the film, retrieving the identifier of each person in the very same way as the country code was retrieved. The only difference is that, whereas it was obvious that not finding the country in table *countries* was an error condition making the whole registration impossible, you could take a more lenient view of not finding in the *people* table one of the persons. Some products allow the issuing of warnings besides generating errors. My feeling, but the opposite opinion could be upheld as validly, is that, as the procedure is designed, not finding a person is an unexpected case and should be handled as an error more than as a mishap. Under these assumptions, if I fail to find (for instance) the director after having successfully inserted a row in table *movies*, I should roll back my change and not keep the new row in *movies*.

Not all products allow transaction statements (beginning a transaction and **commit** or **rollback**) in a stored procedure. With PostgreSQL, if a function doesn't successfully complete, the successful changes it has performed are automatically undone. With the other products, you should consider whether the procedure will be called from within a transaction, or whether you want to turn the procedure into a single transaction, complete with **commit** if it succeeds or **rollback** if something goes wrong. It's a program design choice, the question is whether there may be cases when the procedure is called in the context of a larger all-or-nothing-passes transaction, or if it can always be considered as an atomic business operation, in which case it could include (if allowed) transaction statements. If I were to call the procedure several thousand times when reading a file for instance, I would remove references to transactions because **commit** statements slow down operations, and I would manage transactions outside the procedure.

NOTE **commit** statements require writing to a file to ensure that the change will not be lost even if the database server crashes, an operation comparatively much slower than changes in memory, where most database operations happen.

Coding Cleverly

What we have to do for the director and for the two (at most) actors is pretty much the same processing, the only differences are the value inserted in column *credited_as* and the parameter that is handled. Most people who lack deep familiarity with SQL would probably repeat the same pattern four times (the pattern is the same when we insert a row in table *movies*):

1. Retrieve either the country code or the people identifier
2. If not found, quit
3. Insert data in either *movies* or *credits*

At this point you should remember Tom Kyte's recommendation of doing as much as possible in one SQL statement – or what I would express as doing as much as possible with a minimal number of database accesses. The procedure needs to query two tables (*countries* to retrieve the country code and *people* to retrieve the identifiers of the director and of the actors) and to insert rows into two tables (*movies* and *credits*). The magic of **insert ... select** means that we can retrieve from one table and insert into another one, in a single operation. To insert into table *credits* the row that corresponds to the director, I can run an **insert into credits select ... from people ....**, and I can do the same for each one of the two actors.

But do we need to run three separate **insert** statements into table *credits*? The answer is no. We can try to insert all people at once; the only problem is that we must check that the number of rows inserted (the number of people we have found) actually matches the number of rows we want to insert. We must know beforehand how many parameters are not null out of three possible, director, first actor and second actor. SQL can do the counting for us: we need to build a virtual three row table, with the director surname on one row and the surnames of the two actors on the other rows (I am using surnames, indicated by the *_sn* suffix in parameter names because they are mandatory in table *people* – the *@* prefix is specific to SQL Server, it would be something like a *p_* prefix with other products):

```
select @director_sn as surname   ← 'from' needed for Oracle and DB2
union all
select @actor1_sn as surname    ← 'from' needed for Oracle and DB2
union all
select @actor2_sn as surname    ← 'from' needed for Oracle and DB2
```

Unlike other products, Oracle and DB2 always want a **select** to be **from** a table; you should use the dummy tables provided by these products and add **from dual** with Oracle and **from sysibm.sysdummy1** with DB2 to each **select** statement in the **union**.

If we count the rows in this virtual table, as aggregate functions ignore nulls, we'll count how many not null parameters were passed to the procedure. If we store into a variable the result of the following query

```
select count(surname)
from (select @director_sn as surname ← from dual/sysibm.sysdummy1 with Oracle/DB2
      union all
      select @actor1_sn as surname   ← from dual/sysibm.sysdummy1 with Oracle/DB2
      union all
      select @actor2_sn as surname   ← from dual/sysibm.sysdummy1 with Oracle/DB2
     ) provided
```

we'll get what we want.

> **NOTE** SQL Server issues warnings when an aggregate function skips null. You can of course add `where surname is not null` to the preceding query to silence it, even if it isn't technically required. You can also add the condition with other DBMS products; it may help you to understand the purpose of the query.

Now we have several possibilities for retrieving from zero to three identifiers from table *people*. We can use **or** conditions in the **where** clause, we can use the **union** of three **select** statements – or we can turn the parameters into a kind of virtual table that will be joined to table *people*. You have this virtual table in the preceding query to count how many people we want to insert; all we need to do is add a *credited_as* column:

```
select coalesce(@director_fn, '*') as first_name,
       @director_sn as surname,
       'D' as credited_as          ← from ... with Oracle/DB2
union all
select coalesce(@actor1_fn, '*') as first_name,
       @actor1_sn as surname,
       'A' as credited_as          ← from ... with Oracle/DB2
union all
select coalesce(@actor2_fn, '*') as first_name,
       @actor2_sn as surname,
       'A' as credited_as          ← from ... with Oracle/DB2
```

> **NOTE** I have also replaced null first names with an asterisk. This will ease comparisons with what is stored in *people* if I am looking for someone with no first name – a null is never equal to a null but when you replace nulls with asterisks, an asterisk is equal to an asterisk.

Let's now see how this procedure can be written with SQL Server (you'll find details for other products in Appendix D). You may need to add Errol Flynn (1909-1959) to your *people* table for testing the procedure with the example I give.

In a SQL Server procedure, unlike other products, parameters and variables all have a name that starts with @. Variable declaration takes place with SQL Server (and MySQL and DB2) inside the main **begin ... end** block and each declaration is preceded by the **declare** keyword (with Oracle and PostgreSQL, variables are declared before the main **begin** ... **end** block, in a special section). I'm going to use two variables, one to store the value of *movieid* when I have inserted a new row in table *movies*, which I retrieve from the special system variable **@@identity** using the syntax

```
set @movieid = @@identity;
```

and one to count how many names are provided, using the syntax

```
set @people = (select count(name)
               from (select @director as name
```

```
              union all
              select @actor1 as name
              union all
              select @actor2 as name) specified_people
        where name is not null);
```

NOTE Other products use **select** ... **into** *<variable name>* **from** ... to assign the result of a query to a variable.

Immediately after the variable declarations I start a transaction – which I'll have to terminate in the procedure, by a **commit** if everything goes according to plans, or by a **rollback** if anything fails.

Another special system variable, **@@rowcount**, tells us how many rows were affected by the latest database change. After each **insert** statement, this value is checked with an **if** test and, if the condition is satisfied, the statements between the **begin** and **end** that follow are executed (SQL Server doesn't use **if** ... **then** ... **end if** as other products do). If no rows were inserted, I end the transaction with a **rollback** to undo whatever may have succeeded between the start of the procedure and the failure;. Then I call **raiserror()** that takes three parameters; a message preceded by an *N* that simply says that it may contain characters not necessarily from the Latin alphabet; a first value that indicates the severity (the higher the number, the more severe, up to 18); and a second value that is just here to help identify the database where the problem occurred, for people who monitor many databases. Once the error is generated, I explicitly quit the procedure with **return**.

Simple movie registration, SQL Server version

```
create procedure movie_registration
          (@title        varchar(200),   ← Parameter names start with @
           @country_name varchar(50),
           @year         int,
           @director_fn  varchar(30),
           @director_sn  varchar(30),
           @actor1_fn    varchar(30),
           @actor1_sn    varchar(30),
           @actor2_fn    varchar(30),
           @actor2_sn    varchar(30))
as
begin
  declare @movieid   int;   ← Variable names start with @ too
  declare @people    int;
  --
  begin transaction;          ← Explicit transaction start
  insert into movies(title, country, year_released)
  select @title, country_code, @year
  from countries
  where country_name = @country_name;
  if @@rowcount = 0           ← Get the number of inserted rows
```

```
begin
  raiserror(N'Country not found in reference table', 15, 1);
  rollback;
  return;      ← raiserror doesn't return
end;
set @movieid = @@identity;    ← Get the movie identifier
set @people = (select count(surname)        ← No select into with T-SQL
               from (select @director_sn as surname
                     union all
                     select @actor1_sn as surname
                     union all
                     select @actor2_sn as surname) specified_people
               where surname is not null);    ← To avoid a warning
insert into credits(movieid, peopleid, credited_as)   ← Insert credits
select @movieid, people.peopleid, provided.credited_as
from (select coalesce(@director_fn, '*') as first_name,
             @director_sn as surname,
             'D' as credited_as
      union all
      select coalesce(@actor1_fn, '*') as first_name,
             @actor1_sn as surname,
             'A' as credited_as
      union all
      select coalesce(@actor2_fn, '*') as first_name,
             @actor2_sn as surname,
             'A' as credited_as) provided
     inner join people
       on people.surname = provided.surname
      and coalesce(people.first_name, '*') = provided.first_name;
if @@rowcount <> @people    ← Check that everything is OK
  begin
    raiserror(N'Some people couldn''t be found', 15, 1);
    rollback;
    return;
  end;
commit;
end;
```

When the procedure is created, you can call it as follows:

```
execute movie_registration 'The Adventures of Robin Hood',
                           'United States', 1938,
                           'Michael', 'Curtiz',
                           'Errol', 'Flynn',
                            null, null
go
```

Deeper into Programming

In this section I am going to give you a little more than a glimpse of what can be achieved with user-defined functions and procedures (and perhaps more importantly what can but shouldn't be done). If you have no prior experience of programming or if the result of your struggle against **if ... then ... else ....** loops and error handling is still uncertain, I suggest you skip this section for the time being and jump directly to triggers. What I am talking about here certainly belongs to the database eco-system but is tangential to SQL.

If you know a programming language, you'll probably be interested by many of the features implemented by the various procedural extensions to SQL. You'll find all the details online in the reference documentation of the various products but I'm going to give you a brief overview before discussing what to use and what not to use, and giving a couple of examples.

Flow Control

Any procedural extensions to SQL implement the control flow statements that you find in all programming languages: you have seen in the preceding examples **if** blocks which are just a subset of the general case of **if ... then ... else if ... else** blocks, and you can loop. As usual, syntax varies:

ORACLE AND POSTGRESQL

Conditions are tested with either **if** *condition* **then ... elseif** *condition* **then else ... end if**, or a **case ... end case** not exactly similar to what you would use inside an SQL statement, since it is terminated by **end case** and not by **end** and, while the conditions are expressed in the same way, what follows **then** or **else** is a statement, not a value or an expression. Iterative processing is performed inside a **loop ... end loop** block, out of which you break with an **if** followed by a condition and an **exit** command inside the loop, or, alternatively, by **exit when** *condition*. You have also two other ways to iterate, one is

```
while condition loop
...
end loop;
```

and the other is

```
for variable in lower_bound .. upper_bound loop
...
end loop;
```

variable is an integer variable that is automatically declared by the **for** statement; *lower_bound* and *upper_bound* are two integer constants, variables or expressions, separated by two dots, and *variable* takes, successively, the values *lower_bound*, *lower_bound* + 1, *lower_bound* + 2 ... up to and including *upper_bound* (it is possible to increase each step value by more than one).

You can also say `for` *variable* `in reverse` *upper_bound* `..` *lower_bound* if you want *variable* to take decreasing values.

MYSQL AND DB2

Conditions are tested with either **if** *condition* **then ... elseif** *condition* **then else ... end if**, or a **case ... end case** not exactly similar to what you would use inside an SQL statement, since it is terminated by **end case** and not by **end** and, while the conditions are expressed in the same way, what follows **then** or **else** is a statement, not a value or an expression.

Iterative processing is performed by a block

label: **loop**

...

end loop *label*;

out of which you break with an **if** followed by a condition and a **leave** *label* command inside the loop; rather than a crude **loop ... end loop** block, you can use either

```
while condition do
  ...
end while;
```

or

```
repeat
  ...
until condition end repeat;
```

depending on whether you wish to test a condition before or after the loop body. In all cases, there is no semi-colon after what indicates the beginning of the block but there is one after what indicates its end (just like with **begin ... end**).

SQL SERVER

SQL Server knows of no **else if** - you need to nest series of

```
if condition
  begin
    ...
  end;
else
  begin
    ...
  end;
```

There is a single construct for loops:

```
while condition
begin
  ...
end;
```

from which you can optionally exit with a **break** statement.

WHEN TO USE LOOPS

In user-defined SQL functions, the most common use of loops is for processing character strings. I mentioned in Chapter 6 that to search movies by title we shouldn't proceed through strict equality between user input and stored title but instead, by splitting both user input and stored titles into normalized words and by looking for the best match between sets of words. This kind of processing can be performed in any programming language - and in particular in procedural extensions to SQL. As a first step, I'm going to write a MySQL function that "cleans up" a title by replacing accented characters with their unaccented equivalent and replaces everything that isn't a letter or a digit with a space.

There are two ways to replace accented letters, dumb replacement of *é* by *e* or *ü* by *u*, and more intelligent, culture-sensitive replacement matching local habits, for instance replacing *ü* by *ue*, or *å* by *aa*. Actually, even though dumb replacement would probably raise eyebrows in German-speaking countries (among others), if our aim is to replace a title with a series of normalized tags, the only thing that matters is applying the same transformation to user input during a search, as to what is stored inside the database. If in a title such as *Der Himmel über Berlin* we transform *über* into *uber* (instead of the correct *ueber*), as long as a user doesn't enter the correct unaccented form we won't have any problem at all; and if a German using an American keyboard types *ueber*, we can hope to match on *Himmel* and *Berlin* and retrieve the film anyway. Trying to be too clever is often counter-productive with everything that is language-dependent because several languages may use the same letters and transcribe them differently when accents aren't available: what will be correct in one language may not be correct in another.

Oracle, DB2 and PostgreSQL implement a useful function called **translate()** that takes three arguments, firstly some text to process, secondly a string of characters to replace and thirdly, a string of replacement characters that has at most the same length as the string of characters to replace. The first character in the second parameter is replaced by the first character in the third parameter, and so on. Rather than a long series of nested calls to **replace()**, loops can easily provide the same functionality with SQL Server or MySQL.

MySQL Title Clean-up Function

```
delimiter $$      ① Change the delimiter
create function cleanup(p_title varchar(200))  ← Specify the varchar length
returns varchar(200)      ← here too
begin
  declare v_result     varchar(200);
  declare v_accents    varchar(50);
  declare v_noaccents  varchar(50);
  declare n_len        int;
  declare n            int;
  declare n_pos        int;
  declare c            char(1);
  --
  set v_result = trim(lower(p_title));   ② Conversion to lower case
```

```
  set v_accents   = 'àâçéèêôöùûü';        ③ Letters to replace
  set v_noaccents = 'aaceeeoouuu';        ← Replacement
  set n_len = length(v_result);
  set n = 1;
  while (n <= n_len) do          ← Main loop
    set c = substr(v_result, n, 1);  ④ Process each character in turn
    if (c not between 'a' and 'z'
        and c not between '0' and '9')
    then
      if ascii(c) < 128   ⑤ Check the internal code
      then     ← Punctuation sign
        set v_result = replace(v_result, c, ' ');
      else
        set n_pos = position(c in v_accents);  ⑥ Look for known accented letters
        if (n_pos > 0)
        then
          set v_result = replace(v_result, c,
                                 substr(v_noaccents, n_pos, 1));
        else
          set v_result = replace(v_result, c, '');  ⑦ Suppress what is unknown
          set n_len = length(v_result);
        end if;
      end if;
    end if;
    set n = n + 1;
  end while;
  return trim(v_result);
end;
$$    ⑧ Send to the database server
```

I first change the delimiter ① (what tells the command line client 'send to the server for execution) from the default semi-colon to something I am sure not to have to type in the body of my function. Accents are (on the keyboards I know) easier to type in lower case than in upper case, which is why, to work on accents, I first convert the title to lower case ②. I have limited my choice of characters to replace ③ to what is easy to type on a French keyboard (guess what I'm using) but the list can of course be expanded at will - with a replacement list that matches. I loop on all characters in the title, picking one character ④ each time. If this character is neither a letter between a and z nor a digit, I check if the internal code of the character is less than 128 ⑤, using a function called **ascii()** that returns the internal code of a character. Accented characters always have a code greater than 128; if the character is neither a letter nor a digit and has a code that is less than 128, then it is a punctuation sign that I replace with a space. Otherwise if I find the character in my list of accented letters ⑥ I replace it with its unaccented equivalent; if I don't find it I suppress the character ⑦. I suppress it, rather than replace it with a space, to keep words as one chunk even if they contain unexpected characters. When the function is finished I enter what I have defined as delimiter ⑧ to send it to the server (I can change the delimiter back to a semi-colon afterwards).

By applying this function to all titles with country *fr*, accents will magically disappear - and punctuation will vanish whichever the country.

Catching Errors

If you already know programming, you are probably accustomed to handling errors, for instance trying to avoid an inelegant crash in a program when it tries to open, for reading, a file that doesn't exist. Failures are usually detected by testing the return value of a function but there is, in many modern languages, an alternative mechanism, *exceptions*. Errors fire an exception that can be caught and processed. When you issue an SQL statement in a procedure, the mechanism for handling errors is trapping them through exceptions. As in a well-defined database, data controls are extremely strict and as much of the boring work of checking input, consistency, existence, is delegated to the database, you may discover that procedural SQL is more prone to generate runtime errors than other languages that you know. Even if a program that accesses a database checks input to some extent (most do), it's usually the database that will tell you that Feb 29th is not valid for 1927 because it wasn't a leap year, or that the data that you are trying to insert violates referential integrity. When you write to a file that you can access, you can happily write inconsistent or invalid data to your file but few things can go wrong in the program (a corrupt disk or a full file system, possibly). The occurrence of a write failure is rare and a graceful handling of the error is a nice-to-have rather than a must-have feature. By contrast, many database errors must be anticipated as being possible or even likely and cannot (or should not) result in a cryptic message in a pop-up box, or the display in the console of an error stack that looks like Armageddon, only more serious.

Errors such as not finding data that satisfies a **select** statement or violating a unique constraint are so common that their handling is a staple feature of most stored procedures; less common errors can also be handled, as well as your own error conditions - you can generate errors as you have seen in the *movie_registration* procedure example. All errors, whether they are "native" or user-defined, are handled in the same way.

There are two approaches to exception handling. With MySQL and DB2, you define in a procedure (or function) an error handler which is a sub function that is automatically called if the corresponding error happens in the function. With PostgreSQL, Oracle and SQL Server, you can define a single error handler that is global to the function, or you can isolate fragments of code as **begin** ... **end** blocks, each one with its own exception handler; those blocks can be nested.

In all cases, when an error occurs and isn't trapped in the block or procedure, it interrupts processing and ripples out either to an external block that would catch it, or to the caller.

I am going to illustrate exception handling with a minor improvement to procedure *movie_registration()*, to associate more than one director or more than two actors with a film, I'll call the procedure several times for the same film but with different people names. At the second (and subsequent) call, I'll fail to insert the movie because it is already registered and would violate the unique constraint on the title, country and year of release. What I need to do is ignore this error, retrieve the *movieid* value and go on with the registration of people.

NOTE I adopt this approach because I consider that adding more people to a movie by repeated calls to *movie_registration()* will be an exceptional case affecting only a small percentage of the registered movies. Otherwise, it would be more efficient to try to retrieve the identifier of the movie, and when none is found insert the film before proceeding.

With SQL Server (you'll find the code for other DBMS products in Appendix D), sections where errors can occur are enclosed by a **begin try ... end try** block immediately followed by a **begin catch ... end catch** block; **end try** mustn't be followed by a semi-colon. If no error occurs in the first block, the second one is skipped. However, behavior depends on the severity level of the error (a number between 0 and 18 - there are higher values but they are reserved for really serious system errors). To be caught, an error must be sufficiently serious (a level higher than 10; lower numbers are understood as information or warnings) but not critical enough to terminate the session and disconnect the user. Inside the **begin catch ... end catch** block, some functions allow us to retrieve information about the error (**error_number()**, **error_message()**, **error_severity()**, **error_procedure()**, **error_line()** ... the name of which is self-explanatory) and handle it as it should be handled. If the error is completely unexpected, it should be propagated. With versions of SQL Server older than SQL Server 2012 you propagate the error by calling **raiserror()** that was described earlier in this chapter; with later versions a simple **throw** propagates the error without any need to retrieve message, severity and state. Be careful that **raiserror()** doesn't like to be passed functions such as **error_message()**, hence variables to retrieve the result of these functions before calling **raiserror()**.

Flow Change

In a **begin try** ... **end try** block the statement that follows a **raiserror()** isn't executed - flow is immediately diverted to the **begin catch ... end catch** block. Which is why I have removed the **rollback** and **return** if I discover that I have inserted no rows because the country is unknown. We return from the procedure in the **begin catch ... end catch** block.

```
begin try     ① Beginning of the "protected" section
  insert into movies(title, country, year_released)
  select @title, country_code, @year
  from countries
  where country_name = @country_name;
```

```
  if @@rowcount = 0
  begin
    raiserror(N'Country not found in reference table', 15, 1);  ② Regular error
  end;
  set @movieid = @@identity;
end try
begin catch     ③ Beginning of the 'catch' block
  if error_number() = 2627    ④ Tolerated error
  begin
    set @movieid = (select m.movieid
                    from movies m
                         inner join countries c
                         on c.country_code = m.country
                    where m.title = @title
                      and m.year_released = @year
                      and c.country_name = @country_name);
  end;
  else  ⑤ Not the expected error
  begin
    declare @errormsg nvarchar(1000) = error_message(); ← Retrieve error information
    declare @errorsev int = error_severity();
    declare @errorstate char(5) = error_state();
    raiserror(@errormsg, @errorsev, @errorstate);       ⑥ Propagate
    rollback;
    return;
  end;
end catch;
```

To ignore a duplicate attempt to insert a movie in SQL Server, I put all the statements between the first **'insert'** and the retrieval of the latest inserted *movieid* value in a **begin try ... end try** block ①. The error I was handling previously ② is no longer followed by **return**: the call to **raiserror()** redirects the flow to the following **catch** block ③ that is skipped when nothing goes wrong. In the adjacent **begin catch ... end catch** block, I test the error number ④: if it's what I expect then I retrieve the *movieid* previously affected to the film and processing will continue with the statement that follows **end catch**. In other cases ⑤, I retrieve the error information and propagate it ⑥ before returning.

Collections and Composite Data types

MySQL only recognizes scalar (simple) variables but the other products accept arrays (where values are indexed) or tables of values, user-defined types that are row-like associations of values of different types, and arrays or tables of user-defined types. We are coming here to topics that are relatively advanced but I'd just like to point out that when you can make a function return an array or a table, this function can be used (sometimes after calling a conversion function) in a **from** clause, as if it were a small table. Let's consider, again, the problem of splitting a movie title into tags that can be separately searched and counted to perform the type of fuzzy search shown in Chapter 6.

Once you have a cleaned-up title, clear of accents and punctuation, it's easy to loop on the string, looking for spaces, using a function such as **substr()** to extract the first word, insert it with the movie identifier into the table that contains the various words, get the trimmed remainder of the processed title and iterate. But each word will require a separate **insert** statement, which will not be a problem for a film such as *Jaws*, but is slightly more painful with *Dr. Strangelove or: How I Learned to Stop Worrying and Love the Bomb*. If you transform a title in a series of words at the same time as you insert a film in table movies, each separate **insert** adds up and makes the whole operation heavier. Every **insert** statement has a kind of fixed cost; the analysis of a repeated statement by the SQL engine may be performed only once (more about this in Chapter 11) but each execution requires some kind of dialogue between the procedure and the core of the database, even if the procedure is executed by the SQL engine. When you can insert several rows at once you add much less overhead. It may not be very noticeable; for a movie database where we can expect insertions to be rare operations after the initial load, it would really be a minor concern but it can make a difference in an e-commerce environment for instance, with many people creating purchase orders corresponding to multiple articles: it will be much more efficient to process one "basket" at a time than each article separately. Same story on a popular video-sharing site if you can insert all the tags that users associate with their videos at one go.

Transforming a title into an array of tags that can be inserted at once in a single **insert ... select** statement illustrates a technique that can sometimes boost performance.

I am going to give you a SQL Server example, assuming the existence of the *cleanup()* function previously shown for MySQL and which is given in Appendix D for SQL Server.

A SQL Server Function to Return Words from a Title as a Table

```
create function get_tags(@title varchar(200))  ← Specify the varchar length
returns @tag_list table(word varchar(50))  ① The return type is special
as
begin
  declare @pos int;

  set @title = dbo.cleanup(@title);  ← Remove accents and punctuation
  set @pos = charindex(' ', @title, 1);
  while @pos > 0
  begin
     insert into @tag_list(word)     ② Not a real heavy-weight insert
     values(upper(rtrim(substring(@title, 1, @pos))));
     set @title = ltrim(substring(@title, @pos, len(@title)));
     set @pos = charindex(' ', @title, 1);
  end;
  insert into @tag_list(word)  ← Don't forget the last piece
```

```
    values(upper(@title));
    return;  ③ Don't return anything, it's implicit
  end;
  go
```

We define not only the return type ① (a table, defined as a regular table – it could have several columns) but also the name of the variable *(@tag_list)* that will hold what we want to return. We search all the spaces in a loop and insert each word (converted to uppercase) in the loop inside the table variable ②. However, while the syntax looks like a regular **insert** statement, in reality it is a "fake" **insert** statement in as much as there is no interaction with the database. It's a light, memory-only, operation that by-passes all the logging, locking and numerous security mechanisms required by a standard **insert** into a table. When we leave the function ③ we mustn't say what to return: actually, we said it at the beginning of the function ①.

This function in action looks like what is shown in Figure 8.1. Using it in an **insert ... select** construct allows the insertion of all the tags at once instead of iterating.

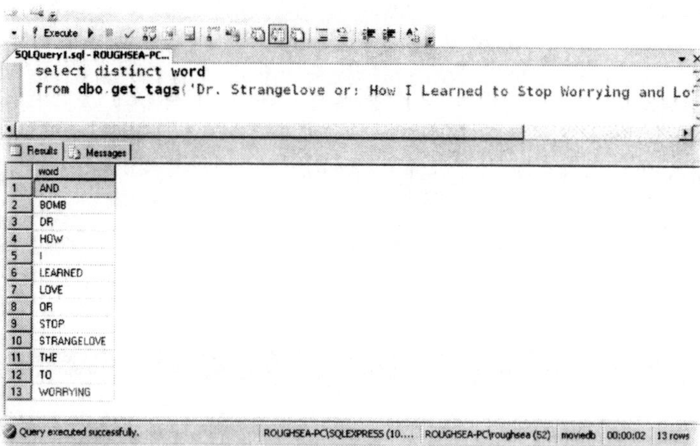

Figure 8.1: A SQL Server function that returns a table and can be used in a from clause.

A table-valued function (this is the official SQL Server name of a function that returns a table) is an elegant way to transform a list into a table; it isn't, though, the only way. Some alternative methods are shown in Appendix D.

Cursors

In the context of procedural extensions to SQL, *cursors* are the equivalent of file-handlers in other languages: a cursor is declared as a variable and, instead of being associated with a file name, is associated with an SQL statement (usually a **select** statement). I have shown you **select ... into ...** and explained that **select ... into ...** can only be used when the query returns a single row (if not, you get an exception that you can of course catch and process). If you want to retrieve an indeterminate number of rows into your procedure's variables, cursors are the solution.

You create a cursor with for instance

```
declare my_cursor cursor for select title, year_released
                             from movies where country = 'us';
```

Cursors names don't start with @ in SQL Server.

> NOTE There is a good reason for not requiring a special name. Special prefixes (such as @) are here mainly to distinguish variables from columns in statements that are embedded in a procedure. You cannot refer to a cursor in another statement.

In the same way as you open a file, you open a cursor, in the same way as you fetch records from a file you fetch rows into local variables, and with cursors as with files, when there is nothing more to fetch a status variable is set, and you close the cursor.

For instance, after having declared the cursor as I have done, as well as suitable variables into which to fetch the values, you can retrieve all the titles and years of release of American movies by doing with SQL Server:

```
open my_cursor;
fetch my_cursor into @title, @year;
while @@fetch_status = 0
begin
   ... do stuff ...
  fetch my_cursor into @title, @year;
end;
close my_cursor;
deallocate my_cursor;
```

It would hardly be different with Oracle:

```
open my_cursor;
loop
  fetch my_cursor into v_title, n_year;
  exit when my_cursor%notfound;
 .. do stuff ...
end loop;
close my_cursor;
```

(no deallocation with Oracle; **close** does it).

> NOTE Oracle also implements shorthand notations, such as **for** loops applied to cursors.

Dos and Don'ts

There are a few simple rules that you should follow if you want to use correctly stored functions and procedures. Like with all rules, you can always find exceptions but by sticking to them you'll write much better code than the average developer.

- **Use functions for implementing data transformations that require a complex usage of built-in functions.**

  Many bugs come from simple errors when using built-in functions (such as a failure to take nulls or other fringe values into account). Functions written by the best developers in a team can save a lot of time for everyone. They may also help people when they switch from one DBMS product to another. Not retrieving in a product, a function that is convenient and that one has grown accustomed to, may be frustrating. Don't hesitate to implement in one DBMS product, good ideas stolen from another one. That's what DBMS vendors do...

- **Don't query the database in a function that you call in an SQL query (unless the function returns a table and is used in the *from* clause.)**

  If you need to retrieve information from the database in a statement, you should use a join, a set operator or a subquery, certainly not a function. If you want to make a complicated SQL expression re-usable by people who aren't too comfortable with SQL, you shouldn't provide them with stored functions that access the database but with *views*, which you will see in Chapter 10.

- **Use stored procedures to implement business work units.**

  Whenever you can easily identify a "business transaction" which modifies the database and takes a well defined input, you have a good candidate for a stored procedure. It's an even better candidate if this business transaction can be executed from different environments (for instance interactively from a web-based application and in nightly batch programs). Having the process in one place -- in the database - will ease maintenance and its execution in the database will make it faster.

- **Be careful with transactions.**

  As pointed out earlier, committing is an operation that involves writing to files and takes a noticeable amount of time when executed often. If you are certain that a procedure will always be called in isolation, you can commit changes in it (if the DBMS allows it). If it can be called repetitively in a program for groups of operations, it is safer to let the caller handle transactions and commit changes globally.

- **Keep away from cursors.**

  This piece of advice will probably come as a shocker, as cursors figure prominently in all books and courses on procedural extensions to SQL but the reality is that you should avoid them. There are places where you should loop on the results that you retrieve from a database: in programs that access the database, when they have to write to files or network messages, to screens, to web pages, and you'll see plenty of examples in Chapter 12. In fact, the concept of cursor first appeared (as early as System-R, the IBM database system prototype that also was the first implementation of SQL) in programs that were embedding SQL statements, long before procedural extensions. Cursors belong to the border zone between the database and the world of languages or other data storage methods that don't know how to handle data sets. Stored procedures, as the name says, belong to the database, which is a place where you work on data sets, not on individual rows, and where you should process data sets globally. You *really* need to loop on a query result inside a stored procedure in very few cases; you need it if your procedure accesses the world outside the database (it's sometimes possible to write to files or to send network messages from inside a stored procedure), you need it if you are building and executing on the fly statements based upon the current structure of the database (yes, you can do this, I'll show you how in Chapter 10). But cursors are unnecessary in the vast majority of regular applications. Most people use them because they haven't been told about **insert ... select** or because they lack the skills to update a table from the data contained in another table. Cursors and loops certainly "work" as far as they produce the expected result but they are slower than plain SQL by an order of magnitude or two - which means factors that can be anywhere between 5 and 100.

Triggers

Stored procedures can be used in a mechanism that you find in all databases, the mechanism of *triggers*. A trigger is a (usually small) program that is attached to a table by a statement

```
create trigger trigger_name ...
```

followed by specifications about which specific change operations fire the trigger (**insert**, **update**, **delete**), the name of the table to which the trigger is attached, and the program to run next, written with the same syntax as stored procedures, and sometimes reduced to the call of a stored procedure that performs all the work. Each time the specified change happens, the program is automatically executed.

NOTE The change operation refers to a type of operation, not to a specific SQL statement. For instance we've seen in Chapter 7 that we can use statements other than **insert** to load data into a table. If they don't by-pass the SQL engine (some commands operate directly at the file level) they would fire a trigger defined on insert operations as well as a regular **insert** statement. A **merge** statement could fire insert and update triggers.

Triggers have no life independently of a table. When a table is dropped, all triggers that were attached to it are automatically dropped as well.
You never commit changes in a trigger, they belong to the same transaction as the statement that fired them. You can however roll back changes in a SQL Server trigger.

The most tricky point with triggers is probably when they are activated; it must be specified with the change operation and it depends on the DBMS.

- Oracle, PostgreSQL and DB2 let you choose whether to fire a trigger before or after the triggering change is applied to the table (for instance `create trigger movies_ins_trg before insert on movies ...`), and whether the code must be run once per statement, or once per row that is changed (with an **insert ... select ...** or an **update** or **delete** that affects many rows, for instance), which is specified by the expression **for each row**.

  When you are running the code of a **for each row** trigger, you can access two dummy rows called *old* and *new* that have the same columns as the table to which the trigger is attached. These dummy rows respectively contain the values held in the current row before and after the change (you access a particular column by referring to, for instance, *new.column_name* - *:new.column_name* with Oracle). It is possible in a **before** trigger, to assign values to *new* before actually inserting them, which is how some people simulate auto-increment columns in Oracle prior to Oracle12c (the reference to *seq_name*.**nextval** is in the trigger instead of being in the **insert** statement - I personally find the latter simpler and better.)

  Additionally, DB2 lets you access (in triggers that are fired for each row as well as triggers that are fired only once per statement) two virtual tables named *old table* and *new table* that contain the modified rows.

  If an error is generated in a **before** trigger, the actual change operation isn't performed.

- SQL Server fires triggers only once after the change was applied to the table, and gives access to two virtual tables called *inserted* and *deleted* that respectively contain all the rows inserted by the change and all the rows deleted by the change (an update operation is considered as the deletion of a row followed by the insertion of a row with the same key but different attribute values). SQL Server cannot prevent a change but a trigger can roll back a change when it discovers that the change violates the rules.

- MySQL and SQLite only allow triggers that are fired for each row, before or after the triggering statement and like Oracle, PostgreSQL and DB2, give access to the before-change and after-change values of the current row in pseudo rows called *old* and *new*.

What Triggers are Useful For

Triggers are mostly used for three different purposes:

- You can use triggers for modifying data on the fly to insert, either a default value, or a value different from what was originally entered. It's probably better to avoid this kind of trigger when creating a new application.

  NOTE As usual, there are cases when what you should normally avoid happens to be the best available solution. Modifying data on the fly may be useful when you want for instance, to force input to uppercase in an existing application and don't have access to the source code of the program that modifies table content, or if users may use any SQL client to insert or update data.

  A case when you might be tempted to use triggers for modifying data on the fly is the case of Scottish surnames, which I touched on briefly in Chapter 5 when I talked about sorting names. By "Scottish surnames" I don't mean here Gordon, Stewart, Campbell, or Scott but all the Scottish (and Irish) surnames that start with Mc. If you remember, I said in Chapter 5 that for sorting purposes, those surnames would better be stored as Mac*Someone* rather than Mc*Someone*. In fact, normalizing names is important, not for sorting - a minor concern - but primarily for data consistency, as no kind of unique constraint will prevent you from storing a *Steve MacQueen* alongside a *Steve McQueen* - with one associated with some movies, the other associated with other movies, and possibly conflicting biographical data. One way to ensure that Mc*Someone* is stored as Mac*Someone* would be a **before insert/before update** trigger that would stealthily replace *Mc* at the beginning of a surname by *Mac*. The problem is that I find disturbing, the idea that someone might successfully execute

  ```
  insert into people(first_name, surname, born, died)
  values('Steve', 'McQueen', 1930, 1980)
  ```

  then get nothing when running

  ```
  select * from people
  where surname = 'McQueen'
  ```

  because a trigger modified input on the fly. I much prefer a **check** constraint that forbids entering a name that starts by *Mc* and demands *Mac* instead. At least you are warned.

- Triggers can also be used for checking data consistency and aborting operations if there is something wrong.

  Historically, before you could define foreign key constraints (people sometimes talk about *declarative referential integrity* - *declarative* means that you state the constraint and have nothing to code), you could use triggers to implement them. An **insert** into the *movies* table would trigger a **select** on the *countries* table to check if we recognize the code, and generate an error as we have seen happen in the procedure examples of this chapter when the code was unknown. It was better to use triggers than to code checking in programs because the control is in the database and always applies independently of the program used to access the tables.

Checking Data Types in SQLite

I have mentioned, more than once, SQLite's rather disdainful attitude to data types; even if you declare a column to be of type **integer**, SQLite will not generate an error if you store 'Hello World' into it (and it will be correctly stored). You can however straighten up SQLite, by using the property that when you add 0 to text in SQLite, you obtain 0 as a result (and no error). SQLite implements a function called **raise()** that can be used in triggers and takes two parameters. The first one specifies the action to take (I'll use *ABORT* to interrupt the statement) and the second is the message to display.

You can for instance create a trigger to check that the year of release of a film is indeed numerical:

```
create trigger movies_year_trg
before insert on movies
begin
  select raise(ABORT, 'Invalid year')
  where new.year_released + 0 <> new.year_released;
end;
```

You'll notice that there is a **where** clause in the **select** but no **from** ... If the **where** condition is satisfied, this **select** returns one row and generates an error. Otherwise the insertion goes through.

You can however achieve exactly the same effect with a named **check** constraint:

```
create table movies (....,
                     year_released int not null
                         constraint year_validity
                         check(year_released + 0 = year_released),
                      ...)
```

which I think is a better way. I might have thought differently if it were possible to pass to the **raise()** function as second parameter `'Invalid year ' || new.year_released` but at the time of writing only a constant message is accepted, not an expression.

Today, you can use triggers to implement complex business rules that are hard to describe with constraints alone. This is where things sometimes get a bit murky because when you look closer, you often discover that the "complex business rules that cannot be implemented with constraints" are a direct consequence of a poor database design. When people don't respect Bill Kent's rule "non-key attributes are facts about the key, the whole key, and nothing but the key" they suddenly have a lot of rules saying that if this attribute has this value, then another attribute must have that value, or that out of a pair of attributes only one must be null - which you cannot sometimes say with constraints but is first of all an indication that non-key attributes depend on each other, which they shouldn't.

I have to qualify strict rules about dependencies. If you consider for instance the *people* table, birth and death year aren't related, strictly speaking, nevertheless checking that the death year, if defined, is greater than the birth year (and no more than 120 years greater, and not greater than the current year) makes a lot of sense and can protect against typos. All products allow you to control these conditions through **check** constraints, which are a lighter, and therefore better, mechanism than triggers. When you can't use a **check** constraint, a trigger can do the job.

- Finally, you can use triggers for writing to the database, information that is related to the information explicitly handled in the statement.

Once again, some applications of these triggers are perfectly legitimate, while others are more dubious. Among good trigger usage, you find auditing - some DBMS products feature built-in auditing features but they aren't always available and sometimes you want something more precise than the standard built-in feature. Every time data is changed, you can collect through information functions, data such as the name of the account that was used, or the IP address of the person who made the change - you could automatically record in table *movies* itself (for instance) when a row was last modified and by whom but you would have no information if a row were deleted instead of being updated as "no longer active". A journal with timestamp, identification of who made the change, type of change, previous value, and new value can be useful for fraud detection.

Using a Journal to Migrate a Database

A journal of changes created by triggers can also be useful for a completely different purpose - when you move a big database from one server to another, you may minimize downtime by stopping the database, backing it up locally, setting up triggers to record changes, restarting the database, copying the files while new changes are recorded by triggers, then replaying the changes, and only them, once everything is almost ready, just before switching servers.

You also find a number of cases when somewhat redundant information is stored, which is a kind of grey area where the use of triggers can sometimes be justified and is sometimes more questionable.

I mentioned in Chapter 6 that for searching movies by title, it was better to process titles and store the significant words in the title, once normalized, into a separate table. This is something that can be done by programs running in the background (what most "true" full-text search engines do); this is something that you can do in a special program for entering films in the database but this is also something that you can do in triggers, with the advantage, compared to the special data-entry program, that even if someone manually inserts a movie under an interactive SQL client, the title will still be processed.

For a forum, you often want to display next to the various topics the number of posts, as well as the date of the latest post and the name of the person who wrote it. Especially if your DBMS lacks window functions, a trigger to associate with each topic the identifier of the last post related to this topic may help to find the information much faster.

A MySQL Audit Trigger Example

To illustrate triggers, I shall populate by trigger, an auditing table to record who changed something in table *people* and when. There are different ways to design a log table; you can store the primary key column, plus two columns per non-key column in the audited table ("before" and "after" values), then information about who performed the change. Or you can decide to store "before" and "after" values in different rows of a log table with a structure very similar to the audited table, plus the "whodunit" data.

I am going to use another type of log table, in which I will only record columns that are actually modified, with one row per column, with the following structure in this MySQL example:

```
create table people_audit
          (auditid          serial,              ① Auto-generated identifier
           peopleid         int not null,     ← Primary key of the changed row
           type_of_change   char(1) not null,       ② Operation
           column_name      varchar(30) not null,
           old_value        varchar(250),         ← All data is coerced to text
           new_value        varchar(250),         ← Ditto
           changed_by       varchar(100) not null,
           time_changed     datetime not null)      ③ Date/time information
```

The auto-generated identifier ① is mostly used to help restitute the exact sequence of operations, as the date/time information that is stored ③ may not be precise enough. The operation that caused the changed ② is recorded as I, U or D depending on its being an insert, update or delete. For an insert *old_value* will necessarily be null, for a delete *new_value* will necessarily be null.

Log and audit tables are probably the only ones for which you can tolerate the absence of a primary key or of any constraints. Strictly speaking, there should be a primary key defined as for any table; the natural key is *peopleid*, *column_name*, plus the identifier of who performed the change and the timestamp. Adding a system-generated identifier is pointless, unless - and it can be critical in some cases - you want to monitor the sequence of operations more precisely than the *time_changed* column allows. For reasons I shall explain in a later chapter, a primary key slows down (a little) inserts. By themselves, triggers add overhead to regular operations. I want them as fast as possible, even if I have (with some remorse) to omit constraints in the tables to which triggers write; in that case, having no constraint is a forgivable sin, and the lighter triggers are, the better.

NOTE With MySQL, log and audit tables should also be created with the default MyIsam storage engine instead of InnoDB; the MyIsam storage engine is faster for plain writing to tables. It lacks critical features such as the enforcement of referential integrity but these features aren't required for logging.

Such a table structure could be easily modified to log changes applied to several tables - which can be a good idea, or a very bad one. It could be a good idea if we want to log changes applied to tables linked by foreign keys, and if recording the actual sequence of operations applied to different tables is critical. It would be a very bad idea if the database is heavily modified by several concurrent processes because then the processes would jam when writing into the log table, even if they were originally affecting different tables, and logging would quickly turn into a major performance bottleneck. As always, there is no good or bad solution, just a solution that works best in your case.

When I audit, I am interested by the details of operations - if someone runs a massive update against table *people*, I need to know what happened to each row, and I need triggers that will be fired for each row.

NOTE SQL Server is an exception, as triggers cannot be fired for each row but the detail if changes occurred is available through the two virtual tables **inserted** and **deleted**.

I only want to record values that have changed and must be very careful with non-mandatory columns and testing anything against null; for simplifying conditions, I'll make ample use of the **coalesce()** function to transform a possible null into a value that is invalid but has the right data type, '*' for instance for the first name or -1 for a year.

Some products accept the creation of triggers that are fired by several different events and have special variables that record in the trigger, what type of event fired it. Others (including MySQL at the time of writing) demand one separate trigger by type of event (but different triggers could very well call the same procedure). In this MySQL example I'll only show the trigger associated with an update, which is the most complicated case.

Logging and auditing triggers should be run as **after** triggers. There is no point recording an operation that hasn't yet succeeded.

Inside the trigger, *new* and *old* give access to the data being changed.

Audit trigger (update only), MySQL version

```
delimiter $$      <- Change the delimiter from the default semi-colon
create trigger people_u_trg
after update on people        <- Only one event
for each row
begin
  insert into people_audit(peopleid,
                           type_of_change,
                           column_name,
                           old_value,
                           new_value,
                           changed_by,
                           time_changed)
  select peopleid, 'U', column_name, old_value, new_value,
         user(), current_timestamp()        <- Auditing data
  from (select old.peopleid,
               'first_name' column_name,
               old.first_name    old_value,
               new.first_name     new_value
        from dual                              ① Special trick
        where coalesce(old.first_name, '*')
                   <> coalesce(new.first_name, '*')
        union all
        select old.peopleid,
               'surname'   column_name,
               old.surname old_value,
               new.surname new_value
        from dual                               ① Special trick
        where old.surname <> new.surname
        union all
        select old.peopleid,
               'born'   column_name,
               cast(old.born as char) old_value,
               cast(new.born as char) new_value
        from dual                               ① Special trick
        where old.born <> new.born
        union all
        select old.peopleid,
               'died'   column_name,
               cast(old.died as char) old_value,
```

```
                 cast(new.died as char) new_value
          from dual
          where coalesce(old.died, -1) <> coalesce(new.died, -1)) modified;
end;
$$
delimiter ;
```

MySQL accepts, unlike Oracle or DB2, a **select** statement without any **from** clause; however, unlike PostgreSQL or SQL Server, a **from** clause becomes mandatory as soon as the statement contains a **where** clause, even if no data is actually retrieved from the database. In that case one uses (as with Oracle) the dummy one-row, one-column table called *dual*.

As usual, you'll find the same trigger written for other products in Appendix D.

After having created triggers to handle at least insertions and updates I can run for instance, the following SQL statements:

```
insert into people(first_name, surname, born)
values('George', 'Clooney', 1961);
insert into people(first_name, surname, born)
values('Frank', 'Capra', 1897);
update people
set died = 1991
where first_name = 'Frank'
  and surname = 'Capra';
```

NOTE There should be references to *people_seq.nextval* with Oracle and references to *next value for people_seq* with DB2 when inserting into table *people*.

If after having run these statements, I query table *people_audit* I would find in it rows looking like the following ones:

```
AUDITID PEOPLEID T COLUMN_NAME OLD_VALUE NEW_VALUE CHANGED_BY TIME_CHANGED
------- -------- - ----------- --------- --------- ---------- ------------
      1      137 I born                  1961      SFAROULT@  ... 10:08:08
      2      137 I surname               Clooney   SFAROULT@  ... 10:08:08
      3      137 I first_name            George    SFAROULT@  ... 10:08:08
      4      138 I born                  1897      SFAROULT@  ... 10:08:08
      5      138 I surname               Capra     SFAROULT@  ... 10.08.08
      6      138 I first_name            Frank     SFAROULT@  ... 10:08:08
      7      138 U died                  1991      SFAROULT@  ... 10:08:08
```

Of course, identifiers may vary and depending on the DBMS the various columns from the same row may be inserted in a different order but it would allow forensic investigation about all changes applied to the table.

Triggers and Quantum Physics

You should be most careful with triggers that are fired with each row; in a row trigger you mustn't try to look at rows other than the current one. In one respect, changes applied to a table are somewhat like quantum physics - you switch from one stable state to another stable state but nobody has the slightest idea of what happens during the transition.

I don't need a trigger to illustrate that during an update, strange things happen. Create a simple table *test* with a numerical column *id* on which you define a unique constraint and a text column (a simple **char** column could do); populate this table with values 1 and 2 in *id* and distinct values in the other column. If you run

```
update test
set id = 2
where id = 1
```

you will violate the constraint and get an error, as expected but if you run

```
update test
set id = case id
           when 1 then 2
           else 1
          end;
```

the update will run smoothly, and when you query the table you will see that what was once associated with *id* 1 is now associated with 2 and vice-versa. You have violated no constraint because in every case the values in column *id* were unique before the update, and are still unique after the update.

If you keep a row-by-row mindset, you have to think that at one point, during the update, column *id* in one row took the same value as in the other row; and yet no errors are generated. During the update you are, so to speak, in a case of "quantum jump" where you don't really know what any rows, other than the current one, contain. If in a trigger that is fired for each row, you observe the other rows, results could be meaningless; you shouldn't attempt in the midst of an **update** statement to enforce constraints across several rows, any more than the DBMS enforces a unique constraint. When a trigger is fired once per statement, though, whether it is before or after the statement, you have no such issue because then the table is in a stable state and you can consider it as a whole.

When to Use Triggers

You should always keep in mind that when you add triggers to a table, instead of running one **insert**, **update** or **delete** statement, you will run this statement, plus all the statements in the triggers, multiplied by the number of rows affected when triggers are fired for each row. They can easily put a significant strain on your system; with triggers that are fired for each row, the strain may be much worse than running separately queries that are applied to full datasets. Triggers that change the database can also cause locking issues, when they aren't carefully written (locking is the mechanism used to ensure that changes applied by concurrent database users remain globally consistent).

The purpose of triggers is to perform a number of operations stealthily. The flip side is that triggers can be deactivated (they sometimes are for maintenance operations) and a failure to re-activate them may pass unnoticed for quite a while. This is unfortunate but not critical with operations such as auditing - you can survive a gap in an audit log. It may have much more serious consequences when triggers ensure data consistency.

When a number of operations are closely related and must be run together, it is much better to group them as a stored procedure than to use triggers that cascade changes to the database. Stored procedures are easier to understand and maintain; even auditing can be performed in stored procedures, if people have no other way to perform changes.

The strength of triggers is that they ensure that rules are respected, even if people are accessing the database with an interactive SQL client instead of an application that checks everything, and if people have a direct access to tables, triggers can act as the last line of defense. In places where developers happen to fix problems directly on the production databases (which happens more often than it should), triggers can sometimes prevent big mistakes. For instance, I once created triggers that wouldn't allow changes to a table other than through a scheduled task that was updating the table from an external source; as several people could access the account, it ensured that any accidental manual update could not occur.

My advice, though, is that unless you need to implement integrity constraints in a database which doesn't let you do it in a declarative way, you'd better keep away from triggers as long as you lack many years of experience with SQL. Very often triggers are used for reasons that aren't very sound in the first place (maintaining consistency in a badly normalized database, for instance), they are difficult to write well, as said above it is easy to encounter logical issues that cause internal locking, and even without locks they can severely impact performance. It's good to know about triggers but they should be used with extreme caution.

To Remember

- All products allow you to add your own functions, the definition of which is (except with SQLite) stored in the database. They also allow you to store procedures grouping several SQL statements into a logical entity and to run a procedure automatically, when a table is changed through the trigger mechanism.
- Although they are not the only way to create stored functions and procedures, proprietary procedural extensions to SQL are often used for this purpose.
- You should not code in a procedural way what you can write in SQL.
- Don't query the database in functions.

- Stored procedures allow us to test a number of conditions and generate errors. They should be used to implement operations that correspond to a single business operation.
- Triggers can usually run specific code after or before the event that fires them, for each row and sometimes once per statement. They can give access to modified values. They should be used very carefully.

Exercises

NOTE If you are using SQLite, jump straight to the trigger exercise (the last one).

1. Create a function *unaccent()* that removes à, é, è, ê, ö, ô, ü from the text that is passed as parameter and replaces them respectively with a, e, e, e, oe, o, ue.
2. Create a function *age()* that takes as input a birth year and a death year and returns either the current age of a person or '+' followed by the age at the time of death if this person is dead.
3. Create a function *numwords()* that takes as input, a sentence (... or a title) and counts how many words are present. Ignore punctuation (which can be suppressed by writing a function similar to the function in exercise 1) and assume that words are separated by one space.
4. A web site aggregates for statistical analysis, the number of visits, hour by hour, in a table that was created as follows (adjust data types for your DBMS):

   ```
   create table webstats(interval_start   datetime,
                         interval_unit    char(1),
                         page             varchar(255),
                         hits             int)
   ```

   interval_unit is H for an hour, D for a day; *page* is a page of the site that was requested; hits counts how many times the page was requested between *interval_start* and *interval_start* + the time corresponding to *interval_unit*. We want to keep detailed recent information, but we want to aggregate per day for each page, all data that is older than three months. Write a procedure (which will be run weekly) to aggregate old data and purge details that are too old (you may need to check Appendix B or the DBMS documentation for date arithmetic.)
5. Create a trigger on table *people* that prevents the insertion of a row into this table outside business hours (you may need to check the DBMS documentation for date functions). Ignore public holidays.

Speeding Up Queries 9

Any simpleton can write a book, but it requires high skill to make an index.

- Rossiter Johnson (1840-1931)

This chapter covers

- Understanding how you can speed up queries by indexing column values
- Identifying columns worth indexing
- Checking whether indexes are used in SQL statements
- Understanding how indexes can influence how we write statements

Now that we have seen how to retrieve and modify data that is stored in a database, it's time to turn to a topic of the utmost practical interest: how to do all this quickly. Writing a query that answers a problem and returns the right result should certainly be your prime concern, there is no point in returning the wrong result quickly, but speed often comes a poor second to accuracy and end-users demand data that is both accurate and timely. The relational theory and all we have seen about the problems raised by nulls and duplicates were all about accuracy. Everything that you will see in this chapter is about how implementation can help performance.

When you have few things to search, speed is rarely a problem; if you just have a few books on a bookshelf and look for a particular title, you just scan the spines until you find the title you want. When your bookshelf becomes bigger, it's usually time to organize your books if you want to find them quickly and very often you'll organize them by category – art books here, novels there, travel guides elsewhere.

In a bookshop, where you really have a large number of books and customers with various demands to satisfy, a broad categorization isn't enough. Within one category, there will be a secondary ordering – for instance, history books will be ordered by period, from the Antiquity to modern times, and very often there will be a tertiary ordering. Travel guides may be ordered by continent and alphabetically by country within a continent, and history books may be ordered by country too. Ordering is what allows you locating a book reasonably fast.

When Physical Ordering is Not Enough

If you have a really, really large number of books, like a big library, then the physical ordering of books as practiced in a bookshop no longer works for finding books. There is a good reason for the failure of exclusive reliance on physical ordering: when you physically order books, you favor one type of search over all the others and you would have trouble searching in a bookshop, for a history book by author name alone. In general, bookshops cheat by using different ordering in different sections: for instance, cookbooks will be ordered by type of cuisine, technical books will be ordered by technology but literature will probably be ordered by author. In libraries, people may want to find a book by theme, by title or by author; and unless you have as many copies of each book as you have ways to order them, there is no way to satisfy every search need. Librarians found a solution. Several centuries ago they were writing down their inventories in catalogs; more recently they used card indexes. You can have several card indexes, one by author and one by title for instance; you can find the location of a book using cards, as many times as you have pre-defined ways to search for it. Today's cataloging modules of library automation software are directly descended from card indexes. Whether the books are physically stored by topic and author or ordered by publisher, size, cover color or number of pages becomes irrelevant – in other words, the way books are physically arranged, bears much less relation to how long it takes to locate them with a card index than in a bookshop. The library search gives you a book reference that takes you (or a librarian) directly to the right shelf.

Searching specific rows in a table is the same type of challenge as searching specific books in a library. As you can see, speeding up searches is a concern that far predates computers and databases; and as the techniques that are used for books are well proven, it will come as no surprise that related techniques are used with databases. This is also a similar indexing technique that I used in Chapter 6 when I was associating with a word, the identifier of a film containing that word in its title but then I wasn't storing the precise location of the information about the film. I was operating at a logical level, relying on the DBMS to find title, year of release and country when provided with a *movieid.* To speed up searches on the rows of a table, you index column values but at a more physical level.

What Are Table Indexes

Instead of the shelf location codes used for books in libraries, rows in a table are located by physical addresses. These addresses or *row locators* may for instance be a compound of a file identifier (remember that database management systems handle files transparently for you), of a *page* or *block* number within that file and an offset within the block to the beginning of the row.

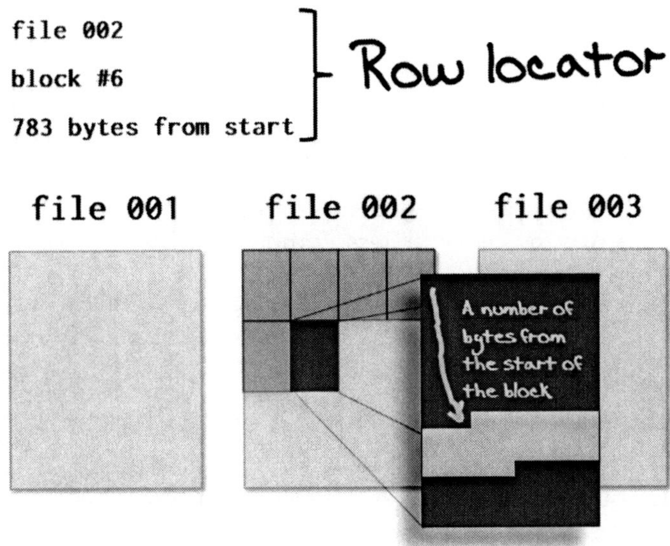

Figure 9.1: How a DBMS can record the location of a row.

Database indexes are indeed more "filesical" than "physical"; references are within files, not locations on disk (which means that when you copy the files elsewhere, locators remain valid). Row locators are for internal DBMS usage.

NOTE Database files are usually organized as an integer number of pages (sometimes called blocks) which have a fixed size. A page is the minimum addressable unit of data that a DBMS will transfer between disk and memory.

When you want to find rows quickly for any given value (for instance a person's surname) you can accelerate searches by collecting, prior to any search, all the values in the column with their corresponding row locator, and to prepare something that is comparable to a book index. Instead of being written down on pages at the end of a book or on pieces of cardboard inside drawers, the information that a value can be found in this column, of that row, located at this particular place in this file, is stored in a database object other than a table, which is called an *index*.

An index points to rows from only one table. Like triggers, indexes are subordinated to tables and have no independent existence - drop the table and the associated indexes disappear with the table. However, whereas you usually need special rights (I shall talk more about the topic of rights in the next chapter) to create a trigger, anybody who is allowed to create a table, is allowed to create indexes on this table.

NOTE MySQL is an exception in this area; unless you have a special right you can create indexes at the same time as you create a table but not later.

How indexes are physically built depends on the product; implementation detail may vary wildly, it may be more or less complicated but the basic ideas behind indexes can be explained simply. Most often, the (value, locator) pairs are stored by increasing or sometimes decreasing values. A tree structure, which is nothing more than a number of redirections saying 'if your value is between this and that, look into this area of the index', is plugged over the list to speed-up searches in the index itself. You must remember that the value that is stored is just the collection of bytes found in the column at the row indicated by the locator - the actual meaning of these bytes depends on the data type of the column (you will see later in this chapter that this is important).

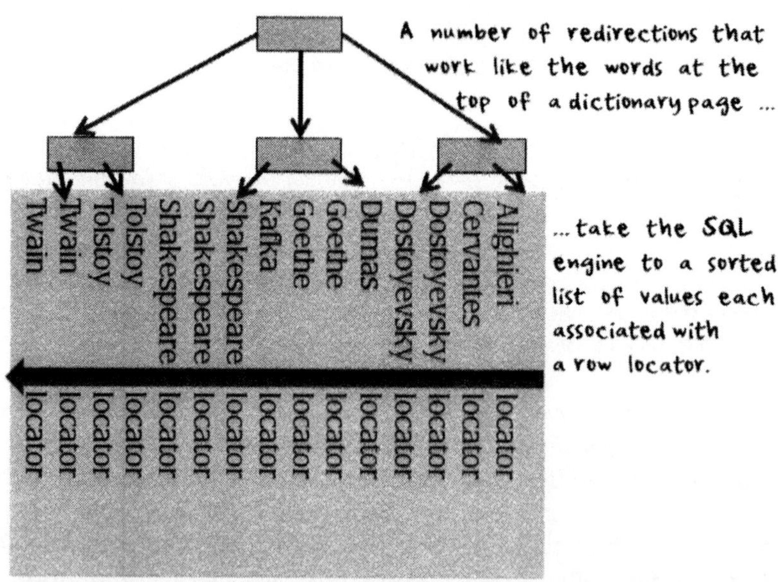

Figure 9.2: What a library book index might look like in a database system.

Tree searches are the closest a computer can get, to the type of searches you perform manually in a dictionary or a phone book - what I'm looking for is before the value at the top of this page ... but after this one ... got it! This type of search is hardly sensitive to the number of values that are indexed - searching for a word in a large multi-volume dictionary may take you a little more time than a search in a compact edition but not in the same proportion as to the ratio of the number of pages.

I need to stress, you'll see very soon that it's important, the fact that index searches are based on comparisons. If you search a person by surname, for instance

```
select *
from people
where surname = 'Depp'
```

and if the surname has been indexed, the SQL engine will first enter the index, looking for the surname the way you would look for it in a dictionary, and will discover that a row locator for a *Depp* in the *people* table should be found somewhere between the locator for *Christie* and the locator for *Ford*. In a split second the SQL engine will know if there is a *Depp* in the table, and if there is at least one will find the exact location of the row in *people* - row or rows, as several people may bear the same surname. The DBMS will be able to fetch the relevant data immediately without inspecting all the rows in table *people* (inspecting all of the rows is an operation usually called *table scan*).

Creating an Index

The basic syntax to create an index is very simple:

```
create index <index name> on <table name>(<col1>, ... <coln>)
```

Some products may allow along with indexes (as well as with tables), other clauses to specify more precisely storage details linked to the implementation; there are always reasonable default values.

You'll notice that you can create an index on several columns at once. Very often, queries associate the same attributes in **where** clauses; for instance, if you want to book tickets for a trip, whether you travel by plane, train, coach or boat, you will always specify a place of departure, a place of arrival and a date. A search makes no sense if any of the three criteria is missing.

When criteria are always (or very often) used together, you create what is called a *composite index* on several columns. The value associated with a row locator in a composite index is the concatenation of the values found in the columns of the index. A composite index is more precise than several single-column indexes on the same columns.

Indexes and Constraints

It's important to know that whenever you define, as you should, a primary key for your tables, or state that the values in some columns should be unique, you implicitly create an index (some products such as PostgreSQL issue notices about implicitly created objects when you run a **create table** statement). There is a simple reason for that: with an index, the database management system can immediately check whether the key value is already present in the table, and raise an error if that is the case. Otherwise, the bigger the table, the longer the check would take, and the longer the time required to insert a row.

You should note that very often, the column that is indexed is called the index *key*. Don't confuse constraint keys and index keys, even though indexes are important for implementing constraints. While constraint keys are also index keys, the reverse isn't true. It's common to create indexes on columns that contain the same value several times and for which no constraint is defined but which are important search criteria.

Index Overhead

In the same way as a newly acquired book is immediately cataloged in a library and their card indexes, or their electronic equivalent, are updated if some books are discarded, indexes on tables are automatically maintained each time a row is inserted or deleted, or when an indexed column is updated in a row. Indexes are always up-to-date but keeping up-to-date has a price and each index potentially means a little extra work. Whenever you update a value that is indexed, the DBMS needs to change the index too, and the change in the index may prove more complex than in the table: as values are ordered in an index, the DBMS must remove the row locator from the place corresponding to the old value in the index, and insert it at the place corresponding to the new value.

Insertion can also cause issues, when rows are inserted from different sources at the same time (a multitude of active users, for instance) and indexes are on columns that take close values, such as a system-generated identifier or the current timestamp. All **insert** statements will result in addition of locators at the same end of the index, and as several processes cannot simultaneously write bytes at the same place, operations will have to be regulated, one after the other, which may slow down the global insertion operation.

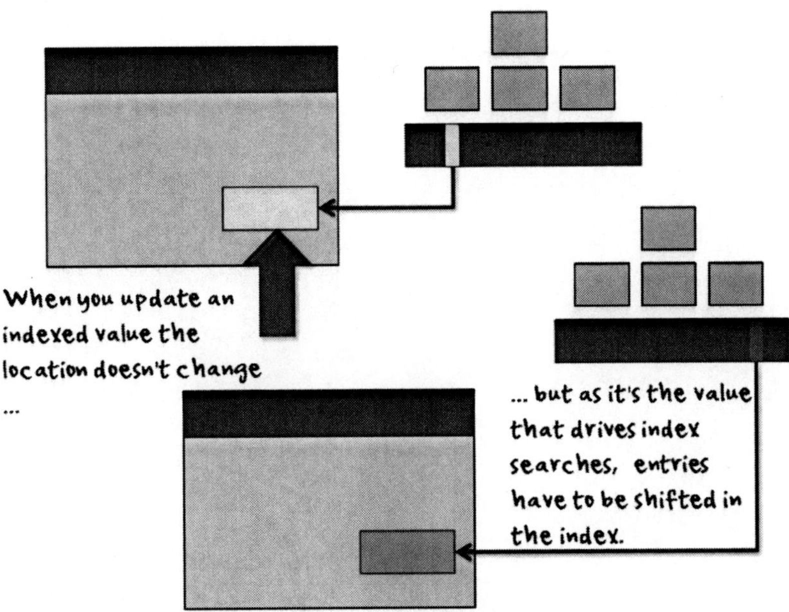

When you update an indexed value the location doesn't change ...
... but as it's the value that drives index searches, entries have to be shifted in the index.

Figure 9.3: How updating an indexed value affects the index.

When you add one or several indexes to a big existing table, the table has to be scanned to find the values to store in the index, their locations have to be recorded, and everything must be sorted before creating the index proper. On very big tables, creating an index can take several hours; the database may in many cases remain accessible to ordinary users but sorts are heavy operations and performance takes a hard knock.

Indexes also consume a significant amount of storage; remember that indexes hold values and locations - data that can be derived from the content of tables but still data that has to be stored somewhere. An index usually takes much less storage than the associated table but when you multiply indexes on different columns of the same table, storage requirements add up. Very often, the total storage used by indexes in a database is more than half the total storage used by tables proper. Some tables use less space to store their rows than what their indexes consume.

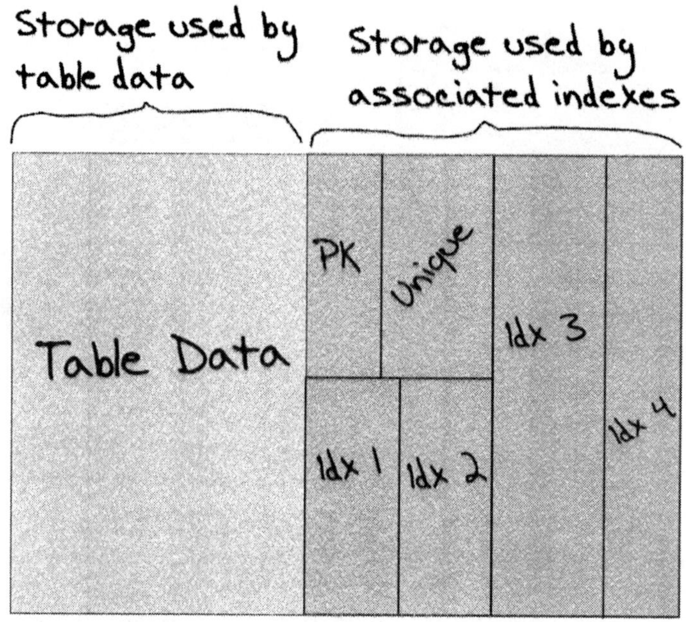

Figure 9.4: It happens that all indexes together use more storage than the table.

Unique Indexes

Optionally, you can specify that only one row should match each index value as defined by the set of columns (column value if a single column is indexed, combination of column values for composite indexes). You do this by writing

```
create unique index
```

instead of

```
create index
```

Creating a **unique** index on a number of columns is, in practice, equivalent to defining a **unique** constraint on these columns. My advice is that you create unique constraints rather than unique indexes. Actually, a unique constraint will create a unique index in the background, and one could argue that it doesn't make a lot of difference but it makes a lot of difference in terms of database design: a unique constraint is something that helps you to define your data. It's part of the model, the representation in a database of the data managed by an application. Constraints belong to the design in almost the same way as data types. Indexes are part of the physical implementation. They are very important but they are dependent on the way the DBMS physically organizes the data; they are more "nuts and bolts" than constraints.

> NOTE There are exceptions to the rule of using unique constraints rather than unique indexes but they are due to SQL syntax limitations. I'll discuss before the end of the present chapter, a case when I'd use a unique index rather than a unique constraint.

Index Naming

On a practical note, one usually assigns to indexes a name that indicates clearly their nature. Tables and indexes are all described in the data dictionary, which is a set of tables that record the objects (tables, indexes, sequences, triggers, stored procedures and functions ...) that populate the database. I shall briefly talk in the next chapter about the data dictionary. It's usual to give to indexes a name that indicates the table they relate to, and that also says 'this is an index'. Some people have the habit of prefixing index names with *i_* or *idx*. Although using a prefix is legitimate, I'd rather advise you, unless some different naming standards are already firmly established at your site, to start with the table name, followed by either a number or a reference to the columns, and suffix with *_i* or *_idx* - for instance if you want to create an index on column *country* of table *movies*, you could call it *movies_country_idx*. The advantage of this method is that you can order tables and indexes by name and still find a table and its associated indexes together. This is largely a matter of personal preference: the naming standards you are using are not, by themselves, very important. What matters is to have naming standards, and to stick to them.

Index Efficiency

There is one thing that you must be conscious of, which is that a modern DBMS scans tables very fast. So fast, that a failure to index tables properly may pass unnoticed until it hurts. For instance, I have artificially grown the *people* table from the sample movie database, up to about 400,000 rows, and I have run, on a fairly modest server, two searches, one using an index, and one scanning the table. I've run the queries a large number of times to get an average time per execution, and got 0.1 millisecond when finding rows using the index, and 0.4 seconds when scanning all the rows - inspecting 400,000 rows in 0.4 seconds isn't bad in itself. Table scan performance can be much, much better on high-range machines with state-of-the-art disks - or, even better, most of the data already in memory.

On a single query, with a comfortably sub-second response time in both cases a human being will hardly notice much of a difference - even if we extract the result from the database 4000 times faster in one case than in the other. The problem becomes noticeable, and very noticeable, as soon as queries are repeated a large number of times, for two reasons:

- First, the simple cumulative effect acts as a magnifying glass. If you repeat the operation one hundred times in a program, between 0.01 second and 40 seconds there is a large difference for a human being.
- Second, the fact that if to simplify we say that out of the 0.4 seconds required when scanning the table 0.3 are pure computer processing (the remainder being various delays such as waiting for the completion of disk access operations) you can only perform three such operations per second and per processor. If queries are issued at a higher rate, for instance by many web-users accessing the same site simultaneously, the various queries will be entered into a waiting line by the DBMS until they can be executed by one of the computer's processors, and the response time seen by users will be the sum of the actual execution time (one third of a second) and of the time spent waiting, which can be very long. Perceived performance will crash all of a sudden, as soon as the load exceeds a limit that depends on the power of the machine, even if unitary testing gave acceptable response times - in practice, performance will crash as soon as queries arrive faster than they can be executed (it's exactly the same phenomenon as traffic jams at toll gates: when cars arrive faster than the time required to pay, lines grow).

There is another point to consider. I have so far compared fetching one row using an index to fetching one row by scanning a table, and when I talked about repeating the operation in a loop, I was talking about scanning a table repetitively. If we have many different rows to fetch, we can probably fetch them in a single sweep of the whole table. If fetching one row using the index is, as in my example, about 4,000 times faster than inspecting all rows, when a query returns 4,000 rows it makes no difference whether we are using the index to fetch rows one by one, or scanning the table and returning rows as we find they match the search criteria - the time will be the same. And if we want to return 40,000 rows out of 400,000, then it will take 4 seconds if we use the index to locate each of them individually, while the full scan will still take 0.4 seconds - the time required to scan the table is the same whether we ultimately return zero, one, or several thousand rows. With indexes, the more rows we return, the longer it takes. It really is a question of using the right algorithm for the right volume of data.

This is why determining which columns really require indexing is of the highest practical importance.

Choosing Which Columns to Index

Determining which columns would benefit from indexing other than those automatically indexed by constraints requires some thought - in fact, quite a lot of thought. The columns that are the best candidates for indexing must satisfy a number of conditions:

- Firstly, they must often be used as search criteria.

  A typical example would be a table that contains currency exchange rates. Your criterion for searching such a table will never be "which are the rows corresponding to an exchange rate of 2.5678". Although the rate itself is what you really want from the table, it's the currency code and, if the table stores historical values, the date, which will drive the searches. And when you think 'index' for this table you should think 'currency code' and 'date' (which are likely to be the primary key).

  A column that is only rarely used as the main search criterion isn't necessarily a good candidate either; unless 1) it's critical that the queries that rely on this column return very fast and 2) the index really makes a difference. Performance gains for occasional queries must be balanced against the overhead induced by index maintenance when inserting, deleting and perhaps updating, as well as against the extra storage required. Good overall performance is often a question of compromise.

- Secondly, the columns must contain values that are selective enough to help the DBMS engine to focus fast enough on the final result set.

  Once again, a comparison with libraries may help to clarify. In the library of the Computer Science department of a University, it makes little sense to index books that mention the word "computer" – all the books will probably contain it. Words like "memory" or "disk" are unlikely to be much more helpful; even "SQL" will probably get a mention in many books. The value of a search criterion is inversely proportional to its frequency – you have experienced it with web search engines. The rarer the value you are looking for, the faster it allows the DBMS to identify the result set you want to see and the more sense it makes to index it.

I just want to point out, briefly, a potential snag; if I take the example of table *movies* in the movie database, should column *country* be indexed for searches? The problem is that some countries produce thousands of movies every year, and for them the country alone isn't a very selective criterion. It's likely that the query will involve other search criteria, and that some of those will be more effective for helping the DBMS shape the final result set. Even if the country is the only search criterion, it is quite possible that simply scanning all the rows in the table will be more efficient than finding references in the index and then fetching rows one by one (a full table scan will certainly be faster if the country is *us*).

On the other hand, the very same "country" criterion that isn't very significant for countries with a buoyant movie industry, may be very selective for countries where film-making is still an art or a craft and not an industry, and where very few films are produced.

The "big" database management systems have sophisticated optimizers and usually collect statistics about the distribution of values. They know which values are "popular" - a popular value is a value that you find very often and which isn't very selective. When the SQL engine evaluates how best to run a query, it checks whether indexes can be used to speed up the search, and if this is the case, a second check can be performed to verify that the value that is searched, is rare enough to make the index search faster than a plain table scan. A DBMS may decide not to use an existing index because the value that is searched is too common.

Column *country* in table *movies* is also a foreign key (referencing column *country_code* in table *countries*). Many people recommend always to index foreign keys (some DBMS products require foreign keys to be indexed); I have mixed views on this topic.

The main rationale for indexing foreign keys is linked to an aspect of referential integrity that people often forget: while foreign keys prevent you from inserting into the referencing table, a row with a value that cannot be found in the referenced table, they also prevent you from deleting from the referenced table, a row that matches rows in the referencing table because the disappearance of this row would make data inconsistent. For instance, you cannot delete a row from table *countries* if *movies* contains films from this country. If I try to delete one row from *countries*, the SQL engine must first look into *movies* (and possibly other tables) to see if there is a row referencing it. In the absence of any index on column *country* of *movies* (the foreign key column) this will require scanning table *movies* until either the DBMS finds a film for this country - which would prevent deletion - or it has checked all films, which may take a long time if the table is really big. Moreover, while doing this, the SQL engine will need to prevent other users from inserting rows into table *movies* because someone might want to insert the first film for a small country, at the same time as the DBMS checks whether another session can safely remove this country from table *countries*. An index on column *country* of table *movies* allows the checking of consistency very quickly.

But this particular concern with foreign keys only occurs if we want to delete some countries. For many reference tables, *countries* is a good example, we'll never want to delete rows (even if the uncertainties of geopolitics redraw the map, if some countries disappear and other countries are created, we may want to keep references to the state of the world when a movie was released). The problem with indexing all foreign keys is that some tables have many foreign keys. I could for instance add other attributes to table *movies* such as genre, main language, company owning the rights to the film and so on, all of which would probably be foreign keys. As I have just said, indexes are maintained as tables are changed. If your database is a read-only decision-support system, you can happily index all columns in your tables. If your tables undergo many changes, whether you insert, delete or update many rows, the additional work required to maintain indexes, consumes processor time as well as, very often, disks accesses and slows down, very significantly, change operations to the database. I'll want to index some of the columns - those that are important for searches - but not all of them.

The Cost of Indexes

This is a test you can easily replicate. I have inserted 100,000 rows into a table of a dozen columns.

In the same time I could insert 100 rows without any index.

- After creating a primary key index I inserted 65,
- After adding a second index I was down to 22,
- After adding another index I could only insert 15
- And a last index brought my throughput down to 5.

The actual numbers you get may differ with the DBMS, variations can be more or less dramatic but since indexes are maintained in real time, each index inflicts a performance penalty and it can be verified with any database management system. It's not a concern in a read-only decision support system. It can be one in an operational system with a lot of insertions.
I certainly want some indexes besides those that are required to ensure data integrity. Only if they are worth the cost.

Even worse, when a large number of processes are concurrently inserting into a table, it is common to see concurrent accesses to indexes being the biggest bottleneck.

It means the benefits that are expected of each index must be carefully assessed against the predictable overhead. Contrary to what I have seen advised more than once in forums by well-meaning but unenlightened advisors, you shouldn't index all columns that appear in **where** clauses: once again, you should only index columns that are important to searches and would benefit from an index.

Checking That Indexes Are Used

Before I discuss further a number of important index-related issues, it's time to introduce an SQL command that is a part of the standard but the output of which is highly dependent on the underlying DBMS, and which tells you (broadly) how a DBMS processes a statement. This command is **explain** and is used as such with DB2 and Oracle:

```
explain plan for <SQL statement>
```

NOTE Prior to running an explain statement with DB2, you must install some system tables which are created by a script named `EXPLAIN.DDL` located in the DB2 directories. You can run the script with the following command:

```
db2 -tf EXPLAIN.DDL
```

With PostgreSQL, MySQL and SQLite it's simply:

```
explain <SQL statement>
```

NOTE Actually, with SQLite `explain` *<query>* returns a very detailed trace for the developers of the product but SQLite also supports `explain query plan` *<query>* that shows summarily in an intelligible way, for people like you and me, how the query was run.

explain doesn't exist in SQL Server but you can obtain the same result by running

```
set showplan_all on
```

prior to running the query (better still, you have an icon *Display Estimated Execution Plan* a few icons away from *Execute* in SQL Server Management Studio).

For instance you can check how a DBMS runs a simple query by typing, depending on the product you are using

```
explain plan for select * from movies where country = 'gb'
```

or

```
explain select * from movies where country = 'gb'
```

or

```
explain query plan select * from movies where country = 'gb'
```

When an SQL statement is preceded by **explain**, it isn't executed. Instead, it's analyzed by the SQL engine that determines how best to run the statement and produces what is called the *execution plan*. The execution plan, among other things, gives the names of the tables and indexes that are accessed to run a query. With some products **explain** immediately displays some output; with some other products, it just stores the plan somewhere and the plan has to be queried from some temporary table as a second step.

Displaying the Execution Plan

Products that store the plan in tables, use column names which aren't really self-explanatory nor an ideal of user-friendliness. This is why I would warmly recommend for this purpose, using IBM Data Studio for DB2 (the 'Open Visual Explain' icon is located next to the 'Run SQL' icon) or SQL Developer (the 'Explain Plan' icon is two icons away from the 'Run Statement' icon), with Oracle. With these tools there is no need to type the **explain** command - just type the SQL statement and click on the button that generates the execution plan.

If you really, really want to display an Oracle execution plan under SQL*Plus, you should run after the **explain** statement

```
select plan_table_output
from table(dbms_xplan.display());
```

You can try **explain** immediately with two queries (adapt the syntax to your DBMS):

- First, try `explain select * from movies`
- Then, try `explain select * from movies where movieid = 1`

  The second execution plan shows that the SQL engine would use the index associated with the primary key.

Just a word about execution plans: don't try to assign to them any "good" or "bad" qualifier. Some people are obsessed by execution plans and particularly tables that are accessed without passing by an index. There are times when using an index is a pretty dumb thing to do, not a smart one, and what matters is not how but how fast statements are run. Besides, execution plans are particularly difficult to read (except for very simple queries) and based on information - such as how data is physically stored in the files - that have nothing to do with the logic of a business or an application. Even senior database administrators often have a hard time with them. Study your queries more than execution plans.

As the tables in the sample database are small, using an index or not using an index makes no perceptible difference in terms of response time; it would be different with large tables. **Explain** (or equivalent) will help you see when a DBMS uses indexes - indexes on which you are relying for performance cannot always be used, as we are going to see now.

Keeping Indexes Usable

When you are introduced to indexing, you usually think that if a column that is referenced in a query is indexed, then everything is fine, the SQL engine will use the index and the query will run fast. Reality is more complicated. First of all, as I have told you, sometimes you need indexes, sometimes you don't and you need to determine which columns require indexing. A DBMS will not create indexes for you.

NOTE A DBMS will not create indexes but sometimes it can suggest them. Corporate grade DBMS products usually include (or let you buy as an expensive additional option...) automated "performance advisors" that can tell you where additional indexes might improve performance by analyzing queries that are run. Beware that the analysis is based on existing queries and that often rewriting queries is more efficient than adding more indexes, as you will see in this section.

While the existence of an index is a prerequisite to indexed access, it's far from the only condition. I have already mentioned that an optimizer may choose not to use an index because the value being searched is too common and scanning the table is overall faster than searching the index, then retrieving rows one by one. There are also cases when an index exists but the query is written in such a way that the index cannot be used. This is what we are going to see now. If you want to shine when optimizing queries, you need to understand what can get in the way of the tree search that is applied to indexes when the DBMS tries to locate the locators of rows that contain a particular value.

Using Composite Indexes Correctly

Composite indexes, indexes for which the index key is, in fact, the combination of several columns, demand that several conditions are satisfied to be correctly used. What you must understand is that when an index is built on several columns (most products allow at least 16 columns in an index but in practice composite indexes usually involve 2 or 3 columns) it's like having an index on a single column that would be the concatenation of all the columns in the index. A real-life example of composite index would be a phone book, in which the key to find a phone number is composed of the surname, the first name, and the address, in this order. The interesting point is that to be able to find a number, you don't need to know all components in the index key but you absolutely need the first one. If you have met at a party, people whom you would like to meet again and who told you their first name and the street where they live but not their surname, a phonebook will be useless for finding their number (unless you read the phone book from A to Z, which you might call a full phone book scan); your best chance of getting their phone number would be to ask a common acquaintance, to whom the first name might mean something (in a way, the common acquaintance will act as an index on the first name).

The same is true with indexes in relational databases. If you don't provide, either directly or indirectly (that is, by providing the value through a join), the value that the first column in the index must match, the index will be unusable. But if you provide only the value for the first column, then the index will help you to locate rows that are candidates for the final result set – in the same way that if you only have a surname and an address, assuming the surname isn't too common, you can scan in the phone book, all the entries for that surname until you find the right address, ignoring first names in the process. That means that whenever you create a composite index, you must be extra careful about the order of the columns because it will determine when the DBMS will or will not be able to use the index. Columns that will always be referred to in the **where** clause must come first. Columns that might not appear in the **where** clause must come last. Of course, it's always possible (and commonly done) to index separately, columns that are already part of a composite index but not in the lead position, when they can appear as the only search criterion. Remember however that the additional cost of maintaining an index must be justified.

You can test this behavior with **explain** in the sample database by querying all columns from table *people*, which has a composite index on the surname and the first name, in this order. A condition that will include the surname will use the index, with or without a condition on the first name but a condition on the first name without the surname will not use it (or will use it much less efficiently).
You can recognize the same problem pattern on searches such as

```
where surname like '%man%'
```

that don't provide the beginning of the string to match, or conditions that use regular expressions; if the column that is searched is indexed, you have exactly the same issue as with composite indexes. This is why in Chapter 6 I have shown you how you could transform an approximate search for a title, into a precise search on keywords because any search on chunks of text will ultimately translate into some kind of scanning, unless another criterion is provided that allows an efficient index search.

Not Applying Functions to Indexed Columns

The other important point for performance is related to functions and the problem comes from the tree structure that is used to find row locators quickly. I told you that the tree structure is what allows the DBMS to mimic the type of search you would perform with a dictionary, and I insisted on searches being based on comparisons. Let's say that instead of asking you to find the definition of a word in the dictionary, I ask you to give me the definition of all words that contain A-T-A as 2nd, 3rd and 4th letter respectively. There is no option when searching the dictionary, other than to try all possibilities for the first letter one by one because the words that match the search criterion can be found anywhere in the dictionary, *cataclysm*, *fatal*, *matador*, or, *satay*, among others – not forgetting **data** and *database*. Having a condition applied to the 2nd, 3rd and 4th letters instead of the full word prevents alphabetical comparisons.

If I reword the problem definition in SQL syntax with a mock table,

```
select word_definition
from word_dictionary
where word = 'database'
```

is quick and easy if column *word* is indexed,

```
select word_definition
from word_dictionary
where substr(word, 2, 3) = 'ata'
```

is slow and painful, even with the same index.

Isolating three letters – in other words, using function **substr()** - completely breaks the order upon which we rely to find words. Whenever we apply a function and transform values, the key ordering that is assumed when searching the index becomes moot; even in the rare cases when the function or expression doesn't affect order – this is what would happen for instance if you were extracting the first three letters of a word - many DBMS products play safe, assume that order *may* be changed, and won't search the index. In some cases the DBMS might find it more efficient to scan the index than to scan the table (an index is usually smaller than the table it's built upon) but in any case it will not be an efficient index search.

I told you in Chapter 3 that functions (and expressions) shouldn't be applied to columns in the **where** clause and the reason why I said that is precisely because functions 'break' indexes. If you apply a function to a column that isn't indexed, it doesn't really matter but I routinely see functions or expressions that are applied to indexed columns.

One common reason for applying functions to columns in **where** clauses is when we are performing searches that are not sensitive to case. If the DBMS product is case-sensitive for text and you don't force case when inserting data, then a case-insensitive search will usually become a condition such as

```
where upper(surname) = upper('some input')
```

Because internally uppercase letters come before lowercase letters (and accented letters after them), when case isn't consistent, a DBMS that is case-sensitive would, for instance, order surnames like this, with uppercase characters first (because this is how internal codes that represent letters have been assigned):

```
MILES      ← Uppercase letters first, sorted
O'Brien
Stewart
marvin     ← Lowercase letters next, sorted
wayne
```

Values would be ordered like this in an index too.

NOTE If you are using a case-sensitive operating system such as Linux, you also get the same type of ordering when you list files in a directory.

Imagine now that you have a dictionary in which words and names are ordered as in the preceding example, with a random, unpredictable case and that you are looking for the name which, once in upper case, is MARVIN (in other words, `where` `upper(surname) = 'MARVIN'`). If you open the dictionary at random and land on the 'Stewart' page, because of the upper case transformation you are unable to say whether the value you are looking for will be before this page (which would be the case if the name had been entered as 'Marvin') or after, as it is here. The same thing happens, for the same reason, with an index. Apply **upper()** to the searched column and you won't be able to perform a search in the index and use it to locate rows.

How functions such as **upper()** or **substr()** (**substring()** with SQL Server) prevent the use of indexes is again something you can try with **explain**.

Another common reason for applying functions to columns is type conversion, particularly with dates. Many people, looking for all rows related to June this year, would for instance, use twice a function such as **extract()**, to say that the month must match 6 for June and that the year must match the current year:

```
where extract(month from date_column) = 6
  and extract(year from date_column) = extract(year from current_date)
```

extract() is a conversion function, as here it converts the date into two different integer values. If *date_column* is indexed, the index becomes unusable because an index on a date column relies on a chronological order to store the indexed values. In such a case, the proper way to write the query is to replace the conditions by a range condition and say that the values of *date_column* must fall between June 1st and June 30th (inclusive) of the current year. In that case you are comparing a date column to date values and you can use the index to locate the first row at or after June 1st, then collect the locations of rows corresponding to the following dates, up to June 30th.

Avoiding Implicit Conversions

You also sometimes have implicit conversions between for instance, character columns that only contain digits and number constants.

Suppose that you store in a table, student or employee numbers, stored as character strings. It makes sense to store them as characters, they don't represent amounts or quantities, just strings of digits. I told you at the beginning of this chapter, that the value in the index that is associated with a locator, is just the collection of bytes found in the column at the row indicated by the locator - and that the actual meaning of these bytes depends on the data type of the column. For instance, here is how 12345 is stored in Oracle, depending on the data type:

```
SQL> select 'Number' as datatype, dump(12345) as storage from dual
  2  union all
  3  select 'Varchar2', dump('12345') from dual;

DATATYPE STORAGE
-------- ----------------------------
Number   Typ=2 Len=4: 195,2,24,46
Varchar2 Typ=96 Len=5: 49,50,51,52,53

SQL>
```

If you store in Oracle the *number* 12345, it will be internally represented by four bytes that will take respectively the values 195, 2, 24 and 46. If you store the *character string* '12345', internally it will be five bytes, each one corresponding to the ASCII code of a digit (in that case, 49 to 53). The internal representation of the number will be different in another DBMS but in all cases the internal representation of a number and of a string of characters will be wildly different.

Now, imagine that you write in a query, a condition such as

```
where studentid = 12345
```

If the DBMS looks for the four bytes 195, 2, 24 and 46 in the index, it won't find them – or if it ever finds the bytes corresponding to a number, those bytes will not correspond to the representation of the number as a string. The DBMS cannot compare apples and oranges; it knows that the *studentid* column stores character strings and that it is compared with a number. It might have been decided to say "if people compare values of different types, return an error". However, SQL was initially designed as a user-friendly language for non-developers – even if that was wishful thinking. The user-friendly way to cope with impossible comparisons is to convert one of the two values so that we can compare values with identical data types. Which one should we convert? We could say "let's convert 12345 to a string" and run under the hood

```
where studentid = '12345'
```

Then, we have a major problem. What if the student identifier was entered in the table as 0000012345? It's not uncommon to pad string identifiers composed of digits with zeros to the left, it ensures that they are sorted properly and that we don't have student 2345 appearing AFTER student 12345. If you take a string equivalent of a number, values that are numerically equal will no longer be: 100 is the same as 100.00 but '100' isn't the same as '100.00'.

If the student identifier was entered as '0000012345' and we search for '12345', the query will tell you "not found", which is true at the byte level but not from a real life standpoint. Not user-friendly. So, the reasonable thing to do is to convert the string value found in the column to number. It's not risk free – we may encounter values that aren't entirely composed of digits and get a conversion error but then we will have tried, at least, and the user will be warned; better to say "we couldn't convert" than to give a wrong answer as with the reverse conversion. Unfortunately, with the conversion the index will become moot as the byte order of values will change and it will become impossible to descend the index tree.

So, the comparison will result in a full table scan because the philosophy of a DBMS is "better to be slow and right than quick and wrong" – which makes sense. In such a case, a developer should enter the value as a correctly formatted string (as stored in the table). Of course, what happens here between column and constant can also happen when comparing two columns of different data types, in a join for instance.

Avoid data type conversion and if you need data type conversion make it explicit with a function such as **cast()**, don't let it be implicit. You'll understand better why an index isn't used when you see the function.

In all cases, when an index cannot be used, it boils down to the fact that the tree that was built over the list of (value, row locator) pairs can no longer be descended efficiently.

Indexing Expressions

The incompatibility between applying functions to columns in search conditions and using indexes is often a major hindrance. You can store some data in uppercase to avoid calls to **upper()** in the queries because it's possible to massage data on retrieval to make it look better and because (most often) converting to uppercase doesn't lose any information. Unfortunately, if you want to use function **soundex()**, which we saw in Chapter 6, to run an approximate search on the names in table *people*, then you have a big problem because you cannot from the soundex value, reconstruct a name; actually, **soundex()** was precisely devised so that many names may have the same soundex value. If for instance you want to find people who have a name sounding like *Stuart*, you will find yourself writing

```
where soundex(surname) = soundex('Stuart')
  and ...
```

which cannot use the index on the surname. One option is to add to the table another column, say *surname_soundex* and either insert the soundex value of the surname each time you insert a row, or, if you cannot modify all the programs that insert actors and directors, populate the column with a trigger each time a new person is added to the *people* table (solutions that involve triggers are always complicated and shouldn't be your first choice for solving an SQL problem). You can then index this column, and write

```
where surname_soundex = soundex('Stuart')
  and ...
```

An expression referring to *surname_soundex* (no function here) could use the index on the new column and allow searching the table very fast.

This solution isn't completely satisfying; we are managing, with the soundex value, data that end-users will never see (it will only appear in **where** clauses of queries). If we ever need to correct a misspelled surname, we may have to change the soundex value as well and clearly the soundex value is redundant information that adds nothing to what we already know: the soundex value of the surname is fully determined by the surname. We are here violating, only for performance reasons, Bill Kent's rule that says that non-key attributes (such as the soundex value) must depend on the full key that identifies a row in table *people*; even if in queries we may use *peopleid*, surname plus first name do compose the real life key. The surname is only a part of the key.

When no other possibility is available, bending the rules of good design can be a solution. There may be however a much better way that conciliates clean database design and performance. Some products, but not all, allow creation of an index on the result of an expression or a function; for instance

```
create index people_surname_soundex_index on people(soundex(surname));
```

When such an index exists, if you write

```
where soundex(surname) = soundex('Stuart')
  and ...
```

the SQL engine will recognize the same expression as was used to create the index – and use this index, thus locating the rows with the correct **soundex()** value extremely quickly.

Creating an index on the result of a function isn't always possible, the expression or function has to be *deterministic*. What does "deterministic" mean? Simply that when you call the function several times with the same parameters, it should return the same result. Always. This is the case with a function such as **soundex()** but a surprisingly high number of functions are not deterministic, especially date conversion functions because they depend on machine or database settings. Typically, a function such as **datename()**, a SQL Server function that may return among other things the name of the month, is not deterministic because if you change the language settings then the name that will be returned will change. The problem is that indexed values are stored in the index. If some settings are modified and all of a sudden, applying a function to a column no longer returns the same value as the pre-calculated value that was stored in the index, it becomes impossible to retrieve the data. If you could index the function that returns the name of a month (SQL Server will prevent you from doing this) you would store, in the index, key values that a different language setting would make irrelevant. Clearly, this isn't acceptable: the purpose of indexes is to provide an answer faster, not to change the answer by saying *no data found* (or perhaps more to the point something such as *¡No se ha encontrado ningun dato!*) when you search for *Enero* in an index that was built when the current language was English and refers to a lot of rows for *January*.

NOTE *Enero* is Spanish for *January*.

You can be on a shifting ground even with date functions that return numerical values, which you might believe language-neutral: the number of the day in a week is counted differently in different countries. If you ship to several countries, a program that uses the number of the day of the week, you cannot guarantee that the behavior will be the same everywhere.

Figure 9.5: functions that depend on regional settings such as the number of the day in the week cannot be indexed.

When you can create indexes on functions, the functions can of course be functions that you (or a colleague) have created – as long as they are deterministic. Functions that return the result of database queries are never deterministic, as an update to the database is all that is required to change what they return but of course after what I told you in the preceding chapter, you'll never want to create one.

Although I find legitimate to create (once again if the database allows it), an index on **soundex(***surname***)** or on **upper(***surname***)** to speed up case insensitive searches, I have also seen many cases when slightly changing how the query is written, is the only step that is necessary to make an existing index usable.

Suppose for instance, that you have a very big table with people from the US and their phone numbers, stored as text in the format *(XXX)-XXX-XXXX* and that you usually access this table by area code, possibly for geographically targeted telemarketing. Let's say that you want phone numbers in Manhattan, New-York (area codes 212, 646 and 917).

You could write a condition such as

```
where substr(phone_number, 2, 3) in ('212', '646', '917')
```

It's very likely that a unique constraint will exist on the phone number and therefore, that it will be indexed. Applying function **substr()** to the number prevents the use of the index. The lazy solution is to say 'all right then, let's create an index on `substr(phone_number, 2, 3)`, all my queries refer to the second to fourth digits'. This additional index (which has a maintenance cost and a storage cost) is not needed if you simply write the query

```
where (phone_number like '(212)%'
       or phone_number like '(646)%'
       or phone_number like '(917)%')
```

Here you have conditions on the beginning of the column, the same case as with a composite index when you only provide the value for the first column in the index. You can perfectly use the existing index associated with the **unique** constraint.

To be quite candid about function-based indexes, they are often used as duct-tape by database administrators desperate to improve performance when the problem is well identified but the code is not available to them. As a developer, it's much better to design solutions, when possible, that don't require indexing expressions or functions. I certainly prefer an indexed expression to an additional indexed column maintained by trigger; simpler is always better but keep in mind that all indexes add overhead, especially those based on expressions as the computation of the expression requires a little extra processing. Very often columns that people want to index through an expression are already indexed directly. Therefore, try whenever possible to devise code that only needs plain indexes - forcing for instance, the case of character strings when you insert them and possibly embellishing them (with initial capitals, for instance) when you retrieve them or display them to the end-user.

Revisiting Queries

A point that is interesting to note, is that most often indexes are presented as a way to accelerate existing queries. True enough but in fact most queries are written *after* indexing has been defined. Creating an index specifically for a query, although it happens, is more the exception than the rule (as creating an index on a big table can take hours, requiring new indexes usually raises little enthusiasm among database administrators, especially if you just *think* that the new index *might* improve performance - you need a very strong case). When you write a query, you should know which indexes exist on the tables involved in the query because even though theory says that in SQL you just state what you want and let the DBMS retrieve the data, in practice existing indexes influence the way queries are (or should be) written.

You may remember that in Chapter 4 I showed you that joins, correlated, and uncorrelated subqueries, were all functionally equivalent and that choosing one over the other was dependent on circumstances. I can now be more precise and say that circumstances are actually existing indexes and the volume of data examined.

Let's take a simple example and say that you want to find the number of films in the database in which Tom Hanks has performed. There are several ways to write the query and we can consider a regular join:

```
select count(c.movieid)
from credits c
     inner join people p
            on p.peopleid = c.peopleid
where c.credited_as = 'A'
   and p.surname = 'Hanks'
   and p.first_name = 'Tom'
```

but an equivalent query can also be written with a correlated subquery or an uncorrelated subquery and studying those alternative versions may help us to understand better, the work performed by the join. In one way, the two queries with subqueries might represent different options for performing the join operation. A correlated subquery would be written:

```
select count(c.movieid)
from credits c
where c.credited_as = 'A'
   and exists (select null
               from people p
               where p.peopleid = c.peopleid
                 and p.surname = 'Hanks'
                 and p.first_name = 'Tom')
```

which suggests scanning *credits* and then, for each row from *credits*, finding the matching row in *people*. Since most rows in *credits* contain the value *A* in the *credited_as* column, indexing this column would be rather pointless and therefore no index will be used to access *credits*. Now, to find the matching row in *people*, the DBMS can use the primary key index on *peopleid*. The index on *surname* and *first_name* will not be used - simply because a one-column primary key index is for a DBMS a dream index, small and guaranteed to associate one value with one row only. It will make no noticeable difference if a function such as **upper()** or **soundex()** is applied to *surname* or *first_name*, as they won't drive the search. Interestingly, if the name of a non-existent actor is provided, if you have mistyped the name for instance, it makes no difference either, every row that matches an actor in *credits* will be checked. This query is rather inefficient because we have no selective filter to apply to table *credits* before checking *people*. It might be different if we had say, another join with *movies* and a very selective condition on the film, which would leave us with very few rows from *credits* before checking table *people*.

The query can be written differently: it can also be written with an uncorrelated subquery that first retrieves the identifier assigned to Tom Hanks, and then uses this identifier to search *credits*:

```
select count(c.movieid)
from credits c
where c.credited_as = 'A'
   and c.peopleid in (select peopleid
                      from people p
                      where p.surname = 'Hanks'
                        and p.first_name = 'Tom')
```

(In that case, we know that more than one row won't be returned because there is only one *peopleid* associated with Tom Hanks so we could use = instead of **in**)

This query is probably the query that should be run if we focus exclusively on actors; if the question had been "in which American films released in 1994 did Tom Hanks play?", with an additional join on table *movies*, the optimizer might have decided – or not – that getting the movie identifiers first, based on the country and year condition, would be more efficient.

When you just want to find in how many films one can find Tom Hanks, the query with an uncorrelated subquery would execute very differently from the query with a correlated subquery. Here, the query calls for using the index on *surname* and *first_name* to retrieve the person identifier, then finding the matching rows in *credits*. If we have been fat-fingered and typed something such as

```
where p.surname = 'Hnaks'
```

the fact that the nested query returns no rows will immediately be noticed by the DBMS and it could return an empty result set instantly. If we code with calls to **upper()**, the difference will be felt too: unless we have indexed **upper(***surname***)**, that would mean scanning table *people* (without using an index) simply to retrieve Tom Hanks's identifier.

When we have retrieved the person identifier, it all depends on the existing indexes on *credits*. When I created this table, I specified that the primary key was (*movieid, peopleid, credited_as*), in this order. The index associated with the primary key constraint is a composite index – and I provide in the **where** clause, returned by the subquery, the value for the second column in the index, without providing anything for the first column. I am in exactly the same position as searching the dictionary for words that contain some letters, without knowing the first ones. The index cannot be used efficiently for the search. If I had defined the primary key as (*peopleid, movieid, credited_as*) then I could have used the primary key index (more on the subtle links between constraints and indexes in the next section).

Having no efficient index available could induce us to create a separate index on *peopleid* in table *credits* because we know that the number of movies an actor played in, will be very small relatively to all the movies in the database or to rethink the way we have defined our constraints.

Revisiting Constraints

We have just seen an example query that couldn't use the existing primary key index, simply because the value we were (indirectly, by a subquery) feeding into the query, corresponded to the second column of the index associated with the constraint, rather than the first one. Sometimes, a table has very few indexes besides those associated with primary keys and unique columns. It's interesting to review constraints in the light of what you have seen in this chapter.

Defining Constraints With an Eye to Performance

I have said repeatedly, that order is a notion foreign to the relational theory; it's foreign to integrity constraints too. Whether I say that (*first_name, surname*) is unique or (*surname, first_name*) is unique, it's six of one and half a dozen of the other. Relational theory is one thing, implementation another and index usage is all about the order of columns. I want unique constraints - they guarantee I have clean data. If the order in which I define the constraint doesn't matter, it also means that I can define the constraint in the way that best benefits my queries. When users are going to search for an actor or director, what will they specify? Probably *Steven Spielberg* or *Spielberg*, not *Steven*: either first name and surname or surname alone. If I say that (*first_name, surname*) is unique, the index will be created in this order and will be unusable if users only specify the surname. If I say that (*surname, first_name*) is unique, the range of queries for which the index will be usable will be much wider. Sold! This is much better than creating an additional index on the surname alone.

There is a similar case with table *movies*, for which (*title, country, year_released*) should be unique. Is this the ideal order for defining the constraint? Having the title as the first column in an index isn't very interesting if whenever I search for a title I use the fuzzy search that I have described in Chapter 6 - I'll use an index on the words from the title, stored separately in another table, not the title as a whole. Even if I don't use this mechanism, it's likely that searches on titles will use **like** and wildcard characters that will make using the index impossible anyway. We can move the title to the last position. Then the question becomes of which, of the country and year, is the most likely to be the driving force of a query and appear without the other in a **where** clause. I have seen in shops, books on Italian or Japanese cinema or books on French cinema in the 1930s - I have never seen (yet) a book on all the movies produced in the world between 1970 and 1975. Even if the case for having an index on the country isn't absolutely compelling as I have mentioned in this chapter, the constraint, which is mandatory if I want a clean database, offers it to me at no extra cost, if I simply say that there is a unique constraint on (*country, year_released, title*) in this order.

Now, what about the primary key on *credits*? It says that *movieid, peopleid* and *credited_as* are unique. The column that defines in which capacity people intervened in a movie, *credited_as*, is not selective – most rows will have *A* in it, all the others will have *D*, if I want a list of all the directors scanning table *credits* would probably be the best solution. Obviously, *credited_as* can come last in the primary key definition, queries will be driven either by the movie (who played in or directed *Duck Soup*) or by a person (what are the movies in which Marilyn Monroe performed); queries in which you must retrieve persons when the movie is specified or retrieve movies when a person is specified are all likely. This is typically a case where you can have either *peopleid* or *movieid* as the leading column in the constraint but you should also create an index on the second column in the constraint.

When Unique Indexes Replace Constraints

I mentioned at the beginning of this chapter, that in some exceptional cases (and due to SQL syntax limitations rather than an appetite for bending the rules), you might want to use unique indexes rather than declarative constraints, to ensure integrity. This curious case can happen with DBMS products such as Oracle, DB2 or PostgreSQL, which store text data in a case-sensitive way. I have told you that, in that case, you should force the case of input before storing it, for instance to upper case. However, not all data can be used in upper case; few things make me feel like a number as much as receiving a cheerful pseudo-targeted letter starting with 'Dear Mr. FAROULT'. Data has to be beautified, for instance with a function such as **initcap()** (available in Oracle, DB2 and PostgreSQL) which converts the first letter of every word to upper case and every letter that follows another letter to lowercase, turning for instance *O'CONNOR* into *O'Connor* (as *C* doesn't follow a letter it is considered the first letter of a word).

But if **initcap()** is more than satisfactory with most text data, some surnames are initcap-proof. Whether you store *VON STROHEIM* or *STROHEIM (VON)*, you ultimately want to see *von Stroheim*, not *Von Stroheim*. You want to see *Ewan McGregor* or *MacGregor*, not *Macgregor*. You can try to devise a function of your own, saying that if a name is preceded by *von* then *von* should all be in lower case, and if the first three letters in a name are *M-A-C*, then the fourth one should be in uppercase. If there is one thing that my many years in Information Technology have taught me, it's that it doesn't matter how cleverly you design a function to handle special cases, it will not be long before oddities appear and you will see the Italian actor *Erminio Macario* rendered as *Erminio MacArio* and so on. Correctly rendering a capitalized surname is near impossible to process faultlessly, and the wiser solution is to let people who manage the data store it as they want; except for one thing, we don't want duplicates.

If reference data is managed by very few people, who stand by the same rules when it comes to storing data, it's reasonable simply to create a unique constraint on (*surname, first_name*) and nothing more, leaving the full responsibility of using consistent case to data administrators – if they ever enter an Audrey Hepburn and an Audrey HEPBURN, that will be their problem, and they will need to carry out a number of updates to clean-up the data. If reference data is maintained by a growing web community of enthusiasts, you can no longer rely on consistent data entry and you must become more restrictive, even if you don't want to force names to uppercase systematically.

The only thing that we really want is to ensure that first name and surname are unique, independently of the case – as would be ensured by a unique constraint in a DBMS that isn't case-sensitive for text such as SQL Server or MySQL. Alas, you cannot say with Oracle (nor SQL Server, by the way) that there is a unique constraint on (**upper(***surname***)**, **upper(***first_name***)**); this isn't supported by the SQL syntax, you cannot refer to functions in the constraint definition. However, you can create a unique index on (**upper(***surname***)**, **upper(***first_name***)**). In such an exceptional case, I would create this unique index and not define a unique constraint (which would create an additional, useless index), but only because I want to implement uniqueness and the SQL syntax doesn't allow me to do it satisfactorily.

Indexes and Physical Ordering

Even though indexing makes the physical ordering of rows irrelevant, it may make sense to keep rows physically ordered, just like it might make sense in a library to store books by author name or by title, rather than dumping them haphazardly on shelves and recording their location.

Physically ordering rows in the same way that books may be physically ordered on a shelf, is something that most database management systems implement; the way you are going to organize rows is specified when you create the table and before it contains any data.

If you want to reorganize an existing table, in which rows were not ordered or were ordered differently, then you have actually to copy the data to a new table.

A table that isn't ordered in a particular way is called a *heap-organized table* with most systems; names for tables that are physically ordered vary more, for instance SQL Server will talk about a *clustered index* while Oracle will call it *index-organized table*. Whatever the name the principle is still the same: physically, the table looks like an index except that where you would find a locator in an index, you directly get the row data.

There are a number of benefits and a number of drawbacks to forcing rows to be ordered. Interestingly, storing tables as indexes is a standard practice with SQL Server for instance, and rather uncommon with Oracle. If you are using the InnoDB storage engine with MySQL, the primary key always dictates how rows are ordered. You have to understand both benefits and drawbacks of row ordering to know when or how to use such a type of storage.

On the positive side, whenever you insert or delete one row you save the maintenance of one index, since the table doubles as one index (or vice-versa). Of course there may be other indexes to maintain.

When you are looking for data using the column used for ordering the rows, you save the cost of using the locator to fetch the data, since you go straight to the data, and not to a locator.

This is particular beneficial when you want the data for many successive rows in the order of the index key, which is called a *range scan*. Typical queries that want to retrieve a succession of rows are queries on dates (retrieve all the sales between this date and that date) but not only them. If you often want to retrieve films by country, it might make sense to try to keep rows in table *movies* ordered by *country*.

On the negative side, when you update an indexed value in a regular table, you just have to move a value and a locator. Here you have to move a full row to keep everything ordered and you have to displace more bytes. This is why it's usually recommended (and often mandatory), to use the primary key as the ordering key, since primary key columns are not updated.

Finally, inserting rows "at the right place" may prove a little more costly than dumping them anywhere room is found, especially if the row is large. Besides, if the row is very large, many benefits of the physical proximity of rows will vanish for reasons out of our scope.

In brief, clustered indexes are better used with tables with many rows but few columns, in which the natural order of key, matches natural searches.

Let's just consider the three tables in the sample database, *movies*, *people* and *credits*. The primary keys of both tables *movies* and *people*, is a number that is used for convenience and has no "real life" meaning. A user will never search for movies with a *movieid* between 350 and 427 and it's the same with table *people*. Would some kind of physical ordering be more useful with a real life key, such as the country, release year and title, or someone's name? It's also unlikely that someone will ever want to retrieve all people with a name between *Farrell* and *Ford*. Search by country may be more conceivable but for countries with few movies a regular index search will be very fast anyhow, and for countries with a very large number of movies a full table scan will be as fast. In fact, there isn't much benefit to expect in retrieval performance from storing the rows of *movies* or *people* in one particular order, unless perhaps, this order matches how a result set is usually sorted before being returned.

The picture is different with table *credits*. For one thing, its primary key comprises all its columns. There is no reason why we should store the data twice, once in the table and once in the primary key index. And although all the numbers that are stored in table *credits* are artificial identifiers that are unlikely ever to be shown to the end-user, if we make the primary key start with the movie identifier, then fetching all the rows that start with a particular *movieid* value makes a lot of real life sense – it's getting the identifiers of all the people who worked on the movie. But ordering by *peopleid* may make even more sense, if we expect that most queries will be based on actor or director name rather than title – that would allow to access quickly all the movies in which one particular person was involved. In other words, *credits* is a perfect candidate for a clustered index – but finding precisely how to cluster it is something that depends on the search patterns that we expect and we must decide whether we must tilt the balance in favor of movies or of people. It's one or the other, not both. This illustrates again that when a primary key is a composite key, the order of the columns in the key, which is irrelevant from a theoretical standpoint, isn't neutral in practice.

Any topic that is relevant to storage usually needs to be discussed with a database administrator, who knows better how tables are physically stored. As database administrators rarely have much detailed knowledge of applications and SQL statements that are run, it's really through collaboration between administrators, business analysts and developers that the best architecture choice for a particular application can be determined.

I must mention, without getting into details, that data can be physically organized by ways other than storing tables as indexes. The best known of them is partitioning, which means instructing the DBMS to store together, rows for which the same condition is true for the values in some columns – for instance, storing together all the rows for which values in a date column belong to the same month. This is an advanced notion that is used with very big tables (tens of millions of rows and above) and is out of the scope of this book.

To Remember

- You speed up access to rows that contain some values for one or several columns by creating indexes on the columns. Indexes store values and the associated row locators.
- Indexes are automatically created when you define a primary key or unique constraint. You should have frequent queries in mind when you define the order of columns in a constraint, so as to take advantage of the index.
- Indexes add overhead to data maintenance. You should only index columns that drive important searches and contain a large number of different values.
- If you apply functions to indexed columns, you make indexes unusable. You must be very careful about how you write your conditions. Many DBMS

products allow you to create an index on the result of a function but you should look first for other solutions.

- All DBMS products let you see the *execution plan* of queries that tell you whether indexes are used. It's sometimes faster not to use an index.
- Existing indexes often dictate how best to write a query when there are several ways to write it.

Exercises

1. A site hosts videos that can be downloaded on demand and a special *video_language* table stores a video identifier *videoid*, a language code *lan*, and a code *lan_type* that is S for subtitles, M for monaural audio, D for Dolby stereo audio, etc.

   We want to display language information when we search for a video on other criteria (such as actors, director, or genre) but a significant number of queries are also based on the languages available.

   - How would you define the primary key for *video_language*?
   - Would you create an additional index besides the primary key index? If so, on which column(s)?

2. We have seen in other chapters that it might be interesting to add to table *movies*, other film attributes such as genre, black and white or color, duration; we might also think of the original language, of audience rating (family, teens, adults) and of a mark from 0 to 10 assigned by members on a website, with how many people have given a mark. Suppose we add all of these attributes. Which ones, if any, would you index? Try to justify your answer.

3. The following queries all return information about the Italian films of the 1960s stored in table *movies*. I remind you that there is a unique constraint on (*country*, *year_released*, *title*) in this order, and no index other than the index associated with this constraint needs to be considered here. Can you rank the queries from the one that makes the best use of the existing index to the one that makes the worst use of it (there are ties)?

   Query A

   ```
   select year_released, title
   from movies
   where year_released like '196%'
     and country = 'it'
   ```

   Query B

   ```
   select year_released, title
   from movies
   where year_released >= 1960
     and year_released < 1970
     and country = 'it'
   ```

<u>Query C</u>

```
select year_released, title
from movies
where upper(country) = 'IT'
  and year_released between 1960 and 1969
```

<u>Query D</u>

```
select year_released, title
from movies
where 'italy' like country || '%'
  and year_released in (1960, 1961, 1962, 1963, 1964,
                        1965, 1966, 1967, 1968, 1969)
```

4. The following queries on table *people* retrieve those whose surname starts with S and whose first name starts with R. I remind you that there is a unique constraint on (*surname, first_name*), in this order. - read **substring()** instead of **substr()** if you are using SQL Server. Index-wise, which query(-ies) do you prefer?

   <u>Query A</u>

   ```
   select *
   from people
   where substr(surname, 1, 1) = 'S'
     and substr(first_name, 1, 1) = 'R'
   ```

   <u>Query B</u>

   ```
   select *
   from people
   where surname like 'S%'
    and substr(first_name, 1, 1) = 'R'
   ```

   <u>Query C</u>

   ```
   select *
   from people
   where surname like 'S%'
    and first_name like 'R%'
   ```

   <u>Query D</u>

   ```
   select *
   from people
   where substr(surname, 1, 1) = 'S'
     and first_name like 'R%'
   ```

   <u>Query E</u>

   ```
   select *
   from people
   where first_name like 'R%'
     and surname >= 'S'
     and surname < 'T'
   ```

Views, Privileges and Security

10

God has given you one face, and you make yourselves another.

- William Shakespeare (1564-1616)

This chapter covers

- How you can reuse complex queries by creating views
- How security between user accounts is managed in a database
- How views and procedures can protect data
- How a set of special system views lets you see what the database contains

Views

We have seen in Chapter 8 that you can hide the complexity of an expression (such as the one used for displaying full names) by recording it in the database as your own function. Creating a function allows its re-use in numerous queries, without having the bother of writing something complicated over and over again - a common programming practice.

SQL queries, seen as a whole, are also expressions, applied to tables rather than text, numbers or dates. Instead of using numerical operations, concatenation or date operations, we will use **where** clauses, joins, aggregates, subqueries, **union** ... but it's still the same idea of combining two or more "values" to obtain new "values", with values that are actually datasets contained in tables or returned by queries. An SQL query can be described as a table expression, in the same way as $b * b - 4 * a * c$ is a number expression if *a*, *b* and *c* all represent numbers. You must by now be convinced that table expressions can also be very complex.

Creating a View

In SQL, you can record a complex query for re-use by creating a *view*. The syntax for creating a view is simple:

```
create view <viewname> as
select ...
```

For instance, you can create a very simple view over the *movies* table (I am going to call it *vmovies*) that substitutes the full name of the country retrieved from table *countries* for the country code:

```
create view vmovies
as select m.movieid,
          m.title,
          m.year_released,
          c.country_name
   from movies m
        inner join countries c
          on c.country_code = m.country
```

Optionally, you can assign names to the columns as a comma separated list between parentheses after the view name. Naming columns in a list between parentheses has exactly the same effect as defining aliases for column names in the **select** statement.

Both

```
create view vmovies as
   select m.movieid,
          m.title,
          m.year_released,
          c.country_name country
   from movies m
        inner join countries c
          on c.country_code = m.country
```

and

```
create view vmovies(movieid, title, year_released, country) as
   select m.movieid,
          m.title,
          m.year_released,
          c.country_name
   from movies m
        inner join countries c
          on c.country_code = m.country
```

will result in a view in which the country name appears as *country* (but if you rename a column in the **select** statement and provide a different name for the column in the list in parentheses after the view name, the column will take the name given in the list).

When you write a query, you aren't compelled to give a name to an expression (if you don't mind having columns with weird headers) and you can return two columns with the same name. It's mandatory in a view, that each column returned by the **select** statement has a unique name that respects the rules for column names in a table.

Once you have created the view, querying it is equivalent to using in the **from** clause as a subquery the **select** that defines the view:

```
select * from vmovies
where year_released = 1994
```

is the same as

```
select *
from (select m.movieid,
             m.title,
             m.year_released,
             c.country_name country
      from movies m
           inner join countries c
             on c.country_code = m.country) vmovies
where year_released = 1994
```

The only difference is that the view is a permanent object that is stored in your database and can be reused at will, in many queries. Because it's a permanent object, while the data returned by the view will evolve over time, its structure will not. If you create a view as `'select *'` from one table (never recommended, always use an explicit list of columns), the list of columns in the view will be the list of columns in the table at the time when you create the view and it won't change, even if you later add columns to the table. You can get the description of the columns of a view in the same way as you can get the description of the columns of a table. Views have a life of their own, unlike triggers and indexes. Even if the view refers to a single table, it will survive if you drop the table. It will simply become invalid and querying it will return the error you get when you refer in any query, to a non-existent table.

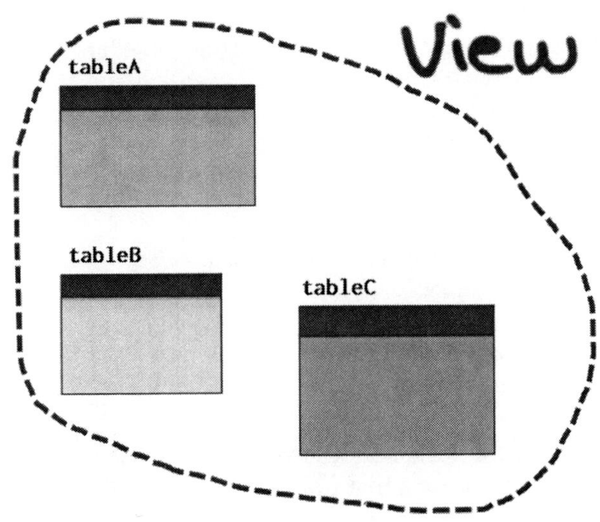

Figure 10.1: Building views over tables

A view is used in queries, exactly as a table, which explains why you can't give a view the same name as an existing table (you would no longer know to what you are referring). It's better to give special names to views (using a *v* prefix as I have done is one possibility among many) so that anyone who reads a query in which a view is used, understands that we have here, not a plain table but a named table expression that may be complex.

NOTE There may be cases when you want views to have names similar to table names. It can happen when a database is undergoing structural changes (for instance when you change some tables to improve their design and make them able to handle cases that had not been foreseen). In that case you may want to give a new name to the redesigned tables and create on them, views bearing the same name and looking the same as the old tables. It allows old queries in programs that haven't been rewritten yet, to run as before - although possibly not as fast.

Unlike a function in a program for which you define explicitly, a list of parameters, the parameters are implicit in a view: they are the rows contained in the tables referenced in the view. If rows are modified in the underlying tables of the view, the result that is displayed changes when you query the view.

NOTE 1 Some products, SQL Server in particular, allow the creation of *parameterized views* which aren't views in the sense I use here but special functions that can return a table (I have given an example of such a function when I created function *get_tags()* in Chapter 8). If you ever see something like

```
select ... from parameterized_view(123)
```

it's usually nothing more than another way of writing something that you could have written as `select ... from regular_view where some_col = 123`. Depending on the query involved, and depending on how the optimizer processes the query, the advantage of the parameterized view is that it may allow you to inject the value deeper into the query but this is a rather advanced discussion...

NOTE 2 Views should not be confused with the *materialized views* available in several DBMS products, which aren't views but tables in which you store snapshots of the result of a query. Those snapshots are usually automatically refreshed at regular intervals such as every two hours or every night and are used for purposes such as pre-computing aggregates that may be slow to obtain on the spot.

If a view respects the two basic conditions that allow the relational theory to work its magic (the existence of columns that uniquely identify one row and no duplicates), then of course you can combine views in queries. You can (which doesn't mean that you should) even build views over views, in the same way as you can create a function that refers to another function that you have created. Properly designed views (views without duplicates) are just an alternative way to look at the same data, as if the database were designed in a different way (hence the name of *view*, suggesting that you are observing the data from a different standpoint). In theory, views are indistinguishable from tables. In practice, reality isn't so rosy.

NOTE For instance, an **order by** can with some DBMS products be added to the query used to define a view; it's a departure from theory and from the fundamental principle that the order of rows shouldn't matter. Fortunately, it's still possible to query from an ordered view and add an **order by** clause that sorts rows in another way.

Strengths and Weaknesses of Views

The fact that views look like tables is both a strength and a weakness. The strength is that views allow you to hide a lot of complexity from programs. Many software development frameworks, for web applications in particular, can easily generate code to query one table. As soon as you have joins it becomes more complicated and many of the automated generation features apply to single tables only. If you need to generate web-reports, rather than coding queries in the program, you can create a view that returns data as you want users to see it and let the generator handle filtering, ordering and display. Views also allow leveraging the skills of the best SQL coders on the team.

The weakness is that views hide complexity from people who will usually learn a bit of SQL soon enough and will try slightly more ambitious queries than `select *` with sometimes calamitous consequences.
Suppose for instance that a view has been created over table **credits** to make its content more user-friendly and that this view uses the *full_name()* function that we have created in Chapter 8:

```
create view vmovie_credits
as select m.title,
          m.year_released,
          case c.credited_as
            when 'A' then 'Actor'
            when 'D' then 'Director'
            else '?'
          end duty,
          full_name(p.first_name, p.surname) name
from movies m
     inner join credits c
          on c.movieid = m.movieid
      inner join people p
          on p.peopleid = c.peopleid
```

NOTE The name of the user-defined function is prefixed by *dbo.* with SQL Server.

When a developer refers to the view, he or she will see something that looks like a table and will be able to run simple queries as if it were a table. The name *vmovie_credits* is of course a hint that we have here a view and not a table but this isn't a detail that you pay attention to when you start to learn SQL and are more concerned by getting the syntax right. A condition on the name that will look perfectly innocent such as

```
where name = 'Humphrey Bogart'
```

will actually mean an ugly

```
where full_name(p.first_name, p.surname) = 'Humphrey Bogart'
```

in which *full_name()* is not only a function but a relatively complex function. Such a filtering condition turns into SQL-fiction, an intelligent use of existing indexes as we have seen in the preceding chapter. If you are not convinced, you can try to use **explain**.

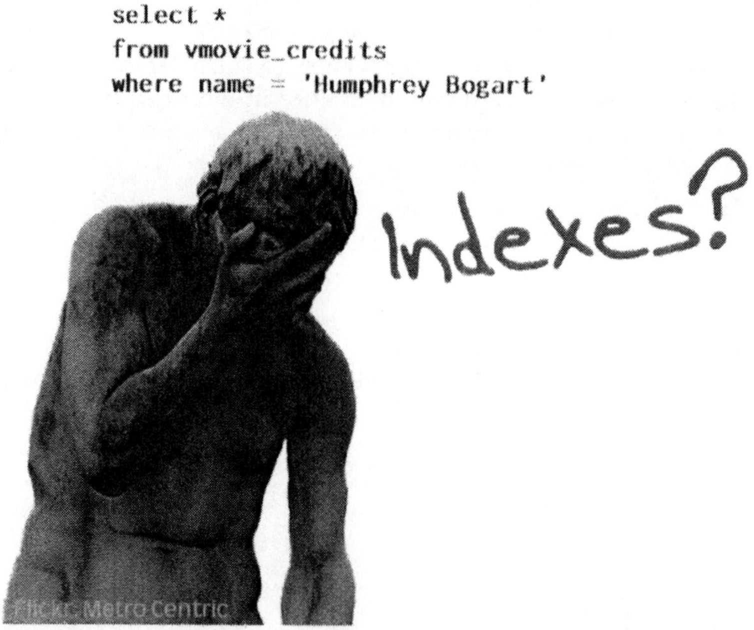

```
select *
from vmovie_credits
where name = 'Humphrey Bogart'
```

Indexes?

Flickr: Metro Centric

Figure 10.2: Applying conditions in views to what looks like a column but is an expression

As views are hardly more than named queries, you cannot create indexes on their columns – the rows they return aren't stored as such, they have no physical address that can be recorded in an index. The only indexes available are those on the underlying tables. In the particular circumstance of a search on a prettified full name, some products would allow you to create an index on function *full_name()* applied to the columns of table *people* because function *full_name()* is deterministic.

NOTE Reminder: *deterministic* means that the same input always produces the same output. Oracle and DB2 require you to state it when you create the function, though - `create function full_name(...) returns ... deterministic ...`

However, such a new index on table *people* is clearly unnecessary: you only need it if you query through the view. Besides, you often encounter a similar problem in views in which dates have been formatted to conform better to local date representation standards - remember that date formatting functions are not deterministic, as changing language settings may, with the same input, change the output.

Any filter applied to columns of a view that aren't straight columns from underlying tables but user-friendly expressions will not (except when function-based indexes have been created) use indexes. It's not necessarily an issue: the view may return few rows or it's just possible that using an index would not be very efficient anyway. Sometimes, however, it hurts, and when it does, it hurts badly.

The potential for performance issues, though, reaches another level when our emboldened young developers, now mastering the **where** clause, discover joins and decide that the country or the age of the director, are also required in the resulting dataset - if they build their queries around the friendly *vmovie_credits* view instead of the unfriendly *credits* table, the same tables that could be referenced only once will appear several times, sometimes explicitly, sometimes hidden in the view, and joins will be performed on apparent columns that actually are expressions.

Another unhappy possibility is that our young programmers find *vmovie_credits* so convenient that when asked to list all the film titles the first thing that jumps to their mind is

```
select distinct title
from vmovie_credits
```

It certainly "works" as far as it returns film titles but even if you omit the fact that the join will screen-out movies for which we have neither director nor actor name, it will perform two joins that are perfectly useless for the result we want, plus just as useless calls to the function that massages people's names, and we would have avoided all this unnecessary work by simply scanning the *movies* table. Perhaps that compared to a query against the table, a query against the view will be 4 or 5 times slower; it may not be that terrible for users, it may still run in a fraction of a second but even if it looks reasonably fast during unitary tests, it means that at peak time we will be able to process 4 or 5 times fewer queries than we might otherwise run on the same machine. We'll also have the same phenomenon of sudden loss of performance that I discussed in the preceding chapter, when queries arrive faster than they can be processed.

The biggest risk is possibly that one day, people will start building views upon views, compounding all the performance issues I have just mentioned until the whole edifice crumbles...

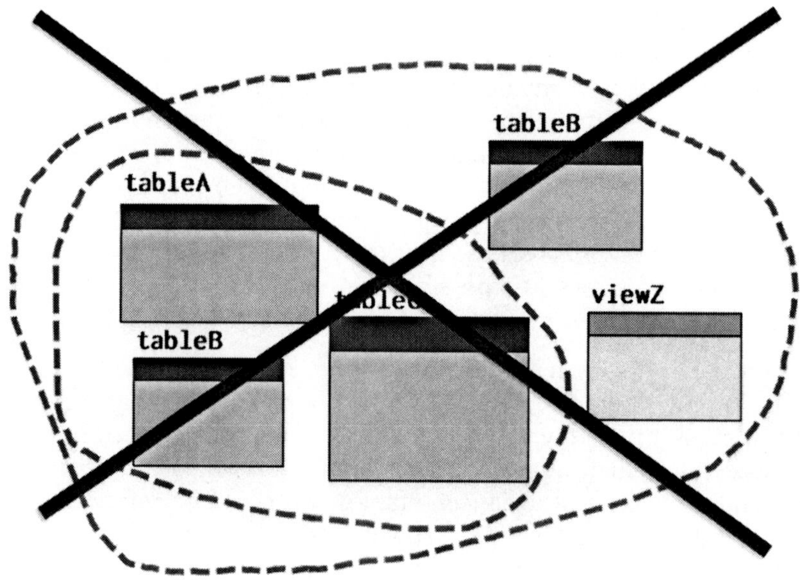

Figure 10.3: You don't want to build views over complex views. Really.

It's an area where it's difficult to give any hard and fast rules but in my opinion, views belong to a phase where you want to display data in a certain way but where you no longer need "data crunching" - or at least, where most data crunching is behind you, not ahead. In any case, resist as much as you can, creating views atop complex views even if it makes creating the final view much easier; by complex view I mean any view that returns the result of functions (including aggregate functions) or is based on a set operator such as **union**. Copy the text of the views that you would like to use as subqueries in **from** clauses, remove ruthlessly everything that isn't needed to obtain the final dataset and you will get something efficient.

Views as they have been defined here are mostly for convenience - convenience of writing simpler queries over views, convenience of maintenance as changing a view will automatically affect all queries that use it. If you make the view more efficient, or change in a view, how data is formatted, for instance replacing a simple concatenation of first name and surname by a call to function **full_name()**, you won't have to change several programs. There is however an area where views are even more useful and it's as security devices. Using views for security is particularly important in environments where users connect with personal accounts, have some relatively free access to the database and are able to issue queries either directly, using an interactive SQL client, or with the help of a reporting or data mining tool.

Security, Rights and Data Organization

Before I show you how views can help make data more secure, I must tell you how DBMS products manage security and how you should usually organize your tables, indexes and procedures when you create a database application.

Connection and Rights

To connect to a database server, you need a database account, which, usually, is either protected by a password or requires that you are already identified by the operating system of your computer (the fact that you have already successfully entered a password to log into the computer is deemed to prove your identity). This is a process known as *authentication*. It's important to understand that with most products database account and system account are different; several people can be connected at once to a database using the same database account and they can sometimes do it from different system accounts.

NOTE DB2 is the exception here: you don't create database accounts in DB2, it relies on existing system accounts.

However, most DBMS products allow us to associate closely, one database account with one operating system.

Connection rights are tightly controlled. You may be allowed to connect to a database server from some but not all machines in the network. Identification by the operating system often demands

- that you are connecting from the same machine where the DBMS software is running,
- and that a relationship exists between the system account (which you use to open a session on the machine) and a database account; this relationship is often derived from similar account names at the operating system level and in the database

NOTE Sometimes an administrator explicitly maps a system account to a database account to which it will be able to connect without a password.

Being able to connect to a database, though, is just the beginning. You need special rights (often called *privileges*) to do more and you have two categories of rights:

- System rights, which broadly correspond to the Data Definition Language (DDL) part of SQL, in other words everything that is linked to creating, altering or dropping objects in the database. Not everyone can create tables; you must have the right to do so. You need an additional, special right to create stored procedures and triggers, which often call stored procedures, also require a special right, independent of both the right of creating tables and the right of creating stored procedures.

  NOTE With all products except MySQL, you don't need any special right to create indexes on tables that you have created. With MySQL, while you can define primary keys and unique constraints when you create tables, and therefore create indexes to implement the constraints, you need a special right to add indexes later.

  System rights are granted by administrators, who create accounts for developers, create accounts that will own the tables used by one application, and create accounts for regular users. They grant rights by connecting to the database through a privileged account, created during the database installation. I won't say any more about system rights, the important thing to know is that if you get an error message saying that you have insufficient privileges, the person who can help you is the database administrator.

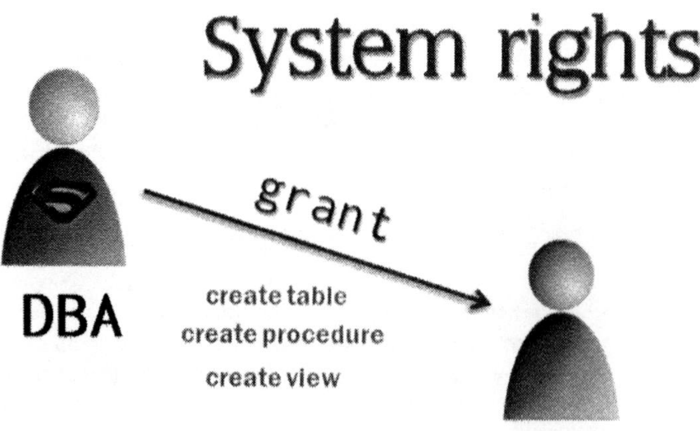

Figure 10.4: Database Administrators grant system rights to users.

- Data rights, also called object rights or *table rights*, correspond to the Data Manipulation Language (DML) part of SQL, **select**, **insert**, **update**, **delete** (to which we can add **merge** that combines **insert** and **update**). When you create tables, you have all rights over them: you can insert rows, update any column, delete any row, as well of course, as select any data from a table that you have created. You can even drop the table if this is your pleasure. Nobody wants to give such wide-ranging powers to all database users but almost everybody wants to share data: if data is located on a database server, it's precisely so that many people can access it. Access it, but in a controlled way. While any identified user on an e-commerce website can create a new order and insert rows in a table to add articles to a "shopping basket", you only want some members of the staff to add new articles for sale, update prices or create deals of the week, and you want nobody to be able to drop tables. To data rights I can add the right to call a procedure, or a function.

NOTE The association of DDL with system rights and of DML with data rights is broadly correct but some system rights, rarely given to someone who isn't a database administrator, allow you to access or modify data in all tables, currently existing or which will be created later. They are blanket privileges.

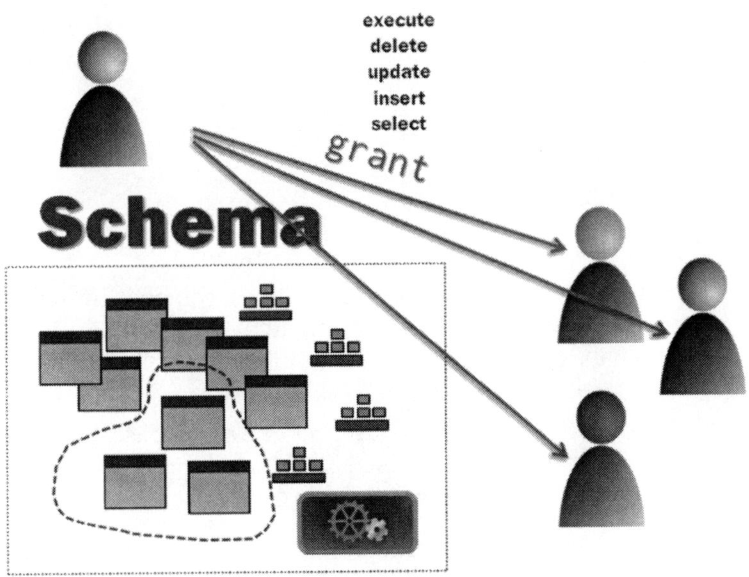

Figure 10.5: Schema owners grant access rights on their tables, views and procedures to other users.

The keyword used in SQL to give rights (whether they are system or data rights) is **grant**. If I am connected to the database as the creator of tables *countries*, *movies*, *people* and *credits* and want to give to someone connected under the database account *john_doe* the right to query table *countries* I'll issue the command

```
grant select on countries to john_doe
```

I can give several rights at once as a comma-separated list:

```
grant select, insert on movies to john_doe;
grant select, insert, delete on credits to john_doe;
grant select, insert, update(died) on people to john_doe;
```

The right to update a table can be restricted, as in the preceding example, to one column between parentheses (or several columns separated by commas). A statement such as

```
grant select, insert, update on people to john_doe
```

would allow *john_doe* to update all of the columns in the table. To allow other users to run your functions or procedures, you grant them the **execute** privilege on your functions or procedures.

NOTE You don't give rights on triggers or indexes – they are inherited from the rights given on tables (remember that triggers and indexes have no independent life, they are automatically dropped when you drop tables). However, if you are using sequences and people need them to insert new rows in tables, you must grant the **select** right on the sequences.

Rights can be taken off at any time by using `revoke ... from` instead of `grant ... to`:

```
revoke delete on credits from john_doe
```

Transmitting Rights

When a user is given a right to access a database object, the right can be passed on by the original receiver of the right to another user on one condition: the initial right must be given with the **with grant option** qualifier:

```
grant select on movies to john_doe with grant option
```

Giving such a privilege would allow user *john_doe* to pass on the right to someone else. This feature is rarely used; it's much simpler and more secure to have only the owner of objects, grant rights on them.

The *john_doe* database account will probably have no other system right than the right to connect to the database; it won't need to create any object in the database, just to query or modify data in tables that already exist. How the person connected as *john_doe* will refer in practice to my tables depends on the DBMS used and how data is organized.

Data Organization

When you write a real-life database application, you don't only think about tables and programs; you also think about how you must organize your tables and everything to help install your application on the computers where it will run, which are usually different from the computers where you developed it. This is especially true if you are creating a software package that you want to sell to many companies. Most often, you cannot demand a dedicated machine to host your dedicated database server that will only manage your application. Your customers may already have machines, database servers, disks, and staff monitoring everything, ensuring backups, and ready to solve incidents when they occur. You must fit in and organize your data in a way that makes it reasonably easy to plug your application into an existing database server running the same DBMS software that you have been using (you won't make SQL Server run an application written for Oracle ...)

All products broadly agree that the set of database objects that are required by one application, tables, views, indexes, procedures and functions, possibly sequences and triggers, should be called a *schema*. Objects are created within a schema, which has a name, and table names are unique within the schema (you can have identically named tables as long as they belong to different schemas). Generally speaking, whenever a user who has been granted the right to access a table wants to refer to this table, he or she will do it by prefixing the table name by the schema name and a dot. For instance, if I have initially created table *movies* in a schema called *moviedb*, the user connected as *john_doe* and who has been granted the right to select from table *movies*, will write queries such as

```
select title, year_released
from moviedb.movies
where country = 'jp'
```

Specifying the schema isn't necessarily something that you want to do in your application, for several reasons:

- Prefixing tables by schema names in SQL statements is tedious (this isn't a very good reason but it's a practical one).
- There is always a risk, when designing a new application for sale, of assigning a schema name that will conflict with an existing schema name (most software companies name their schemas after themselves for this reason); if you have to change the schema name, you'd rather not rewrite all the SQL statements.
- You may want to use the same application against different schemas. A case commonly encountered, is when you install a new application and want to train people on using it. Obtaining a dedicated database server for training isn't easy. People usually set up a schema dedicated to training, on either a production database server or a database server used for testing. This schema

> will be populated with a small sample of data representative of the production database, without any confidential information. If your application refers to the schema in each and every statement, there will be no way to switch to alternative data for training.

All products provide ways either to change the default schema of a user or to create aliases replacing the full, schema-qualified, name of a table.

The exact, practical meaning of *schema* varies with each DBMS product and you'll find details about each of the products I mention in Appendix A. What is important to know, is that a schema is always owned by a database account and that this database account can give other accounts, the rights to access or modify the tables in the schema, or run the stored procedures in the schema. In practice, if there is a large number of database accounts, database administrators create groups of rights called *roles*, which in turn are granted to database accounts (or other roles). You can create roles very simply, for instance with Oracle, DB2 or Postgres:

```
create role moviedb_user
```

Or, with SQL Server (7 and above)

```
sp_addapprole 'moviedb_user'
```

Several products also allow granting of privileges to **public**, a name that represents all users; existing accounts as well as accounts that will be created in the future.

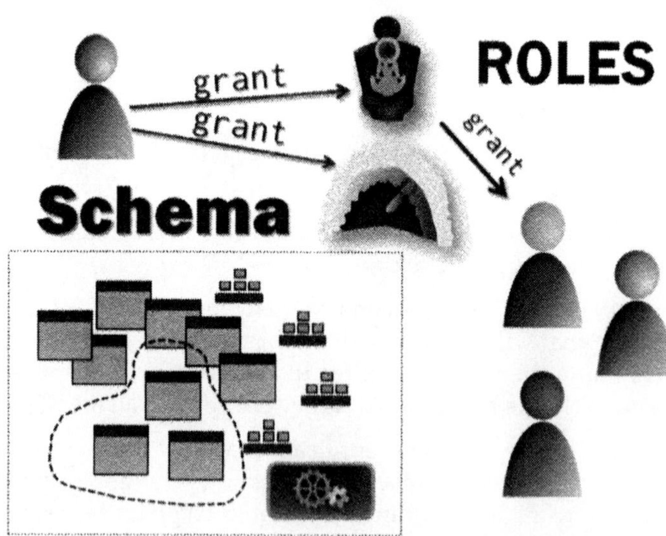

Figure 10.6: With large numbers of users you grant privileges to roles, and then you grant roles to users.

Views and Security

It's time, after having presented schemas and how accounts are given access to data, to discuss how views contribute to security. Although the role of views as the equivalent of functions, short-hand notation for complex queries, is no doubt important, they also play an essential part in ensuring data access control.

Excluding Columns from what Users Can See

I told you that the right to update columns in a table can be limited to certain columns. While **insert** and **delete** necessarily affect a full row in a table, limiting **select** to only some columns, is a legitimate requirement; you often find in the same table, data of varying degrees of confidentiality. Some personal information or data such as credit card numbers is highly sensitive. Let's say that we consider that the year of birth in table *people*, is a somewhat sensitive piece of data and that we don't want to show it to everybody. The **grant** command doesn't allow you to give a **select** right on only some columns. Rather, what you are going to do is create a view:

```
create view vpeople
as select peopleid,
          first_name,
          surname
from people
```

and then, if the *john_doe* account should only have a partial access to data available in table *people*:

```
grant select on vpeople to john_doe
```

By granting the right to query a view instead of the underlying table, you effectively limit what users can see.

Figure 10.7: Granting the right to select from views is the way to hide columns from tables.

NOTE Beware that if you aren't the owner of a table but were only granted the right to select from it, you cannot create a view on that table and grant the right to select from the view to someone else; if that were the case, there would be a security breach because the one who gave you the right to access the table may not want anyone else to access the data. You can create a view, which you own, and grant access to this view to someone else only if you own the base tables or if the right to access them has been given to you **with grant option**.

This method provides a lot of flexibility; you can for instance decide that you only want to hide the year of birth for people who are still alive (a common rule in genealogical databases). All you need to do is to define the view differently:

```
create view vpeople
as select peopleid,
          first_name,
          surname,
          case
            when died is not null then born
            else null
          end as born,
          died
from people
```

This view will return null instead of the value in *born* when the person is recorded as alive.

Excluding Rows from what Users Can See

As any query (preferably one that doesn't return duplicate rows) can be used to create a view, we can naturally exclude rows with a **where** condition as well as exclude columns. What makes filtering in a view really interesting is that it's possible to create a single view that doesn't show the same rows to all users.

All DBMS products implement functions that are usually classified under 'information functions', 'security functions', or 'other functions' in the documentation (for DB2 you need to look under 'Special Registers'). I am using here "function" very loosely; sometimes the information is available through a function call, sometimes it's a special variable, sometimes a pseudo-column.

NOTE A pseudo-column is simply something that looks like a column in a query but is in fact, a kind of function that takes no parameters and is called without parentheses. With Oracle for instance you can use a pseudo-column such as **rownum** (which numbers rows as they are returned) in any query.

The syntax may vary slightly between products but what you get is the same. One particularly notable function returns the name under which the user is connected – I mentioned it briefly in Chapter 8 when discussing triggers, as a way to audit user actions. In an environment where all database users have their own account, this function allows us to show selectively, some rows to some users and other rows to other users, when everybody is querying the same view.

Suppose that we only want to display to users, films that were produced on one continent - preferably their continent.

> **NOTE** In practice filtering would sooner be applied for instance to user age and movie rating, so that grandmothers remain blissfully unaware of the films watched by their teenage grandchildren.

I need an additional table that I am going to call *user_scope* and that contains two columns, a username (which is supposed to match a database account name) and the name of one continent; this also allows me, if needed, to give access to several continents, to one user.
Let's say that this table contains the following data:

```
Username     Continent
------------ ------------
HUIZHONG     ASIA
PAVEL        EUROPE
IBRAHIM      AFRICA
AMINATA      AFRICA
MICHAEL      EUROPE
JUAN_CARLOS  AMERICA
SANDEEP      ASIA
PATRICIA     AMERICA
PATRICIA     EUROPE
```

I can take the view I have created at the beginning of this chapter:

```
create view vmovies
as select m.movieid,
          m.title,
          m.year_released,
          c.country_name
   from movies m
        inner join countries c
           on c.country_code = m.country
```

and recreate it so as to show only the films that the currently connected user can (or want to) see:

```
create or replace view vmovies      ① Redefine the view
as select m.movieid,
          m.title,
          m.year_released,
          c.country_name
   from movies m
        inner join countries c
           on c.country_code = m.country
```

```
        inner join user_scope u
           on u.continent = c.continent
    where u.username = user         ② Filter on the account
```

I have used here something that I haven't used so far, the ① **create or replace** construct which is commonly used for views and stored functions and procedures; it simply redefines an existing object. If I had dropped and recreated the view, all the rights granted on the view would have been lost; with **create or replace** they are preserved. There is no **create or replace** with SQL Server, use **alter view** instead. I refer to a kind of pseudo-column ② **user** that is actually a very special parameter-less function returning the database account to which you are currently connected. With SQL Server you should rather use **system_user**; **user** also exists but returns the schema name. With MySQL, you must refer to **user()** and the function also returns the name of the user's computer, which should be stripped for the comparison.

The amount of information that you can retrieve about a connected user varies; you can always access the name of the account and the name (or address) of the computer from which the user is connected. I invite you to check the documentation of your favorite DBMS to find out everything that it offers. I must however mention function **sys_context()** in Oracle, which may not immediately attract your attention in the documentation. It takes two parameters, the first one will be 'USERENV' and the second one, the name of the piece of information that you want to obtain – there is a large collection of values you can obtain, from the classic account or computer names to the edition of the database that is running or how you were authenticated.

You can now see how you can combine views and privileges to guarantee the privacy of data: instead of granting to users the **select** privilege on table *movies* (or whatever), you grant them **select** on views, which only show them what you want them to see. And they will only be able to see their own data even if they use an SQL client or a spreadsheet to access the database.

Basing access controls on views that refer to the name of the database account supposes that, either all users have their own private account or that at least all users aren't connected under the same database account. In the preceding example, we could imagine having a database account called EUROPEAN_USER systematically used whenever someone from Europe wants to connect to the database. Personal database accounts are much used in the corporate world, especially when data is highly confidential and when there is both a need to limit what users can see and to audit who did what.

NOTE When sharing accounts means sharing passwords, you can be sure that the wrong person will know the password sooner or later. The only way to ensure security with passwords is through personal passwords that are checked for strength and regularly changed.

When you connect to a website you connect to a special server (an HTTP server), which in turn connects to the database server, using usually, a single database account for all HTTP requests and relays queries that are generated by web interactions. It would of course be possible, to connect people to different database accounts based on their geographical location, which can be guessed rather precisely. As users have no direct access to the database and filtering can safely be applied in the queries issued by the HTTP server, the use of views as a security device, is however less interesting with web applications than their use as an object that can be readily mapped to a web page.

NOTE It is possible to have session-specific views, even when everybody is connected to the database through the same account, by assigning before running a query, values to session variables (MySQL, DB2, SQL Server) or what is called a *context*, which is just another name for something very similar (Oracle, SQL Server), or to a temporary table automatically dropped at the end of the session (PostgreSQL) and by then referring to this session-specific data in a view. The problem is that views, which are static objects in the database, then depend on dynamic operations (suitable assignments before querying the view) independent from what the database contains. I don't find such a dependency very clean but it can sometimes save the day.

Both views-as-convenience-device and views-as-security-device raise an interesting question: if views are convenient for looking at data, what about changing data? What about granting, not only the right to **select** from a view but also to **insert**, **update** or **delete** by referencing the view instead of the base tables?

Views and Updates

Updating a view means nothing more than updating the underlying tables. There are cases when some changes are impossible through a view:

- If a view is built upon a single table and excludes mandatory columns that have no default value, it is impossible to insert a row by only referring to the view. For instance, if a view of the *people* table excludes the mandatory *born* column, you cannot insert rows into the view and expect to retrieve them in *people*. It can only fail.
- A view that includes an aggregate, for instance a view that would return the number of movies per country, is also a case where any chances of changing meaningfully the underlying data are severely impaired - inserting a new country with a new film count straight through the view would be impossible, as well as updating the aggregate value. Aggregates lose information and you need the finer grain of detail to change tables.
- If a view includes a column that is the result of a computation or of a function call, you may not be able to reconstruct the original data from which was derived what the view shows. Suppose that a view on table *people* uses

> function *full_name()* of Chapter 8 to display first name and surname as a single column. How could we insert *Tommy Lee Jones* into such a column? There is no way for the SQL engine to decide whether *Tommy Lee* should be inserted into the *first_name* column and *Jones* into the *surname* column (as it should) or whether *Tommy* should be inserted into *first_name* and *Lee Jones* in *surname*.

Even with a view that presents a relatively unaltered vision of the original columns, the problem of updates isn't a simple one. Let's consider again the view that simply substitutes the actual country name for the country code in table *movies*:

```
create view vmovies
as select m.movieid,
          m.title,
          m.year_released,
          c.country_name
   from movies m
        inner join countries c
          on c.country_code = m.country
```

Let's now suppose that the Austrian documentary *We Feed the World* has been entered into table *movies* and that the person who inserted it, possibly confused by the original English title, entered as country code *au*, the code for Australia, instead of the correct *at*, the code for Austria. Another person, who only has access to the view, notices the mistake and wants to correct it, trying to update the view to replace, in the *country_name* column, Australia by Austria. But if the country name is actually pulled from table *countries*, it's not table *countries* that you want to modify - you don't want to rename Australia into Austria. What you really want to do is to change the country code, which isn't shown in the view, in table *movies*. All of this is reasonably easy to understand for a human being, much less so for an SQL engine.

Changing the country

```
create view vmovies
as select m.movieid,
          m.title,
          m.year_released,
          c.country_name     <- NOT this
   from movies m
        inner join countries c
          on c.country_code = m.country
                                 ^ THIS
```

Figure 10.8: Changing a value in a view may not be what it appears.

At the time of writing, I know of no DBMS that effects the country code change that a human being could perform.

The preceding examples illustrate a number of issues that make updating views a tightrope walking exercise. When they have to cope with view updating, you can class the DBMS products into three categories:

- The shy, which refuse to change data through views (SQLite)
- The cautious, which allow changing of views only if they satisfy a number of requirements (no join or only join on the primary key columns, no **distinct**, no aggregation) (Oracle, DB2, PostgreSQL, with some degrees of variation in tolerance)
- The bold, which attempt whatever they can, even if it's not necessarily what was initially intended (SQL Server)

NOTE By "changing data" I mean inserting or deleting rows as well as updating them.

If you try to change Australia into Austria for one particular film by updating view *vmovies* as I have defined it, the cautious will notice something fishy and generate an error, the bold will try to update the country name in table *countries* – which will fail because of the unique constraint on country names. Without the unique constraint on the country name, all Australian films would appear as Austrian (however, country codes would remain untouched and reversing the change would be easy but you could expect a moment of panic).

Direct View Change

In practice it often happens that the purpose of views is simply to hide columns and rows from some users, without any complicated transformation. If the view can be mapped to one table, the rules to make it updatable are relatively simple:

- No mandatory column should be omitted in the view, unless it has a default value.
- With cautious products, rows should be filtered through simple conditions or subqueries.

This last condition is an interesting one. I hope you remember that in Chapter 4 I showed you that joins and subqueries in the **where** clause, could be used equally in queries. However, I mentioned at the end of the chapter that in some cases, subqueries had to be used instead of a join, and I can now illustrate such a case.

I'm going to create a view that shows exactly the same columns as table *movies* but restricts the rows to the films produced in continents associated in table *user_scope* with the current user (note that I am returning the country code here, and no longer the country name). Here is the creation of the view with Oracle:

```
create or replace view vmy_movies
as select m.movieid,
          m.title,
          m.year_released,
          m.country
   from movies m
        inner join countries c
           on c.country_code = m.country
        inner join user_scope u
           on u.continent = c.continent
   where u.username = user
```

I have limited the rows that my database account can see, to films from Asia and Oceania. If I try to insert a new row in table *movies* across view *vmy_movies*, for instance:

```
insert into vmy_movies(movieid, title, year_released, country)
values (movies_seq.nextval, 'In the Mood for Love', 2000, 'hk')
```

I get the following error:

```
insert into vmy_movies(movieid, title, year_released, country)
                                *
ERROR at line 1:
ORA-01779: cannot modify a column which maps to a non key-preserved table
```

(One of those legendary head-scratchy Oracle error messages - in plain English Oracle has noticed that for one table in the join several rows can match one row in the other table, and it doesn't like it.)
But if I rewrite my view as follows, with a query that is strictly equivalent to the previous one:

```
create or replace view vmy_movies
as select m.movieid,
          m.title,
          m.year_released,
          m.country
   from movies m
   where m.country in
     (select c.country_code
      from countries c
           inner join user_scope u
              on u.continent = c.continent
      where u.username = user)
```

then my insert is successful - simply because the SQL engine no longer sees any join. With SQL Server (assuming you replace **user** by **system_user** in the view) the insert will be successful with both ways of writing the view.

While we can in some cases, change data through views, there remains one problem. Even if I am connected to the database with an account that can only see films from Asia and Oceania through *vmy_movies*, nothing prevents me from inserting an American or French film - which I won't be able to see afterwards. As long as I don't violate any unique or foreign key constraint, there will be nothing to prevent such an illogical operation to succeed.

We need therefore a new, special constraint that guarantees that the view is, for a user, a "closed world" - that if I am only able to see films from Asia and Oceania, then I am allowed to insert Chinese, Japanese, Korean, Indian films, or to change a country code from New Zealand's *nz* to Australia's *au* or the reverse but not to perform a data modification that would make a film immediately disappear from what I see. This special constraint for views, supported by most DBMS products, is called **check option** and ensures that we aren't allowed to apply, through the view, any change that would make rows vanish from the view. The constraint is added at the end of the view definition:

```
create or replace view vmy_movies
as select m.movieid,
          m.title,
          m.year_released,
          m.country
   from movies m
   where m.country in
     (select c.country_code
      from countries c
           inner join user_scope u
              on u.continent = c.continent
      where u.username = user)
with check option
```

Of course, if an Austrian movie was wrongly created as Australian, only someone operating on the base tables or allowed to see both Australian and Austrian films will be allowed to correct the mistake.

Change through Procedures

Views with subqueries and **check option** solve some of the problems but not all of them. If you remember, when I was returning not the country code but the country name retrieved by a join with table *countries*, not only were Oracle and DB2 preventing me from changing the country name but SQL Server, which was allowing it, was attempting a wrong operation.

And yet, the change isn't very complicated; when I type

```
update vmovies
set country_name = 'Austria'
where title = 'We Feed the World'
```

I actually mean nothing worse than

```
update movies
set country = (select country_code
               from countries
               where country_name = 'Austria')
where title = 'We Feed the World'
```

There is a simple solution: create three procedures, one for insertion, one for update and one for deletion, which take as parameters, the columns that appear in the view. These procedures will operate on the underlying tables, executing statements that correspond to what should really take place. When people fill a form on screen, the program that receives the data when they click on the *submit* button (or whatever it is called), will call these procedures instead of directly running SQL statements. Access rights with procedures are similar to access rights with views: when you create a view, you can grant the right to query the view, to someone who isn't allowed to query from the tables that appear in the view definition. You can write a procedure that inserts into tables, deletes rows from them, updates them, and grant the right to execute this procedure to someone who isn't even allowed to query the tables modified by the procedure. As I have said earlier in this chapter, granting the right to execute a procedure is as easy as granting the right to select from a table:

```
grant execute on proc_insert_movie to john_doe
```

Not only do procedures guarantee that complex business processes are properly applied but they can also be the only means that users have to change the tables.

Fake Direct View Change

Ensuring security (where security is needed) by only granting the right to query data through views and to change it through stored procedures, can satisfy the most stringent confidentiality requirements but, depending on the programs used to access your database (the topic of the next chapter), it may not be the most convenient. Most programming languages make calling a stored procedure as easy as executing an **insert** or an **update** statement but many programmers use development environments that automatically churn out for them, forms for querying, inserting, updating and deleting data. The development environments generate **insert**, **update**, and **delete** statements, not calls to stored procedures. It's possible to replace manually, code that was generated by something else; it's also possible with most DBMS products (MySQL is the exception) to keep untouched, what tools generate and automatically substitute for an **insert**, **update**, or **delete** statement applied to a view, a call to the procedure that changes the underlying tables independently from application-building tools.

This substitution is performed by a special type of trigger that can be applied to views and called an **instead of** trigger (when you create the trigger, the words **instead of** replace **before** or **after**.)

NOTE: Although SQLite doesn't support stored procedures, it supports **instead of** triggers and they are the only way to make a SQLite view writable.

Here is a SQL Server example; I remind you that with SQL Server, triggers populate two pseudo tables called **deleted** and **inserted**, containing respectively, rows that were deleted and inserted by the statement (updates are considered like a **delete** followed by an **insert**):

```
create trigger vmovies_trg
on vmovies
instead of insert, update, delete      ← Note the instead of
as
begin
  declare @cnt int;
  set @cnt = (select count(*)          ① Count how many rows were updated
              from inserted i
                   inner join deleted d
                      on i.movieid = d.movieid);
  if (@cnt > 0)
  begin
    update movies
    set title = i.title,
        year_released = i.year_released,
        country = c.country_code
    from inserted i                    ② Join inserted and deleted (plus countries)
         inner join countries c
         on c.country_name = i.country
         inner join deleted d
         on d.movieid = i.movieid
    where i.movieid = movies.movieid;
    if @@rowcount != @cnt              ③ Anticipate what can go wrong
    begin
      raiserror(N'Country not found in reference table', 15, 1);
    end;
  end;
  delete from movies                   ④ True deletes
  where movieid in
    (select movieid from deleted
     except
     select movieid from inserted);
  set @cnt = (select count(*)          ⑤ Check if there are true inserts
              from inserted i
                   left outer join movies m
                      on m.movieid = i.movieid
              where m.movieid is null);
  if (@cnt > 0)
  begin
    insert into movies(title, year_released, country)
    select i.title, i.year_released, c.country_code
    from inserted i
         inner join countries c
         on c.country_name = i.country
    where i.movieid not in (select movieid from movies);
```

```
      if @@rowcount != @cnt              ← Handle errors
      begin
        raiserror(N'Country not found in reference table', 15, 1);
      end;
    end;
  end;
```

Inserts and updates can fail if you enter the name of a country that doesn't exist in table *countries*. The trigger starts with updates and checks ① how many rows will be updated. For updates you must be careful to check that you only affect rows that are both in pseudo tables **inserted** and **deleted** ②. If the number of changed rows is less than the number of rows to be updated ③ the only possible reason is that one (or more) of the updated countries didn't exist, and we raise an error. For true deletes ④ we cannot have any foreign key issue, we just need to be careful not to delete rows that were actually updated. For inserts, we need, as for updates, to check how many rows ⑤ are supposed to be inserted and to raise an error if our expectations aren't met.

NOTE **instead of** triggers are incompatible with **check option** in SQL Server. As far as they replace (and enhance) **check option**, it's not a real limitation.

Needless to say, if a view loses some information from the base tables (aggregates, and so on), no procedure or trigger magic will in general allow you to create missing data out of thin air. However, when views are merely a more user-friendly representation of data as is the case with view *vmovies* here or in view *vmovie_credits* at the beginning of this chapter, at least some partial data update can be effected through views, by users who have no access to the underlying tables.

I consider a combination of views and stored procedures for changes, to be a cleaner solution than **instead of** triggers; **instead of** triggers can be abused and there is something uncomfortable in the thought of seeing a vehicle head to the right when you turn the steering-wheel to the left because a different action was substituted for what you were doing. Besides, while triggers on views are quite acceptable in an interactive usage (users manually entering data in a form), they nevertheless slow down operations, to a point that can be extremely harmful to massive loads. **Instead of** triggers have to be used discerningly and as I have already said, their main (and important) benefit is that they allow us to take full advantage of the SQL-generating capacities of a development tool, when a single view can be associated with a screen or a web page.

I should add that what I said about triggers in general remains true: software developers have a notorious dislike of documenting what they do and when the original culprits have left the scene of the crime, stealth operations can make diagnosing malfunctions rather difficult. There is however a place we can look for information about triggers (and actually everything about the database), which also happens to be a perfect illustration of views: the data dictionary.

The Data Dictionary

In this book we have been dealing with films, people, and the association of people with films. When we create database objects, the DBMS has to deal with tables, columns, constraints, triggers, indexes and to keep track of associations between them. All this data about the structure of our database (usually called *meta-data*) is also stored in tables, system tables that constitute the *data dictionary* (sometimes called *catalog*, or *system catalog*). Each data definition language statement (**create**, **alter**, **drop**, to which we can add other commands such as **grant** or **revoke**) actually translates into **insert**, **update** and **delete** statements applied to system tables. Needless to say, you should NEVER EVER operate against system tables directly but always do it using the data definition language, as you could completely corrupt your database otherwise.

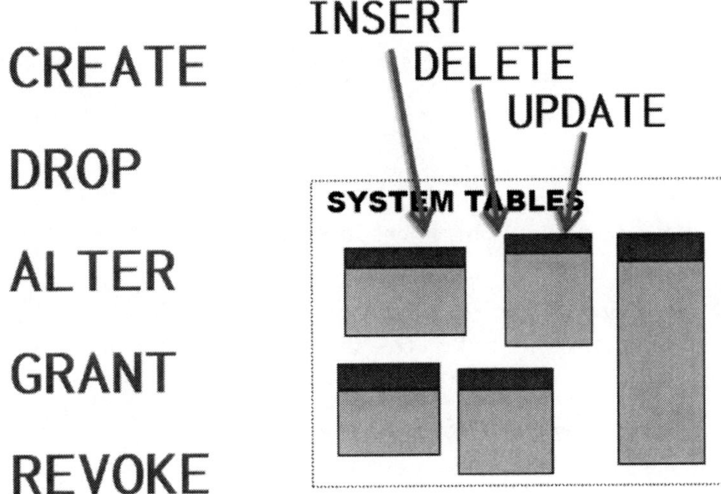

Figure 10.9: Data definition statements translate behind the scenes into data manipulation statements on system tables.

The data dictionary that is accessible to users is a set of views that, thanks to functions returning the current user's identity, only show the objects created by the user, or on which the user has been granted some rights. We can query these views using regular SQL statements. This self-describing feature of database management systems was an early requirement of Ted Codd and is very handy - you have already used it without even knowing it.

The humble **describe** (or equivalent) command to show the name and data type of each column in a table, is nothing more than a data dictionary query in disguise. Most database tools, such as SQL Server Management Studio in Figure 10.10 or phpMyAdmin allow you to browse the definitions of tables and see the names and types of all columns without having to run a **select ***.

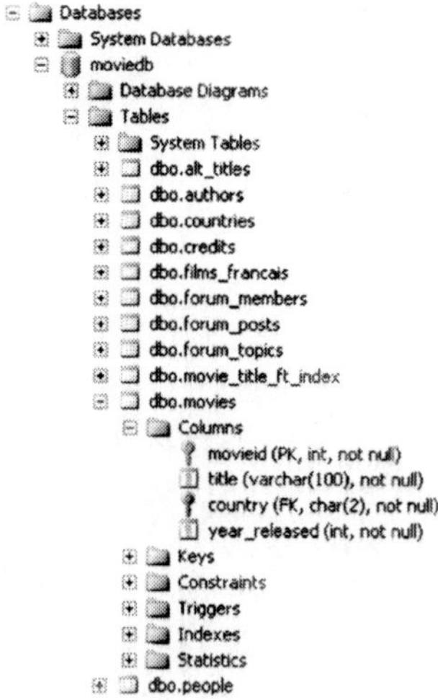

Figure 10.10: How SQL Server Management Studio displays data dictionary information

Dictionary views also let you see which columns are indexed and in what order, when the index is a composite index. This is of course invaluable information when you write a query.

The Data Dictionary in the Different Products

As usual, while the data dictionary contains at least the same fundamental information in all products, its implementation varies significantly from DBMS to DBMS.

SQL Server, MySQL, and PostgreSQL

SQL Server, MySQL, and PostgreSQL all use a special schema called *information_schema* to present data about tables, views and so on (meta-data) to users. Because products have a different definition of "schema" and of "database" (see Appendix A), with MySQL *information_schema* describes meta-data for all databases managed by the server; while with SQL Server and PostgreSQL, you have one *information_schema* within each database.

The views in *information_schema* are just the tip of the iceberg. For instance, there is a view called *information_schema.tables* that lists the tables and the views in the database with minimal information. It only contains, in SQL Server, the four "standard" columns, *table_catalog* (for SQL Server, the database where the table resides), *table_schema*, *table_name* and *table_type* (which can be VIEW). The PostgreSQL version contains these columns plus twice as many that are specific to PostgreSQL, and the MySQL version contains an even more copious number of specific columns than PostgreSQL; however, with MySQL *table_catalog* is null and the database name is in *table_schema*.

In fact, SQL Server also has views such as *sys.tables* and *sys.views* that are referred to as *object catalog views* and which contain much more internal information than *information_schema*; in the same way, you have in PostgreSQL *pg_class*, *pg_tables*, *pg_views* and all their family that can provide much more information than you would normally dream (or perhaps nightmare) of. You can say that you have with SQL Server and PostgreSQL, two levels of data dictionary: a relatively user-friendly *information_schema* that describes the database from a data organization point of view and is of interest to developers, and a second level with more details about physical implementation, to quench the thirst for information of database administrators. In MySQL both levels are grouped in an extended *information_schema*.

Unfortunately, the limits between the various levels of data dictionary aren't always as clear cut as I have presented them above. Both PostgreSQL and MySQL have a view named *information_schema.triggers*; this view is conspicuously absent from SQL Server 2012 or earlier versions, for instance (but there is a *sys.triggers*). Worse, there is neither in SQL Server nor in PostgreSQL, an *information_schema* view showing indexes that aren't associated with constraints - and in MySQL you have to look for this information in a view called *statistics*, which may not be what you would have thought of. What you will always find in *information_schema* is mostly data about tables, views, columns, constraints and stored procedures - there is much interesting data in *information_schema*, but not necessarily everything you want. Rather than list the tables, I'm going to give you in the next sections (and in the exercises at the end of the chapter) a handful of examples showing what you can get from *information_schema* - or elsewhere. These examples and the exercises will use the most important data dictionary views.

DB2

DB2 has a data dictionary for every taste. The "native" DB2 data dictionary isn't in a schema named *information_schema* but in a schema named *syscat*, in which names (views and columns) are similar, although not identical, to what you can find in *information_schema* in other products. You can get the list of all *syscat* views by querying *syscat.tables*:

```
select tabname
from syscat.tables
where tabschema='SYSCAT'
order by tabname
```

What is *table_name* elsewhere is *tabname* in the DB2 catalog (*catalog* is used preferably to *data dictionary* in DB2) and *table_schema* becomes *tabschema*, but the translation is easy. Don't be overwhelmed by the long list of views: most of your needs will probably be satisfied by fewer than ten of them.

However, there is also a schema named *sysibm* in which view and column names are equivalent to what you find in *information_schema* in MySQL, PostgreSQL or SQL Server; and you also find in DB2 a schema named *sysibmadm* in which views are similarly named as in Oracle (which follows) - with DB2 prefixing the name of views with the name of the schema is not necessary for views in *sysibmadm*. Remember that views are just alternative sights of the same data, and DB2 exploits this characteristic.

Oracle

Oracle presents a vision of the data dictionary that is significantly different from the other products, DB2 excepted, but presents similar information. Even if the views are in the *sys* schema, you don't need to prefix the view names by *sys.* as the Oracle installation creates aliases (Oracle calls then *synonyms*) for all of them. Most views are declined in three versions; for instance the list of tables (which doesn't include views) is available from three different views:

- *dba_tables*, which as the name implies is for database administrators and lists all the tables that the database contains,
- *all_tables*, which lists the tables owned by the currently connected user, plus the tables on which some rights have been granted to the currently connected user, directly or through roles, plus the tables that everybody is allowed to see,
- *user_tables*, which only lists the tables created by the currently connected user (the table owner being implicit, it doesn't appear in this view).

The full list of data dictionary views is available from a view called *dictionary*. If the list of views is impressive in DB2, it's frankly scary with Oracle - there are more than 350 *user_...* views alone. Once again, in practice only a handful of them are regularly used, and some examples follow that will introduce them to you.

SQLite

If there is one area where SQLite is really up to its name, it's the data dictionary: with SQLite the data dictionary is limited to a single view called *sqlite_master*, which contains one row for each object in the datafile, its type (table, view, trigger, index), its name, the table it relates to (only meaningful for indexes and triggers), an indication to its location in the file and the full statement used to create it. There is no view, for instance, to query the columns of a particular table as in all the other products. There is, however, a command called **pragma** to return information in a tabular format; for instance

```
pragma table_info(movies)
```

will display something like

```
cid  name          type          notnull dflt_value pk
0    movieid       integer             1             1
1    title         varchar(100)        1             0
2    country       char(2)             1             0
3    year_released int                 1             0
```

Similar **pragma** commands exist to return information about indexes or constraints, among other things. The only major annoyance is that while these **pragma** commands display what looks like the result of a **select** statement, they aren't **select** statements; there is no way to filter with a **where** condition nor join the result of two **pragma** commands. You can do something with them, only if you are ready to program with a programming language other than SQL. You can get the list of indexes or triggers associated with a table by querying *sqlite_master* but that's about the most sophisticated queries you can do. I'll therefore forget about SQLite in what follows.

Using the Data Dictionary

In practice, people query the data dictionary for two purposes:

- **Gathering information**. Most people use graphical tools to get a description of the database, and graphical tools query the data dictionary for you. However, sometimes you have no graphical tool available, sometimes the graphical tool is good for interactive work but not for generating documentation for a project, and sometimes graphical tools don't display what you want to see. In all cases, knowing how to manage your way through data dictionary views is a useful skill to have.
- **Generating SQL statements**. Statement generation is particularly valuable for database administrators but can be useful to most developers as well. Very often, you have to execute a large number of DDL statements such as **create**, **drop**, **alter** or **grant** as a part of migrations, upgrades, or installations. Either you painfully write them all, one by one in a script, with the risk of forgetting something and the pending liability of maintaining the script when something changes in the future, or you use data dictionary queries to generate the script.

I am going to give you examples of both cases.

Gathering Information - Constraints

If when you have one table, for instance *movies*, finding which tables it references through foreign keys is usually easy, finding the reverse information - which are the tables that reference *movies* - is, in the best case harder and sometimes impossible to obtain from user-friendly graphical tools. Yet this is important information to have because some data reorganization operations require the switching of foreign key references from an old table to a new table, then dropping the old table. You need to find which tables reference the old table, to make them refer to the new table instead. You can obtain the list of tables from the data dictionary.

With SQL Server, MySQL, PostgreSQL and DB2 you can get the information about foreign keys from two views in *information_schema* (*sysibm* for DB2).

- The first view is *information_schema.table_constraints* that associates tables, identified by the pair (*table_schema, table_name*) with constraints, which are identified by (*constraint_schema, constraint_name*) and qualified by a type (PRIMARY, UNIQUE, FOREIGN KEY, ...)

> NOTE There are also columns in the *information_schema.table_constraints* view for *table_catalog* and *constraint_catalog* but they are not very meaningful because you cannot have referential integrity constraints between tables belonging to different catalogs.

- The second view is *information_schema.referential_constraints* that is associated with a foreign key constraint identified by (*constraint_schema, constraint_name*) either a primary key or a unique constraint identified by (*unique_constraint_schema, unique_constraint_name*).

> NOTE The MySQL version of *information_schema.referential_constraints* includes both the table name and the name of the referenced table (without any indication of schema) but this information is absent from this view for SQL Server, PostgreSQL, and DB2.

With MySQL you can get all the dependencies between tables from *information_schema.referential_constraints* alone. For the other products, you need to join this view twice to *information_schema.table_constraints* to obtain the name of the table for which the foreign key is defined and the name of the table that it references.

For instance with SQL Server you can write something such as

```
select pk.table_schema+'.'+pk.table_name table_name,          } SQL Server specific
       fk.table_schema+'.'+fk.table_name referenced_by        } concatenation
from (select unique_constraint_name    pk_name,
             unique_constraint_catalog pk_cat,
             unique_constraint_schema  pk_schema,
             constraint_catalog        fk_cat,
             constraint_schema         fk_schema,
             constraint_name           fk_name
      from information_schema.referential_constraints
      where unique_constraint_catalog = db_name()) r
                 ↑ ① Restriction to the current schema or database
```

```
    inner join information_schema.constraint_table_usage pk
      on pk.constraint_catalog = r.pk_cat        ② Not for MySQL!
     and pk.constraint_schema = r.pk_schema
     and pk.constraint_name = r.pk_name
    inner join information_schema.constraint_table_usage fk
      on fk.constraint_catalog = r.fk_cat        ② Not for MySQL!
     and fk.constraint_schema = r.fk_schema
     and fk.constraint_name = r.fk_name
order by table_name, referenced_by
```

I am limiting my query to tables in the current database ①; how I refer to the current database depends on the product; **db_name()** with SQL Server, **current server** with DB2, **current_database()** with PostgreSQL. For MySQL *catalog* columns is sometimes null (or *def*, depending on versions) which is why you should omit this column in joins ② as null is never equal to null (actually, the joins are unnecessary with MySQL as *information_schema.referential_constraints* contains the table names), and the condition on the line indicated by ① should be **unique_constraint_schema = database()**

If you want the detail of the columns that are involved in the constraints, you should take a look at *information_schema.key_column_usage*.

With Oracle (and DB2), information about constraints is accessible through a view called *user_constraints*. This view contains among other things the owner (schema), the constraint name, a one-letter constraint type (**P**rimary, **U**nique, **R**eferential, **C**heck...), the name of the table it applies to and, for constraints of type *R*, the schema *r_owner* and the name *r_constraint_name* of the constraint that is referenced (a primary key or unique constraint). The name of the referenced table, however, isn't directly provided. To fetch it, we simply need to join *user_constraints* to itself and fetch the name of the referenced table thanks to the constraint name:

```
select pk.owner || '.' || pk.table_name table_name,
       fk.owner || '.' || fk.table_name referenced_by
from user_constraints fk
     inner join user_constraints pk
       on pk.owner = fk.r_owner                          } Join on constraint names
      and pk.constraint_name = fk.r_constraint_name      }
where pk.constraint_type in ('P', 'U')  ← Referenced constraint can be unique
                                          or primary
  and fk.constraint_type = 'R'
  and pk.owner = user       ← Take referenced tables in the current schema
order by table_name, referenced_by
```

Columns which are involved in the constraints can be found in view *user_cons_columns*.

Gathering Information – Indexes

Finding information about constraints is important but it's even more important to know how to find information about indexes when you write SQL statements. As we have seen in previous chapters it may tilt the choice in favor of correlated queries versus uncorrelated queries or the reverse (even if the query optimizer lurks in the background). When a function is required in the comparison of two columns, if one is indexed and the other one isn't, you'll want to apply the function to the unindexed column.

While all graphical interfaces for database developers make listing the indexes on one table an easy operation, it may be more convenient, for working on queries in which many tables are involved, to refer to some project documentation that lists all indexes on all tables in the schema. The best way to generate such documentation is to query the data dictionary. I am going to generate a simple list of indexes with their columns with one column per row. This list can be improved, more or less easily, depending on the product, by giving the columns as a suitably ordered comma-separated list; I'll let you do it (I'll generate comma-separated lists of names in Chapter 12). For the sake of simplicity, I'll also forget, with products that allow indexing deterministic expressions, about indexes on the result of functions and will only consider the much more common indexes on regular columns.

Rather strangely, as I have already said when introducing the data dictionary, of all DBMS products that support *information_schema*, only MySQL stores detailed information about indexes in this schema, and you find this information in the rather improbably named view *information_schema.statistics*.

First of all, remember that while all tables in a schema should in theory have a primary key (which implies an index), this isn't always the case, as the presence of a primary key isn't enforced by SQL when you create a table. And while the absence of any index is sometimes voluntary (to limit overhead when inserting into audit tables, for instance), it's sometimes an unfortunate oversight that only reveals itself when tables have grown and irate users become vocal about the slowness of applications. Listing all tables, including those that aren't indexed, is therefore important and we should start from the *information_schema* view *tables*, which contains not only tables but also views. We are only interested by tables, which have BASE TABLE as value in column *table_type*. To the full list of tables, we can outer join view *statistics*, which contains table name, index name, whether this index is unique and points to only one row per key, column name – and position of the column in the index, an important piece of information if you remember the preceding chapter.

```
select t.table_name,
       case s.non_unique
         when 0 then 'U'
         else ' '
       end u,
```

```
       s.seq_in_index pos,
       coalesce(s.column_name,
                '--- NO INDEX ---') column_name   ② Prepare for the worst
from information_schema.tables t
     left outer join information_schema.statistics s
       on s.table_schema = t.table_schema
      and s.table_name = t.table_name
where t.table_schema = database()     ③ Current schema
order by t.table_name,
         s.non_unique,
         s.index_schema,
         s.index_name,        ④ Index name needed for ordering
         s.seq_in_index
```

I don't return ① the index name – I don't need it to write my queries. However, when I sort my output, I must group columns by index and therefore the index identifier must be referred to in the **order by** clause ④. Knowing if the index is unique, though, is important. If there is no index, the outer join will return null and I try to shout at ② the absence of index. As usual, I restrict my query ③ to the current schema.

With SQL Server, PostgreSQL or DB2, the information is there but not in *information_schema*. For SQL Server, we'll get it from schema *sys*. I get the list of tables from *sys.tables* (I could get it from *information_schema.tables* but *sys.tables* is closer to what SQL Server internally manages, and it's more efficient to query *sys.tables*). Indexes are to be found in *sys.indexes* and their columns in *sys.index_columns*; finally I must join with *sys.columns* to get the column name. All joins are outer joins to keep unindexed tables in the result set and through numerical identifiers. Although *sys* tables may superficially look complicated, they are cleanly and methodically organized, and getting familiar with them is relatively easy.

```
select t.name table_name,     ← I return the same data as with MySQL
       case i.is_unique
         when 1 then 'U'
         else ''
       end as u,
       ic.key_ordinal pos,
       coalesce(c.name, '--- NO INDEX ---') column_name
from sys.tables t
     left outer join sys.indexes i
        on i.object_id = t.object_id      ① Join on internal identifiers
     left outer join sys.index_columns ic
        on ic.index_id = i.index_id
        and ic.object_id = i.object_id
     left outer join sys.columns c
        on c.object_id = ic.object_id
        and c.column_id = ic.column_id
where t.schema_id = schema_id()   ② Internal identifier for the schema too
order by t.name,
         i.name,
         ic.key_ordinal
```

All database objects are internally identified by a numerical identifier ① which I use in joins; *object_id* in *sys.indexes* and *sys.index_columns* refers to the table. Like objects and columns, the current schema is identified not by name but by a numerical identifier ②, and there is a function to return the right value.

For PostgreSQL we have access to the full data dictionary with table names like *pg_class*, *pg_namespace*, *pg_attributes* and so on. Although they are well-documented, I would certainly not advise a beginner to tackle those tables which require a rather abstract view of the database and make use of specific PostgreSQL data types (which include true/false values or arrays). Fortunately there are a handful of views also prefixed by *pg_* that you should use, unless you intend to write an application to browse the PostgreSQL data dictionary.

Among these views, two are of interest to identify indexes: *pg_tables* which is equivalent to *information_schema.tables* and *pg_indexes*, which contains the names of indexes and of the tables they are referring to, as well as a column called *indexdef* which is a reconstruction of the **create index** statement. The fact that it is a reconstruction means that it isn't the statement entered by the person who created the index but a statement that follows a standard template and from which, it's easy to extract the two pieces of information that really interest us:

- Whether the index is unique or not
- What are the columns in the index

The first point is checked by verifying whether the statement starts with CREATE UNIQUE and the second one by extracting what we find between parentheses in the reconstructed statement - a very different tactic from the one adopted with other products but no less effective to obtain our list.

```
select t.tablename table_name,
       case
         when i.indexdef like 'CREATE UNIQUE%' then 'U'    ← Check for UNIQUE
         else ''
       end U,
       coalesce(rtrim(substr(i.indexdef,
                             1 + position('(' in i.indexdef)),
                                              ↑ ① Extract column names
                   ')'), '--- NO INDEX ---') column_names
from pg_tables t
     left outer join pg_indexes i
     on i.schemaname = t.schemaname
     and i.tablename = t.tablename
where t.schemaname = current_schema    ← Limit to the current schema
order by table_name,
         u,
         columns
```

To extract the column names ① I locate the first opening parenthesis and take everything that follows it. A call to **rtrim()** removes the closing parenthesis. As usual, if the left outer join returns null I make it clear.

For Oracle and DB2 the information is to be found in *user_...* views and we can use exactly the same query with both products. This query looks for the list of tables in *user_tables* (which, unlike *information_schema.tables*, only lists tables, not views) and left outer joins it with *user_indexes* that relates indexes to tables, and finally *user_ind_columns* that shows for every index, which columns belong to it. There is no need to add a restriction to get the current schema, as by default, *user_* views only show what is in the current schema.

```
select t.table_name,
       substr(i.uniqueness, 1, 1) U,
       c.column_position,
       coalesce(c.column_name, '-- NO INDEX --') column_name
                                     ↑ Show when there is no index
from user_tables t
     left outer join user_indexes i
       on i.table_owner = user
      and i.table_name = t.table_name
     left outer join user_ind_columns c
       on c.index_name = i.index_name
      and c.table_name = i.table_name
order by t.table_name,
         i.uniqueness,
         i.index_name,     ← Use the index name for sorting (only)
         c.column_position
```

Generating SQL Statements

Data dictionary queries are also frequently used for automatically generating series of SQL statements. To give you one simple example, it often happens when you aggregate data from heterogeneous sources and need to massage it energetically, that you load files into many work tables with different structures (we did such operations in Chapter 7). All products allow the creation of temporary tables that are either emptied or dropped when you disconnect from the database (or when you commit) but you sometimes need work tables that are less volatile than temporary tables. The only trouble is that when all the data has been merged, you no longer need these work tables, which can be big.

NOTE The problem with big unused tables is that they are backed up with useful tables. Backup operations become longer, backup files are bigger too and if the database crashes you don't want to waste time restoring data you don't need.

If you are consistent in your naming, calling for instance every work table *something_wrk*, you can easily run a query such as

```
select 'drop table ' + table_name + ';' drop_stmt ① SQL Server concatenation
from information_schema.tables
where table_catalog = db_name()  ② DBMS specific condition
 and table_type = 'BASE TABLE'
 and table_name like '%wrk'
```

With MySQL you should piece the parts of the statement together ① with function **concat()** and use || instead of + with PostgreSQL. The condition ② should be **where table_catalog = current_database()** with PostgreSQL and **where table_schema = database()** with MySQL

or with Oracle or DB2

```
select 'drop table ' || table_name || ';' drop_stmt
from user_tables
where table_name like '%WRK' ← names are in uppercase in user_tables
```

Redirect the output of the query to a file, or simply paste and copy it somewhere and you have a clean-up script ready to run.

To take another example, let's say that when you create the movie application, you decide that user Alex will be in charge of maintaining tables. As the schema owner you run statements such as

```
grant select, insert, update on movies to alex;
grant select, insert, update, delete on credits to alex;
grant select, insert, update on people to alex;
```

As the application evolves new tables are added to the schema, new privileges are granted to Alex and things go on until poor Alex becomes unable to cope with the maintenance of all the reference tables and asks for someone to help (and for a well-deserved vacation).

At that point you realize that rather than granting all the rights to one user, it would have been smarter to grant them to one role, for instance *movie_admin* and to grant the role to Alex - and to Robin who will assist Alex. The question then becomes of copying all the table (or view or procedure) privileges granted to Alex to the role *movie_admin* (which must have been created by a database administrator, creating a role requires special system rights). This can be very tedious unless you get the information from the data dictionary.

NOTE I'll assume to simplify that the **update** right is granted on full tables, not on specific columns and I ignore any **grant option**. I'll also only consider table privileges; there may be rights to execute some procedures as well.

Information about rights is in *information_schema.table_privileges* with SQL Server and MySQL, in *information_schema.role_table_grants* for PostgreSQL, in *syscat.tabauth* for DB2, and in *user_tab_privs* for Oracle (and DB2). All these views refer both to the *grantor* (the database account that gave the right, usually the table owner) and the *grantee*, who received the right.

With these views, generating grant statements is easy, for instance with Oracle or DB2:

```
select 'grant ' || privilege || ' on ' || table_name
       || ' to movie_admin;' grant_stmt
from user_tab_privs
where grantee = 'ALEX '
```

Once the generated script has been run, you just need to generate a similar script to revoke the table rights from Alex, and have the database administrator execute

```
grant movie_admin to alex;
grant movie_admin to robin;
```

All the privileges have been transferred from user to role without too much effort.

At this point, you know most of what matters to use SQL professionally. I have tried to give you a solid foundation, to explain to you both the why and the how. There remains only one important question: how do we use SQL in programs? This is the topic of the next chapter.

To Remember

- A view is the SQL equivalent of a function. The parameters are the datasets contained in the tables involved.
- Views look like tables but can cause performance issues especially when columns are the result of operations on the columns of the underlying tables.
- Don't create views that depend on complex views. It's a sure recipe for performance disaster.
- Security is based on rights that you grant to users or roles; views are a great way to control and to customize what people see. Updates, however, may not be trivial with views and are sometimes impossible.
- Table, indexes, views and all objects are described in a set of views called catalog or data dictionary. You can extract important information from the data dictionary and use it to generate repetitive SQL statements automatically.

Exercises

1. Create a view called *people_alive* that, as its name implies, only shows people who are alive.
2. Create a view that displays the movie title, the surname of the director and the release year for all movies from a European country.

3. For each one of the following views, assuming no **instead of** trigger that would do tricky things behind your back, would it be possible or not possible to insert new rows through the view:

```
create view v1 as
select title, country
from movies
where year_released>1980

create viev v2 as
select born, count(*) number_of_births
from people
group by born

create view v3 as
select peopleid, surname, born
from people
where died is not null

create view v4 as
select peopleid, surname, born
from people
where died is not null
with check option
```

4. One important data dictionary view that I haven't talked about in this chapter is the view that contains all the columns (for tables and views).

   In *information_schema.columns* for SQL Server and MySQL you find columns such as *table_catalog*, *table_schema*, *table_name*, *column_name*, *ordinal_position* (integer) and *data_type*.

   For DB2, in *syscat.columns* the value of *table_catalog* is implicit and the equivalent names for the other columns are respectively *tabschema*, *tabname*, *colname*, *colno*, *typename*.

   For Oracle it's *user_tab_columns*; there is no equivalent of *table_catalog*, the schema is implicitly the current one and you find *table_name*, *column_name*, *column_id* and *data_type*.

   Using the view of your choice, write a query that returns table name, column name and data type for columns that have the same name but different data types in different tables (which can be a design error).

   NOTE To be exhaustive, one should also compare lengths of varchar columns and precision of numbers but it's not requested in this exercise.

5. Starting with the data dictionary query shown in this chapter, which lists indexes, write a query that lists all single column indexes for which a multi-column index starting with the same column exists (you can get rid of the single-column index, as the multi-column index can be used for the same purpose).

 > **NOTE** Unnecessary indexes are often encountered when people generate schemas with design tools that systematically index foreign keys. When the leading column of the primary key also happens to be a foreign key, as is the case for table *credits*, you usually end up with an index you can drop without regret.

Using SQL in Programs 11

The thorns which I have reap'd are of the tree
I planted; they have torn me, and I bleed.
I should have known what fruit would spring from such a seed.

- George Gordon Byron (1788-1824)

This chapter covers

- How programs access databases
- Why you should care about the number of interactions with the server
- Why you should care about passing values as parameters to queries
- How to build queries dynamically
- Two examples in Java and PHP (more in the next chapter)

At this stage in the book I have told you everything I wanted to tell you about SQL; all you need is some practice and you'll understand easily by yourself what I have omitted. You now have in your hands, everything you need to translate a question about data into an SQL query that returns that data from a database, correctly and efficiently.

However, we have used so far SQL clients; programs that, whether they are run in a console or have a graphical user-interface, allow you to issue SQL statements and get a result. Those tools are only used by

- database administrators who execute administrative statements such as **create user** or **grant** and query the data dictionary to get a database health check,
- and developers when they are designing and testing queries.

Most people who access a database, very often unwittingly, do it through various programs that run SQL statements for them. How do we query a database from inside a program? This is the topic of the present chapter. I won't start immediately with code samples that show you in practice how to do it; I'll start with an explanation about how a program and a database interact, and even though you may be extremely eager to start coding, please don't skip these explanations. I hope that they will give you a much better grasp of how the database server responds to queries in any language, and that you'll get much more from them, than from a mere description of a handful of functions with their parameters.

I'll give you two simple examples in this chapter. The next chapter contains more developed examples in the same languages, plus many more and provides you with a basic program structure that you can use as the foundation for more ambitious projects. Before the specifics and studying the examples, let's see some important principles that are valid with any language.

Accessing a Database from a Program

The general pattern to access a database in a program is relatively simple.

- You pass to a function, all the connection information that is required. This function fails or returns a valid database handler, usually an object or a pointer to an opaque structure, that you will use later when communicating with the database server. By connecting to the database, you open a *session* that will end when you disconnect.
- You send SQL commands to the database as text, calling a method of the database object or passing to a function the handler and the text as parameters, depending on whether you're using an object-oriented language or not. Several outcomes are possible:
    - If the command is a data definition language command such as **create table**, the function returns success or failure (executing DDL statements in an application program is usually a bad idea but you can do it).
    - If the command is an **insert**, **update**, or **delete** statement, it will usually return either a failure code or the number of rows affected by the command (which can be zero); sometimes the number of rows affected by the last SQL statement can be retrieved by an independent function.
    - If the command is a **select** statement, the function returns either failure or a result set handler allowing you to fetch the rows retrieved, one by one, or sometimes in batches.

Add a few functions to disconnect, free resources and get error information, and in many languages that's about all you need. And like almost everything that relates to databases, it's deceptively simple.

When you are accessing a database from a program, you are connecting two completely different worlds: on the one hand a world in which you handle sets of data that may be gigantic (some tables store billions of rows) and on the other hand a world in which you manipulate either simple variables or more complex objects.

NOTE The expression *impedance mismatch* is sometimes used to refer to the differences in perspective between SQL and programming languages.

Even though these variables or objects can be organized in collections that range from modest fixed-size arrays, to more sophisticated hash-maps, sets, trees or whatever, and even though some languages let you operate globally on a collection, you always reach a point in a program where you have to iterate on the elements of a collection, picking them one by one.

The switch from a world in which you operate on sets to a world in which you operate on set elements, practically means that your program will have to loop on what corresponds to table rows, whether it's for retrieving data or for storing data. I warned you in Chapter 8 against using loops in stored procedures because very often you don't need them. With a traditional programming language, it's different: you have to use loops. Iterating means that you are going to interact a lot with the database, calling database functions many times.

Round-Trips

All servers, whether they are database servers or another type of server such as HTTP servers, share one characteristic: a network usually sits between them and the clients they serve. Even though data travels very quickly in networks, there is an absolute physical speed limit (the speed of light). In practice, it takes data about 5 microseconds (five millionths of a second) to travel one kilometer (or if you prefer, eight millionths of a second to travel one mile). This travel time is known as *network latency*. This is a notion completely separate from *bandwidth*, which says how much data you can send over the network per unit of time. To give you an analogy, latency is how long it takes to drive from A to B, independently of the number of lanes and traffic conditions; bandwidth says how many cars can drive simultaneously from A to B without a traffic jam.

Whenever you issue a database call, you need to send a request to the server which processes it, then returns either a status or data - communication requires a *round-trip* to the server. If you are running a database application locally that queries a database physically located in a data center 100 miles away (160km), the 200 miles round-trip adds about 1.6 thousands of a second to every interaction with the database. This elapsed time in itself is quite negligible but when you iterate and retrieve or load many rows, it adds up. If a program inserts 10,000 new rows (which is by no means a large number of rows) into a database located 100 miles away, one row at a time, it wastes 16 seconds in network latency alone for an operation that would execute in a flash if run as an **insert** ... **select** ... statement on the server. When accumulated latency far exceeds execution time on the server, you have a problem.

There are many cases when the actual distance between the client application and the database server is much greater than in the previous example; it may strike you as a weird idea to operate against a database in Tokyo when you are in London, or vice versa but it's relatively frequent in multinational companies, to centralize some data in a single database, which is accessed by all subsidiaries worldwide, to ensure data consistency or confidentiality. The same application that may be responsive when run in one office may be insufferably slow elsewhere if it wasn't coded carefully enough. Table 11-1 gives you an idea of what distance adds to response times. It can be worse if you're on a ship in the middle of the ocean and the signal is beamed up to a satellite 22,000 miles above before being beamed down to earth.

Approximate round-trip times (source: AT&T)	
London - Paris	10ms
Dallas - Chicago	25ms
Rio de Janeiro - Santiago	50ms
Los Angeles – New York	70ms
New York - London	75ms
Singapore - Tokyo	75ms
San Francisco - Tokyo	95ms
Hong Kong - Sydney	120ms
Singapore - Los Angeles	180ms
Tokyo - London	240ms

Table 11-1: Network latency (in ms, aka thousandths of a second)

Applications that run across the world are obviously an extreme and striking case but even when your application is running on a computer physically close to the database server or even on the same machine, and when latency is very low (which is usually the case with web-based applications in which SQL statements are fired from the HTTP server), each database call adds noticeable overhead. You can check it by comparing the performance of a single (well written) SQL statement to a stored procedure that performs the same process by issuing multiple statements.

Network latency and the cost of database calls are the main reasons why it's much better, when you have a succession of database operations to run in sequence, to embed them in a procedure that will be run on the server. You can execute all the operations in one single call instead of invoking them one by one, one round-trip at a time, from the client. It's even better to run a single SQL statement, for instance an **insert** ... **select** ... statement, than to loop on the result of a query and insert rows one by one, even in a stored procedure. What about queries, now? In order to limit the number of round-trips, some database functions used to fetch data, will attempt to get all the rows returned by a query at once. When you retrieve the different rows in the result set one by one, you don't usually issue a call to the database server each time, even if you are calling a "database function". You are actually retrieving the data from a buffer area that is local to your machine. There are also cases when a fixed number of rows are fetched and the buffer is transparently refilled when you have retrieved all the rows returned in the previous batch.

The use of buffers on the client side raises a number of questions. First of all, even if the client computer is equipped with a comfortable amount of memory, it's unlikely it will be able to hold the full result set when you query the biggest table in the database, without any filtering conditions. Additionally, all this memory to hold the rows must be allocated (reserved) before you actually retrieve them. This is done transparently for the application programmer in most cases but to understand better how to code, you should have some ideas about what goes on behind the scenes.

Memory Requirements

Retrieving even a reasonably large number of rows, will rarely be a problem on a modern computer - unless, which can happen on a web server, many different sessions are doing it at the same time. In a language such as PHP, there is a memory limitation for every script which, in practice, restricts the number of rows you can retrieve at once. In all cases, you should write your SQL queries in such a way that they return the data you need in your program and nothing more. Any row that your program discards and doesn't process is one row too many. The situation is particularly difficult with text or binary columns that have no maximum length specified and are used to store large multimedia documents because with them, the number of rows that you will be able to retrieve at once, will necessarily be much reduced.

I have read in some product documentation, a suggestion to fetch data row by row when retrieving a large number of rows (some settings allow row-by-row operations). I am sorry to say that this is a poor piece of advice. Firstly, it's not so much the number of rows, as the number of rows times the average size in bytes of a row that matters. Although indeed the plain number of rows could be an issue, as retrieved rows are held in arrays and some languages don't allow arrays with more than two billion elements, it's likely that you'll hit a memory limit before you have a problem with the sheer number of rows.

Secondly, when you don't know how many rows you will ultimately return but you expect them to be numerous, it's sometimes possible (it depends on the language and the DBMS), to fetch the rows from the server in successive batches that contain a fixed numbers of rows. If the library functions don't allow you to fetch from a result set by successive batches, you can do it in SQL. There is nothing to prevent you from paging through the result as I have shown to you in Chapter 5, using either **row_number()** or **limit ... offset ...** to retrieve the full result set through several executions. If you run repeatedly, a query that returns successive batches of 1,000 rows until you have retrieved everything, latency will be one thousandth of what it would be working row-by-row. Unless your query is so terrible that it takes hours to run, this is how you should proceed. Working row-by-row is something that you only want to do when one row can be very big, when you are retrieving very large multimedia documents.

Parameters

I have explained that you send SQL commands to the database as text. Let me rephrase that slightly. A database server receives from applications, the *text* of statements to execute. In the case of SQL, the name *statement* is a bit misleading. Indeed, an SQL query states what you want but it's not a simple statement in the same league as a programming language statement such as

```
a = b + 3;
```

An SQL statement is much more complicated. In fact, an SQL statement is more like a program and, like any program, it must be analyzed and transformed before it can be run. The database server must check that the syntax of the statement is correct. By querying the data dictionary that we saw in Chapter 10, it must check that tables exist and that you are connected as a user who has the right to query or change the tables. It must check that columns also exist and that you are applying functions to them that are compatible with their data types. Finally, it must check indexes, check whether they can be used, whether it would be beneficial to use them, and decide on a data access strategy that a command such as **explain** (that we saw in Chapter 9) will reveal. All of this must be performed before executing the statement proper. This phase of analysis and preparation is known as *parsing* and can take up a significant part of the overall execution time.

Preparing Statements

In real life, it very often happens that, not only the same query may be executed repeatedly by the same user but that many queries submitted by different users in different sessions will be identical. Everybody who visits a blog will unknowingly execute the same query that displays the last articles. Many queries will follow exactly the same pattern (people who look for films starring Jennifer Lopez, Maggie Smith, Zac Efron or Chiranjeevi may not have much in common but it will be the same query, looking for different values in the same index and if you apply **explain** to the different queries you'll see the same steps).

As the purpose of a database server is to serve as many queries as possible as quickly as possible, there is no point consuming processing power while repeating again and again, the same parsing operations.

When you know that you are going to execute repeatedly, the same statement in your program with different values, you use a *prepared statement*. A prepared statement requires one more call than its non prepared equivalent but parses a statement only once instead of doing it for each execution.

NOTE A prepared statement requires one more call but not necessarily one more round-trip. Functions are often clever enough to postpone some operations and only communicate with the database server when really necessary.

Instead of sending to the database server:

```
select m.title, m.year_released, m.country
from movies m
     inner join credits c
        on c.movieid = m.movieid
     inner join people p
        on p.peopleid = c.peopleid
where c.credited_as = 'A'
  and p.first_name = 'Ryan'
  and p.surname = 'Gosling'
```

You send something like this:

```
select m.title, m.year_released, m.country
from movies m
     inner join credits c
        on c.movieid = m.movieid
     inner join people p
        on p.peopleid = c.peopleid
where c.credited_as = 'A'
  and p.first_name = :first_name
  and p.surname = :surname
```

in which `:first_name` and `:surname` are placeholders for actual values that are passed separately. We have a generic query "find the films in which an actor or actress appears", and it can be reused.

NOTE Conventions for placeholder names vary with the language, as you will see in the examples.

The function that prepares the statement will return to you (if it succeeds) a statement handler, then you will be able to assign, for this handler, *Ryan* to `:first_name` and *Gosling* to `:surname` (an operation usually referred to as *variable binding*), pass the handler to a function that will execute it, and then retrieve the result set. Once the statement is prepared, you can also execute it a second time after having associated *Natalie* with `:first_name` and *Portman* with `:surname`, and a third time, and so on, only changing bound variables before executing the already parsed statement.

You'll notice that I have left a constant in my sample query to specify that I am looking for actors. I could also use a placeholder there to be able to use the same query when looking for directors but as a general rule, when a column can take only very few different values, constants are used in queries. The reason is that some values may be very common, others much less so, and if the column is indexed, knowing the exact value can be critical in the optimizer decision on whether to use the index or not. Suppose that you are a big online retailer; in your *orders* table, which stores millions of rows, only orders that are in the "ready to ship" state are of any interest to the shipping department. There may be perhaps four or five different possible states for orders, with the vast majority of rows in the "shipped" state. Compared to the bulk of the table, especially after a few years of frantic sales, there are very few "ready to ship" rows and indexing the status makes sense. If you pass the status as *:status*, the optimizer may assume that the five states correspond to a roughly equal number of rows and not use the index. If you write the status explicitly, it will know the frequency of the value and make the right choice.

NOTE Oracle and SQL Server are able to extract constant values and replace them with placeholders before starting processing a query. When done aggressively (which isn't the default option) it can lead the optimizer to unfortunate choices.

Some products (Oracle, DB2, SQL Server) go much further than preparing and reusing statements for one session and keep a number of frequently executed prepared statements in server memory. They can recognize statements that are identical and hit the same tables when they are executed at different times and in different sessions. If two people who have accounts in the same bank both take money out of automated tellers, they won't enter the same personal identification number. Different amounts of money will be subtracted from different accounts but the same SQL statements will be executed by the database servers of the bank.

When the DBMS product caches SQL statements globally in server memory and not by session, actual parsing by a session is only performed when the statement isn't found already parsed in memory. This means that, even when you take into account the slight overhead required by the preparation of the statement, with such a product it's better to prepare statements that will be executed by many sessions, even if each session runs them only once - as usually happens when you withdraw money from an ATM.

SQL Injection

There is a reason other than performance for preparing statements: user input is sometimes dangerous. Suppose that in a website you retrieve authentication data in variables and check that people can access the member section by executing a statement that is built in your program (I am using PHP here, where concatenation is indicated by a dot and variable names start with a dollar sign):

```
$query = "select memberid from members where username='"
       . $entered_username
       . "' and password = '" . $entered_password . "'";
```

You expect to find in `$entered_username` something such as *Mickey* and in `$entered_password` something like *Mouse* or, which would be much better, an encrypted password looking like *3#(ag89zhost]=89* so that in the end you get in `$query`

```
select memberid from members
 where username='Mickey'
 and password='3#(ag89zhost]=89'
```

But suppose that the user has passed as username *Pete* and as a password *hack' or 'hack'='hack*. Then you are going to build

```
select memberid from members
 where username='Pete'
 and password='hack' or 'hack'='hack'
```

There is no user in your database with username *Pete* and password *hack* but remember that the logical operators **and** and **or** have different precedence: what is linked by **and** is evaluated first. The condition on username and password is false and it doesn't matter whether there is a user named *Pete* or not. As the condition `'hack'='hack'` is always true, this condition combined with an **or** ensures that the global condition in the **where** clause is always true. If the program just fetches the first row returned and assumes that if one row is returned then the user is authenticated, anybody can access the member section. Entering into input variables, fragments of SQL code so as to change queries, is known as *SQL injection*. To avoid this type of attack, you must either sanitize user input by applying functions that escape quotes (doubling them, for instance), making quotes truly part of the data and not part of the statement or, which is even better, use placeholders. The choice between sanitizing input and using placeholders with bind variables depends, in that case, on the DBMS that you are using. As authentication is the typical query that is executed only once per session but by many sessions, using bind variables makes more sense with a DBMS that keeps parsed queries in server memory, and energetically sanitizing input makes more sense with a DBMS that doesn't share queries between sessions.

Dynamic Statements

Finally, while most database programs execute repeatedly the same statements with different search (or update, or insert) values, there is also a growing number of advanced programs that need to execute statements that are relatively dynamic and depend on user input - and as surprising as it may seem, my simple application in the next chapter will belong to that group.

When you are first told about parameters and placeholders, you sometimes think that writing

```
order by :user_choice      ← It doesn't work
```

is the way to let people specify how they want to see data sorted - for instance by relevance, price, or customer rating on a merchant site. Unfortunately that isn't how it works. You can't use placeholders just anywhere in a query. The general rule is that you only can have a placeholder in a query where you can have a constant. You cannot substitute a table or column name by a placeholder. You cannot substitute a whole condition in a **where** clause or an **order by** clause by a placeholder. You cannot even write in a program

```
select title, country, year_released
from movies
where country in (:list)      ← It doesn't work either
```

and associate *'us','gb'* with `:list`. The SQL engine would look for movies the country of which is the single value *'us','gb'*. In such a case, the program must build the query by concatenating pieces of text.

Dynamic Queries and Parameters

When the program builds the query, the temptation is often very strong to concatenate user input to the text, before passing the resulting string to the database server. You should resist this temptation for several reasons: one is the ever present risk of SQL injection; another is the fact that even when queries are dynamically built, the global number of query patterns is usually limited (or can be limited) and among the various patterns, some will usually be very popular and there will be ample scope for query reuse if you employ placeholders. Suppose that a program displays a form that allows us to search for movies on many criteria: title, actors, directors, country, year, genre, duration, producer, spoken language ... Depending on the criteria that are entered, the resulting queries will be very different. However, it's likely that most searches will be by title, actors and directors, and that these three search patterns will be repeatedly executed with different titles and names.

More or Less Dynamic

There are many differing degrees of dynamism. First of all, it's not because the number of criteria that can be entered may vary that the query needs to be dynamic. If you have a form in which you search films and can specify year of release or country or both, if unspecified criteria become nulls in your program something such as

```
select title, year_released, country
from movies
where year_released = coalesce(:year, year_released)
  and country = coalesce(:country, country)
```

allows us to ignore criteria that haven't been entered. What is happening here? Suppose that only the year is specified (let's say 1970). In the condition on *year_released*, function **coalesce()** returns the value passed, 1970, which isn't null; in the condition on the country, if no value is provided and therefore if *:country* is undefined, **coalesce()** returns the value of country for the current row. As a country is always equal to itself, the condition is always true and doesn't matter: the only condition that matters is the condition on the year. Of course, I am assuming:

- That unspecified criteria are received as nulls, as said previously
- That the columns are mandatory. As `null = null` is never true, you would have a problem otherwise, which you could work around. If *year_released* could be null for instance, you could write a condition such as `where coalesce(year_released, 0) = coalesce(:year, year_released, 0)`

At the bottom of the scale of dynamism, you find queries where you simply change the **order by** clause (without any placeholder). If users want the result sorted by title, or by year, or by country, or by country and year, it's just a matter of appending `order by title` or `order by year_released` or `order by country, year_released` to the query before passing it to the DBMS.

Dynamism increases when the number of input criteria may vary. Suppose that users select, in the preceding example, year and country through drop-down boxes that don't just allow one but multiple choices. In that case you need a variable geometry **where** clause, with a variable number of parameters. This is the most commonly encountered type of dynamic query.

A higher degree of dynamism, much less common than the preceding one, is when users can choose which information to display. You can decide to fetch everything that can be selected and manage in the host program, what to show and what to hide; but if some rarely needed information demands complicated joins to be fetched, you are better off building dynamically the *select list* and the **from** clause. As you need to fetch the data into program variables, your program must then know what to expect. In that case you pass the query to the DBMS server that analyzes it, then you call another function to ask the DBMS server to describe the select list and provide information (number of columns fetched, data types, maximum byte size) that allows your program to receive the data.

The highest degree of dynamism is demonstrated by SQL clients that pass what you type to the DBMS and display feedback, error message or result.

If the columns you return are always the same ones, building dynamic queries in programs isn't particularly difficult when you know exactly what you want to build. You just need to be very careful because when you concatenate chunks, it's easy to forget a space, a comma or a parenthesis somewhere and generate a syntactically incorrect query in the end. Debugging takes usually longer than when you can try your query in an SQL client, then copy and paste the query in your program with few changes; you must carefully test all possible combinations.

It's worth noting that when you build queries in a program, some constructs are easier to code in programs than other equivalent ones. Uncorrelated subqueries are easier than correlated subqueries and set operators such as **intersect** or **except** (**minus** with Oracle) are easier than joins. To give an example, suppose that you can enter various criteria and want to find the British films that are directed by Ang Lee. You can try to build a big complicated join between *movies, countries, credits* and *people*, then add the conditions on *first_name* and *surname* in *people*, and on *country_name* in *countries*. Or you can write first a simpler join between *movies* and *countries* to retrieve the identifiers of British films, then another simple join between *credits* and *people* to retrieve the identifiers of films directed by Ang Lee, and take the intersection of the two sets of identifiers by concatenating one query, `intersect`, and the other query. If there is an additional condition on actors, you just plug in one more simple query, without having to completely rethink a big join. Perhaps the resulting query will be a little less efficient than a big query (if the optimizer does its job well, it may make no difference) but your program will be much simpler and much easier to maintain.

A Couple of Examples

I am going to show you in this section only two simple examples, one using Java and the JDBC interface (**J**ava **D**ata**B**ase **C**onnectivity) with Oracle, and the other using PHP and the PDO interface (**P**HP **D**ata **O**bjects) with MySQL. I have chosen these two languages, firstly because they are popular and secondly because the interfaces that I am using are independent of the accessed DBMS (needless to say, the SQL code, which is seen as plain text by the programming language, remains dependent on the DBMS, unless it's very simple as in this case). Both database interfaces rely on drivers that are DBMS dependent but after loading the driver you use the same functions with the same parameters with all DBMS products. If you have a suitable driver installed on your machine, you can run these examples with any DBMS by simply changing the driver and the connection information. For the Java example you will need on your machine, either the Java Development Kit (JDK) or an Integrated Development Environment (IDE) such as Eclipse for Java Developers (both are free). For the PHP example, PHP is usually bundled with Linux distributions and if you are on a Windows or Mac OS X you can easily install XAMPP, a distribution of the Apache web server that includes everything that you'll need (including MySQL.)

A very simple Java/Oracle Example

There are several prerequisites if you want to write and run a sample Java program on your machine.

The first prerequisite, if you aren't using an IDE, is that you must make sure that you can run the javac command (which translates a .java source program into a .class file that can be executed by the Java virtual machine). You probably won't have any issue under a Linux system. If however, you open a Windows console and type javac at the prompt, it's likely that you will get a message saying that the command is not found. You must add its location to the *path*, the list of directories where commands are searched. You will normally find the javac.exe program in C:\Program Files\Java\jdk*<version>*\bin with *<version>* depending on which version of the JDK is installed on your machine. Typing the following

```
set PATH=C:\"Program Files"\Java\jdk<version>\bin;%PATH%
```

before running javac should solve the problem.

Secondly, as I said, you need to load in your Java program a JDBC driver that is specific to your DBMS before you can connect to the database. Not only is the JDBC driver dependent on the version of Java running on your machine and on the DBMS but there are also four types of drivers available, that depend on how the driver is written. For instance, some JDBC drivers are written using the specific C client libraries of a DBMS, which allows a stronger integration with the product and opens access to DBMS-specific features. Unfortunately, it also means that they require as a prerequisite the installation of DBMS libraries on the client computer. The most commonly used drivers are the so-called "type 4", pure Java drivers (called "thin driver" with Oracle) which don't require anything more on the client computer than a .jar file and are extremely easy to deploy.

Sometimes drivers are installed with the DBMS software and in that case you will find them in the installation directories of products. For instance, for Oracle on Linux, you'll find the driver under $ORACLE_HOME/jdbc/lib and the .jar file will be named ojdbc*n*.jar (*n* is a number that depends on the JDK). In Windows and with Oracle Express, you will find the same driver under

C:\oraclexe\app\oracle\product*<oracle version>*\server\jdbc\lib.

Sometimes JDBC drivers have to be installed separately and in that case you can obtain them from several sources: the *download* section on the web sites of DBMS vendors, independent software providers, and even Open Source projects that try to write ever more efficient drivers buffering data cleverly, or drivers that provide additional functionality (for debugging, for instance). A very good example of a third-party JDBC driver is the jTDS driver (an Open Source project at http://jtds.sourceforge.net) available for SQL Server and its close relative Sybase.

The first thing to do is to make sure that a suitable .jar file for your DBMS is present on your computer. The second thing to do is to make sure that Java knows where it is.

Prior to running the program, you must check that the .jar file is listed in your CLASSPATH environment variable (unless you specify where to look for it on the command line with the -classpath option to the java program). Beware that *both* the .jar file containing the driver and the directory where the .class file generated by javac resides, must appear in CLASSPATH; the latter one is usually the current directory, represented by a dot in CLASSPATH.

The easy way to check CLASSPATH is correctly set and that the driver is accessible to the Java engine is to type on the command line in a console

```
java <driver name>
```

for instance (depending on the driver and the DBMS that you are using)

```
java oracle.jdbc.OracleDriver
```

or

```
java org.sqlite.JDBC
java net.sourceforge.jtds.jdbc.Driver
java com.microsoft.sqlserver.jdbc.SQLServerDriver
java org.postgresql.driver
java com.ibm.db2.jcc.DB2Driver
java com.mysql.jdbc.Driver
```

If CLASSPATH is properly set, any of the previous commands should either give you information about the driver (such as, for instance, its version) or a message

```
Error: Main method not found in class <driver name>
```

If CLASSPATH is not properly set, the message will be

```
Error: Could not find or load main class <driver name>
```

I am going to give you here, a very simple example with a Java program that you will run in a console (there is a much more sophisticated example, with a graphical user interface, in the next chapter). My example simply reads from the command line, a username and a password (which we need to connect to the database), then the two-letter code of a country and lists title and year of release for films from this country, from the oldest to the most recent. Here is my program Example.java:

```
import java.util.Properties;
import java.sql.*;
import java.util.Scanner;

class Example {
  static Connection    con = null; ← Database connection object

  public static void main(String arg[]) {
    Properties info = new Properties();
```

```
String     url = "jdbc:oracle:thin:@localhost:1521:orcl";
```

↑ The url is where you pass connection information and the actual format (after "jdbc:") depends on the DBMS you are accessing. Check the docs.

You can recognize after @ the name of the server, the port, and the name of the instance (which would be *XE* instead of *orcl* if I were using Oracle Express).

```
Scanner    input = new Scanner(System.in);
try {
  Class.forName("oracle.jdbc.OracleDriver"); ← Load the driver
} catch(Exception e) {
  System.err.println("Cannot find the driver.");
  System.exit(1);    ← CLASSPATH isn't properly set
}
try {
    System.out.print("Username: ");
    String username = input.nextLine();
    System.out.print("Password: ");
    String password = input.nextLine();  ← BEWARE the password isn't hidden
    info.put("user", username);
    info.put("password", password);
    con = DriverManager.getConnection(url.toString(), info);
```

↑ Here is where we connect.

We pass to the **getConnection()** method the URL and username and password as properties. It can fail if authentication is wrong, if the URL is incorrect, or if the database or (for Oracle) the listener is down.

```
    con.setAutoCommit(false);
```

↑ I HATE autocommit (JDBC default). First thing I deactivate when I connect. Even when I don't intend to change data.

```
    System.out.println("Successfully connected.");
} catch(Exception e) {
    System.err.println(e.getMessage());
    System.exit(1);
}
System.out.print("Enter the two character country code: ");
String country = input.nextLine();
try {
   PreparedStatement stmt =
        con.prepareStatement("select title, year_released"
                           + " from movies"
                           + " where country = lower(?)"
                           + " order by year_released");
```

↑ The prepareStatement() method of the Connection object returns a PreparedStatement object.

Note the question mark in the query, it's the placeholder for the parameter.

```
        stmt.setString(1, country);
              ↑ Bind the parameter to the PreparedStatement.
```

If you ever want to re-execute the query with a different parameter, that's all you'll have to change. There is one method per data type. "1" just says that it's associated with the first (and in this case only) question mark.

```
        ResultSet rs = stmt.executeQuery();
                         ↑ You run the executeQuery() method of the
                           PreparedStatement and get a ResultSet on which
                           you'll loop
        while (rs.next()) {
           System.out.println(rs.getString(1) +  "\t" + rs.getString(2));
                                   ↑ Like the methods to bind variables,
                                     the methods to retrieve data depend
                                     on data types.
                                    The number refers to the column in the
                                    result set.
        }
        rs.close();  ← Always close. Especially if you want to re-execute
                        the PreparedStatement
     } catch(Exception e) {
         System.err.println(e.getMessage());
         try {
            con.close();     ← close the connection to the database
         } catch(SQLException sqlE) {
            // Ignore
         }
         System.exit(1);
     }
     try {
         con.close();     ← close the connection to the database
     } catch(SQLException sqlE) {
         // Ignore
     }
   }
}
```

With java.util.Scanner, the password will be shown. If you want to hide the password, you must use java.io.Console, which unfortunately doesn't work in an integrated development environment (IDE) such as Eclipse. The Console class implements a method called readPassword() (a version of this program with Console is available from http://edu.konagora.com.)

Here is what the program gives in action (when CLASSPATH is correctly set):

```
$ javac Example.java  ← Generate the .class file (no Eclipse here)
```

```
$ java Example
Username: moviedb
Password: sqlsuccess     ← It's shown with a Scanner object
Successfully connected.
Enter the two character country code: gb
The Man Who Knew Too Much    1934
The Third Man          1949
Lawrence Of Arabia   1962
$
```

Chapter 12 contains a more complicated Java program with a graphical interface and a proper Login window.

A very simple PHP/MySQL Example

PHP is usually associated with web servers (or HTTP servers, after the name of the protocol used by browsers to request pages), even though I am going to write a program that you can run from the command line. That will allow you to test it if PHP is installed on your machine but you have no HTTP server running or aren't allowed to write files where the HTTP server reads them.

In web applications, databases are accessed through server-side scripting. Application users provide, through forms, data that is used in queries. Sanitizing input to protect against SQL injection and keeping databases safely away from would-be hackers is of particular importance in the case of web programming.

PDO, *PHP Data Objects*, is, like JDBC, a generic library that loads a DBMS-specific driver but uses identical functions with all DBMS products (even though the SQL statements that are passed to each DBMS are usually slightly different). One way to check PDO drivers are installed on your system is to call the **phpinfo()** function, which you can do even from the command line, for instance here on Linux (you can of course also open the file I have called `info.php` in a browser):

```
bash$ echo '<?php phpinfo(); ?>' > info.php ← create the script to check drivers
             ↑ You can also create a new file with a text editor,
               write into it what is between quotes and save it
               under the name info.php
bash$ php info.php | grep -i 'pdo driver'    ← filter only interesting lines
  < You'll get here several lines of warning saying it's not safe to rely
    on the system's timezone settings. Ignore them.                    >
PDO drivers => dblib, mysql, odbc, pgsql, sqlite
PDO Driver for FreeTDS/Sybase DB-lib => enabled
PDO Driver for MySQL => enabled
PDO Driver for ODBC (UNIXODBC) => enabled
PDO Driver for PostgreSQL => enabled
PDO Driver for SQLite 3.x => enabled
bash$
```

If you have installed XAMPP on your machine and have created `info.php`, you should launch the XAMPP Control Panel and click the "Shell" button on the right. It will open a console in which the environment will be properly set to run PHP from the command line, and

```
# php info.php
```

will display a lot of information in which you'll have to scroll back to locate for instance

```
PDO

PDO support => enabled
PDO drivers => mysql, sqlite
```

Let's now see my script, which I have unimaginatively called `Example.php`.

```
<?php
```

I am starting with a trick that will allow me to run the script directly on the command line or by requesting it through a HTTP request. I expect a parameter to be passed on the command-line as **country=<some code>**. If I find a command line parameter, I assign it to the $_GET array, which means that after the assignment it will be exactly as if the page had been called in a browser as `http://localhost[:port]/Example.php?country=<some code>`

```
if (isset($argv) && (count($argv) > 1)) {
   parse_str(implode('&', array_slice($argv, 1)), $_GET);
}
if (isset($_GET['country'])) {  ← Check that we have the required parameter
   $country = $_GET['country'];
} else {
   echo 'You must provide a country code' . PHP_EOL;
   exit;
}
$db = new PDO('mysql:host=localhost;dbname=moviedb', ← DBMS-specific
              'moviedb',     ← Username
              'SQLsuccess', ← Password
              array(PDO::MYSQL_ATTR_INIT_COMMAND=>"SET NAMES utf8"));
                   ↑ Initial settings (DBMS-specific and optional)
```

I instantiate a PDO object that represents my database connection. The first parameter is the most DBMS-product specific; it starts with the specification of the DBMS, followed by key connection information. Username and password are classic but I can also pass specific settings, in that case I want to work in UTF8.

```
if ($db === false) {
   echo 'Connection to database failed' . PHP_EOL;
   exit;
}
```

```
$query = 'select title, year_released'
       . ' from movies'
       . ' where country = lower(:country)'
       . ' order by year_released';
```

Note that in the query, the placeholder is a colon followed by the name that we'll use to refer to the parameter.

```
$stmt = $db->prepare($query);
```

The **prepare()** method of the PDO object returns a prepared statement (called a **PDOStatement** object) or false if it fails – for instance if the SQL syntax is incorrect.

```
if (($stmt !== false)
    && $stmt->execute(array('country'=>$country))) {
```

↑ when I call the execute() method of the PDOStatement object, I pass an array that contains the values to bind.

The array that is passed is an associative array, indexed by the names I have given to the parameters in the statement. It's also possible to have numbered parameters but the code becomes more difficult to read.

```
    $film_list = $stmt->fetchAll(PDO::FETCH_ASSOC);
```

↑ the fetchAll() method returns all rows at once as an array of arrays.

The parameter specifies that I want an associative array, indexed by the names of the columns that are returned (legibility, once again).There are other methods to retrieve tens of thousands of rows (which is rare in a web application).

```
    $cnt = 0;
```

In the loop I'll output an HTML table. Needless to say, there should be more HTML than that. I am assigning a class to each row in case we want to alternate the background colors of rows.

```
    foreach ($film_list as $film) {
       if ($cnt == 0) {
          echo '<table>'
             . '<tr><th>Title</th><th>Year</th></tr>' . PHP_EOL;
       }
       $cnt++;
       echo '<tr class="' . ($cnt % 2 == 0 ? 'even' : 'odd') . '">'
          . '<td>' . $film['title'] . '</td>'
          . '<td>' . $film['year_released'] . '</td>'
          . '</tr>' . PHP_EOL;
    }
```

```
        if ($cnt > 0) {
           echo '</table>' . PHP_EOL;
        } else {
           echo '<span class="error">No movies found</span>';
        }
    } else {
```

Depending on where the failure occurs, I need to call the **errorInfo()** method of either the **PDO** object or the **PDOStatement** object, both implement this method. It returns an array, the message is at index 2.

```
        if ($stmt === false) {
           $flop = $db->errorInfo();
        } else {
           $flop = $stmt->errorInfo();
        }
        echo '<span class="error">' . $flop[2] . '</span>';
    }
    unset($db);  ← Close the connection
?>
```

Here is what I obtain when I run the script from the command line:

```
$ php Example.php country=de
<table><tr><th>Title</th><th>Year</th></tr>
<tr class="odd"><td>Das indische Grabmal</td><td>1959</td></tr>
<tr class="even"><td>Der Tiger von Eschnapur</td><td>1959</td></tr>
<tr class="odd"><td>Das Boot</td><td>1985</td></tr>
<tr class="even"><td>Good Bye Lenin!</td><td>2003</td></tr>
<tr class="odd"><td>Das Leben der Anderen</td><td>2006</td></tr>
</table>
$
```

These two examples are very simple and just here to show you the basic interactions between a program and a database. For more solid examples, both for Java and PHP, as well as other programming languages, please proceed to Chapter 12...

To Remember

- Programs that access databases transmit SQL statements as text and, for queries, need to loop on results. Some libraries may make storing database results into components that can be displayed more or less transparently
- Because of latency, time lost in networks, what is sent must do as much as possible in one shot; you should avoid multiple exchanges between client program and database.
- Because of latency, only the necessary data must be returned, in as few iterations as possible. Unnecessary data mustn't be discarded in the program; it mustn't be selected.

- Statements that are repeatedly executed must be prepared because they are analyzed only once for multiple executions. Analysis adds to the execution time.
- Beware of SQL injection. User input must always be sanitized or passed as parameters to the query.

Project Launchpad 12

Dimidium facti, qui coepit, habet.

He who has begun has half done.

- Horace (65-8BC)

This chapter covers

- How to write a shell-script that accesses a database
- How to write database accesses in a command-line program with embedded SQL or C functions
- How to write a graphical database client program in Java or Python
- How to write a .NET database application with C#
- How to write a database-driven web application with PHP and AJAX
- How to use an embedded SQLite file in a mobile application written with Cocoa and Objective C

This chapter describes in detail, a moderately complex application, programmed with various DBMS products and programming languages. Books as thick as this one have been written on most of the types of programs that I'll talk about so don't expect each example to be a full course, teaching everything you need to know to become a professional developer, in a language that you had so far only heard about. My purpose isn't to teach you any particular language other than SQL in this book, I will only underscore in this chapter, the finer points that I think are important. I'll assume each time, that you have some knowledge but not expert knowledge, of the programming language I am talking of. If I am not using as an example, the DBMS/programming language combination of your choice, focus on the programming language and don't worry; whatever the section title says, I may give a few hints about other DBMS products where applicable. The idea in this chapter is to provide you with a basic program structure for something that is much more substantial than the "hello world" type of demonstration program, with at its core, a relatively complex SQL statement that is partly built by the program. If you want to benefit fully from the examples given in this chapter, download the full code from http://edu.konagora.com and start playing around.

The sample program offers a lot of scope for improvement and enhancements. I'll suggest several at the end of this chapter and I hope that you will be able to build upon the examples to turn them into projects of your own. It's impossible to learn new programming techniques without practice and very often, you have to jump directly from simple and basic code snippets, to horribly complex real life projects. I have tried to provide a stepping-stone on the learning curve, with examples that are reasonably hard but that I have commented copiously, and which you can modify and improve until you really "get it".

Before the examples proper, I am going to describe the sample application.

The Sample Application

The sample application will be a simple search in the movie database for the films in which an actress or an actor plays.
We shall display the result of queries against the database as follows:

```
Title   Country,Year of Release     Director(s)        Actors
```

People names will be represented as comma-separated lists.

Although the description is simple, you will see that in most cases, the resulting program will be much more complicated than the examples commonly used in tutorials. Before considering what we shall do in the host language (the one that sends SQL statements to the database), let's discuss how the criteria input by users will take us to the final result.

Getting the Result

A mistake very commonly made by beginners, is to focus on what will be displayed and to start thinking "how I am going to build these lists of names?" I'll discuss this later but you must understand that it's of second importance, in spite of the SQL "challenge" (which you don't necessarily need to solve in SQL, as you are going to see shortly). A beginner often tries to write a query that transforms the base tables into a result set that looks like what we want to obtain, then screens the rows that are wanted. One of the many difficulties of SQL development is that on a small database, almost anything can work and that a wrong approach rarely looks obviously wrong (if it did, everyone would see it and find a better way). If you create for instance, a view that returns film information as desired and apply a **where** clause with a **like** condition to the list of actors in the view, you won't use a single index when filtering but as long as the database isn't too big, it will work satisfactorily. The day when the database becomes really large, queries will become painfully slow. It's something that happens frequently in the professional world, when developers have only tested their queries against small datasets or when they are alone working on the database. When an application works well on a small dataset or with few users and is sluggish on a large one accessed simultaneously by many users, you usually hear that it doesn't *scale* (some people are quick to blame the database rather than programming). I want to show you how to design an application that scales.

What do I want, really? I want something that will not be shown to end-users: I want a list of *movieid* values. If I provide a *movieid* value to someone who has even a cursory knowledge of SQL, that person will be perfectly able to obtain the title, country name, year of release, as well as who directed and played in that particular film. Perhaps it will mean more queries than I'd like to see but we'll get the information. The real difficulty isn't in retrieving all the information that gravitates around a *movieid* value: the real difficulty is to find *movieid* values. How do I obtain these *movieid* values? They are the identifiers of films in which someone played. I can easily find the information in table *credits* - provided that I have the identifier of the person. In the end, the real challenge is to retrieve the identifier of one person when provided with a name, not necessarily typed as it's stored in the database. Everything else is cosmetic.

Searching on people's names is an interesting problem. First of all, in a program for a wider public, you probably won't require the entering of first name and surname separately; the single "search box" is a familiar feature of web sites and it's more natural for a casual user to type the full name in a single input field. You will find a single input field in all examples with the exception of the C# one that illustrates "entering surname and first name separately" - but assumes that users can get it wrong. It's a safe rule to say that the easier a program is for the end-user, the harder it is to code, and the simple requirement of entering the full name in one field can easily cause headaches. You'll get input values that will look like *Clint Eastwood*, as one string of characters. Your program will have to split this single field and match each part against columns *first_name* and *surname* in table *people*. That would be fine if all people were named Clint Eastwood or Cameron Diaz but there are also Edward G. Robinson, Jamie Lee Curtis, Benicio Del Toro, Josef von Sternberg and Ewan McGregor, for all of whom, you will recognize problems I have already addressed in previous chapters. Chow Yun-Fat and Gong Li are known, as is usual in Chinese, surname first which isn't the case of Michelle Yeoh, Jacky Chan or Andy Lau. In the sample programs, I assume that the name may be incomplete ('Eastwood') or that first name and surname may be inverted but otherwise I'll assume that names are typed as they should be - there is no provision in the sample programs for mistyped names, and a name with an accented letter won't be found if it's typed without the accent. I'll simply focus here on matching input to several columns in the database and finding the best match.

Knowing where to "cut" when there are more than two space-separated parts in a full name is not something that can be easily coded.

Different strategies can be applied. One is to split on spaces, the full name as entered by the user and compare each one of the chunks thus obtained with both the first name and the surname. For instance, if the user has entered *Jamie Lee Curtis*, we can have as condition

```
where ((first_name = 'Jamie' or surname = 'Jamie')
       or (first_name = 'Lee' or surname = 'Lee')
       or (first_name = 'Curtis' or surname = 'Curtis'))
```

I am in fact using each one of the components of the full name as a tag here, as in the search on titles of Chapter 6. You will notice that if the first name is stored in the database as *Jamie Lee*, only the surname will match but that's enough. The problem is that the query will also return Jamie Lee's father, Tony Curtis and Jamie Foxx, and also people whose first name is Curtis, and Lee will match the first name of Lee Marvin, and the surname of Bruce Lee – among others. With any search, there is always the question of not only finding what we are looking for but also of getting rid of "noise", irrelevant data. We must be ready to rank the rows that satisfy the conditions by relevance. Even with a simpler name we can get noise, as the condition

```
where ((first_name = 'James' or surname = 'James')
       or (first_name = 'Stewart' or surname = 'Stewart'))
```

would certainly find James Stewart but also James Cagney, James Cameron and Stewart Granger. We cannot here, count a number of hits as with tags in Chapter 6 because irrespective of whether we have a match on both first name and surname or only one of them, a single row will be returned per actor. A possible solution would be to remove (with a function such as **replace()**) the input from what we have found and check the length of what remains:

```
coalesce(
         length(
           trim(
             replace(
               replace(coalesce(first_name,'')||surname,
                       'James', ''),  ← Remove 'James' from the concatenation
               'Stewart', '')  ← Remove 'Stewart' from whatever remains
             )  ← Remove spaces, just in case / you may use rtrim(ltrim(    ))
         ), 0)  ← if length is null, say zero
```

NOTE The **coalesce()** is required by Oracle, and Oracle alone, for which the length of an empty string is null and not zero as with other products.

This is an expression that we can use to sort people by relevance. However, minor misspellings may derail the replacement. Better strategies are possible, based on functions such as **translate()** that are available in some DBMS products only, and you'll see some examples in the sample programs. Whatever the tactics, the strategy remains the same: in all cases you need what we can call a *scoring expression* to qualify how well what you have found, matches the user input. Once you can rank people and identify the most likely candidate, you can build a query that returns the *movieid* values (what we ultimately want) for the films that person was involved in, for instance with a query like

```
select q2.movieid
from (select q1.movieid,
             rank() over (order by q1.score) as rnk
      from (select c.movied, <scoring expression> as score
            from people p
                 inner join credits c
                 on c.peopleid = p.peopleid
            where c.credited_as = '...'
              and ...) q1) q2
where q2.rnk = 1
```

NOTE If the DBMS doesn't support rank(), we'll use a substitute such as **limit**...

A few points are worth noting:

- As already stated, I am showing here one tactic among several possible ones. When a full name is composed of more than two parts, it would be possible to find a match by trying different combinations, for instance

  ```
  where ((first_name = 'Jamie' and surname = 'Lee Curtis')
         or (first_name = 'Jamie Lee' and surname = 'Curtis'))
  ```

- If we design a good method for filtering out "noise", then we can try to cast our net wider and use **like** *<input>* **|| '%'** instead of plain equality. If the percent sign trails the input, indexes will still be usable.
- In the tactic in which you compare each part of the name that is entered by the user to *first_name* and *surname* in turn, you are using both columns symmetrically, which is perfectly legit with regard to relational theory. But there is also implementation and from an implementation standpoint, both columns aren't interchangeable. The difference is in the unique constraint, and the index that implements it. As you have seen in Chapter 9, I had specified that (*surname*, *first_name*), in this order, is unique because I had speculated that searches on the surname alone would be more common (and more useful) than searches on the first name alone. If I write

  ```
  where ((first_name = 'James' or surname = 'James')
         or (first_name = 'Stewart' or surname = 'Stewart'))
  ```

  I can use the index to find quickly, people whose surname is either James or Stewart because the surname is the leading column in the index but I cannot find quickly, people whose first name is either James or Stewart because the index cannot be used for a column that appears in the second position. It would be different if the condition on *first_name* and the condition on *surname* were linked by an **and** as in the alternative tactic suggested in the first point; it would mean that I should find them on the same row. Using **or** means that the condition can be true for different rows. The DBMS will have to scan the table to find first names that match the condition; hence, it's unlikely it will use any index at all for table *people*, since if the table has to be scanned anyway, everything can be checked in the same pass. Unless of course we create an additional index on column *first_name* alone, restoring symmetry between the two columns.

If you conclude that the tactic in the first point is better because of the **and** demanding that a condition on both *first_name* and *surname* is true for the same row, the tactic isn't flawless either, and I'll let you guess where it can go wrong (hint: think of Chow Yun-Fat). If we want to cover all possible cases, we may end up with a lot of combinations to try.

Alternatively, we can search first on the surname alone and only use the full user input for removing noise. To give you an example you can simply search on

```
where (surname like 'Jamie%'
       or surname like 'Lee%'
       or surname like 'Curtis%')
```

which will return less noise than the preceding example. Then you can compare the user input to the combination of first name and surname in the rows that were found to get rid of Tony Curtis and of Bruce Lee. This assumes of course that the surname hasn't been mistyped but if the correct surname was entered by the user, we don't need an additional index. I'll adopt this tactic in most sample programs; the exception is the .NET program, where input is compared in the same way with *first_name* and *surname*, which suggests an additional index on the first name.

Once again, my goal is primarily to show you how programs interact with the database and I'll keep my examples relatively simple. I invite you to modify the programs and try to improve searches. Searches on people names are very common and studying different techniques may sharpen your skills. I have used different tactics in the different programs, trying to take advantage of the built-in functions of each DBMS.

As we don't know how many pieces of name we'll need to compare (user input can be *Bogart*, *Marilyn Monroe* or *Tommy Lee Jones*) and how many conditions and variables we'll have in the **where** clause, we'll need to build some part of the query in the program, when we know the input.

NOTE It's possible to split a string variable in SQL but it isn't easy.

Presenting the Result

As I have said earlier, getting the film identifiers (after having found the identifier of the actress or actor) is what really matters. Let's turn our attention now to comma-separated lists of names. Most DBMS products feature an aggregate function that concatenates strings. For instance, with MySQL you can obtain a comma-separated list of the actors who played in *Citizen Kane* with (knowing that I only have one *Citizen Kane* in my database, I have somewhat simplified conditions):

```
select group_concat(trim(concat(coalesce(p.first_name, ''),
                                ' ', surname))) actors
from movies m
     inner join credits c
        on c.movieid = m.movieid
     inner join people p
        on p.peopleid = c.peopleid
where m.title = 'Citizen Kane'
  and c.credited_as = 'A'
```

This function is often known under a different name, such as **listagg()** in Oracle and DB2, or **string_agg()** in PostgreSQL.

> NOTE **listagg()** has a more complicated syntax than **group_concat()**. There is an example on page 372.

When a product (possibly an older version) has no aggregate function, there are usually three ways to obtain a comparable result in SQL:

- Write one's own function (usually the worst idea, unless the DBMS offers facilities for writing your own aggregate function).
- Use a complicated recursive **with** expression that also uses a **row_number()** window function to rank and relate the elements to order, then apply a **group by** that simply keeps the longest strings, to what the **with** expression returns. Tough.
- Use an existing function that is able to return, as one row, data from several rows, and play with it. Many DBMS products allow retrieving, as a long **XML** string, all the rows returned by a query. In case you don't know it, XML (e**X**tensible **M**arkup **L**anguage) is a popular data exchange format in which the various pieces of data are surrounded by tags in the form *<tag>* before the data, and *</tag>* after it; these tags can be nested. A full table can therefore be exported as something like **<dataset><row><col1>**col1 value**</col1><col2>**col2 value**</col2> ... </row><row> ... </row> ... </dataset>.** Many utilities can understand such a format and load it into another database. By stripping the tags you can also use XML functions in a query to obtain, on a single line, the concatenation of pieces of text found in several rows.

Clever tricks and SQL contortion are popular on database forums. You mustn't forget nevertheless, that when you are retrieving data in a program, there is one place other than SQL where you can process data for presentation purposes: the program itself. You can indeed let SQL return a concatenated list of director names and a concatenated list of actor names. You can also retrieve one row per person, suitably ordered, with the information telling how the person is credited and concatenate each name to one list or another inside the program, before displaying the information (I shall give you one example in the DB2 program with embedded SQL).

I am touching here on an important point when you execute SQL queries from within a program: deciding on what should be done in SQL and what should be done in the programming language. Some people consider that SQL must retrieve the data and that the presentation of data should be the exclusive territory of the calling language. I am insisting on *presentation*, in the strictest sense of presenting the set returned from the database. I have seen people fetching many rows and deciding in their programs, with simple conditions applied to the data retrieved, which rows they wanted to show (it should have been done in the **where** clause; there is no point returning data you don't want) and others loading all the rows in sophisticated data structures, before engaging in what amounted to the equivalent of a **group by**, only much slower. Real presentation operations such as number formatting, concatenating strings, displaying data in rows or in columns, can often be equally performed in SQL or in the calling language.

I would say that it depends on the programming language that is used to access the database, the SQL dialect, your skills with both SQL and the programming language, and the final destination of the data. What matters, as I have already mentioned, is the number of calls, or round-trips, to the database (as well as the amount of data you process). When the ultimate destination of data is another table in the database, and if the data transfer is expected to be a frequent operation that must be fast, I wouldn't hesitate a moment. I would write either a stored procedure or (preferably) an SQL expression, even a very complicated one, simply to be able to run an **insert** ... **select** ... statement and avoid having a lot of rows received by my program, only to be inserted back into the database. If the data must simply be written to screen or to a file, if the programming language is very rich, with many libraries and functions, and if it allows the performance of some operations more easily than in SQL, then, all other things being equal, you are probably better off using the programming language for the final layer of polish before presenting the data to users. There are also cases to consider where SQL is probably easier for massaging data, I am thinking of string manipulation in SQL compared to C, for instance.

If there must be a rule, it would rather be

- to compare efficiency (returning different names on several rows rather than one row with all names doesn't make much of a difference if you don't return a very large number of films),
- to adjust for the frequency factor (remember that if a program runs once a week, it can be less efficient than if it runs every hour),
- and go for the easier, of SQL or of the programming language - easier for you and for people who will come after you, because some languages, C and Perl spring to mind, lend themselves to obfuscated code as much as SQL.

The main focus of SQL is on retrieving data and operating on it, as correctly and as efficiently as possible. Further than this, the choice is yours whether you want to do everything in SQL or not.

Sample Programs

That was a lengthy introduction; but I hope you found it interesting and that you now see the numerous difficulties involved in what might look at first sight like a simple program, and have ideas about how to cope with those difficulties. It's time to see how we can code the sample application in various environments and languages. Although functionally all of the various programs correspond to the same application, I have tried each time to take advantage of features available in the DBMS and have also adopted different tactics, sometimes doing more in SQL, and sometimes more in the programming language. Once again, the full source code for all examples can be downloaded from http://edu.konagora.com. You shouldn't consider these examples as anything more than illustrations - they aren't tutorials and won't spare you the trouble of reading the relevant reference documentation. I have tried to illustrate what the description of a function in a reference manual and a two-line example often leave in the dark.

You will find in this section:

Command-Line Programs

Command-line programs are often non-interactive programs, launched by schedulers, that operate on massive amounts of data (you can find command-line programs in other contexts - for instance, Web CGI programs arguably belong to the same family). My sample program is a poor example of a command-line program, as no application that targets end-users would ever be released without some kind of graphical interface but it's a good way for me to demonstrate techniques.

One common issue to all non-interactive programs is authentication: how should we provide hostname, port, database, username, and password that are required to connect to the database server when there is no login window?

> NOTE Many products implement more secure and sophisticated authentication mechanisms than password authentication but passwords still remain the most common method.

What you should **not** do is hard-code everything in the program. Database passwords, like all passwords, should be changed from time to time (some products implement optional password policy mechanisms) and you don't want to have to modify programs when passwords are changed. Besides, even when the program is compiled, it's easy to look for strings of characters in an executable file and anybody who can read the program, can potentially read the password.

A better option is to pass connection parameters as command-line arguments, as all SQL command-line clients do. The password, however, is still an issue. If you type the password on the command line, on many systems while the program is still running, another user will be able to see which arguments you passed (on a UNIX system, you just have to issue the *ps* command with the right flags). Command line history in consoles is also a security problem. If somebody comes to your workstation while you are away and presses the up arrow the right number of times, your password will become public knowledge. The right way to connect is to provide as command-line arguments, non-sensitive data (hostname, database name, username - although one could debate the sensitivity of the username), and let the program prompt for the password. But if the program is launched by a scheduler at 2am, there will be no one around to enter a password.

- The best way to connect in a batch program is to use trusted connections - I mentioned them in Chapter 2. You can set-up database accounts so as to associate them with an operating system account; if you are running the program and accessing the database from this operating system account, then the database server considers that you have already proved who you are and connects you without a password.

- Trusted connections usually require (unless you want to open a big security hole in your system) that program and database server are running on the same machine. Alternatively, the second best solution would be to store connection information in a (preferably hidden) file at a well-known location and to make this file readable by its owner only. This configuration file can either be included (by scripting languages) or read (by compiled programs) to obtain connection data. It's the method commonly used by web servers, which can access database servers on other machines.

Accessing Oracle with bash/ksh

The bash scripting language (or its close relative ksh) is typical of UNIX systems, which includes Linux and Mac OS X. What I am showing in this section can, however, be practiced on a Windows system, if you install a free Linux-like environment such as Cygwin. Coding database access in a shell script is a bit special, as it doesn't follow the general pattern I gave in Chapter 11 (many other scripting languages though, such as perl or Python, *do* follow that pattern); you simply wrap calls to the command-line interactive SQL client in a shell script. It will be here `sqlplus` with Oracle, it would be `clpplus` (with the `nw` option so that it doesn't open a new window) with DB2, `psql` with PostgreSQL, `mysql` with ... I think you can guess. It's rather common to use the traditional scripting languages of the UNIX/Linux world to access databases. You don't use them to write an application such as my sample application, which in this context isn't a realistic example but shell scripts are very often used by database administrators for a wide array of operations that require database accesses. These tasks range from monitoring, to routine administrative tasks, and scripts that access databases are also very much used in undertakings that involve data transfer from one system to another, for instance regularly uploading data from an operational database to a decision support system. Shell scripts are also perfect for some mundane tasks such as generating and emailing weekly, a CSV file that some manager will use to generate charts to include in a report (sometimes you need very little to make a manager happy). It's possible to access a database from a spreadsheet with ODBC or OLE objects but the weekly email has a nice personal touch and allows us to ensure that several people receive exactly the same data, instead of collecting slightly different figures at different times.

I assume in my examples that I'm using a database account that is associated with an operating system account. In that case authentication is implicit and doesn't require a password.

NOTE With Oracle, if you are connected to the operating system as *username* and if a database account called *ops$username* exists, no password is required to connect to this database account. The *ops$* prefix is the default and can be changed by database administrators (it's possible to have identical operating system and database account names).

I assume furthermore, that the account I am accessing has been granted the suitable rights to access the tables (owned for instance by the *moviedb* account) and that aliases (synonyms) have been created, allowing me to refer to *movies* instead of the qualified name *moviedb.movies*.

With Oracle, private synonyms can be created by an account that has such a privilege

```
create synonym movies for moviedb.movies
```

Alternatively, public synonyms, valid for all accounts across the database, can be created by even more powerful accounts, for instance by a database administrator

```
create public synonym movies for moviedb.movies
```

In a script, everything revolves around passing queries to the SQL client. There are different ways in a script to "feed" the command line client. One is to store queries in a .sql file and invoke this file from the command line (Oracle example):

```
sqlplus  s / < my_query.sql
```

(the -s flag is for *silent* and suppresses the banner and the prompt; the / is how you connect from a trusted operating system account).

The inconvenience of the external file is that it's one more file to maintain, deploy, pass parameters to, and keep in the right directory. Besides you lose the global vision when you read the script.

Another method is to write something like this

```
sqlplus  s / <<EOF
   Your query here;
   exit 0
EOF
```

Alternatively you can use

```
echo "Your query here;
      exit 0" | sqlplus  s /
```

The second version is slightly less efficient (it forks an additional process) but it's what I usually write - I simply find it easier to combine with other commands.

What I have always found painful when running **select** statements in shell scripts is that, unless you return one word per line, you completely lose the notion of row. What I mean is that if you run

```
for row in $(echo "select title from movies;
                   exit 0" | sqlplus  s /)
do
   echo $row
done
```

Your script won't display one line per row as you might expect but something like this:

```
TITLE
--------------------------------------------------------------------------------
All
About
Eve
Annie
Hall
Blade
Runner
...
```

There is the same issue when you return several columns. The shell doesn't differentiate between space and carriage return. Once again, there are several possibilities. One is to redefine the separator (variable IFS), which by default can equally be a space, a tab or an end of line marker, as a carriage return only:

```
oldsep=$IFS
IFS=$'\n'
```

This solution works best if you are returning a single column that may contain spaces. If you want to return several columns, you must have a special separator for columns and add it to IFS. Alternatively, you can use something that is brutish but works well, applying **replace()** to substitute a special character for all spaces in the output of your query, concatenating if necessary, multiple columns with separators of your choice, then cleaning up rows in the script. For instance:

```
for row in $(echo "select replace(title, ' ', '_') from movies;
                   exit 0" | sqlplus  s /)
do
   echo $row | sed 's/_/ /g'
done
```

I won't have this problem in my sample script, as I'll merely display what SQL*Plus returns. Here is the annotated shell script:

```
#
#   Usage : films_starring.ksh <actor name>
#
#   Written by Stephane Faroult for "SQL Success"
#
if [ $# -eq 0 ]
then
  echo 'An actor name is required' >&2
  exit 1
fi
actor_name=''          ① Don't expect quoted names
spaceless_name=''
while [ $# -gt 0 ]     ② Process all command line parameters
do
  actor_name="${actor_name} $1"
```

```
    spaceless_name="${spaceless_name}${1}"
    shift
  done

  spaceless_name=$(echo ${spaceless_name} | sed 's/ //g')
```

③ Handle quoted arguments

④ Start the query

```
  query="select m.title, cast(m.year_released as varchar2(4))||',' \
         ||ctry.country_name origin, \
```

⑤ Build name lists as nested queries

```
   (select listagg(trim(coalesce(d.first_name,' ')||' '||d.surname),',') \
          within group(order by d.surname,d.first_name) \
         from credits c \
              inner join people d \
              on d.peopleid=c.peopleid \
         where c.credited_as='D' \
         and c.movieid=m.movieid) directors, \
       (select listagg(trim(coalesce(a.first_name,' ')||' '||a.surname),',') \
          within group(order by a.surname,a.first_name) \
         from credits c \
              inner join people a \
              on a.peopleid=c.peopleid \
         where c.credited_as='A' \
         and c.movieid=m.movieid) actors \
         from movies m \
           inner join countries ctry \
           on ctry.country_code=m.country \
         where movieid in \
        (select q2.movieid \
         from (select q1.movieid, \
                      rank() over (order by q1.score) as rnk \
               from (select c.movieid, \
```

⑥ Scoring function of death

```
                            coalesce(\
                              length(\
                                replace(\
                                  translate(\
                                    replace(\
                                      lower(\
                                        trim(first_name||surname)), \
                                      ' ',''),\
                                    lower(trim(replace('${spaceless_name}', \
                                                  '''', '''''')))),\
                             rpad('*',length(trim('${spaceless_name}')),\
                                        '*')),\
                                  '*','')),0) as score\
                     from people p \
                          inner join credits c \
                          on c.peopleid=p.peopleid \
                     where c.credited_as='A' \
                       and ("
  cnt=0
  cond=''
```

```
for part in $actor_name    ⑦ Shell substitution, not bind variable
do
  if [ $cnt -gt 0 ]
  then
    cond="$cond or"
  fi
  cond="$cond p.surname like initcap(replace('${part}','''',''''''))||'%'"
  cnt=$(( $cnt + 1 ))
done
cond="${cond})) q1) q2\
      where q2.rnk=1)"
query="$query ${cond}"
# If you want to see what the query looks like ..
#echo $query
echo "set feedback off         ⑧ A bit of formatting and we are done
      set recsep off
      set linesize 180
      col title format A40
      col origin format A25
      col directors format A30
      col actors format A70
      ${query};
      exit" | sqlplus -s /
```

The name provided on the command line may, or may not, be quoted. If it isn't, I reconstruct it ① by concatenating the various command line arguments ②. At the same time, I am building a name without spaces, which I will use in the scoring function. As the name may be quoted, I need to make really sure ③ that the "spaceless" name is really spaceless. I then start building my query ④, of which the major part doesn't depend on user input. A complex expression to aggregate names ⑤ appears twice, for directors and for actors. Another tough expression is the scoring function ⑥, which isn't as bad as it looks. The dynamic part of the query is built by taking in turn, each component in the full name ⑦ and adding it to the query, escaping quotes in the process. Finally the query is passed to SQL*Plus, with some formatting ⑧ to make the output look better. We first suppress the message saying how many rows were selected, then we suppress empty lines that are usually added when data wraps around in columns, then we set a large line-width. The other commands set the width of each column.

The script probably looks tough at first sight but while the SQL part isn't entirely trivial, the wrapping around it isn't difficult. Let me comment the query.

- The first complexity in the query lies in the subqueries in the *select list*, which use the **listagg()** function also available in DB2. I almost never use subqueries in the select list because each subquery (both subqueries in the present case) fire with each row returned (unless the optimizer savagely rewrites everything). In this particular case I know that I won't return many rows and it's not an issue.

- The second complexity is in the (admittedly challenging) scoring function. The idea behind the function is simpler than its expression. Its goal is to suppress from the full name of "candidates" (i.e. people whose surname matches one of the components in the name provided by the user), all letters that can be found in user input, and then compute the length of what remains. Letter suppression is performed in two steps because in Oracle, **translate()** cannot replace a character by nothing (see Appendix B, where an example is provided). First we replace all characters in the user input by a asterisk (constructing a string of asterisks as long as what we want to replace), then we replace asterisks by an empty string (this works) and check the length of what remains. I have built a special "spaceless name" merely for these substitutions.
- You should also notice the replacement of every single quote by two single quotes; as this replacement is done in SQL, in which quotes must be doubled (and are themselves between quotes); we end up with an impressive collection of quotes. This replacement firstly protects against SQL injection and secondly allows searching for names such as *O'Hara* or *O'Toole*, which would produce syntactically incorrect SQL otherwise.

I would like to point out that when I insert the different parts that comprise a full name in the query, a shell substitution occurs. This is pure text replacement, not parameter-passing in the sense of bind variables and you shouldn't mistake one for the other. What will be passed to the SQL engine, ultimately, is a query in which all values are hard-coded, not passed as parameters as I would do with a query that is executed repeatedly. You can echo the query before it's executed if you aren't completely convinced. It would be possible to assign values to variables and pass those variables to queries, even with shell scripts but as shell scripts are mostly used to execute very occasional SQL processes, true SQL variables are rarely used in them.

Accessing DB2 with Embedded SQL and C

DB2, Oracle and PostgreSQL allow one to type SQL commands directly into a host language, with a simple syntax and no explicit function call. Old versions of SQL Server used to support embedded SQL as well but it has been deprecated. If you want to retrieve how many films you have in your database, you can write with embedded SQL in a C program (several host languages are supported, C is just one of them):

```
EXEC SQL SELECT COUNT(*) INTO :number_of_films FROM MOVIES;
```

(it's customary to write SQL in upper case in an embedded C program)
If an integer variable named *number_of_films* was properly declared in the program, you'll assign the value returned by the query to the variable, with this command.

Embedded SQL is very interesting for several reasons:

- Historically, it's the very first devised method to access SQL databases from a program. Embedded SQL was actually created by the folks who invented SQL, the System/R team at IBM.
- Because it was there from the beginning, embedded SQL has strongly influenced the procedural extensions that were later developed for creating stored procedures. You have already seen **select ... into ...** in Chapter 8 but it originally came from embedded SQL. In the same way, *cursors*, a simple way to inspect a result set row by row, were born in embedded SQL (where they are necessary) and found their way into procedural extensions to SQL (where people often make questionable use of them). If you are comfortable with SQL and its procedural extensions, you'll find the learning curve gentler with embedded SQL than with function calls.
- Embedded SQL requires lesser mastery of the host language than direct function calls; programs are simpler.
- Embedded SQL is the best way to access a database from a programming language that doesn't permit instantiating objects or allocating memory dynamically, such as COBOL or FORTRAN (old languages that have long lost their dominance but are still much in use). This having been said, embedded SQL is much used with C and there is a direct descendent called SQLJ available for Java.

The key point to understand with embedded SQL is that it's basically a macro processor. User-friendly SQL commands in the program code are processed in a special pass, commented out and replaced by actual function calls, so as to obtain a pure source code in the host language that is later compiled, then linked with the client DBMS libraries to obtain the executable program. EXEC SQL statements are exactly similar to predefined macros in a C program.

Let's suppose that a developer writes a program that mixes C with embedded SQL statements; the extension given to programs depend on the DBMS product (with DB2 it's usually **.sqc**, with Oracle, for which the C processor is called Pro*C, the usual extension is **.pc**, and PostgreSQL, the processor of which is called ECPG, prefers **.pgc**). If this program is called `myprog.sqc` the various steps with DB2 to obtain the executable program will be

```
db2 connect to <dbname>          ① Connect to the database
db2 prep myprog.sqc bindfile     ② Transform the .sqc into a .c
db2 bind myprog.bnd              ③ Associate with stored procedures
cc  o myprog myprog.c  ldb2      ④ Compile and link
```

One of the strengths of embedded SQL, is that many operations that involve the database are performed when you prepare the program and not at run time (not with

> PostgreSQL). It requires that you are connected ① to the database (with Oracle you pass connection information as a parameter when you process the .pc file). Note that this connection is simply for preparing the program, you still need to connect inside the program. The preprocessing ② transforms the original file into a pure .c file. In the particular case of DB2, it also prepares a kind of stored module associated with the program which is loaded ③ into the database. As a result, you obtain an industrial-strength program in which SQL operations that have already been prepared and stored in the database, are just called by the program, compiled ④ as any C program and linked with the DB2 client libraries (I assume the system knows where they are).

To show you the result of preprocessing, I have written, with DB2, a small program which I have called *demo.sqc*, in which I just count the number of films in table *movies* using the example **select** statement shown at the beginning of this section. Once processed, the single command

```
EXEC SQL SELECT COUNT(*) INTO :number_of_films FROM MOVIES;
```

becomes the unattractive piece of C code that follows:

```
/*
EXEC SQL SELECT COUNT(*) INTO :number_of_films FROM MOVIES;
*/

{
#line 28 "demo.sqc"
  sqlastrt(sqla_program_id, &sqla_rtinfo, &sqlca);
#line 28 "demo.sqc"
  sqlaaloc(3,1,2,0L);
    {
      struct sqla_setdata_list sql_setdlist[1];
#line 28 "demo.sqc"
      sql_setdlist[0].sqltype = 496; sql_setdlist[0].sqllen = 4;
#line 28 "demo.sqc"
      sql_setdlist[0].sqldata = (void*)&number_of_films;
#line 28 "demo.sqc"
      sql_setdlist[0].sqlind = 0L;
#line 28 "demo.sqc"
      sqlasetdata(3,0,1,sql_setdlist,0L,0L);
    }
#line 28 "demo.sqc"
  sqlacall((unsigned short)24,1,0,3,0L);
```

Macros add the original line number (in the .sqc file) as well as the original file number, which allows the file that was written by the developer to be referred to in error messages. The simple SQL statement is commented and replaced by several not-so-user-friendly calls to functions from the DB2 client library.

An embedded SQL program always contains two special EXEC SQL elements that have no real equivalent in other programming environments.

- The first one is a statement

  ```
  EXEC SQL INCLUDE SQLCA;
  ```

  SQLCA stands for **SQL C**ommunication **A**rea. How do you check that a **select ... into** ... succeeds and that you really retrieve the value you wanted? So many things can fail ... The SQLCA is simply a structure that is used as context and stores information about the outcome of each SQL command. You can inspect it directly in your program or you may, which is much more convenient, use

  ```
  EXEC SQL WHENEVER <event> <action>;
  ```

  in which the event is usually `SQLERROR` or `NOTFOUND` and the action is either the call of a procedure or a jump to a label in your C program (embedded SQL is an environment in which you sometimes have to compromise with the best practices of structured programming ...). Such an `EXEC SQL` statement automatically adds tests of the suitable SQLCA fields and the action, to all SQL commands that follow. Beware that by "follow", I really mean "on the following lines in the file". The preprocessor has no knowledge of functions and blocks in your program.

- The second one is a block called the `DECLARE SECTION` (between `EXEC SQL BEGIN DECLARE SECTION` and `EXEC SQL END DECLARE SECTION`) in which you declare the variables that are known to both your C program and to the SQL statements: variables in which you return values or that are used to pass criteria values to the database. The `DECLARE SECTION` is often global but it's not obligatory. Beware that only a subset of all the C data types is supported; however, some special data types are available to support binary data, for instance (structures that include the length).

  You also declare in this section, with the **short** type in C, what is known as *indicator variables*. Indicator variables are always associated with another variable. When present, indicator variables are used by the DBMS libraries to indicate whether what we find in the associated variable is valid (the indicator is set to 0), was truncated because the program variable wasn't big enough to accommodate what was in the database (the indicator is set to a positive value) or is invalid because the value was null in the database and the bytes of the variable weren't overwritten with data (the indicator is set to a negative value). You'll see indicator variables in use in the sample program.

Let's now see the program. I have created, and use, a structure called *STRBUF* which contains three fields; a `char *` pointer called *s*, the current length of what *s* points to and the current maximum size of what *s* can accommodate. Such a structure must be initialized by a call to **strbuf_init()**, text is appended by **strbuf_add()** which takes care of memory allocation and resizing, and memory is freed by calling **strbuf_dispose()** (another function, **strbuf_clear()**, resets to an 'empty' state without freeing memory). It's similar to *String* objects in C++ and even more similar to a Java

StringBuffer. Everything else in the code is standard. Note that I have added a lot of tabs (\t) to the SQL statement which are unnecessary but make the statement more readable if you want to display it and check what the program generates.

```
#include <stdio.h>
#include <stdlib.h>
#include <string.h>
#include <errno.h>

#include <sql.h>      ① DB2 header file

#define   MAX_PARAMETERS   250

#include "strbuf.h"

EXEC SQL INCLUDE SQLCA;     ② Communication area (error codes)
EXEC SQL INCLUDE SQLDA;     ③ Descriptor area (for parameters)

static char  *G_parameters[MAX_PARAMETERS];  ④ To hold parameters
static short  G_paramcnt = 0;

static void print_usage() {
   fprintf(stderr,
           "Usage:\n  films_starring <name>\n");
}
```

I first start by including **sql.h** ① which is the header file for the DB2 client library. I assume that I won't have more than 250 parameters, which is hugely oversized for this particular program. I include the SQLCA ② (mandatory) in which I'll get the status after each interaction with the database. I also include ③ the optional descriptor area; I'll use it to describe to the database the parameters I'll pass. The same structure is also used to retrieve from the database, the description of columns that are returned when this isn't known in advance. I also declare as a global variable, an array that will hold the parameters I pass ④, as well as a short integer value to record how many parameters I have.

```
void  main(int argc, char *argv[]) {

   EXEC SQL BEGIN DECLARE SECTION;   ⑥ C variables known by SQL
   char          *stmt;
   char           film_title[500];
   char           origin[200];
   char           who[100];
   short          whoind;
   char           credited_as;
   short          creditind;
   int            rn;
   int            cnt;
   EXEC SQL END DECLARE SECTION;

   char           errmsg[1025];
```

```
int          i;
char        *p;
STRBUF       query;
STRBUF       searched_name;
STRBUF       director_list;
STRBUF       actor_list;
char         start;

struct sqlda *da = (struct sqlda *)NULL;  ⑥ Declare an SQLDA

if (argc < 2) {
   print_usage();
   exit(1);
}
strbuf_init(&searched_name);
for (i = 1; i < argc; i++) {          ⑦ Concatenate command-line parameters
   strbuf_add(&searched_name, argv[i]);
   strbuf_add(&searched_name, " ");
}
```

Another mandatory piece of any embedded SQL program is ⑤ the DECLARE SECTION which contains the declaration of C variables that will appear in the EXEC SQL statements. It includes the pointer to the SQL statement I'll pass, and all the variables I will fetch results into, as well as two indicator variables (*whoind* and *creditind*) that you will see in use. If I were passing to the statement values in static C variables as bind variables, they would also appear in the DECLARE SECTION. However, I'll pass them in a descriptor area, to which I declare a pointer ⑥ outside the DECLARE SECTION. Beware that only a subset of C data types can appear in the DECLARE SECTION. It includes most usual data types but nothing fancy. I concatenate ⑦ all command line arguments as a single string.

```
//
strbuf_init(&query);
strbuf_add(&query,                  ⑧ THE query
          "select m.title,\n"
          "\tc.country_name||','||cast(m.year_released as char(4)),\n"
          "\ttrim(p.first_name||' '||p.surname)  as who,\n"  ⑨ Return names
          "\tcr.credited_as,\n"      ⑩ Return involvement in the film
          "\trow_number()\n"         ⑪ Return a rank in the film
          "\t\tover (partition by m.movieid\n"
          "\t\torder by p.surname, p.first_name) rn,\n"
          "\tcount(*)\n"             ⑫ Return a count per film
          "\t\tover (partition by m.movieid) cnt\n"
          "from movies m\n"
          "\tinner join countries c\n"
          "\ton c.country_code = m.country\n"
          "\tleft outer join credits cr\n"
          "\ton cr.movieid = m.movieid\n"
          "\tand cr.credited_as in ('A', 'D')\n"
          "\tleft outer join people p\n"
          "\ton p.peopleid = cr.peopleid\n"
```

```
              "where m.movieid in\n\t(select movieid\n"
                                       ⑬ Subquery to identify films
              "\tfrom (select movieid,\n"
              "\t\t\trank() over (order by score) rnk\n"
              "\t\tfrom (select c.movieid,\n"
              "\t\t\tcoalesce(length(replace(\n"
"\t\t\ttranslate(lower(replace(trim(p.first_name||p.surname),' ','')),\n"
 "\t\t\t\trepeat('*',length(replace(trim(cast(? as varchar(100))),' ',''))),\n"
 "\t\t\t\tlower(replace(trim(cast(? as varchar(100))),' ',''))),\n"
              "\t\t\t\t\t'*','')), 0) as score\n"  ⑭ Scoring function
              "\t\t\tfrom people p\n"
              "\t\t\t\tinner join credits c\n"
              "\t\t\t\ton c.peopleid=p.peopleid\n"
              "\t\t\twhere c.credited_as='A'\n"
              "\t\t\tand (");
   if (G_paramcnt > (MAX_PARAMETERS - 2)) {  ⑮ Paranoid test
      fprintf(stderr,
              "Maximum number of parameters (%d) exceeded (%d)\n",
              MAX_PARAMETERS, (int)G_paramcnt);
      exit(1);
   }
   G_parameters[G_paramcnt++] = strdup(searched_name.s);
   G_parameters[G_paramcnt++] = strdup(searched_name.s);
```

The query ⑧ is once again challenging but I adopt a tactic that is different from what I have done in shell with Oracle and from what I'll do with PostgreSQL next. I return all names one by one ⑨, as well as how they were credited ⑩ and I'll build the name lists in the program. To help me in this exercise, I return an order number ⑪ for each person, as well as ⑫, how many people I have for this film. It will allow me to know when I have everything and can display information for the film. A subquery ⑬ identifies the films in which an actor played, with a scoring expression ⑭ very similar to the Oracle one in ksh, except that the order of parameters of function **translate()** isn't the same with DB2. A completely paranoid test ⑮ precedes the assignment to the array of parameters of the searched name to associate with the two place-holders in the scoring expression.

```
   p = strtok(searched_name.s, " ");   ⑯ Split names
   start = 1;
   while (p) {
      if (!start) {
         strbuf_add(&query, "\n\t\t\t\tor ");
      } else {
         start = 0;
      }
      strbuf_add(&query, "surname like initcap(?)||'%'");
      G_parameters[G_paramcnt++] = strdup(p);      ⑰ Add each part as parameter
      if (G_paramcnt == MAX_PARAMETERS) {
         fprintf(stderr,
                 "Maximum number of parameters(%d) exceeded\n",
                 MAX_PARAMETERS);
         exit(1);
      }
```

```
    p = strtok(NULL, " ");
}
strbuf_add(&query, ")) p1) p2\n"        ⑱ Terminate the query
                   "\twhere rnk=1");
strbuf_add(&query,
          ")\norder by m.title,m.movieid,p.surname,p.first_name");
```

I then start tokenizing ⑯ the actor name I have been provided, adding a condition for each part and copying the value (an actual copy) to the parameter array ⑰. When all tokens have been added, I finish up the query ⑱.

```
if ((da = (struct sqlda *)calloc((size_t)1, SQLDASIZE(G_paramcnt)))
            == (struct sqlda *)NULL)    ⑲ Allocate a suitably sized descriptor
   perror("calloc()");
   strbuf_dispose(&searched_name);
   strbuf_dispose(&query);
   if (G_paramcnt > 0) {
      short i;

      for (i = 0; i < G_paramcnt; i++) {
         free(G_parameters[i]);
      }
   }
   exit(1);
}
populate_sqlda(da);    ⑳ This comes later
```

Before I can execute the query, I must prepare the SQL Descriptor Area (SQLDA) in which I'll describe the parameters in my query to the SQL engine. I only have declared a pointer to the descriptor area. I must allocate it ⑲, passing the number of parameters I want to describe to a library macro that computes the correct size for the descriptor. The description is done in a function ⑳ that you'll see shortly.

```
stmt = query.s;

EXEC SQL WHENEVER SQLERROR GOTO flop;    ㉑ Error handling
EXEC SQL CONNECT TO MOVIEDB;
EXEC SQL PREPARE S FROM :stmt;
EXEC SQL DECLARE C CURSOR FOR S;
EXEC SQL OPEN C USING DESCRIPTOR :*da;

EXEC SQL WHENEVER NOT FOUND GOTO done; ㉒ To exit the loop
```

We are now ready to access the database. First of all, I declare a label to which I want to branch ㉑ if an error occurs. It will save me the trouble of checking the SQLCA myself. Next, I connect to the database. With Oracle or PostgreSQL the syntax for connecting would be slightly different. Then I prepare the statement. The name *S* I assign to it is arbitrary. I associate a cursor *C* (another arbitrary name) with the statement to allow me to fetch data and I open the cursor, providing it with the SQLDA that describes the parameter. Note that the syntax here is particular to DB2, other products pass a pointer to the SQLDA, not the SQLDA itself (in other words, only DB2 uses **:*da**, it would be **:da** with another product). Before entering the loop I tell it to where to jump when all data has been fetched ㉒.

```
  strbuf_init(&director_list);
  strbuf_init(&actor_list);

  printf("%-30s\t%-20s\tDirected By\tStarring\n", "Title", "Origin");
  while (1) {
     EXEC SQL FETCH C                     ㉓ Get one row
     INTO :film_title, :origin,
          :who:whoind, :credited_as:creditind,
          :rn, :cnt;
     if (whoind >= 0) {        ㉔ Check for nulls (unnecessary here)
        if (credited_as == 'D') {
           if (director_list.curlen) {
              strbuf_add(&director_list, ",");
           }
           strbuf_add(&director_list, who);
        } else {
           if (actor_list.curlen) {
              strbuf_add(&actor_list, ",");
           }
           strbuf_add(&actor_list, who);
        }
     }
     if (rn == cnt) {
        printf("%-30.30s\t%-20.20s\t%s\t%s\n", film_title, origin,
                                  director_list.s,
                                  actor_list.s);
        strbuf_clear(&director_list);
        strbuf_clear(&actor_list);
     }
  }
done:
  EXEC SQL WHENEVER NOT FOUND CONTINUE;
  EXEC SQL CLOSE C;
  goto finish;
```

I fetch in the loop ㉓, the various columns into C variables declared in the DECLARE SECTION and known both from the DBMS and from the C program. Note that for the name and *credited_as* I have appended to the name of the variable that receives the column value, the name of an indicator variable. In the strict context of this particular program these indicator variables are useless, as I will always have at least the actor I am looking for associated with the movie. If I could search on the title of the film only, or on the country, I could imagine returning films for which director and actors are unknown, in which case testing ㉔ if I get a name would make sense. If the test is satisfied, I concatenate the name to one list or another, depending on the value of *credited_as*. I compare the number of the person in the film to the number of people involved, to decide whether I should output the line or not. I could have done it without the window functions, returning for instance *movieid* and checking for changes in values. Then I would have had to display a row AFTER the loop (last non displayed film) – or perhaps not. The window functions simplify the logic in the program a lot. After the loop, first (IMPORTANT!) I deactivate the jump to the *done* label and then I close the cursor before going to the end of the program (skipping the error handling section). I know, it's not structured programming...

```
flop:
   sqlaintp(errmsg, 1024, 0, &sqlca);    ㉕ Display error
   fprintf(stderr, "%s\n", errmsg);

 finish:
   EXEC SQL WHENEVER SQLERROR CONTINUE; ㉖ I don't care if disconnect fails
   EXEC SQL CONNECT RESET;
   strbuf_dispose(&query);
   strbuf_dispose(&searched_name);
   if (da) {
      free_sqlda(da);
   }
}
```

With DB2 you must call a special function to display the error message, as the sqlca doesn't contain a user-friendly error message (unlike some other products). I deactivate ㉖ (IMPORTANT) error handling before disconnecting from the database – otherwise, launching the program when the database server isn't started could result in an infinite loop. EXEC SQL CONNECT RESET is specific to DB2, Oracle uses EXEC SQL COMMIT (or ROLLBACK) WORK RELEASE and PostgreSQL EXEC SQL DISCONNECT but the functionality is the same. I free memory, there is a special function for freeing the descriptor area.

```
static void populate_sqlda(struct sqlda *da) {  ① Prepare to pass parameters
  short  nvar = 0;
  struct sqlvar *var;

  if (da) {
     memcpy(da->sqldaid, "SQLDA   ", sizeof(da->sqldaid));
     da->sqldabc = SQLDASIZE(G_paramcnt);
     da->sqln = G_paramcnt;    ② Tell how many
     da->sqld = G_paramcnt;
     var = da->sqlvar;
     for (nvar = 0; nvar < G_paramcnt; nvar++) {
        var[nvar].sqldata = G_parameters[nvar];
                              ③ Make each structure point to the data
        var[nvar].sqltype = SQL_TYP_CSTR;  // Defined in sql.h
                              ④ Tell it's a C string
        var[nvar].sqllen = strlen(G_parameters[nvar]);  ⑤ Give length
     }
   }
}
```

Here is the function ① where I assign to the SQLDA the parameter values stored, during the building phase of the query, in the global array G_parameters. The SQLDA has multiple fields, the names of which aren't the same with all products. What is important is that I must say how many parameters I have ②; then, as a special structure describes each parameter, for every parameter I must set a pointer to the data I input ③; say what is the type of what I am pointing to ④; and say how many bytes ⑤, I have to consider (not really necessary with 0 terminated C strings). I am only passing strings here. Note that passing strings is quite convenient; you can use **cast()** to change them to other data types inside the SQL statement.

```
static void free_sqlda(struct sqlda *da) {
  short          i;
  struct sqlvar *var;

  if (da) {
     for (i = 0; i < da->sqln; i++) {
        var = (struct sqlvar *)&(da->sqlvar[i]);
        if (var->sqldata) {
           free(var->sqldata);
        }
     }
     free(da);
  }
}
```

In the function where I free the SQLDA, I free memory that was allocated by **strdup()** when I copied the values to G_parameters. In other words, I have allocated memory when assigning values at one place and I am freeing it elsewhere. Just to make sure you have clear ideas about pointers...

Accessing PostgreSQL in C with the Client Library

When you directly use C functions, calls are sometimes more complicated (especially with Oracle) but you have more control in the program. I am using here again the **strbuf_...** functions I have described on page 377 in the previous section on embedded SQL with DB2.

Most functions with PostgreSQL return a pointer to an opaque structure called *PGresult* which contains both the status (whether the command succeeded or failed) and meta-data for queries (how many columns and rows were retrieved among other things), as well as the result set. This structure must be freed by calling function **PQclear()** when it's no longer needed. Placeholders for variables in the query are named **$*n***, with *n* varying from 1 to the total number of parameters.

```
#include <stdio.h>
#include <stdlib.h>
#include <string.h>
#include <locale.h>
#include <errno.h>
```

```
#include <libpq-fe.h>        ① Header file for the PostgreSQL C client library

#define  MAX_PARAM   50

#include "strbuf.h"

#define CONNECT_STRING   "host=localhost dbname=moviedb"
                                 ② Connection information

③ Simple utility functions
extern void DBerror(PGconn *con, PGresult *res, char *msg);
extern void error_terminate(PGconn *con, PGresult *res, char *msg);
```

First I include the header file ① that is required for the PostgreSQL client libraries. I am using a trusted connection but I specify the name of the database and the host – this won't change and I can hard-code it in the program ②. I also define ③ two utility functions for displaying errors. They have nothing special, and I won't comment on them here but they are available in the source code in file util.c.

```
static void print_usage() {
   fprintf(stderr, "Usage:\n  films_starring <name>\n");
}

int  main(int argc, char *argv[]) {
   PGconn     *con;        ④ Database handler
   PGresult   *res;        ⑤ What most database functions return
   int         i;
   char       *p;
   STRBUF      searched_name;
   STRBUF      query;
   short       paramcnt = 0;
   char       *param_array[MAX_PARAM];
   char        placeholder[10];
   int         rows;

   if (argc < 2) {
      print_usage();
      exit(1);
   }
   strbuf_init(&searched_name);
   for (i = 1; i < argc; i++) {    ⑥ Concatenate command line arguments
      strbuf_add(&searched_name, argv[i]);
      strbuf_add(&searched_name, " ");
   }
   con = PQconnectdb(CONNECT_STRING);    ⑦ Try to connect
   if (PQstatus(con) != CONNECTION_OK) {
     DBerror(con, (PGresult *)NULL, "Connection");
     return 1;
   }
   (void)setlocale(LC_ALL, "");    ⑧ For the conversion of UTF8 characters
```

There are two variables that you will find in every C program that accesses a database: a database handler ④, that materializes your connection to the database server and a fairly complicated structure, which represents the result ⑤ of the statements that you pass to the server. I first start by concatenating everything I find on the command line, into a single string ⑥, and then I try to connect to the database ⑦. This function always returns something but the connection isn't always successful (the database server may be stopped, the connection string may be wrong, authentication may fail ...). The **setlocale()** call ⑧ is merely intended to make accented characters look better when displayed after being retrieved from the database.

```
strbuf_init(&query);
strbuf_add(&query,    ⑨ THE query
           "select m.title,"
           "       c.country_name||','"
           "        ||cast(m.year_released as char(4)) as origin,"
           "       string_agg(case cr.credited_as"   ⑩ Aggregate names
           "         when 'D' then trim(coalesce(p.first_name,'')"
           "                       ||' '|| p.surname)"
           "         else null"
       "       end,',' order by p.surname,p.first_name) as directors,"
           "       string_agg(case cr.credited_as"
           "         when 'A' then trim(coalesce(p.first_name,'')"
           "                       ||' '|| p.surname)"
           "         else null"
           "       end,',' order by p.surname,p.first_name) as actors"
           " from movies m"
           "      inner join countries c"
           "      on c.country_code = m.country"
           "      left outer join credits cr"
           "      on cr.movieid = m.movieid"
           "      and cr.credited_as in ('A','D')"
           "      left outer join people p"
           "      on p.peopleid = cr.peopleid"
           " where m.movieid in"
           " (select q2.movieid"
           "  from (select q1.movieid,"
           "               rank() over (order by q1.score) as rnk"
           "        from (select c.movieid,"
           "                     length(translate(upper("  ⑪ Scoring
           "replace(coalesce(first_name,'')||surname,' ',''),"
           "         upper(replace($1,' ','')),'')) as score"
           "              from people p"
           "                   inner join credits c"
           "                   on c.peopleid=p.peopleid"
           "              where c.credited_as='A'"
           "              and (");
```

Another query of death ⑨, which manages to be different both from the Oracle version in the shell script and from the DB2 version in the embedded SQL program, and not only because of differences in function names. Here I combine the use of a function that aggregates strings (named **string_agg()** ⑩ in PostgreSQL), with the approach '*I get all names and dispatch them to one list or the other one*' that I used with DB2, except that instead of separating names in the programs, I do it in the query with a **case ... end** clause. The scoring function ⑪ that works like the Oracle and DB2 versions is (slightly) simpler than the Oracle version because **translate()** can, unlike its Oracle namesake, suppress a single character in PostgreSQL.

```
param_array[paramcnt++] = strdup(searched_name.s);
                                  ⑫ First argument: the searched name
p = strtok(searched_name.s, " ");
paramcnt = 1;
while (p) {
   if (paramcnt > 1) {
      strbuf_add(&query, " or ");
   }
   param_array[paramcnt++] = strdup(p);    ⑬ Add each subpart of the name
   if (paramcnt == MAX_PARAM) {
      fprintf(stderr, "Maximum number of parameters (%s) exceeded\n",
                      MAX_PARAM);
      exit(1);
   }
   (void)sprintf(placeholder, "$%d", paramcnt);  ⑭ Prepare the placeholder
   strbuf_add(&query,
              "p.surname like initcap(");
   strbuf_add(&query, placeholder);
   strbuf_add(&query, ")||'%'");
   p = strtok(NULL, " ");
}
strbuf_add(&query, ")) q1) q2"    ⑮ Finish up the query
                   " where q2.rnk=1)"
                   " group by m.title,c.country_name,m.year_released"
                   " order by m.year_released,m.title");
```

I first add to the list of parameters ⑫, a copy of the searched name, which will be substituted for the $1 placeholder that appears in the scoring function. Then I loop of the various "parts" that constitute the name, adding each one of them to the list of parameters ⑬, and adding the corresponding placeholder ⑭ to the query, which I terminate ⑮, when I exit the loop.

```
res = PQexecParams(con,        ⑯ Execute the query
                   (const char *)query.s,
                   (int)paramcnt,
                   (const Oid *)NULL,
                   (const char * const *)param_array,
                   (const int *)0,
                   (const int *)0,
                   (int)0);
if (PQresultStatus(res) != PGRES_TUPLES_OK) {  ⑰ Check the outcome
  DBerror(con, res, "Query");
  return 1;
}
```

```
    rows = PQntuples(res);    ⑱ Get the number of rows returned
    if (rows == 0) {
       printf("No data found.\n");
    } else {
       printf("%-30s\t%-20s\tDirected By\tStarring\n", "Title", "Origin");
       for (i = 0; i < rows; i++) {      ⑲ Loop and display
          printf("%-30.30s\t%-20.20s\t%s\t%s\n",
                 PQgetvalue(res, i, 0),
                 PQgetvalue(res, i, 1),
                 PQgetvalue(res, i, 2),
                 PQgetvalue(res, i, 3));
       }
    }
    PQclear(res);  ⑳ Free the result set
    PQfinish(con);  ㉑ Disconnect
    strbuf_dispose(&query);
    strbuf_dispose(&searched_name);
    for (i = 0; i < paramcnt; i++) {
       free(param_array[i]);
    }
    return 0;
}
```

Although I am passing parameters separately from the query, I am not preparing the statement, which will be executed only once in the session ⑯; most parameters can be 0 when you pass parameters as strings of characters as I am doing here. You need nothing but the database handler, the number of parameters, and the array of values. The function returns a pointer to a **PGresult** structure which must be checked ⑰. Commands that return nothing (DDL, insert/update/delete ...) return **PGRES_COMMAND_OK** when they succeed. A function that returns data returns either **PGRES_TUPLES_OK** (full result set) or, sometimes, **PGRES_SINGLE_TUPLE** (row by row, rare and not recommended). *Tuple* is the relationally correct word for *row*, as *relation* is the relationally correct word for *table*; you usually hear this word when people try to sound serious and academic. I retrieve the number of rows in the result set ⑱, and retrieve in a loop ⑲, all the data that I just display "as is". **PQgetvalue()** takes as parameters the **PGresult** pointer followed by the row number and the column number (in the select list); both numbers start from 0, not from 1. When I'm done I free the result set ⑳ and disconnect from the database server ㉑.

Client Applications with a Graphical Interface

I am going to give you here, three examples of classic database applications, with a graphical client (first nothing but a graphical client with a SQLite application, then a graphical Java client that connects to a database server, then a .NET example). I'll use Python, Java and C# as programming languages. With Python and Java, database interfaces are pretty much the same with all DBMS products. Graphical client/server applications, which used to be very common, have often been replaced by web-based applications (of which an example will follow) because in a big company when a new version of a program is released, it's much easier to update a single web server than to install a new client on possibly thousands of workstations – an operation known as *deployment*. Most companies prefer to have on workstations, only one browser to update with the latest version when needed, rather than ten different applications, even though deployment operations can often be automated.

Client/Server applications are still used when the client needs to be a sophisticated program, such as computer-aided design programs in engineering for instance – or some games or educational programs.

As graphical interfaces tend to require a significant number of lines of code, I will skip most of what doesn't relate to the interaction between the languages and the database. I remind you that the full code can be downloaded from `http://edu.konagora.com`.

Accessing SQLite with Python

In this example, I'll show you not only how you can execute SQL commands from Python but also how one can add a function written in the host language to SQLite. I am doing it here with Python3 but it can be done as easily with, among other languages, C, Java, or PHP (I also give examples in C and PHP at the end of Appendix B in this book.).

At the beginning of my program I need to import a few modules:

```
#! /usr/bin/python3.2              ① Linux stuff
# -*- coding: iso-8859-1 -*-       ② If you need accents
import tkinter                     ③ For the GUI
import sys                         ④ sys and os are for launching
import os
import sqlite3                     ⑤ You mustn't miss this one
```

I'm first saying which Python interpreter ①, I am using. This will allow me, if I make the script executable, to run it under Linux by invoking its name instead of calling *python3 <script>*. I specify that I'm using a character set ② that allows me to use accents in the program code. I need the GUI module ③ (not necessarily installed by default, beware) – **tkinter** is just one among several options. Two modules, **sys** and **os** ④, are only needed when bootstrapping the program. And of course we need the SQLite interface ⑤.

SQLite has some built-in functions which cover the bare minimum – but nothing more. However, as there is no security concern of sandboxing a database server from bugs introduced by application developers, adding one's own function is extremely easy and I'm going to illustrate it here with my own scoring function written in Python. My function is used to rank by relevance, a number of people whose surname matches one of the 'parts' in the user input (if I use the **like** operator it may not be strictly identical). I am going to apply therefore, scoring to a small number of rows; this is important because I am going to write a computation-intensive function that I wouldn't want to apply to a very large number of rows. What I am going to do is first to get rid of what is identical in the input and in the person's full name. Then I'll use the Levenshtein distance I mentioned in Chapter 6 to evaluate how much what remains on one side, matches what remains on the other side. You may have seen these word games in which you are given one word (for instance *row*) and must obtain another word by changing a single letter in it (for instance you turn *row* into *mow*, then *mew*, then *men*, then *ten*, and so forth). Sometimes you are given one start word and one end word and must work out all the intermediate steps. That's very much how the computation of the Levenshtein distance works: it counts how many steps are required to go from one word to another word, changing (or adding, or subtracting) one letter at a time - except that there is no requirement that the intermediate words can be found in a dictionary. I just searched "levenshtein python" on the web and found the following function on `www.hetland.org`.

NOTE Magnus Hetland is the author of a book on Python algorithms.

I just copied Magnus Hetland's code:

```
def levenshtein(a,b):
    "Calculates the Levenshtein distance between a and b."
    # Found on hetland.org
    n, m = len(a), len(b)
    if n > m:
        # Make sure n <= m, to use O(min(n,m)) space
        a,b = b,a
        n,m = m,n

    current = range(n+1)
    for i in range(1,m+1):
        previous, current = current, [i]+[0]*n
        for j in range(1,n+1):
            add, delete = previous[j]+1, current[j-1]+1
            change = previous[j-1]
            if a[j-1] != b[i-1]:
                change = change + 1
            current[j] = min(add, delete, change)

    return current[n]
```

I have wrapped it up in my own function because I am not sure of the order of the different parts that constitute the name as typed by the user, nor whether the user gave the complete name (it may be *Jamie Curtis* instead of *Jamie Lee Curtis*, or even *Curtis Jamie*). I compute the Levenshtein distance between one chunk on one side and all the other chunks on the other side, and keep the smallest value. Here is what it gives:

```
def score(name, searched_name):
    name_array = name.split()      ① Transfom names into lists
    searched_name_array = searched_name.split()
    for part in name_array:
       try:
         searched_name_array.remove(part)  ② Remove what is common
         name_array.remove(part)
       except ValueError:
         pass
    score = 0
    n = len(searched_name_array)
    if n > 0 :            ③ Evaluate how far apart is what remains
       for searched_part in searched_name_array:
           lev = []
           for part in name_array :
               lev.append(levenshtein(searched_part, part))
           score += min(lev)
    return score
```

I first transform into lists, both the (full) name found and the name given ①; then I try to remove everything that is common ② and, if something remains ③, compute the Levenshtein distance of every remaining chunk that was provided with each of the chunks that remain from the name found. I only count the smallest value and add it to the score. The lower the final score the better.

My algorithm isn't especially efficient but once again I am not going to compute all this for many rows and I don't need to be obsessed by performance. Function **score()** is the one I am going to hook into SQLite and use as if it were a regular SQL function.

Now for the bulk of the program, which is basically one class:

```
class Movieapp_tk(tkinter.Tk):
    def __init__(self, parent, location):  ① Where to find the SQLite file
        tkinter.Tk.__init__(self,parent)
        self.parent = parent
        self.location = location
        self.initialize()       ② Method that starts the GUI
```

The initialization method passes the name of the directory in which to find the SQLite file ① as *location*, and the graphical interface is created in another method ②.

```
    def close_dbfile(self, event):  ③ Called when the window is closed
        self.conn.close()           ④ Close the SQLite file
```

One method to exit cleanly when the window is closed ③. All I do is "close the database connection" which is just closing the file with SQLite ④. Note that it doesn't commit changes (not a concern here)

```
    def initialize(self):
        self.conn = sqlite3.connect(os.path.join(self.location,
```

```
                                    'movies.db'))   ⑤ Open the SQLite file
        self.conn.create_function("score", 2, score) ⑥ Add the function
```

I first open the SQLite file ⑤, expected to be found in the directory specified by *location*. If I were doing things well, I would put this in a **try** block but as SQLite creates files that don't exist, it's not critical. Next ⑥, I hook my Python function to SQLite. The first parameter is the name I will call my function in SQL, the second is the number of parameters it wants, the third is the name of the function in Python.

I skip a lot of graphical stuff which is mostly about defining a layout and placing various graphical elements (also known as *widgets*) in my window, entry fields, labels, buttons ... I'll call the field where users will input the name *actor_entry* and I'll call the scrollable area where I'll display the films I have found starring this actor or actress, *listbox*.

Now let's see the method that is called when a name has been entered and the "Search" button clicked:

```
    def SearchFilms(self):
        actor = self.actor_entry.get().strip().title()
                        ⑦ Get the actor or actress name
        query = """select m.title,       ⑧ Build the query
                     c.country_name || ', ' || m.year_released,
                     group_concat(case cr.credited_as
                                    when 'D' then
                                      trim(coalesce(p.first_name, '')
                                           || ' '
                                           || p.surname)
                                    else null
                                  end),
                     group_concat(case cr.credited_as
                                    when 'A' then
                                      trim(coalesce(p.first_name, '')
                                           || ' '
                                           || p.surname)
                                    else null
                                  end)
                   from movies m
                        inner join countries c
                          on c.country_code = m.country
                        left outer join credits cr
                          on cr.movieid = m.movieid
                        left outer join people p
                          on p.peopleid = cr.peopleid
                   where m.movieid in
                        (select cc.movieid
                         from credits cc
                              inner join
                                (select p2.peopleid
                                 from  people p2
                                       inner join credits c2
                                       on  c2.peopleid = p2.peopleid
```

```
                                         and c2.credited_as = 'A'
                                    where """
```

I first get the name ⑦ (the "Search" button remains deactivated as long as the field is empty), then I build a query ⑧ that resembles all the other queries in that chapter. Note that with SQLite you cannot order strings you concatenate with **group_concat()**, but that's a minor problem.

```
parameters = []     ⑨ Create an empty parameter list
cnt = 0
name_list = actor.split()  ⑩ Explode the name into a list of parts
for n in name_list:
   if cnt > 0:
      query += ' or '
   else:
      cnt += 1
   query += "p2.surname like ? || '%'"
   parameters.append(n)       ⑪ Add parameter to the list
query += """ order by score(p2.first_name
                            || ' ' || p2.surname, ?)
                                                 ⑫ Call our function
             limit 1) pp
            on pp.peopleid = cc.peopleid
            where cc.credited_as = 'A')
          group by m.title,
                   c.country_name,
                   m.year_released
          order by m.year_released, m.title"""
parameters.append(actor)     ⑬ Parameter to the score() function
try:
   cur = self.conn.cursor()          ⑭ Open a cursor
   cur.arraysize = 20                ⑮ Set the batch size
   cur.execute(query, parameters)   ⑯ Execute the query
   found = 0
   rslt = cur.fetchmany()        ⑰ Get a batch of rows
   while len(rslt) > 0:
      for row in rslt:
         self.listbox.insert(tkinter.END,   ⑱ Add rows to the display area
                                  format(row[0], '35.35s')
                            + ' ' + format(row[1], '20.20s')
                            + ' ' + format(row[2], '30.30s')
                            + ' ' + row[3])
         found += 1
      rslt = cur.fetchmany()
   if found == 0:
      self.listbox.insert(tkinter.END, '*** No films found ***')
except:
    print("Unexpected error:" + str(sys.exc_info()))
```

I first create a list ⑨, to which I'll add the parameters I'll pass with the query. After splitting the name ⑩, on spaces to get all the parts of the name, I loop on the name and add the suitable condition to my query, not forgetting each time to add to my list of parameters ⑪, what I want the SQL engine to substitute for my placeholder, the question mark. I finish the subquery by sorting by my scoring function ⑫ and only retaining the first person. Before finishing up the query, I mustn't forget to add the name that was input to the parameters ⑬, as I need to pass it to the scoring function. Then I open a cursor ⑭, define the batch size when I fetch rows ⑮ (this is important: it usually defaults to one), execute the query with the parameters ⑯ and use **fetchmany()** ⑰, to get a first batch of rows. You can specify the batch size or let as here Python use, which is best, the default cursor size. There are also **fetchone()** (don't use it, unless you know that the query can only return one row or none), and **fetchall()** (which I could use in this case but might be dangerous if I return a large number of rows). Function **fetchmany()** is a good compromise in terms of performance versus memory usage; I iterate on batches until all rows have been retrieved and display them ⑱, on the screen.

Accessing Oracle with Java (*Program refactored by Laurent Fourrier*)

In Chapter 11 I gave you a simple Java program and introduced you to JDBC, drivers, and CLASSPATH. I won't repeat (too much) here what I showed in the previous chapter and I'll try to focus on the peculiarities of this particular program.

If you want to access a DBMS other than Oracle, you need to load a different driver and provide in your program, the suitable URL, the syntax of which depends on the DBMS that is accessed. Afterwards all the Java calls when interacting with the database are identical with whichever DBMS flavor you are interacting. Needless to say, SQL statements themselves (which are just plain text when seen from Java) will be significantly different from one DBMS to another. If you want to run this program and access a DBMS other than Oracle though, you just need to copy the suitable SQL queries from another program in this section, load a different driver and that will be it.

In this example I am using Swing for the graphical user interface. You may be more likely to meet Java accesses to a database in "Java Beans" or in an Android application; once again, as my focus is on Java interactions with the database, I'll skip most of the graphical stuff to comment on my real interest.

The code is organized into three directories corresponding to packages:

- **db** contains some really generic database code
- **ui** contains the user-interface, some of which is generic (the login window), and some of which is very specific to the application
- **tools** contains a class that stores the result of a query in a table that can be displayed, and is also generic

The entry point of the application is the class *FilmsStarring* that follows:

```
package ui;

import javax.swing.JOptionPane;    ← Just to display an error window

public class FilmsStarring {

  public static void main(String arg[]) {
    try {
      Class.forName("oracle.jdbc.OracleDriver");  ① Load the Oracle driver
    } catch(Exception e) {
      System.out.println(
      "Cannot find the Oracle JDBC driver. Check the value of CLASSPATH.");
      System.exit(1);
    }
    try {
      new Login();       ② Call the login window
    } catch(Exception e) {
      JOptionPane.showMessageDialog(null, e.getMessage());
    }
  }
}
```

I remind you that whichever DBMS you want to access, all you have to do is load ①, the corresponding driver (found in a `.jar` file). Prior to running the program, you just need to check that the suitable `.jar` file is listed in your CLASSPATH environment variable (unless you specify where to look for it on the command line). Once the driver is loaded, I call a login window ②, which will in turn call the main window if connection is successful. There are several ways to deal with the login window, another frequent method is to load the main window and make the login window a *modal window* that prevents any interaction with the main window until the user is successfully authenticated.

I'll comment on only some fragments of `Login.java`. Firstly, of all the information that is required to connect to a database (name of the server machine, port number, name of the database or database instance, username and password), only the username and password are really meaningful to an end user. This is why I have decided to store all the remaining information to a file named here `config.cfg` that would ideally be located on a shared disk if many users can run the application; if the application database is ever moved to another server (it happens) there will only be one file to modify. If no configuration file is found, I use default values that I hope I have chosen cleverly (default DBMS port number, and so on). The URL depends on the DBMS in use. Note that this type of connection necessarily uses the network layers, even when the application program and the DBMS software are running on the same machine. As a consequence, you cannot be authenticated by the operating system and you <u>must</u> provide a username and a password to connect to the database.

```
prop = new Properties();
String fileName = "config.cfg";
url = new StringBuffer("jdbc:oracle:thin:@");
try {
    InputStream is = new FileInputStream(fileName);
                                  ↑ Open the configuration file
    prop.load(is);
    url.append(prop.getProperty("host")).append(":");
    if (prop.getProperty("port") == null) {
       url.append("1521:");
    } else {
       url.append(prop.getProperty("port")).append(":");
    }
    url.append(prop.getProperty("instance"));
} catch (Exception e) {
    System.err.print("Warning : ");  ← Warn that no file was found
    System.err.println(e.getMessage());
    String orasid = System.getenv("ORACLE_SID");
                                   ↑ Trying to get the name of the Oracle
                                     instance from the environment (on Windows
                                     you could set it in a .bat file launching
                                     the application)
    if (orasid != null) {
       url.append("localhost:1521:").append(orasid);
    } else {
       System.err.println("Missing connection information");
       System.exit(1);
    }
}
```

The real connection work is done in the method called by clicking on the "Login" button:

```
public void actionPerformed(ActionEvent ae) {
   String username = usrField.getText();
   String password = new String(pwdField.getPassword());
   Properties info = new Properties();
   info.put("user", username);    ← Retrieve data that was input
   info.put("password", password);
   info.put("defaultRowPrefetch", "20");  ① Adjust connection parameters
   try {
      DBConnection.setConnection(url.toString(), info);
                              ② Connect to the database
      new SearchWindow();  ③ Call the main window
      this.dispose();
   } catch (Exception conE) {
      JOptionPane.showMessageDialog(this, conE.getMessage(), "Error",
            JOptionPane.ERROR_MESSAGE);
      // conE.printStackTrace();
   }
}
```

As I know that I'll probably retrieve for each actor, a few dozens of films at most, I set ① the default batch size to 20. This is particularly important with the Oracle driver that defaults to 10, much too small in many cases and the cause of avoidable round-trips. When the program fetches rows, it actually retrieves them from what it has "pre-fetched" until stocks are depleted and it has to pre-fetch another batch. I connect ② using a class defined in the **db** package, which follows. It throws an exception if it fails; if it succeeds, then we open ③ the main window where we can enter an actor name and search for films.

The *DBConnection* class is rather simple:

```
public class DBConnection {
   static Connection connection = null;

   public static Connection getConnection() {
      return connection;
   }

   public static void setConnection(String url,Properties info)
         throws SQLException {
      DBConnection.connection = DriverManager.getConnection(url, info);
      connection.setAutoCommit(false);
   }
}
```

The only notable feature is that, as in the Chapter 11 example, I immediately disable the "autocommit" feature which was initially designed for people who had no idea of transactions; you should think your transactions and manage them in your programs. In the example there will only be a search and no data change but remember that this class is generic.

The *SearchWindow* class is by far the biggest, with a lot of graphical stuff and the same impressive Oracle query as in the shell programming example (as long as it's the same database, it's usually the same queries). Here, however, parameters will really be passed separately from the query. In JDBC, a question mark is used as a place-holder for a parameter in a query. In the program an ArrayList is used to hold parameters:

```
private ArrayList<String> parameters = null;
```
← not an SQL null

This list will be populated at the same time as we build the query, as you can see here:

```
   private String buildQuery() {
      StringBuffer  s = new StringBuffer(100);
      StringBuffer  refname = new StringBuffer();
```

```
String[]      nameArray = actor.getText().trim().split(" ");
```

↑ Retrieve whatever was input and turn it into an array by splitting on spaces

```
for (int i = 0; i < nameArray.length; i++) {
    refname.append(nameArray[i].toLowerCase());
```

↑ build a name without spaces that will be used for scoring. We'll suppress all the letters in refname from whatever we find. The name with the fewest remaining letters wins.

```
}
if (parameters == null) {
   parameters = new ArrayList<String>();
} else {
   parameters.clear();   ← launching a new search
}
// Tabs are added for mere legibility if you want
// to display the query that is generated
s.append("select m.title,\n\tctry.country_name||','||");
s.append("to_char(m.year_released) as origin,\n\t");
```

Using listagg() for building both the list of directors ↓ and the list of actors

```
s.append("listagg(case c.credited_as\n\t\t");
s.append("when 'D' then trim(p.first_name||' '||p.surname)\n\t\t");
s.append("else null\n\t\tend,',')\n\t\t");
s.append("within group(order by p.surname,p.first_name)");
s.append(" as director,\n\t");
s.append("listagg(case c.credited_as\n\t\t");
s.append("when 'A' then trim(p.first_name||' '||p.surname)\n\t\t");
s.append("else null\n\t\tend,',')\n\t\t");
s.append("within group(order by p.surname,p.first_name) as starring\n");
s.append("from movies m\n\t");
s.append("inner join countries ctry\n\t");
s.append("on ctry.country_code=m.country\n\t");
s.append("left outer join credits c\n\t");
s.append("on c.movieid=m.movieid\n\t");
s.append("left outer join people p\n\t");
s.append("on p.peopleid=c.peopleid\n");
s.append("where m.movieid in\n\t(");
s.append("select q2.movieid\n\t\t");
s.append("from (select q1.movieid,\n\t\t\t");
s.append("rank() over (order by q1.score) as rnk\n\t\t");
s.append("from (select c.movieid,\n\t\t\t");
```

Scoring expression. Removes all letters ↓ found in refname.

```
s.append("coalesce(length(replace(translate(");
s.append("replace(lower(trim(first_name||surname)),' ',''),");
s.append("?");
parameters.add(new String(refname.toString()));
s.append(",rpad('*',length(");
s.append("?");
```

```
        parameters.add(new String(refname.toString()));
                                  ↑ refname is the first parameter
        s.append("),'*')),'*',''")),0) as score\n\t\t");
        s.append("from people p\n\t\t\t");
        s.append("inner join credits c\n\t\t\t");
        s.append("on c.peopleid = p.peopleid\n\t\t");
        s.append("where c.credited_as = 'A'\n\t\t");
        s.append("and (p.surname like initcap(?)||'%'\n\t\t\t");
        parameters.add(new String(nameArray[0]));
        for (int i = 1; i < nameArray.length; i++) {
            s.append("or p.surname like initcap(?)||'%'\n\t\t\t");
            parameters.add(new String(nameArray[i]));
                   ↑ For every chunk found in user input add one place
                     holder and the value to the array of parameters
        }
        s.append(")) q1) q2\n\t");
        s.append("where q2.rnk=1\n");
        s.append(")\ngroup by m.title,\n\t");
        s.append("ctry.country_name,\n\t");
        s.append("m.year_released\n");
        s.append("order by m.title, m.year_released");
        return s.toString();
    }
```

Each time a place-holder is added to the query that is built when we click on the "Search" button, the corresponding value is appended to the ArrayList. Once the query is built (as a string) it can be used in a **try** block and here we strictly follow the pattern that I described at the beginning of this chapter:

```
try {
   stmt = DBConnection.getConnection().prepareStatement(query);
                         ↑ Instantiate a PreparedStatement object
   for (int i = 0; i < parameters.size(); i++) {
      stmt.setString(i + 1, parameters.get(i));
            ↑ Bind the parameters to the PreparedStatement
   }
   ResultSet rs = stmt.executeQuery();
      ↑ Call the executeQuery() method that returns a ResultSet object
   ResultSetModel rsModel = new ResultSetModel(rs);
            ↑ Use the ResultSet to instantiate our own ResultSetModel
   JTable filmInfo = new JTable(rsModel);
```

Finally, the *ResultSetModel* class in our tools package shows how to handle what we retrieve from the database:

```
public class ResultSetModel
            extends DefaultTableModel {

      public ResultSetModel(ResultSet rs) {
         super();
```

```
            try {
               ResultSetMetaData rsmd = rs.getMetaData();
                                          ① Get information about the ResultSet
               // Populate the model
               for (int i = 1; i <= rsmd.getColumnCount(); i++) {
                                                    ② how many columns
                  this.addColumn(rsmd.getColumnLabel(i));  ③ ... and their names
               }
               Object[] data = new Object[rsmd.getColumnCount()];
               while (rs.next()) {
                        ↑ there will be a new round-trip when
                          we have returned all the pre-fetched rows
                          but only then
                  for (int i = 0; i < rsmd.getColumnCount(); i++) {
                     data[i] = rs.getObject(i + 1);
                                 ④ Transfer from the ResultSet to our buffer
                  }
                  this.addRow(data);
               }
            } catch(SQLException e) {
               e.printStackTrace();
               System.exit(1);
            }
         }
}
```

The final operation consists of transferring the data from the **ResultSet** into program objects. The **ResultSet** object can provide a **ResultSetMetaData** object ①, that implements methods that describe the columns returned – their number ②, their names ③, but also their data types and a lot of information primarily useful when you have no idea about what the query returns (when the query is very dynamic). The actual transfer is done with method **getObject()** ④.

Accessing SQL Server in a Microsoft .NET Environment with C# (*Program by Rudi Bruchez*)

The .NET environment is now the most widely used development environment with Microsoft Windows. Microsoft offered several database access libraries over time. The first one was ODBC (Open Database Connectivity) that became a de facto standard to access multiple SQL databases. ODBC was later phased out by Microsoft in favor of OLEDB, a layer implementing the Component Object Model (COM) and giving access in a consistent manner, to a wider variety of data sources than ODBC (it added Object Oriented databases as well as spreadsheets to SQL databases). Then came ActiveX Data Objects (ADO), a set of more abstract components built on top of low level libraries like ODBC or OLEDB. Finally, Microsoft released the .NET framework (a huge set of libraries and a run-time virtual machine to run applications). They adapted ADO to the framework and it became ADO.NET. ADO.NET is today sometimes hidden behind Object-Relational Mapping (ORM) tools like Entity Framework or LINQ for SQL. ORM tools are available for all environments and all object-oriented languages; their goal is to map application objects to relational tables and make the database almost transparent to developers. This approach only works for very simple interactions with a database; as operations become complex, ORM tools multiply queries and basic operations, and perform far more database accesses than are required, making latency issues worse. Avoid ORM tools and stick to real SQL queries, with ADO.NET in a Microsoft environment.

We will see here, a short example of a graphical application querying our movies database and showing a list of movies in a .NET control. The graphical interface is handled by WPF (Windows Presentation Foundation); WPF contains graphical controls that can bind to a data source and easily display the result of a query.

```
public partial class MainWindow : Window
{
    private SqlConnection cn;
    private string strConnexion = "Data Source=localhost;"
                                + "Integrated Security=SSPI;"
                                + "Initial Catalog=moviedb";
                                 ↑ The connection string relies on authentication
                                   by the operating system

    public MainWindow()
    {
        InitializeComponent();
    }

    private void Window_Closed(object sender, EventArgs e)
    {
        if (cn.State == System.Data.ConnectionState.Open) { cn.Close(); }
    }

This is where it becomes interesting
      ↓
    private void btnSearch_Click(object sender, RoutedEventArgs e)
    {
        if (txtSearchFirstName.Text.Trim().Length        ← Any input?
            + txtSearchLastName.Text.Trim().Length > 0)
        {
            try
            {
                cn = new SqlConnection(strConnexion); ① Instantiate a connection
                cn.Open();                            ② Actually connect
                SqlCommand cmd = cn.CreateCommand();  ③ Statement to prepare
```

Connection to the database is effected ①, by instantiating a **SqlConnection** object, to which is passed connection information: a session is created by calling ②, the **Open()** method of the connection; next we instantiate with the **CreateCommand()** method a **SqlCommand** object ③, that will be our vehicle for communicating with the database.

```
string sqlcmd = @"with cte as (        ④ Common Table Expression
      select ',' + ltrim(coalesce(d.first_name,' ')
             + ' ' + d.surname) as name,
            c.credited_as, d.surname, c.movieid
      from dbo.credits c
      inner join dbo.people d on d.peopleid=c.peopleid
      where c.credited_as IN ('A', 'D')
   )
   select m.title,
   cast(m.year_released as char(4))
       + ',' + ctry.country_name origin,
   substring((select c.name as [text()]
              from cte c            ← Note reference to cte
              where c.credited_as='D'
              and c.movieid = m.movieid
              order by c.surname
              for xml path('')), 2, 4000) as directors,
                     ⑤ Use xml
   substring((select c.name as [text()]
              from cte c           ← cte again
              where c.credited_as='A'
              and c.movieid = m.movieid
              order by c.surname
              for xml path('')), 2, 4000) as actors
                     ⑤ Use xml
   from dbo.movies m
   inner join dbo.countries ctry
   on ctry.country_code = m.country
   where m.movieid in (select movieid
       from dbo.credits
       where credited_as = 'A'
       and peopleid in
       (select top 1 p.peopleid  ⑥ get best match
       from dbo.credits c
       inner join dbo.people p
       on p.peopleid = c.peopleid
       cross join (";
```

The query uses an interesting feature ④. I have mentioned briefly Common Table Expressions (or CTEs) defined in a **with** clause, in a note in Chapter 5, when I talked about recursive queries (mentioning that you could have a non-recursive **with** clause). The goal of CTEs is to "factorize" a dataset that will be used several times in the query, sometimes in different part of a **union** statement or in different subqueries like here. The optimizer may or may not decide to run the CTE separately and use it as a virtual, temporary dataset. Another interesting point is the use of **xml path** ⑤. As mentioned earlier in this chapter, XML functions or constructs that return a full data set as a single string are a way to "aggregate" character strings. In this case, the empty string in **path('')** says that we don't want any tags, and we get what is returned by the CTE as one big piece of text. The **substring()** is only here to remove the first comma. There is also a subquery that tries, with a **top** clause ⑥, to identify the actor whose name matches the input best

```
↓ Complete the query, based on input
if (txtSearchFirstName.Text.Trim().Length > 0) {
    sqlcmd += "select '{0}' as name ";
                          ↑ Place-holder
                           There will be two parameters,
                           First one (first name) is represented
                           by {0}, second one (surname) by {1}
    if (txtSearchLastName.Text.Trim().Length > 0) {
        sqlcmd += "union all ";
    }
}
if (txtSearchLastName.Text.Trim().Length > 0) {
    sqlcmd += "select '{1}' as name ";
}
sqlcmd += @") entered
        where c.credited_as = 'A'
        and (1 = 0";                              ⑦ Trick
⑦ Never trust what end-users enter
if (txtSearchFirstName.Text.Trim().Length > 0) {
    sqlcmd += " or p.first_name like '{0}%'
               or p.surname like '{0}%' ";
}
if (txtSearchLastName.Text.Trim().Length > 0) {
    sqlcmd += " or p.first_name like '{1}%'
               or p.surname like '{1}%' ";
}
```

We are adding here, place-holders for user input. We cannot trust users to enter first name and username where they belong, for entering *Kajol* as the surname and for knowing that *Gong Li*'s surname is *Gong*, so we check all possibilities. To avoid checking whether we are handling the first bit of the condition (no **or**) or any subsequent bit (**or** required) we use a trick ⑦, a dummy condition `1 = 0` that is always false and won't alter the final result – after which we can systematically precede each condition by **or**.

```
sqlcmd += @")
    group by p.peopleid
    order by sum(
        case                    ⑧ Try to score candidates
            when difference(coalesce(p.first_name, ''),
                     entered.name) <
                      difference(p.surname, entered.name)
                then difference(coalesce(p.first_name, ''),
                                    entered.name)
            else difference(p.surname, entered.name)
        end)
    ))
    order by origin;";
```

At this point we try to score ⑧, the various candidates by using a function that is specific to SQL Server, **difference()**, that gives a number which measures how much the soundex value of a column differs from the soundex value of another column (see Chapter 6). The higher the value, the greater the difference. We take each time, the lower difference that we find between first name or surname and what is entered, sum everything up, and decide that the lowest-scoring individual in our database is probably the right one. Note that we don't use **soundex()** (not very reliable) to *find* suitable candidates, only to *rank* candidates in a short list.

```
            sqlcmd = String.Format(sqlcmd,      ⑨ Sanitize input and add it
                txtSearchFirstName.Text.Replace("'", "''").Trim(),
                txtSearchLastName.Text.Replace("'", "''").Trim()
            );
            SqlDataAdapter da = new SqlDataAdapter(sqlcmd, cn);
                                    ⑩ Create a DataAdapter for getting data
            DataTable dt = new DataTable();
                                   ⑪ Data storage on the client side

            da.Fill(dt);      ⑫ Fetch data and fill buffer
```

Finally, we carefully sanitize ⑨ user-input, duplicating quotes and removing spaces, before substituting it in the query. At this point, we can instantiate ⑩ a **SqlDataAdapter** object that corresponds to what is called a cursor or statement handler in other languages, instantiate ⑪ a **DataTable** object to hold in our program, the result set returned by the **SqlDataAdapter** and call ⑫, the **Fill()** method of the **SqlDataAdapter** to bring at one go, all the data in the program. Here, loops are implicit.

```
            if (dt.Rows.Count == 0)     ⑬ Anything?
            {
                MessageBox.Show("no result !");
                return;
            }

            listViewMovies.DataContext = dt.DefaultView;   ⑭ Ready to display

        }
        catch (Exception err)
        {
            Console.WriteLine("Error at connection :" + err.Message);
        }

    }
}
```

A quick check ⑬, that anything is returned and ⑭, we are ready to hand data to WPF for display.

Before I give a web programming example with PHP, I need to point out that with .NET, switching from a graphical client program to a web program isn't a major effort and that database accesses remain unchanged. You need to switch to a webform ASP.NET project and draw graphically the visual part, with the same type of components as in WPF, to which event-driven code is attached.

Web Programming

As I said in the previous chapter, Web applications, especially when they are publicly accessible by anybody, must be carefully protected against SQL injection. In Chapter 11, I gave an example consisting of a simple, single PHP script. This time I am going to give a more realistic example in which the PHP script is called when users submit an HTML form.

Accessing MySQL with PHP

There are multiple libraries that allow access to databases from PHP:

- DBMS-specific libraries and sometimes multiple libraries for one DBMS product (this is the case with MySQL)
- Generic libraries that, similarly to JDBC in Java, load a DBMS-specific driver but use identical functions with all DBMS products (even though the SQL statements that are passed to each DBMS are usually slightly different)

I used PDO (PHP Data Objects), a generic library, in Chapter 11 and I am going to use it again. As we saw in Chapter 11, even though in my example, I'll be accessing a MySQL database all you have to do, is to use another driver and change the text of the query, to make the program run against another database product.

My application mostly consists of an HTML page that will be called in a browser (`index.html`), a few lines of JQuery that associate actions with buttons and in particular an AJAX call, and a short PHP script that is invoked by the AJAX call. Saying AJAX (**A**synchronous **J**avascript **A**nd **XML**), is a bit of a stretch in this case, as there isn't the slightest hint of XML in the program. I am, in fact, using AJAH; my PHP script merely outputs a piece of HTML which is simply inserted by the client-side script (the JQuery part) into the HTML page when it is returned.

There isn't much to say about the HTML page, which basically contains one input field for entering the name of an actress or actor and is identified by *id-name*, one button identified by *id-btn-search* to trigger the AJAH call, one button identified by *id-btn-clear* to erase the result of the previous search and start a new one, and finally a `<div>` block identified by *id-result* that is the place where the output of the PHP script is inserted. The page includes a style sheet, the JQuery library and the following client-side JQuery script:

```
$(function(){
  // Define button actions
  $("#id-btn-clear").attr('disabled', 'disabled');
```

↑ Start by disabling the clear button

```
                         ↓ Action performed when clicking Search
$("#id-btn-search").click(function(e){
  e.preventDefault();   ← We take control of everything
  $("#id-result").html(
      '<img src="img/ajax-loader.gif" alt="working"/>');
                       ↑ An animated GIF to suggest action
  $("#id-btn-search").attr('disabled', 'disabled'); ← Prevent double clicks
  $.get("ajax/moviesearch.php",   ← AJAH call
        {name:$("#id-name").val()}, ← Pass input value
        function (data) {   ← What to do when data arrives
           $("#id-result").html(data);  ← Insert the data where it belongs
           $("#id-btn-clear").removeAttr('disabled'); ← Activate Clear button
        });
});
// Clear button (simpler)
$("#id-btn-clear").click(function(e){ ← I let you work out this one
  e.preventDefault();
  $("#id-result").html('');
  $("#id-name").val('');
  $("#id-btn-clear").attr('disabled', 'disabled');
  $("#id-btn-search").removeAttr('disabled');
  $("#id-name").focus();
});
});
```

The PHP code isn't particularly complicated. It includes dbsetup.php, a very short PHP script that must be even more protected than everything else (readable by the HTTP server only) and assigns to constants, the information required to connect to the database:

```
<?php
  require_once('../inc/dbsetup.php');

  if (isset($argv) && (count($argv) > 1)) {  ① A trick for testing
     parse_str(implode('&', array_slice($argv, 1)), $_GET);
  }
  if (isset($_GET['name'])) {    ② Basic control
     $fullname = $_GET['name'];
  } else {
     echo '<span class="error">You must provide a name</span>';
     exit;
  }

              ③ Database connection
  $db = new PDO('mysql:host=' . DB_HOST . ';dbname=' . DB_NAME,
                DB_USER,
                DB_PASS,
                array(PDO::MYSQL_ATTR_INIT_COMMAND=>"SET NAMES utf8")); ④ Options
  if ($db === false) {
     echo '<span class="error">Connection to database failed</span>';
     exit;
  }
```

In order to be able to test the Ajax program by running it from the command line (debugging is painful otherwise), I check ① if I have been provided parameters on the command line, and if this is the case, I fake that they have been provided by a GET call by using the parameters to populate the $_GET array. This allows me to run **php moviesearch.php name=Bogart** and see what it returns (I did something similar in the Chapter 11 example). The mechanism is identical to the Chapter 11 PHP program: I check ②, that a name has been entered (I should but I haven't, done it in Javascript as well) and output an error message otherwise. I then instantiate a PDO object ③, specifying (it's specific to MySQL) ④, that I want to work in UTF8.

```
$query = 'select m.title,concat(c.country_name,'   ⑤ MySQL query
       . " ', ', cast(m.year_released as char)) as country_year,"
        ↑ I enclose with double quotes when the string contains
          single quotes, otherwise I enclose with single quotes.
       . ' group_concat(case cr.credited_as'
       . "     when 'D' then trim(concat(coalesce(p.first_name,''),' ',"
       . '                             p.surname))'
       . '     else null'
       . '     end'
       . '     order by p.surname) as directed_by,'
       . ' group_concat(case cr.credited_as'
       . "     when 'A' then trim(concat(coalesce(p.first_name,''),' ',"
       . '                             p.surname))'
       . '     else null'
       . '     end'
       . '     order by p.surname) as starring'
       . ' from '
       . '   (select cr2.movieid'
       . '    from credits cr2'
       . '    inner join'
       . '      (select p2.peopleid'
       . '       from people p2'
       . '       where (1=0';    ⑥ Trick
$parameters = array();    ⑦ Prepare parameters to pass
foreach(explode(' ', $fullname) as $name_part) {   ⑧ First loop (search)
   $query .= " or p2.surname like concat(?,'%')";
   $parameters[] = ucwords($name_part);   ⑨ Normalize input
}
$query .= ')'
       . ' order by length(trim(';
$replexpr = "upper(concat(coalesce(p2.first_name,''),p2.surname))";
foreach(explode(' ', $fullname) as $name_part) {   ⑩ Second loop (scoring)
   $replexpr = 'replace(' . $replexpr . ",?,'')";
   $parameters[] = strtoupper($name_part);
}
```

I enter a complicated MySQL query ⑤, to return film information, to which I dynamically add one condition per part in the entered name. One trick worth mentioning ⑥, as I don't want to test each time, if I want to add **or** (general case) or not (first condition), I add a condition that is always false and will not affect the series of **or** conditions (with a series of **and** conditions, I would use something that is always true such as 1=1). I create an array to hold parameters ⑦, and loop ⑧, to add a condition for each part. Each time I add a '?' to the query I append the corresponding value to the parameters array ⑨. As MySQL's SQL has no **initcap()** function, I use an equivalent PHP function before passing the data to SQL. A second loop ⑩ is required to build a condition allowing me to rank possible candidate actors.

```
$query .= $replexpr . ')) limit 1) act'
        . '     on act.peopleid = cr2.peopleid'
        . "     where cr2.credited_as='A') f"
        . '    inner join movies m'
        . '    on m.movieid = f.movieid'
        . '    inner join countries c'
        . '    on c.country_code = m.country'
        . '    inner join credits cr'
        . '    on cr.movieid = m.movieid'
        . '    inner join people p'
        . '    on p.peopleid = cr.peopleid'
        . ' group by m.title,c.country_name,m.year_released'
        . ' order by m.year_released';

$stmt = $db->prepare($query);  ⑪ Create a statement object

if (($stmt !== false)
    && $stmt->execute($parameters)) {   ⑫ Execute / pass parameters
    $film_list = $stmt->fetchAll(PDO::FETCH_ASSOC);
                                ⑬ Get the result set, all at once
    $cnt = 0;

    foreach ($film_list as $film) {  ⑭ Loop on rows in the result set
       if ($cnt == 0) {
          echo '<table>'
              . '<tr><th>Title</th><th>Country, Year</th>'
              . '<th>Directed By</th><th>Starring</th></tr>';
       }
       $cnt++;
       echo '<tr class="' . ($cnt % 2 == 0? 'even' : 'odd') . '">'
          . '<td>' . htmlentities($film['title']) . '</td>'
                         ⑮ Beware of what the tables contain
          . '<td>' . htmlentities($film['country_year']) . '</td>'
          . '<td>' . htmlentities($film['directed_by']) . '</td>'
          . '<td>' . htmlentities($film['starring']) . '</td>'
          . '</tr>';
    }

    if ($cnt > 0) {
       echo '</table>';
    } else {
       echo '<span class="error">No movies were found starring '
           . htmlentities($fullname) . '</span>';
    }
```

```
  } else {
     if ($stmt === false) {     ⑯ Handle errors
        $flop = $db->errorInfo();
     } else {
        $flop = $stmt->errorInfo();
     }
     echo '<span class="error">' . $flop[2] . '</span>'; ⑰ For debugging
  }
  unset($db); ⑱ Disconnect
?>
```

The **prepare()** method ⑪ of the **PDO** object returns a **PDOStatement** object that will be executed later. It's also possible, when statements don't take a parameter, to pass their text directly to methods of the **PDO** object. The **execute()** method of the **PDOStatement** object ⑫ takes an array of parameters. I have used **?** as place marker; the elements of the array will be associated in sequence with each place marker. It's also possible to have named parameters in the query (as *:name*). In that case, the array of parameters must be indexed by the various names. If the execution is successful, I fetch all rows at once ⑬ (I know that I won't get tens of thousands of rows). The parameter specifies that I want rows to be indexed by the names of the columns in the query ("associative array"); other options are the use of numerically indexed arrays (less convenient for maintenance, if you ever add columns to your query) or (the default) returning all row values twice, once indexed numerically and once indexed by column name. I loop on the result set ⑭, inspecting each row in turn. As I am turning my result set into HTML, I am careful to escape ⑮ any character that may cause trouble in an HTML page with the **htmlentities()** PHP function. I handle errors ⑯, through return codes; it's also possible to set-up PDO so as to generate exceptions. Both the **PDO** and **PDOStatement** objects implement an **errorInfo()** method that returns an array; the error message is in the third position (other elements include error code, etc.). Returning the actual error message ⑰, helps debugging but I would avoid it in a production application and return a sober "Database error" or a flat apology. There is no need to advertise too wildly, which DBMS you are using and tease hackers in quest of an exploit. I disconnect ⑱, by simply discarding the **PDO** object.

Here is my dbsetup.php:

```
<?php
 define('DB_USER', 'moviedb');
 define('DB_PASS', 'sqlsuccess');
 define('DB_HOST', 'localhost');
 define('DB_NAME', 'moviedb');
?>
```

Mobile Application Programming

Mobile applications can also store data in a SQLite file queried with SQL. As Android uses Java as its programming language, please refer to the Java/JDBC example given earlier in this chapter. We are going to see here, how you can code database accesses with Objective-C, with an example kindly provided by Eddie McLean.

ACCESSING SQLITE WITH OBJECTIVE-C/COCOA (*PROGRAM BY EDDIE MCLEAN*)

The program is organized according to the Model/View/Controller pattern made popular by web development frameworks and is split into seven main files (I ignore header and ancillary files):

- `AppDelegate.m`
- `main.m`
- `ViewController.m`
- `DB.m`
- `DBStatement.m`
- `DetailView.m`
- `MovieTableView.m`

I'll skip the first two files that are just here for launching the application. The real action starts in the `ViewController.m` file which defines the implementation of the class by the same name. When the **ViewController** is loaded, the database file is opened and copied from the bundle if not found:

```
@implementation ViewController
@synthesize movieActor;
@synthesize movableView;

NSString *indexedDBPath;

- (void)viewDidLoad
{
    [super viewDidLoad];

    NSFileManager *fileManager = [NSFileManager defaultManager];
    NSError *error;
    NSArray *paths = NSSearchPathForDirectoriesInDomains(NSDocumentDirectory,
                                    NSUserDomainMask, YES);
    NSString *documentsDirectory = [paths objectAtIndex:0];
    indexedDBPath = [documentsDirectory
                    stringByAppendingPathComponent:@"movies.db"];

    if ([fileManager fileExistsAtPath:indexedDBPath] == NO) {
        NSString *unindexedDBPath = [[NSBundle mainBundle]
                              pathForResource:@"movies" ofType:@"db"];
        [fileManager
         copyItemAtPath:unindexedDBPath toPath:indexedDBPath error:&error];
    }
}
```

The most important method is **prepareForSegue** that takes the name entered in the *movieActor* field and builds the query to retrieve the films in which the actor or actress had a leading part:

```
- (void) prepareForSegue:(UIStoryboardSegue *)segue sender:(id)sender {
   MovieTableView *mtv = [segue destinationViewController]; ① for the result

   [self dismissKeyboard:nil];

   DB *db = [DB alloc];    ② We'll see the DB object next

   if ([db openWithPath:indexedDBPath]) {

       NSMutableString *query =  ③ Start building the query
         [NSMutableString stringWithString:@"select m.title as title,\
           c.country_name||','||m.year_released as country_year,\
               group_concat(case cr.credited_as\
                   when 'D' then trim(coalesce(p.first_name,'')
                                   ||' '||p.surname)\
                   else null\
                   end) as directed_by,\
               group_concat(case cr.credited_as\
                   when 'A' then trim(coalesce(p.first_name,'')
                                     ||' '||p.surname)\
                   else null\
                   end) as starring\
               from\
                 (select cr2.movieid\
                  from credits cr2\
                  inner join\
                    (select p2.peopleid\
                     from people p2\
                         where (1=0 "];    ④ Trick
```

For subtle details about the SQLite query ③, see the prior Python example, which also accesses a SQLite file. It's almost the same query, except that here we are using the trick ④ of starting a series of **or** conditions with a condition that is always false (we would start a series of **and** conditions with a condition that is always true): the dummy condition allows us to concatenate **or** ... without having to test for the first condition (which should not preceded by an **or** without the dummy false condition).

```
      NSMutableArray *parameters = [[NSMutableArray alloc] init];
                                       ⑤ Parameters
      if (movieActor.text.length > 0) {
          NSArray *name = [movieActor.text
  componentsSeparatedByCharactersInSet:[NSCharacterSet whitespaceCharacterSet]];
                                    ⑥ Split input field on spaces
          for (NSString *n in name) {
              [query appendString:@"or p2.surname like ?||'%%'"];
              [parameters addObject:[n capitalizedString]];
                              ⑦ Add condition to query and value to parameters
```

```
            }
        }

        [query appendString:@")\          ⑧ limit to actors and find best candidate
            and exists (select null from credits cr3\
            where cr3.peopleid = p2.peopleid\
            and cr3.credited_as = 'A')\
            order by length(trim("];

        NSString *replexpr = @"upper(coalesce(p2.first_name,'')||p2.surname)";

        if (movieActor.text.length > 0) {
            NSArray *name = [movieActor.text
   componentsSeparatedByCharactersInSet:[NSCharacterSet whitespaceCharacterSet]];
            for (NSString *n in name) {
                replexpr = [NSString stringWithFormat:@"replace(%@,?,'')",
                          replexpr];
                [parameters addObject:[n uppercaseString]];
            }
        }

        [query appendFormat:@"%@)) limit 1) act\          ⑨ Finish the query
                          on act.peopleid = cr2.peopleid\
                          where cr2.credited_as='A') f\
                        inner join movies m\
                        on m.movieid = f.movieid\
                        inner join countries c\
                        on c.country_code = m.country\
                        inner join credits cr\
                        on cr.movieid = m.movieid\
                        inner join people p\
                        on p.peopleid = cr.peopleid\
                      group by m.title,c.country_name,m.year_released\
                      order by m.year_released", replexpr];

        mtv.results = [db queryFetchAllAsDicts:query parameters:parameters];
                              ⑩ Coming next!
        [db close];
    }
    else {
        NSLog(@"Could not open database");
    }
}
```

As with any language, it's just about building a dynamic SQL query, adding simultaneously place holders and values to an array of parameters that is passed when executing the query. Let's take a closer look at database interactions. DB.m implements a *DB* class the methods of which simply call the C SQLite functions. I'll just focus here on a couple of methods (download the code from http://edu.konagora.com for the full picture), for instance *openWithPath* which is a wrapper around **sqlite3_open()**.

```
- (BOOL) openWithPath:(NSString *)path {
    return (sqlite3_open([path UTF8String], &db) == SQLITE_OK);
}
```

Another example is *prepare*, which prepares the statement, binds the variables and returns a *DBStatement* object, itself a wrapper for the various C SQLite3 functions that take as argument a **sqlite3_stmt** pointer:

```
- (DBStatement *) prepare:(NSString *)query parameters:(NSArray *)parameters {
    sqlite3_stmt *stmt;
    if (sqlite3_prepare_v2(db, [query UTF8String], -1, &stmt, nil)
                == SQLITE_OK) {
        if (parameters != nil && parameters.count > 0) {
            for (int i=0; i<parameters.count; i++) {
                sqlite3_bind_text(stmt, i+1,
                      [[parameters objectAtIndex:i] UTF8String],
                      -1, SQLITE_TRANSIENT);
            }
        }
        DBStatement *statement = [[DBStatement alloc] initWithStmt:stmt];
        return statement;
    }
    else {
        NSLog(@"Error!");
        return nil;
    }
}
```

Method *queryFetchAllAsDicts* encapsulates calls to methods of the *DBStatement* class and to the preceding method to fetch all the result set at once (we don't expect more than a few dozen rows at most) and return it as a dictionary:

```
- (NSArray *)queryFetchAllAsDicts:(NSString *)query
                                 parameters:(NSArray *)parameters {
    DBStatement *statement = [self prepare:query parameters:parameters];
    if (statement == nil) {
        NSLog(@"Error!");
        return nil;
    }

    NSArray *results = [statement fetchAllAsDicts];
    [statement finalize];
    return results;
}
```

Here are the three key *DBStatement* methods, found in DBStatement.m:

```
- (id) getElement:(sqlite3_stmt *)stmt column:(int)column {
    switch (sqlite3_column_type(stmt, column)) {
        case SQLITE_INTEGER:
            return [NSNumber numberWithInt:sqlite3_column_int(stmt, column)];
```

```
        case SQLITE_FLOAT:
            return [NSNumber
                     numberWithDouble:sqlite3_column_double(stmt, column)];
        default:
            return [[NSString alloc]
                initWithUTF8String:(char *)sqlite3_column_text(stmt, column)];
    }
}
```

The SQLite C interface uses different functions to return values of different types; function **sqlite3_column_type** takes a pointer to a structure that represents a prepared statement and the number of the column.

```
- (NSDictionary *) getRowAsDict {
    if (sqlite3_step(statement) != SQLITE_ROW) return nil;   ← Loop on rows

    NSString *colNameStr;
    id colVal;
    int numCols = sqlite3_data_count(statement);

    NSMutableDictionary *rowDict = [[NSMutableDictionary alloc] init];
    for (int col = 0; col < numCols; col ++) {
        char *colName = (char *) sqlite3_column_name(statement, col);
        colNameStr = [[NSString alloc] initWithUTF8String:colName];
        colVal = [self getElement:statement column:col];

        [rowDict setObject:colVal forKey:colNameStr];
    }
    return rowDict;
}
```

Function **sqlite3_data_count** shows how many columns the data set contains.

```
- (NSArray *) fetchAllAsDicts {
    NSDictionary *row;
    NSMutableArray *results = [[NSMutableArray alloc] init];
    while ((row = [self getRowAsDict]) != nil) {
        [results addObject:row];
    }
    return results;
}
```

Once the result set is loaded into a dictionary, it becomes GUI, not database, programming ...

Suggested Improvements

NAME SEARCH

When I presented the sample application at the beginning of this chapter, I stressed that my programs wouldn't try to solve all the issues associated with name searches, and that names containing accented letters, would have to be input as they are stored to be found. Special characters are challenging, especially with people such as Hardy Krüger whose surname may be as validly searched as *Kruger* or *Krueger*, you encounter a similar problem with abbreviations, as the program won't find Steve McQueen if his surname is stored as *MacQueen*, nor will it recognize *Sternberg* as being the same as *von Sternberg*. Furthermore when working with traditionally case sensitive DBMS products, I have applied the **initcap()** function that transforms *MacGregor* into *Macgregor* and *von Stroheim* into *Von Stroheim*. Although that would work, you should not code

```
where upper(surname) = upper('user input goes there')
```

which would make the index unusable (unless you have indexed `upper(surname)`). Did I mention accents and German *umlauts*? You may either want to write your own stored function for matching user input to database content - or process the user input in the host programming language before binding the values to SQL queries. Additionally, you always have fat-fingered users. A feature that can help when searching on names is function **soundex()** presented in Chapter 6, especially if applied to "normalized" names from which accented letters have been removed. If your DBMS supports indexing expressions, let's assume that you have written a deterministic function called *normalize()* that replaces accented characters by their accent-less equivalent, turns names starting with *Mc* into *Mac*, deals with *von*, *van* and *de*, and puts everything into a standard case if needed. If you index both `soundex(normalize(first_name))` and `soundex(normalize(surname))` in table *people*, referring to these expressions in a condition will use the indexes. Once again, you'll need to check the relevance of what you retrieve, as by design **soundex()** returns identical values for different names. As you can see, there are multiple trails to explore, challenging indexing issues and the permanent difficulty of retrieving what was entered badly while not returning too much noise.

Extended Search

You can go further than improving name searches and the sample programs provide a good base for more ambitious applications. You could allow a search on several names ("What are the films starring Fred Astaire and Ginger Rogers?").

You could also allow a search on directors ("Anything directed by Tim Burton?"), or a search on titles, using the technique shown in Chapter 6. All those searches must return *movieid* values. If a user enters several search criteria, it seems logical to understand that we need to retrieve the films for which all criteria are satisfied - if director and actor are specified, we'll retrieve films directed by one and starring the other. That means that we must only retain the *movieid* values that are common to the list of *movieid* values of films directed by one and to the list of *movieid* values of the films in which the other played: in mathematical parlance, the intersection. As I mentioned earlier, in a program, **intersect** is often easier to use than complex joins in programs. If you had more criteria, you'd need to change the interface but also to build a query dynamically, that can be much more complicated, while still trying to keep decent performance for all possible combinations of criteria. This is a type of challenge regularly encountered by professional developers.

Conclusion

Now, this is not the end, this is not even the beginning of the end, but it is, perhaps, the end of the beginning.

- Winston Churchill (1874-1965)

In this book, I have tried to teach you not only how to access a database programmatically but also to explain why databases need to be carefully designed, how the leading ideas behind data modeling flow into the way queries are written, and how to manage data correctly and efficiently. Most software developers need SQL; whether you write financial or health care or travel applications, develop websites, even games, you need to handle a lot of structured data finally stored in an SQL database. What this book teaches has an almost unlimited range of applications and is as fundamental as operating systems principles.

Database programming is relevant to most IT specialists, even to system engineers who need to administer databases (as database audits often consist in querying the database dictionary and internal tables with SQL). This being so, I would like to suggest a number of "further readings" that you might find valuable. I wouldn't necessarily advise you to read these books immediately after this one. In fact I believe that you will get much more benefit from most of them after you have digested the contents of this book and practiced database programming for at least a few months.

A word of warning: as I mentioned in the preface, when I learned SQL and databases, there were very few books available. The topic of databases was introduced to me, and soon forgotten, when I was a student. My first real contact with SQL was a one-day course at IBM during an internship in the early 1980s, followed a few years later, by a 3-day refresher course when I joined Oracle France. From then on, I mostly learned from the documentation; practice; what you could globally describe as "experience", which includes my mistakes as well as the mistakes of others; and from many exchanges over the years with colleagues, at work or on the web. When books on SQL began to become numerous, I had little to learn from most of them and therefore my knowledge of existing books is narrow and limited. I am talking here of books I know; because I was a technical reviewer for them; because I have knowledge of the authors and I trust both their expertise and their capacity to transmit it; or because I have seen these books recommended by people I professionally respect. For these reasons, you'll notice that I'll often mention authors more than particular titles. I certainly don't mean to say that the names I give are the only good books and authors on the topic of databases, I just mean that from them, you can learn beyond what the present book teaches. There are other good books but with some significant overlap with this one. There are also even more advanced books that are extremely good but which I would only recommend to senior DBAs, a different audience.

Another point worth noting is that, although it is customary in IT to look for the latest book on any given topic, principles remain constant. "How To" books age fast and badly; books on fundamentals can remain fresh twenty years after having been first published. Surprisingly, many good books on DBMS architecture that don't focus on precise commands, remain 95% relevant many years after the version they were written for is no longer supported. You must understand that, even though application programs evolve over time, they have a long life in production; software always outlives hardware. When DBMS vendors introduce new features, programs written for previous versions must still run with the newer one. As a result, major upheavals that affect development are rare. Most changes are additional features of varying importance, or are internal performance improvements, or affect manageability (database administrators need to be much more aware of new features than developers). My message is that you'll probably benefit more from a good older book than from a more recent but average one.

For people who are more career oriented, I have already mentioned in Chapter 1 Clare Churcher's short and good book on database design, *Beginning Database Design*. If you plan for instance, to create a website and are uncertain how you should organize your data, this book will guide you and help you to avoid mistakes. If you need to work on performance issues, I have written a book called *Refactoring SQL Applications* that shows how to analyze query slowness and what you can do to remedy these problems, from easy solutions to more challenging ones.

If you have to develop database programs professionally, you will probably be interested in a book that gives specific details about the DBMS that you are using. I'd advise you to read a book about "architecture" that will give you a wider vision of how the DBMS is implemented, rather than a book about a particular SQL dialect (which would add little to this book, plus the odd visit to online documentation). Beware though, unless of course you are particularly interested by administration, that many books about "architecture and internals" are more targeted at DBAs than at developers; have a quick glance at the table of contents, if half of the book is about backups and recovery, it's a book for DBAs. If you are using Oracle, check Tom Kyte's books; for SQL Server, Itzik Ben-Gan wrote highly rated books (the T-SQL *Fundamentals* book covers more or less the same ground as this one but you'll probably learn a lot from his *Inside* books); the books of Ken Henderson (who sadly died in 2008) are well regarded, and I must also mention the names of Kalen Delaney, Grant Fritchey and Adam Machanic. For DB2 you may want to take a look at books by Philip Gunning, Craig Mullins and Grant Allen. With MySQL and PostgreSQL, there isn't the same division between DBA and developer books as with the other products. The good books have a strong DBA flavor – I can mention *High Performance MySQL* by Baron Schwartz, Peter Zaitsev and Vadim Tkachenko. For SQLite, the book by Mike Owens and Grant Allen covers how the product works internally and gives more examples than this book.

If you have to work with several DBMS products, I am sure that you will find, as I have, Jonathan Gennick's short *SQL Pocket Guide*, extremely handy.

Whether you are career oriented or have a more academic inclination, you may be interested, when you have gained some experience, by Fabian Pascal's *Practical Issues in Database Management*. Fabian has a website, http://www.dbdebunk.com/, which is somewhat disputatious but very interesting, and where he also uploads papers that are worth reading. On SQL proper, I have seen my own *The Art of SQL* used as textbook for graduate courses but it was written for developers with two to five years' experience. A slightly more difficult read than the previous titles, Chris Date's *Database in Depth* or his more recent (and twice as thick), *SQL and Relational Theory* should be accessible to anyone who has assimilated *SQL Success*. If your type of computer book is a cookbook, you probably won't like Chris's writing (you probably didn't like this book either). Some people find Chris meandering. He uses a precise and sometimes unusual vocabulary that you need to become accustomed to. Chris makes no mystery of his dislike of SQL (mostly for reasons presented in the book you are holding) and of his dislike of nulls (ditto). He prefers using a relational language of his own but he has a vision of relational databases that you probably won't find anywhere else. Alternatively to the books, Chris has also recorded (for O'Reilly) some of his seminars as video presentations, which are more expensive than books but can be worth considering for group training. As someone who has attended (live) some of his seminars, I can assure you that whatever your level is, it will give you food for thought.

If you intend to pursue advanced database studies, you will be asked to buy a textbook but you should probably read *Database Design and Relational Theory*, by

Chris Date again. It's all about design theory, full of terms I have carefully avoided in the present book but as far as theory goes Chris is probably the author who explains it the most lucidly.

Setting Up a Work Environment

Appendix

A

Although downloading and installing a DBMS on your personal computer is relatively easy, by installing the product you become the database administrator, even if it's the very first time you've played with a database. Database administration is a topic outside the scope of this book but I will attempt, in this appendix, to give you a few ideas about how a database is organized; it's something that even a software developer ought to know a little bit about. I shall also guide you in setting up an environment that resembles what a developer can reasonably expect to have when developing in a professional capacity, even though I'll assume that we're using the free version (usually called "Express") for all commercial products.

NOTE Don't underestimate free versions of commercial products. They have limits on database size and lack some advanced features but can be used quite professionally. You can't run a multi-billion dollar multinational corporation on them but they can be sufficient for a small company if well used.

I'll be mostly relying on default options and completely ignoring settings that are often important to database and system administrators for production systems. What I'll show here is fine for installing a small sample database relatively cleanly, not for setting up a one Tera-byte mission critical production database.

First of all, and however weird it may look, the very name of *database* has a completely different meaning with Oracle from SQL Server or MySQL, for instance. For Oracle, at least until version 12c, a database is, to put it simply, a collection of files that are managed by an Oracle database server program.

NOTE Sometimes several Oracle database servers running on different machines can co-manage files on shared disks all belonging to the same database.

For most other products, a database is a collection of related tables (and ancillary database objects) and the database server provides access to several databases. The focus is more on data than on files, as it is with Oracle. Moreover, in products such as SQL Server or DB2 (from version 12 Oracle takes this route as well) databases can be "unplugged" from a server and "plugged" into another server; a corollary is that databases that have an independent life must be self-contained units.

With all DBMS products, the collection of tables managed by one application is called a *schema*. It often happens that one application references tables that belong to another schema. For example, in a company, the table that stores the name of all employees will be managed by an application of the Human Resources department and may belong to a schema called HR but as these employees need to be paid, the Finance Department, which manages its own accounting tables, will need to access the table of employees but only to read from it. Related schemas must belong to the same database. Schemas define, in a way, who is responsible for keeping data up-to-date in each functional domain.

I am going to show you here, how to create a schema (a database in several cases) called *moviedb* (the name is arbitrary) to store the sample data used in this book. No set-up is required with SQLite, all you need to do is open *moviedb.sqlite* - a file will be created and initialized automatically if it doesn't already exist.

Oracle

For Oracle, a schema is synonymous with a database account that owns tables. It's easy to extract all the objects owned by one account (there are utilities for that purpose).

Once you have installed Oracle on your machine, and if this isn't already done, start the database (the Oracle Express installation adds *Start Database* and *Stop Database* to the menus in your environment). Then, rather than using a graphical user interface, we are going to use the command line, which will make it easier to explain what we are doing. On Windows and Linux, the installation should create *Run SQL command line* in the menu, which opens a Window with the **SQL>** prompt. Alternatively, open a console window and type *sqlplus /nolog*.

- At this stage you aren't connected. We are first going to connect as an administrator, which you can do, without entering any password, from the (operating system) account that has installed Oracle.

  Type at the prompt

```
SQL> connect system as sysdba
```

  You will be asked for a password - none is required, hit return and you should see 'Connected.' If you see the error 'TNS:protocol adaptor error' it means that Oracle wasn't properly started. If you see the error 'insufficient privileges' it means that you are on Linux and connected to a Linux account that doesn't belong to the *dba* Linux group; use another account in this group (e.g. *oracle*) or have your account added to the *dba* group (you must also belong to the *dba* group to be able to start or stop the database).

- Tables have to be stored somewhere; they are stored in files, and files, for convenience, are grouped in sets that constitute *tablespaces*. Usually, especially with large corporate databases, there is one or several tablespaces associated with each application (having everything that relates to one application grouped in a limited number of files makes it easier to backup, restore or move to another database on a per-application basis). We aren't going to create a tablespace but simply use for our schema, a tablespace called *users* that is created by default when you install Oracle and is fine for small applications. We are also going to specify a tablespace to use for temporary storage (which may be required for sorting huge amounts of data), once again using a tablespace that is created when Oracle is installed. Type what is printed in bold in the following:

```
SQL> create user moviedb
  2  identified by sqlsuccess        ① password assigned to the user
  3  default tablespace users        ② where tables will be created
  4  quota unlimited on users        ③ don't assign any limit
  5  temporary tablespace temp;      ④ for sorts
```

① The password can be up to 30 characters long; I am using *sqlsuccess*, you can use anything you want. Unless you are using an old version of Oracle (Oracle 10 and earlier), the password is case-sensitive. By default, this password will expire and will have to be changed by the user in six month's time (with a command `alter user moviedb identified by` *new_password*).
② We specify where tables will go, but
③ we can only create tables in a tablespace, if we are allocated a storage quota on this tablespace. Quotas can be a number of megabytes or gigabytes but a set limit is very rarely used and most often accounts are granted an unlimited quota. This means that they can create tables and that their tables can grow, as long as there is room in the files that constitute the tablespace (database administrators can control how much storage is used in files and how files grow).
④ Finally, we specify a tablespace for temporary operations. No quota is needed here, it's handled by the DBMS internally.

- Contrary to what you probably think, having defined a database account and assigned a password to this account, isn't enough to allow a connection to this database account; we must also explicitly give the right to connect (to create a session, in Oracle-speak). Besides, having associated the account with a tablespace and having unlimited quota on this tablespace isn't enough to allow us to create tables; the right to create a table must also be given explicitly, as well as some other rights that will be needed for various sections of this book.

```
SQL> grant create session,     ← The minimun you need!
  2    create table,           ← Required for Chapter 2
  3    create sequence,        ← Required for Chapter 7
  4    create procedure,       ← Required for Chapter 8
  5    create trigger,         ← Required for Chapter 8
```

```
create view
to moviedb;
```

This command will give to the *moviedb* account, everything that it needs for this book – and nothing more.

At this stage, you are ready to go. You can connect as *moviedb* with (in my example) password *sqlsuccess* and start working.

SQL Server

In SQL Server you have two levels: you have databases, which regroup tables but you also have schemas, which are, in SQL Server, subdivisions of databases. Databases are self-contained and can be detached from one database server and attached to another one. Different schemas inside a database are linked, and require each other. You could imagine, for instance, having one database to store information for a subscription-based movie streaming business, and have one schema to store data about films proper, and another one for accounting, recording what was watched and by whom, separating reference data (the films) from operational data (your customers, and what they buy).

For this book we will have a very simple organization, with all the data in a dedicated database and there will be no schema other than the default database schema that is called *dbo* (for **d**ata**b**ase **o**wner).

If the database server isn't already running, start it with SQL Server Configuration Manager. Then start SQL Server Management Studio (SSMS) and connect using Windows Authentication. If you are connecting from the account that installed SQL Server in the first place, no password will be asked of you. Once you are connected, your current database is by default, a database called *master*, that contains tables and objects used internally by SQL Server. You don't want to create your tables in this database and we are going to create our special database by clicking on *New Query* and issuing

```
create database moviedb
```

This will create the database but you will need to type

```
use moviedb
```

after connection, unless you change your default connection options. On the left-hand side of SSMS, in the hierarchy under Object Explorer, click on *Security*, then *Logins*, then right-click on the name that corresponds to your login, and click on *Properties*. At the bottom of the (default) *General* page, you will find *Default Database* – choose *moviedb* in the drop-down list and you are done.

You can perform the same operation with one SQL command:

```
alter login [domain\account]
with default_database = moviedb
```

NOTE The square brackets are required and *domain\account* is what is returned by the command `select system_user`

When you create a new query in SSMS the name of the current database appears in a drop-down list (from which it can be changed) just under *New Query*. You can also check your current database by executing the query

```
select db_name()
```

MySQL

Although MySQL superficially looks similar to SQL Server, a MySQL schema is the same as a MySQL database and there is no sub-grouping possible. For the tables used in this book we are going to create a database called *moviedb*. On Linux, you can connect as the master MySQL account *root* without any password after the installation. Open a terminal window, and type

```
mysql  uroot
```

The first thing to do, is to assign a password to this account, by executing

```
mysql> set password = password('enter a password of your choice here');
```

On Windows, you will normally have assigned a password to the MySQL *root* account during the installation. If you search the menu, under *MySQL* and then *MySQL Server*, you should find a command that runs SQL command lines. You will be prompted for a password - the password of *root*.

We are now going to create a special database in which to store the sample data used in this book and we'll name it *moviedb* (an arbitrary name):

```
mysql> create database moviedb;
```

When you work in a company, only database administrators ever connect as *root*. We need to create a user account that will be used for development. You could give your own name to this account. However, as it will be used to store the tables of an application and will "own" these tables, it's common to give the owner of the tables, the same name as the application. I am going to create a user account that has the same name as the database (it could be different) and assign to it the password *sqlsuccess* (you can use whatever you want):

```
mysql> create user moviedb identified by 'sqlsuccess';
```

Once this user is created, we must give special rights to allow the account to create tables and various database objects that we'll need in this book:

```
mysql> grant create,         ← Required for Chapter 2
    ->  create routine,      ← Required for Chapter 8
    ->  trigger,             ← Required for Chapter 8
```

```
-> index,           ← Required for Chapter 9
-> create view      ← Required for Chapter 10
-> on moviedb.* to moviedb;
```

You now have an account that you can safely use for work, which only has the rights that are needed for practicing what is shown in this book. From now on you will connect to the MySQL *moviedb* database using the account *moviedb*. With the command line tool you'll need to type

```
mysql  u moviedb  p  D moviedb
```

`-u` specifies the user account, `-p` requires a password prompt, and `D` is followed by the name of the database to which we want to connect. If you are using a tool such as MySQL Workbench and create a connection, you'll specify *moviedb* as the default schema (remember that in MySQL, schema and database are synonyms).

DB2

Like with SQL Server, with DB2 you can have one separate database for each application, or you can have multiple schemas grouping a number of tables inside one database (the choice is mostly a question of coupling between applications - you can copy databases to different servers, if applications are strongly linked, it makes sense to store them as separate schemas inside one database). Like with SQL Server, I'll go here for the simpler option and create a *moviedb* database rather than a *moviedb* schema inside an existing database.

On Windows, everything that follows can be done from the account from which you installed DB2. On Linux, you should first connect to the *db2inst1* account that is created during the installation.

Start the command interpreter from the menu (alternatively, open a console window and run *db2*); it will display the following prompt

```
db2 =>
```

If the DBMS isn't already running begin with

```
db2 => start database manager
```

and once you have a message telling you that the command has succeeded you can issue

```
db2 => create database moviedb using codeset utf-8 territory us
```

if you plan to use non Latin character sets (note that what follows `territory` should be the code for your country, not necessarily *us*); if not, you can just type

```
db2 => create database moviedb
```

With DB2, you don't connect generically to the database server but you connect to a specific database. Use `connect to moviedb` with the command-line interpreter or create a connection with IBM Data Studio; the user name and password are those that you used to connect to your operating system account, as DB2 relies on operating system accounts.

On a system such as Linux, you probably want to work from a different account from the *db2inst1* account; let's say that the Linux account you are using is called *jgarcia*. You must then, after having created the database and connected to it, give to *jgarcia* the right to connect to this database, the right to create tables in it, the right to ask DB2 how it processes queries (we'll use it in Chapter 9) and the right to load data:

```
db2=> grant connect, createtab, explain, load on database to user jgarcia
```

Once this is done, we still have a few things to do at the Linux level: the user needs for instance to have DB2 directories added to the list of directories where executable commands and libraries are searched. Let's first disconnect (as *db2inst1*) from the database:

```
db2=> disconnect moviedb
db2=> quit
```

If you are in the home directory of user *db2inst1*, check the `.bashrc` file. You'll find in this file something like the following lines:

```
# The following three lines have been added by UDB DB2.
if [ -f /home/db2inst1/sqllib/db2profile ]; then
    . /home/db2inst1/sqllib/db2profile
fi
```

Add them to the `.bashrc` file of user *jgarcia*, and you'll be able to run command `clpplus` from this account. By default, tables will be created in a schema named after the system account but in upper case (JGARCIA in this example).

PostgreSQL

PostgreSQL understands both application-focused databases and schemas within databases like DB2 and SQL Server. For a simple database such as the sample database used in this book, schemas are an overkill. I'm simply going to create a dedicated database, which I can do by running in a console window, the `psql` command from the account that installed the DBMS and initialized the database. At the psql prompt, type

```
create database moviedb;
```

and hit return.

Next, we must create a user account that will own the tables of the application. You could give any name to this account (including yours) but for a project, on which people come and go, it's probably better to give this account, which will stay, a name relating to the project itself, rather than the name of an individual working on the project. I am going to give this user the same name as the database. This is rather convenient, as by default, PostgreSQL connects to a database that bears the same name as the user account. I'll give the account the password *sqlsuccess* (feel free to use a different one):

```
create user moviedb password 'sqlsuccess';
```

You will notice that PostgreSQL echoes CREATE ROLE: role and user are synonyms in PostgreSQL, a user is simply a role that has the right to login.

Finally, you must give the newly created user, the right to create tables and other database objects in the *moviedb* database:

```
grant create on database moviedb to moviedb;
```

Tables created in the database will by default belong to a schema called *public*.

At this stage, you can connect to the database as user *moviedb*. If you are running the following command from the machine where PostgreSQL was installed:

```
psql  U moviedb
```

you will connect directly to the database from any system account, without ever being asked for a password. If this makes you feel as uneasy as it does myself on anything other than a personal workstation, you should modify the file named pg_hba.conf that is located in the data directory of PostgreSQL. You will find in this file the following lines:

```
# TYPE  DATABASE        USER            ADDRESS                 METHOD
# "local" is for Unix domain socket connections only
local   all             all                                     trust
# IPv4 local connections:
host    all             all             127.0.0.1/32            trust
# IPv6 local connections:
host    all             all             ::1/128                 trust
```

The trust at the end of each line basically means 'no password required'. On a server, for instance a Linux server, I am ready to allow a password-less connection to the *postgres* user – this user can already do whatever it wants with PostgreSQL at the system level. I am therefore going to say trust for the *postgres* user, and nobody else. For the mixed bunch of other users I am going to change the authentication method to md5 (it means a password that is transmitted encrypted):

```
# TYPE  DATABASE        USER            ADDRESS                 METHOD
local   all             postgres                                trust
host    all             postgres        127.0.0.1/32            trust
host    all             postgres        ::1/128                 trust
# "local" is for Unix domain socket connections only
local   all             all                                     md5
# IPv4 local connections:
host    all             all             127.0.0.1/32            md5
# IPv6 local connections:
host    all             all             ::1/128                 md5
```

Once my `pg_hba.conf` file is modified, I must issue the command

```
pg_ctl reload
```

to bring that fact to the attention of the running programs. From there on

```
psql  U moviedb
```

will prompt for the password assigned to the *moviedb* user when the account was created.

A Selection of Useful Functions

Appendix
B

With the exception of SQLite which has a minimalistic approach to functions[1] all DBMS products come with a somewhat bloated list of built-in functions. As often happens, 20% of the available functions (or less) will cover 80% of your needs (or more).

In this appendix, I will list a number of frequent transformation problems, with the functions commonly used to solve them. This list isn't meant to be exhaustive and doesn't pretend to be a substitute for the full list, which you will find in the documentation of each product. See it as a cheat-sheet to point you in the right direction to solve frequent issues.

Taking Care of Nulls

Unless specified otherwise, a function applied to a null, returns null. Taking care of nulls is therefore usually one of the very first concerns.

Function **coalesce()** takes an indefinite number of parameters and returns the value of the first one that isn't null. This function is available with all products covered in this book.

If you want to concatenate strings in SQL and one of them happens to be null, the result is null.

For instance

```
select first_name || ' ' || surname as name, born
from people
```

May return something such as

```
name                    born
...
Karan Johar             1972
Milla Jovovich          1975
                        1974   ← No first_name / resulting name is null
Heather MacComb         1977
Rani Mukherjee          1978
...
```

[1] It is easy with SQLite, to plug one's own functions into the product, I'll give you one example at the end of this appendix.

If you use instead

```
select coalesce(first_name || ' ' || surname, surname) as name, ...
```

the surname (which is mandatory) will be used when the expression is null and you'll see a name only comprising the surname.

```
name                    born
...
Karan Johar             1972
Milla Jovovich          1975
Kajol                   1974
Heather MacComb         1977
Rani Mukherjee          1978
...
```

For historical reasons, you may also encounter with the different products, other equivalent functions that take a fixed number of parameters: **nvl()** (two parameters) and **nvl2()** (three parameters) with Oracle, **isnull()** (two parameters) with SQL Server (not to be confused with a MySQL function of the same name), **ifnull()** (two parameters) with MySQL.

Working with Numbers

Although most products feature an impressive number of mathematical functions, for most real life applications you need very few. Except for the computation of sums and averages (that you'll find under ***Aggregating*** page 457 in this appendix), you rarely need much more than rounding besides simple numerical operations.

Rounding to the nearest integer

Function **round()** is available in all dialects and rounds to the nearest integer when passed a value; for instance

`round(3.141592)` yields 3 with all products.

This function takes additional optional parameters that allow interesting variations as you will see.

Rounding up

Rounding up means getting the nearest integer value bigger than the parameter, or the parameter itself if it's an integer (beware with negative numbers, bigger for them means closer to zero). Rounding up is useful for operations as diverse as computing the maximum value to assign to an axis when preparing data for a chart, or computing how many storage units you need to archive your database files.

There is a function that returns the nearest higher integer; this function is called **ceil()** in Oracle, **ceiling()** in SQL Server and either name in DB2, PostgreSQL or MySQL. Alternatively, you can use **round(*val* + 0.5)**.

`round(3.141592)` returns 3 but if you add 0.5 it becomes `round(3.641592)` that returns 4.

Rounding down

Rounding to the nearest smaller integer value (once again, beware with negative values) can be useful for computing lower bounds or threshold values. The function that corresponds to this operation is called **floor()** in all products, except SQLite. SQLite doesn't natively implement **floor()** but you can use **round(*val* – 0.5)**.

If you subtract 0.5 from 2.71828 you get 2.21828 that rounds to 2.

Rounding to a precise decimal

Function **round()** always takes an optional second parameter that specifies to how many decimal points you want to round: omitting this parameter is the name as specifying 0. Thus

`round(3.141592, 2)` yields `3.14`

and

`round(3.14159, 4)` yields `3.1416`

Rounding to a number of decimal points is most commonly used with money (for instance to display an amount to which a tax or fee percentage has been applied) and to beautify the result of aggregate functions such as **avg()**.

SQL Server is the only product that allows you to round down (but not up) to one particular decimal, which is done by passing a third, optional, parameter to the **round()** function. If this parameter is 0, regular rounding occurs. If it's a non-zero integer value, then rounding down occurs. Thus

`round(3.14159, 4, 1)` yields `3.14150` with SQL Server

With other products (and for rounding up) you can play with **floor()** and **ceil*[ing]*()** and powers of 10; for instance

```
floor(3.141592 * 10000)/10000
```

will give you the same result as the SQL Server expression above. With SQLite you can use

```
round(3.141592 * 10000 - 0.5)/10000
```

Rounding to the nearest hundred (or thousand)

In all products, it is possible to pass to **round()**, a negative number as the second parameter. For SQLite3 (at least until version 3.7), a negative number has the same effect as zero. For other products; -1 rounds to the nearest multiple of 10; -2 to the nearest multiple of 100; -3 to the nearest multiple of 1000 and so on.

For instance:

```
select round(123456.78, -2)
```

returns 123500.

For rounding up and down, you can also use expressions such as

```
select floor(123456.78 / 100) * 100
```

which returns 123400.

Checking the sign of a number

A shortcut to using a **case** expression for testing whether a value is positive or negative (for instance for dispatching it to a *credit* or to a *debit* column in the result set) is the function **sign()**. Available in all products except SQLite, **sign()** returns 1 if the value is positive, 0 if it's zero, and -1 if it's negative.

```
sign(val)
```

is equivalent to

```
case
  when val > 0 then 1
  when val < 0 then -1
  else 0
end
```

Getting the remainder of integer division

You may occasionally need to check if an integer value is a multiple of another integer. The easiest way to do this is by dividing the first integer by the second one, and checking the remainder. If the result is zero, we have a multiple. The function that returns the remainder of the division of two integers is **mod()**. It's available in all products, except SQL Server and SQLite which instead, use the **%** operator found in many programming languages.

`mod(val, 2)` or `val % 2` (SQL Server and SQLite) will return 1 if the number is odd, 0 if it's even.

This function can also be used to extract a more or less random sample of data from your database. For instance you may decide that you want to contact, for marketing research, 1% of your customers. Applying a filter such as

```
where mod(customerid, 100) = <any number of your choice between 0 and 99>
```

will give you the sample that you want.

Working with Text

Applying functions to text is, at least in my experience, rather more common than applying functions to numerical values. One applies functions to character strings partly for good reasons (standardizing data on input, trying to make it look better when retrieving it) and partly for not-so-good ones, usually imposed by questionable database design choices.

Computing the length

A commonly used function is **length()**, called **len()** in SQL Server. Computing the length of character string is useful when importing data into tables (does it fit?). This function can never return 0 with Oracle, which considers that an empty string such as '' is the same as null (a questionable choice from a theoretical standpoint but understandable from a practical one). Therefore, **length('')** returns null with Oracle, and 0 with all the other products. With all products, Oracle included, **length(null)** returns null.

A less common but interesting use of a function such as **length()** is, with help from a judicious choice of codes, the management of hierarchies and subgroups. For instance, for statistical purposes, the United Nations subdivides the world countries into various regions: *Americas* is composed of *Latin America and the Caribbean*, and of *Northern America*. The former is itself divided into *Caribbean*, *Central America* and *South America*. The United Nations uses a three-digit code for all regions and sub regions (*Americas* is 019, *Central America* 013). Now, imagine that instead of a three-digit code you use mnemonics, for instance AM for *Americas* and that the code of each sub region is composed of the code of the parent region plus a two-letter specific code – AMSA for *Americas/South America*, or AFNA for *Africa/Northern Africa*. With such a coding scheme, the length of the code immediately gives you the aggregation level – if the length is two, then it's a continent, if it's four we have a sub region.

Changing the case

Functions **lower()** and **upper()** can be found in every product and return their parameter in lowercase and uppercase respectively. Thus

`upper('SQL Success')` returns `SQL SUCCESS`

and

`lower('SQL Success')` returns `sql success`

PostgreSQL, DB2 and Oracle also implement **initcap()** that returns the argument in lowercase with the first letter of every word capitalized:

```
initcap('SQL Success')
```

returns

```
Sql Success
```

Changing pieces of text

All products implement function **replace()** that takes three parameters, a string to change, a string to search for and a replacement string (optional with some products). In many cases, SQL is explained merely through syntax, which is pretty boring, and many students end up thinking that "SQL sucks". I hope that this book will convince you that very little is needed to make SQL interesting, as little as is needed by **replace()** as shown with Oracle:

```
SQL> select replace('SQL sucks', 'k', 'ces') from dual;

REPLACE('SQ
-----------
SQL success
```

All occurrences of the searched string (which may be any length) will be replaced by the specified replacement string. If there is no replacement string or if the replacement string is empty, the searched string will be removed. Function **replace()** is a case with Oracle in which a third parameter passed as null or '' (empty string) doesn't cause the function to return null but simply to remove the second parameter from the first one.

DB2, Oracle and PostgreSQL also implement a function called **translate()** that takes three arguments. This function only operates on single characters, unlike **replace()** that can change full strings of characters.

This function is easier to explain with an example than in words. The following expression for instance

```
translate('meeting', 'egmnt', 'oscek')
```

returns

```
cookies
```

with Oracle or PostgreSQL. What has happened here is that the first argument has been examined character by character to see if any of its characters are represented in the second argument. Where there is a match, the character in the first argument is replaced by the character in the third argument which occupies the same position as the matching character in the second argument; **translate()** replaced every occurrence of *e* with *o*, every *g* with *s*, every *m* with *c*, every *n* with *e*, every *t* with *k*.

Note that the meaning of the second and third arguments isn't the same in DB2 as in Oracle and PostgreSQL. In DB2 the second argument is the list of characters that we want in the result and the third one the characters that must be replaced. It's the opposite with Oracle and PostgreSQL.

This function can be useful to check patterns in **check** constraints. For instance, if you want to accept in the US, only phone numbers in the same format as (311) 555-2368 (which isn't very nice for people who don't live in the US), you can replace each of the digits in the phone number between 1 and 9 inclusive, by 0 using the following expression with DB2

```
translate('(541) 555-3010', '000000000', '123456789')
```

or, with Oracle and PostgreSQL

```
translate('(541) 555-3010', '123456789', '000000000')
```

You can then check if the resulting pattern is indeed `(000) 000-0000`. If there are fewer characters in the list of replacement characters than in the list of characters to replace, they are suppressed with Oracle and PostgreSQL; they are replaced in DB2 by a space by default, or any character that can be specified as an optional fourth parameter, including an empty character ''. Thus, with Oracle or PostgreSQL

```
translate('allowance', 'ow', 'i')
```

returns

```
alliance
```

(*o* is replaced by *i* and *w* is suppressed)

With DB2

```
translate('allowance', 'i', 'ow')
```

returns

```
alli ance
```

but

```
translate('allowance', 'i', 'ow', '')
```

returns

```
alliance
```

With Oracle you cannot directly use **translate()** only to remove characters - if the third parameter is an empty string (identical to null for Oracle), the function returns null. Suppose that with Oracle, you want to remove every *t*, *r*, and *a* from *illustration*. The following query doesn't return what you would expect:

```
SQL> select translate('illustration', 'tra', '') from dual;
                                              ↑ same as null for Oracle

T
-

    ← and you get null

SQL>
```

The workaround is to translate at least one of the characters to be suppressed, to a real character (for instance #):

```
SQL> select translate('illustration', 'tra', '#') from dual;
```

```
TRANSLATE(
----------
illus##ion     ← t is replaced, other letters disappear

SQL>
```

then apply **replace()** to the resulting string of characters:

```
SQL> select replace(translate('illustration', 'tra', '#'), '#', '') from dual;

REPLACE(
--------
illusion

SQL>
```

Trimming

It's important when inserting data to ensure that no extraneous characters are inserted. Data can be cleaned up in the host language, or directly by calling appropriate functions in **insert** statements. Sometimes you also want to remove prefixes from displayed data (such as the international phone code for your country) even though they are stored in the database.

Oracle, DB2, PostgreSQL and SQLite provide a function **ltrim()** and a function **rtrim()** that remove respectively from the left and the right of their first argument, all the characters from their second argument. PostgreSQL also has a similar function called **btrim()** that operates at both ends (the same function is simply named **trim()** in SQLite). Be careful that the second argument is understood as a list of independent characters: **ltrim(***value*, **'abc')** will not only remove 'abc' from the start of *value* but will actually remove all the letters until a letter that is neither *a* nor *b* nor *c* is encountered. Thus

```
ltrim('www.some-url.com', 'w.')
```

returns

```
some-url.com
```

ltrim() and **rtrim()** as implemented by MySQL and SQL Server only take one parameter (the string to process) and only remove spaces.

Oracle and DB2 also implement **trim()**, which can take different forms:

- **trim(***value***)** removes leading and trailing spaces
- **trim(***character* **from** *value***)** removes leading and trailing occurrences of *character*.
- **trim(leading** *character* **from** *value***)** only removes *character* on the left.
- **trim(trailing** *character* **from** *value***)** only removes *character* on the right.

Unlike the second argument of **ltrim()** and **btrim()**, *character* in that case is a <u>single</u> character.

MySQL implements a version of **trim()** that works as in Oracle and DB2 but can trim a string instead of a single character. Thus

```
trim(leading 'www.' from 'www.some-url.com')
```

returns

```
some-url.com
```

Be careful to note that with MySQL, it's a full string that is trimmed, not a collection of independent characters. Compare the following MySQL example with the preceding **ltrim()** case:

```
trim(leading 'w.' from 'www.some-url.com')
```

returns

```
www.some-url.com
```

as the string doesn't start with 'w.'.

trim() (or a combination of **ltrim()** and **rtrim()**), **len*[gth]*** () and **coalesce()** are useful for ensuring that data is clean when loaded from a tab-separated file as shown in Chapter 7. It's relatively frequent in this type of file to have extra spaces between two tabs in place of empty fields. Loading spaces may cause many problems in queries. If you expect the column to be null and apply a condition `where my_col is null,` rows for which the column contains one or several spaces won't be retrieved as technically speaking a space isn't the same as null. There is an additional difficulty with empty strings (containing no space at all), which aren't the same as null, except for Oracle. Thus with MySQL for instance you get this when you have spaces:

```
mysql> select '  ' as two_spaces,
    ->        length('  ') as length_of_two_spaces,
    ->        length(trim('  ')) length_of_trim;
+------------+----------------------+----------------+
| two_spaces | length_of_two_spaces | length_of_trim |
+------------+----------------------+----------------+
|            |                    2 |              0 |
+------------+----------------------+----------------+
1 row in set (0.02 sec)
```

With Oracle you get a different result in the third column:

```
SQL> select '  ' as two_spaces,
  2         length('  ') as length_of_two_spaces,
  3         length(trim('  ')) length_of_trim
  4  from dual;

TW LENGTH_OF_TWO_SPACES LENGTH_OF_TRIM
-- -------------------- --------------
                      2                    ← length after trimming is null, not 0
```

You can suppress "empty values" and set them to null with a statement such as

```
update my_table
set my_col = null
where my_col is not null
   and coalesce(length(trim(my_col)), 0) = 0
```

NOTE **coalesce()** is here for Oracle only, as a trimmed ' ' (not null) becomes '' (null). It doesn't hurt with other products.

Padding

Mostly for the record because this type of operation is often better performed in the host language, Oracle, MySQL, PostgreSQL and DB2 implement functions **lpad()** and **rpad()** that perform the opposite operation to **ltrim()** and **rtrim()**: they take two or three arguments, a string to transform, a length, and an optional padding string (which defaults to space). If the string to be transformed is shorter than the length, then it is padded either to the left or to the right with the padding string the number of times required to obtain the required length. If the string to be transformed is longer than the length provided, it's truncated. These functions are often used for indentation in hierarchical lists, or for generating crude character-based histograms (I far prefer the HTML version shown in Chapter 5).

Extracting substrings

There are several functions for extracting a substring. The most generic one is **substr()** available in Oracle, DB2, MySQL and SQLite that takes two or three parameters, first the string to which the function is applied, then the position from which to start the extraction and, optionally, how many consecutive characters to extract (if unspecified, the substring till the end of the original string is returned). A similar function called **substring()** is implemented in SQL Server but requires the third parameter (if you want everything to the end of the string, you can use the length of the original string – it doesn't matter if the third parameter is greater than the length of what is ultimately returned). In MySQL, **substr()** and **substring()** are in fact synonyms.

PostgreSQL uses a function also called **substring()** but with a syntax that is very different from the syntax of the similarly named SQL Server function (a **substring()** function similar to the PostgreSQL one, is also implemented in DB2 and the same syntax is supported by MySQL). In PostgreSQL, DB2 and MySQL you can use

```
substring(some_string from start_position)
```

which returns everything from *start_position*, or

```
substring(some_string from start_position for a_number_of_characters)
```

Two other functions, available in all products except Oracle and SQLite are **left()** and **right()** that take two parameters, a string of characters and a number of characters to return from, respectively, the left or the right of the first parameter.

Writing `left(some_string, 4)` is the same as writing `substr(some_string, 1, 4)`, with a difference - some query optimizers can easily know that we are only looking at the first characters and use an existing index (see Chapter 9). Saying

```
left(some_string, 3) = 'abc'
```

is the same as saying

```
some_string like 'abc%'
```

Writing `right(some_string, 4)` is the same as writing `substr(some_string, length(some_string) - 3)`. With **right()**, no hope of using an existing index efficiently (unless perhaps you are using a language that writes from right to left).

Locating a substring

Very often the position from which we want to extract a substring, is determined by a special character that we must locate, such as @ in an email address. Locating a character (or a string of several characters) that I'll call *needle* in a string that I'll call *haystack* is done with a function called **instr()** in Oracle, DB2 and MySQL; **instr(***haystack, needle***)** returns the position of *needle* in *haystack*, numbering the leftmost character as character 1. If *needle* isn't found, the function returns 0.

In the case of Oracle, **instr()** can take up to four parameters; the third one (1 by default) indicates the position from which to search. This position can be negative, in which case the string is searched backwards (but the position returned is still given by counting characters from the left). The fourth parameter tells which occurrence (first one by default) to locate. The DB2 version, otherwise similar to the Oracle version, can take an optional fifth parameter that specifies whether we are working with single, two-byte or four-byte characters (the default is determined by the data being searched).

ORACLE NOTE If your data contains non-Latin characters (Cyrillic, Japanese or Chinese characters, among others) there are with Oracle variants such as **instrc()**, similar to **instr()** but which can consider a multi-byte unicode character as a single character.

Function **instr()** only takes two parameters in MySQL; however the equivalent **locate(***needle, haystack***)** - beware, parameters are inverted - can optionally take a third parameter that specifies a starting position for the search (this parameter must be positive). Another synonym that you may meet with MySQL is **position(***needle* **in** *haystack***)**, also available in DB2 and PostgreSQL. There is no way to specify a starting position with **position()** (you can cheat by searching a substring). Both DB2 and PostgreSQL support synonyms for this function, **strpos()** for PostgreSQL, **locate_in_string()** and **posstr()** for DB2. The order of parameters in the synonyms is sometimes reversed.

The equivalent function in SQL Server is **charindex(***needle, haystack*[, *start_position*]). A negative start position or 0 are the same as 1. SQL Server also implements a **patindex()** function that only takes two parameters (no starting position) but allows us to search for patterns that use the % wildcard character (as with **like**).

SQLite3 has no function for searching strings. I'll show you how to implement it at the end of this chapter.

All products except Oracle and SQLite implement a **reverse()** function which returns its input backwards – thus

```
select reverse('stressed')
```

returns the more enjoyable

```
desserts
```

This function can be used to perform a backward search.

I am going to illustrate searches by finding the position of the various dots in a moderately complex domain name such as

```
cs.cam.ac.uk
```

We have a dot in 3rd position, another one in 7th position and still another one in 10th position.

Finding the position of the first dot is easy; depending on the product, you can obtain it by

```
position('.' in 'cs.cam.ac.uk')
```

or

```
instr('cs.cam.ac.uk', '.')
```

or

```
charindex('.', 'cs.cam.ac.uk')
```

Finding the position of the last one can be effected with DB2 or Oracle with

```
instr('cs.cam.ac.uk', '.', -1)
```

For SQL Server you need

```
1 + len('cs.cam.ac.uk') - charindex('.', reverse('cs.cam.ac.uk'))
```

With MySQL and Postgres you can use

```
1 + length('cs.cam.ak.uk') - position('.' in reverse('cs.cam.ac.uk'))
```

To find the position of the second dot, with Oracle and DB2 it will be

```
instr('cs.cam.ac.uk', '.', 1, 2)
```

With SQL Server

```
charindex('.', 'cs.cam.ac.uk', 1 + charindex('.', 'cs.cam.ac.uk'))
```

With MySQL

```
locate('.', 'cs.cam.ac.uk', 1 + position('.' in 'cs.cam.ac.uk'))
```

Locating the position of the second dot with PostgreSQL requires much more back-bending than with other products. First we must check that we have more than one dot in the string that is searched, which we can do by checking the length of the string minus the length of the same from which we have removed all dots:

```
length('cs.cam.ac.uk') - length(replace('cs.cam.ac.uk', '.', ''))
```

If this value is less than two, we should return 0. Next, we can use an interesting function that exists in no other product, called **split_part()**, which takes three arguments, a string to split, a string that describes on what to split (in this case it will be '.') and the number of a part.

> POSTGRESQL NOTE Function **split_part()** derives more or less directly from the implementation in PostgreSQL of a generic "array" data type, of many functions that apply to arrays, and of functions to convert strings to arrays and back (if you have any knowledge of PHP, think of **explode()** and **implode()**). These functions are non-standard.

If we split the domain on dots and obtain 'cs', 'cam', 'ac', 'uk' in this order, the position of the second dot can be obtained by summing up the length of the first two parts, plus the length of the separator (one in this case). Thus, the final expression becomes

```
case
  when length('cs.cam.ac.uk')
        - length(replace('cs.cam.ac.uk', '.', '')) < 2 then 0
  else length(split_part('cs.cam.ac.uk', '.', 1) + 1
           + length(split_part('cs.cam.ac.uk', '.', 2) + 1
end
```

The PostgreSQL expression may look complicated (actually it is complicated) but very often locating various separators in a string is necessary to isolate parts between two separators - which you can do with **split_part()** much more conveniently than with other DBMS products.

> NOTE Several products other than PostgreSQL implement functions for retrieving portions of delimited data. I could mention **parsename()** in SQL Server or **substring_index()** (in combination with other functions) with MySQL, which also implements a function called **find_in_set()**. Please refer to the relevant documentation.

It's also possible to perform this type of operation with recursive queries (see Chapter 5) and when expressions become too complicated, it's advisable to create user-defined functions (see Chapter 8).

Working with Dates

Date functions are commonly used in SQL - and commonly misused. First, always keep in mind that when you search on a date you should generally express the condition as a search on a range of values (see Chapter 9 for the reason why). I'll start with tables summarizing how to obtain the current date or time (or both) with the various products. When we talk about time, there are two possible times: the local time where the database server is located, and what is called *universal coordinated time* (or UTC for short), formerly known as *Greenwich Mean Time* or GMT. UTC also affects the date, as people in places like the Western Samoa and French Polynesia spend the best part of the day with a different date on the wall calendar.

NOTE You may be surprised by an acronym that doesn't match what it is an acronym for (Universal Coordinated Time should be UCT). The Universal Coordinated Time is computed in France from a world network of atomic clocks; French acronyms are usually the reverse of English ones (ONU for UNO, OTAN for NATO, FMI for IMF, and so on). UTC matches neither Universal Coordinated Time nor Temps Coordonné Universel, so it was considered a good compromise. Diplomatic logic.

The problem with local time is that it isn't dependent on geography alone but also on political whim, and the desire to have more or less the same time as important trading partners - or to the contrary, the desire to stress independence. Moreover, daylight saving time can be suppressed or decreed by law. All this doesn't really matter for most people, who follow the official time of the place where they live, whatever it is. When you need to record sequences of operations across several time zones in different countries, it becomes much more difficult, hence the need for a time that can be used as a reference, UTC. I'll discuss how to work with time zones later.

Current date and time

The following tables show how to obtain local and UTC date and time with the various products covered in this book; **current_date** is supported by most products to obtain the local date.

DB2

Result wanted	Function or expression	Precision

Local date and time	`current timestamp`
	or
	`sysdate`
		0.000001s
		(by default)
		1s

UTC date and time	`current timestamp - current timezone`
	or
	`sysdate - current timezone`
		As above

Local date	`current date`	
UTC date	`trunc(sysdate - current timezone, 'DD')`	
Local time	`current time`	1s
UTC time	`current time - current timezone`	1s

MySQL

Result wanted	Function or expression	Precision

Local date and time	`now()`
	or
	`current_timestamp()`
		1s

UTC date and time	`utc_timestamp()`	1s

Local date	`curdate()`
	or
	`current_date()`	

UTC date	`utc_date()`	

Local time	`curtime()`
	or
	`current_time()`
		1s

UTC time	`utc_time()`	1s

Oracle

Result wanted	Function or expression	Precision

Local date and time	`localtimestamp`
	or
	`sysdate`
		0.000001s (by default)
		1s

UTC date and time	`current_timestamp at time zone 'UTC'`	0.000001s (by default)
Local date	`trunc(sysdate)`	
UTC date	trunc(`current_timestamp at time zone 'UTC'`)	
Local time	N/A as such . Apply formatting to date + time. with function `to_char()`	
UTC time	N/A as such . Apply formatting to date + time.	

PostgreSQL

Result wanted	Function or expression	Precision
Local date and time	`localtimestamp`	0.000001s (by default)

UTC date and time	`current_timestamp at time zone 'UTC'`
	or
	`now() at time zone 'UTC'`
		0.000001s (by default)

Local date	`current_date`	
UTC date	`date_trunc('day', now() at time zone 'UTC')`	
Local time	`localtime`	0.000001s (by default)
UTC time	`localtime at time zone 'UTC'` *or* `current_time at time zone 'UTC'`	0.000001s (by default)

SQL Server

Result wanted	Function or expression	Precision
Local date and time	`sysdatetime()` *or* `getdate()`	0.0000001s 0.003s
UTC date and time	`sysutcdatetime()` *or* `getutcdate()`	0.0000001s 0.003s
Local date	`cast(getdate() as date)`	
UTC date	`cast(getutcdate() as date)`	
Local time	`cast(sysdatetime() as time)`	0.0000001s
UTC time	`cast(sysutcdatetime() as time)`	0.0000001s

cast() is a function to change data types that is described in more detail starting on page 459; `cast(getdate() as date)`. It may seem surprising but in spite of its name, **getdate()** returns a datetime, and casting it as a date suppresses the time part

SQLite

Result wanted	Function or expression	Precision
Local date and time	`datetime('now', 'localtime')`	1s by default
UTC date and time	`datetime('now')`	1s by default
Local date	`date('now', 'localtime')`	
UTC date	`date('now')`	
Local time	`time('now', 'localtime')`	1s by default
UTC time	`time('now')`	1s by default

Beware that `date('now')` returns either UTC time, in which case you get the localtime by adding a second parameter `'localtime'` as indicated here, or it returns the localtime, in which case you get the UTC time by specifying the second parameter as `'utc'`. I have seen identical behavior on Linux and Windows (`datetime('now')` returning the UTC time) but there is no guarantee of consistency across all platforms and software versions.

Formatting (input/output)

Even though most object oriented languages implement a *Date* class, dates that are inserted into a database are usually provided as text or, occasionally, as a UNIX timestamp (a number of seconds since Jan 1st, 1970) that must be converted into a datetime data type. Conversely, dates are displayed to users in a format that depends on local habits (such as the *month/day/year* format in the US and *day/month/year* in Britain or France, a regular source of misunderstandings). Even if the ultimate date formatting is performed in the program that queries the database, dates must be returned in a format understood by the functions of that language. As a result, using dates (and who doesn't need them?) means copiously using formatting/conversion functions for transforming text into database dates (these functions fail when provided with an invalid date), and the reverse. Database products implement basically two functions, one that returns an SQL date and takes as parameters a string that represents a date and usually another string that describes a format, and the reverse function that returns a character string and takes as input an SQL date and a format. See the product documentation for the format, there are tons of options and if DB2, Oracle and PostgreSQL use the same formats, it can be either subtly different (as with SQL Server) or clearly different with the other products. There is a default format (which often can be changed by a database administrator) when no format is specified. When you want to obtain a single component, such as the month, from a date, see also functions **extract()** and **datepart()** page 450.

Date conversion and formatting

Product	Text to date	Date to text
DB2	**to_date(***text*, *fmt***)**	**to_char(***date*, *fmt***)**
MySQL	**str_to_date(***text*, *fmt***)**	**date_format(***date*, *fmt***)**
Oracle	**to_date(***text*, *fmt***)**	**to_char(***date*, *fmt***)**
PostgreSQL	**to_date(***text*, *fmt***)** **to_timestamp**(date, fmt)	**to_char(***date*, *fmt***)**
SQL Server	**convert(date,** *text*, *fmtcode***)**	**format(***date*, *fmt***)** *(SQL Server 2012 and above)* *or* **convert(varchar,** *date*, *fmtcode***)**
SQLite	**strftime(***fmt*, *text***)**	

NOTE With DB2 and Oracle, **to_date()** can transform the time component in a string. With PostgreSQL you need **to_timestamp()**, as **to_date()** only deals with the date component.

NOTE For converting a date or datetime to text, you can also use the conversion function **cast()** that is described from page 459; with **cast()** the value will be represented using the default format.

The case of SQLite is somewhat special, as it has no real datetime data type; dates can be stored internally as correctly formatted strings or UNIX timestamps.

The following table presents frequently used formats (parameter *fmt* in the previous table). For instance if you want to display the number of the day and the name of the month for a date expression, you can use

- `to_char(<date expression>, 'DD MONTH')` with Oracle or PostgreSQL,
- `format(<date expression>, 'dd MMMM')` with SQL Server (2012 and above)
- `date_format(<date expression>, '%d %M')` with MySQL.

Commonly Used Date Formats

Component	DB2, Oracle, PostgreSQL	SQL Server (2012 and above)	MySQL	SQLite
Year	YYYY	yyyy	%Y	%Y
Month *(number)*	MM	MM	%m	%m
Month *(name)*	MONTH *(N/A in DB2)*	MMMM	%M	*N/A*
Month *(short name)*	MON *(N/A in DB2)*	MMM	%b	*N/A*
Day *(num. in month)*	DD	dd	%d	%d
Day *(num. in year)*	DDD	*Use* ***datepart()***	%j	%j
Day *(num. in week)*	D	*Use* ***datepart()***	%w	%w
Day *(name)*	DAY *(N/A in DB2)*	dddd	%W	*N/A*
Day *(short name)*	DY *(N/A in DB2)*	ddd	%a	*N/A*
Hour *(24 hour clock)*	HH24	HH	%H	%H
Hour *(12 hour clock)*	HH	hh	%h	*N/A*
am/pm	AM	tt	%p	*N/A*
Minutes	MI	m	%i	%M
Seconds	SS	ss	%s	%S

NOTES

- With Oracle and PostgreSQL, names of weekdays and months are padded with spaces up to the length of the longest name. For instance, if the language is set to English, the longest weekday name is Wednesday (9 characters) and all weekday names will be returned as a nine character string. For shorter names such as Monday, the right number of spaces, in this case three, will be appended.
- When returning names, beware of language settings, which can vary independently of programs. Oracle allows using a third optional parameter with **to_char()**, for instance `'nls_date_language=english'`. You should use this parameter in programs, if you want to compare what the value returns to a constant, to ensure that you will get the same result with different language settings.
- Beware of the number of the day in the week, conventions vary and are sometimes dependent on language settings.

Additionally, some products provide some functions for direct conversion to and from UNIX timestamps (number of seconds since January, 1st 1970 at 00:00:00).

Adding (or subtracting) time units

Deriving a datetime value from another datetime value usually means adding or subtracting a time interval; for instance, adding four hours or three days.

- In DB2 you can add to a date, time or timestamp, a numerical value followed by a time unit (**years**, **months**, **days**, **hours**, **minutes** ...)
- With PostgreSQL you add to a date, **interval** '*time specification*' where the (quoted) time specification is something like '2 hours' or '3 days'.
- Oracle considers that every number that you add to a date is a number of days (which can be fractional). Thus to add one week, you add 7 to a date, to add two hours you add 1/12 (in other words, two divided by 24) and to add one second you add 1/86400. With Oracle there is a problem with months, as when you want to add one month to a date it might mean adding anything between 28 and 31 days; hence a function **add_months()** that takes two parameters, a date and an integer number (possibly negative) of months to add.
- What Oracle uses for months is used for all time units with SQL Server, with function **dateadd(***interval_unit, number, date***)**.
- MySQL takes a similar approach with **date_add(***date*, **interval** *number interval_unit***)** and **date_sub(***date*, **interval** *number interval_unit***)**. It also supports a syntax **+/- interval** *<value> time_unit*.

- With SQLite, optional parameters passed to functions **date()** or **datetime()** fulfill the same purpose.

Intervals between dates

There are also ways to compute the interval between two dates.

- With Oracle, subtracting two dates (which, I remind you, include time in Oracle) will return a decimal number which is a fractional number of days.
- SQL Server uses **datediff(***interval_unit, date1, date2***)** which returns, as a signed integer, the number of units (month, day, year, hour, week, and so forth) between the two dates.
- MySQL also implements a function called **datediff(***date1, date2***)** which returns, as a signed integer, the number of days between *date1* and *date2* (positive if *date1* is posterior to *date2*, negative otherwise); the MySQL function that is similar to the SQL Server **datediff()** is called **timestampdiff(***interval_unit, date1, date2***)**.
- DB2 also implements a **timestampdiff()** function, needless to say different from the MySQL one. With DB2, **timestampdiff()** takes two arguments, the first one is a numerical code for the interval unit (2=seconds, 4=minutes, 8=hours, 16=days, 32=weeks, 64=months, and so forth), the second one is an expression, the result of a difference between two timestamp values.
- PostgreSQL returns an integer number of days when you subtract one date from another, and a special **interval** data type when you subtract a timestamp from a timestamp (or combine a date and a timestamp); an interval is displayed as a number of hours, minutes, seconds and fractions of a second, which can be preceded by a number of days.
- These operations require a lot of imagination and creativity with SQLite.

Date components

There are also functions for specifically extracting, as a number, the day, hour, month or year (for instance) from a date. There are some product-specific functions but the function **extract(***partname* **from** *date_value***)** is implemented in Oracle, MySQL, PostgreSQL and DB2. SQL Server has the equivalent function **datepart(***partname, date_value***)** (as well as dedicated functions to return year, month or day ...). In functions **extract()** and **datepart()**, *partname* isn't quoted.

SQL SERVER NOTE Replacing a date value by 0 in a SQL Server function is understood as January, 1st 1900 (which was a Monday):

```
select datepart(year, 0) as year_0,
       datepart(month, 0) as month_0,
       datepart(day, 0) as day_0
```

returns

year_0	month_0	day_0
1900	1	1

Commonly Used Date Components

Function **datepart()** in SQL Server also supports some less readable abbreviations.

Component	extract() partname	datepart() partname	Comment
Year	year	year	
Month *(number)*	month	month	
Day *(num. in month)*	day	day	
Day *(num. in year)*	doy *(PostgreSQL only)*	dayofyear	
Day *(num. in week)*	dow *(PostgreSQL only)*	weekday	dow: Sunday=0,Saturday=6 weekday: depends
Hour *(24 hour clock)*	hour	hour	
Minutes	minute	minute	
Seconds	second	second	

SQL SERVER NOTE With **datepart()** the value of what is returned when *partname* is specified as weekday, depends on an internal parameter that can be changed for your session with `set datefirst` *<value>*, for instance, `set datefirst 7` defines that Sunday=1 and Saturday=7 (it's the default value in the US).

ORACLE NOTE Function **extract()** exhibits strange behavior with Oracle and **sysdate**. Although **sysdate** returns the current date and time, `extract(hour from sysdate)` fails but **extract()** succeeds for parts, such as the day in the month or month, which apply to a pure date. However, `extract(hour from localtimestamp)` returns the expected result.

MYSQL NOTE MySQL implements a function called **weekday()** that returns the number of the day in the week (Monday=0, Sunday=6) and a function called **dayofyear()**.

DB2 NOTE DB2 implements functions **dayofweek()** (Sunday=1, Saturday=7) and **dayofyear()** to get numerical values for days other than the number in the month.

Finding the first date in a period

Sometimes you have a need, for aggregation purposes, to round down a date or datetime value to other dates or datetimes that are used as milestones: the round hour, the day at 00:00, the date of the beginning of the week, of the month, of the quarter, of the year ... It may be more convenient than extracting separately month, year, date and so forth.

Some of these rounded down values are easy to obtain (once you have extracted the year, you can build a string for the corresponding January, 1st, then convert it to a date). For other milestones, such as the first date in the week, it can be more difficult.

- Oracle and DB2 allow applying function **trunc()**, that we have seen for numbers, to date (or datetime) values; instead of specifying as second parameter a number of decimals, you specify a date part name which is usually similar to a date format; when no date part name is specified, the default is `'DD'`, which means truncating the date to the same day at 00:00:00 by removing the time part.
- PostgreSQL provides a similar function **date_trunc()**, but this function takes the date precision (always mandatory and different from formats) as first parameter and the datetime value as second parameter, the opposite of Oracle and DB2.
- SQL Server provides no special function but you can compute your milestones relatively easily by using the fact, mentioned in the note page 450 that 0 means Monday, January 1st, 1900 for SQL Server. By combining **datediff()** with **dateadd()** to first compute the integer number of periods between 0 and the date processed, then adding this number of periods back to 0, you can obtain almost anything you want.
- For MySQL and SQLite, it's, like with SQL Server, by using date arithmetic that one obtains, more or less painfully, what one wants. SQLite implements modifiers to the date functions that make some operations easy; for some other operations you have to err on the wild side.

The following tables summarize possible methods used to obtain common rounded down datetime values, based on the current date or datetime. The expressions can of course be applied to any date, not only the current one. Rounding down to the week is understood as returning the date of the last Monday for any other day of the week (and the current date for Mondays); beware that the behavior of functions can in some cases be affected by localization settings.

DB2

Round down to	Function or expression
The hour	`trunc(current timestamp, 'HH24')`
The day	`trunc(current timestamp)`
The week	`trunc(current date, 'W')`
The month	`trunc(current date, 'MM')`
The quarter	`trunc(current date, 'Q')`

MySQL

Round down to	Function or expression
The hour	`date_add(date(now()), interval extract(hour from now()) hour)`
The day	`date(now())`
The week	`date_sub(curdate(), interval weekday(curdate()) day)`
The month	`date_sub(curdate(), interval extract(day from curdate()) - 1 day)`
The quarter	`date_add(date_sub(curdate(), interval dayofyear(curdate()) - 1 day), interval (extract(quarter from curdate()) - 1) * 3 month)`

I have used `date(now())` deliberately in the hour and day expressions rather than `curdate()`, to emphasize the fact that we are processing a datetime value.

Oracle

Round down to	Function or expression
The hour	`trunc(sysdate, 'HH24')`
The day	`trunc(sysdate)`
The week	`trunc(sysdate, 'W')`
The month	`trunc(sysdate, 'MM')`
The quarter	`trunc(sysdate, 'Q')`

Oracle only displays the date part and hides the time by default. With SQL*Plus if you want to see the time you must change your session settings with

```
alter session set nls_date_format='DD-MON-YYYY HH24:MI'
```

(or any other format to your liking)

PostgreSQL

Round down to	Function or expression
The hour	`date_trunc('hour', now())`
The day	`date_trunc('day', now())`
The week	`date_trunc('week', now())`
The month	`date_trunc('month', now())`
The quarter	`date_trunc('quarter', now())`

SQL Server

Round down to	Function or expression
The hour	`dateadd(hour, datepart(hour, getdate()),` `cast(cast(getdate() as date) as datetime))`
The day	`cast(cast(getdate() as date) as datetime)`

The week	`dateadd(week,`
	`datediff(week, 0, getdate()),`
	`0)`

The month	`dateadd(month,`
	`datediff(month, 0, getdate()),`
	`0)`

The quarter	`dateadd(quarter,`
	`datediff(quarter, 0, getdate()),`
	`0)`

cast() is a function to change data types that is described in more details starting page 459; a double change of data type allows us to obtain a datetime with the time set to 00:00:00. As 0 (January 1st, 1900) was a Monday, the first day in a month and the first day in a quarter, it's a very convenient reference for finding the beginning of the week (if you consider that the first day of the week is Monday, subtract one day for Sunday), the month, or the quarter.

SQLite

Round down to	Function or expression

The hour	`datetime('now', 'localtime',`
	`'start of day',`
	`'+' ||`
	`strftime('%H',datetime('now', 'localtime'))`
	`|| ' hours'`

The day	`datetime('now', 'localtime',` `'start of day')`

The week	`case strftime('%w', 'now')`
	`  when '1' then datetime('now',`
	`                          'localtime',`
	`                          'start of day')`
	`  else datetime('now', 'localtime',`
	`                        'weekday 1',`
	`                        '-7 days',`
	`                        'start of day')`
	`end`

The month	`datetime('now', 'localtime',` `                'start of month')`

The quarter	`datetime('now', 'localtime',`
	`                'start of year',`
	`                '+' ||`
	`    cast(cast((strftime('%m', 'now',`
	`                  'localtime')-1)`
	`               /3 as int)*3 as char)`
	`                || ' months')`

All operations are based on using date modifiers, which are sometimes built from other expressions. Please refer to the SQLite documentation for details. Function **cast()**, described in more detail starting on page 459, makes more explicit conversions between numerical values and text.

Working with time zones

Any computer has a built-in clock and knows in which time zone it is located, for this is information that is set by systems engineers when the operating system is installed. The computer also stores system files that say when daylight saving time (DST) is applied all over the world, which allows automatic adjustment of the clock when necessary. When you get the current or UTC date and time from a database, it's the system underneath that provides the data. In most cases, database applications use the current (local) time kept by the computer.

Difficulties arise when a database stores datetime information that originates from several different time zones, especially if you still want to keep track of chronology. Working across time zones is common in large countries ("wide" countries would be more correct), or in international applications. You may need to aggregate in one database, data initially entered into several local databases in different time zones. In a number of business sectors, time zones are a permanent concern: telecom companies for long distance calls, banks for financial operations executed on the stock exchanges of several continents – among others. In these cases, there are essentially two options: either only working with UTC time in all time zones (I have shown you how to obtain current UTC time with all DBMS products), or using, with products such as DB2, Oracle, PostgreSQL or SQL Server, special datetime data types that *also* record the current time zone with the date and time information (these types are called **datetimeoffset** in SQL Server, **timestamp with time zone** with the other products).

NOTE Remember that the **timestamp** data type in SQL Server isn't a time value but a serial number. You don't need it.

Whether you store UTC or local times with or without time zone information, it happens that you need to convert times from one time zone to another. Very often, conversion to display the time in the user's time zone is performed in the application program. When the application runs on the user's workstation, the application can pull the local time zone information from the workstation and adjust an UTC (for instance) time retrieved from the database. It's slightly more complicated with web applications but there are different solutions (using Javascript in the browser to get the local time zone, deriving the location and therefore the time zone from the user's IP address ...). Sometimes, time zone conversions have to be performed in the database: airlines must display schedules in local time, both at the airport of departure (better to catch your flight) and at the airport of arrival (it makes it easier for friends or family to know when to welcome you). However, airlines also need to tell you the duration of the flight, which requires a common time base between departure and arrival. Let's see how to convert between time zones with the various products.

When you are using a datetime data type that records the timezone, you can convert easily with DB2, Oracle or PostgreSQL by querying, instead of *date_col*, *date_col* **at time zone** '*time zone specification*'; with SQL Server, you use **switchoffset(***date_col*, '*time zone specification*'**)**. The time zone can often be specified in different ways:

- By a signed time difference with UTC, for instance '+02:00'. In that case, you have to manage DST by yourself. DB2 and SQL Server only support this format.
- By a standard code such as 'UTC' or 'WST'. These codes may be ambiguous, as you have a Central Standard Time both in North America and in Australia, for instance; you may also have DST issues.
- By a name combining continent and (most often) city name, such as 'Asia/Shanghai', which takes care of DST.

When you are using a datetime data type that *doesn't* store the time zone information, you need to specify the original time zone before converting. I'll assume in all the following examples that we have in a table, a column called *date_col* that stores UTC time without any explicit specification of the time zone, and that I want to translate it to Eastern Daylight Time (EDT), which is four hours behind UTC.

You must be very careful with Oracle, PostgreSQL and DB2 because when you write for instance *date_col* **at time zone 'UTC'** with a regular datetime data type without time zone information, you aren't converting it – you are just stating that its time zone is UTC and transforming a value into a datetime value with time zone information which can now be converted. Thus, if a datetime column stores UTC data but without any time zone information, you can convert it to EDT by writing:

```
date_val at time zone 'UTC' at time zone 'EDT'
↑ Assign time zone UTC ↑
↑        Convert the UTC date time to EDT     ↑
```

Conversion of a plain datetime is slightly less confusing with SQL Server, which uses function **todatetimeoffset()** to assign a time zone to a datetime without timezone. Thus, the previous example would be written with SQL Server:

```
switchoffset(todatetimeoffset(date_val, '+00:00'), '-04:00')
                                         ↑ UTC     ↑ EDT
```

With MySQL that doesn't store time zones in dates, function **convert_tz()** takes three arguments, a datetime, the time zone that corresponds to this datetime, and the target time zone:

```
convert_tz(date_val, '+00:00', '-04:00')
                      ↑ UTC     ↑ EDT
```

NOTE It's possible with MySQL to read the operating system time zone information with a provided utility and to load it into the database so as to use time zone names.

With SQLite, timezone conversion is just a special case of date arithmetic and the simplest is probably to convert the target time zone to a number of minutes, relative to the time zone of the column (in our example EDT is minus 240 minutes relative to UTC) and write

```
datetime(date_val, '-240 minutes')
```

Aggregating

I'll list in this section both classical aggregation functions (used with **group by**, or as window functions with **over** (...)), and functions that are only used as window functions.

The classic SQL aggregate functions are **count()**, **min()**, **max()**, **avg()** (average) and **sum()**, which are available with all products. The first one applies to any type of column and can take * as an argument to mean "count the number of rows"; **min()** and **max()**, apply to any data type that can be ordered; **avg()** and **sum()** only apply to numerical columns. These functions ignore nulls; however, all of them except **count()**

can <u>return</u> null if applied to rows that only contain nulls or to an empty dataset. If you count no rows or only nulls, you get zero.

In addition to these functions, all products with the exception of SQLite, implement several statistical functions such as **stddev()** to compute standard deviation (**stdev()** with SQL Server) or **variance()** (**var()** with SQL Server). DB2, Oracle and PostgreSQL also implement regression functions.

Finally, all products except SQL Server (for which one can use an XML clause, see an example in Chapter 12) allow aggregating columns as a delimited list.

- Oracle and DB2 use **listagg(**<*column name*>, <*delimiter*>**) within group (order by ...)**
- PostgreSQL uses **string_agg(**<*column name*>, <*delimiter*>**)**
- MySQL uses **group_concat(**<*column name*> **order by ... separator** <*delimiter*>**)**
- SQLite uses **group_concat(**<*column name*>, <*delimiter*>**)**

Neither SQLite nor PostgreSQL, provide a way to order the character strings in the list. Although applying the function to the output of an ordered subquery in the **from** clause may work, it shouldn't be considered a reliable solution. As shown in Chapter 12, concatenations can also easily be performed in the program that interacts with the database server. It should be noted that, although these functions return a character string and are most commonly used with character strings, they can be applied to numerical or date columns as well (numbers are implicitly converted to strings of digits).

Aggregate functions can be used with a **group by** clause, or they can be followed in DB2, Oracle, PostgreSQL and SQL Server by an **over (partition by ...)** clause. In this case the aggregate is computed for all the rows that belong to the same group, defined by the **over ()** clause, as the current row (window function, called analytic function in Oracle and OLAP function in DB2). The **over ()** clause can be empty to mean "compute for all the rows in the table".

Additionally, the same products support **row_number()**, **rank()** and **dense_rank()** to classify rows within groups (see Chapter 5). DB2, PostgreSQL, Oracle and SQL Server (2012 and above) support other interesting functions such as **lead()** or **lag()** that allow us to return values that "follow" or "precede" the value in the current row, respective to the **order by** specified in the **over ()** clause. They may be useful for computing differences between chronologically successive rows when columns store cumulative values.

Miscellaneous

Changing data types

Data type conversion can be useful in results, to apply functions or operators normally associated to another data type (for instance for concatenating a numerical value to a string of characters) and for normalizing data from heterogeneous sources (for instance for relating an identical Information Technology course referenced as a numerical 2407 here, CS2407 there and IT-2407 elsewhere). Changing the data type can also be useful for **union** statements, including for specifying that a null in the select list is a placeholder for a value of a particular data type.

Although for historical reasons, multiple data type conversion functions co-exist in most products, the function that is found everywhere is **cast()**, a function generally used to convert between text and numbers (text to date conversion and the reverse, are better handled by date functions if you want to have a fine control on formats). Unfortunately, if the general format is **cast(**<*column or value*> **as** <*data type*>**)**, the way data types are used isn't consistent across products.

- With MySQL, the data type that is used is a *generic* data type that you wouldn't necessarily use in a **create table** statement. For instance, to convert a numerical value to a character string, you can write `cast(12345 as char)`. If you specify a length for **char**, for instance **char(3)**, the function will only return 123, the three left-most digits. Without any length specification, all digits are returned. Interestingly, `cast(12345 as varchar(10))` returns an error. Conversely, you convert a string of digits to a numerical value with something such as `cast('12345' to decimal)` or `cast('12345' to signed)` (or **unsigned**; **signed** and **unsigned** are short for **signed integer** or **unsigned integer**, which are also valid).
- DB2, Oracle and PostgreSQL all expect the data type to be the data type used to define, in a **create table** statement, a column that would store the converted value. There are some minor differences, though; for instance `cast(12345 as char)` with PostgreSQL returns 1 (the leftmost character, as **char** is understood as **char(1)** as it would be in a **create table** statement). With DB2 you get the same value, plus a warning about truncation; Oracle returns an error. An expression such as `cast(12345 as varchar(10))` (`varchar2(10)` recommended with Oracle) works as advertised with all products.
- SQL Server holds a kind of middle-of-the-road position; `cast(12345 as char)` returns 12345 as does MySQL. So does `cast(12345 as varchar(10))` as with DB2 or PostgreSQL. Rather strangely, `cast(12345 as char(3))` succeeds without any warning but returns * (an asterisk). Text to number conversion works like with DB2, Oracle and PostgreSQL (no **signed** nor **unsigned** as with MySQL, although **decimal** is valid).

Note that SQL Server (2012 and above) implements a **try_cast()** function that works like **cast()** but returns null when the conversion (typically, character string to number) fails.

NOTE **cast()**, also supported by SQLite, is rather futile with this product, which doesn't wink at `cast(12345 as bongobongo)`, nor at `cast('12345' as bongobongo)` (result is 12345 in both cases). However, casting text to a numerical value or the reverse, with simple data types such as **int**, **numeric** or **char** in an expression improves readability and removes some guesswork for the SQLite engine.

Information

All products except SQLite, for which it would be meaningless, provide functions to obtain information about the current session. I'll just show you how to obtain current user, current schema, current database and database server host name with Oracle, DB2, SQL Server, MySQL and PostgreSQL (other information may be available). Note that for MySQL there is no difference between schema and database (see Appendix A). Some functions are implemented as virtual columns and don't require parentheses, other functions do require parentheses.

DB2

Current User	`current user`
Current Schema	`current schema`
Current Database	`current server`
Hostname	`select host_name from table(sysproc.env_get_sys_info())`

MySQL

Current User	`substr'(user(), 1, position('@' in user()) - 1)`
Current Schema	`database()`
Current Database	`database()`
Hostname	N/A (client hostname is available in `user()`)

Oracle

Current User	`user`
Current Schema	`sys_context('USERENV', 'CURRENT_SCHEMA')`
Current Database	`sys_context('USERENV', 'INSTANCE_NAME')`
Hostname	`sys_context('USERENV', 'SERVER_HOST')`

PostgreSQL

Current User	`current_user`
Current Schema	`current_schema`
Current Database	`current_database()`
Hostname	`N/A. inet_server_addr() provides the remote IP address, but only when you are remotely connected.`

SQL Server

Current User	`system_user`
Current Schema	`schema_name()`
Current Database	`db_name()`

Hostname	`host_name()`
	or
	`@@SERVERNAME`

Adding a Function to SQLite

Let me conclude this appendix by showing you how to add your own function to SQLite. I have chosen to implement a function called **position()** to locate a substring in a string, similar to the equivalent functions described on page 441; this function is probably the one I miss the most in SQLite.

There are two ways to add one's own functions to SQLite.

- The most elegant one consists of writing the functions in a language such as C, and creating a dynamically loadable library (a file with the extension `.DLL` under Windows, `.so` under Linux and other UNIX systems). Immediately after opening the SQLite file, this library is loaded in memory by calling a special SQLite function and then all functions defined in the library can be used.
- The second option consists of implementing separately, each function in a host language that calls SQLite and plugging them one by one into the SQL engine just after having opened the SQLite file. There is just such an example in Chapter 12, with a **score()** function written in Python and used in queries to identify the actor or actress whose name best matches user input. I'll give here another example in PHP (I could have used Java as well).

The advantage of the first option, besides elegance and the efficiency usually associated with the C language, is that it's the only way to use your own functions with `sqlite3`, the command-line SQL client provided with SQLite. There are two drawbacks; the first one is C, not the easiest of computer languages and not necessarily the one you feel the most comfortable using. The other drawback is that if you want to use SQLite on a PHP-driven website for instance, dynamically loading a library presents a big security risk, and is an operation rarely allowed by hosting companies. The second option requires a full program or script accessing the SQLite file instead of the `sqlite3` utility but asks for no special privilege.

Creating a Dynamically Loadable Library

I'll first write a C function with a big disclaimer: my very basic function makes the (wrong) assumption that one character is equal to one byte. This is obviously wrong with UTF8 encoding (used by SQLite) in which one character may be encoded by several bytes; it works with the Latin alphabet, it won't work in Japanese. This being said, my purpose isn't to make you discover the joys of working with wide chars, and

I leave to you the task of turning the naïve function that follows into a robust, UTF8-aware function. I have created a single file named `my_sqlite_functions.c` as follows:

```
#include <stdio.h>
#include <stdlib.h>
#include <ctype.h>
#include <errno.h>            Usual stuff
#include <locale.h>

#define __USE_GNU      ← required for function strcasestr()
#define _GNU_SOURCE    ← but some environments seem to want that instead
#include <string.h>

#include <sqlite3.h>  ← ① IMPORTANT

extern void posFunc(sqlite3_context  *context,   ② where the result will go
                    int               argc,      ③ classical list of parameters
                    sqlite3_value   **argv){
  char          *haystack;
  char          *needle;
  char          *p;
  size_t         nlen;
  size_t         hlen;
  int            pos;

  if (argc != 2) {     ④ This is only for a variable number of arguments
     sqlite3_result_error(context,            ⑤ Error function
                          "position() takes two arguments",
                          -1);
     return;
  }
  haystack = (char *)sqlite3_value_text(argv[0]); ⑥ Retrieve values passed
  needle = (char *)sqlite3_value_text(argv[1]);
  if ((haystack == (char *)NULL)
      || (needle == (char *)NULL)) {
     sqlite3_result_null(context);    ⑦ Don't forget this case
  } else {
     if (((hlen = strlen(haystack)) == 0)
         || ((nlen = strlen(needle)) == 0)) {
        sqlite3_result_int(context, 0);    ⑧ To behave like other products
        return;
     }
     if ((p = strcasestr((const char *)haystack,
                         (const char *)needle)) == (char *)NULL) {
        sqlite3_result_int(context, 0);     ⑨ Not found
     } else {
        pos = (int)(p - haystack) + 1;      ← Completely naive
        sqlite3_result_int(context, pos);  ⑩ Set the result
     }
  }
}
```

Add-on functions use SQLite functions and structures extensively; the inclusion ①, of the `sqlite3.h` file is required. The function as implemented in C ② doesn't need to have the name it will have in SQL, returns nothing and uses an opaque context to communicate with the SQL engine; return values or error messages are passed through this context. Arguments to the functions ③ are passed through a classical (*argc, argv*) mechanism, in other words a number of arguments followed by an array holding their values, which allows the passing of a variable number of arguments (more on the topic later); note that in this case the array is composed of "sqlite3_value" elements. At the beginning of the function ④ I tested the number of arguments, which is completely moot in that case (more later) but is here to show you what you ought to do, if you wanted to handle optional parameters, such as an offset from where to start the search. It also shows you how to return an error which will become the SQL error, by using ⑤, **the sqlite3_result_error()** function that takes the context as the first parameter, the error message as the second parameter, and as the third parameter, how many bytes from the second parameter should be used as the error message; a negative value such as -1 means all of them. I convert the values passed as parameters ⑥, to the suitable C type with a function **sqlite3_value_*xxx*()** that depends on the expected data type of the argument (text, int, double ...). SQL nulls are returned as null pointers; I must handle the case when one or the parameters is null and ⑦, return null with function **sqlite3_result_null()** in that case. Like with the **sqlite3_value_*xxx*()** series of functions, there is a **sqlite3_result_*xxx*()** series of functions to return a result of the suitable data type – with the function I am implementing, the result will be either null or an integer. I have been careful ⑧, to check the behavior of similar functions in other products with "extreme cases" such as empty strings (not null – Oracle makes no difference) and I have tried to be consistent with them. I have used the GNU case insensitive search, to be consistent with SQLite case-insensitivity and I return 0 when nothing is found ⑨. Finally, when I have found a position, I set the result ⑩, using once again pointer arithmetic that assumes that one byte is equal to one character, something that is wrong with the character sets used by many human languages. A proper function should use wide characters and take into account the fact that one character can be represented by several bytes. You know what you have to do.

```
#include <sqlite3ext.h>  ← IMPORTANT

SQLITE_EXTENSION_INIT1      ⑪ Initialization macro

extern int sqlite3_extension_init(sqlite3                    *db, ⑫ Entry point
                                  char                 **pzErrMsg,
                                  const sqlite3_api_routines *pApi) {
  SQLITE_EXTENSION_INIT2(pApi)              ⑬ Other initialization macro
  (void)setlocale(LC_ALL, "en_US.UTF-8");  ⑭ Define the context
  sqlite3_create_function(db, "position", 2, SQLITE_UTF8,
                          0, posFunc, 0, 0);  ⑮ "Hook" the function
```

```
  return 0;
}
```

I have written what is used by the SQL engine as the "entry point" in the same file. With a real-life library of add-on functions this part would probably be a distinct `.c` file. I need to include another, special SQLite header file that contains the definition of functions and macros that are only used for adding functions to the engine. First ⑪, an initialization macro is required and the entry point for all my functions ⑫, will be **sqlite3_extension_init()**. It starts with another required macro ⑬, I then set the locale ⑭ because I feel bad about multi-byte characters and take a weak line of defense, in stating that I work with the subset of UTF8 used for English in the US. Then I call for each function I want to add to SQLite core functions ⑮, **sqlite3_create_function()** that takes as parameters: the database handler, then the name under which I want to invoke this function in SQL, then the number of arguments. If the number of arguments can be variable (for instance if I want to add an optional offset from which to start the search), I should pass this parameter as -1 and the number and types of the parameters should be controlled in the function (which I have started to do but which is useless if I say that the function takes two parameters – SQLite will control it). The next parameter isn't very useful when you have several parameters, it's supposed to say what kind of characters parameters are using. You can safely use **SQLITE_ANY**. I skip the fifth parameter for a moment, the sixth one is the function that implements 'position' in the C code. The fifth, seventh and eighth parameters are all 0 in my example; they are useful when you define an aggregate function, which is also possible with SQLite but much less useful than defining regular, scalar functions unless you are writing a statistical application. The fifth parameter is an optional pointer to a user-defined context, a structure where intermediary results are stored. The seventh one is, with aggregate functions, an intermediate function that is called at each step, returns nothing but performs some computations and stores the result into the user-defined context. The last parameter is a function that "finalizes" the operation, gets the result, possibly frees some memory, and returns the final result to SQLite. With an aggregate function, the "official function" (sixth parameter) is in charge of initializing the process and possibly allocates the user-defined context that will be freed during finalization.

To create the .so file under Linux, you can use a makefile similar to the following one:

```
SQLITE=<path to the SQLite amalgamation>
CFLAGS=-I$(SQLITE) -fPIC

all: my_sqlite_lib.so

my_sqlite_lib.so: my_sqlite_functions.o
     gcc -g -shared -o my_sqlite_lib.so my_sqlite_functions.o

my_sqlite_functions.o: my_sqlite_functions.c
     gcc $(CFLAGS) -c -o my_sqlite_functions.o my_sqlite_functions.c
```

Here is how I can use my new function in practice:

```
sqlite> .load ./my_sqlite_lib.so        ← Add my functions to SQLite
sqlite> select position('john_doe@some_address.net', '@');
9
sqlite> select position('john_doe@some_address.net', 'u');
0
sqlite> select position('john_doe@some_address.net');
Error: wrong number of arguments to function position()     ← Handled by SQLite
sqlite>
```

Under the interactive command-line tool, I use the **.load** command to load the dynamic library; in a program I would use a special function call. That's all that is needed to make my function known to SQLite and use it. If I pass only one parameter to a function that expects two, I get an error; you'll notice that the error message I get is not the error message I set in my function. The reason is that when I "hooked" my function into SQLite, I said explicitly that it was expecting two parameters and the control is performed by SQLite before it calls the function. If instead of saying "2", I had passed "-1" to say that the function can take a variable number of parameters, SQLite would have called the function and I would have seen my own message – you can try it.

Creating a Function in PHP

As I said at the beginning of this section, dynamically loaded libraries are often perceived, in particular by web hosting companies, as a security risk and the feature may be deactivated. In that case, you can write functions in the host language that you are using to access the database, Python as in Chapter 12 or PHP as here. Scripting languages often come with extremely rich libraries and adding a function to SQLite, is often nothing more than writing a wrapper function for an existing function – such as here **mb_strpos()**, a PHP function that handles, unlike my preceding C examples, multi-byte characters (once told which character set is used) and allows you to find for instance that **習** is the fourth character in **學而時習之、不亦說乎**. Writing the function is also much easier than in C, as it takes the parameters that the SQL function will take and returns what the SQL function will return. There is no opaque context to ensure communication between the function and the SQL engine.

```
function sqlite_position($haystack, $needle) {
   if (isset($haystack)
       && ($haystack != null)
       && isset($needle)
       && ($needle != null)) {
      if (($p = mb_strpos($haystack, $needle, 0, "UTF-8")) === false) {
         return 0;
      } else {
         return 1 + $p;    ← the SQL convention isn't the same as the PHP one
      }
   }
   return null;
}
```

To "hook" the function to the SQL engine, you only need to call, after having for instance, opened your SQLite file with PDO (you'll find something similar in all languages and with all interfaces) the method called **sqliteCreateFunction()**:

```
$db->sqliteCreateFunction('position', 'sqlite_position', 2);
```

The first parameter in the name of the function in SQL, the second parameter (passed as a string of characters, which is different from C) is the name of the PHP function, and the third parameter, the number of arguments. Note that it's also possible to create aggregate functions with another method.

While the closeness of the PHP function to the SQL function makes programming easier in many cases, it also makes it (slightly) more complicated in more advanced cases. For instance, what happens if the function should fail because, for instance, it receives some text when a numerical value is expected? Failure will be indicated by returning **false**. However, there is no way to set the error message. Possibly the best thing to do, is to have a global context in which to store the message; you mustn't forget that in a PHP application, it's your program that normally retrieves the error set by the SQL engine. You can also check in the code, whether one of your functions did set something.

For a variable number of parameters (indicated by passing -1 in third position to **sqliteCreateFunction()**), you only need to use standard facilities provided by the scripting language. With PHP it will be functions **func_num_args()** and **func_get_args()**. Thus, if you want to implement the Oracle version of **instr()** (described on page 441) which can take 2, 3 or 4 parameters, your PHP function could start as follows:

```
function sqlite_instr() {
  global $G_SQLctx;
  $numargs = func_num_args();   ← Retrieve the number of arguments
  if ($numargs < 2) {
     $G_SQLctx['errmsg'] = 'not enough arguments for function'; ← Set message
     return false;
  }
  if ($numargs > 4) {
     $G_SQLctx['errmsg'] = 'too many arguments for function';
     return false;
  }
  $arg_list = func_get_args();   ← Retrieve arguments
  $str = $arg_list[0];
  $substr = $arg_list[1];
  if ($numargs > 2) {
     $start_pos = $arg_list[2];
  } else {
     $start_pos = 1;
  }   ... and so on.
```

Answers to Exercises

Appendix
C

SQL is infamous for the number of different ways that you have of obtaining the same result. Sometimes a query returns the right result by chance, simply because tables don't currently contain the data that would expose logic flaws. My answers in this appendix are much more verbose than what is expected of you. I hope that detailed answers will help you to assess better what you have done, especially as it's rare that there is one indisputable "correct answer". I'll try to give some order of preference where several answers are possible and to justify my choice (sometimes it will be for objective reasons, sometimes it will depend on some hypotheses, and sometimes it will simply be a matter of style or taste, which is often as debatable as choices in matters of colors - there are design rules but ultimately you decide). I am not even trying to give all possible variants, just the opinion of a seasoned database professional.

Don't be disappointed if your answer is different from mine, as I am also taking the opportunity with these exercises, to show you some savvy that a database student cannot have (and that some professional developers haven't either). If by and large, you are following the same trail, even if some subtle detail has escaped you, you can consider that you have fully succeeded. It's the reasoning that matters, not whether the result is more or less polished.

Chapter 1: Introduction to Databases

1. *You want to put on-line on a website, the movie database that has been discussed in this chapter. You wish to build a community by letting people register as members on the site.*
    a. *Based on your own experience of websites, what type of information would you try to record for members and how would you identify them? In other words, what would a members table look like for the site? Specify which attributes would be mandatory and which would be optional.*
    b. *You want to allow members to post movie reviews and/or to assign from one to 5 stars to a movie. Someone can review without rating or rate without posting a review. However, a member cannot rate or review a given movie more than once. How would you organize data?*

a. Members on a website need at least an identifier, a freely chosen name that will be the assumed identity on the site and a password to sign in. The identifier, by definition, needs to be unique. Now, there are a number of problems that may occur: what happens when people forget their password? Usually they expect to be sent a new password, which means that the website needs their email address (some professional web sites use the email address, necessarily unique, as an identifier but you can't sign posts on a forum with an email address). As an identifier can be a relatively long string that you won't want to repeat in other tables whenever you reference a member, you will probably also need a numerical member identifier that will be assigned to people as they register.

   Those four attributes (numerical member id, chosen username, email address and password) are what you ought to have thought of immediately and should all be mandatory.

   You can also have an "avatar" attribute, the name of an image that will be associated with one user, who will have uploaded it. The avatar should be optional because when people register they usually enter minimum information (username, email address and password), and everything else is added later.

   Next there are two broad categories of information that may be useful to you:

   - Demographic information. Who are your members? Every website wants to know that to target contents and advertising effectively. You can ask of your members their birthdates, their gender, their country, possibly other information about education and so forth (beware that collecting identifiable personal information is often regulated by law). None of this can be mandatory and you should always let people choose whether or not to give any information about who they are (and as already stated, people must already have an account to be able to provide information about themselves).
   - Information that is directly related to member activity on the website. You may first want to know how long they have been members, which means a registration date (mandatory). You may want to record their number of visits, possibly when they last connected (all this can be mandatory too). You may or may not know this but a website receives the network address (the famous "IP address") of every visitor, which is sent by the browser. IP addresses are regulated and assigned very precisely, and can be used for locating, sometimes at the city level (search the web for "IP geolocation"). You can find free data that tells you at least the country.

Even if people don't volunteer their location, the location for the IP address is something that you can record, if not at each visit, at least when people register.

Members can provide reviews, which might be voted up or down by other users. All this will probably translate into points gained or lost, which will represent the "reputation" of a member. Point counters can be mandatory, if when you create an account you systematically assign 0 to them.

- o Finally, there may be other information that you would like to register, for instance about the tastes of members (favorite film genre, favorite films, actors and actresses, directors ...), or the "friendships" they can have with other members. However, for each of these categories, the number of entries per member can be highly variable (one can have one or twenty favorite movies and some members will probably say nothing about their tastes) and cannot be stored in the members table. Points if you have thought of recording this type of information; negative points if you planned to store it in the *members* table.

b. If you want to prevent users from voting for the same film twice, or from reviewing the same film twice, there is only one solution: **each time a member votes or reviews a film, you must store the identifier of the member and the identifier of the film, and create a constraint that forces the combination to be unique**.

2. *You are working for an association that allows its members to borrow DVDs for a few days. We want to focus only on recording suitable DVD information. Firstly, you think that it would be a good idea to have several copies of popular movies so that several people can borrow different DVDs of the same movie at once. Secondly, at the back of a DVD box you typically find this kind of information:*

Special Features

** Behind-the-scenes mini-documentary*

** Interactive Menus*

** Theatrical Trailer*

** Cast/Filmmaker Profile*

** Scene access*

LANGUAGES: English DTS 5.1 & Español Stereo Surround

SUBTITLES: English for the hearing impaired, Français, Português, Deutsch, Chinese, Thai & Korean

Color/118 Mins

Aspect-ratio: Widescreen

Not Rated

a. *What information from the above would you choose to store in your database?*

b. *How would you organize the information that you want to manage?*

a. Some of the characteristics can obviously be very important and would in many cases affect your decision about borrowing the DVD - as far as I am concerned I wouldn't borrow a film in Mongolian with subtitles in Quechua and Wolof even if I'd love to watch it. **Languages and subtitles are obviously information that needs to be recorded** and the same is true of the **duration** (sometimes you want to watch something short), and of the **rating** when available if you plan to watch something with your family.

There is a second category of characteristics that have some importance but would probably not be used as a primary search criterion - color, for instance, sound quality (DTS 5.1, Stereo Surround) or aspect ratio (the later probably being even less important - you could as legitimately chose to keep it or to forget about it).

Now, what about the bonus features? The list in the example (taken from the back of a real DVD) is an interesting example: it contains items that look like copy-filler - How many DVDs have no interactive menus nor direct scene access? Very few. It's something that you normally expect and not worth noting - it's just like specifying that headlights, seatbelts and a windshield are part of the equipment of a car. Cast and film-maker profile? You'll probably learn more on Wikipedia. Trailer? Unless you are studying how trailers are made, it's unlikely that you will watch it. The only feature that can be interesting here is the behind-the-scenes documentary. You sometimes have other bonus features that are worth recording - interviews, full film commentary by the director, deleted scenes - and yet this will probably interest very few people.

Modeling bonus features isn't easy and several approaches could be taken:

- A micro-minimalist (and lazy) approach would be to say "bonus features: yes/no" but this would hardly be interesting, as almost all DVDs come with some bonus feature of a kind and it would be unfair to some editions which come with a lot of interesting material.

- A minimalist approach that would simply rate the amount and quality of bonus features available; for instance 'none', 'minimum' (trailers, filmography), 'medium' (interviews, comments), 'important' (documentaries, etc.), 'extensive' (additional bonus DVD)
- An extensive approach would require compiling a list of bonus features commonly available (to which it would be careful to add 'Other', just in case), storing them in a reference table and specifying for each DVD which of the bonus features it includes.

Both the second and third options are perfectly acceptable.

b. *The question of how to organize data is mostly the question of knowing how many tables are required and which columns they should contain. The question states that you want several copies for popular movies. You cannot, therefore, have a single table that records movies and say that this movie is on loan. You need a table in which every row represents a physical DVD. However, you aren't going to repeat information such as title or year of release, for every DVD that corresponds to the same film: you are going to associate with each DVD the identifier of the film that is burnt on this DVD. The DVD table will therefore be composed of:*

- A DVD identifier (a number), which will probably be printed as a barcode on the DVD and will be the primary key
- A film identifier (another number), a foreign key
- Optionally the year of release of the DVD (not of the film, which is a characteristic of the film), and the company that published it
- Rating
- Duration. It wouldn't be foolish to say "the duration is a characteristic of the film, not of the DVD". However, it's common that some films were cut by producers when they were released because they were too long, or because some scenes were then too daring, politically or otherwise, or because the ending wasn't commercial enough. Some DVD producers try faithfully to restore the film as initially intended by the director and release a "Director's Cut" DVD that may be longer (much more often than shorter) than the theatrical release. You may therefore have two DVDs of the "same" film, one with the film as it was released in theaters, one with the director's cut, which have different durations.
- Color. It's the same story as for duration here. You can consider that it's a characteristic of the film but some popular black and white films (for which the choice of black and white was more a budget constraint than an aesthetical choice) have been colorized by

computer. You can imagine having two DVDs of the same film, one in the original black and white and the other in color.

- Aspect ratio. More likely to be a true characteristic of the film but instinctively I'd rather associate it with the DVD as it's more directly linked to viewing.
- Depending on the approach adopted for recording bonuses, you can have (micro-minimalist approach) an attribute that will say Yes/No or (minimalist approach) a code to rate amount and quality. If you adopt the extensive approach the information will be stored in another table (as you will see shortly).

It would be a mistake to store information about audio quality, soundtracks and subtitles in the DVD table. Why? Because you usually have *several* soundtracks and subtitles, an indefinite number of them (just like actors in films), and because for one language you'll have several DVDs with this language as soundtrack or subtitle; it's a typical many-to-many (or m-n) relationship. We must have a table that associates one soundtrack with one DVD, in the same way as table *credits* associates one actor with one film.
You need one reference table for languages, which will relate a language code such as 'en' to the name of the language ('English').
Then you have a *dvd_language* table that contains, for each language available for a DVD, the identifier of the DVD and the code of the language. Additionally, a type code can specify the sound quality if it's an audio-track, or the subtitle type if it's a subtitle (regular, or for the hard-of-hearing, which includes indications about ambient noises that are important for the plot).
Optionally (I'd rather have it) an additional table can store the values of the type codes and their meaning (for instance 'MO' for 'Monaural', 'DS' for 'Dolby Stereo', 'ST' for 'Subtitle', 'SH' for 'Subtitle for the hard-of-hearing', ...)
It would be possible to have one table for audio languages and one for subtitles, each one associating a language code with a DVD identifier but I find the single-table solution more elegant. In this table, the primary key would be the combination (DVD identifier, language code, type code) as an audio language may also be available as subtitle, or there may be two audio tracks for the same language with different sound quality.

If you have decided to describe bonuses extensively, then you must have a reference table that lists all possible types of bonuses (with a bonus type identifier and a description) and a table to implement the many-to-many relationship, with one row relating a DVD identifier to a bonus type identifier for each bonus available in this DVD.

Chapter 2: Introduction to SQL

1. *To enhance the database, it has been decided to add, as a one letter code, an indication about the genre of the movie – Drama, Comedy, Musical, Thriller, Action, ... with a reference table called* movie_genres *storing the acceptable codes and their meanings.*
   a. *Write the create statements for* movie_genres *and the modified* movies *table.*
   b. *Write two or three insert statements to add genres into* movie_genres.

This exercise is a simple exercise and if you could run successfully, the statements you wrote, you probably have everything right. Needless to say you can give any valid name to columns.

a. Tables

```
create table movie_genres(code    char(1) not null primary key,
                          meaning varchar(50) not null,
                          unique(meaning));
create table movies2(movieid        int not null primary key,
                     title          varchar(60) not null,
                     country        char(2) not null,
                     year_released  numeric(4) not null,
                     genre          char(1) not null,
                     unique (title, country, year_released),
                     foreign key(country)
                        references countries(country_code),
                      foreign key(genre)
                        references movie_genres(code));
```

A few comments:

- If you are using Oracle, use **varchar2** instead of **varchar**, and **number(4)** instead of **numeric(4)**.
- If you are using MySQL, don't forget to add `engine=InnoDB` after the last closing parenthesis of both **create** statements (before semi-colons).
- The actual length of columns *meaning* and *title* doesn't really matter – anything between 40 and 500 is alright for the title, anything between 20 and 100 could be right for the meaning.
- I haven't added any **check** constraint but adding reasonable **check** constraints could be a good idea.
- There is no need for a numerical *genre_id* in table *movie_genres*; many people systematically add a numerical identifier but it's a bad practice. Unless you are working with a software development framework that requires a numerical identifier for every column (some do), the one letter code is a perfectly good identifier, exactly as

the country code is a perfectly good identifier for the table of countries.

- Declare all columns as mandatory, there is no reason for any column to be optional.

b. Insertion

```
insert into genres(code, meaning) values('C', 'Comedy');
insert into genres(code, meaning) values('D', 'Drama');
insert into genres(code, meaning) values('A', 'Action');
insert into genres(code, meaning) values('T', 'Thriller');
```

Naming the columns after the table name isn't mandatory but it's better because new columns can later be added to the table, or it can even be re-created with columns listed in a different order.

2. *We want to design the tables for a forum. We have a table of members that stores a member id, a password, a screen name and a registration date. There must be one table that defines various broad categories (for instance, Database Topics, HTML, Javascript ...); a table of questions that will specify the forum to which the question relates; which member posted the question; when it was posted; the actual text of the question; and an indicator which shows whether the original poster considers the question answered or not. Finally, there is a table of answers, with a reference to the question that is answered; who (which member) answered it; when the answer was posted; the text of the answer; and an indicator (which may be set by the original poster of the question) which shows whether this answer helped the original poster. Write the create statements for these four tables, if you need to make assumptions for data types justify them, identify primary keys, unique columns and foreign keys (ignore check constraints - all columns are mandatory).*

Other than Oracle

```
create table members
            (member_id     int not null primary key,
             screen_name   varchar(30) not null,
             password      varchar(50) not null,
             registration  date not null,
             unique(screen_name))
engine=InnoDB   ← MySQL only
;
create table forum_categories
            (category_id   int not null primary key,
             description   varchar(30) not null,
             unique(description))
engine=InnoDB   ← MySQL only
;
create table forum_questions
            (question_id   int not null primary key,
             category_id   int not null,
             asked_by      int not null,
             date_posted   datetime not null,
```

```
            question      varchar(2000) not null,
            answered      char(1) not null,
            unique(category_id, asked_by, date_posted),
            foreign key(category_id)
                    references forum_categories(category_id),
            foreign key(asked_by)
                    references members(member_id))
engine=InnoDB   <- MySQL only
;
create table forum_answers
           (question_id   int not null,
            answered_by   int not null,
            date_posted   datetime not null,
            answer        varchar(2000) not null,
            helpful       char(1) not null,
            primary key(question_id, answered_by, date_posted),
            foreign key(question_id)
                    references forum_questions(question_id),
            foreign key(answered_by)
                    references members(member_id))
engine=InnoDB   <- MySQL only
;
```

Oracle

```
create table members
           (member_id     number not null primary key,
            screen_name   varchar2(30) not null,
            password      varchar2(50) not null,
            registration  date not null,
            unique(screen_name))
;
create table forum_categories
           (category_id   number not null primary key,
            description   varchar2(30) not null,
            unique(description))
;
create table forum_questions
           (question_id   number not null primary key,
            category_id   number not null,
            asked_by      number not null,
            date_posted   date not null,
            question      varchar2(2000) not null,
            answered      char(1) not null,
            unique(category_id, asked_by, date_posted),
            foreign key(category_id)
                    references forum_categories(category_id),
            foreign key(asked_by)
                    references members(member_id))
;
create table forum_answers
           (question_id   number not null,
            answered_by   number not null,
            date_posted   date not null,
            answer        varchar2(2000) not null,
            helpful       char(1) not null,
```

```
    primary key(question_id, answered_by, date_posted),
    foreign key(question_id)
          references forum_questions(question_id),
    foreign key(answered_by)
          references members(member_id))
;
```

Some comments:

- For non Oracle databases I have defined the registration date as a **date** data type, which means without any time component; it could be a **datetime** as well but I don't think it necessary ("member since Sept 23rd, 2005, 21:07"). However, I have used the **datetime** data type for post times because as a member can post several questions or answers during the day, the time matters to get the chronology of answers. No problem with Oracle as the **date** type includes the time.
- I haven't' assigned any numerical identifier *answer_id* to table *forum_answers*; most people would probably do it but it's not necessary as no table references *forum_answers* (my position would be different if there were the possibility to vote for answers, which might mean a separate table referencing this one). If you have added one in view of future enhancements, that's good. If you have added one just to have the table look like the others, it's not so good.
- You must be very careful, whenever you have a numerical identifier that has no meaning outside the database tables, always to have a unique constraint on columns that do have a meaning. For instance, I have a unique constraint on the screen name in table *members* because I cannot have two members known by the same name. I also have a unique constraint on (*category_id, asked_by, date_posted*) in table *forum_questions* because one person cannot possibly ask two different questions in the same second. If you have chosen (and it can be legitimate to do so) to add a column *answer_id* to table *forum_answers*, then the combination of columns I have defined as composing the primary key must be specified as unique. That's important.
- Make certain that you haven't forgotten any foreign keys. This is also important.
- Some people prefer, even with Oracle, to use data type **int** for identifiers; the only difference is that **int** is a synonym for **number(38)**, which doesn't accept decimal values (**number** could store a decimal value). As long as I just want those identifiers to be numerical and unique, I don't really mind.

Chapter 3: Retrieving Data From One Table

1. *List the titles and years of release for all Indian movies released before 1985.*

```
select title, year_released
from movies
where country = 'in'
and year_released < 1985
```

Once you have understood that the order of clauses is **select** followed by **from** and followed by **where**, and once you have understood where you need commas and where you don't need them, there are few difficulties here. You must just be careful to note that the country column contains a country code, not a country name, so it's 'in' and not 'India', and to enclose text between single quotes (some products accept double quotes but the standard is single quotes); the country code is text. Another thing to take care about with some products is case, which must match the case of what is stored in the database. The condition on the year can also be specified as

```
and year_released <= 1984
```

The order of the condition on the country and the condition on the year doesn't matter (and `select year_released, title` is as good as `select title, year_released`)

If you have struggled on this one, repeat it for various countries and years, replace *before* by *after* (or search for films that were released a specific year, such as the year you were born), retype the statement fully (rather than simply changing the values) four or five times and you'll be OK.

2. *What are the titles of the American movies that we have in the database for the 1970s?*

```
select distinct title
from movies
where country = 'us'
and year_released between 1970 and 1979
```

It's good if you have thought "ah, but we could have two films with the same title released different years, there should be **distinct**"; if not, I can tell you that many professionals would probably forget about it (until they have a problem); there can be remakes within a decade (several films entitled *Carmen* were released in the 1980s).

The use of **between** is the most compact way to write the query but the condition on the year can be written in different ways, all equally valid:

```
and year_released in (1970, 1971, 1972, 1973, 1974,
                      1975, 1976, 1977, 1978, 1979)
```

```
and year_released >= 1970 and year_released <= 1979
```

```
and year_released > 1969 and year_released <= 1979
```

```
and year_released >= 1970 and year_released < 1980
```

```
and year_released > 1969 and year_released < 1980
```

The conditions on the two years can also occur in any order (not with **between**, for which the earliest year must come first), and in the list of years with **in()** they can also appear in any order (and if a year appears several times, it won't change the result at all).

3. *How many different people have a surname that starts with a K?*

```
select count(*)
from people
where surname like 'K%'
```

Note that there is an aggregate function but no **group by** because we count all people in the table and we aren't regrouping them by subcategories.

If you are using a DBMS that isn't case-sensitive, `like 'k%'` is also valid. Using **like** is the best way to write the query. With the exception of the function called **left()** (quickly mentioned in the body of the book) using a function such as **substring()** (with SQL Server) or **substr()** (with all the other products) to isolate the first character in the surname would work, but would be a bad idea in a real world application. As the reason is explained in Chapter 9, you can be forgiven for using this function at this stage.

4. *Write:*

   a. *A query to find how many people have the first name 'Peter' in the database.*

   b. *A query to find how many people have no first name.*

   c. *A query that returns two values, how many people have 'Peter' for first name and how many people have no first name.*

   We have in all cases, counts that apply to the whole table, which means no **group by**.

   a. Finding the number of Peters:

   ```
   select count(*) as number_of_Peters
   From people
   Where first_name = 'Peter'
   ```

   The alias to have a more meaningful title for the column is a nice touch but of course nothing changes in the validity of the result.

   b. Finding people with no first name:

   ```
   select count(*) as no_firstname
   from people
   where first_name is null
   ```

What is expected here, is the **is null** condition. If you write `first_name = null` you won't get a syntax error, the query will run but return zero as the condition is never true, even when no first name is provided. Note that if you are using DB2, when there is no first name it is set to an empty string '' in the sample database. Therefore the solution for the sample DB2 database, and in this case only, is:

```
select count(*) as no_firstname
from people
where first_name = ''
```

(DB2 knows **is null** perfectly well but wants all columns that are involved in a unique constraint, which is the case for *first_name*, to be mandatory)

c. The last one is really more difficult. If you have come up with

```
select count(*)
from people
where first_name = 'Peter'
or first_name is null
```

you deserve some credit (note that `first_name in ('Peter', null)` will not work because it's the same as `first_name = 'Peter or first_name = null`, and the second condition is never true. However, if you are using DB2, `in ('Peter', '')` is correct as the table is defined)

The trick here, which is what you do when you want to dispatch data between two or more columns, is to use several **case ... end** constructs, each one only returning what we want to count, and null for anything else. There is an additional difficulty in that case, as one of the things we want to count are actually nulls. Starting point: retrieving first names for Peters and people who have none:

```
select first_name
from people
where first_name = 'Peter'
or first_name is null
```

The second step consists of trying to distinguish one case from the other (as it's necessarily, with the **where** clause, one or the other). If we write

```
select count(first_name) as cnt
from people
where first_name = 'Peter'
or first_name is null
```

We'll get in *cnt* the number of Peters: null first names will be ignored and only Peters will be counted, which answers half the question. Let's forget about the **count()** just for a moment and let's add a **case** construct to mark null first names with something other than null:

```
select first_name,
       case
         when first_name is null then 'None'
         else null
       end as no_first_name
from people
where first_name = 'Peter'
or first_name is null
```

We now have as our second column, an expression that returns 'None' when there is no first name, and null in the other cases (which means, in that case, when the first name is Peter). We could have just as well written:

```
case first_name
  when 'Peter' then null
  else 'None'
end as no_first_name
```

Pick the one that you find easier to understand (note that, as stated in Chapter 3, `case first_name when null ...` wouldn't work). Whichever way you chose to write the query, it will return something like the following table, with either 'Peter' or 'None' in one column and null in the other, thus dispatching data between the two columns:

first_name	no_first_name
	None
	None
Peter	
	None
Peter	
	None
	None
Peter	
	None
	None

At that point, the only thing you have to do is use **count()** to ignore nulls and return how many values are displayed in each column:

```
select count(first_name) as Peters,
       count(case
               when first_name is null then 'None'
               else null
             end) as no_first_name
from people
where first_name = 'Peter'
or first_name is null
```

(You can use a query in the **from** clause if you find it more legible).

If you are using DB2 for which the first name cannot be null, a correct answer for this exercise would be:

```
select count(case first_name
                when 'Peter' then 1
                else null
              end) as Peters,
       count(case first_name
                when '' then 1
                else null
              end) as no_first_name
from people
where first_name = 'Peter'
or first_name = ''
```

5. *A variant on the last example in the chapter: how many people have played in a movie that they have directed?*

It's in table *credits* that we find the information that we need: identifiers of people and in which capacity they participated to a film. We need not only people for whom we find two different values in column *credited_as* but for whom we find two different values for the same film. The first operation consists as a consequence, in counting how many different values for *credited_as* we find, per person and per movie.

```
select peopleid, movieid, count(*) as different_credits
from credits
where credited_as in ('A', 'D')  ← Not necessary if we only have actors
group by peopleid, movieid             and directors but precautionary
```

The next step is simple: we only want to retain people and movies for which we have TWO different credits; such a condition, applied to a result of an aggregate, is expressed by a **having** clause:

```
select peopleid, movieid, count(*) as different_credits
from credits
where credited_as in ('A', 'D')
group by peopleid, movieid
having count(*) = 2
```

At this point we need to think a little bit (or watch what the query returns so far, if it can help). When we have a **group by**, the key to the result becomes the column by which we are grouping - in this case *peopleid* AND *movieid*. If we consider only one, the person identifier, we'll have duplicates - indeed, when a director has played in one of his or her own films, it's often in more than one. The question is "how many people have played in a movie they have directed", not "how many times has a person directed a film that same person was playing in". We don't want to count the same person twice. Two solutions: either first only picking distinct people from the previous result:

```
select distinct peopleid
from (select peopleid, movieid, count(*) as different_credits
      from credits
      where credited_as in ('A', 'D')
      group by peopleid, movieid
      having count(*) = 2) as films_where_director_played
```

Then counting the rows:

```
select count(*) played_and_directed
from (select distinct peopleid
      from (select peopleid, movieid, count(*) as different_credits
            from credits
            where credited_as in ('A', 'D')
            group by peopleid, movieid
      having count(*) = 2) films_where_director_played) actors_directors
```

or a more compact but otherwise equivalent coding with **count(distinct ...)**:

```
select count(distinct peopleid) as played_and_directed
from (select peopleid, movieid, count(*) as different_credits
      from credits
      where credited_as in ('A', 'D')
      group by peopleid, movieid
      having count(*) = 2) as films_where_director_played
```

(Both solutions are quite good)

Chapter 4: Retrieving Data From Several Tables

1. *Which actors in the database appear in at least two movies?*

   First step: finding the identifiers of actors that appear in at least two movies. We find all the information in table *credits*:

```
select peopleid   ← We don't need to return count(*) here but having it is OK
from credits
where credited_as = 'A'
group by peopleid
having count(*) >= 2
```

   From here we can retrieve first name and surname from the *people* table; two main options, either of them is good:

   a. A join (the order in the join doesn't matter as it's an **inner join**):

```
select p.first_name, p.surname
from (select peopleid
      from credits
      where credited_as = 'A'
      group by peopleid
      having count(*) >= 2) q
     inner join people p
     on p.peopleid = q.peopleid
```

   b. An **in ()** uncorrelated subquery:

```
select first_name, surname
from people
where peopleid in
     (select peopleid
      from credits
      where credited_as = 'A'
      group by peopleid
      having count(*) >= 2)
```

2. *Write a query that only returns the oldest movie in the database (hint: you need a subquery on the same table as the outer query)*

   First retrieve the earliest release year from table *movies*:

```
select min(year_released) as min_year
from movies
```

   Next retrieve from the same table, the films (there may be several) that were released that year:

```
select title, year_released, country
from movies
where year_released = (select min(year_released) as min_year
                       from movies)
```

   (**in** or = are equivalent in this case, as the subquery returns a single value). As in the previous example you can also write a join, for instance:

```
select m.title, m.year_released, m.country
from movies m
     inner join (select min(year_released) as min_year
                 from movies) m2
     on m2.min_year = m.year_released
```

   There are other ways to answer the same question which are presented in Chapter 5.

3. *Write a query that returns the people involved in the oldest movie, with their role (actor/director)*

   First we need the year of the oldest movie, as in the previous question:

```
select min(year_released) as min_year
from movies
```

   Still, as in the previous question, we must use this result to retrieve the identifier of the oldest film(s), which we will join with credits to get the identifiers of people involved, then to people to get their names; there are, as usual, several ways to write the query but most of them should be close to this one:

```
select m.title,
       case c.credited_as
         when 'D' then 'Director'
         when 'A' then 'Actor'
       end as credit,
       p.first_name,
       p.surname
from movies m
     inner join credits c
     on c.movieid = m.movieid
     inner join people p
     on p.peopleid = c.peopleid
where m.year_released = (select min(year_released) as min_year
                         from movies)
```

I have chosen, even though it wasn't explicitly required, (and don't worry if you didn't) to return the film title. There isn't necessarily ONE oldest movie, we may have several films released the same year and it's more cautious to be able to see who was involved in which film. Another point worthy of note, is that I have listed explicitly `when 'D'` and `when 'A'` in the **case** construct. With only two distinct values, I could have used for instance `when 'D' ... else ....` but what would happen if other credits were added to the database later, for instance producers? I don't want the producer to be listed as an actor. With my **case** construct, a producer (*P* value) would have nothing next to the name; not madly informative perhaps but at least not wrong.

4. *Of all the people in the database who are no longer alive, who died the oldest?*

   First I find the age at death of all people who are known to have died:

```
select died - born age_at_death
from people
where died is not null
```

   Then I find the greatest value:

```
select max(age_at_death) as oldest
from (select died - born age_at_death
      from people
      where died is not null) a
```

   Finally, I join this result (I could also use a subquery) with *people*, to find who was or were this or these persons. Note the unusual join condition:

```
select p.first_name, p.surname, b.oldest age_at_death
from people p
     inner join (select max(age_at_death) as oldest
                 from (select died - born age_at_death
                       from people
                       where died is not null) a) b
     on p.died = p.born + b.oldest
where p.died is not null
```

   The final `where p.died is not null` isn't necessary, as the join condition would fail for someone who is alive. It doesn't hurt and it reminds the reader of the query that we are only interested in people who have passed away.

5. *Who are the actors who played in films from different countries?*

   As usual, let's start with something simpler, and identifiers: with each *peopleid* value that identifies an actor, how many different countries can I associate?

```
select c.peopleid, count(distinct m.country)
from credits c
     inner join movies m
     on m.movieid = c.movieid
where c.credited_as = 'A'
group by c.peopleid
```

Of these, I only want those for which the count of countries is greater than one:

```
select c.peopleid
from credits c
     inner join movies m
     on m.movieid = c.movieid
where c.credited_as = 'A'
group by c.peopleid
having count(distinct m.country) > 1
```

At this stage, the problem is solved: all that remains to be done is joining the result of the previous query with table *people* (or using it as a subquery as in my query) to find out who are these actors:

```
select first_name, surname
from people
where peopleid in
   (select c.peopleid
    from credits c
         inner join movies m
         on m.movieid = c.movieid
    where c.credited_as = 'A'
    group by c.peopleid
    having count(distinct m.country) > 1)
```

Chapter 5: Ordering and Reporting

1. *List all the people who are recorded as alive in the database and were born in 1965 or later by age, from oldest to youngest.*

   Not a difficult exercise but one which can be handled in different ways. First you write a query that returns the age for all people alive born in or after 1965:

   ```
   select first_name, surname, <current year> - born as age
   from people
   where born >= 1965
     and died is null
   ```

   You can either write the current year as a constant (which you would do for an instant, one-of-a-kind query) or you can use an expression such as `extract(year from ...)`, with the function (dependent on the DBMS that you are using) that returns the current date (`datepart(year, getdate())` with SQL Server); this is of course what you should do for a query in a program. You have two options to sort from the oldest to the youngest:

   a) Either you refer to the *age* alias in the **order by** clause, something you can do because the **order by** clause is evaluated after the *select list* and column aliases are known to the **order by** clause (contrarily to the **where** clause). Oldest to youngest means sorting by age descending, indicated by **desc**:

```
select first_name, surname, <current year> - born as age
from people
where born >= 1965
  and died is null
order by age desc
```

b) Or you simply refer to the birth year and as older people were born before younger people, in that case the sort is ascending, which is the default:

```
select first_name, surname, <current year> - born as age
from people
where born >= 1965
  and died is null
order by born
```

2. *List continents with the number of movies per continent, ordered by decreasing number of movies.*

   As usual before sorting data we must retrieve it. The name of the continent is in table *countries*, therefore we need to join *countries* with *movies*, group, then sort:

```
select c.continent, count(m.movieid) movie_count
from countries c
     inner join movies m
     on m.country = c.country_code
group by c.continent
order by movie_count desc
```

3. *Who are the three actors who appear in the most movies in the database? (warning: trick question)*

   The first operation consists in counting how many times each actor appears (as an actor, we mustn't count appearances as director)

```
select peopleid, count(*) appearances
from credits
where credited_as = 'A'
group by peopleid
```

   Where is the trick? The obvious, easy answer that most people would provide would be something such as

```
select peopleid, count(*) appearances
from credits
where credited_as = 'A'
group by peopleid
order by appearances desc
limit 3
```

   with a DBMS that supports **limit** then join with table *people*.

   NOTE Please refer to the chapter for Oracle and SQL Server - you could use `offset 0 rows fetch next 3 rows only` with Oracle12c or above and SQL Server 2012 or above, **rownum** with previous versions of Oracle and **top** with previous versions of SQL Server.

What if other people appear as many times as the actor who appears the least number of times in the top 3? There is no particular reason to favor one particular actor or actress over the others. With this query, what is shown depends on what the DBMS encounters first when it scans data. This can be a worrying problem because you may take your data, copy it to a different database server for testing, and the same query can return different results, depending on how the copy was done (when you dump and reload, the data is physically reorganized, unlike what happens when files are copied) or on minute differences in the release of the DBMS (and the optimizer choosing a slightly modified execution path).

So, what is the correct course of action? There is the lazy solution and the correct solution. The lazy solution simply consists in ensuring that even if we have ties, the "top three" will be strictly determined, something which can be easily achieved by sorting on more columns than the number of appearances alone - for instance, sorting by decreasing number of appearances, then arbitrarily by *peopleid* value. This will ensure that whatever happens, the same query against the same data will return the same result, even if there are ties.

The lazy solution might be acceptable for some applications but the correct solution is more complicated. First you must find the minimum number of appearances among the top three:

```
select min(appearances)
from (select peopleid,
             count(*) appearances
      from credits
      where credited_as = 'A'
      group by peopleid
      order by appearances desc
      limit 3) a
```

Then you must retain people who appear that number of times or more:

```
select peopleid,
       count(*) appearances
from credits
where credited_as = 'A'
group by peopleid
having count(*) >=
      (select min(appearances)
       from (select peopleid,
                    count(*) appearances
             from credits
             where credited_as = 'A'
             group by peopleid
             order by appearances desc
             limit 3) a)
```

This query returns at least three people – more if other people appear as many times as the third one.

Once you have found the identifiers of the people you want to return (whether you adopt a lazy or a correct solution), you can join with *people* to get their names:

```
select p.first_name, p.surname, b.appearances
from (select peopleid,
             count(*) appearances
      from credits
      where credited_as = 'A'
      group by peopleid
      having count(*) >=
         (select min(appearances)
          from (select peopleid,
                       count(*) appearances
                from credits
                where credited_as = 'A'
                group by peopleid
                order by appearances desc
                limit 3) a)) b
    inner join people p
    on p.peopleid = b.peopleid
order by b.appearances desc, p.surname
```

If you are working with a DBMS that supports window functions, there is another, more elegant and efficient way to return a correct result with a ranking function (in the previous example we are multiplying aggregates and relatively heavy operations). We need everyone who will make it to the podium, even if there are ties. **rownum()** ignores ties, it's not what we need; so, **rank()** or **dense_rank()**? Let's say that four different people appear as many times and that all the others appear fewer times; although the question said "top three", if we want to give a truly correct answer we want all these people, and as they are already more than three, we want none of the other actors. With **rank()** these four top people will be numbered 1, and the following one 5; with **dense_rank()**, the following one will be numbered 2. It's **rank()** that we need use because all the people we want will have as rank 1, 2 or 3, and those we don't want will have a higher rank. So here is the query, counting appearances deep inside, then ranking appearances, then only keeping ranks at most equal to 3:

```
select p.first_name, p.surname, b.appearances
from (select peopleid,
             appearances,
             rank() over (order by appearances desc) rnk
      from (select peopleid,
                   count(*) appearances
            from credits
            where credited_as = 'A'
            group by peopleid) a) b
     inner join people p
     on p.peopleid = b.peopleid
where b.rnk <= 3
order by b.appearances desc, p.surname
```

The query can also be written in a more compact (but less legible) way:

```
select p.first_name, p.surname, b.appearances
from (select peopleid,
             count(*) appearances,
             rank() over (order by count(*) desc) rnk
      from credits
      where credited_as = 'A'
      group by peopleid) b
     inner join people p
     on p.peopleid = b.peopleid
where b.rnk <= 3
order by b.appearances desc, p.surname
```

4. *List all directors alphabetically and the title of their earliest movie.*

   Let's start by listing the identifiers of directors and the titles and years of the films they have directed:

```
select c.peopleid,
       m.title,
       m.year_released
from credits c
     inner join movies m
     on m.movieid = c.movieid
where c.credited_as = 'D'
```

By using aggregate function **min()** as a window function, we can also display the year of the earliest movie for each director (alternatively, you could use **rank()** to assign each film a number; if you order them by year, 1 will be the oldest. In fact, **min()** is better because it's simpler to compute for the DBMS):

```
select c.peopleid,
       m.title,
       m.year_released,
       min(m.year_released) over (partition by c.peopleid) min_year
from credits c
     inner join movies m
     on m.movieid = c.movieid
where c.credited_as = 'D'
```

At this stage, we are almost done; we just have to filter and only keep the row for the film, the year of which is the minimum one, join on *people* to get the director's name, and order:

```
select p.first_name, p.surname, q.title
from (select c.peopleid,
             m.title,
             m.year_released,
             min(m.year_released) over (partition by c.peopleid) min_year
      from credits c
           inner join movies m
           on m.movieid = c.movieid
      where c.credited_as = 'D') q
     inner join people p
     on p.peopleid = q.peopleid
where q.min_year = q.year_released
order by p.surname
```

If your DBMS doesn't support window functions, you need an additional subquery that returns, for each director, the year of release of the earliest film:

```
select c.peopleid,
       min(m.year_released) as earliest
from credits c
     inner join movies m
     on m.movieid = c.movieid
where c.credited_as = 'D'
group by c.peopleid
```

Then you need to join this result to a join on *people*, *credits* and *movies*:

```
select p.first_name, p.surname, m.title
from credits c
     inner join people p
     on p.peopleid = c.peopleid
     inner join movies m
     on m.movieid = c.movieid
     inner join
        (select c.peopleid,
                min(m.year_released) as earliest
         from credits c
              inner join movies m
              on m.movieid = c.movieid
         where c.credited_as = 'D'
         group by c.peopleid) q
      on q.peopleid = p.peopleid
      and q.earliest = m.year_released
where c.credited_as = 'D'
order by p.surname
```

NOTE In the unlikely case that a director has two "earliest films" released in the same year (with only the year, we cannot say which one was truly the earliest), the same director name may be listed several times, with a different title each time.

5. *The following query:*

```
select c.country_name,
       m.title,
       m.year_released
from countries c
       inner join movies m
      on m.country = c.country_code
order by c.country_name, m.title, m.year_released
```

would return something that looks like this:

```
country_name title                          year_released
------------ ------------------------------ -------------
...
France       La belle et la bête                     1946
France       Le cinquième élément                    1997
France       Les Visiteurs du Soir                   1942
Germany      Das Boot                                1985
Hong Kong    Ying hung boon sik                      1986
```

```
India        Pather Panchali                    1955
India        Sholay                             1975
Italy        Il buono, il brutto, il cattivo    1966
Italy        Ladri di biciclette                1948
Japan        Shichinin no Samurai               1954
New Zealand  The Lord of the Rings              2001
...
```

How would you write the query to display the country name only, for the first film of each country? The goal is to obtain

```
country_name title                              year_released
------------ ------------------------------ -------------
...
France       La belle et la bête                1946
             Le cinquième élément               1997
             Les Visiteurs du Soir              1942
Germany      Das Boot                           1985
Hong Kong    Ying hung boon sik                 1986
India        Pather Panchali                    1955
             Sholay                             1975
Italy        Il buono, il brutto, il cattivo    1966
             Ladri di biciclette                1948
Japan        Shichinin no Samurai               1954
New Zealand  The Lord of the Rings              2001
...
```

We want to display the country name for the first film of each country and nothing (which means null) for the others. Let's first identify the title of each "first film". I am using **rank()** this time, I could have used **min()** as in the previous exercise but **rank()** is better because it also allows me to order by year when two films have the same title (I can have the same order for the window function as I have for the whole of my query).

```
select c.country_name,
       m.title,
       m.year_released,
       rank() over (partition by c.country_name
                    order by m.title, m.year_released) rnk
from countries c
       inner join movies m
      on m.country = c.country_code
order by c.country_name, m.title, m.year_released
```

So, I want to show the country name when *rnk* is one and null otherwise. I wrap the query (without an **order by**) in a subquery, add a **case ... end** construct, order properly and mission accomplished:

```
select case rnk
         when 1 then country_name
         else null
       end as country,
       title,
       year_released
from (select c.country_name,
```

```
            m.title,
            m.year_released,
            rank() over (partition by c.country_name
                         order by m.title, m.year_released) rnk
        from countries c
             inner join movies m
             on m.country = c.country_code) q
  order by country_name, title, year_released
```

(if you have ordered by year instead of title and year in the window function, it may cause unexpected results in some cases).

As in the previous exercise, if your DBMS doesn't support window functions you need an additional query to retrieve the first film to display for this country. You could think of

```
select country,
       min(title) as first_title
from movies
group by country
```

but there is a problem if the first title is shared by two films, an original one and a later remake; we must be able to distinguish between the two and only retain the earliest film. Aggregate functions only take one parameter. The (ugly) solution in that case is a correlated subquery in the *select list*, which allows us to order by both title and year, and only retain the first row. It's not only ugly, it would probably be inefficient on large volumes (I discuss performance in Chapter 9):

```
select c.country_code as country,
       (select m.movieid
        from movies m
        where m.country = c.country_code  ← Note the correlation
        order by m.title,
                 m.year_released
        limit 1) as first_movie      ← Can be null if there is no film
from countries c                       for this country
```

Alternatively, if you are working with MySQL, you can build a suitably ordered list of film identifiers per country with the (non-standard) aggregate function **group_concat()**:

```
select country,
       group_concat(movieid order by title, year_released) as list
from movies
group by country
```

Join this result set to the other tables and function **find_in_set()** - also non standard - will tell you for each film whether it's the first one in the series or not:

```
select case find_in_set(m.movieid, q.list)
         when 1 then c.country_name
         else null
       end as country_name,
```

```
        m.title,
        m.year_released
from (select country,
             group_concat(movieid
                   order by title, year_released) as list
      from movies
      group by country) q
     inner join countries c
     on c.country_code = q.country
     inner join movies m
     on m.country = q.country
order by c.country_name, m.title, m.year_released
```

6. *JSON (JavaScript Object Notation) is a popular data exchange format on the web.*

> *NOTE See http://www.json.org/*

The general format for dumping a table (or the result of a query) in JSON is

```
{"tablename":[
   {"column_name1":value, "column_name2":value, ..., "column-namen":value},
  ...
   {"column_name1":value, "column_name2":value, ..., "column-namen":value}
 ]}
```

Curly brackets surround the whole table output, which includes the table name. The whole set of rows is between square brackets and the values on each row are returned between curly brackets, as a comma-separated list of "column name":value pairs. String values must be between double quotes like the column names.

Basing your query on the HTML-generating queries and writing explicitly in the query, the table name and the column names, can you write a query to output table countries *in JSON format?*

Each row will appear as

```
{"country_code":"..","country_name":"...","continent":"..."}
```

which is easy to generate with a query such as

```
select '{"country_code":"' || country_code || '","country_name":"'
       || country_name || '","continent":"' || continent || '"}'
from countries
```

(Use **+** for string concatenation with SQL Server; function **concat()** can also be an alternative to the concatenation operator **||**).

Now, we have to distinguish between three cases:

- The first row, for which the name of the table must appear, as well as opening curly and square brackets,
- Regular rows, terminated (as the first one) by a comma
- The last row, at the end of which instead of a comma, we have closing brackets.

The simplest way to identify which case we have is to assign an arbitrary row number to each row and to count at the same time, how many rows we have in the result set. This will tell us whether a row is the first one, the last one, or in between. Those computations can be performed with functions **row_number()** and the window version of **count()** (I'll discuss shortly what to do when you have no window functions):

```
select '{"country_code":"' || country_code || '","country_name":"'
      || country_name || '","continent":"' || continent || '"}' as row_data,
      row_number() over(order by country_code) as rn,  ← assign a row number
      count(*) over () as cnt  ← count the rows
from countries
```

Finally, all we have to do is to wrap the preceding query in another query that tests the different row number values and outputs what is required. We mustn't forget to add an **order by** clause to be certain that the rows will be returned in the order that matches the numbers we have assigned (there is no guarantee otherwise that the order will always be respected and if it weren't the result would be messed up).

```
select case rn
         when 1 then '{"countries":['   ← First row only
         else ''
       end || row_data
       || case rn
            when cnt then ']}'       ← Last row only
            else ','
          end as json_data
from (select '{"country_code":"' || country_code || '","country_name":"'
             || country_name || '","continent":"'
             || continent || '"}' as row_data,
             row_number() over(order by country_code) as rn,
             count(*) over () as cnt
      from countries) c
order by rn  ← Important
```

If you are working with a DBMS that doesn't support window functions, you also need to identify the first and the last country in the series; in this particular case, it's relatively easy and you need a **cross join** (shown in the chapter) to combine countries with the query that returns the minimum and maximum country code values it contains:

```
select '{"country_code":"' || c.country_code
        || '","country_name":"' || c.country_name
        || '","continent":"' || c.continent || '"}' as row_data,
       c.country_code,   ← You need this one too for comparisons
       c2.min_code,
       c2.max_code
from countries c
     cross join
       (select min(country_code) as min_code,
               max(country_code) as max_code
```

```
            from countries) c2
```

This query can be nested and instead of comparing on numerical ranks, you can compare on country codes – not forgetting to order the result set by country code:

```
select case q.country_code
          when q.min_code then '{"countries":['
          else ''
        end ||
        q.row_data
        || case q.country_code
            when q.max_code then ']}'
            else ','
          end as json_data
from (select '{"country_code":"' || c.country_code
             || '","country_name":"' || c.country_name
             || '","continent":"' || c.continent || '"}' as row_data,
             c.country_code,
             c2.min_code,
             c2.max_code
      from countries c
           cross join
             (select min(country_code) as min_code,
                     max(country_code) as max_code
              from countries) c2) q
order by q.country_code  ← Important
```

Chapter 6: Fuzzy Searches – Method

1. *Blogs, picture and video sites commonly use tags, which are very similar in their usage to words extracted from a title – for instance, a table picture_tags will contain a picture identifier pic_id, and a text column tag that contains a word used to qualify the picture. The same picture will be associated with several tags.*

   How would you write a query to retrieve the identifiers of all pictures associated with tags WINTER and FOG but not associated with tag SNOW?

   Queries on tags are conveniently processed with set operators (**union**, **intersect**, **except/minus**). There are subtleties, though. The following query, for instance, is wrong:

   ```
   select pic_id
   from picture_tags
   where tag in ('WINTER', 'FOG')
   except   ← minus with Oracle
   select pic_id
   from picture_tags
   where tag = 'SNOW'
   ```

   The problem is that a picture associated with WINTER or FOG alone will be returned. We must check that *both* WINTER and FOG are associated with the picture. You can do it with set operators only, using **intersect** to ensure that we have both WINTER and FOG, then **except** to eliminate pictures associated with SNOW:

```
select pic_id
from picture_tags
where tag ='WINTER'
intersect
select pic_id
from picture_tags
where tag = 'FOG'
except     ← minus with Oracle
select pic_id
from picture_tags
where tag = 'SNOW'
```

My favorite way to do it, however, would include an aggregate and a check that I have indeed, retrieved the number of tags I wanted:

```
select pic_id
from picture_tags
where tag in ('WINTER', 'FOG')
group by pic_id            } We need this to check that
having count(*) = 2        } we have both tags
except     ← minus with Oracle
select pic_id
from picture_tags
where tag = 'SNOW'
```

Other tactics are possible; if your DBMS has no **except**, you can use a left outer join:

```
select a.pic_id
from (select pic_id
      from picture_tags
      where tag in ('WINTER', 'FOG')
      group by pic_id
      having count(*) = 2) a
     left outer join
       (select pic_id
        from picture_tags
        where tag = 'SNOW') b
     on b.pic_id = a.pic_id
where b.pic_id is null   ← Only keep when SNOW isn't found
```

Alternatively, you can also only use an aggregate function:

```
select pic_id
from picture_tags
where tag in ('WINTER', 'FOG', 'SNOW')
group by pic_id
having sum(case
             when tag in ('WINTER', 'FOG') then 1
             else 10    ← very different value for SNOW
           end) = 2
```

The **having** condition is designed to ensure that we do indeed have both WINTER and FOG but not SNOW; we collect everything associated with all three tags, including the one we don't want (to check it's not there). Of all possible combinations, the sum will give either 1 or 10 for pictures associated with only one tag, 12 for pictures associated with all three tags, 11 for pictures associated with SNOW and either WINTER or FOG, and 2 for pictures associated with WINTER and FOG only. As a side note, the version that combines **intersect** and **except** would probably be the easiest to generate in a program (I talk about the generation of SQL statements by program in Chapter 11.)

2. *As stated, the third example demonstrating the application of a sound method for writing a query has been taken from a forum. Here are the comments by (presumably) the project manager who posted the query, and the query he or she posted (slightly massaged – I have renamed some tables and columns and removed an ancillary condition):*

   As my developer hasn't completely mastered SQL and its subtleties, I am posting this query here looking for help.

   This query displays the 10 first videos having the greatest number of categories which are similar to the video being watched (in this example video 81). The current query takes 3 seconds with 2,700 videos on a rather powerful server, we find this a bit slow.

```
SELECT DISTINCT          ← I don't like this
       video_id,
       video_type,
       video_title,
       video_description,
       video_idPartner,
       video_urlMini,
       video_dateValid,
       partner_valid,
       partner_redirection,
        ( SELECT COUNT(Y.v_belongs_c_idVideo) AS NbSimilar
          FROM  v_belongs_c  Y
          WHERE Y.v_belongs_c_idVideo=81
            AND Y.v_belongs_c_idCategory IN
              (SELECT Z.v_belongs_c_idCategory    ← subquery in subquery
               FROM v_belongs_c Z
               WHERE Z.v_belongs_c_idVideo=video_id)) as Counter,
        ( SELECT category_singular
          FROM category,              } That's the old type of join, with
               v_belongs_c X          } join conditions in the where clause
          WHERE X.v_belongs_c_idVideo=video_id
            AND X.v_belongs_c_default=1
            AND category_id=X.v_belongs_c_idCategory )
                as category_singular
FROM category,
     v_belongs_c A,       } Old joins again
     video
     LEFT JOIN partner      ← New type of join
            ON video_idPartner=partner_id
WHERE (A.v_belongs_c_idCategory IN
        (SELECT W.v_belongs_c_idCategory
```

```
            FROM v_belongs_c W
            WHERE W.v_belongs_c_idVideo=81)
        AND video_id=A.v_belongs_c_idVideo)
  AND (video_idPartner=0
       OR (partner_valid=1
           AND partner_redirection<>1))
  AND video_valid=1
  AND video_id<>81
 ORDER BY Counter DESC
 LIMIT 10
```

There are in this query, a number of things that are plainly wrong, even though the syntax is correct. Can you see the big mistake which means that many more rows than expected by the developer are processed and how it was "fixed" (as in "sweeping the dirt under the rug")?

That's what happens when people try to throw everything into the query at once.

Whenever I see a **distinct** at the beginning of a complex query, I check the joins – and here first we have a mix of old and new syntax (bad), and a dismal absence of join conditions in the **where** clause, which would be needed with the old join syntax. In other words, the developer, who not only hasn't mastered SQL but struggles with the basics, noticed lots of duplicates, and used a **distinct** to hide the problem. Cascading subqueries in the *select list* (executed for each row returned, before the **distinct** suppresses a lot of rows) aren't very helpful for performance either.

There are tons of things that are plainly wrong with this query. If I understand the schema well, there is a table of videos (*video*), to which presumably, belongs all the attributes named *video_*xxx; there is the table of categories, *category*; there is a table *v_belongs_c* that associates a video identifier with one or several category identifiers (similar to the role of *credits* in the sample database used in this book); and there is table *partner*. Apparently one video is associated with at most one partner, as there is a column called *video_partnerid* that looks like an attribute of table *video*. The following figure presents what I could call an artist's rendition of my understanding of the schema.

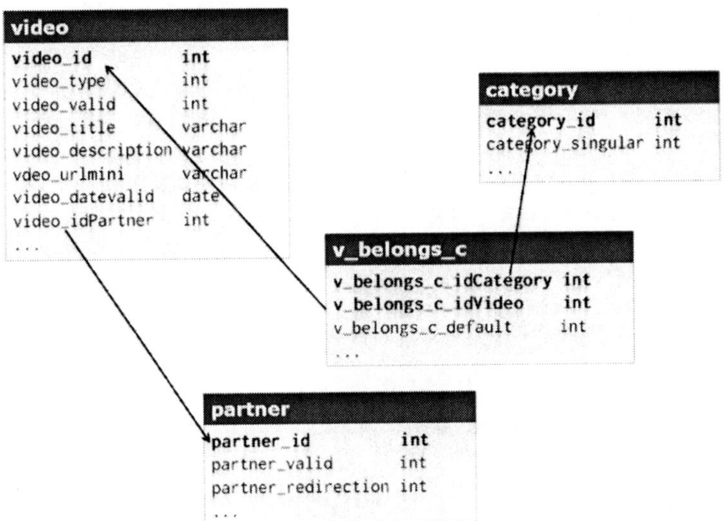

This being said, take the first table in the **from** clause, *category*. I don't see, either in the *select list* or in the **where** clause, any column name starting with *category*. Actually, there is a subquery in the *select list* to return *category_singular* but this subquery applies (again) to *category* and doesn't return data from the table listed in the main **from** clause. In other words, we have here a completely useless reference to table *category* (or the subquery in the *select list* is useless - you just need one reference to *category* in the whole query).

I presume that the developer tried to adopt some kind of top-down approach, starting with the columns that had to be returned. This approach is heading straight for the wall with complex queries and there is an almost palpable panic in the style in which this query is written, with subqueries thrown in indiscriminately, pieces of syntactically correct SQL brought together haphazardly, and finally the **distinct** to get rid of the innumerable duplicates brought by joins without any join conditions, some of them useless.

How would I have built the query? (This wasn't asked in the exercise, it's just a reminder about how you should proceed.)

First, the categories associated with the video being watched:

```
select v_belongs_c_idCategory as catid
from v_belongs_c
where v_belongs_c_idVideo = 81
```

Then the videos that have categories in common with this one; we can use either an **in()** subquery or a join:

```
select b.v_belongs_c_idVideo as videoid,
       b. v_belongs_c_idCategory as catid
from (select v_belongs_c_idCategory as catid
```

```
      from v_belongs_c
      where v_belongs_c_idVideo = 81) a
    inner join v_belongs_c b
      on b.v_belongs_c_idCategory = a.catid
     and b.v_belongs_c_idVideo <> 81      ← don't take the video being watched
     and b.video_valid = 1
```

At this point, it's easy to count the number of categories per video, order, and only keep the top 10 videos (I am using here **limit** as in the original query but not at the same place):

```
select b.v_belongs_c_idVideo as videoid,
       count(b.v_belongs_c_idCategory) as common_cats
from (select v_belongs_c_idCategory as catid
      from v_belongs_c
      where v_belongs_c_idVideo = 81) a
    inner join v_belongs_c b
      on b.v_belongs_c_idCategory = a.catid
     and b.v_belongs_c_idVideo <> 81
     and b.video_valid = 1
group by b.v_belongs_c_idVideo
order by common_cats desc, videoid     ← additional sort key
limit 10
```

Note that we don't really worry about ties in this example; I have added *videoid* as second sort key, to ensure that the same data will always produce the same result set, even if physically rows are stored differently. Now that we have the 10 video identifiers we are interested in, we can join *video*, *category* and *partner* to obtain whatever we need:

```
select v.video_id,
       v.video_type,
       v.video_title,
       v.video_description,
       v.video_idPartner,
       v.video_urlMini,
       v.video_dateValid,
       p.partner_valid,
       p.partner_redirection,
       q.common_cats as counter,
       c.category_singular
from (select b.v_belongs_c_idVideo as videoid,
             count(b.v_belongs_c_idCategory) as common_cats
      from (select v_belongs_c_idCategory as catid
            from v_belongs_c
            where v_belongs_c_idVideo = 81) a
           inner join v_belongs_c b
             on b.v_belongs_c_idCategory = a.catid
            and b.v_belongs_c_idVideo <> 81
            and b.video_valid = 1
      group by b.v_belongs_c_idVideo
      order by common_cats desc, videoid
      limit 10) q
      inner join video v
      on v.video_id = q.videoid
```

```
        left outer join v_belongs_c vc
        on vc.v_belongs_c_idVideo = v.video_id
        and vc.v_belongs_c_default = 1
        left outer join category c
        on c.category_id = vc.v_belongs_c_idCategory
        left outer join partner p
        on p.partner_id = v.video_idPartner
where (v.video_idPartner=0
        or (p.partner_valid = 1
            and p.partner_redirection <> 1))
order by q.common_cats desc
```

← Not sure that one category is defined as default

I haven't had any opportunity to test this query against the original data but I am confident that it runs much faster – and returns a correct result, which I doubt in the original query.

Chapter 7: Changing Data

1. *Write (and if possible execute) the statements required to add to the movies database information about* The Sea Hawk, *a 1940 American movie directed by Michael Curtiz (1886-1962), starring Errol Flynn (1909-1959), Brenda Marshall (1915-1992), and Claude Rains (1889-1967). Try to do it in as few statements as possible.*

NOTE Some of the people (Michael Curtiz, Claude Rains) normally belong to all sample databases and are ignored here. If you try to insert them again, it's not a mistake, this kind of thing happens. That's what unique constraints are there for.

To insert people, if your DBMS supports inserting several rows at once, you can insert people in one query (it wouldn't be a mistake to have two insert statements):

```
insert into people(first_name, surname, born, died)
values ('Errol', 'Flynn', 1909, 1959),
       ('Brenda', 'Marshall', 1915,1992)
```

No value is specified for *peopleid* because I suppose that I'm using a DBMS that automatically generates a value (actually, an explicit value would generate an error in that case).

If your DBMS doesn't support inserting several rows at once, either you insert them one by one or cheat with an **insert ... select**. Don't forget to use sequences explicitly, if your DBMS uses sequences instead of auto-generated values, for instance with Oracle:

```
insert into people(peopleid, first_name, surname, born, died)
select people_seq.nextval,
       first_name,
       surname,
       born,
       died
from (select 'Errol' as first_name,
             'Flynn' as surname,
```

```
               1909 as born,
               1959 as died
        from dual
        union all
        select 'Brenda',
               'Marshall',
               1915,
               1992
        from dual)
```

NOTE Oracle complains if you are referring to a sequence in a **union** statement, which is why I have used a nested query and the sequence reference at the higher level.

You need one separate insert statement to insert the movie itself (once again, don't forget the sequence if you are using one).

```
insert into movies(title, country, year_released)
values('The Sea Hawk', 'us', 1940)
```

It's with insertions in table *credits* that it becomes interesting. Although you could possibly use the latest generated identifier for the film (and yet - what if the previous **insert** statement failed, telling you that the film is already present? Some credits may be missing), it's impossible for people because several people need to be credited, some of whom may already be in the *people* table because they are associated with other films. We need to retrieve the identifiers assigned by the system using the "real life identifiers" (title, year and country for films, first name (which can be null) and surname for people) and use an **insert ... select** statement, which will minimize the number of statements.

```
insert into credits(movieid, peopleid, credited_as)
select m.movieid,
       p.peopleid,
       case p.surname
         when 'Curtiz' then 'D'
         else 'A'
       end
from movies m
     cross join (select peopleid, surname
                 from people
                 where (first_name = 'Michael'
                        and surname = 'Curtiz')
                    or (first_name = 'Errol'
                        and surname = 'Flynn')
                    or (first_name = 'Brenda'
                        and surname = 'Marshall')
                    or (first_name = 'Claude'
                        and surname = 'Rains')) p
where m.title = 'The Sea Hawk'
  and m.country = 'us'
  and m.year_released = 1940
```

As I have nothing to link *movies* to *people*, I am using a **cross join** (mentioned in Chapter 5), that returns all the possible combinations of the films I return from *movies* (a single film in that case) and of the people selected.

Alternatively, I could have used a subquery in the *select list* to retrieve the movie identifier:

```
insert into credits(movieid, peopleid, credited_as)
select (select movieid
         from movies
         where title = 'The Sea Hawk'
         and country = 'us'
         and year_released = 1940) as movieid,
       peopleid,
       case surname
         when 'Curtiz' then 'D'
         else 'A'
       end
from people
where (first_name = 'Michael'
       and surname = 'Curtiz')
   or (first_name = 'Errol'
       and surname = 'Flynn')
   or (first_name = 'Brenda'
       and surname = 'Marshall')
   or (first_name = 'Claude'
       and surname = 'Rains')
```

2. *Make everybody in the* people *table three years younger ... and cancel the change!*

   If you are using a DBMS that starts transactions explicitly, **begin** (or **start**) **transaction** must be the first statement (if you don't issue it, the only solution to cancel the update will be a second update making everyone three years older – which in this particular case will not be too difficult but some changes can be considerably more complex, and sometimes impossible, to cancel without **rollback**)

   ```
   begin transaction
   ```
   ← "start transaction" with MySQL
   not needed with Oracle or DB2

   Next, to make everybody three years younger, we just need to make the date of birth three years later:

   ```
   update people
   set born = born + 3
   ```

   You can query and check, then cancel the change:

   ```
   rollback
   ```

3. *Which sequence of statements would you apply to remove from the database, anything that refers to France?*

   The problem with deletions is of course the problem of foreign keys. We cannot delete the row that refers to France in table *countries* as long as there is a French film in table *movies*, since column *country* of table *movies* is a foreign key that references table *countries*. We cannot delete French films from table *movies* as long as there is a row in table *credits* that references them. The order of deletion therefore needs to be:

a. Table *credits*

```
delete from credits
where movieid in (select movieid from movies where country = 'fr')
```

b. Table *movies*

```
delete from movies where country = 'fr'
```

c. Table *countries*

```
delete from countries where country_code = 'fr'
```

You needn't delete rows from table *people*. For one thing, no information is stored about citizenship in that table. Besides, it frequently happens that the citizenship of directors or actors doesn't match the official country of a film; it's more frequent between countries that share the same language but for many talented directors and actors language is no barrier. If you really want to, you can delete people who are no longer credited:

```
delete from people
where not exists (select null
                  from credits
                 where credits.peopleid = people.peopleid)
```

4. *Many sources of reference data are available on the web – including from Intelligence agencies. The NGA provides geographical information on several countries, in the format specified on this page:*

   http://earth-info.nga.mil/gns/html/gis_countryfiles.html

   Create a suitable table, and then pick one country on this page:

   http://earth-info.nga.mil/gns/html/namefiles.htm

   Download the data and load it in your database.

   There isn't much to say here in terms of "solution", as the exercise is a straight application of what is shown in the chapter (and is very dependent on the DBMS that you are using). I'd like however, to comment on the table that you need to create.

   First of all, when you don't really know the data that you are going to load (it might be different if you were doing it on a regular basis), don't assume that you are going to load the data into the final table but instead, into a staging table: a temporary data container, useful for analyzing and possibly processing data before copying to its final storage place. In staging tables, you can be lax; don't define a primary key if the primary key isn't obvious, make most columns optional (you

will be able to check afterwards in which ones values are actually missing). Don't be over-scrupulous now.
In this particular case, when the field description says "unique feature identifier' or "unique name identifier" you can safely choose one as primary key and say that the other one is unique.
Another important point is the choice of data types. A few signs suggest that downloadable data comes from Oracle: the use of NUMBER, and more particularly the field width of 38 for numbers – when you declare a column as **number** without any further precision in Oracle, it can store up to 38 digits (which is very, very big). If you are using a DBMS other than Oracle, you'll be safe with a **numeric** or **decimal** data type. It's quite possible that a regular **int** would be quite enough to store the value, a **bigint** will most certainly be. When you see CHARACTER, it must obviously be a varchar or varchar2, unless it is obvious that the length is fixed (1, or when the description says "two letter code" or "three letter code"). For dates, you can choose in a staging table, to load them as character strings – you'll convert them to a true date type later. Or you can try to load them directly into a date column but you must make sure that your settings are such that the format to load corresponds to the default format.

Chapter 8: Functions, Procedures and Triggers

NOTE If you are using SQLite, jump straight to the trigger exercise (the last one).

1. *Create a function unaccent() that removes à, é, è, ê, ö, ô, ü from the text that is passed as parameter and replaces them respectively with a, e, e, e, oe, o, ue.*

   Function *unaccent()* is basically a wrapper for built-in functions. If you are using Oracle, PostgreSQL or DB2 you can use function **translate()** for some transformations but not all of them, as one character must sometimes be replaced by two characters (**translate()** is a one-for-one transformation); it's probably easier to use cascading calls to function **replace()** with all products). Here is how you can write it.

SQL SERVER

```
create function unaccent(@string varchar(max))
returns varchar(max)
begin
  return replace(
           replace(
             replace(
               replace(
                 replace(
                   replace(
                     replace(@string, 'à', 'a'),
                     'é', 'e'),
```

← You could use a high value instead of max (eg 1000)

```
                'è', 'e'),
              'ê', 'e'),
            'ö', 'oe'),
          'ô', 'o'),
        'ü', 'ue');
end;
```

MySQL and DB2

With MySQL you must first issue

```
delimiter $$
```

The function is identical with MySQL and DB2:

```
create function unaccent(p_string varchar(1000))
returns varchar(1000)
return replace(
         replace(
           replace(
             replace(
               replace(
                 replace(
                   replace(p_string, 'à', 'a'),
                     'é', 'e'),
                   'è', 'e'),
                 'ê', 'e'),
               'ö', 'oe'),
             'ô', 'o'),
           'ü', 'ue');
```

To create the function with MySQL you must type:

```
$$
delimiter ;
```

With DB2, under clpplus type / at the beginning of the line and hit return.

PostgreSQL

```
create function unaccent(p_string varchar)
returns varchar
as $$
begin
  return replace(
           replace(
             replace(
               replace(
                 replace(
                   replace(
                     replace(p_string, 'à', 'a'),
                       'é', 'e'),
                     'è', 'e'),
                   'ê', 'e'),
                 'ö', 'oe'),
               'ô', 'o'),
             'ü', 'ue');
end;
$$ language plpgsql;
```

ORACLE

```
create function unaccent(p_string varchar)
return varchar
as
begin
  return replace(
           replace(
             replace(
               replace(
                 replace(
                   replace(
                     replace(p_string, 'à', 'a'),
                       'é', 'e'),
                     'è', 'e'),
                   'ê', 'e'),
                 'ö', 'oe'),
               'ô', 'o'),
             'ü', 'ue');
end;
/
```

In case you have some experience of programming and couldn't resist the temptation of writing, with loops, your own scanner to find and replace characters, I would advise you to write a small procedure that repeats your function and the function above that corresponds to your DBMS, perhaps 5,000 or 10,000 times and compare execution times. If your function is faster you've won. If not, you'll have learned that using built-in functions as much as you can is very often the best option because they are optimized.

2. *Create a function* age() *that takes as input a birth year and a death year and returns either the current age of a person or '+' followed by the age at the time of death, if this person is dead.*

For syntactical details for each DBMS product I refer you to exercise 1 above. What is interesting in this exercise is the data type of the function. Although an age should be, logically, numerical, if we want to display a plus sign before the age at the time of death of deceased people, we need to store the result in a string. For a DBMS, numerical values such as 83 and +83 are identical; of course if we ever need to run computations on ages, the function will be useless; its purpose is limited to displaying information.
The expression to return will be something such as

```
case
   when p_death_year is null then
         cast(extract(year from <current date>)
                   - p_birth_year as <string type>)
  else '+' || cast(p_death_year - p_birth_year as <string type>)
end
```

I have called the parameters *p_death_year* and *p_birth_year*, they should be *@death_year* and *@birth_year* with SQL Server. Please check functions in

Appendix B, as both the function to obtain the current date and the type to pass to function **cast()** are product-specific (needless to say, || should be a plus sign with SQL Server and replaced by a call to function **concat()** with MySQL)

3. *Create a function* numwords() *that takes as input a sentence (... or a title) and counts how many words are present. Ignore punctuation (which can be suppressed by writing a function similar to the function in exercise 1) and assume that words are separated by one space.*

   If your first thought was to set up a counter, scan a piece of text character by character and increment the counter each time you encounter a space, then you are probably looking at this from a traditional programming perspective. You could do that, of course but you don't need to, and it's likely that by doing as indicated here, the function will be much more efficient.
   You only need two functions: the function that computes the length of a string of characters, **length()** (**len()** with SQL Server), and function **replace()**. Let's take as an example a title such as

   `The Lord of the Rings: The Return of the King`

   We have here 10 words, separated by 9 spaces (I assume that there is never a space between the end of a word and punctuation such as the colon). In all cases, we'll have one more word than we have spaces. Instead of counting words, we are going to count spaces. How? Simply by comparing the length of the title (45 characters) with the length of the same, without the spaces. If we apply a `replace(..., ' ', '')` to the title, we obtain something such as

   `TheLordoftheRings:TheReturnoftheKing`

   which has a length of 36 characters – the difference between the two lengths is the number of spaces. So, all you need to return is:

   ```
   1 + length(p_string) - length(replace(p_string, ' ', ''))
   ```

   Or, with SQL Server

   ```
   1 + len(@string) - len(replace(@string, ' ', ''))
   ```

4. *A web site aggregates for statistical analysis the number of visits, hour by hour, in a table that was created as follows (adjust data types for your DBMS):*

   ```
   create table webstats(interval_start   datetime not null,
                         interval_unit    char(1) not null,
                         page             varchar(255) not null,
                         hits             int not null,
                         primary key(interval_start, page, interval_unit))
   ```

   interval_unit is H for an hour, D for a day; page is a page of the site that was requested; hits counts how many times the page was requested between interval_start and interval_start + the time corresponding to interval_unit. We want to keep detailed recent information but we want to aggregate per day, for each page, all data that is older than three months. Write a procedure (which will be run weekly) to aggregate old data and purge details that are too old (you may need to check Appendix B or the DBMS documentation for date arithmetic.)

There are aspects in this exercise that have to do with what happens in real life; to some extent, having a syntactically correct procedure is almost ancillary.
The most important point is that if, when you write a procedure, you may have some usage pattern in mind, you mustn't take this usage pattern for granted. You shouldn't assume, for instance, that the procedure will be run on Sundays at 00:00 – unless you code something that exits the procedure when the time isn't Sunday, 00:00 (and yet you cannot be sure that it will ever been run when it should). Even if you plan to have it run every Sunday at 00:00, it may be launched, on purpose or by mistake, at another time, for good or bad reasons (a new important process may be scheduled to run in place of your procedure, infrastructure operations such as a system upgrade may prevent regular operations for the best part of a week-end ... Anything can happen).
What does it mean in practice? If the procedure is run say at 5am and we want to aggregate per day everything that is older than three months, if we strictly take what happened three months earlier than now, the "cut-off" date will be three months earlier ... at 5am. For the last day, the 5 first years of the day will be aggregated as (incomplete) daily stats, and not the remainder of the day.
There is a question of choice and both options are perfectly valid: either we choose to process only complete days when aggregating, or we accept having incomplete daily stats for the last (chronological) day, with the understanding that these stats will be updated and completed the next time the procedure is run. As the second option is possibly slightly more complex to process, this is the one I have adopted here.
When you take the route that I am taking, which is aggregating even incomplete days, there is another point that needs to be taken into account and which people often forget. The process may be something like:

a. Create the daily entries that don't exist yet for statistics older than three months

b. Update these entries with the hourly statistics older than three months

c. Delete the hourly statistics older than three months

The problem is that you should not take as reference, the current date at each step because none of these operations will be instant. Suppose that we are June, 10th, it's 23:57 and we start the procedure. Step (a) will create all the required entries up to, and including, March, 10th. Step (a), that day, takes 140 seconds. We start step (b) shortly after 23:59, and aggregate all the entries up to March, 10th at 23:00; we won't aggregate anything after 23:00 because we process hourly statistics and if we say 'before 23:59' then it can only be the preceding round hour. This step takes 15 minutes. Then we start step (c) on June, 11th at 00:14 or thereabouts, and then delete hourly statistics up to and excluding March, 11th at 00:00. The statistics for March 10th between 23:00 and midnight are gone, and weren't processed. The solution is easy: get the current date and time when the procedure starts and keep them as reference for all the duration of the process. This is what you should always do with complex, multiple steps processes that take "some time" to run.

That being said, here is how you could use the procedure with the various products; when the **merge** command is available, I have used it. Otherwise I have first inserted rows for the new aggregated statistics I wanted, then updated them; proceeding like this with a product that knows **merge** is perfectly acceptable. There is much date arithmetic in the procedure, please refer to Appendix B or to product documentation if you don't really understand how the various functions work. Please note that in order to limit the amount of data I'll have to process in the future, I don't process everything that is older than three months but everything that is older than three months and (arbitrarily) more recent than one year old, assuming that everything older than one year is necessarily processed.

DB2

```
create procedure aggregate_stats()
language sql
begin
  declare d_ref_date    timestamp;

  set d_ref_date = current timestamp;
  merge into webstats w
  using (select trunc(interval_start) interval_start,
                'D' interval_unit,
                page,
                sum(hits) hits
         from webstats
         where interval_start <= d_ref_date - 3 months
           and interval_start > d_ref_date - 1 year
           and interval_unit <> 'D'
         group by trunc(interval_start), page) x
  on (x.interval_start = w.interval_start
      and x.interval_unit = w.interval_unit
      and x.page = w.page)
  when matched then
       update set w.hits = w.hits + x.hits
  when not matched then
       insert(interval_start,interval_unit,page,hits)
       values(x.interval_start,x.interval_unit,x.page,x.hits);
 delete what has just been aggregated
  delete from webstats
  where interval_start <= d_ref_date - 3 months
    and interval_start > d_ref_date - 1 year
    and interval_unit <> 'D';
```

```
end;
```

MYSQL

```
delimiter $$
create procedure aggregate_stats()
begin
  declare d_ref_date    datetime;

  set d_ref_date = now();
  insert missing days
  insert into webstats(interval_start, interval_unit, page, hits)
  select distinct date(w.interval_start),
         'D',
         w.page,
         0
  from webstats w
       left outer join webstats w2
       on w2.interval_start = date(w.interval_start)
       and w2.interval_unit = 'D'
       and w2.page = w.page
  where w.interval_start <= date_sub(d_ref_date,
                                    interval 3 month)
    and w.interval_start > date_sub(d_ref_date,
                                   interval 1 year)
    and w.interval_unit <> 'D'
    and w2.interval_start is null;
  update
  update webstats w
         inner join
            (select date(interval_start) as interval_start,
                    page,
                    sum(hits) hits
             from webstats
             where interval_start <= date_sub(d_ref_date,
                                              interval 3 month)
             and interval_start > date_sub(d_ref_date,
                                          interval 1 year)
             and interval_unit <> 'D'
             group by date(interval_start),
                      page) w2
         on w2.interval_start = w.interval_start
         and w2.page = w.page
  set w.hits = w.hits + w2.hits;
  delete what has just been aggregated
  delete from webstats
  where interval_start <= date_sub(d_ref_date, interval 3 month)
    and interval_start > date_sub(d_ref_date, interval 1 year)
    and interval_unit <> 'D';
end;
$$
delimiter ;
```

ORACLE

```
create or replace procedure aggregate_stats
as
  d_ref_date    date;
```

```
begin
  d_ref_date := sysdate;
  merge into webstats w
  using (select trunc(interval_start) interval_start,
                'D' interval_unit,
                page,
                sum(hits) hits
         from webstats
         where interval_start <= add_months(d_ref_date, -3)
           and interval_start > add_months(d_ref_date, -12)
           and interval_unit <> 'D'
         group by trunc(interval_start), page) x
  on (x.interval_start = w.interval_start
      and x.interval_unit = w.interval_unit
      and x.page = w.page)
  when matched then
       update set w.hits = w.hits + x.hits
  when not matched then
       insert(interval_start,interval_unit,page,hits)
       values(x.interval_start,x.interval_unit,x.page,x.hits);
  delete what has just been aggregated
  delete from webstats
  where interval_start <= add_months(d_ref_date, -3)
    and interval_start > add_months(d_ref_date, -12)
    and interval_unit <> 'D';
end;
/
```

POSTGRESQL

```
create or replace function aggregate_stats()
returns void
as $$
declare
  d_ref_date    timestamp;
begin
  d_ref_date := localtimestamp;
  insert missing days
  insert into webstats(interval_start, interval_unit, page, hits)
  select distinct date_trunc('day', w.interval_start),
         'D',
         w.page,
         0
  from webstats w
       left outer join webstats w2
       on w2.interval_start = date_trunc('day', w.interval_start)
       and w2.interval_unit = 'D'
       and w2.page = w.page
  where w.interval_start <= d_ref_date - interval '3 months'
    and w.interval_start > d_ref_date - interval '1 year'
    and w.interval_unit <> 'D'
    and w2.interval_start is null;
  update
  update webstats
  set hits = hits + w2.newhits
  from (select date_trunc('day', interval_start) interval_start,
               page,
```

```
                sum(hits) newhits
        from webstats
        where interval_start <= d_ref_date - interval '3 months'
          and interval_start > d_ref_date - interval '1 year'
          and interval_unit <> 'D'
        group by date_trunc('day', interval_start), page) w2
  where w2.interval_start = webstats.interval_start
    and w2.page = webstats.page;
  delete what has just been aggregated
  delete from webstats
  where interval_start <= d_ref_date - interval '3 months'
    and interval_start > d_ref_date - interval '1 year'
    and interval_unit <> 'D';
end;
$$ language plpgsql;
```

SQL SERVER

```
create procedure aggregate_stats
as
begin
  declare @ref_date    datetime;

  set @ref_date = getdate();
  merge into webstats w
  using (select cast(interval_start as date) interval_start,
                'D' interval_unit,
                page,
                sum(hits) hits
         from webstats
         where interval_start <= dateadd(month, -3, @ref_date)
           and interval_start > dateadd(year, -1, @ref_date)
           and interval_unit <> 'D'
         group by cast(interval_start as date), page) x
  on (x.interval_start = w.interval_start
      and x.interval_unit = w.interval_unit
      and x.page = w.page)
  when matched then
       update set w.hits = w.hits + x.hits
  when not matched then
       insert(interval_start,interval_unit,page,hits)
       values(x.interval_start,x.interval_unit,x.page,x.hits);
  delete what has just been aggregated
  delete from webstats
  where interval_start <= dateadd(month, -3, @ref_date)
    and interval_start > dateadd(year, -1, @ref_date)
    and interval_unit <> 'D';
end;
```

5. *Create a trigger on table people that prevents the insertion of a row into this table outside business hours (you may need to check the DBMS documentation for date functions). Ignore public holidays.*

I am assuming in what follows that business hours are Monday to Friday, 9am to 6pm; if in your country standards are different, then adapt the triggers, the exact boundaries are unimportant. The whole idea is that when the trigger is fired by an **insert**, the current date and time are checked. If they fall outside the allowed time slots, an error is generated, which cancels the operation. With products that allow **before** triggers, the trigger should be fired before the **insert** statement is executed; and once again with products that allow it, the trigger doesn't need to be fired for each row.

DB2

```
create trigger people_ins_trg
before insert on people
for each row
begin
  if (dayofweek(current date) not between 2 and 6
          ↑ Sunday = 1, Saturday = 7
      or extract(hour from current timestamp) not between 9 and 17)
  then
    signal sqlstate '70000'
       set message_text = 'Operation impossible now';
  end if;end;
/
```

MySQL

Identical to DB2.

```
delimiter $$
create trigger people_ins_trg
before insert on people
for each row
begin
  if (dayofweek(now()) not between 2 and 6
          ↑ Sunday = 1, Saturday = 7
      or extract(hour from now()) not between 9 and 17)
  then
    signal sqlstate '70000'
       set message_text = 'Operation impossible now';
  end if;end;
$$
delimiter ;
```

With older MySQL versions, you can call a procedure that doesn't exist and give it the name of the message that you want to communicate:

```
delimiter $$
create trigger people_ins_trg
before insert on people
for each row
begin
  if (dayofweek(now()) not between 2 and 6
      or extract(hour from now()) not between 9 and 17)
  then
    call Error_Operation_impossible_now;  ← Doesn't exist but the name
                                            will be displayed in the error
  end if;end;
$$
```

```
delimiter ;
```

ORACLE

```
create trigger people_ins_trg
before insert on people
declare
  n_dummy number;
begin
  if (to_char(sysdate, 'DY', 'nls_date_language=english')
```

↑ This parameter is here to ensure that the function will always return a short name in English even with different language settings

```
          in ('SAT', 'SUN')
      or extract(hour from localtimestamp) not between 9 and 17)
  then
     raise_application_error(-20000, 'Operation impossible now');
  end if;
end;
/
```

How days are numbered depends on localization settings. To have code that runs independently from localization settings, I retrieve the shortened day name and force language to English in the function. This is particularly important for software programs that can be shipped to different countries (not so in college labs).

POSTGRESQL

```
create or replace function check_insert_fn()
returns trigger
as
$$
begin
  if (extract(dow from current_timestamp) not between 1 and 5
```

↑ Day Of Week – Sunday = 0, Saturday = 6

```
      or extract(hour from current_timestamp) not between 9 and 17)
  then
    raise exception 'Operation not allowed now';
  end if;
  return null;
end;$$ language plpgsql;

create trigger people_ins_trg
before insert on people
execute procedure check_insert_fn();
```

SQL SERVER

```
create trigger people_ins_trg
on people
after insert
as
begin
  declare @df int;
```

```
  set @df = @@datefirst;       ← get current settings
  set datefirst 7;             ← set Sunday=1, Saturday=7
  if (datepart(weekday, getdate()) not between 2 and 6
      or datepart(hour, current_timestamp) not between 9 and 17)
  begin
    raiserror(N'Operation not allowed now', 15, 1);
    rollback;
  end;
  set datefirst @df;           ← restore original settings
end;
```

The only notable feature, is that I first retrieve current settings for day numbering, then set day numbering to something I know how to check, and finally restore original settings. It's not too important for a small application used at only one place, for which you can assume standard local settings (although documenting assumptions is usually a good idea). If you want to ship your program all over the world, you'd better be careful.

SQLite

```
create trigger people_ins_trg
before insert on people
for each row
begin
  select raise(abort, 'Operation not allowed now')
  where strftime('%w', 'now') in ('0', '6')      ← Sunday=0, Saturday=6
    or cast(strftime('%H', 'now') as int) not between 9 and 17;
end;
```

With SQLite we have to run a **select** statement that returns one row if there is an error and no rows if the statement can proceed. There is no built-in procedural language with **if** conditions.

Chapter 9: Speeding Up Queries

1. *A site hosts videos that can be downloaded on demand and a special video_language table, stores a video identifier videoid; a language code lan; and a code lan_type that is S for subtitles, M for monaural audio, D for dolby stereo audio, etc.*

   We want to display language information when we search for a video on other criteria (such as actors, director, or genre) but a significant number of queries are also based on the languages available.

   - *How would you define the primary key for video_language?*
   - *Would you create an additional index besides the primary key index? If so, on which column(s)?*

   I am going to answer both questions at once. The columns that uniquely identify each row in table *video_language* are those listed in the exercise – the video identifier *videoid*, the language code *lan* and *lan_type*, as for each video there can be several soundtracks in the same language (DTS and Dolby Stereo, for instance), or the same language can be available both as soundtrack and as subtitles (some people prefer dubbed movies and may prefer to watch an Italian movie in, for instance, German, others will prefer keeping the original Italian soundtrack with German subtitles). The real question isn't so much 'what are the columns in the primary key?' but 'in which order should they be listed in the primary key?'

It's said that 1) we want to display language information when a film is found, from other criteria (which means that other criteria such as title or director name have determined the film, and therefore the video identifier – in other words, the entry point is *videoid*), 2) there can be searches based on the language as well. That means that we necessarily need two indexes, one starting with column *videoid*, and one starting with column *lan*. Which one is the primary key and which one is the "additional" index is up to you. Let me just say that while all three columns that uniquely identify a row must be part of the primary key, not all of them need necessarily appear in the additional index.

- One possibility is:

  PK (*videoid, lan, lan_type)*

  Additional index : *lan*, or (*lan, lan_type*), or (*lan, lan_type, videoid*)

  (*lan, lan_type*) is probably slightly better than *lan* alone because whether the language is for an audio-track or subtitles may be important (for subtitled Italian comedies you'd better be a fast reader). (*lan, lan_type, videoid*) is a combination that some professionals would use to find the identifier of the video in the index without requiring an additional access to the table row. As this kind of table is unlikely to be much changed, we may have more and bigger indexes to favor queries. Note that (*lan_type, lan*) would be a wrong choice because queries will either be on the language alone (videos that you can watch when you only speak – and read – Spanish) or on the language and type (videos for which a Spanish soundtrack is available). You'll never query on the type alone. This is also why *lan* comes before *lan_type* in the primary key. Any of the three choices for the additional index is correct, although the second and third are slightly better.

- The other option is:

  PK (*lan, lan_type, videoid)*

  Additional index : *videoid*

  In this case, there is no real need for more than one column in the additional index. The primary key is used when looking for videos based on a language criterion, and the additional one to find the language information associated with a video.

My personal favorite is the second option because I like to keep indexes as small as I can but all possibilities listed are acceptable as correct answers.

2. *We have seen in other chapters that it might be interesting to add to table* movies, *other film attributes, such as genre, black and white or color, duration; we might also think of the original language, of audience rating (family, teens, adults), and of a mark from 0 to 10 assigned by members on a website, with how many people have given a mark. Suppose we add all of these attributes. Which ones, if any, would you index? Try to justify your answer.*

   Let's see, even before discussing indexing, which of the additional attributes are likely to be used as search criteria:

   - Genre: yes. There are days when you'd rather watch light entertainment than a documentary on the industrial food chain.
   - B&W/Color: probably no. Perhaps you'll prefer to watch the recent color remake rather than the old black and white original, and it will help you narrow your choice but it's unlikely that you'll absolutely want to watch a B&W film (or a color film, for that matter). Besides, with only two possible values, it would be a very bad candidate for indexing anyway.
   - Duration: once again, a useful secondary criterion for these days when you want to go to bed early but not a primary one. If it ever appears in a **where** clause, it will probably be in combination with another criterion; it may be useful as a sort key.
   - Original language: no. Available languages, as discussed in the previous exercise, will be a criterion but the original one isn't so important if the film is dubbed in a language that you understand (or subtitled, if you aren't averse to subtitles).
   - Rating: yes. It can be important for some people, parents in particular.
   - Mark/number of raters: important as a secondary criterion and for sorting. Could appear, though, as the main criterion.

   Ultimately, my analysis is that among the attributes above, only genre, rating and mark are really likely to be used as the primary search criterion. Should we index them? Rating, probably not. There are few categories, and moreover when you are looking for a film suitable for a teenage audience, there is no reason to exclude 'family' films. When you specify a rating, it usually means "this rating, or something suitable for an even wider audience". In other words, it won't be very selective and an index probably won't improve performance. For marks, it's a different matter. The problem with marks is that their significance depends on the number of people who have assigned a mark. If only one person rated a film and assigned it 10, the top mark, it's not as meaningful as an average of 8.7 based on the ratings of thousands of people. We cannot dissociate the mark from the number of raters. We could contemplate an index on (mark, number_of_raters) that could be used on conditions such as

```
where mark >= 8
  and number_of_raters >= 200
```

However, the index that is most likely to be useful is an index on genre - if there are enough of them, or if some genres are rare enough to be significant.

3. *The following queries all return information about the Italian films of the 1960s stored in table movies. I remind you that there is a unique constraint on (country, year_released, title) in this order, and no index other than the index associated with this constraint needs to be considered here. Can you rank the queries from the one that makes the best use of the existing index to the one that makes the worst use of it (there are ties)?*

   Query A

   ```
   select year_released, title
   from movies
   where year_released like '196%'
     and country = 'it'
   ```

   Query B

   ```
   select year_released, title
   from movies
   where year_released >= 1960
     and year_released < 1970
     and country = 'it'
   ```

   Query C

   ```
   select year_released, title
   from movies
   where upper(country) = 'IT'
     and year_released between 1960 and 1969
   ```

   Query D

   ```
   select year_released, title
   from movies
   where 'italy' like country || '%'
     and year_released in (1960, 1961, 1962, 1963, 1964,
                           1965, 1966, 1967, 1968, 1969)
   ```

   Best usage of the index (uses the two first columns): query B.

   Second best usage: query A. It uses the first column in the index. However, it implicitly converts *year_released* to a character string in the comparison.

   For queries C and D, it depends on the collation and the optimizer; if the collation is not case-sensitive and the optimizer understands that **upper()** changes nothing, query C will be as good as query B. If data is case sensitive,

upper() will prevent the use of the index and query C will be less efficient than query B The question with query D is whether the optimizer will be able to understand that

```
'italy' like country || '%'
```

is the same as

```
country = left('italy', 2)
```

You may be lucky but you are taking a risk, including the risk that your query is quick with some versions of the DBMS and slow with other versions. In all cases, the safe way to write the query is query B.

4. *The following queries on table* people *retrieve those whose surname starts with S and whose first name starts with R. I remind you that there is a unique constraint on (surname, first_name), in this order. – read* ***substring()*** *instead of* ***substr()*** *if you are using SQL Server. Index-wise, which query(-ies) do you prefer?*

Query A

```
select *
from people
where substr(surname, 1, 1) = 'S'
  and substr(first_name, 1, 1) = 'R'
```

Query B

```
select *
from people
where surname like 'S%'
 and substr(first_name, 1, 1) = 'R'
```

Query C

```
select *
from people
where surname like 'S%'
 and first_name like 'R%'
```

Query D

```
select *
from people
where substr(surname, 1, 1) = 'S'
  and first_name like 'R%'
```

Query E

```
select *
from people
where first_name like 'R%'
  and surname >= 'S'
  and surname < 'T'
```

Query C and E are the best ones. With most products, using **substr()**, even to retrieve the leftmost character, disables the index. Damage is limited with query B, as **substr()** is only applied to the second column in the index. Query A and D are equivalent, index-wise.

Chapter 10: Views, Privileges and Security

1. *Create a view called people_alive that, as its name implies, only shows people who are alive.*

```
create view people_alive
as select *
   from people
   where died is null
```

   Not much to say here...

2. *Create a view that displays the movie title, the surname of the director and the release year for all movies from a European country.*

   Note that the country isn't requested in the view but the country is part of the primary key. The fact that the country is a European one isn't, strictly speaking, enough. I am therefore adding the country name to the view (if you don't want it later on, don't select it from the view – but then use **distinct** to prevent nasty surprises).

```
create view european_films as
select m.title,
       v.surname,
       m.year_released,
       c.country_name as country
from countries c
     inner join movies m
     on m.country = c.country_code
     and c.continent = 'EUROPE'      ← It's here to filter early. It can
                                       also be in the where clause.
     left outer join                 ← Director not necessarily known
      (select cr.movieid,            ← Retrieve all directors
              p.surname
       from credits cr
            inner join people p
            on p.peopleid = cr.peopleid
            and cr.credited_as = 'D') v
     on v.movieid = m.movieid
```

3. *For each one of the following views, assuming no **instead of** trigger that would do tricky things behind your back, would it be possible or not possible, to insert new rows through the view:*

```
create view v1 as
select title, country
from movies
where year_released>1980
```

```
create viev v2 as
select born, count(*) number_of_births
from people
group by born

create view v3 as
select peopleid, surname, born
from people
where died is not null

create view v4 as
select peopleid, surname, born
from people
where died is not null
with check option
```

v1: No, because the year of release is mandatory and, if it's used for restricting the rows, it doesn't appear in the view.
v2: No, because the view returns an aggregate.
v3: yes. The columns that are omitted (*first_name* and *died*) aren't mandatory but if you insert a row, you won't see it through the view as you will insert null into *died*.
v4: No, **check option** prevents insertion of a row that the view wouldn't display.

4. *One important data dictionary view that I haven't talked about in this chapter, is the view that contains all the columns (for tables and views).*

   In information_schema.columns for SQL Server and MySQL you find columns such as table_catalog, table_schema, table_name, column_name, ordinal_position (integer) and data_type.

   For DB2, in syscat.columns the value of table_catalog is implicit and the equivalent for the other columns are respectively tabschema, tabname, colname, colno, typename.

   For Oracle it's user_tab_columns; there is no equivalent of table_catalog, the schema is implicitly the current one and you find table_name, column_name, column_id and data_type.

   Using the view of your choice, write a query that returns table name, column name and data type for columns that have the same name but different data types in different tables (which can be a design error).

NOTE To be exhaustive, one should also compare lengths of varchar columns and precision of numbers but it's not requested in this exercise.

The first step consists in identifying the names of columns for which several distinct data types appear in the data dictionary (in bold), then the result is joined another time to the view that describes columns and ordered.

With *information_schema*:

```
select c2.column_name,
       c2.data_type,
       c2.table_name,
       c2.table_schema,
       c2.table_catalog
from (select column_name
      from information_schema.columns
      group by column_name
      having count(distinct data_type) > 1) c1
     inner join information_schema.columns c2
     on c2.column_name = c1.column_name
order by c2.column_name,
         c2.table_name,
         c2.table_schema,
         c2.table_catalog
```

With *syscat*:

```
select c2.colname,
       c2.typename,
       c2.tabname,
       c2.tabschema
from (select colname
      from syscat.columns
      group by colname
      having count(distinct typename) > 1) c1
     inner join syscat.columns c2
     on c2.colname = c1.colname
order by c2.colname,
         c2.tabname,
         c2.tabschema
```

As many oddities are spotted in the multiple data dictionaries maintained in DB2, it's probably better to limit the query to the current schema, which is equivalent to the query (which follows) with the *user_* view:

```
select c2.colname,
       c2.typename,
       c2.tabname,
       c2.tabschema
from (select colname
      from syscat.columns
      where tabschema = current schema      ← Note the restriction
      group by colname
      having count(distinct typename) > 1) c1
     inner join syscat.columns c2
     on c2.colname = c1.colname
where c2.tabschema = current schema         ← Restricted again
order by c2.colname,
         c2.tabname,
         c2.tabschema
```

With the *user_* view :

```
select c2.column_name,
       c2.data_type,
       c2.table_name
from (select column_name
      from user_tab_columns
      group by column_name
      having count(distinct data_type) > 1) c1
    inner join user_tab_columns c2
    on c2.column_name = c1.column_name
order by c2.column_name,
         c2.table_name
```

5. *Starting with the data dictionary query shown in this chapter which lists indexes, write a query that lists all single column indexes for which a multi-column index starting with the same column exists (you can get rid of the single-column index, as the multi-column index can be used for the same purpose).*

> *NOTE Unnecessary indexes are often encountered when people generate schemas with design tools that systematically index foreign keys. When the leading column of the primary key also happens to be a foreign key, as is the case for table credits, you usually end up with an index you can drop without regret.*

The data dictionary query that lists indexes returns, for all DBMS products, columns to which I have given exactly the same name with all products:

- *table_name*, the name of the indexed table,
- *u*, an indicator that says whether the index is unique and that I won't need here,
- *pos*, the position of each column in the index,
- *column_name*

> NOTE FOR POSTGRESQL The PostgreSQL version of the view returns all columns on the same row. To have one column per row, please check the two product-specific functions **string_to_array()** and **unnest()**. Alternatively for this exercise you can simply consider the first column name and the number of columns in the index.

As my purpose was only to see which columns were indexed and in which position, I didn't return the index name, which is irrelevant to a software developer. In the particular case of the present exercise, I need the index name: I want to identify indexes that I can safely drop. I'll let you drop and recreate view *v_indexing* and add to the columns that it returns the name of each index as *index_name*. I'll suppose, for simplicity and convenience, that we have created, after removing the **order by** clause, a view named

v_indexing, based on the modified query (you don't need to create a view; you could use a nested query in the **from** clause as well), which will allow me, for once, to have a single query independent from the underlying DBMS.
With the view, I can write my query. First I need to find out which are the columns that can be found in first position of several indexes on the same table:

```
select table_name,
       column_name
from v_indexing
where pos = 1
group by table_name,
         column_name
having count(*) > 1
```

By joining this result to *v_indexing* again, I can get the names of the exact indexes on the table, which have the same column in the first position:

```
select b.index_name,
       b.table_name
from (select table_name,
             column_name
      from v_indexing
      where pos = 1
      group by table_name,
               column_name
      having count(*) > 1) a
     inner join v_indexing b
     on b.table_name = a.table_name
     and b.column_name = a.column_name
     and b.pos = 1
```

Among these, I can safely get rid of indexes with a single column (the case is less clear-cut otherwise):

```
select b.index_name,
       b.table_name
from (select table_name,
             column_name
      from v_indexing
      where pos = 1
      group by table_name,
               column_name
      having count(*) > 1) a
     inner join v_indexing b
     on b.table_name = a.table_name
     and b.column_name = a.column_name
     and b.pos = 1
where not exists (select null
                  from v_indexing c
                  where c.table_name = b.table_name
                  and c.index_name = b.index_name
                  and c.pos > 1)
```

Create a useless one-column index and this query should single it out...

Procedural Variants

Appendix

D

Procedural extensions are a peripheral area to SQL and it's probably in procedures that differences between the various DBMS products are the most glaring. I have chosen in Chapter 8, to illustrate functions, procedures and triggers with only one product each time - what follows is commented code showing you how to write the same thing with the other products.

Simple Function to Format Names

PostgreSQL

The syntax used by PostgreSQL for stored user-defined functions is rather close to the syntax used by Oracle and shown in Chapter 8.
However, where Oracle wants

```
return <data type>
```

PostgreSQL wants, like all other products I am talking of in this book, an **s** at **returns**:

```
returns <data type>
```

After **as** PostgreSQL delimits the body of the query between a pair of identical tags, usually *$$*, the last one being followed by **language plpgsql** (since, remember, functions can be written in different languages, of which the procedural extension to SQL is just one). Those tags, which are specific to PostgreSQL, act like a wrapper to the actual body of the function. Semi-colons between the tags are not understood, as they would normally be, as a sign that the statement is complete and must be sent to the server. For both Oracle and PostgreSQL the body of the function is between **begin** and **end** and limited in that case, to a simple **return** (without an **s** in both cases) followed by the expression.

Simple user-defined function, PostgreSQL version

```
create function full_name(p_fname varchar, p_sname varchar)  ① Parameters
returns varchar          ② Data type of what the function returns
as $$     ← Start of the function body wrapper
begin
  return case                      ③ Returned expression
           when p_fname is null then ''
           else p_fname || ' '
         end ||
```

```
          case position('(' in p_sname)
            when 0 then p_sname
             else trim(')' from substr(p_sname,
                                       position('(' in p_sname)
                                                          + 1))
                       || ' ' || trim(substr(p_sname,
                                            1,
                                            position('(' in p_sname)
                                                          - 1))
          end;        <- End of the 'case' clause
end;        <- End of the function
$$ language plpgsql;  <- End of the function body wrapper
```

Like with other products, parameters ① must be given special names; as with Oracle, lengths don't need to be specified. Like most products, PostgreSQL says **returns** with an s when defining the data type of the returned value ② but **return** without an s when it actually returns it ③.

MySQL and DB2

The syntax for creating functions with DB2 is very similar to the syntax used with MySQL. As with Oracle and PostgreSQL, arguments are defined in a function as a name followed by a data type but in that case you need to specify the length of a **varchar** (this is also true for the value that is returned). You give the type of what is returned with **returns**, followed by the data type, immediately followed by the body of the function between **begin** and **end**. In this particular case however, the function has no real 'body' and you only need to return the expression, and neither MySQL nor DB2 requires any **begin** ... **end**; the syntax of the expression itself varies significantly between the two products, as functions and string concatenation are different.
If with MySQL, you are creating the function with the `mysql` client you must first change the delimiter that says that a statement is finished and must be sent to the server. You can redefine it from the default semi-colon to something else, for instance $$, by issuing:

```
delimiter $$
```

Once you have entered the function, you type `$$`, hit the return key, the function is sent and created and you can change the delimiter back to a semi-colon.

Simple user-defined function, MySQL version

```
create function full_name(p_fname varchar(30),
                          p_sname varchar(30))       ① Parameters
returns varchar(61)         ② Data type of what the function returns
return concat(case        ③ Returned expression
                when p_fname is null then ''
                else concat(p_fname, ' ')
              end,
```

```
            case position('(' in p_sname)
              when 0 then p_sname
              else concat(trim(')' from substr(p_sname,
                                            position('(' in p_sname)
                                                   + 1)),
                              ' ', trim(substr(p_sname,
                                             1,
                                            position('(' in p_sname)
                                                   - 1)))
            end);
```

The length of parameters ①, (with a special name) and of the value returned by the function ②, must be specified as they would be when creating a table. As the function returns only an expression ③, it isn't necessary to put the **return** statement between **begin** and **end**.

Only the expression returned is different with DB2:

Simple user-defined function, DB2 version

```
create function full_name(p_fname varchar(30), p_sname varchar(30))
returns varchar(61)
return case
         when length(coalesce(p_fname, '')) = 0 then ''
         else p_fname || ' '
       end ||
       case locate('(', p_sname)
         when 0 then p_sname
         else trim(')' from substr(p_sname, locate('(', p_sname) + 1))
                || ' '
                || trim(substr(p_sname, 1, locate('(', p_sname) - 1))
       end;
/ <- with clpplus a slash sends the function to the server
```

Unlike MySQL, there is no need to change the command terminator in a script. If you are using clpplus, the same conventions apply as with Oracle's SQL*Plus: **create function** deactivates the command-line client's understanding of a semi-colon as a signal to send what has been typed to the database server. To signify that the function is complete and can be created, you simply type a slash at the beginning of the line and press *<return>*.

SQL Server

SQL Server has a peculiarity: arguments and variable names in a procedure must have a name that starts with @. Like with MySQL and DB2 specifying the length of **varchar** columns is mandatory but **begin** and **end** are required, as with Oracle and PostgreSQL, even for a very simple function.

NOTE If you don't specify the length of a varchar parameter, SQL Server generates no error but assumes that the length is one character.

Simple user-defined function, SQL Server version

```
create function full_name(@fname varchar(30),
                          @sname varchar(30))      ① Parameters
returns varchar(61)    ② Data type of what the function returns
begin
  return case
           when @fname is null then ''
           else @fname + ' '
         end
         + case charindex('(', @sname, 1)
             when 0 then @sname
             else replace(substring(@sname,
                                    1 + charindex('(', @sname , 1),
                                    len(@sname)), ')', ' ')
                  + rtrim(substring(@sname, 1,
                                    charindex('(', @sname, 1) - 1))
           end;
end;
```

The name of function and procedure parameters must start with @ with SQL Server ①, which ensure that they can be safely used in SQL statements if need be. The length of what is passed must be specified as in a "create table" statement and the length of what is returned ②, must be specified as well.

Simple Procedure To Register Films

Oracle

We need one variable in the procedure, *n_people*, to count how many names are provided, using the syntax

```
select count(surname)
into n_people                          ← Note
from (select p_director_sn as surname
      from dual
      union all
      select p_actor1_sn as surname
      from dual
      union all
      select p_actor2_sn as surname
      from dual) specified_people;
```

(**select** ... **into** ... is a construct that you retrieve in most procedural extensions to SQL. You can retrieve several values from the same row with `into variable1, variable2, ...` It only works if the query returns a single row.)

I am also going to use another variable, *n_movieid*, to store the sequence value attached to the film after I have successfully inserted a new row into table *movies*. I assign the value to the variable with

```
n_movieid := movies_seq.currval;
```

It would be quite possible to refer to *movies_seq.currval* everywhere I refer to *n_movieid*, which is shorter to type and more convenient.
Variables are declared before the main **begin ... end** block that defines the function, just after **as**.

> NOTE Unlike PostgreSQL, there is no **declare** keyword in an Oracle function or procedure; however you may encounter what is called "anonymous PL/SQL blocks", in other words, procedures with no name that aren't stored on the server, in which the first keyword is either **begin** if no variables are needed, or **declare** followed by variable declarations.

The number of rows affected by the last **insert**, **update** or **delete** is retrieved from a system variable named **sql%rowcount**. This value is compared with the number of people to insert in an **if ... then ... end if** block:

```
if sql%rowcount <> n_people
then
  raise_application_error(-20001, 'Some people couldn''t be found');
end if;
```

Errors are generated by a call to **raise_application_error()** that takes two arguments, first a negative number that is the code associated to the error (user-defined codes are in the -20000 range) and second the error message. A call to **raise_application_error()** aborts the procedure; it also automatically generates a **rollback**.
You can commit in an Oracle procedure, which is done here. Transactions are started automatically with Oracle.

Simple movie registration, Oracle version

```
create procedure movie_registration
          (p_title         varchar2,
           p_country_name varchar2,
           p_year          number,
           p_director_fn  varchar2,
           p_director_sn  varchar2,
           p_actor1_fn    varchar2,
           p_actor1_sn    varchar2,
           p_actor2_fn    varchar2,
           p_actor2_sn    varchar2)
as
  n_movieid  number;          <- Variable declaration
  n_people   number;
begin
  insert into movies(movieid, title, country, year_released)  <- Insert the film
  select movies_seq.nextval, p_title, country_code, p_year
  from countries
  where country_name = p_country_name;
```

```
    if sql%rowcount = 0                     <- Check we inserted something
    then
      raise_application_error(-20000,
                              'country not found in table COUNTRIES');
    end if;
    n_movieid := movies_seq.currval;  <- Retrieve the movie identifier
    select count(surname)              <- Count people to insert
    into n_people
    from (select p_director_sn as surname
          from dual
          union all
          select p_actor1_sn as surname
          from dual
          union all
          select p_actor2_sn as surname
          from dual) specified_people
    where surname is not null;          <- Dispensable but doesn't hurt
    insert into credits(movieid, peopleid, credited_as)      <- Insert credits
    select n_movieid, people.peopleid, provided.credited_as
    from (select coalesce(p_director_fn, '*') as first_name,
                 p_director_sn as surname,
                 'D' as credited_as
          from dual
          union all
          select coalesce(p_actor1_fn, '*') as first_name,
                 p_actor1_sn as surname,
                 'A' as credited_as
          from dual
          union all
          select coalesce(p_actor2_fn, '*') as first_name,
                 p_actor2_sn as surname,
                 'A' as credited_as
          from dual) provided
         inner join people
           on people.surname = provided.surname
          and coalesce(people.first_name, '*') = provided.first_name
    where provided.surname is not null;
    if sql%rowcount <> n_people       <- Check everything was OK
    then
      raise_application_error(-20001, 'Some people couldn''t be found');
    end if;
    commit;
  end;
  /    <- Send to the database server (with sqlplus)
```

An environment such as SQL*Plus allows us to call a procedure with

```
execute procedure_name(...)
```

It needs to be written on a single line (or using a dash at the end of the line to indicate that the command continues on the next line). Execute is actually an SQL*Plus command and is in fact a short-hand notation for the only proper way to ask an

Oracle server to run a procedure, which is inside a **begin** ... **end** block (in which you can of course have other statements):

```
begin
   movie_registration('The Adventures of Robin Hood',
                      'United States', 1938,
                      'Michael', 'Curtiz',
                      'Errol', 'Flynn',
                      null, null);
end;
/
```

PostgreSQL

Postgres doesn't know about "procedures" but it knows about functions that return nothing, which is specified by **returns void**. The body of the function is surrounded by an arbitrary tag (*$$* is commonly used) that inhibits the understanding of a semi-colon as a sign to send the command for execution to the SQL engine. Like with Oracle, variables are declared in a special section that precedes the main **begin ... end** block that defines the function; in the case of PostgreSQL this section must start with **declare**.

We need three variables:

- one variable, *n_movieid*, to store the value of *movieid* after inserting a new row in table *movies*, a value retrieved by calling **lastval()** using the syntax

  ```
  n_movieid := lastval();
  ```

  (alternatively it would be possible to refer to the underlying sequence as with Oracle).
- one variable, *n_people*, to count how many names are provided, using the syntax

  ```
  select count(surname)
  into n_people
  from (select p_director_sn as surname
        union all
        select p_actor1_sn as surname
        union all
        select p_actor2_sn as surname) specified_people;
  ```
- and finally one variable, *n_rowcount*, to retrieve how many rows were inserted, using

  ```
  get diagnostics n_rowcount = row_count;
  ```

  This construct to retrieve the number of rows affected by the last **insert**, **update** or **delete** operation, is also used by DB2 and MySQL (5.6 and above). It is supposed to be "standard", whatever that means in the baroque context of procedural extensions to SQL.

As you see, you have three different variables and you have three different ways to assign a value to each of these variables. I don't know who had the bright idea for the

get diagnostics syntax but I would have far, far preferred a function like *get_diagnostics('row_count')* and a regular assignment.
The variable *n_rowcount* allows us to control with an **if** followed by a condition, if something didn't go as planned. When that is the case, we execute what is between **then** and **end if**, in that case a single statement that generates an error:

```
raise exception 'Error message'
```

Transaction statements such as **start** (or **begin**) **transaction** and **commit** or **rollback** have no place in a PostgreSQL procedure; generating an error automatically cancels what the function has successfully done since it was last called, and causes the function to return to the caller.

Simple movie registration, PostgreSQL version

```
create function movie_registration      ← PostgreSQL only knows functions ...
           (p_title         varchar,
            p_country_name varchar,
            p_year          int,
            p_director_fn  varchar,
            p_director_sn  varchar,
            p_actor1_fn    varchar,
            p_actor1_sn    varchar,
            p_actor2_fn    varchar,
            p_actor2_sn    varchar)
returns void                            ← ... but some functions return nothing
as $$            ← Start tag for the wrapper
declare                ← Start of declarations
  n_rowcount  int;
  n_movieid   int;
  n_people    int;
begin
  insert into movies(title, country, year_released)
  select p_title, country_code, p_year
  from countries
  where country_name = p_country_name;
  get diagnostics n_rowcount = row_count;  ← Retrieve how many rows were inserted
  if n_rowcount = 0
  then
    raise exception 'country not found in table COUNTRIES';
  end if;
  n_movieid := lastval();        ← Save the movie identifier
  select count(surname)          ← Count the people
  into n_people
  from (select p_director_sn as surname
        union all
        select p_actor1_sn as surname
        union all
        select p_actor2_sn as surname) specified_people
  where surname is not null;     ← Dispensable but doesn't hurt
  --
```

```
  insert into credits(movieid, peopleid, credited_as)    ← Insert credits
  select n_movieid, people.peopleid, provided.credited_as
  from (select coalesce(p_director_fn, '*') as first_name,
               p_director_sn as surname,
               'D' as credited_as
        union all
        select coalesce(p_actor1_fn, '*') as first_name,
               p_actor1_sn as surname,
               'A' as credited_as
        union all
        select coalesce(p_actor2_fn, '*') as first_name,
               p_actor2_sn as surname,
               'A' as credited_as) provided
       inner join people
         on people.surname = provided.surname
        and coalesce(people.first_name, '*') = provided.first_name
  where provided.surname is not null;
  get diagnostics n_rowcount = row_count;
  if n_rowcount != n_people       ← Check everything is OK
  then
    raise exception 'Some people couldn''t be found';
  end if;
end;
$$ language plpgsql;      ← End tag for the wrapper
```

There are two ways to call a PostgreSQL procedure (void function).

- If it is called from another function you call it with:

```
perform movie_registration('The Adventures of Robin Hood',
                           'United States', 1938,
                           'Michael', 'Curtiz',
                           'Errol', 'Flynn',
                           null, null);
```

- Otherwise you simply run

```
select movie_registration('The Adventures of Robin Hood',
                           'United States', 1938,
                           'Michael', 'Curtiz',
                           'Errol', 'Flynn',
                           null, null);
```

  which returns null - or an error message if anything fails.

MySQL

We need, like with PostgreSQL, three variables:

- one variable, *n_movieid*, to store the value of *movieid* when I have inserted a new row in table *movies*, a value which I retrieve with function **last_insert_id()** using the syntax

```
set n_movieid = last_insert_id();
```

- one variable, *n_people*, to count how many names are provided, with

```
select count(name)
into n_people
```

```
from (select p_director as name
      union all
      select p_actor1 as name
      union all
      select p_actor2 as name) specified_people;
```

- and finally one variable, *n_rowcount*, to retrieve how many rows were inserted, using either function **row_count()** in the same fashion as **last_insert_id()** or, for MySQL 5.6 and above

```
get diagnostics n_rowcount = row_count;
```

  a construct shared with PostgreSQL and DB2.

Unlike what happens in Oracle and PostgreSQL, variable declaration with MySQL (and DB2 and SQL Server) occurs inside the main **begin ... end** block and each declaration is preceded by the **declare** keyword.
The number of rows inserted into *credits* will be tested for inequality against the number of people provided to the function. With MySQL and all products except SQL Server, statements to execute whenever an **if** test succeeds, are between **if** *condition* **then ... end if**; success of the test means in that case, failure of the operation and I generate an error with

```
signal sqlstate 'xxxxx'
       set message_text = 'message text';
```

xxxxx are five characters (digits often but not always) that indicate the type of error. The first two characters indicate a 'class of errors' and with MySQL *02* indicates that we haven't found what we were looking for, which is the case here. It is important to follow established standards with error codes and messages; very often whenever you issue a message it's automatically logged somewhere. Logged messages and error codes are analyzed by monitoring programs used by people who check that production is working smoothly.
The **signal** statement also interrupts the procedure and we must roll back the explicitly started transaction before calling it.

Simple movie registration, MySQL version

```
delimiter $$
create procedure movie_registration
           (p_title         varchar(200),     ← Specify parameter length
            p_country_name varchar(50),
            p_year          int,
            p_director_fn  varchar(30),
            p_director_sn  varchar(30),
            p_actor1_fn    varchar(30),
            p_actor1_sn    varchar(30),
            p_actor2_fn    varchar(30),
            p_actor2_sn    varchar(30))
begin
  declare n_rowcount  int;     ← Variable declaration after "begin"
```

```
    declare n_movieid   int;
    declare n_people    int;
    --
    start transaction;           ← Explicit transaction start
    insert into movies(title, country, year_released)
    select p_title, country_code, p_year
    from countries
    where country_name = p_country_name;
    set n_rowcount = row_count();       ① Retrieve how many rows were inserted
    if n_rowcount = 0
    then
      rollback;             ② End transaction
      signal sqlstate '02000'     ③ Generate an error
             set message_text = 'country not found in table COUNTRIES';
    end if;
    set n_movieid = last_insert_id(); ← Save the movie identifier
    select count(surname)             ← Count the people
    into n_people
    from (select p_director_sn as surname
          union all
          select p_actor1_sn as surname
          union all
          select p_actor2_sn as surname) specified_people
     where surname is not null;    ← Not necessary but doesn't hurt
    insert into credits(movieid, peopleid, credited_as)  ← Insert credits
    select n_movieid, people.peopleid, provided.credited_as
    from (select coalesce(p_director_fn, '*') as first_name,
                 p_director_sn as surname,
                 'D' as credited_as
          union all
          select coalesce(p_actor1_fn, '*') as first_name,
                 p_actor1_sn as surname,
                 'A' as credited_as
          union all
          select coalesce(p_actor2_fn, '*') as first_name,
                 p_actor2_sn as surname,
                 'A' as credited_as) provided
         inner join people
           on people.surname = provided.surname
          and coalesce(people.first_name, '*') = provided.first_name
    where provided.surname is not null;
    set n_rowcount = row_count();
    if n_rowcount != n_people     ← Check that everything is OK
    then
      rollback;
      signal sqlstate '02000'     ③ Generate an error
             set message_text = 'Some people couldn''t be found';
    end if;
    commit;
  end;
$$
```

Starting with MySQL 5.6, retrieving the number of inserted rows ①, can also be performed with **get diagnostics** like PostgreSQL and DB2. If no rows were inserted, the transaction must be terminated ②, even if in truth there is nothing to undo. Please note ③, that **signal** appeared in MySQL 5.5 and you may find in older versions (or in code written by people who learned the ropes with older versions), other ways to generate an error.

Generating an Error with MySQL

signal appeared in MySQL 5.5. With older versions you could define a char(2) variable *c_country_code* and run something such as

```
select country_code
into c_country_code
from countries
where country_name = p_country
```

It would generate a similar error to the first **signal** at the cost of an extra query. Alternatively, in your procedure you can call a non-existent procedure, for instance replace **signal** by

```
call dummy_not_found;
```

In that case, you need to declare at the beginning of the procedure, just after the declaration of variables, a handler to trap the error generated by a call to a non-existent procedure, which you identify by the *sqlstate* value 42000:

```
declare exit handler for sqlstate '42000'
   select 'Expected data not found';
```

The handler is the "clean" way to generate an error. The flip-side is that your procedure can generate only one user-defined error message. The dirty way to generate an error is to have no handler but give to the non-existent procedure a name that <u>is</u> the error message. A call to this procedure will then result into something looking like:

```
ERROR 1305 (42000): PROCEDURE test.Error_You_shouldnt_have_done_that does not exist
```

Not elegant, but the message gets across.

signal allows us to return much more precise (and helpful) error messages.

Once the procedure is created, you run it as follows:

```
call movie_registration('The Adventures of Robin Hood',
                        'United States', 1938,
                        'Michael', 'Curtiz',
                        'Errol', 'Flynn',
                        null, null);
```

DB2

The syntax is close to the syntax used by MySQL and I'll mostly point out the peculiarities of DB2. The first peculiarity is that **begin** must be preceded by **language sql** as stored procedures can be written in several languages. I use with DB2, explicit sequences as with Oracle,; the reason is that I make an intense use of **insert ... select**, with which the function in DB2 that is supposed to return the last generated identifier, returns null. A **select** always requires with DB2 (as with Oracle) a **from** clause and for counting how many people names were provided, you must refer to *sysibm.sysdummy1*.

DB2 shares with PostgreSQL and versions of MySQL greater than 5.5, the **get diagnostics** construct to retrieve how many rows were affected by the last statement. Like with MySQL I generate an error with

```
signal sqlstate 'xxxxx'
       set message_text = 'message text';
```

where *xxxxx* are five characters that indicate the type of error, the first two being a general "error class". I use a class '70' that is available for user-defined errors.

NOTE The sqlstate patterns in DB2 are rather nightmarish.

The **signal** statement also interrupts the procedure and I roll back changes before issuing it. You will notice that there is no explicit beginning of transaction: it is implicit with DB2 (as with Oracle.)

Simple movie registration, DB2 version

```
create procedure movie_registration
          (p_title        varchar(200),
           p_country_name varchar(50),
           p_year         int,
           p_director_fn  varchar(30),
           p_director_sn  varchar(30),
           p_actor1_fn    varchar(30),
           p_actor1_sn    varchar(30),
           p_actor2_fn    varchar(30),
           p_actor2_sn    varchar(30))
language sql           <- A language mention is required with DB2
begin
  declare n_rowcount  int;
  declare n_movieid   int;
  declare n_people    int;
  --
Implicit transaction starts here
  ↓
  insert into movies(movieid, title, country, year_released)
  select next value for movies_seq, p_title, country_code, p_year
  from countries
```

```
    where country_name = p_country_name;
    get diagnostics n_rowcount = ROW_COUNT;
    if n_rowcount = 0
    then
      rollback;
      signal sqlstate '70000'
             set message_text = 'country not found in table COUNTRIES';
    end if;
    set n_movieid = previous value for movies_seq;
    select count(surname)
    into n_people
    from (select p_director_sn as surname
          from sysibm.sysdummy1                    <- Dummy table required
          union all
          select p_actor1_sn as surname
          from sysibm.sysdummy1
          union all
          select p_actor2_sn as surname
          from sysibm.sysdummy1) specified_people
    where surname is not null;
    insert into credits(movieid, peopleid, credited_as)
    select n_movieid, people.peopleid, provided.credited_as
    from (select coalesce(p_director_fn, '') as first_name,
                         ① Convert null to empty string
                 p_director_sn as surname,
                 'D' as credited_as
          from sysibm.sysdummy1
          union all
          select coalesce(p_actor1_fn, '') as first_name,
                 p_actor1_sn as surname,
                 'A' as credited_as
          from sysibm.sysdummy1
          union all
          select coalesce(p_actor2_fn, '') as first_name,
                 p_actor2_sn as surname,
                 'A' as credited_as
          from sysibm.sysdummy1) provided
         inner join people
           on people.surname = provided.surname
          and people.first_name = provided.first_name
    where provided.surname is not null;
    get diagnostics n_rowcount = ROW_COUNT;
    if n_rowcount != n_people
    then
      rollback;
      signal sqlstate '70000'
             set message_text = 'Some people couldn''t be found';
    end if;
    commit;
  end;
  /      <- Send to the server (with clpplus)
```

In the sample database the unique constraint makes the first name mandatory; instead of null we store an empty string, which is why a null parameter must be transformed into an empty string ①.

The procedure is called like with MySQL:

```
call movie_registration('The Adventures of Robin Hood',
                        'United States', 1938,
                        'Michael', 'Curtiz',
                        'Errol', 'Flynn',
                        null, null)
```

Exception Handling

Exception handling is illustrated by a minor improvement to movie registration – unique constraint violation is ignored when adding a film, which allows linking more than one director and more than two actors to a movie by calling *movie_registration()* several times for the same film.

Oracle and PostgreSQL

You must enclose critical sections where errors can occur between **begin ... end** keywords and add before the **end**, a new section called **exception**, in which you analyze the error that was generated and try to handle it. As a procedure or function is by construction between a pair of **begin ... end** keywords, in many cases you have a single global **exception** clause for the stored procedure but you can have the exception handling closer to where errors have strong odds of occurring. When an error happens, execution jumps to the **exception** clause of the current **begin ... end** block. If the error is handled by this clause, processing continues in sequence after the **end** that terminates the block in which the exception was processed. If not, or if there is no **exception** clause in the block, the exception ripples out and is propagated to the nearest enclosing **begin ... end**, or to the caller if the exception ripples across the full procedure without being caught.

To ignore duplicate attempts to register the same film in Oracle, I need to enclose the following section of the *movie_registration()* procedure in a block with an exception clause:

```
insert into movies(movieid, title, country, year_released)
select movies_seq.nextval, p_title, country_code, p_year
from countries
where country_name = p_country;
if sql%rowcount = 0
then
raise_application_error(-20000, 'country not found in table COUNTRIES');
end if;
n_movieid := movies_seq.currval;
```

which gives:

```
begin
   insert into movies(movieid, title, country, year_released)
   select movies_seq.nextval, p_title, country_code, p_year
   from countries
   where country_name = p_country;
```

```
    if sql%rowcount = 0
    then
      raise_application_error(-20000,
                              'country not found in table COUNTRIES');
    end if;
    n_movieid := movies_seq.currval;
exception                              ← It happens here
    when dup_val_on_index then         ← the exception that occurred is tested
         select m.movieid
         into n_movieid
         from movies m
              inner join countries c
                 on c.country_code = m.country
         where m.title = p_title
           and m.year_released = p_year
           and c.country_name = p_country;
end;
```

The construct is the same with PostgreSQL, with the difference that the name of the exception is a logical *unique_violation* rather than the mysterious *dup_val_on_index* of Oracle.

NOTE The name of the Oracle exception refers to how unique constraints are implemented, as you will see in Chapter 9.

When the **insert** statement succeeds, the **exception** block is skipped and processing continues in sequence with the insertion into table *credits*. If the **insert** statement fails, processing jumps to the **exception** block and if the exception that occurred is processed in this block, processing resumes after the block, with the insertion into table *credits*. Otherwise, the error ripples to the nearest enclosing block and its **exception** block if there is one, as long as the error isn't caught. If you try to insert a movie for an unknown country, the error that is raised will take execution to the **exception** block too but as the only exception that is handled is the violation of unique constraints, it will ripple out.

DB2 and MySQL

MySQL has extended the SQL language so as to specify inside an **insert** statement, that primary key violations can be ignored but it also shares with DB2's SQL PL, a more general way of managing errors through the declaration of *handlers*. A handler is declared at the beginning of the procedure with the variables and defines a course of action to take when an error occurs (the error is defined by either its error number, its *sqlstate* value, or a condition name arbitrarily assigned by the developer). To ignore an error, you can add to the beginning of your procedure

```
declare continue handler for sqlstate '...'
begin
     ...
end;
```

and specify between **begin** and **end**, operations to perform (which may be as simple as incrementing a counter, or retrieving an identifier). Instead of **continue**, you can have **exit**, which allows some error management before quitting.

Audit Trigger

Oracle

The name of the trigger is followed by either **before** or **after**, the triggering operation(s) (several operations can be listed, for instance `after insert or update or delete` as in this example) and **on**, followed by the name of the table to which the trigger is attached. By default a trigger is only fired once per statement and for a logging trigger, you must specify **for each row** before the **begin** that starts the trigger body. As the trigger can be fired by several events, we must check inside the trigger true/false values **inserting**, **updating** or **deleting** to know which event occurred.

Inside the **insert** statement, information about the current user is retrieved with the special **sys_context()** built-in function; the predefined **USERENV** context (the name of which is passed as first parameter) contains much information. The previous value of the current row must be referred to as *:old* and the new one as *:new* inside the statements; the colons are mandatory (Oracle is the only product to require them, although DB2 has an Oracle-compatible mode in which references are identical). It's an error to refer to *:old* or *:new* in a trigger that is fired only once per statement (even if the statement affects a single row).

Audit trigger, Oracle version

```
create trigger people_trg
after insert or update or delete on people  ← The trigger is fired by multiple events
for each row
begin
  if updating   ① Event control
  then
    insert into people_audit(auditid,
                             peopleid,
                             type_of_change,
                             column_name,
                             old_value,
                             new_value,
                             changed_by,
                             time_changed)
    select people_audit_seq.nextval,        ← Sequence required with Oracle
           peopleid, 'U', column_name, old_value, new_value,
           sys_context('USERENV', 'OS_USER')||'@'||        ← Auditing data
                    sys_context('USERENV', 'IP_ADDRESS'), ← Auditing data
           current_timestamp
    from (select :old.peopleid   peopleid,
                 'first_name'    column_name,
                 :old.first_name old_value,
```

```
                :new.first_name new_value
          from dual
          where coalesce(:old.first_name, '*')
                      <> coalesce(:new.first_name, '*')
          union all
          select :old.peopleid peopleid,
                 'surname'     column_name,
                 :old.surname  old_value,
                 :new.surname  new_value
          from dual
          where :old.surname <> :new.surname
          union all
          select :old.peopleid peopleid,
                 'born'        column_name,
                 cast(:old.born as varchar2(250)) old_value,
                 cast(:new.born as varchar2(250)) new_value
          from dual
          where :old.born <> :new.born
          union all
          select :old.peopleid peopleid,
                 'died'        column_name,
                 cast(:old.died as varchar2(250)) old_value,
                 cast(:new.died as varchar2(250)) new_value
          from dual
          where coalesce(:old.died, -1)
                      <> coalesce(:new.died, -1)) modified;
  elsif inserting then   ① Event control
    insert into people_audit(auditid,
                             peopleid,
                             type_of_change,
                             column_name,
                             new_value,
                             changed_by,
                             time_changed)
    select people_audit_seq.nextval,   ← Sequence required with Oracle
           peopleid, 'I', column_name, new_value,
           sys_context('USERENV', 'OS_USER')||'@'||
                sys_context('USERENV', 'IP_ADDRESS'),
           current_timestamp
    from (select :new.peopleid   peopleid,
                 'first_name'    column_name,
                 :new.first_name new_value
          from dual
          where :new.first_name is not null
          union all
          select :new.peopleid peopleid,
                 'surname'     column_name,
                 :new.surname  new_value
          from dual
          union all
          select :new.peopleid peopleid,
                 'born'        column_name,
                 cast(:new.born  as varchar2(250)) new_value
          from dual
          union all
          select :new.peopleid peopleid,
```

```
                'died'        column_name,
                cast(:new.died  as varchar2(250)) new_value
          from dual
          where :new.died is not null) inserted;
  else                                              ← necessarily a delete
    insert into people_audit(auditid,
                             peopleid,
                             type_of_change,
                             column_name,
                             old_value,
                             changed_by,
                             time_changed)
    select people_audit_seq.nextval,   #B
           peopleid, 'D', column_name, old_value,
           sys_context('USERENV', 'OS_USER')||'@'||
                sys_context('USERENV', 'IP_ADDRESS'),
           current_timestamp
    from (select :old.peopleid   peopleid,
                 'first_name'    column_name,
                 :old.first_name old_value
          from dual
          where :old.first_name is not null
          union all
          select :old.peopleid peopleid,
                 'surname'     column_name,
                 :old.surname  old_value
          from dual
          union all
          select :old.peopleid peopleid,
                 'born'        column_name,
                 cast(:old.born  as varchar2(250)) old_value
          from dual
          union all
          select :old.peopleid peopleid,
                 'died'        column_name,
                 cast(:old.died  as varchar2(250)) old_value
          from dual
          where :old.died is not null) deleted;
  end if;
end;
/
```

Inside triggers, **inserting**, **updating** ①, (and **deleting**, not shown) are true/false values that tell which event fired the trigger.

PostgreSQL

PostgreSQL is different from all other DBMS products, as it associates with each trigger, a special function that takes no parameters and says `returns trigger`. What this function should actually return depends on the trigger. A *for each row* **before** trigger should end with **return new** for **insert** and **update** triggers, **return old** for **delete** triggers. If it returns null the operation that should normally follow (the actual change) is skipped. All triggers other than a *for each row* **before** trigger (as this example) should return null. Inside the trigger function I use two specific built-in functions (**current_user** - no parenthesis - and **inet_client_addr()**), to retrieve information about the current user. Pseudo one-row tables *old* and *new* give access to the data. Inside trigger functions, several system variables called **tg_**... provide information about the context, as the same trigger function can be called by several different triggers. For instance, **tg_op** says whether the triggering statement was an **insert**, **update** or **delete**.

The trigger itself is very simple; like with Oracle, it starts with the specification after the trigger name of **after** or **before** followed by a type of event or several types of events linked by **or**, **for each row** if this is what you want and simply **execute procedure** followed by the name of the trigger function.

Audit trigger, PostgreSQL version

```
create or replace function people_audit_fn()  ← Special trigger function
returns trigger                               ← Note!
as
$$
begin
  if tg_op = 'UPDATE'     ① Event control
  then
    insert into people_audit(peopleid,
                             type_of_change,
                             column_name,
                             old_value,
                             new_value,
                             changed_by,
                             time_changed)
    select peopleid, 'U', column_name, old_value, new_value,
           current_user||'@'                                ← Auditing data
               || coalesce(cast(inet_client_addr() as varchar),
                           'localhost'),
           current_timestamp
    from (select old.peopleid,
                 'first_name'   column_name,
                 old.first_name old_value,
                 new.first_name new_value
          where coalesce(old.first_name, '*')
                      <> coalesce(new.first_name, '*')
          union all
          select old.peopleid,
                 'surname'   column_name,
                 old.surname old_value,
                 new.surname new_value
          where old.surname <> new.surname
          union all
          select old.peopleid,
                 'born'   column_name,
                 cast(old.born as varchar) old_value,
                 cast(new.born as varchar) new_value
          where old.born <> new.born
          union all
          select old.peopleid,
```

```
               'died'   column_name,
               cast(old.died as varchar) old_value,
               cast(new.died as varchar) new_value
         where coalesce(old.died, -1) <> coalesce(new.died, -1)) modified;
elsif tg_op = 'INSERT' then
  insert into people_audit(peopleid,
                           type_of_change,
                           column_name,
                           new_value,
                           changed_by,
                           time_changed)
  select peopleid, 'I', column_name, new_value,
         current_user||'@'
             || coalesce(cast(inet_client_addr() as varchar),
                         'localhost'),
         current_timestamp
  from (select new.peopleid,
               'first_name'   column_name,
               new.first_name new_value
        where new.first_name is not null
        union all
        select new.peopleid,
               'surname'   column_name,
               new.surname new_value
        union all
        select new.peopleid,
               'born'   column_name,
               cast(new.born  as varchar) new_value
        union all
        select new.peopleid,
               'died'   column_name,
               cast(new.died  as varchar) new_value
        where new.died is not null) inserted;
else
  insert into people_audit(peopleid,
                           type_of_change,
                           column_name,
                           old_value,
                           changed_by,
                           time_changed)
  select peopleid, 'D', column_name, old_value,
         current_user||'@'
             || coalesce(cast(inet_client_addr() as varchar),
                         'localhost'),
         current_timestamp
  from (select old.peopleid,
               'first_name'   column_name,
               old.first_name old_value
        where old.first_name is not null
        union all
        select old.peopleid,
               'surname'   column_name,
               old.surname old_value
        union all
        select old.peopleid,
               'born'   column_name,
```

```
                cast(old.born  as varchar) old_value
         union all
         select old.peopleid,
                'died'   column_name,
                cast(old.died  as varchar) old_value
         where old.died is not null) deleted;
  end if;
  return null;
end;
$$ language plpgsql;

create trigger people_trg    <- Actual trigger definition
after insert or update or delete on people
for each row
execute procedure people_audit_fn();
```

Inside triggers, the special variable **tg_op** ①, indicates which event fired the trigger (many other *tg_* ... variables are available to check the trigger context.)

DB2

Besides the usual specific system variables to collect information about the current user, the peculiarity of DB2 triggers compared with (for instance) Oracle, is that before **for each row** you must provide aliases for **old** and **new** with a special clause **referencing old as ... new as ...**; you cannot reference them directly in the trigger body like with other products.

NOTE Other products support the **referencing** clause if you want to alias **new** and **old** but with them it's optional.

Like with Oracle, PostgreSQL and SQL Server, a DB2 trigger can be fired by several events; inside the trigger you must use the same true/false variables as with Oracle (**inserting**, **updating**, **deleting**) to find out which event fired the trigger.

Audit trigger, DB2 version

```
create trigger people_trg
after insert or update or delete on people  <- The trigger is fired by multiple events
referencing old as o new as n               <- old and new must be aliased
for each row
begin
  if updating              ① Event control
  then
    insert into people_audit(auditid,
                             peopleid,
                             type_of_change,
                             column_name,
                             old_value,
                             new_value,
                             changed_by,
                             time_changed)
```

```
 select next value for people_audit_seq,    ← Sequence used with DB2
        peopleid, 'U', column_name, old_value, new_value,
        system_user ||'@'|| current client_wrkstnname,  ← Auditing data
        current timestamp
 from (select o.peopleid   peopleid,
              'first_name'    column_name,
              o.first_name old_value,
              n.first_name new_value
       from sysibm.sysdummy1                    ← Dummy table required
       where o.first_name <> n.first_name    ② DB2 peculiarity
       union all
       select o.peopleid peopleid,
              'surname'     column_name,
              o.surname  old_value,
              n.surname  new_value
       from sysibm.sysdummy1                    ← Dummy table required
       where o.surname <> n.surname
       union all
       select o.peopleid peopleid,
              'born'        column_name,
              cast(o.born as varchar(250)) old_value,
              cast(n.born as varchar(250)) new_value
       from sysibm.sysdummy1                    ← Dummy table required
       where o.born <> n.born
       union all
       select o.peopleid peopleid,
              'died'        column_name,
              cast(o.died as varchar(5)) old_value,
              cast(n.died as varchar(5)) new_value
       from sysibm.sysdummy1                    ← Dummy table required
       where coalesce(o.died, -1) <> coalesce(n.died, -1)) modified;
elseif inserting then     ① Event control
  insert into people_audit(auditid,
                           peopleid,
                           type_of_change,
                           column_name,
                           new_value,
                           changed_by,
                           time_changed)
  select next value for people_audit_seq,
         peopleid, 'I', column_name, new_value,
         system_user ||'@'|| current client_wrkstnname,  ← Auditing data
         current timestamp
  from (select n.peopleid   peopleid,
               'first_name'    column_name,
               n.first_name new_value
        from sysibm.sysdummy1                  ← Dummy table required
        where length(n.first_name) > 0    ② DB2 peculiarity
        union all
        select n.peopleid peopleid,
               'surname'     column_name,
               n.surname  new_value
```

```
         from sysibm.sysdummy1          ← Dummy table required
         union all
         select n.peopleid peopleid,
                'born'        column_name,
                cast(n.born  as varchar(5)) new_value
         from sysibm.sysdummy1          ← Dummy table required
         union all
         select n.peopleid peopleid,
                'died'        column_name,
                cast(n.died  as varchar(5)) new_value
         from sysibm.sysdummy1          ← Dummy table required
         where n.died is not null) inserted;
   else    ← Necessarily a delete
     insert into people_audit(auditid,
                              peopleid,
                              type_of_change,
                              column_name,
                              old_value,
                              changed_by,
                              time_changed)
     select next value for people_audit_seq,
            peopleid, 'D', column_name, old_value,
            system_user ||'@'|| current client_wrkstnname,  ← Auditing data
            current timestamp
     from (select o.peopleid   peopleid,
                'first_name'    column_name,
                o.first_name old_value
         from sysibm.sysdummy1     ← Dummy table required
         where length(o.first_name) > 0     ② DB2 peculiarity
         union all
         select o.peopleid peopleid,
                'surname'     column_name,
                o.surname  old_value
         from sysibm.sysdummy1     ← Dummy table required
         union all
         select o.peopleid peopleid,
                'born'        column_name,
                cast(o.born  as varchar(5)) old_value
         from sysibm.sysdummy1     ← Dummy table required
         union all
         select o.peopleid peopleid,
                'died'        column_name,
                cast(o.died  as varchar(5)) old_value
         from sysibm.sysdummy1     ← Dummy table required
         where o.died is not null) deleted;
   end if;
 end
 /
```

Inside triggers, **inserting**, **updating** ①, (and **deleting**, not shown) are true/false values that indicate which event fired the trigger.

In the DB2 case, the unique constraint on (*first_name, surname*) requires *first_name* to be mandatory. When someone only has a surname, an empty string ('') is stored instead of null, which explains conditions ②, that are different from the conditions used with other products.

SQL Server

The syntax for triggers is significantly different from other products with SQL Server. The trigger name is directly followed by **on** and the table, and the specification of the triggering event(s), follows the table name, preceded by **for** or **after** (no **before**). If you specify several events, they must be separated by commas, not by **or** like other products. Modified rows are to be found in virtual tables *deleted* and *inserted* - which can be empty. Those tables can be used like any other table in a query, for instance joined to the table to which the trigger applies.

Audit trigger, SQL Server version

```
create trigger people_audit_trg
on people                          ← Specify the table first
after insert, update, delete       ← Specify events next
as
begin
  with z as                    ① Common Table Expression (CTE)
     (select 1 as n
      union all
      select 2 as n
      union all
      select 3 as n
      union all
      select 4 as n)
  insert into people_audit(peopleid,
                           type_of_change,
                           column_name,
                           old_value,
                           new_value,
                           changed_by,
                           time_changed)
  select peopleid,
         type_of_change,
         column_name,
         old_value,
         new_value,
         system_user, sysdatetime()
  from (select p.peopleid,
               'I' as type_of_change,
               case z.n                        ② Using the CTE
                  when 1 then 'first_name'
                  when 2 then 'surname'
                  when 3 then 'born'
                  when 4 then 'died'
               end column_name,
```

```
            null as old_value,
            case z.n                    ② Using the CTE
               when 1 then p.first_name
               when 2 then p.surname
               when 3 then cast(p.born as varchar(5))
               when 4 then cast(p.died as varchar(5))
            end new_value
        from inserted i
             inner join people p
               on p.peopleid = i.peopleid
             cross join z        ← Reference to the CTE
        where i.peopleid not in (select peopleid    ← Only inserted rows
                                 from deleted)
        union all
        select d.peopleid,
            case
              when p.peopleid is null then 'D'
              else 'U'
            end type_of_change,
            case z.n                    ② Using the CTE
               when 1 then 'first_name'
               when 2 then 'surname'
               when 3 then 'born'
               when 4 then 'died'
            end column_name,
            case z.n                    ② Using the CTE
               when 1 then d.first_name
               when 2 then d.surname
               when 3 then cast(d.born as varchar(5))
               when 4 then cast(d.died as varchar(5))
            end old_value,
            case z.n                    ② Using the CTE
               when 1 then p.first_name
               when 2 then p.surname
               when 3 then cast(p.born as varchar(5))
               when 4 then cast(p.died as varchar(5))
            end new_value
        from deleted d
             left outer join people p      ← Updated and deleted rows
               on p.peopleid = d.peopleid
             cross join  z) modified
  where coalesce(modified.old_value, '*')
             <> coalesce(modified.new_value, '*');
end;
go
```

In this trigger I am using something special, a Common Table Expression ①, that is nothing more than an alias for a virtual table that returns, as 'n', values 1 to 4 – one per non-key column in the table. Those values are used at different places ②, for inserting into different rows, values that were in different columns of the same row. Other techniques exist to achieve the same result, in particular a SQL Server operator named **pivot** which I find more complicated to use.

SQLite

Auditing in the case of SQLite is rather futile as users usually have access to the file and can do whatever they want with it. Nevertheless, let's illustrate SQLite triggers with the same example as with true DBMS products to help comparison. SQLite triggers are very close to MySQL triggers - except that as SQLite implements no procedural extension to SQL, they can only be composed of a simple succession of SQL statements without any conditional logic. As shown on page 252 in this book, function **raise()** can generate an error if needed when called in a **select** statement that returns one row. There is no function in SQLite to retrieve information about the current user; it would be possible though, to write a function that retrieves information from the operating system.

Audit trigger (update only), SQLite version

```
create trigger people_u_trg
after update on people      <- Only one event per trigger
for each row
begin
  insert into people_audit(peopleid,
                           type_of_change,
                           column_name,
                           old_value,
                           new_value,
                           changed_by,
                           time_changed)
  select peopleid, 'U', column_name, old_value, new_value,
         '-- Current User --', datetime('now')
  from (select old.peopleid,
               'first_name' column_name,
               old.first_name    old_value,
               new.first_name     new_value
        where coalesce(old.first_name, '*')
                   <> coalesce(new.first_name, '*')
        union all
        select old.peopleid,
               'surname'   column_name,
               old.surname old_value,
               new.surname new_value
        where old.surname <> new.surname
        union all
        select old.peopleid,
               'born'   column_name,
               cast(old.born as char) old_value,
               cast(new.born as char) new_value
        where old.born <> new.born
        union all
        select old.peopleid,
               'died'   column_name,
               cast(old.died as char) old_value,
               cast(new.died as char) new_value
        where coalesce(old.died, -1) <> coalesce(new.died, -1)) modified;
end;
```

Index of Directors, Actresses, Actors and Films mentioned

Sometimes one remembers better an example than the precise technical term it was trying to illustrate. If this is your case, I hope that this index will help.

Numbers

A

B

C

D

E

F

G

H

I

J

K

L

M

N

O

P

R

S

T

V

W

Y

General Index

Special Characters

Numbers

A

B

C

D

E

F

G

H

I

J

K

L

M

N

O

P

Q

R

S

T

U

V

W

X

Y

Z

About the Author

Stéphane Faroult is a French consultant who first discovered relational databases and the SQL language in 1983, shortly before graduating from the École Centrale de Paris, a French "Grande École" of engineering. Stéphane joined Oracle France in its early days (after a brief spell with IBM and a period of time teaching at the University of Ottawa) and developed an interest in performance and tuning topics, on which he soon started writing training courses. After leaving Oracle in 1988, Stéphane briefly tried going straight and did a bit of operational research but after only a year, he succumbed again to the allure of relational databases. For his sins, Stéphane has been performing database consultancy continuously ever since and founded RoughSea Ltd in 1998. In recent years, Stéphane has had a growing interest in education, which has taken various forms; books (*The Art of SQL*, soon followed by *Refactoring SQL Applications*, both published by O'Reilly); a series of seminars in Asia; and video tutorials (http://www.youtube.com/user/roughsealtd).

CPSIA information can be obtained at www.ICGtesting.com
Printed in the USA
LVOW11s1331180713

343539LV00004B/14/P